Monitoring

Stream

and

Watershed

Restoration

Partial financial support for this publication provided by

NOAA National Marine Fisheries Service

Monitoring Stream and Watershed Restoration

Edited by Philip Roni
Northwest Fisheries Science Center
National Marine Fisheries Service

Ed Quimby
Technical Editor

American Fisheries Society
Bethesda, Maryland, USA
2005

Suggested citation formats follow.

Entire book

Roni, P., editor. 2005. Monitoring stream and watershed restoration. American Fisheries Society, Bethesda, Maryland.

Chapter within the book

Medina, A. L., J. N. Rinne, and P. Roni. 2005. Riparian restoration through grazing management: considerations for monitoring project effectiveness. Pages 97–126 *in* P. Roni, editor. Monitoring stream and watershed restoration. American Fisheries Society, Bethesda, Maryland.

Printed in the United States of America on acid-free paper.

Library of Congress Control Number 2004111531
ISBN 1-888569-63-8

American Fisheries Society website address: http://www.fisheries.org

American Fisheries Society
5410 Grosvenor Lane, Suite 110
Bethesda, Maryland 20814-2199
USA

Distributed exclusively outside North and Central America by CABI Publishing
CAB International, Nosworthy Way, Wallingford, Oxon OX10 8DE, UK
http://www.cabi-publishing.org
ISBN 0 85199 907 7

Table of Contents

Acknowledgments

This book would not have been possible without the assistance and support of many individuals. First and foremost, I thank Ed Quimby for technical editing of this book. His tireless attention to structure, formatting, and detail helped improve the organization, accuracy, and readability of the chapters. Moreover, I learned a great deal about writing and editing while working with Ed on this project, and his effort saved me countless hours. Ed Quimby, Karrie Hanson, and Jeff Cowen assisted with developing graphics for various chapters. Karrie provided reference checking and other editorial support. I also thank the numerous anonymous scientists who peer reviewed earlier drafts of chapters and provided detailed and useful recommendations for improving the content. George Pess, Tim Beechie, and Ed Quimby offered helpful suggestions on the organization of chapters within this volume. Drs. John Stein and Bob Iwamoto, my supervisors at the Northwest Fisheries Science Center, deserve special thanks for recognizing the importance of this project, allowing me to spend hours working on it, and authorizing financial support when needed. Finally, I thank the American Fisheries Society for seeing the value of this book and supporting its publication.

Preface

Growing up fishing the waters of the western United States, I witnessed the continual degradation of these waters by development and other land uses. Thus, the need for restoration of streams, rivers, and estuaries was apparent to me at an early age. When I began my career as a fisheries scientist, I became acutely aware of the need not just for restoration of aquatic habitats but also the need to evaluate the effectiveness of restoration actions. Over time, it became clear that guidance on the most effective restoration techniques and on how to monitor restoration actions was sorely needed. I was not alone; scientists have been calling for more information on restoration and monitoring for several years. Moreover, during the last decade, several manuals for restoration and several books on restoration in general have been published. Numerous books on monitoring also have been published, yet none have focused exclusively on evaluating restoration. Many are texts on statistical and experimental design, often not easily digested by scientists, restoration practitioners, and resource managers, or not easily translated to a restoration ecology context.

In my current position, directing a salmon habitat research program in the Pacific Northwest, I am frequently reminded of the need for guidance on monitoring of restoration actions and occasionally am presented with opportunities to provide such guidance. In 1999, my employer, the U.S. government, asked me if our researchers could develop guidance on how to monitor and evaluate restoration actions for threatened and endangered salmon. The federal government was planning on distributing approximately $100 million a year to state agencies and local communities along the West Coast to fund salmon restoration and recovery actions and was searching for guidance on monitoring to provide to restoration practitioners. I saw the opportunity to fill a long-standing need; however, a number of financial and political hurdles ultimately prevented us from initiating the project and writing a guidance document. Realizing that our initial efforts perhaps had larger significance, I proposed to the American Fisheries Society (AFS) a more general book on the topic of monitoring stream and watershed restoration. The AFS agreed, and the book you are about to read represents an outgrowth of discussions with the AFS and various entities and individuals involved in recovery of threatened and endangered salmonids throughout the United States and Canada.

Symbols and Abbreviations

The following symbols and abbreviations may be found in this book without definition. Also undefined are standard mathematical and statistical symbols given in most dictionaries.

A	ampere	eq	equivalent
AC	alternating current	et al.	(et alii) and others
Bq	becquerel	etc.	et cetera
C	coulomb	eV	electron volt
°C	degrees Celsius	F	filial generation; Farad
cal	calorie	°F	degrees Fahrenheit
cd	candela	fc	footcandle (0.0929 lx)
cm	centimeter	ft	foot (30.5 cm)
Co.	Company	ft³/s	cubic feet per second (0.0283 m³/s)
Corp.	Corporation	g	gram
cov	covariance	G	giga (10⁹, as a prefix)
DC	direct current; District of Columbia	gal	gallon (3.79 L)
D	dextro (as a prefix)	Gy	gray
d	day	h	hour
d	dextrorotatory	ha	hectare (2.47 acres)
df	degrees of freedom	hp	horsepower (746 W)
dL	deciliter	Hz	hertz
E	east	in	inch (2.54 cm)
E	expected value	Inc.	Incorporated
e	base of natural logarithm (2.71828...)	i.e.	(id est) that is
e.g.	(exempli gratia) for example	IU	international unit

J	joule		*R*	multiple correlation or regression coefficient
K	Kelvin (degrees above absolute zero)		*r*	simple correlation or regression coefficient
k	kilo (10^3, as a prefix)		rad	radian
kg	kilogram		S	siemens (for electrical conductance); south (for geography)
km	kilometer			
l	levorotatory		SD	standard deviation
L	levo (as a prefix)		SE	standard error
L	liter (0.264 gal, 1.06 qt)		s	second
lb	pound (0.454 kg, 454g) > 454g		T	tesla
lm	lumen		tris	tris(hydroxymethyl)-aminomethane (a buffer)
log	logarithm			
Ltd.	Limited		UK	United Kingdom
M	mega (10^6, as a prefix); molar (as a suffix or by itself)		U.S.	United States (adjective)
			USA	United States of America (noun)
m	meter (as a suffix or by itself); milli (10^{23}, as a prefix)		V	volt
			V, Var	variance (population)
mi	mile (1.61 km)		var	variance (sample)
min	minute		W	watt (for power); west (for geography)
mol	mole		Wb	weber
N	normal (for chemistry); north (for geography); newton		yd	yard (0.914 m, 91.4 cm)
N	sample size		α	probability of type I error (false rejection of null hypothesis)
NS	not significant			
n	ploidy; nanno (10^{29}, as a prefix)		β	probability of type II error (false acceptance of null hypothesis)
o	ortho (as a chemical prefix)			
oz	ounce (28.4 g)		Ω	ohm
P	probability		μ	micro (10^{26}, as a prefix)
p	para (as a chemical prefix)		'	minute (angular)
p	pico (10^{212}, as a prefix)		"	second (angular)
Pa	pascal		o	degree (temperature as a prefix, angular as a suffix)
pH	negative log of hydrogen ion activity			
ppm	parts per million		%	per cent (per hundred)
qt	quart (0.946 L)		‰	per mille (per thousand)

Chapter 1
Overview and Background

Philip Roni

Northwest Fisheries Science Center, National Marine Fisheries Service
2725 Montlake Boulevard East, Seattle, Washington 98112, USA
phil.roni@noaa.gov

Introduction

The degradation and simplification of aquatic systems from anthropogenic activities has led to large efforts throughout the world to restore aquatic habitats for economic, cultural, and environmental reasons (NRC 1992). Nowhere is this more evident than in temperate streams, rivers, and estuaries of North America, where hundreds of millions of dollars are invested annually in restoring or improving habitat to increase both resident and anadromous fish populations. For example, between 2000 and 2003, the U.S. government distributed more than $170 million to the states of Washington, Oregon, California, and Alaska, to fund restoration of salmon habitat under the Pacific Coastal Salmon Recovery Fund (Joe Scordino, National Marine Fisheries Service, Seattle, personal communication). Millions more are invested by other federal, state, provincial, and local programs throughout Canada and the United States to restore aquatic ecosystems for salmonids and other coolwater biota.

These restoration efforts are largely in response to impacts on watersheds and estuaries that occurred following European settlement of North America. Forest practices have negatively impacted many streams by increasing fine and coarse sediment, altering stream hydrology, disrupting delivery of woody and organic debris, and simplifying habitat (Salo and Cundy 1987; Meehan 1991; Murphy 1995). Improving the navigation of rivers and estuaries through dredging and snagging (removal of wood), still widely practiced today, has greatly simplified many rivers (Sedell and Froggatt 1984; Collins et al. 2003). Agricultural activities have had detrimental effects on estuaries, floodplains, wetlands, and low-gradient tributaries through dredging, draining, filling, pollution, and channelization of waterways (NRC 1992). Irrigation and the overappropriation of water rights, particularly in arid regions, has led to reduced stream flows, which can lead to higher water temperatures, changes in hydrology, reduced total wetted habitat, reduced ability to transport sediment, and other deleterious effects (Orth 1987; Hill et al. 1991). Mining and other extraction industries have had many negative effects on streams, from direct alteration and removal of substrates to pollution and release of toxic substances (Nelson et al. 1991). Residential development, industrialization, and urbanization have lead to a suite of problems for aquatic habitats, including filling and channelization, changes in hydrology from increased impervious surface area, pollutants from point and nonpoint sources, elimination of riparian zones, and simplification of habitat (Booth 1990; Booth et al. 2002; Conrad 2003). All these factors have contributed to the degradation and simplification of aquatic habitats across entire ecosystems and are the basis for the development of numerous rehabilitation techniques and comprehensive restoration efforts underway.

Hundreds of millions of dollars are allocated to watershed and estuarine restoration annually, yet rigorous monitoring to evaluate effectiveness occurs infrequently and often is inadequate to quantify physical and biological responses (Reeves and Roelefs 1982; Reeves et al. 1991a, 1991b; Beschta et al. 1994; Chapman 1996; Roni et al. 2003). The lack of adequate monitoring of restoration actions has been noted for many decades (e.g., Tarzwell 1934; Reeves and Roelefs 1982; Reeves et al. 1991a). Given the considerable debate within the scientific community about the effectiveness of various restoration techniques (Reeves et al. 1991a; Kondolf 1995; Kauffman et al. 1997; Roni et al. 2002) and the financial investment in restoration, it is almost incomprehensible that monitoring is not an essential component of designing any restoration project. Monitoring and evaluating the effectiveness of a project is a common practice in science, business, and numerous other fields. Biotechnology companies would not invest hundreds of millions of dollars in a drug without monitoring for effectiveness. In restoration ecology, however, monitoring has not been adequately funded, designed, implemented, or even reported—if it is conducted at all. Moreover, little guidance exists on how to design and implement monitoring programs for restoration projects.

Historically, monitoring of aquatic restoration has focused on changes in physical habitat or vegetation and has been limited to individual projects or case studies that do not necessarily have broadly applicable results. Most monitoring has focused on various instream restoration techniques (e.g., log structures, boulders), with inadequate monitoring of other techniques that seek to restore basic watershed and ecosystem processes. Occasionally, fish response to instream techniques has been evaluated, but monitoring of macroinvertebrates and other aquatic biota is relatively rare (NRC 1992; Frissell and Ralph 1998; and others). The paucity of rigorous monitoring and clear results is due to a variety of reasons, including but not limited to inadequate funding for research and monitoring, the potentially long time frame needed to detect a response, and the lack of knowledge on how to evaluate different restoration techniques at site, reach, and watershed scales. Moreover, only a small fraction of funds spent on restoration activities are allocated for monitoring or research on restoration projects. For example, the U.S. Army Corps of Engineers generally allocates 1% of restoration project construction funds to monitoring and evaluation (Fred Goetz, U.S. Army Corps of Engineers, Seattle, personal communication). While scientific validation of most restoration techniques is sparse, economic or cost–benefit analyses of different restoration techniques are almost nonexistent. Given the current status of many coolwater fishes, vertebrates, and invertebrates as depressed, or threatened or endangered under the Endangered Species Act, and the large sums of money being allocated to habitat restoration to recover vertebrate and invertebrate populations, the need for evaluation of restoration efforts is particularly pressing.

Poorly designed restoration and monitoring programs are costly in terms of potentially negative impacts to the ecosystem from ineffective restoration and in terms of financial resources allocated to ineffective monitoring (Downes et al. 2002). It is important to fully recognize that restoration actions are, in essence, experiments, and, without monitoring and evaluation, society cannot determine which techniques are effective, worthwhile investments. Active adaptive management, which is a key component of most land management, endangered species recovery, and habitat restoration plans, depends on rigorous monitoring to modify or adapt future management decisions. Without well-designed and implemented monitoring and evaluation, adaptive management of restoration ecology is impossible. All these factors emphasize the need for this volume, dedicated to monitoring of stream and watershed restoration.

Book Objective and Scope

This book provides a comprehensive, practical resource for developing monitoring and evaluation programs for restoration activities at various scales—from individual, site-specific actions to multiple projects throughout a watershed. Previous publications have reviewed the effects of anthropogenic activities on aquatic ecosystems (Salo and Cundy 1987; Meehan 1991; Naiman and Bilby 1998), the need for restoration of aquatic ecosystems (NRC 1992; Williams et al. 1997; Montgomery et al. 2003), and techniques for restoration (Hunter 1991; Slaney and Zaldokas 1997; Cowx and Welcomme 1998; FISRWG 1998). The unique emphasis of this book is on how to monitor the effects of various restoration actions at habitat unit (site), reach, and watershed scales (Figure 1). Evaluating restoration actions at multiple scales is critical, because many restoration actions may occur locally but have effects throughout a watershed. The chapters describe monitoring design and sampling considerations, and parameters and techniques needed to design effective physical and biological monitoring of restoration efforts at various scales. While restoration occurs throughout diverse regions and climates, the focus here is on temperate North American streams and estuaries, with emphasis on restoration activities for coolwater biota and salmonid fishes. This focus allows the authors to treat the specific topic in adequate detail. However, the basic principles discussed in this book also will be useful for developing monitoring and evaluation of aquatic restoration in other ecoregions and continents.

Methods are described for monitoring physical (e.g., sediment, habitats, woody debris), chemical (nutrients), and biological (e.g., primary productivity, macroinvertebrates, fishes) responses to habitat restoration and

Watershed/catchment

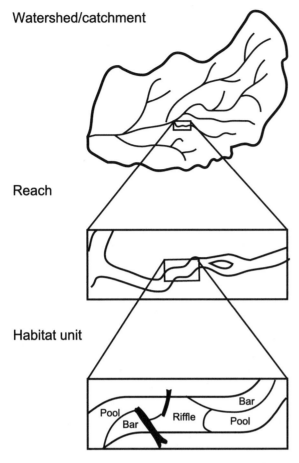

Reach

Habitat unit

Figure 1.
Three levels of scale commonly addressed in this book (modified from Montgomery and Buffington 1998). A watershed can vary in scale from 50 km² to as large as the Columbia, Sacramento, or Colorado River basins. A reach typically is 100 m to several kilometers, and a habitat unit (site) is from a few meters to 100 m, depending on the size of the stream and the habitat classification system used. (Classification of estuarine habitat is discussed in Chapter 7.)

enhancement techniques that restore watershed processes, habitat complexity, and stream productivity. While terrestrial amphibians, birds, mammals, and other wildlife certainly use aquatic ecosystems and are affected by restoration activities, we do not discuss monitoring their response to restoration activities in detail. Other topics not covered in this book include contaminants, impervious surfaces, water withdrawal, and fish passage at hydropower facilities. Contaminants and toxicology are major factors impacting many waterways and often are the focus of restoration efforts in urban and industrial areas. Impervious surfaces in urban watersheds impact the hydrology and deliver various pollutants to streams, from industrial chemicals to motor oil and gardening wastes. These topics are addressed only briefly because they are covered in more detail in texts specifically dedicated to toxicology, such as Ballantyne et al. (1993), Calow (1994), Rand (1995). Likewise, water quality is addressed only in terms of the effects that different restoration actions may have on sediment, nutrients (N and P), and water temperature. While water quality, instream flows and water withdrawal, and toxic pollutants impair aquatic ecosystems in many areas, it would be difficult to cover these topics comprehensively in this book. Similarly, while monitoring fish response to reconnection of isolated habitat is discussed, the engineering and ecological effects of fish passage facilities are not discussed.

Intended Audience

This book is designed to provide useful guidance and information on restoration monitoring and evaluation to three major, diverse groups: (1) scientists evaluating restoration techniques, (2) technicians and watershed groups implementing restoration, and (3) agencies and entities funding restoration. Biologists and scientists often are called upon to develop a monitoring and evaluation program, either for restoration actions they design or for actions funded by their employers. Many of the federal, state, and provincial dollars are being distributed to local community groups, such as watershed councils, local environmental groups, or chapters of national environmental groups. Many agencies and organizations funding restoration are asking the entities to conduct project monitoring. These funding entities are struggling with determining how various projects should be monitored; how many projects to monitor, at what frequency, duration, and intensity; the parameters to measure; and how to develop consistency among restoration projects and monitoring programs.

No one monitoring approach fits all project types or scenarios. Each watershed has unique attributes (e.g., geology, hydrology, climate, plant and animal communities). Developing an effective monitoring program depends on considering many questions and factors (including scientific, logistic, and economic), and on making decisions specific to that monitoring program and restoration project. Thus, each chapter provides questions and guidelines for different project types and scenarios at various scales, rather than a one-size-fits-all approach.

Although we strive to provide lucid descriptions and examples that can be understood by a broad spectrum of natural resource professionals, this book is not intended for the layperson. It is assumed that the reader has some knowledge of aquatic and watershed ecology, restoration ecology, and common restoration practices. If not, good introductory texts on these topics include Hauer and Lamberti (1996), Naiman (1992), Naiman and Bilby (1998), and many others.

Book Organization

The book is organized into 12 chapters based mainly on major types of restoration techniques, including road improvements, riparian silviculture, fencing and grazing, floodplains, estuarine, instream, nutrient enrichment, reconnection of isolated habitats, and acquisitions and conservation easements (Table 1). These chapters, on specific techniques, are organized similarly to assure a certain level of consistency among chapters, to aid reader comprehension, and to highlight differences among restoration techniques. However, because the steps for monitoring or study design are so important and similar for many project types, Chapter 2 is dedicated to monitoring design and common steps needed to develop an effective program regardless of project type.

Many restoration programs include the acquisition of property or conservation easements to protect or to restore both terrestrial and aquatic ecosystems. This is an increasingly popular approach, because protecting high-quality habitat often is cheaper than restoring degraded habitat (Cairns 1993; Roni et al. 2002). Evaluating the efficacy of land acquisitions and conservation easements, which often requires an economic evaluation of other potential restoration actions, is particularly difficult and has seldom been attempted. To address these important components of monitoring and evaluation, there are chapters both on monitoring acquisitions and conservation easements (Chapter 11) and on conducting economic or cost–benefit analyses (Chapter 12). While this book is organized mainly around individual techniques, the reader should recognize the importance of not treating each restoration action separately. That is why Chapter 2 also discusses the importance of integrating restoration monitoring with other monitoring programs into a comprehensive program to examine multiple project types across a watershed or watersheds.

Table 1.
Major categories of restoration covered in this book and examples of specific restoration actions. Chapters covering the different categories are listed in parentheses. Other chapters cover steps for designing restoration monitoring (Chapter 2) and economic evaluations (Chapter 12). Examining multiple actions throughout a watershed or multiple watersheds is discussed in Chapter 2.

Major restoration category	Selected examples of specific actions
Roads and hydrology (Chapter 3)	Road removal, resurfacing, regrade or upgrade stream crossings
Riparian silviculture and forests (Chapter 4)	Vegetation replanting, thinning, removal of invasive plants
Grazing management (Chapter 5)	Fencing, removal of ungulates, rest-rotation, or other grazing management strategy
Floodplains (Chapter 6)	Levee removal or set back, grade control structures, dam removal, beaver reintroduction
Estuarine restoration (Chapter 7)	Reconnect estuarine areas, excavation of fill materials, additions of gravel or substrate, planting of aquatic vegetation
In stream habitat enhancement (Chapter 8)	Log structures and large woody debris placement, engineered log jams, boulder and gravel placement, cover structures/brush bundles, gabions
Nutrient enrichment (Chapter 9)	Addition of organic or inorganic fertilizers, placement of salmon carcasses
Reconnection of isolated freshwater habitats (Chapter 10)	Culvert replacements, barrier removal, reconnection of isolated sloughs and other off-channel habitats
Habitat protection (Chapter 11)	Conservation easements, land acquisitions

Entire texts are dedicated to protocols for measuring various physical and biological parameters; these protocols and parameters often vary by geographic province and agency (see Johnson et al. 2001), and are periodically updated. An overview of some key protocols and references to the many regional reports that outline standards for collecting data on various parameters is provided within each chapter. Finally, a glossary is provided to define the terminology used in this volume, because many unique or specialized terms are defined differently by various converging disciplines that are part of restoration ecology.

A key point to emphasize is that development of a monitoring program such as discussed in the subsequent chapters is best done as an integral part of the design phase of restoration (Thom and Wellman 1996). The objectives of individual restoration programs and projects vary, as do the objectives of monitoring programs. Numerous decisions that need to be made in designing a monitoring program often are interrelated with those that need to be made in developing a restoration project. With this in mind, the following chapters were prepared to help guide the reader through these decisions, elucidate key points and questions, and provide guidance on monitoring stream and watershed restoration.

Background for All Chapters

Before launching into this series of detailed chapters on how to monitor and evaluate various restoration activities, it is necessary to provide some common background. The proceeding subsections discuss restoration terminology, the importance of understanding ecological processes in designing restoration and monitoring, and the types of monitoring.

What Is Restoration?

Efforts to improve or restore aquatic habitat generally are called restoration. There are many different definitions of restoration, however, and the scientific community is in considerable disagreement over its definition and the use of related terminology (Table 2). Cairns (1988) proposed three levels: full restoration (to the original, undisturbed state), partial restoration (enhancement, rehabilitation, improvement, and related terminol-

Table 2.
Commonly used restoration terminology and general definitions. In this book, we apply the term restoration to encompass all these activities, with the exception of mitigation. Where appropriate, we distinguish between the different types of restoration. Definitions were modified from Gore (1985), Cairns (1988), Koski (1992), NRC (1992), and Kauffman et al. (1997).

Term	Definition
Restoration	To return an aquatic system or habitat to its original, undisturbed state. It can be further divided into passive (removal of human disturbance to allow recovery) and active restoration (active manipulations to restore conditions) or more generally defined to include any of the activities below excluding mitigation
Rehabilitation	To restore or to improve some aspects of an ecosystem but not fully restore all components
Enhancement or Improvement	To improve the quality of a habitat through direct manipulation (e.g., placement of instream structures, addition of nutrients)
Reclamation	To return an area to its previous habitat type but not necessarily fully restore all functions (e.g., removal of fill to expose historic estuary, removal of a levee to allow a river to periodically inundate a historic wetland)
Creation	Construction of a new habitat or ecosystem where it did not previously exist (e.g., creation of new estuarine habitat, or excavation of an off-channel pond). This often is part of mitigation activities
Mitigation	Action taken to alleviate or compensate for potentially adverse effects on aquatic habitat that have been modified or lost through human activity (e.g., creation of new wetlands to replace those lost by a land development)

ogy), and habitat creation (mitigation or creating new habitats where none existed). For the purposes of this book, the term restoration is used for all three levels, including many activities that restore, improve, or create habitat. When appropriate, a distinction between full restoration and partial restoration (enhancement or rehabilitation) will be made.

Importance of Understanding Ecological Processes

Both restoration actions and monitoring of restoration require an understanding of the immutable controls (e.g., geology, climate) and processes (e.g., delivery of wood, water, and sediment) that affect and create watershed and estuarine ecosystems and habitats (Figure 2). Land use and other anthropogenic activities can affect habitat by disrupting the processes that form and sustain it, such as the supply and movement of sediment from hillslopes, woody debris recruitment, shading of the stream from the riparian forest, and delivery of water to the stream channel (Roni et al. 2002). Many processes that create habitat operate on time scales of decades or longer (e.g., channel migration and the formation of off-channel habitats). Interrupting these processes (e.g., by stabilizing banks or by constructing roads and levees) can lead to loss of fish habitat over the long term (i.e., decades to centuries; Beechie and Bolton 1999).

While most anthropogenic activities tend to disrupt natural processes that form habitat (e.g., delivery of wood, water, sediment, and nutrients), restoration actions can affect habitat through two major pathways. First, some habitat restoration techniques focus on restoring natural processes (e.g., road removal, riparian replanting)

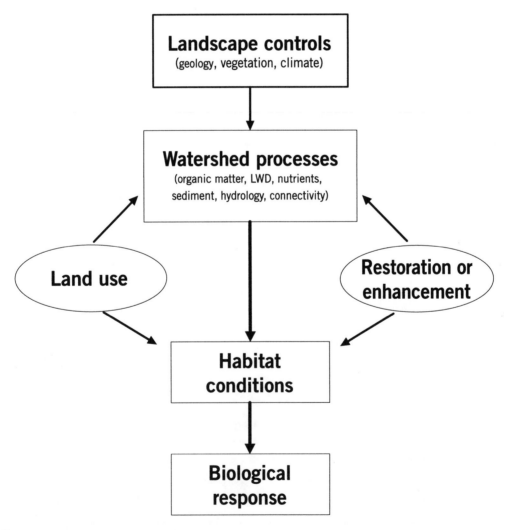

Figure 2.
Simplified model demonstrating linkages between landscape controls and watershed processes, and how land use and restoration or enhancement can influence habitat and biota.

and, thus, affect habitat and biotic production by influencing the underlying watershed processes (e.g., sediment supply, delivery of organic material; Figure 2). In contrast, other techniques focus on actually manipulating or enhancing the habitats themselves (e.g., wood placement, nutrient enrichment, creating new habitats; Table 1). Most habitat-enhancement techniques tend to be relatively short lived (less than a decade) if the underlying process that has been disrupted is not corrected.

This need for a holistic approach to conducting restoration has been noted since at least the late 1970s (Heede and Rinne 1990; NRC 1992; Kauffman et al. 1997; Naiman and Bilby 1998; Beechie and Bolton 1999; and others). Before developing any restoration priorities or strategy, a watershed or ecosystem assessment of current and historical conditions and disrupted processes is necessary to identify restoration opportunities that are consistent with reestablishing the natural watershed processes and functions that create habitat (Beechie and Bolton 1999; Roni et al. 2002). This also provides information on opportunities for habitat enhancement. The assessment of watershed conditions and processes is a critical, obligatory step before developing either a restoration project or a monitoring and evaluation plan.

Consideration of watershed processes also is essential for determining what restoration actions to implement first and how to prioritize actions. Kauffman et al. (1997), Beechie and Bolton (1999), Roni et al. (2002), and others have described restoration prioritization strategies that emphasize restoring physical and biological processes that create healthy watersheds and high-quality habitats (Figure 3). Restoration of watershed processes should precede or be conducted in conjunction with habitat enhancement. That is not to say that habitat enhancement and improvement techniques are inappropriate but rather to emphasize that practitioners be mindful of the broader watershed context and to stress that coupling enhancement efforts with restoration of basic watershed processes that create habitat actually will be the most efficient course for habitat restoration. Clearly, in some heavily managed or urbanized areas, restoration of watershed processes may not be feasible. There are many other scientific, societal, and economic factors to consider when planning and prioritizing restoration. For example, cost, cost–benefit (e.g., fish/dollar, area restored/dollar), habitat quality, location, access and land ownership, endangered species, and other factors often must be considered when planning and prioritizing restoration actions. Notwithstanding, focusing on restoring watershed and ecosystem processes rather than focusing solely on habitat manipulations assures that we will reestablish the naturally diverse and dynamic conditions to which a variety of species are adapted, and, in the long run, this may be the most efficient and cost-effective course of action.

Types of Monitoring

Monitoring technically is defined as systematically checking or scrutinizing something for the purpose of collecting specified categories of data. In ecology, it generally refers to sampling something in an effort to detect a change in a physical, chemical, or biological parameter. MacDonald et al. (1991) reviewed and defined different types of monitoring needed to examine changes in water quality, including baseline, trend, implementation, effectiveness, and validation monitoring (Table 3). Status monitoring, a type of monitoring not discussed by MacDonald et al. (1991), differs from trend monitoring in that it is a snapshot in time and is more concerned with characterizing the condition or status of an organism or physical conditions across an area rather than a trend through time. Baseline, status, and trend monitoring can be helpful in designing monitoring and evaluation programs for restoration effectiveness but generally are not designed to detect the effectiveness of restoration activities. The U.S. Forest Service in the western United States has generally defined three types of monitoring: implementation, effectiveness, and validation (USFS and BLM 1994). Clearly, each type of monitoring is useful for answering different questions, and some combination of these are needed to fully evaluate restoration activities.

Comprehensive monitoring and evaluation of stream and watershed restoration should include physical, chemical, biological, and economic evaluation. Well-designed monitoring should indicate whether restoration measures were designed and implemented properly, should determine whether restoration met objectives, and should provide new insights into ecosystem processes (Kershner 1997). Determining whether a restoration project was implemented correctly (implementation or compliance monitoring) is an important part of understanding why it may or may not have achieved goals and objectives. Implementation monitoring is relatively straightforward, involves quality assurance and project construction management, and may be as simple as a

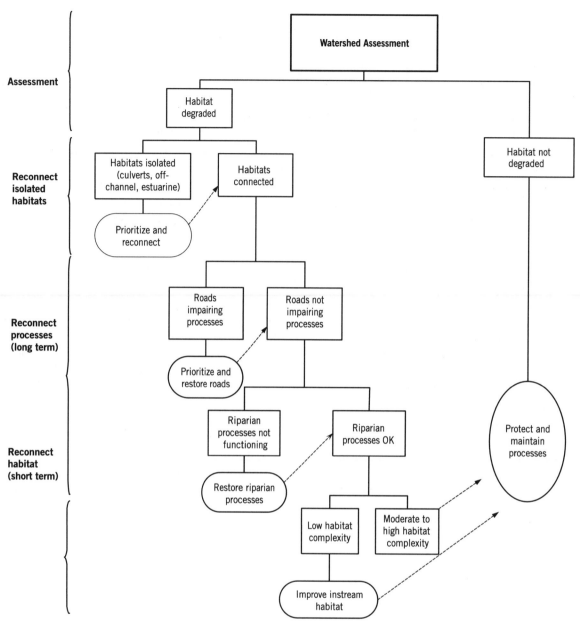

Figure 3.
Example of a strategy for prioritizing specific restoration activities developed for use in streams and watersheds in the Pacific Northwest United States (modified from Roni et al. 2002). Ovals indicate where restoration actions should take place. The strategy was developed as an initial template for prioritizing restoration, with the intent that it be modified as more information becomes available on watershed processes and restoration effectiveness or for use in other regions.

yes–no checklist (Kershner 1997). It is important that those designing monitoring and evaluation programs for restoration activities recognize the importance of implementation monitoring and address it where appropriate. Effectiveness monitoring and validation monitoring, which typically focus on determining whether an action had the desired physical and biological effects (Table 3), often are much more complex, more difficult, and longer term than implementation monitoring, and are the emphasis of this book.

As with other terms in restoration ecology, there is some confusion over the use of monitoring terminology. Effectiveness monitoring and validation monitoring are often confused, and validation monitoring is considered by some as part of effectiveness monitoring. Others think of effectiveness monitoring as physical monitoring and validation monitoring as biological monitoring. For the purposes of this book, when reference is made to monitoring and evaluation of restoration, we generally mean both effectiveness monitoring and val-

Table 3.

Definitions of monitoring types (adapted from MacDonald et al. 1991) and examples of what might be monitored for a wood placement project targeting fish. Effectiveness monitoring and validation monitoring are the focus of this book.

Monitoring types (other names)	Description (key question)	Examples
Baseline	Characterizes the existing biota, chemical, or physical conditions for planning or future comparisons	Fish presence, absence, or distribution
Status	Characterizes the condition (spatial variability) of physical or biological attributes across a given area	Abundance of fish at time x in a watershed
Trend	Determines changes in biota or conditions over time	Spawner surveys and temporal trends in abundance
Implementation (administrative, compliance)	Determines if project was implemented as planned	Did contractor place number and size of logs as described in plan?
Effectiveness	Determines if actions had desired effects on watershed, physical processes, or habitat	Did pool area increase?
Validation (research, sometimes considered part of effectiveness)	Evaluates whether the hypothesized cause and effect relationship between restoration action and response (physical or biological) were correct	Did change in pool area lead to desired change in fish or biota abundance?

idation monitoring. When appropriate, a clear distinction will be made between the two types of monitoring and whether they include physical monitoring or biological monitoring. Many of the design considerations, monitoring techniques, and protocols discussed for effectiveness monitoring and for validation monitoring also are applicable to baseline, status, and trend monitoring programs.

Summary

Hundreds of millions of dollars are invested annually in aquatic restoration, yet little guidance exists on how to monitor aquatic restoration. This book provides a comprehensive, practical resource for developing monitoring and evaluation of restoration activities at various scales—from individual, site-specific actions to multiple projects throughout a watershed. It is designed to provide useful information to scientists evaluating restoration techniques, to groups implementing restoration, and to entities funding restoration. This book is mainly organized around the major types of restoration techniques, including road improvements, riparian silviculture, fencing and grazing management, floodplains, estuarine, instream, nutrient enrichment, reconnection of isolated habitats, and acquisitions and conservation easements. Also included are chapters on monitoring design and economic evaluations. Well-designed restoration and monitoring require an understanding of the natural watershed and ecological processes that create habitat. While there are many types of monitoring, the focus here is on examining the physical and biological effectiveness of restoration actions at different scales. This type of monitoring is critical for determining which restoration techniques are effective, for guiding future restoration and adaptive management efforts, for allocating limited restoration resources wisely, and for moving the field of restoration ecology forward.

References

Ballantyne, B., T. Marrs, and Turner. 1993. General and applied toxicology, New York Stockton Press, New York.

Beechie, T. J., and S. Bolton. 1999. An approach to restoring salmonid habitat-forming processes in Pacific Northwest watersheds. Fisheries 24(4):6–15.

Beschta, R. L., W. S. Platts, J. B. Kauffman, and M. T. Hill. 1994. Artificial stream restoration—money well spent or expensive failure? Pages 76–104 in UCOWR, editor. Proceedings of Environmental Restoration, UCOWR 1994 Annual Meeting, Big Sky, Montana. University Council on Water Resources, University of Illinois, Carbondale.

Booth, D. B. 1990. Stream channel incision following drainage-basin urbanization. Water Resources Bulletin 26:407–417.

Booth, D. B., D. Hartley, and R. Jackson. 2002. Forest cover, impervious-surface area, and the mitigation of stormwater impacts. Journal of the American Water Resources Association 38:835–845.

Cairns, J. Jr. 1988. Restoration and the alternative: a research strategy. Restoration and Management Notes 6(2):65–67.

Cairns, J. Jr. 1993. Is restoration ecology practical? Restoration Ecology 1:3–6.

Calow, P. 1994. Handbook of ecotoxicology. Blackwell, London.

Chapman, D. W. 1996. Efficacy of structural manipulations of in-stream habitat in the Columbia River basin. Northwest Science 5(4):279–293.

Collins, B. D., D. R. Montgomery, and A. J. Sheikh. 2003. Reconstructing the historic riverine landscape of the Puget Lowland. Pages 79–128 in D. R. Montgomery, S. Bolton, D. B. Booth, and L. Wall, editors. Restoration of Puget Sound rivers. University of Washington Press, Seattle.

Conrad, C. P. 2003. Opportunities and constraints for urban stream restoration. Pages 292–317 in D. R. Montgomery, S. Bolton, D. B. Booth, and L. Wall, editors. Restoration of Puget Sound rivers. University of Washington Press, Seattle.

Cowx, I. G., and R. L. Welcomme. 1998. Rehabilitation of rivers for fish. Fishing News Books, London.

Downes, B. J., L. A. Barmuta, P. G. Fairweather, D. P. Faith, M. J. Keough, P. S. Lake, B. D. Mapstone, and G. P. Quinn. 2002. Monitoring ecological impacts: concepts and practice in flowing waters. Cambridge University Press, Cambridge, UK.

FISRWG (Federal Interagency Stream Restoration Working Group). 1998. Stream corridor restoration: principles, processes, and practices. U. S. Department of Agriculture, GPO Item No. 0120-A, Washington, D. C.

Frissell, C. A., and S. C. Ralph. 1998. Stream and watershed restoration. Pages 599–624 in R. J. Naiman and R. E. Bilby, editors. River ecology and management: lessons from the Pacific coastal ecoregion. Springer, New York.

Gore, J. A. 1985. The restoration of rivers and streams, theories and experience. Butterworth Publishers, Stoneham, Massachusetts.

Hauer, F. R., and G. A. Lamberti. 1996. Methods in stream ecology. Academic Press, San Diego, California.

Heede, B. H., and J. N. Rinne. 1990. Hydrodynamic and fluvial morphologic processes: implications for fisheries management and research. North American Journal of Fisheries Management 10:249–268.

Hill, M. T., W. S. Platts, and R. L. Beschta. 1991. Ecological and geomorphological concepts for instream and out-of-channel flow requirements. Rivers 2(3):198–210.

Hunter, C. J. 1991. Better trout habitat: a guide to stream restoration and management. Island Press, Washington, D. C.

Johnson, D. H., N. Pittman, E. Wilder, J. A. Silver, R. W. Plotnikoff, B. C. Mason, K. K. Jones, P. Roger, T. A. O'Neil, and C. Barrett. 2001. Inventory and monitoring of salmon habitat in the Pacific Northwest: directory and synthesis of protocols for management/research and volunteers in Washington, Oregon, Idaho, Montana, and British Columbia. Washington Department of Fish and Wildlife, Olympia.

Kauffman, J. B., R. L. Beschta, N. Otting, and D. Lytjen. 1997. An ecological perspective of riparian and stream restoration in the western United States. Fisheries 22(5):12–24.

Kershner, J. L. 1997. Monitoring and adaptive management. Pages 116–131 in J. E. Williams, C. A. Wood, and M. P. Dombeck, editors. Watershed restoration: principles and practices. American Fisheries Society, Bethesda, Maryland.

Kondolf, G. M. 1995. Five elements for effective evaluation of stream restoration. Restoration Ecology 3:133–136.

Koski, K. V. 1992. Restoring stream habitats affected by logging activities. Pages 343–404 in G. W. Thayer, editor. Restoring the nation's marine environment. Maryland Sea Grant College, University of Maryland, College Park.

MacDonald, L. H., A. W. Smart, and R. C. Wissmar. 1991. Monitoring guidelines to evaluate effects of forestry activities on streams in the Pacific Northwest and Alaska. U. S. Environmental Protection Agency, Region 10, NPS Section, Seattle.

Meehan, W. R., editor. 1991. Influences of forest and rangeland management on salmonid fishes and their habitats. American Fisheries Society, Special Publication 19, Bethesda, Maryland.

Montgomery, D. R., and J. M. Buffington. 1998. Channel processes, classification, and response. Pages 13–36 in R. J. Naiman and R. E. Bilby, editors. River ecology and management. Springer-Verlag, New York.

Montgomery, D. R., S. Bolton, D. B. Booth, and L. Wall, editors. 2003. Restoration of Puget Sound rivers. University of Washington Press, Seattle.

Murphy, M. L. 1995. Forestry impacts on freshwater habitat of anadromous salmonids in the Pacific Northwest and Alaska—requirements for protection and restoration. NOAA Coastal Ocean Program Decision Analysis Series No. 7. NOAA Coastal Ocean Office, Silver Springs, Maryland.

Naiman, R. J. 1992. Watershed management: balancing sustainability and environmental change. Springer-Verlag, New York.

Naiman, R. J., and R. E. Bilby. 1998. River ecology and management: lessons from the Pacific coastal ecoregion. Springer, New York.

Nelson, R. L., M. L. McHenry, and W. S. Platts. 1991. Mining. Pages 426–458 in W. R. Meehan, editor. Influences of forest and rangeland management on salmonid fishes and their habitats. American Fisheries Society, Special Publication 19, Bethesda, Maryland.

NRC (National Research Council). 1992. Restoration of aquatic ecosystems: science, technology, and public policy. National Academy Press, Washington, D. C.

Orth, D. J. 1987. Ecological considerations in the development and application of instream flow-habitat models. Regulated Rivers 1:171–181.

Rand, G. M., editor. 1995. Fundamentals of aquatic toxicology. Chapman and Hall, London.

Reeves, G. H., F. H. Everest, and J. R. Sedell. 1991a. Responses of anadromous salmonids to habitat modification: how do we measure them. Pages 62–67 in J. Colt and R. J. White, editors. Fisheries Bioengineering Symposium, American Fisheries Society, Symposium 10, Bethesda, Maryland.

Reeves, G. H., J. D. Hall, T. D. Roelofs, T. L. Hickman, and C. O. Baker. 1991b. Rehabilitating and modifying stream habitats. Pages 519–557 *in* W. R. Meehan, editor. Influences of forest and rangeland management on salmonid fishes and their habitats. American Fisheries Society, Special Publication 19, Bethesda, Maryland.

Reeves, G. H., and T. D. Roelefs. 1982. Rehabilitating and enhancing stream habitat: 2 field applications. U. S. Forest Service, Pacific Northwest Forest and Range Experimental Station, General Technical Report PNW-140, Portland, Oregon.

Roni, P., T. J. Beechie, R. E., Bilby, F. E. Leonetti, M. M. Pollock, and G. P. Pess. 2002. A review of stream restoration techniques and a hierarchical strategy for prioritizing restoration in Pacific Northwest watersheds. North American Journal of Fisheries Management 22:1–20.

Roni, P., M. Liermann, and A. Steel. 2003. Monitoring and evaluating responses of salmonids and other fishes to instream restoration. Pages 318–329 *in* D. R. Montgomery, S. Bolton, D. B. Booth, and L. Wall, editors. Restoration of Puget Sound rivers. University of Washington Press, Seattle.

Salo, E. O., and T. W. Cundy. 1987. Streamside management: forestry and fisheries interactions. College of Forest Resources, University of Washington, Contribution No. 57, Seattle.

Sedell, J. R., and J. L. Froggatt. 1984. Importance of streamside forests to large rivers: the isolation of the Willamette River, Oregon, U. S. A., from its floodplain by snagging and streamside forest removal Internationale Vereinigung fur Theoretische und Angewandte Limnologie 22:1828–1843.

Slaney, P. A., and D. Zaldokas. 1997. Fish habitat rehabilitation procedures. Watershed Restoration Program, Ministry of Environment, Lands and Parks, Watershed Restoration Technical Circular No. 9, Vancouver, British Columbia.

Tarzwell, C. M. 1934. Stream improvement methods. U. S. Bureau of Fisheries, Division of Scientific Inquiry, Ogden, Utah.

Thom, R. M., and K. F. Wellman. 1996. Planning aquatic ecosystem restoration monitoring programs. U. S Army Corps of Engineers Institute of Water Resources, and Waterways Experimental Station, IWR Report 96-R-23, Alexandria, Virginia, and Vicksburg, Mississippi.

USFS and BLM (U. S. Forest Service and Bureau of Land Management). 1994. Record of decision for amendments to Forest Service and Bureau of Land Management planning documents within the range of the northern spotted owl. Regional Ecosystem Office, Portland, Oregon.

Williams, J. E., C. A. Wood, and M. P. Dombeck. 1997. Watershed restoration: principles and practices. American Fisheries Society, Bethesda, Maryland.

Chapter 2
Steps for Designing a Monitoring and Evaluation Program for Aquatic Restoration

Philip Roni, Martin C. Liermann, Chris Jordan, E. Ashley Steel

Northwest Fisheries Science Center, National Marine Fisheries Service
2725 Montlake Boulevard East, Seattle, Washington 98115, USA
phil.roni@noaa.gov

Introduction

Stream enhancement and watershed restoration methods, such as replanting or fencing of riparian areas, road removal and reduction of sediment, placement of instream structures, and reconnecting isolated channels and sloughs, have been used in North American watersheds for more than 70 years (Tarzwell 1934; White 2002). Despite the large financial investment in aquatic restoration in recent decades, monitoring and research to evaluate project effectiveness occurs infrequently and often is inadequate to quantify biological response (Reeves and Roelefs 1982; Reeves et al. 1991; Beschta et al. 1994; Chapman 1996; Roni et al. 2002). While published evaluations of restoration techniques are scattered throughout the scientific literature, their results often are inconclusive, statistically insignificant, and highly variable (NRC 1992; Minns et al. 1996; Roni et al. 2003). Even fundamental minimum requirements of experimental design (e.g., replication, controls) are rarely met in habitat restoration projects (Minns et al. 1996). Objectives for many restoration projects and associated monitoring often are poorly stated or inappropriate. Moreover, because most evaluations are reach-scale, site-specific case studies, the results are not broadly applicable.

Few rigorous quantitative evaluations exist, in part, because little information has been developed on appropriate restoration monitoring designs. Concurrent evaluations of multiple restoration activities to assess watershed-scale habitat effects on biota, especially fish populations, are extremely rare. Reeves et al. (1997), Slaney et al. (1994), and Solazzi et al. (2000) represent a few of the studies that have examined both physical and biological responses at a broad watershed scale. Although these types of studies can be expensive, they assess the cumulative effect of restoration on watershed-scale recovery of both habitat and populations and, thus, are essential for restoration planning, evaluating, and developing a predictive understanding of restoration effectiveness.

Similar to assessment of the effects of various other anthropogenic activities on aquatic systems (impact assessment), studies evaluating stream, watershed, and estuarine restoration often are hindered by the lack of spatial replication, inadequate pre- and postproject monitoring (temporal replication), and the presence of confounding effects due to a variety of uncontrollable environmental factors (Hurlbert 1984; Walters et al. 1988; Minns et al. 1996; Downes et al. 2002). Guidance for setting up a monitoring program and for determining the appropriate statistical designs for monitoring physical and biological changes at site, reach, watershed, and ecosystem levels is needed. Effective monitoring requires an understanding of the temporal and the spatial scales, the nature of both the restoration actions and the response, and historic and current conditions (Reeves et al. 1995; Downes et al. 2002). Appropriate monitoring and evaluation programs for stream restoration will differ by project type, as well as by region, geomorphology, scale, and a host of other factors.

Aquatic restoration projects, like many management actions, are experiments. As such, they should be implemented according to the standard rules of experimental design, otherwise, little is learned from them (Caughley 1994). A well-designed monitoring and evaluation program is a critical component of any resource management, conservation, or restoration activity. Project-level monitoring is vital to determining whether specific restoration actions have been effective. Broad-scale monitoring is important to assess the success of integrated restoration actions in achieving desired biological goals and in advancing our understanding of restoration. Properly designed monitoring and evaluation programs can help reduce uncertainty about the effects of management actions on the population dynamics of target species and can provide the information needed to adjust management actions. Management and restoration actions can be expensive and time intensive; yet, without monitoring, we are unable to improve our understanding of the potential impacts of individual projects or types of actions on habitat and populations of aquatic biota.

Designing restoration projects as experiments enables tests of hypotheses regarding physical, chemical, and biological responses to different restoration actions and helps us understand cause and effect relationships. This type of monitoring includes both effectiveness monitoring and validation monitoring: determining if the project had the desired physical effect and validating whether basic assumptions about biological responses are correct. As mentioned in Chapter 1, baseline, status, and trend monitoring allow us to establish the context within which restoration actions are performed; effectiveness monitoring and validation monitoring enable us to test hypotheses, to learn from our failures and successes, and to implement adaptive management (a process by which management is initiated, evaluated, and refined; Walters 1986). Thus, linking effectiveness monitoring and validation monitoring to other large-scale (i.e., watershed, basin, or province) monitoring efforts is important.

Our objectives in this chapter are to describe the steps for designing a monitoring program for evaluating the effectiveness of individual or multiple aquatic restoration actions and to set the stage for more detailed discussions of how to evaluate common types of aquatic restoration in subsequent chapters. While there are several types of monitoring, we focus on effectiveness monitoring and validation monitoring throughout this and subsequent chapters.

Regardless of the type, the number, and the scale of aquatic restoration actions, there are several logical steps that should be taken when designing any monitoring and evaluation program. These include establishing project goals and objectives; identifying questions and specific hypotheses; selecting the monitoring design; selecting monitoring parameters, spatial and temporal replication, and a sampling scheme for collecting parameters; implementing the program; and, finally, analyzing and communicating results (Figure 1). In the following subsections, we describe these steps and identify important considerations for each. Because many of these steps are interrelated (monitoring design depends upon questions and spatial scale, just as the number of sites or years to monitor depends, in part, on the parameters selected), some steps could occur simultaneously or in a different order than presented here. For clarity of discussion and to underscore the need to go through a systematic design process, we treat them as sequential steps. We discuss some basic statistical concepts but refer the reader to statistical texts for more detailed information (i.e., Thompson 1992; Sokal and Rohlf 1995; Zar 1999).

Defining Restoration Project Goals and Monitoring Objectives

Before initiating a study to evaluate restoration actions, the overall goals of the restoration project (or projects) and the objectives of the monitoring program must be clearly laid out. Goals typically are broad and strategic, while objectives should be more specific and quantifiable. For example, the goal of a road restoration project may be to reduce fine sediment levels and to improve conditions for aquatic biota. In contrast, the objectives of the monitoring program would likely be to determine if the project reduced levels of fine sediment by some quantifiable amount and if that was followed by any measurable improvement in the survival of aquatic biota. However, the goals and objectives of the restoration project and of the monitoring program could be different, particularly if one were looking at multiple projects. For example, instream structures often are designed with the goal of creating pools, but one objective of the monitoring program could be to test whether instream structures also trapped organic material or increased habitat and fish species diversity. Restoration of riparian vegetation might be undertaken to stabilize banks, increase shading, and lower stream temperatures, but one might also be interested in monitoring the effects of these changes on water chemistry. Ultimately,

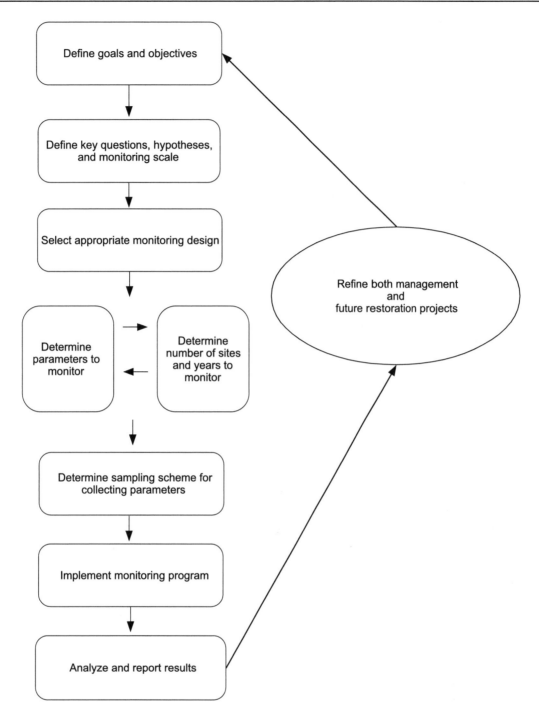

Figure 1.
Diagram of basic steps for setting up a monitoring and evaluation program for stream, watershed, or estuarine restoration. We have placed these steps in a sequential order; however, steps such as determining the length and duration of monitoring, selecting study parameters, and determining the sampling scheme may occur simultaneously.

these subtle differences in goals and objectives will affect the hypotheses, study design, parameters measured, and other factors.

Objectives for monitoring often vary by the agency, the organization, or the individual asking the questions. For example, an organization that funds restoration projects throughout a region will likely want to measure both the short- and long-term collective effects of many projects or the general effects of a specific type of project. Local nonprofit groups or other entities that implement restoration projects often are interested in measuring the effect of individual site-scale projects, such as a culvert replacement or a riparian planting project. Researchers may have objectives in common with both funding agencies and project implementers and proponents. They also may be interested in broader ecological questions (validation monitoring), such as how restoration actions affect migrations or other movements of aquatic vertebrates, whether the restoration action returns sediment transport to historical levels, the degree to which primary productivity is altered, and the long-term effects of restoration actions. Defining what constitutes restoration project "success" thus is a function of who wants to know and their objectives. All participants should be encouraged to monitor both short- and long-term project effectiveness, because the effects of an action are likely to change over time.

Defining Key Monitoring Questions, Hypotheses, and Spatial Scale

After defining monitoring objectives, they need to be further refined into key monitoring questions and hypotheses (MacDonald et al. 1991; Conquest and Ralph 1998; Frissell and Ralph 1998). If objectives have been well defined, they often can be easily translated into questions, then redefined more specifically into testable hypotheses. The key questions and hypotheses will differ among projects and will depend on the overall objectives of the project and monitoring program. In our experience, while there may be many possible specific testable hypotheses, there are only a handful of key or overarching questions. These can be broken into four major questions based on (1) the spatial scale at which one wishes to measure the response (e.g., site, reach, watershed) and (2) spatial replication or the number of projects. These include evaluations of single or multiple reach-level projects and single watershed or multiple watershed-level projects (Table 1). For example, if one is interested in whether an individual restoration action affects local conditions or abundance (reach scale), the key question would be: What is the effect of restoration project x on local physical and biological conditions? In contrast, if one is interested in whether a suite of different project types has a cumulative effect at the watershed scale, then the key question would be: What is the cumulative effect of all restoration actions within the watershed on physical habitat and populations of fish or other biota? While some actions such as riparian plantings or instream wood placement can cover multiple adjacent reaches or occur in patches throughout a geomorphically distinct reach, the initial question is still whether one is interested in examining local- (site or reach scale) or watershed-level effects on physical habitat and biota.

Determining the scale of influence for physical habitat responses requires distinguishing between habitat unit, reach, and watershed-scale effects (Frissell and Ralph 1998; Roni et al. 2003). However, for fishes and other vagile organisms, determining the appropriate scale requires differentiating between changes in local abundance and changes in population parameters at a watershed or larger scale. Most research on habitat and biota, both for restoration and other ecological studies, has focused on reach scale or individual habitat units. This

Table 1.
Overarching questions for monitoring aquatic restoration divided by scale and number of projects of interest. Most appropriate study designs are listed in parentheses. BA = before–after study design, BACI = before–after control-impact, and EPT = extensive posttreatment design. Extensive design refers to a design that is spatially replicated (many study sites, reaches, or watersheds).

Number of Projects	Spatial scale	
	Reach/local	Watershed/population
Single project	Does single project affect local habitat conditions or biota abundance? (BA or BACI)	Does an individual project affect watershed conditions or biota populations? (BA or BACI)
Multiple projects	Do projects of this type affect local habitat conditions or biota abundance? (EPT or replicated BA or BACI)	A. What are the effects of a suite of different projects on watershed conditions or biota populations? (BA or BACI) B. What is the effect of projects of type x on watershed conditions or biota populations? (BA or BACI)

information is important, but uncertainty about movement, survival, and population dynamics of biota prevent these reach-scale studies from addressing watershed- or population-level questions. Studies designed to assess watershed- or population-level effects can provide valuable information but also can face multiple challenges (e.g., upstream–downstream trends, sampling logistics; Conquest 2000; Downes et al. 2002).

Selecting an Appropriate Monitoring Design

There are many potential study designs for monitoring single or multiple restoration actions. None is ideal for all situations, and each has its own strengths and weaknesses. Hicks et al. (1991) distilled these possibilities down to a handful of experimental designs, based on whether data are collected before and after treatment (before–after [BA] or posttreatment designs) and whether they are spatially replicated or involved single or multiple sites (intensive or extensive). They also described the pros and cons of each approach (Table 2). Many variations of these basic study designs have been used or proposed in monitoring of land use, pollution, and habitat alterations (e.g., Johnson and Heifetz 1985; Walters et al. 1988; Bryant 1995), and can easily be modified for use in evaluating restoration actions. However, most of these modifications can be classified as either BA or posttreatment study designs. Below, we discuss these two general study designs, common modifications, and their appropriate applications.

Before–After Studies

Several authors have recommended long-term monitoring by using BA studies as a method for determining biological response to habitat alteration (e.g., Stewart-Oaten et al. 1986; Reeves et al. 1991; Smith et al. 1993).

Table 2.
Summary of advantages and disadvantages of the major study designs used to evaluate stream or watershed restoration or habitat alteration (modified from Hicks et al. 1991 and Roni et al. 2003). Intensive study design generally includes sampling at one or two study sites or streams, extensive at multiple study sites, streams, or watershed. Years of monitoring needed to detect a fish response are general estimates based on juvenile salmonid studies, and extensive study designs assume more than 10 sites are sampled (space for time substitution), thus, fewer years of monitoring are needed. BACI = before–after control-impact. NA = not applicable.

Attribute (pros and cons)	Before and after				Post-treatment	
	Intensive	Extensive	BACI	Staircase	Intensive	Extensive
Includes collection of preproject data	yes	yes	yes	yes	no	no
Ability to assess interannual variation	yes	yes	yes	yes	yes	no
Ability to detect short-term response	yes	yes	yes	yes	no	yes
Ability to detect long-term response	yes	no	ys	yes	yes	yes
Appropriate scale (WA = watershed, R = Reach)	R/WA	R/WA	R/WA	R/WA	R	R/WA
Ability to assess interaction of physical setting and treatment effects	low	high	low	low/high[a]	low	high
Applicability of results	limited	broad	limited	broad	limited	broad
Potential bias due to small number of sites	yes	no	yes	no	yes	no
Assume treatment and controls are similar before treatment	NA	NA	no	no	yes	yes
Results influenced by climate, etc.	yes	yes	yes	no	yes	no
Years of monitoring needed to detect a fish response	10+	1–3	10+	10+	5+	1–3

[a]Depends upon number of treatments and controls

A BA study refers to a design where data are collected both before and after treatment and, thus, generally is replicated in time rather than space. These can be classified into different types, depending upon observation intensity (number of study sites, reaches, or watersheds) and existence of controls (Table 2). The simplest BA study design includes the collection of data before and after treatment within a single stream site, reach, watershed, or estuary. This approach often is used for monitoring individual restoration projects. The most common BA approach, however, is the BA control–impact (BACI) design, in which a control site is evaluated over the same time period as the treatment (impact) site (Stewart-Oaten 1986). The addition of a control (or controls) to the BA design is meant to account for environmental variability and temporal trends found in both the control and treatment areas and, thus, increase the ability to differentiate treatment effects from natural variability (Smith et al. 1993). Additional statistical power to detect treatment effects may be achieved with multiple control sites (spatial replication) and long-term sampling (temporal replication; Underwood 1994). Recent examples of aquatic restoration monitoring using a BACI design include Cederholm et al. (1997) and Solazzi et al. (2000).

While many feel that the BACI design represents an improvement over the BA study design, a BACI design with a poorly chosen control can be less powerful than the uncontrolled BA design (Korman and Higgins 1997; Roni et al. 2003). The BA and BACI designs also suffer from a number of potential statistical problems (Hurlbert 1984; Smith et al. 1993; Conquest 2000; Murtaugh 2000). If the measurements are autocorrelated (i.e., correlated over time), the variance will be poorly estimated, leading to incorrect conclusions about statistical significance and, potentially, about treatment effects. This can be a particular problem if replicate samples are not spaced adequately in time (Stewart-Oaten et al. 1986). For example, in examining nearshore sites impacted and unimpacted from wastewater discharge, Osenberg et al. (1994) found that abundance of white sea urchins *Lytechinus anamesus* followed a seasonal trend and that samples needed to be taken several weeks apart to be independent and to prevent autocorrelation. False conclusions also can occur when the pretreatment trends in the parameter of interest are not similar between treatment and control reaches or watersheds (i.e., they do not track each other well over time). For these reasons, selection of appropriate controls is critical (see the following subsection on controls and references). Conquest (2000) indicated that without replication there is no statistical inference for BA designs. Reeves et al. (1997), Conquest (2000), and McDonald et al. (2000) indicated that interpretation of data from unreplicated BACI studies should include use of graphical analysis and knowledge of ecosystem processes rather than statistical significance to interpret response trajectories.

Downes et al. (2002), in a thorough review of BACI study designs, identified several types, including one with replication (multiple treatment and controls) that they referred to as the multiple BACI or MBACI. Hicks et al. (1991) referred to this design as an extensive BA study but assumed that sampling intensity would be reduced because of the increased number of treatment and control sites. We do not make this distinction by sampling intensity but consider the MBACI described by Downes et al. (2002) as a minor variation of the extensive BACI described by Hicks et al. (1991). A replicated BACI design potentially is the most powerful of all study designs because it includes replication in both space and time (monitoring of multiple treatments and controls before and after restoration) but also potentially is more challenging and costly to implement than other designs (Downes et al. 2002).

Spatially replicating BA and BACI studies would address many of the problems inherent in these designs and would increase the applicability of results to other areas. The ideal BA or BACI design includes many paired treatments and controls across the landscape that are monitored for many years. While this may be challenging to design, implement, and fund, it is the type of monitoring we should strive to develop and implement to examine individual or multiple restoration actions and to quantify population- and watershed-level responses. Spatially replicating the restoration treatment and randomly selecting treatments and controls (ideal situation) often is difficult due to limited resources, logistics, project scale, or location. For example, it would be difficult to replicate dam removals over several comparable rivers or to randomly select rivers on which dams are to be removed. Even where multiple reach-scale restoration projects do exist within a watershed, there may still be only one true replicate if the response of interest is at the watershed scale. Lack of true replication limits the statistical inference and application of results to the study site and prevents extrapolation to other sites. The question of interest becomes, for example: Did this particular habitat modification have an effect on local habitat or fish abundance? Generalizations to effects at other sites are not statistically support-ed. In the absence of true replication, the results of both BA and BACI study designs should be considered case studies and the results interpreted and applied to other areas with caution. Nonetheless, unreplicated BA and BACI studies are useful, because they add to our knowledge of physical and biological processes; the Hub-bard Brook experiments in the northeast United States and the Carnation Creek study in British Columbia are prime examples of key case studies that increased our knowledge about the response of stream and water-shed processes to disturbance (Conquest 2000).

Posttreatment Designs

In many situations, collecting data before treatment is not possible, for example, studies to examine effects of past restoration activities or restoration opportunities that arise as a result of unplanned events such as natu-ral disasters. In these situations, the treated reach or watershed is compared to areas thought to be similar in the absence of restoration activities (a control or reference). In essence, posttreatment designs are retrospective studies, replicated spatially rather than temporally (sometimes called space for time substitution). Some have suggested that only various BACI designs are appropriate for impact or restoration assessment (Downes et al. 2002), but much can be learned from posttreatment designs, and many authors have emphasized the useful-ness of these studies (Hilborn and Walters 1981; Hicks et al. 1991). Hall et al. (1978) and Hicks et al. (1991) defined two types of posttreatment designs: intensive posttreatment (IPT), in which multiple years of data are collected at one or a few paired control and treatment sites (both spatial and temporally replicated); and exten-sive posttreatment (EPT), in which many paired treatment and control sites are each sampled once over a 1- to 3-year period. Thus, the IPT design includes both spatial and temporal replication (albeit limited), while the EPT includes only spatial replication. The IPT is, in essence, a BACI design without preproject data and has a limited ability to draw inferences about the restoration action in the absence of spatial replication (Fig-ure 2). The EPT is more common than the IPT and has been applied to evaluations of different timber har-vest and riparian buffer widths (e.g., Murphy and Hall 1981; Hawkins et al. 1983; Grant et al. 1986). Grant et al. (1986) tested key assumptions of the EPT design and demonstrated that it is effective for examining the influence of habitat modifications on juvenile salmonids. The EPT design is best suited for reach-scale proj-ects, because, at broader scales, it often is difficult to locate suitable controls (Roni et al. 2003). It, however, has been applied at a watershed scale to examine the effects of land use and other habitat modifications on fish communities (e.g., Ralph et al. 1994; Reeves et al. 1993).

Data from an EPT design are particularly flexible. Regression analysis or other correlative techniques can be applied to such data to identify other factors determining physical and biotic responses. For example, by using simple linear regression and data from 30 paired treatment and reference sites, Roni and Quinn (2001) found that juvenile coho salmon *Oncorhynchus kisutch* response to habitat enhancement (abundance) was positively correlated with pool-forming large woody debris (LWD). In contrast, summer juvenile steelhead trout *O. mykiss* numbers, which showed no overall response to restoration when analyzed by using a paired *t* test, were negatively correlated with percent pool area. This ability to correlate differences in responses to other variables is a strength of the EPT design not found in study designs that lack extensive replication. The obvious weak-nesses of most posttreatment designs are the lack of preproject data and the assumption that control reaches or watersheds are similar to pretreatment conditions (see Table 2). As with the BACI design, the selection of appropriate control or reference sites is critical. Randomly selecting treatments and controls would be ideal, though this would be difficult in practice, particularly if sites are to be paired within a stream or watershed.

Other Study Designs

As indicated earlier, there is a suite of modifications of the BA design, which includes modifications in number of sites, random selection of temporal sampling, and differences in intensity of sampling. For example, Bryant (1995) proposed a pulsed monitoring system for evaluating stream restoration in which periods of short-term intensive monitoring are separated by long periods of low-intensity data collection. Another study design, which has rarely been applied, is the staircase design proposed by Walters et al. (1988). This method requires the sequential treatment of several study reaches or watersheds over time (Table 3). Preproject data are collect-ed on all reaches or watersheds, then each reach or watershed is treated sequentially over time, with multiple reaches or watersheds serving as untreated controls. Reaches or watersheds would ideally be selected and treat-ed randomly, though this can be challenging to implement across a watershed or number of watersheds.

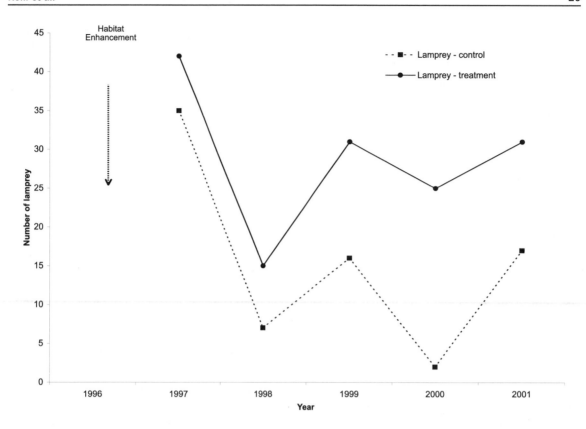

Figure 2.
Results of monitoring of larval lamprey abundance after stream enhancement in Shuwah Creek, Washington, by using the intensive posttreatment design. Treatment, which included habitat enhancement through placement of logs into stream channel, occurred in 1996. Monitoring of fish abundance in treatment and control reaches was not initiated until 1997. Without multiple sites (spatial replication) or preproject monitoring (adequate temporal replication), it is not possible to determine whether the observed differences in fish abundance between reaches is due to habitat enhancement or inherent differences in stream reaches present before treatment.

While the staircase design is more complex than BACI or other designs, data can be analyzed by using general linear models (Walters et al. 1988), and this design reduces the risk of confounding factors that might make data interpretation difficult. For example, a large landslide or flood would not have the same confounding effect on a staircase design as it would on a study in which all the treatments were applied in one perhaps anomalous year and on only one or two watersheds or stream reaches. A variant of the staircase design has been applied to instream structure and to nutrient additions in the Keogh River in British Columbia (McCubbing and Ward 2002). The staircase design shows promise when applied at large scales or to unconnected stream reaches. When applied to multiple reaches within the same watershed, analysis and interpretation of resulting data risks being confounded by factors such as movement of material or biota between reaches and upstream–downstream trends in both physical and biological processes.

The staircase design has some potential advantages over traditional study designs. As previously mentioned, the BACI design typically is replicated solely in time, and, thus, the results generally are not applicable and can be confounded environmental factors. The multiple BACI and EPT designs replicate the treatment in space and, therefore, allow generalization of the results in space (e.g., "this type of restoration increases juvenile coho salmon density in coastal Washington streams"). In contrast, the staircase design requires replication of the treatment in time (the treatment is repeated in different years), as well as space, allowing the results to be generalized in time and space (e.g., "this type of restoration increases juvenile coho salmon density in coastal Washington streams under a variety of environmental conditions experienced in different years").

Other designs or studies might be retrospective or posttreatment studies that examine data collected or reconstructed by others for different purposes, such as comparisons of historical maps or photographs (e.g., Collins

Table 3.
Example of a staircase design proposed to monitor changes before and after restoration in 10 sites, reaches, or watersheds (modified from Walters et al. 1988). Shading represents the treatment and blank cells represent the control years and sites, reaches, or watersheds. Ideally, treatment reaches or watersheds are selected randomly. Application to multiple reaches within a watershed would be confounded if treatments occurred upstream of control reaches (i.e., reaches are not independent).

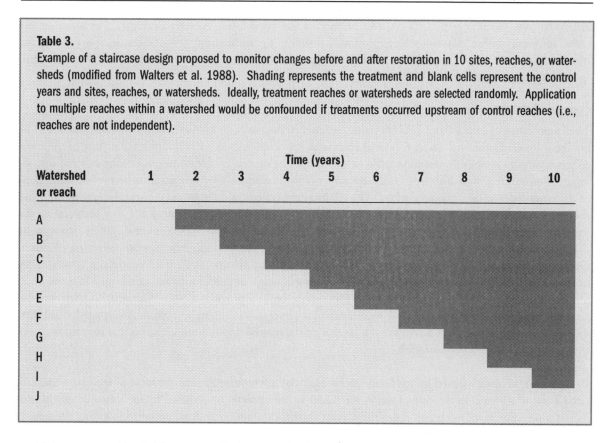

and Montgomery 2001). These typically have involved comparisons of present or restored conditions to historic photos or maps (See Chapters 3, 6, and 8 for discussion of examining channel alterations). For example, Collins and Montgomery (2001) examined the loss of estuarine and floodplain habitat in several Pacific Northwest river basins by using U.S. General Land Office historical land-survey data from the 1800s and comparing that to current information. A similar retrospective study could be particularly useful to examine broad-scale restoration actions.

Another type of analysis would be combining existing small independent studies in a meta-analysis to make inferences at some broader scale. Gurevitch and Hedges (2001) discuss some of the statistical methods for analyzing such data sets. House et al. (1989), Hunt (1988), Binns (1999), and Avery (2004) represent compendiums of monitoring of stream restoration projects in Oregon, Wisconsin, and Wyoming, and attempts at meta-analysis of historic monitoring data. Although meta-analysis has the potential to gleen extra information from existing data, its applicability and relevance are limited when treatments and variables measured differ. Meta-analysis does not, therefore, supplant the need for well-designed and coordinated monitoring of new restoration actions.

In selecting an appropriate monitoring design, it is important to keep in mind that the response to a restoration action may be more than a simple step function (e.g., a change in mean density). Instead, there may be a change in a temporal trend. For example, decreasing abundance may be arrested or reversed due to habitat restoration actions. In this situation, just monitoring immediately before or after the treatment may not be sufficient to detect the change. Longer time series may be necessary, requiring different methods of sampling and analysis for the detection of trends (Urquhart and Kincaid 1999; Larsen et al. 2001).

Appropriate Designs for Different Hypotheses

While many of the specific objectives and associated hypotheses of individual restoration projects and monitoring programs will help determine the study design, the appropriate designs will, in large part, be based on the key questions (Table 1). If one is interested in an individual site, an intensive BA or BACI design of some type will be most appropriate. If one is interested in multiple sites, then an extensive design, either before and after treatment (with or without a control) or an EPT design will be necessary (Table 1). For some project types, only one design may really be appropriate; however, for most monitoring of restoration actions, any number of designs may be appropriate, and the design selection is dependent upon objectives, key questions, specific hypotheses, and available resources.

Controls and References

The importance of control and reference sites, reaches, watersheds, or estuaries cannot be understated. The National Research Council, in its review of ecosystem restoration (NRC 1992), stated that "one of the most effective ways to establish restoration goals is to evaluate the success of stream restoration by comparing biological communities in a disturbed reach to communities in a set of relatively undisturbed reference streams of the same order in the same ecoregion." The distinction between references and controls is a subtle one, and there is some disagreement as to the difference. A control site generally is defined as being identical to the treatment site, with the exception being the treatment or restoration action (Downes et al. 2002). Some argue that no true controls exist in field studies because no two sites, reaches, watersheds, or estuaries are identical. On the other hand, a reference often is defined as the ideal or pristine state, with conditions unaltered by human activities (Downes et al. 2002), or representing a range of predisturbance conditions (Reeves et al. 1995). Regardless of this disparity in views, a reference or control provides a basis of comparison between the restored area and the conditions before restoration and serves as a covariate to account for natural variability. Thus, the control or reference accounts for a portion of the natural background variation that may mask detection of a true response to restoration.

Background variability shared by treatment and controls or reference may take the form of relatively uncorrelated noise or a trend. In the case of noise, the power of the analysis is increased by including a control site. When a common trend occurs in the control and treatment, in addition to potentially increasing the power, the control site prevents the trend from being interpreted as a response to the treatment. For example, if changes in climate caused increased rainfall, stream flow, and decreased water temperatures in a watershed where the effects of riparian and road treatments were being measured, then, in the absence of a control watershed, these changes in flow and in temperature might be erroneously attributed to the treatment (riparian and road restoration) when they are, in fact, the product of changes in climate. However, if the control or reference does not track the treatment well (i.e., follow a similar trend before treatment), the addition of a control can increase the variability, making it more difficult to detect a response rather than easier. Thus, careful and judicious selection of references and controls, while difficult, is extremely important.

Most effective monitoring designs include controls nested at a series of spatial scales (Minns et al. 1996; Poole et al. 1997; Frissell and Ralph 1998), though selection of appropriate controls is, indeed, difficult. For example, Roni and Quinn (2001) examined more than a 100 restoration sites to locate 30 that had suitable paired controls with similar flow, channel slope, channel width, riparian vegetation, geology, morphology, and other features. Controls should be as close as possible to an independent replicate of the treatment and should be as similar as possible in land use, geology, hydrology, biology, and other physical features. Downes et al. (2002) provide a comprehensive list of factors to consider when selecting a control in ecological monitoring. Knowledge of the landscape-scale characteristics of the subbasin or watershed and extensive field investigations often are required to locate suitable control areas (Rosgen 1996; Conquest and Ralph 1998). Status and trend monitoring programs for population and habitat characteristics, such as briefly described earlier, can provide useful physical and biological information for locating and selecting appropriate controls as well as restoration sites. Controls also should be completely unaffected by changes made to treatment areas. This requires an understanding of the mobility of the species of interest and of the spatial scale of the treatment effect.

Whether treatments and controls should be paired is another important consideration, because treatments often, but not always, are paired with similar control reaches. Pairing helps account for some of the variability among sites, because two nearby reaches within a stream often are more similar to each other than to reaches in different watersheds. In studies with paired treatment and control reaches, such as a BACI or an EPT, the measure of interest is the difference between the treatments and the controls (i.e., the analysis is done on the difference between the treatment and the control). Unpaired comparisons typically focus on whether the average, variance, or temporal trends of the control differs from those of the treatment and can result in the need for larger sample sizes than if sites were paired (Roni et al. 2003). Therefore, pairing of similar treatments and controls is recommended when possible to help account for variability, to reduce sample size, and to simplify data analyses.

Determining Appropriate Monitoring Parameters

Determining which metrics, variables, and parameters to monitor and to measure logically follows defining goals and objectives, key questions and hypotheses, definition of scale, and selection of study design. It also goes hand in hand with spatial and temporal replication and sampling schemes discussed below. Parameters and metrics should not be selected arbitrarily or simply because they were used in other studies. Monitoring parameters should be relevant to the questions asked, strongly associated with the restoration action, ecologically and socially significant, and efficient to measure (Downes et al. 2002; Bauer and Ralph 2001; Kurtz et al. 2001). For example, monitoring of riparian restoration will likely be focused on indicators of plant growth and diversity, as well as some channel features, while estuarine restoration may focus on changes in use of estuarine habitats by different members of the vertebrate and invertebrate communities. Moreover, to be useful, the parameter must change in a measurable way in response to treatment, must be directly related to resource of concern, and must have limited variability and not likely be confounded by temporal or spatial factors (Conquest and Ralph 1998).

The appropriate parameters to monitor will differ by types of restoration, as well as specific hypothesis. The choice of a parameter should, in part, be based on the different sources of spatial and temporal variability associated with that parameter. Both observation error and natural variability of a quantity will reduce the precision with which the mean of the quantity is estimated. For example, both electrofishing and snorkeling are used to estimate juvenile fish densities in small streams. While electrofishing may have a smaller observation error, it is more time consuming and, thus, leads to fewer surveyed habitat units. If the variability of fish is high between units, then the marginal reduction in observation error may have a relatively small effect on the precision of the mean density estimate when compared to the increase in precision from snorkeling more units (a more complex comparison would be between electrofishing and snorkel counts corrected by electrofishing a subset of the snorkeled units, e.g., Hankin and Reeves 1988). Moreover, temporal variation within sites and across sites can affect the usefulness of an indicator or parameter for detecting local and regional trends in biota or habitat (Larsen et al. 2001). It is important to consider these different types of error when selecting a parameter.

Several papers have examined the sensitivity of various parameters for detecting changes in physical habitat (Lichatowich and Cramer 1979; Osenberg et al. 1994; Gibbs et al. 1998; Kaufmann et al. 1999; Kurtz et al. 2001; Bauer and Ralph 2001) or biota due to water quality or land use. For example, to examine the sensitivity and precision of habitat parameters commonly used in the U.S. Environmental Protection Agency's Environmental Monitoring and Assessment Program (EMAP), Kaufmann et al. (1999) examined signal-to-noise ratios (S/N): the ratio of variance among streams (signal) with variance between repeated visits to streams (measurement "noise"). They found that many flow sensitive measures such as pool:riffle ratios and qualitative visual assessments had low S/N ratios (<2) and were imprecise. They suggested that parameters should have a S/N ratio in excess of two to be useful in detecting change. This and other studies emphasize the importance of incorporating some type of sensitivity analysis when selecting monitoring parameters and the need to understand the components of variability in the parameters being measured. Subsequent chapters discuss, in detail, parameters to consider for monitoring different types of restoration actions.

Spatial and Temporal Replication

Determining the Number of Sites and Years to Monitor

The ability of a monitoring program to determine change related to restoration action (or actions) will depend upon the variability of the parameter of interest and to what extent the monitoring is replicated across space and time (Green 1979; Kershner 1997). Initiating monitoring without some idea of the ability to detect a change is a poor use of time and resources. Hence, it is important to estimate the sample size (either years, number of sites, or both) needed to detect the level of response of interest before initiating a monitoring program. Detecting small changes in biota, and particularly fish response to habitat alteration, restoration, or management changes, is difficult (Bisson et al. 1997; Minns et al. 1996; Korman and Higgins 1997; Ham and Pearsons 2000; Roni et al. 2003). For example, Ham and Pearsons (2000) examined estimates of mountain whitefish *Prosopium williamsoni*, bull trout *Salvelinus confluentus*, cutthroat trout *Oncorhynchus clarki*, spring and fall chinook salmon *Oncorhynchus tshawytscha*, resident rainbow trout *Oncorhynchus mykiss*, and steelhead in the Yakima River basin and estimated that detecting changes in abundance and population size less than 19% would not be detectable over a short time frame (<5 years). Similarly, Lichatowich and Cramer (1979) examined several abundance, survival, and life history parameters for salmonid fishes and suggested that BA studies of abundance may require 20 to 30 years to produce an 80% chance of detecting a change of 50% or more. All these studies emphasize the need for either long-term monitoring (temporal replication) or sampling multiple sites, reaches, watersheds, or estuaries (spatial replication), or both.

Before one can estimate the appropriate sample sizes in space or time (number of years or sites) or the statistical power (probability of detecting a true difference), we must have some estimate of the variance of the parameter of interest, as well as an understanding of some basic statistical principles. A statistical power analysis before implementing a monitoring project helps determine how many years, locations, or samples will be required to have a reasonable chance of detecting a change in the parameter of interest (Zar 1999). The exact equations for conducting power analyses can be found in basic statistical texts and can be done with a computer software package or by hand with a calculator. Below, we provide a brief overview of power analysis and some examples based on empirical data.

Before conducting a power analysis to estimate the sample size or to calculate statistical power for a particular test, estimates of four of the five following quantities are necessary:
I.   Variance—estimate of the amount of spatial, temporal, or other changes (variability) in a parameter.
II.   Power ($1 - \beta$, β = probability of a type II error)—the probability of detecting a difference or change if it does exist (the probability of rejecting a null hypothesis when it is, in fact, false).
III. Effect size—the difference that you would like to detect between the groups being compared.
IV.   Significance level (α = probability of type I error)—the probability of detecting a difference when it does not exist (probability of rejecting the null hypothesis when it is true).
V.   Sample size—replicates in time or space.

With estimates of any four of these parameters, one can calculate the fifth, though for these examples, we will assume that we have the first four (Zar 1999). A typical analysis might consist of determining the necessary sample size to have an 80% probability of detecting a 50% change, given $\alpha = 0.05$ and variance of X. For example, decreasing the variance, increasing the sample size, or increasing effect size all increase the power. In other words, one is more likely to detect a change when there is less noise (variability), more data, or a large effect. Estimates of the variance often can be calculated by using existing data from similar studies. Ideally, however, a pilot study should be conducted to assure that variance estimates are applicable to the specific situation and the parameter of interest. Finally, power also is determined by the significance or alpha-level set for the test, which generally is determined by the investigator ahead of time and typically is 0.05 or 0.10 in ecological studies (see Zar 1999 or other statistical texts for more detail).

The sample size needed to detect the response of different metrics may be highly variable. To illustrate differences among metrics and the ability to detect different levels of physical and biological responses to restoration, we examined fish and physical habitat data from Roni and Quinn (2001). They used an EPT design to evaluate the response of stream fishes to instream restoration (LWD placement) in 30 streams with paired treatment and control (reference) reaches within each stream. They sampled each pair of sites within a stream once. By using variance estimates from their data, we estimated the number of replicates required to detect a range of increases in coho salmon parr and smolts, pool area, and macroinvertebrate richness (P. Roni, unpublished data), given an alpha level of 0.05 and a statistical power of 0.80. These results indicate that to detect a 50% change in pool area or macroinvertebrate richness (treatment richness:control richness = 1.5), fewer than 10 paired treatment and reference reaches would need to be sampled (Figure 3). In contrast, to detect a 50% change in coho parr abundance would require approximately 30 paired sites (treatment and reference), while a similar change in presmolts would require nearly 50 paired sites. Our analysis here is for illustrative purposes, and specific estimates should be conducted by using data from the region and the parameter of

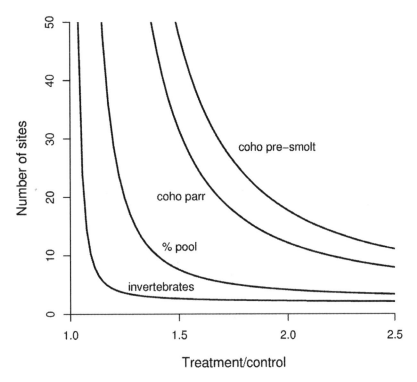

Figure 3.
Sample size to detect change in coho salmon parr and smolts, pool area, and macroinvertebrate richness by using an extensive posttreatment design, a power of 0.80, and an alpha of 0.05. Coho salmon and pool data taken from Roni and Quinn (2001); macroinvertebrate data are unpublished.

interest. The important point is that the variability of a parameter can and does influence our ability to detect changes of different magnitude and will influence the sample sizes needed to detect the change of interest and the utility of a parameter to answer key questions.

The most appropriate allocation of resources to replicate in space and time will depend on the sources of variability. The variability in the estimate of the treatment effect that is attributable to temporal variation depends on the magnitude of temporal variability, the degree to which the control sites track the treatment sites in time, and the variability in the treatment effect when it occurs in different years. Likewise, the influence of spatial variability on the estimate of effect size depends on the magnitude of spatial variability, the degree to which the controls match the spatial patterns seen in the treatments, and the degree to which the treatment effect varies between sites in space. Estimates of these different sources of variability will allow different combinations of spatial and temporal replication to be compared based on the power to detect an effect (or identically, the precision of the estimate of effect size).

As discussed previously, another important consideration is whether treatments and controls or references should be paired. In the data set from Roni and Quinn (2001), examined above, the sites were paired within a stream reach. Not pairing sites, stream reaches, or watersheds, but selecting treatment and reference reaches randomly can result in the need for a larger sample size (Roni et al. 2003; Figure 4). There are many benefits to pairing reaches within a stream, streams within a watershed, or watersheds within a basin, though there also are some drawbacks. Highly mobile organisms, such as fish and other vertebrates, may move between study reaches or watersheds. The longitudinal nature and upstream–downstream gradient of productivity, hydrology, sediment transport, and diversity in streams also may confound the pairing of upstream and downstream reaches. Given estimates of variance for a parameter in both treatment and reference areas, power analysis can help determine benefits of pairing. When there is adequate spatial replication in restoration projects, stratification of study areas by factors like geology, slope, geographic region, or strata may help account for inherent variability among sites. Watersheds are hierarchical systems that lend themselves to stratification by ecoregions, watersheds, channel reaches, habitat units, and other factors (Conquest et al. 1994). This type of strat-

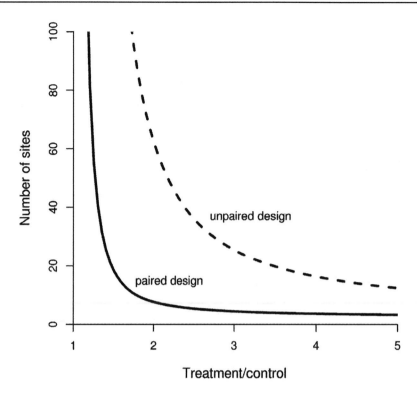

Figure 4.
Example of differences in sample size needed to detect a change in juvenile steelhead numbers by using a posttreatment if reaches are paired within a stream or unpaired. Data from Roni and Quinn (2001).

ification is widely used in broad-scale status monitoring and trend monitoring (Bauer and Ralph 2001; Kershner 1997) and is no less applicable for monitoring to evaluate restoration actions (Frissell and Ralph 1998).

Given the dynamic nature of aquatic and fluvial systems, as we increase the scale and number of sites at which we monitor, additional natural variability (background variability unrelated to the restoration response), as well as sampling and observer error typically are introduced, reducing our ability to detect that portion of change or variability due to restoration. This tends to create a trade-off between the value of the information on population- and watershed-level effects and our current ability to measure and detect these effects with any degree of precision. Thus, detecting local changes in habitat and biota can be easier (or less expensive), but the broader watershed or population level of restoration effects, which require more planning and more spatial and temporal replication (more sites and longer sampling), potentially provide more valuable but less precise information.

The ideal would be to choose the sample size and the monitoring design based solely on statistical considerations. However, financial, logistical, and political boundaries typically constrain the available choices. Choices pertaining to allocation of resources will lead to trade-offs between the number and types of biological and physical characteristics that are measured, the precision with which they are measured, the time period over which they are measured, and the spatial extent of the monitoring. A cost-benefit analysis (e.g., Sokal and Rohlf 1995; Underwood 1997; Downes et al. 2002), along with a clearly defined and prioritized list of questions and an understanding of the boundaries, provides a quantitative method for investigating these tradeoffs. Often, limited resources will prevent the implementation of studies that directly answer the question of interest. Instead, another less costly question is addressed, and inference based not on statistics but expertise will be applied to partially address the original question. For example, a manager may wish to know the impact of a restoration action on freshwater fish survival. However, the resources necessary to answer this question may be unavailable, so, instead, the question addressed statistically becomes: How is local abundance during winter affected by this restoration? Then, based on knowledge of the life history of the species (e.g., seasonal habitat use, limiting factors), the results can be used to make nonstatistical inference about cumulative freshwater survival. It is important to clearly describe where statistical inference ends and inference based on biological expertise begins.

Multiple Restoration Activities and Linking to Other Monitoring Efforts

Restoration actions rarely occur in complete isolation from a larger overall land or natural resource management action. Likewise, local monitoring should not occur in complete isolation from broad-scale monitoring efforts. It is important to know what land and natural resource management actions have occurred and will occur in, or affect, the project area, as well as what other monitoring efforts are ongoing or planned. This information may assist in determining the level of spatial and temporal replication needed or may provide the opportunity to examine multiple restoration actions. For example, if status and trend monitoring programs measure some of the same parameters as the effectiveness monitoring and validation monitoring of restoration projects, extrapolation or interpretation of restoration results to a broader scale may be possible. In addition, if there are ongoing broad-scale status and trend monitoring programs, there should be an existing database and a data framework that restoration monitoring feed into or use. Coordinating restoration activities with other nearby or potentially larger monitoring efforts will lead to greater efficiency in data collection for restoration monitoring.

Knowledge of additional land management or restoration actions planned or underway in the same watershed can influence study design, implementation of restoration actions, and development of monitoring. Land uses and management actions can positively or negatively impact their target biota, confounding the analysis and detection of a single restoration project in a sea of uncoordinated manipulations. While this issue may be resolved with extensive coordination and communication, given the multiple land ownerships and jurisdictions within most watersheds, it is rare that an entire watershed has a regional-scale management plan that includes all actions, restorative or not, and a means for measuring and evaluating these actions. Due to the potential for the unintended consequences of interactions between management activities in different parts of a watershed, the tracking, evaluation, and assessment of projects should be coordinated on a regional or watershed scale. Coordination of this nature, while challenging, allows data to be managed in a manner that facilitates their integration into resource management plans and individual project designs.

Often, many different types of restoration actions occur within a watershed or subwatershed or even stream reach. Actions may occur simultaneously, such as riparian planting and placement of instream structures, or actions may occur sequentially, such as reconnection of isolated habitats before restoration of roads and riparian areas. In addition, some large restoration efforts, such as endangered Atlantic or Pacific salmon species recovery efforts, cover entire basins or states or ecoregions. For example, the Oregon Watershed Enhancement Board has been funding stream and watershed restoration projects throughout the state of Oregon, including multiple project types within an individual basin. The Deschutes River basin provides a good example, where more than a million dollars were spent on road, fish passage, instream, and other types of restoration between 1995 and 2001 (Figure 5). Evaluating the effects of these individual actions requires determining the localized or reach-scale effects of individual actions, the effects of individual actions on the entire watershed, and the effects of all actions together on watershed-scale conditions. Given the number of different actions going on in the basin, other than restoration, that potentially influence physical and biological conditions, this is no small order. The challenge has rarely been attempted because it requires a high level of funding and coordination in both implementation and monitoring of restoration actions.

Regional, statewide, or basinwide monitoring programs provide broad-scale status and trend monitoring programs. Examples include the PACFISH program on federal lands in the interior Columbia River basin or the Northwest Forest Plan Riparian and Aquatic Monitoring Program in the coastal Pacific Northwest; statewide water-quality monitoring plans, such as those of the Delaware, Minnesota, Oregon; and others that use the EMAP probabilistic sampling method (information available at <http://www.epa.gov/NHEERL/arm/index.htm>). While the EMAP and similar approaches can be applied at a regional, state, or watershed level, these monitoring programs initially were not designed to determine the effect of numerous restoration activities within a watershed or basin but to determine regional water quality and aquatic integrity.

The application of EMAP-type probabilistic sampling, coupled with evaluation of restoration actions is being attempted in a few states and areas. For example, to assess the practicality of linking watershed-scale status monitoring and trend monitoring with project-level restoration effectiveness monitoring, pilot projects are underway in the John Day and Wenatchee Rivers subbasins within the Columbia River basin. One of the chal-

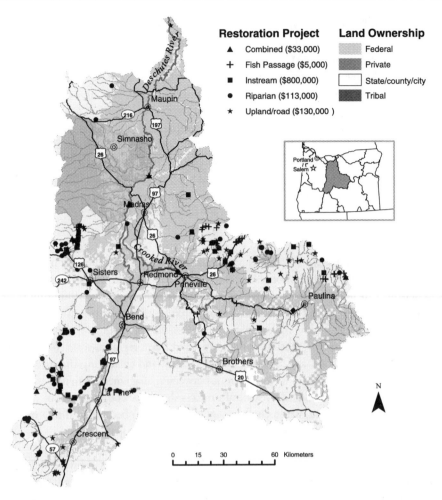

Figure 5.
An example of multiple restoration actions implemented between 1995 and 2001 in the Deschutes River basin in eastern Oregon. Total basin area is 2,787,000 ha (6,886,142 acres). Combined actions represent several activities occurring at one location. (Data provided by Oregon Watershed Enhancement Board, Salem, Oregon; figure courtesy of Jeff Cowen, NOAA, Seattle).

lenges is determining whether spatially representative status and trend data can be linked up with the non-randomly distributed restoration monitoring. The pilot project aims to address this and many logistic and coordination issues by generating a single nested monitoring program that integrates spatial scales of single actions to watersheds efforts (C. Jordan, Northwest Fisheries Science Center, Seattle, personal communication). Another example is the Northwest Forest Plan, which covers most federal lands in northwest California and western Oregon and Washington. The challenge of these programs is to coordinate and combine regional status monitoring and trend monitoring with project-level monitoring. Ringold et al. (2003) propose a similar approach to that being conducted in the John Day and Wenatchee example above: by using both randomly selected sites for status monitoring and selecting another set of sites for monitoring federal land management plans such as the Northwest Forest Plan. The results of these and other new programs will provide great insight into our ability both to design monitoring and to link together individual and multiple restoration projects across watersheds and regions.

Sampling Schemes

In conjunction with selecting appropriate monitoring parameters and determining how long and how many sites to monitor, one needs to determine the methods and spatial allocation of sampling within a site or study area. If the site is a short reach in a small stream, one may survey the entire reach (a census); however, often, the size of the site or study area precludes a census. For example, to survey eel grass *Zostera marina* density after large scale restoration projects in multiple estuaries, it might be impractical to measure density everywhere. Instead, a sampling strategy (scheme) would be necessary, in which case, you would need to decide whether to collect multiple random samples from each site, stratify your samples by depth or another factor, or use some other form of sampling.

Common sampling methods include simple random sampling, stratified random sampling, systematic sampling, cluster sampling, multistage sampling, double sampling, line transects, and capture–recapture (Thompson 1992; Buckland et al. 2001). Downes et al. (2002), for example, discusses a two-stage sampling approach, where the study site is broken into a grid, and simple random sampling is used within each square of the grid. This assures adequate dispersion of samples over the site (i.e., spatial balance), while avoiding some of the potential pitfalls of a completely systematic sample. However, no one sampling design is best for all situations. The optimal sampling strategy will depend on factors such as the spatial distribution of the organism and the logistics of moving between locations and collecting samples or observing the organism. Several methods or sampling schemes exist for spacing samples within a study area—there are pros and cons for each (Table 4; Conquest and Ralph 1998).

Up until now, we have not directly discussed the effects of cost on monitoring and sampling design. Cost will often make it impossible to conduct a complete census of the study areas and will necessitate the use of one of the alternative sampling schemes described in Table 4. Considering the cost also emphasizes the need to prioritize what parameters to monitor (Kershner 1997). If unlimited funding is available, then one might sample the entire study location for all the parameters of interest. However, financial constraints prevent the sampling of all locations, prevent the collection of all parameters, and limit the duration of the monitoring program (see previous discussion on spatial and temporal replication). Therefore, developing a list of which parameters are most important and how much it will cost to collect various parameters by using different experimental and sampling methods will help resource managers allocate monitoring resources. This also will assist the project manager in determining what and which sites to monitor should funding fluctuate from year to year. Complete cost estimates of a monitoring program need to include not only cost of collecting and processing samples but costs of planning, quality assurance, data management, data analysis and interpretation, report preparation, and presentation.

Data Management and Quality Assurance

An often overlooked part of a monitoring and evaluation program is data management, and quality control and assurance. Data acquisition and management are key parts of any monitoring program, large or small (Conquest and Ralph 1998). This includes determining both how the data will be entered and stored in a database, making sure that the database is consistent with the field forms and making sure that field crews are

---

Table 4.
Common methods for collecting samples (sampling schemes) within study sites.

Type of sampling	Description
Census	All units are sampled.
Simple random	A subset of randomly selected units are sampled within the study location in such a way that each subunit has an equal chance of being selected.
Systematic	An initial unit (or units) is chosen randomly and then every kth unit (starting from that unit) is sampled.
Stratified random	The units are broken into strata (categories) based on other available covariates (variables) such as geology, gradient, channel type, etc. Random sampling then occurs in each strata.
Multistage	Sampling units are selected and then the selected units are further divided into units and a subset of those units sampled.
Double sampling	Two samples are collected. For the first, only auxiliary data is collected, while in the second, both the auxiliary data and parameter of interest are collected.
Line transect	An observer walks and makes observation along a predetermined line.

properly trained and collect data consistently. Considerable error can be added to a sampling program because of observer error (Pool et al. 1997; Kaufman et al. 1999; Dunham et al. 2001). Thus, training field crews in both how data are collected and why it is being collected are critical. Periodic follow-up with field crews is often necessary to assure that data continue to be collected consistently within and among crews (Conquest et al. 1994).

Obviously, advances in computer technology have made collection and storing large amounts of data much easier, but they require consistency in data collection and recording. Tools such as electronic measuring boards, flow meters, data loggers, and computer clipboards can greatly simplify entering data into a database, because the data usually can be downloaded directly to a computer. However, this also requires that field crews are trained to use these tools. Regardless of the level of technology used to collect and enter monitoring data, training, quality assurance, and data management are all critical components of a well-designed monitoring program.

Data Analysis

The statistical methods used to analyze data collected from effectiveness monitoring and validation monitoring should, in large part, be based on the monitoring design, the parameters selected, and the data collected. A detailed description of statistical analyses and models is beyond the scope of this book. There are a number of common univariate and multivariate statistical approaches that can be used to test hypotheses regarding restoration activities (Table 5). For example, paired treatment and reference reaches or watersheds used in posttreatment designs are well suited to paired t tests to examine mean differences and linear regression to relate differences in response variables among sites with other parameters measured. Several different analysis of variance (ANOVA) models for comparing data can be applied to BACI designs. As mentioned previously, there is considerable debate over which model is most appropriate and whether statistical models should even be used to analyze data for simple BACI designs. Downes et al. (2002), McDonald et al. (2000), Conquest (2000), and Murtaugh (2000) provide discussions of the recent approaches to analyzing data from BACI designs.

It is important, however, to consider, before collection, how the data should be analyzed and what statistical tests should be used. If those designing the monitoring program are not intricately familiar with statistics, statistical analyses, and statistical design consideration, a statistician should be consulted early in the design process to assist with data analysis.

Statistical analysis, including sample size and power estimates, typically are done with an α of 0.05 (the probability of rejecting when the null hypothesis is true) and power ($1 - \beta$, the probability of rejecting for a given effect size) of 0.80. In research directed at basic ecological theory, scientists have the luxury of a conservative approach where strong evidence is required for general acceptance of a result. In the context of monitoring, however, the cost of inaction due to an incorrect nonsignificant result may be relatively high. This suggests accepting a higher risk of a false rejection (i.e., a larger α value) to increase the probability of detecting an effect if there is one (i.e., higher power; e.g., Gibbs et al. 1998). In fact, as discussed earlier, in many cases, it may be more appropriate to forgo statistical testing and instead resort to graphical analysis of the data (Kershner 1997; Conquest and Ralph 1998; Conquest 2000).

Reporting Monitoring Results

If we are to learn from restoration activities, we must adhere to the basic principles of the scientific method (Minns et al. 1996) and report our findings to both the scientific community and the general public. This requires defining and testing clear hypotheses; appropriate study designs; identification of relevant indicators; and collecting, analyzing, and interpreting data. Scant information on responses to aquatic restoration actions exists in the literature. If collected at all, most information typically is inaccessible or published as gray literature. This may be due, in part, to the lack of time and funds for practitioners to complete their studies or, perhaps, concerns about being embarrassed by reporting their failures (Frissell and Ralph 1998). Regardless of whether a project is deemed a success or a failure, it is important to report the findings and make them available to the scientific community and interested citizens. In fact, given the money spent on and attention paid to restoration actions, it is arguably more important to report failed efforts than the successes. The cliché that we often learn more from our failures than successes is especially true in restoration ecology.

Table 5.
Commonly used statistical tools for stream and river data. Modified from Conquest and Ralph (1998) with permission.

Statistical test/tools	Use	Assumptions	Remarks
Parametric tests (t-tests, confidence intervals, analysis of variance, tests on variances)	Estimation or comparison of means and variances	Normal distribution, equal variances, independent observations	Most powerful to detect changes when assumptions met
Regression and correlation	Linear association, prediction	Independent sampling points, normal distribution	More advanced techniques available for correlated sampling points, comparing regression equations, or non-linear relationships
Nonparametric tests (Mann-Whitney test Wilcoxon paired rank test, Kruskal-Wallis analysis of variance)	Comparison of means without relying on assumption of normal distribution	Independent observations, equal shapes of distributions	Not as powerful as parametric tests, particularly for small sample sizes
Bootstrap techniques	Confidence intervals and parameter estimation (distribution free)	Independent observations	Computer-intensive technique
Multivariate techniques (cluster analysis, principle components analysis, factor analysis, discriminant analysis)	Grouping of sampling units or responses	Normal distribution for any testing	Useful in classification schemes
Multivariate permutation procedures	Nonparametric, multivariate group comparisons	Independent samples	Mann-Whitney test and Kruskal-Wallis test are special cases
Exploratory data analysis (Histograms, box plots, bar, pie, and other charts)	Data display only, no testing	None	Very useful for data visualization interpretation
Geographic information system	Management and display of spatial data	All data require spatial coordinate information (i.e., latitude/longitude or equivalent) from maps, aerial photos, or ground-truthing	Can integrate data from a variety of sources and statistical results to map

Communicating the results of costly restoration actions and equally costly monitoring activities to regulators and to decision and policy makers is critical to affect a change in ecological restoration and management. Effective communication requires reporting results in a format easily interpreted by the audience. Policy makers often find graphical displays and analyses easier to interpret than the statistical analyses favored by scientists and technical experts (Kershner 1997). Some combination of the two is most effective to convey results to a broad interdisciplinary audience, and results also can be made readily available to a very broad audience on the Internet.

Summary

We have outlined and discussed the key steps and issues that need to be followed and addressed when designing a program to monitor the effectiveness of various types of restoration activities. These include determining goals and objectives, defining key questions and hypotheses, as well as monitoring design and project scale, selecting monitoring parameters, determining the spatial and temporal replication and sampling schemes for parameters, and analyzing data and reporting results. While the details of these steps and issues will differ by the type or types of restoration, careful consideration and definition of them are critical for developing an effective monitoring program. Although we have outlined these steps sequentially, many are interwoven and may need to be addressed hand in hand. For example, selecting the monitoring parameters depends upon the hypotheses and scale of the project, and selecting the sampling scheme may effect which and how parameters are measured. Keep in mind that there is no one ideal question, design, sampling scheme, set of parameters, or method of analyses for all projects. These factors will depend upon the specifics of the project and upon addressing the important steps outlined above.

It also is important to try and link monitoring and evaluation of restoration activities to larger monitoring and evaluation programs both to assist in design of restoration monitoring and for evaluating multiple actions at multiple scales. Finally, the monitoring and evaluation of restoration provides information critical for adaptive management. Without analysis and publication of monitoring and evaluation efforts and feedback to decision makers (Figure 1), much of our effort to restore aquatic systems will be in vain, public interest in funding massive restoration efforts such as those for salmon and trout will decrease, and the profession of restoration ecology will lose credibility and support.

Acknowledgments

We thank Ed Quimby, Karrie Hanson, and three anonymous reviewers for helpful comments on earlier version of this manuscript. We would also like to thank Jeff Cowen of the Northwest Fisheries Science Center for assistance with graphics.

References

Avery, E. L. 2004. A Compendium of 58 trout stream habitat development evaluations in Wisconsin—1986-2000. Wisconsin Department of Natural Resources Research Report 187, Madison.

Bauer, S. B., and S. C. Ralph. 2001. Strengthening the use of aquatic habitat indicators in Clean Water Act programs. Fisheries 26:14-24.

Beschta, R. L., W.S. Platts, J. B. Kauffman, and T.M. Hill. 1994. Artificial stream restoration-money well spent or expensive failure? Pages 76-104 in UCOWR, editor. Proceedings of Environmental Restoration, UCOWR 1994 Annual Meeting, Big Sky, Montana. University Council on Water Resources, University of Illinois, Carbondale.

Binns, N. A. 1999. A compendium of trout stream habitat improvement projects done by the Wyoming Game and Fish Department, 1953-1998. Fish Division, Wyoming Game and Fish Department, Cheyenne.

Bisson, P. A., G. H. Reeves, R. E. Bilby, and R. J. Naiman. 1997. Watershed management and Pacific salmon: desired future conditions. Pages 447-474 in D. J. Stouder, P. A. Bisson, and R. J. Naiman. Pacific salmon and their ecosystems. Chapman and Hall, New York.

Bryant, M. D. 1995. Pulsed monitoring for watershed and stream restoration. Fisheries 20(11):6-13.

Buckland, S. T., D. R. Anderson, K. P. Burnham, J. L. Laake, D. L. Borchers, and L. Thomas. 2001. Introduction to distance sampling: estimating abundance of biological populations. Oxford University Press, Oxford, UK.

Caughley, G. 1994. Directions in conservation biology. Journal of Animal Ecology 63:215-244.

Cederholm, C. J., R. E. Bilby, P. A. Bisson, T. W. Bumstead, B. R. Fransen, W. J. Scarlett, and J. W. Ward. 1997. Response of juvenile coho salmon and steelhead to placement of large woody debris in a coastal Washington stream. North American Journal of Fisheries Management 17:947-963.

Chapman, D. W. 1996. Efficacy of structural manipulations of instream habitat in the Columbia River Basin. Northwest Science 5(4):279-293.

Collins, B. D., and D. R. Montgomery. 2001. Importance of archival and process studies to characterizing presettlement riverine geomorphic processes and habitat in the Puget Lowland. Pages 227-246 in J.M. Dorava, D. R. Montgomery, B. B. Palcsak, and F. A. Fitzpatrick, editors. Geomorphic processes and riverine habitat. American Geophysical Union, Washington, D.C.

Conquest, L. L., and S. C. Ralph. 1998. Statistical design and analysis for monitoring and assessment. Pages 455-475 in R. J. Naiman and R. E. Bilby, editors. River ecology and management: lessons from the Pacific coastal ecoregion. Springer, New York.

Conquest, L. L. 2000. Analysis and interpretation of ecological field data using BACI designs: discussion. Journal of Agricultural, Biological, and Environmental Statistics 5:293-296.

Conquest, L. L., S. C. Ralph, and R. J. Naiman. 1994. Implementation of large-scale stream monitoring efforts: sampling design and data analysis issues. Pages 69-90 in S. L. Loeb and A. Spacie, editors. Biological monitoring of aquatic ecosystems. Lewis Publishing, Boca Raton, Florida.

Downes, B.J., L. A. Barmuta, P. G. Fairweather, D. P. Faith, M. J. Keough, P. S. Lake, B. D. Mapstone, and G. P. Quinn. 2002. Monitoring ecological impacts: concepts and practice in flowing waters. Cambridge University Press, Cambridge, UK.

Dunham, J., B. Rieman, and K. Davis. 2001. Sources and magnitude of sampling error in redd counts for bull trout. North American Journal of Fisheries Management 21:343-352.

Frissell, C. A., and S. C. Ralph. 1998. Stream and watershed restoration. Pages 599-624 in R. J. Naiman, and R. E. Bilby, editors. River ecology and management: lessons from the Pacific Coastal Ecoregion. Springer, New York.

Gibbs, J. P., D. Sam, and P. Eagle. 1998. Monitoring populations of plants and animals. BioScience 48:935-940.

Grant, J. W. A., J. Englert, and B. F. Bietz. 1986. Application of a method for assessing the impact of watershed practices: effects of logging on salmonid standing crops. North American Journal of Fisheries Management 6:24-31.

Green, R. H. 1979. Sampling design and statistical methods for environmental biologists. John Wiley & Sons, New York.

Gurevitch, J., and L. V. Hedges. 2001. Meta-analysis: combining the results of independent experiments. Pages 347-370 in S. M. Scheiner and J. Gurevitch, editors. Design and analysis of ecological experiments. Oxford University Press, New York.

Hall, J. D., M. L. Murphy, and R. S. Aho. 1978. An improved design for assessing impacts of watershed practices on small streams. Internationale Vereinigung fur Theoretische und Angewandte Limnologie 20:1359-1365.

Ham, K. D., and T. N. Pearsons. 2000. Can reduced salmonid population abundance be detected in time to limit management impacts? Canadian Journal of Fisheries and Aquatic Sciences 57:17-24.

Hankin, D. G., and G. H. Reeves. 1988. Estimating total fish abundance and total habitat area in small streams based on visual estimation methods. Canadian Journal of Fisheries and Aquatic Sciences 45:834-844.

Hawkins, C. P., M. L. Murphy, N. H. Anderson, and M. A. Wilzbach. 1983. Density of fish and salamanders in relation to riparian canopy and physical habitat in streams of the northwestern United States. Canadian Journal of Fisheries and Aquatic Sciences 40:1173-1185.

Hicks, B. J., J. D. Hall, P. A. Bisson, and J. R. Sedell. 1991. Responses of salmonids to habitat changes. Pages 483-518 in W. R. Meehan, editor. Influences of forest and rangeland management on salmonid fishes and their habitats. American Fisheries Society, Special Publication 19, Bethesda, Maryland.

Hilborn, R., and C. J. Walters. 1981. Pitfalls of environmental baseline and process studies. Environmental Impact Assessment Review 2:265-278.

House, R., V. Crispin, and R. Monthey. 1989. Evaluation of stream rehabilitation projects-Salem District (1981-1988). U.S. Bureau of Land Management, Technical Note T/N OR-6, Portland, Oregon.

Hurlbert, S. H. 1984. Pseudoreplication and the design of ecological field experiments. Ecological Management 54:187-211.

Hunt, R. L. 1988. A compendium of 45 trout stream habitat development evaluations in Wisconsin during 1953-1985. Wisconsin Department of Natural Resources, Technical Bulletin 162, Madison.

Johnson, S. W., and H. J. Heifetz. 1985. Methods for assessing effects of timber harvest on small streams. U.S. Department of Commerce NOAA Technical Memorandum NMFS F/NWC-73, Auke Bay, Alaska.

Kaufmann, P. R., P. Levine, E. G. Robison, C. Seeliger, and D. V. Peck. 1999. Quantifying physical habitat in wadeable streams. U.S. Environmental Protection Agency, EPA/620/R-99/003, Washington, D.C.

Kershner, J. L. 1997. Monitoring and adaptive management. Pages 116-131 in J. E. Williams, C. A. Wood, and M. P. Dombeck, editors. Watershed restoration: principles and practices. American Fisheries Society, Bethesda, Maryland.

Korman, J., and P. S. Higgins. 1997. Utility of escapement time series data for monitoring the response of salmon populations to habitat alteration. Canadian Journal of Fisheries and Aquatic Sciences 54:2058-2067.

Kurtz, J. C., L. E. Jackson, and W. S. Fisher. 2001. Strategies for evaluating indicators based on guidelines from the EPA's Office of Research and Development. Ecological Indicators 1:49-60.

Larsen, D. P., T. M. Kincaid, S. E. Jacobs, and N. S. Urquhart. 2001. Designs for evaluating local and regional scale trends. BioScience 51(12):1069-1078.

Lichatowich, J., and S. Cramer. 1979. Parameter selection and sample size in studies of anadromous salmonids. Oregon Department of Fish and Wildlife, Information Report Series, Fisheries Number 80-1, Salem.

MacDonald, L. H., A. W. Smart, and R. C. Wissmar. 1991. Monitoring guidelines to evaluate effects of forestry activities on streams in the Pacific Northwest and Alaska. U.S. Environmental Protection Agency, Region 10, NPS Section, Seattle.

McCubbing, D. J. F., and B. R. Ward. 2002. The Keogh and Waukwaas rivers paired watershed study for B.C.'s Watershed Restoration Program juvenile salmonid abundance and growth. American Fisheries Society, Canadian Aquatic Resources Section, Bethesda, Maryland.

McDonald, T. L., W. P. Erickson, and L. L. McDonald. 2000. Analysis of count data from before-after control-impact studies. Journal of Agricultural, Biological, and Environmental Statistics 5(3):262-279.

Minns, C. K., J. R. M. Kelso, and R. G. Randall. 1996. Detecting the response of fish to habitat alterations in freshwater ecosystems. Canadian Journal of Fisheries and Aquatic Sciences 53:403-414.

Murphy, M. L., and J. D. Hall. 1981. Varied effects of clear-cut logging on predators and their habitat in small streams of the Cascade Mountains, Oregon. Canadian Journal of Fisheries and Aquatic Sciences 38:137-145.

Murtaugh, P. A. 2000. Paired intervention analysis. Journal of Agricultural, Biological, and Environmental Statistics 5:280-292.

NRC (National Research Council). 1992. Restoration of aquatic ecosystems. National Academy Press, Washington, D.C.

Osenberg, C. W., R. J. Schmitt, S. J. Holbrook, K. E. Agu-Saba, and R. Flegal. 1994. Detection of environmental impacts: natural variability, effect size, and power analysis. Ecological Applications 4:16-30.

Poole, G. C., C. A. Frissell, and S. C. Ralph. 1997. In-stream habitat unit classification: inadequacies for monitoring and some consequences for management. Journal of the American Water Resources Association 33:879–896.

Ralph, S. C., G. C. Poole, L. L. Conquest, and R. J. Naiman. 1994. Stream channel morphology and woody debris in logged and unlogged basins in western Washington. Canadian Journal of Fisheries and Aquatic Sciences 51:37–51.

Reeves, G. H., L. E. Benda, K. M. Burnett, P. A. Bisson, and J. R. Sedell. 1995. A disturbance-based approach to maintaining and restoring freshwater habitats of evolutionary significant units of anadromous salmonids in the Pacific Northwest. Pages 334–349 in J. L. Nielsen, editor. Evolution and the aquatic ecosystem: defining unique units in population conservation. American Fisheries Society, Symposium 17, Bethesda, Maryland.

Reeves, G. H., and T. D. Roelefs. 1982. Rehabilitating and enhancing stream habitat: 2 field applications. U.S. Forest Service, Pacific Northwest Research Station, General Technical Report PNW-140, Portland, Oregon.

Reeves, G. H., F. H. Everest, and J. R. Sedell 1993. Diversity of juvenile anadromous salmonid assemblages in coastal Oregon basins with different levels of timber harvest. Transactions of the American Fisheries Society 122:309–317.

Reeves, G. H., J. D. Hall, T. D. Roelofs, T. L. Hickman, and C. O. Baker. 1991. Rehabilitating and modifying stream habitats. Pages 519–557 in W. R. Meehan, editor. Influences of forest and rangeland management on salmonid fishes and their habitats. American Fisheries Society, Special Publication 19, Bethesda, Maryland.

Reeves, G. H., D. B. Hohler, B. E. Hansen, F. H. Everest, J. R. Sedell, T. L. Hickman, and D. Shively. 1997. Fish habitat restoration in the Pacific Northwest: Fish Creek of Oregon. Pages 335–359 in J. E. Williams, C. A. Wood, and M. P. Dombeck, editors. Watershed restoration: principles and practices. American Fisheries Society, Bethesda, Maryland.

Ringold, P. L., B. Mulder, J. Alegria, R. L. Czaplewski, T. Tolle, and K. Burnett. 2003. Design of an ecological monitoring strategy for the forest plan in the Pacific Northwest. Pages 73–99 in D. E. Busch and J. C. Trexel, editors. Monitoring ecosystems: interdisciplinary approaches for evaluating ecoregional initiatives. Island Press, Washington, D.C.

Roni, P., T. J. Beechie, R. E., Bilby, F. E. Leonetti, M. M. Pollock, and G. P. Pess. 2002. A review of stream restoration techniques and a hierarchical strategy for prioritizing restoration in Pacific Northwest watersheds. North American Journal of Fisheries Management 22:1–20.

Roni, P., M. Liermann, and A. Steel. 2003. Monitoring and evaluating responses of salmonids and other fishes to instream restoration. Pages 318–329 in D. R. Montgomery, S. Bolton, and D. B. Booth, editors. Restoration of Puget Sound rivers. University of Washington Press, Seattle.

Roni, P., and T. P. Quinn. 2001. Density and size of juvenile salmonids in response to placement of large woody debris in western Washington and Oregon streams. Canadian Journal of Fisheries and Aquatic Sciences 58:282–292.

Rosgen, D. 1996. Applied river morphology. Wildland Hydrology, Pagosa Springs, Colorado.

Slaney, P. A., B. O. Rublee, C. J. Perrin, and H. Goldberg. 1994. Debris structure placements and whole-river fertilization for salmonids in a large regulated stream in British Columbia. Bulletin of Marine Science 55:1160–1180.

Smith, P. E., D. R. Orvos, and J. Cairns. 1993. Impact assessment using the before-after-control-impact (BACI) model: concerns and comments. Canadian Journal of Fisheries and Aquatic Sciences 50:627–637.

Sokal, R. R., and F. J. Rohlf. 1995. Biometry: the principles and practice of statistics in biological research. W. H. Freeman, New York.

Solazzi, M. F., T. E. Nickelson, S. L. Johnson, and J. D. Rodgers. 2000. Effects of increasing winter rearing habitat on abundance of salmonids in two coastal Oregon streams. Canadian Journal of Fisheries and Aquatic Sciences 57:906–914.

Stewart-Oaten, A., W. W. Murdoch, and K. R. Parker. 1986. Environmental impact assessment: "pseudoreplication" in time? Ecology 67:929–940.

Tarzwell, C. M. 1934. Stream improvement methods. U.S. Bureau of Fisheries Division of Scientific Inquiry, Ogden, Utah.

Thompson, S. K. 1992. Sampling. John Wiley & Sons, New York.

Underwood, A. J. 1994. On beyond BACI: sampling designs that might reliably detect environmental disturbances. Ecological Applications 4:3–15.

Underwood, A. J. 1997. Experiments in ecology; their logical design and interpretation using analysis of variance. Cambridge University Press, New York.

Urquhart, N. S., and T. M. Kincaid. 1999. Designs for detecting trend from repeated surveys of ecological resources. Journal of Agricultural, Biological, and Environmental Statistics 4:404–414.

Walters, C. J. 1986. Adaptive management of renewable resources. Macmillan Publishing, New York.

Walters, C. J., J. S. Collie, and T. Webb. 1988. Experimental designs for estimating transient responses to management disturbances. Canadian Journal of Fisheries and Aquatic Sciences 45:530–538.

White, R. J. 2002. Restoring streams for salmonids: Where have we been? Where are we going? Pages 1–33 in M. O'Grady, editor. Proceedings of the 13th International Salmonid Habitat Enhancement Workshop, Westport, County Mayo, Ireland. Central Fisheries Board, Dublin, Ireland.

Zar, J. H. 1999. Biostatistical analysis. Prentice Hall, Upper Saddle River, New Jersey.

Chapter 3
Monitoring Treatments to Reduce Sediment and Hydrologic Effects from Roads

Timothy J. Beechie

Northwest Fisheries Science Center, National Marine Fisheries Service
2725 Montlake Boulevard East, Seattle, Washington 98112, USA
tim.beechie@noaa.gov

Curt N. Veldhuisen, Eric M. Beamer

Skagit System Cooperative, 25944 Community Plaza Way, Sedro Woolley, Washington 98284, USA
cveldhuisen@skagitcoop.org, ebeamer@skagitcoop.org

Dave E. Schuett-Hames, Robert H. Conrad

Northwest Indian Fisheries Commission, 6730 Martin Way, Olympia, Washington 98516, USA
dschuett@nwifc.org, bconrad@nwifc.wa.gov

Paul DeVries

R2 Resource Consultants, 15250 NE 95th Street, Redmond, Washington 98052, USA
pdevries@r2usa.com

Introduction

Roads alter hydrologic regimes (Harr et al. 1975; King and Tennyson 1984; LaMarche and Lettenmaier 2001) and sediment supply to streams (e.g., Sidle et al. 1985), which influence channel and habitat characteristics (e.g., Cederholm et al. 1982; Tripp and Poulin 1986a, 1986b; Hicks et al. 1991) and ultimately impact aquatic biota (Waters 1995). Road drainage connections to stream channels (e.g., ditches draining to streams) can alter the amount and the timing of water delivery to streams, as well as the delivery of sediment eroded from hillslopes or road surfaces (Croke and Mockler 2001; Madej 2001). Roads also alter sediment supply through increased frequency of landsliding (Dyrness 1967; Megahan and Kidd 1972; O'Loughlin 1974; Sidle et al. 1985) and increased surface erosion (Packer 1967; Reid and Dunne 1984; Bilby et al. 1989). Actions to reduce sediment delivery from roads can address any of these processes, with the intent of reducing sediment supply to streams and quantities of sediment in channels or in the water column (e.g., Kochenderfer and Helvey 1987; Furniss et al. 1991; Madej 2001). Those actions, however, will require vigorous monitoring to determine their effectiveness.

Throughout this chapter, we distinguish between, and focus on, two basic categories of monitoring for road improvements: effectiveness monitoring and validation monitoring. Effectiveness monitoring evaluates whether actions achieved the desired effect on watershed processes, and validation monitoring evaluates whether hypotheses about the cause-and-effect relationship between the management action and channel, habitat, and biotic responses were correct (MacDonald et al. 1991; USFS and BLM 1994). The distinction between these two types of monitoring is particularly useful for examining road treatments. Monitoring the effectiveness of road improvements involves measuring how well specific actions control the impact of roads on stream discharge or sediment supply to stream channels (e.g., Reid et al. 1981; Madej 2001). Validation monitoring measures resultant responses of stream channels, fish habitat, and biota (e.g., MacDonald et al. 1991), and attempts to elucidate cause-and-effect linkages among them. Several guidelines for determining what and how to monitor have been published recently (e.g., MacDonald et al. 1991), but there has been little treatment of how to predict outcomes of road improvement measures (i.e., identifying the right questions to answer and developing testable hypotheses) or how to design a monitoring program capable of detecting changes in both supply of sediment to streams and the response of channel morphology and fish habitat to altered sediment supply (Reid 2001).

In this chapter, we first review effects of forest roads on streams and common techniques (treatments) for reducing effects of roads on sediment supply and stream hydrology. We then discuss monitoring design for evaluating road improvements, including identification of project goals and monitoring hypotheses, experimental design and monitoring frequency and duration, and selecting study areas. Finally, we describe monitoring parameters and techniques for sediment supply and hydrology (effectiveness monitoring) and channel, habitat, and biological responses (validation monitoring). We do not discuss changes in sediment transport rates, which are extensively treated in Bunte and MacDonald (1999). We only briefly mention monitoring of biota, which is discussed more thoroughly in subsequent chapters.

Background

To devise appropriate monitoring programs for the reduction of erosion and hydrologic effects from forest roads, it is important to understand (1) how forest roads affect supply and routing of sediment and water; (2) how these changes affect channel morphology, aquatic habitat, and biota; and (3) how common techniques for treating landsliding and surface erosion on roads are likely to alter delivery of sediment and water or downstream conditions. In this subsection, we provide a brief background on each of these elements, focusing on physical processes of sediment supply, sediment routing in channels, and the resultant morphological and biological responses in streams. We especially focus on the episodic nature of storms, flooding, and sediment supply, and the problems these present in measuring the relative contribution of roads to flooding or erosion problems. We also describe important time lags (especially with sediment transport to downstream responses reaches) that inhibit our ability to link the results of channel, habitat, or biological monitoring to road treatments.

Road Effects on Sediment Supply and Hydrology

Three main groups of morphological processes deliver sediment from hill slopes to streams: mass wasting (e.g., landsliding), surface erosion (e.g., rainsplash, sheetwash, rilling, and gullying), and soil creep (Dunne and Leopold 1978; see Figure 1). Of these processes, roads influence mass wasting and surface erosion (Figure 2) but, generally, not soil creep. Erosion of road fills around culverts and channel bed or bank erosion downstream of culverts perhaps are best described as intermediate between mass wasting and gully erosion (Knighton 1998) and also are influenced by roads. For the purposes of this chapter, we include these erosion processes under the term gullying, because monitoring designs and techniques are similar between the two.

Mass wasting is the most episodic of the erosion processes, as landslides typically occur during relatively large rainstorms (Rice 1982) and only a small fraction of potential failure sites actually fail during any one storm (Benda and Dunne 1997a). Among the various surface erosion processes, gullying also is episodic, with most erosion also occurring during large storms (Wemple et al. 2001; Croke and Mockler 2001). Surface erosion on bare soils and road surfaces is more predictable, occurring during virtually all rainstorms and snowmelt periods, and the severity of erosion varies with runoff, soil type, and traffic level (Reid and Dunne 1984; Luce and Black 1999). The relative magnitude of each of these processes varies with topography, lithology, and other landscape factors (Gucinski et al. 2000). For example, in mountainous regions, all three processes (mass wasting, surface erosion, and soil creep) are active, whereas surface erosion processes tend to dominate in relatively flat or dry watersheds.

Mass wasting is a dominant process of sediment supply in mountainous regions throughout the world (Bergstrom 1982; Eschner and Patric 1982; Sidle et al. 1985; Roberts and Church 1986), and roads can

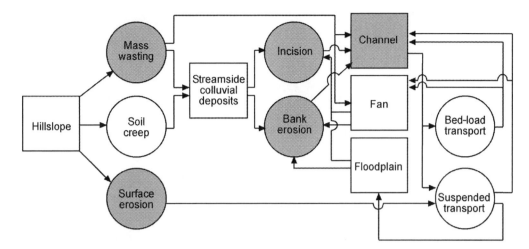

Figure 1.
Simplified schematic diagram of supply and routing processes (circles) that transfer sediment through various sediment storage locations (boxes) in a watershed. Gray circles indicate the hillslope processes altered by roads (mass wasting and surface erosion), as well as channel processes altered by increased discharge from hydrologically connected roads (incision and bank erosion). Surface erosion includes rilling and gullying, along with rainsplash and sheetwash processes. Gray box (channel) indicates the storage location in which we usually attempt to detect effects of altered sediment supply on fish habitat.

increase mass wasting rates by 30–340 times the rate from unroaded areas (Sidle et al. 1985). Mechanisms of road failure include sliding of oversteepened cut and fill slopes (Sidle et al. 1985), collapse of road prisms built upon decaying buried woody debris, saturation of road fills due to interception of springs and seeps or misdirected drainage, and blocked culverts and subsequent failure of stream crossing fills. Roads also can indirectly cause landslides downslope of the road location by concentrating water into areas prone to mass wasting (Sidle et al. 1985; Montgomery 1994). Both new and old roads cause landslides (Harr and Nichols 1993), but failure rates may decrease with road age (Reid and Dunne 1996; Fransen et al. 2001). Although most current road designs attempt to avoid such problems, road failures remain relatively common due to planning errors, poor maintenance, and uncorrected shortcomings of older roads (Robison et al. 1999).

Sediment supply from surface erosion of unpaved roads typically is much lower than from road-related mass wasting in mountainous terrain (Fransen et al. 2001; Wemple et al. 2001). Nonetheless, surface erosion can still substantially increase sediment supply (Reid et al. 1981; Montgomery 1994; Croke and Mockler 2001; Madej 2001). Erosion on cut and fill slopes is primarily a function of slope angle, slope length, slope aspect, vegetative cover, rainfall, and road age (Megahan et al. 2001). Erosion of running surfaces is primarily a function of storm intensity, surfacing material, road slope, and traffic levels (Reid et al. 1981; Bilby et al. 1989; MacDonald et al. 2001; Ziegler et al. 2001). Roads commonly exacerbate gullying, where they accumulate and reroute subsurface flow onto unchanneled hillslopes or channels, or cause erosion around culverts (Montgomery 1994; Croke and Mockler 2001; Madej 2001; Nyssan et al. 2002). This may occur due to poor road drainage design (e.g., long distances between cross drains or routing multiple streams into one culvert) or, more commonly, due to temporary malfunctioning of road drainage features (e.g., plugged culvert or ditch) during intense runoff events (Furniss et al. 1991). For all types of surface erosion, sediment delivery to streams is through direct surface water connections such as ditches, rills, or gullies (Bilby et al. 1989; Croke and Mockler 2001).

Concerns about the hydrologic effects of forest roads have focused mainly on increases in peak streamflow rates below roaded watersheds (e.g., Harr et al. 1975; Jones and Grant 1996). The magnitude and importance of such flow changes varies considerably with drainage area (e.g., Jones and Grant 1996; Thomas and Megahan 1998; Beschta et al. 2000). There is general agreement that natural hillslope runoff processes are modified locally when roads divert runoff and shallow groundwater into roadside ditches (Megahan 1972), then into streams, either directly or via a gully or overland flow path (Wemple et al. 1996). Either case may trigger significant erosion (Dyrness 1967; Montgomery 1994; Madej 2001). The magnitude of change at the water-

Figure 2.
Figure 2. Roads produce sediment by both mass wasting and surface erosion processes. Examples of erosion mechanisms include surface erosion (A, B), failure of stream crossing fills (C, D) and sidecast failure (E, F). Gullying and channel enlargement downstream of culverts (not shown) are intermediate between surface erosion and mass wasting.

shed scale depends on the extent to which (1) runoff becomes more synchronized in arrival to key downstream reaches and (2) total runoff from the contributing watershed is modified. A recent watershed modeling effort suggested that road-related peak-flow increases can occur over a range of peak-flow sizes, including geomorphically significant peak flows of 2- to 10-year recurrence interval (LaMarche and Lettenmaier 2001). However, most empirical studies have only detected peak-flow increases for flow events of less than 1-year recurrence interval (Harr et al. 1975; King and Tennyson 1984; Wright et al. 1990; Beschta et al. 2000).

Channel, Habitat, and Biological Responses

Once sediment has entered the stream network, routing processes transfer sediment downstream. In steeper portions of the channel network (generally, channel slopes > 10%), debris flows episodically transfer large amounts of coarse sediment to lower slope channels, and bed-load transport processes account for a relatively small proportion of the long-term sediment transfer to higher-order streams (Benda and Dunne 1987,

1997a). In lower slope channels where fluvial processes dominate sediment movement (i.e., <10%), coarse sediment is transferred mainly through bed-load transport. Large volumes of bed-load sediment often move in wavelike forms or by dispersion (e.g., Nicholas et al. 1995; Madej and Ozaki 1996; Lisle et al. 2001), with annual travel distances of approximately 20 channel widths per year (Beechie 2001). Fine sediment is transferred as suspended load throughout the channel network and is stored in pools or in the bed between sediment transport events (Beschta 1987).

There often is a time lag of years to decades between a change in sediment supply and a change in morphology of a downstream reach (e.g., Kelsey 1982b; Madej and Ozaki 1996). This lag is due to the time required for sediment to travel from its source to the reach of interest (Kelsey 1982a). Once sediment enters a stream reach, its persistence is, to some extent, a function of the sediment transport capacity of the reach (Benda and Dunne 1997b). Therefore, both the timing and persistence of changes in the morphology of downstream reaches are related to the rate at which sediment moves through a channel network (Madej and Ozaki 1996).

In general, an increased supply of coarse sediments (gravel and larger, >2 mm diameter) in lower gradient reaches can cause fining of the bed surface (Dietrich et al. 1989), reduction of pool depth (Lisle 1982; Madej and Ozaki 1996), channel aggradation (Lisle 1982; Madej 1982), and channel widening (Kelsey 1982b; Madej 1982). Initial increases are accommodated by fining of the bed surface (Dietrich et al. 1989) and by deposition of finer sediments into pools (e.g., Lisle and Hilton 1992, 1999; Lisle and Madej 1992). Larger increases cause aggradation of the channel bed and channel widening (e.g., Lisle 1982; Madej 1982, 1992; Harvey 1987; Pitlick and Thorne 1987; Harvey 1991), and channels may become laterally unstable (Bergstrom 1982; Church 1983). As sediment moves through a reach, the proportion of sediment stored in bars increases rapidly, then decreases over a few years to a few decades (Lisle 1982; Madej 1987, 1992). Pool depths may begin to recover while sediment remains within the reach (Madej and Ozaki 1996) but typically do not fully recover until the sediment pulse passes through the reach (e.g., Lisle 1982; Collins et al. 1994).

Introduction of fine sediments (sand and smaller, <2 mm diameter) alters channel morphology and habitat by different mechanisms than coarse sediments. The smallest particles travel downstream as wash load, while larger particles may travel as bed load (Richards 1982). Suspended particles and fine bed load can accumulate in spaces between gravel particles (Beschta and Jackson 1979; Lisle 1989), restricting the subsurface movement of water through the gravel. Fine sediments also can fill pools and increase turbidity levels during runoff events.

Scour and fill depths may change as a result of changes in local streambed grain size distribution, stream flow, or sediment storage and transport within the monitored reach and upstream (DeVries 2000). Scour and fill measurements reflect two aspects of bed-load transport and storage: (1) the thickness of the bed that is in motion during bed-load transport (bed-load layer thickness) and (2) sediment transport rate imbalances that result in a net lowering or raising of the bed. At the scale of pool and riffle units, scour depth varies, depending on position in the channel (DeVries 2000; Schuett-Hames et al. 2000). Relatively shallow bed disturbance occurs in most areas of a riffle, because there is sufficient material available upstream in the same riffle to replace material transported downstream, so transport rate imbalances have little chance of developing. Deepest scour occurs within and around the margins of pools, where finer material is scoured out as flow strength increases, as well as in partially sheltered locations and transient riffle deposits (Lisle and Hilton 1999; DeVries 2000). Scour also occurs as a result of thalweg migration in meandering, anastomosing, and braided channels. At the reach scale, scour also can reflect the influence of sediment pulses, whereby longer term dispersion of bed-load material can result in a rise and fall of the bed surface elevation over several years (Nicholas et al. 1995; DeVries 2000; Lisle et al. 2001).

These channel and habitat changes have a variety of lethal and sublethal effects on aquatic biota (see also Waters 1995 for a broader review). Changes in supply of coarse sediments alter pool abundance and depth, which alter rates of primary productivity and invertebrate species compositions (Angradi 1999), as well as the quantity and quality of habitat for juvenile and adult salmonids (Tripp and Poulin 1986a; Reeves et al. 1989; Collins et al. 1994). Altered sediment supply and hydrology also may alter scour depth, which can decrease survival of salmonid embryos in spawning gravel (e.g., Tripp and Poulin 1986b). Increased peak flows may alter survival of salmonid embryos in redds or juveniles during freshwater rearing stages, although specific mechanisms of mortality remain undetermined (Beamer and Pess 1999; Spina 2001). Changes in channel geometry and lateral channel movements caused by increased coarse sediment supply also indirectly affect other habitat conditions, such as stream temperature or pool area (e.g., Collins et al. 1994).

A more extensive body of research documents the effects of fine sediments on aquatic organisms (e.g., see reviews by Chapman and McLeod 1987; Waters 1995; Wood and Armitage 1997). Suspended sediments in the water column can degrade water quality and affect aquatic organisms by impairing visibility needed to locate prey and by reducing primary production. Fine sediments that intrude into the gravel bed can reduce the survival of incubating salmonid eggs by decreasing the rate of water movement within redds, reducing the delivery of oxygen-bearing water, decreasing the removal of metabolic wastes, and blocking fry emergence when incubation is complete (Chapman and McLeod 1987).

Road Rehabilitation Techniques

Many techniques and strategies for modifying roads have been developed to reduce sediment delivery and hydrologic effects from roads. However, a broadly accepted terminology for road techniques and strategies is lacking, and various terms with overlapping meanings are used within various agencies and jurisdictions. For the purposes of this chapter, we use the term road technique to identify a single type of site-scale action and the term road treatment to identify a suite of techniques applied to a discrete road segment (Table 1).

For most objectives, a variety of road techniques are available to address the road-related causes of each geomorphic effect (Table 1). Where roads have initiated (or could initiate) significant mass wasting, remedial techniques typically are designed to stabilize soils (e.g., pull back sidecast) or control drainage along unstable portions of the roadway (e.g., remove culverts and fills). Other episodic erosion processes (e.g., gullying) also can be addressed by techniques that improve drainage control or reduce hydrologic connectivity (e.g., increase number of cross drains). Many drainage control techniques are based on a damage reduction strategy that reduces the erosion consequences from unpredictable occurrences (plugged culverts, debris flows) that occur during major runoff events. Projects designed to reduce surface erosion normally protect exposed soils (e.g., rock surfacing, revegetation of cut slopes) or reduce delivery road runoff to streams (Table 1). Modifying road drainage patterns so that most ditch runoff is diverted onto hillslopes rather than into streams (generally termed disconnection) can reduce hydrologic as well as sedimentation effects (Furniss et al. 2000).

Many road restoration projects target more than one of the key geomorphic processes and use more than one of the specific techniques listed in Table 1. Two general treatment types are distinguished by the degree to which vehicle access is modified. The first road treatment category provides continued vehicle access after treatment. Common terms for such treatments include road improvement, upgrading, and storm-proofing. Treated roads that remain accessible experience some level of ongoing surface erosion from traffic and maintenance activities. Although the remaining drainage structures present a continuing risk of erosion from drainage malfunctions, accessibility allows regular maintenance and inspections for erosion activity.

The second road treatment category eliminates vehicle access and encompasses treatments termed abandonment, decommissioning, deactivation, and obliteration. Road treatments that eliminate access typically result in lower erosion rates in the long term because the entire roadway, including the running surface, can revegetate after treatment. However, these benefits may not be entirely realized if deactivated roads receive ongoing use from off-road vehicles. Revegetation and loss of vehicle access makes field inspection and monitoring considerably more difficult than for treated roads that remain accessible.

Monitoring Design

Identification of Project Goals and Monitoring Hypotheses

The first step in developing a monitoring design for evaluating road treatments is to generate hypotheses of (1) how the proposed road treatments will alter sediment supply or hydrologic connectivity (for effectiveness monitoring) and (2) how those changes will affect channels, habitat, and aquatic biota (for validation monitoring). These hypotheses stem from some prior understanding of the problems that need to be addressed, as well as a clear understanding of the goals of road rehabilitation efforts (Table 2).

Table 1.
Overview of road-rehabilitation techniques commonly used to reduce sediment inputs and hydrologic effects.

General objective	Geomorphic process addressed	Site-scale objective	Techniques	Primarily used during[a]:
Stabilize road	Mass wasting	Remove unstable road material	Sidecast removal[b]	B
		Reinforce unstable material	Buttress toeslope[b]	I
			Retaining walls or other geotechnical approaches[b]	I
		Route water away from unstable material	Enhance road drainage control[b]	B
			Subsurface drain pipes or other drainage modifications[b]	I
Protect exposed soil	Surface erosion	Reduce traffic effects	Block vehicle entry with gate	I
			Block vehicle entry with barrier (boulders/tank traps)	D
		Armor running surface	Add rock surfacing to tread[c]	I
			Pave tread (Reid and Dunne 1984)	I
		Vegetate exposed soil surfaces	Seeding and planting[b]	B
			"Rip" (i.e., decompact) tread to improve growth of vegetation	D
		Armor exposed soil surfaces	Cover with rock or other resistant material[c]	B
			Cover with matting[c]	I
Disconnect road drainage from streams	Surface erosion and hydrologic change	Disconnect road runoff from stream	Add more cross drains (e.g., culverts, water bars) between streams (Furniss et al. 2000)	B
			Outslope tread[b]	B
		Filter sediment from road runoff before stream entry	Install settling ponds (Bilby et al. 1989)	I
			Install slash filter windrows[c]	B
Reduce drainage diversion	Surface erosion and mass wasting	Reduce fill erosion at stream crossings	Remove fill at crossing[b]	D
			Replace soil fill with rock or concrete[b]	I
			Armor fill surface with riprap	I
			Plant woody species on fill[b]	B
		Improve stream crossings to minimize potential for plugging or diversion	Replace undersized culverts with adequate structure	I
			Remove culvert or crossing structure (Madej 2001)	D
			Construct drainage dip or hump over structure	I
		Improve road drainage system between stream crossings	Reshape tread (e.g., inslope, crown)[b]	B
			Repair or upsize cross drains[b]	I
			Clear or enlarge ditches[b]	B

Table 1. continued

General objective	Geomorphic process addressed	Site-scale objective	Techniques	Primarily used during[a]:
Reduce drainage diversion	Surface erosion and mass wasting	Improve cross-drainage to minimize diversion	Replace culverts with water bars or dips[b]	D
			Construct dips or backup water bars over culverts[b]	I

[a]Technique primarily used for: D = road decommissioning, I = road improvement, B = commonly used in both decommissioning and improvement projects.
[b]Chatwin et al. (1994)
[c]Burroughs and King (1989)

Ideally, prior watershed analyses and stream surveys will have identified effects of roads on watershed processes, channels, and biota (e.g., USFS 1995; WFPB 1997; Beechie and Bolton 1999; Beechie et al. 2003), and road surveys will have identified specific road sites that cause those problems (Harr and Nichols 1993; Rennison 1998; Flanagan et al. 2000; Luce et al. 2001). In watersheds where such analyses are lacking, hypotheses about the history of road effects on sediment and hydrology and linkages to current habitat conditions can be stated and subsequently tested during the initial phase of monitoring (e.g., by constructing a sediment budget and by identifying channel responses from historical aerial photographs). Either approach yields a problem statement (e.g., roads have increased landslide rates), and the goals of the road treatment should address the identified problem.

The hypothesized treatment effects dictate the types of monitoring to be conducted. Therefore, hypotheses should specify the processes that will be affected (e.g., road surface erosion, hydrologic connectivity, landsliding) and should at least qualitatively estimate the magnitude of changes expected. For example, a typical effectiveness monitoring hypothesis for treatments to control landsliding might state that road treatments in a basin will reduce landslide rates to approximately the rate from mature forests. An associated validation monitoring hypothesis might state that downstream residual pool depths should increase to approximately the same depths as those in reference streams. These hypotheses indicate the types of processes and channel responses that should be monitored and suggest ranges of parameter values that would indicate "success" in a monitoring context.

As described earlier, there are many landscape, land use, and climate processes that make the testing of these hypotheses a complex endeavor. As a general rule, effectiveness monitoring of road treatments will be considerably more straightforward than validation monitoring because there are relatively short lag times between treatment and response, as well as fewer confounding factors to consider. By contrast, establishing cause-and-effect linkages between road treatments and resultant channel responses (validation monitoring) is made difficult by long lag times between treatment and response, and the difficulty increases with increasing distance between the rehabilitation work and the monitored stream reach. Taking the further step of identifying cause-and-effect linkages between road treatments and biological responses (also validation monitoring) is even more problematic, because of additional uncertainties involved in relating biological responses to channel changes. Therefore, effectiveness monitoring is most likely to be cost effective and produce usable results in a short time frame. Validation monitoring should be conducted in a research context with close attention paid to establishing controls and treatments, and with sufficient commitment of funding and effort to sustain monitoring over decadal time periods.

Experimental or Study Design

A monitoring program for road treatment actions requires careful consideration of (1) study design (e.g., before–after control–impact, extensive posttreatment, etc.), (2) parameter selection, (3) study-site selection,

Table 2.
Example of steps to follow in developing a monitoring program for road-related landslide reduction, including both effectiveness monitoring and validation monitoring. Most monitoring should focus on effectiveness monitoring to obtain results in a cost-effective and timely manner, although validation monitoring may be appropriate in some instances.

Step	Effectiveness monitoring	Validation monitoring
Project goal	Reduce sediment supply from road-related landslides to approximate background rate (i.e., sediment supply rate from unroaded mature forests), ultimately increasing pool depths and fish abundance in response reaches to reference reach levels.	
Monitoring hypotheses	Sediment supply from road-related landslides will be reduced to approximately background rates.	Pool depths and fish abundance in response reaches will increase to reference reach levels.
Considerations in choosing effectiveness or validation monitoring	Effectiveness monitoring is most direct, requires less time, and is less expensive.	Validation monitoring results may be confounded by long lag times between treatment and response, influence of other sediment sources, influence of other watershed processes, and other processes affecting biota.
Study design and scale	Watershed-scale project, no adequate control exists, use a before and after design. Use partial sediment budget approach.	Watershed-scale project, no adequate control exists, select several reaches for validation monitoring.
Parameters to monitor	Sediment supply from mass wasting.	Pool frequency, residual pool depth, wood abundance and size, fish abundance.
Select monitoring locations (sites)	Monitor sediment supply from entire watershed, indicating proportions originating from treated road segments, untreated road segments, clearcuts, and mature forests.	Select response reaches (two near treatments, two farther away).
Monitoring frequency and duration	Monitor every 4–5 years for at least two decades after treatment (if using aerial photography alone), reconstruct pretreatment rates from aerial photography. Including field monitoring of gullying may require annual monitoring.	Parameters monitored annually; monitoring duration estimated based on estimated lag times of x and y years; must monitor for at least $x + 10$ and $y + 10$ years to account for sediment transit time plus time to detect changes in monitoring parameters.
Sampling scheme	Complete census of mass wasting in the watershed, including both road and nonroad landslide sources.	Pools and wood—complete census of each study reach; biota—systematic sampling (e.g., every nth riffle or pool unit).
Analysis and reporting	Compare road-related proportion of total mass wasting sediment before and after treatment; road-related portion of total sediment supply should approach zero after treatment if goals are met.	Compare mean pool frequency and depth in study reaches before and after treatment; compare mean fish abundance by species before and after treatment; examine wood data and flood records for potential confounding events (e.g., large floods or large changes in wood abundance).

and (4) monitoring frequency and duration (Table 2). We first discuss study designs in a general context, because they can be applied to either effectiveness monitoring or validation monitoring. Study-site selection and monitoring frequency and duration are discussed here in relation to study designs but depend, in part, on the fourth element, the selection of monitoring parameters. Parameter selection is discussed later in this chapter, along with monitoring techniques. Ultimately, all four elements must be considered simultaneously to develop a sound monitoring plan for road rehabilitation actions.

Choosing a study design for monitoring effects of road treatments depends first and foremost on the questions to be answered. If, for example, the purpose of monitoring is simply to see if the erosion is still occurring and to identify additional corrective actions, there is no need to draw statistical inferences, and the study design focuses on selecting sites from a defined sample pool. By contrast, monitoring that intends to detect differences between treated and untreated roads benefits from thoughtful design of both the restoration plan and the monitoring program. Restoration plans that are structured as experiments improve the likelihood of detecting treatment effects, as well as the ability to generalize results. Monitoring programs then can take advantage of the experimental design to maximize information gained from limited funding.

In general, study designs are distinguished by availability of reference sites, replicates in space or time, and pre-treatment monitoring (see Chapter 2 for details on various designs). Monitoring reference sites as well as treatment sites (either paired or unpaired) allows statistical comparisons between treated and untreated roads. Without replication, statistical inferences are applicable only to the single site and cannot be generalized to other roads. Where both treatment and reference sites are replicated in space (Figure 3), statistical inferences can be generalized to other similar roads. Where replicates in space are not available, monitoring the treated road segment before treatment allows the segment to function as its own control (before–after [BA] design). Adding a reference road segment to the BA design (before–after control–impact [BACI] design) accounts for temporal variability common to both treatment and reference reaches. The addition of spatial replication to this basic design (multiple BACI [MBACI] design), to some degree, controls for both spatial and temporal variability, and results can be generalized to other roads (see also Chapter 2).

One problem of note in choosing a study design for monitoring effects of road treatments is that runoff and erosion are strongly related to rainfall intensity. Because variation in runoff or sediment supply between storms or years often may be much greater than the differences between treatments and controls, replication in time is particularly important to most road monitoring efforts. Monitoring might need to span decadal time frames for rare events (e.g., mass wasting), whereas monitoring during multiple rainfall events over a few years is sufficient for processes such as sheetwash and rilling of road surfaces. Use of analysis procedures that recognize the relationship between rainfall and erosion (e.g., sediment rating curves) can help control for variation due to rainfall intensity and can improve the chance of detecting differences among treatments (e.g., Reid et al. 1981). For the road treatment objective of reducing mass wasting, monitoring designs that lack replication or have small sample sizes do not provide sufficient information for statistical testing, because landslides are relatively rare in both space and time.

Study designs at the watershed scale are similar to those at the site scale, except that the entire road network within a watershed replaces the road segment as the sampling unit. Sampling effort will be considerably greater than for monitoring of individual road segments, and replicate watersheds may be difficult to locate. Therefore, BA monitoring designs (either with or without reference watersheds) are likely to be the only feasible designs for most organizations conducting watershed-scale monitoring. Coordination of efforts among regions or monitoring organizations (i.e., use of similar monitoring designs and protocols) could provide larger data sets over time and eventually could replicate treated and untreated watersheds.

Validation monitoring programs can pair the preceding designs for sediment sources with similar designs for in-channel or biological monitoring. However, we emphasize again that changes in channel morphology, habitat characteristics, or biotic communities will be extremely difficult to link to road treatments due to high natural variation in channel characteristics, long lag times between treatment and response, and the large number of other possible causes of changes in physical or biological characteristics of streams. Moreover, not all sediment produced from hillslopes (including roads) reaches the stream channel, and all sediment in the channel does not originate from hillslopes (Figure 1). Thus, sediment-supply signals from roads may not necessarily reach the channel within a time frame that allows clear conclusions to be drawn, and other sediment sources may overwhelm the signal from roads and mask the cause-and-effect linkage we are trying to demonstrate through monitoring of road sediment reduction projects. These difficulties suggest that validation monitoring will be expensive, of long duration, and may not yield conclusive results. Therefore, validation monitoring generally should be restricted to cases where sample reaches can be selected to minimize lag times and potential confounding factors, and where there is sufficient management control to establish suitable reference and treatment sites.

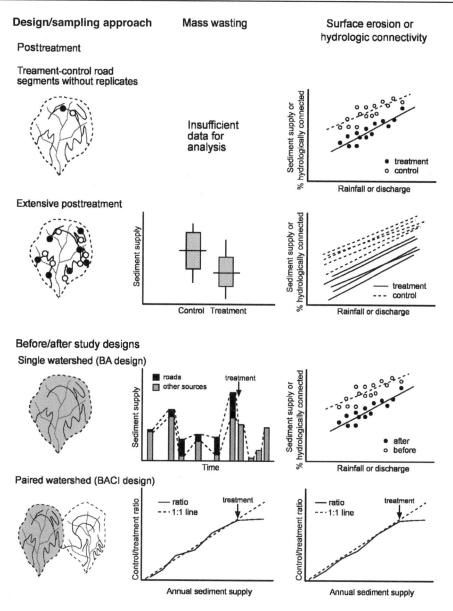

Figure 3.
Examples of alternative sampling approaches and analyses for monitoring effect of road treatments. Watershed illustrations on left show streams as gray lines, roads as black lines, and treatment and control sites as filled and open circles, respectively. Posttreatment designs include a single pair of treatment and control sites (upper row) and an extensive posttreatment design (second row). Replication in time (during storms of various sizes) and use of rating curves can help control for temporal variability in processes. Before-after (BA) and before-after control-impact (BACI) designs control for temporal variation but not spatial variation. Multiple before-after control-impact (not shown) provides some degree of control on both spatial and temporal variability in processes.

Monitoring Frequency and Duration

Effectiveness monitoring

For monitoring mass-wasting sediment supply, sampling intervals for aerial photograph inventories of landslides should be sufficiently short to detect landslides before vegetation recovery. Monitoring frequency (i.e., aerial photograph intervals) should be not more than 5 years in areas of rapid revegetation (e.g., Paulson 1997; Robison et al. 1999), but the interphotograph interval can be longer where scars persist for a decade or more (e.g., Hovius et al. 1997). Field inventories are required to fully account for sediment produced from roads because many small landslides and gullies are not visible on aerial photography. Such inventories should be conducted at least during years when aerial photographs are taken, and additional inventories may be conducted whenever poststorm inspections indicate that road-related landsliding or gullying has occurred. Duration of monitoring for mass-wasting analyses must account for the episodic nature of sediment supply in virtually all climates but particularly where various mass-wasting processes are a dominant source of sediment (e.g., Bergstrom 1982; Rice 1982; Swanson and Fredrickson 1982; Benda and Dunne 1997a; Reid 1998). Thus, monitoring annual supplies of mass-wasting or gully-derived sediment should be conducted over relatively long time frames (i.e., decades) to reflect annual variation in storms and should include monitoring during or after large storms.

Substantial natural variation in stream discharge inhibits conclusive studies of how well road treatments affect hydrologic regimes. Comparison of control and treatment watersheds may be the only practical approach to monitoring downstream changes in stream discharge due to changes in hydrologic connectivity, but detecting such changes in stream discharge requires rigorous controls (e.g., Jones and Grant 1996). However, even controlled designs yield limited results, and conclusively identifying roads as the cause of changes in discharge remains problematic.

More direct monitoring of surface erosion and hydrologic connectivity can be conducted over shorter time frames (i.e., a few years) but must include a wide range of storm magnitudes to develop relationships among rainfall intensity and the measured parameter (i.e., sediment concentrations or proportion of roads that are hydrologically connected). Sampling is conducted opportunistically during storm events (usually several times per year), so monitoring teams should be prepared to sample sites on relatively short notice as storms arrive.

Validation Monitoring

Estimating an appropriate monitoring frequency and duration for channel responses to altered sediment supply is complicated by the lag time between a change in sediment supply and the channel response in downstream reaches (e.g., Kelsey 1982b; Pickup et al. 1983; Madej 1992; Jacobsen and Gran 1999). Numerous studies note that aggradational zones tend to migrate downstream as a sediment wave (Kelsey 1982b; Pickup et al. 1983; Madej and Ozaki 1996; Lisle et al. 2001) and that channel adjustments are related to the downstream migration of channel-stored sediments (Kelsey 1982b; Harvey 1987; Madej 1992; Madej and Ozaki 1996; Miller and Benda 2000). Therefore, the time lag between a change in sediment supply and the channel response increases with increasing distance between the road treatment and the monitored reach. In addition, channel responses in reaches far from the source may be dampened by wave dispersion, attrition, and storage (Dietrich et al. 2001), although large sediment-supply changes may still be detectable as much as 100 km downstream of the sediment source and several decades after the input event (Madej 1992).

The lag time for channel responses can be estimated based on data indicating that annual travel distance of bed load through channel networks increases as a function of stream size. On average, sediment travels about 20 channel widths per year in channels with slope less than 0.03 but can range from approximately 6–50 channel widths per year and varies regionally in relation to the number of bed-load transport days each year (Beechie 2001). Estimated lag time will represent the minimum length of time that a response reach must be monitored to detect a change resulting from the road treatment. In addition to the time lag, the within-reach transit time of sediment pulses tends to range from a few years to about 15 years (Lisle 1982; Collins et al. 1994). A simple illustration of estimated lag time for channel responses at varying distances from the sediment delivery point (meaning the point at which landslides from the treatment road would enter the main channel) indicates that predicted lag time can increase dramatically with increasing distance to the sample reach (Table 3). Thus, monitored reaches should be close to treatment roads to decrease the monitoring period required to observe the treatment effect and to minimize the potential for other events to confound results.

There are fewer problems estimating monitoring frequency and duration for changes in storm flow or suspended sediment because lag times from source to the response generally are only a few hours. Sites should be monitored during all significant rainfall events to establish relationships between rainfall and discharge or suspended sediment concentration (e.g., Reid et al. 1981). Monitoring over a range of storm magnitudes will be required to fully examine treatment effectiveness, because the effect of roads will increase with increasing rainfall intensity and duration. Monitoring should continue at least until several large storms have been captured in the sample, and there is sufficient sample size to detect differences between control and treatment sites.

Table 3.

Example of estimated lag time for channel response after sediment input in streams of the West Coast of North America (based on Beechie 2001). Not shown in this example is the additional within-reach recovery period (discussed in text) or the time required to detect changes in biological parameters. w_{bf} = bank-full width.

	Lag time at L_b = 20 w_{bf}/year (range based on L_b = 6–26 w_{bf}/year)		
	1 km to monitored reach	**5 km to monitored reach**	**15 km to monitored reach**
w_{bf} = 10 m	5 years (4–17 years)	25 years (19–83 years)	75 years (58–250 years)
w_{bf} = 50 m	3 years (2–9 years)	13 years (10–42 years)	38 years (29–125 years)
w_{bf} = 100 m	<1 year (0–2 years)	3 years (2–8 years)	8 years (6–25 years)

For biota, monitoring frequency and time will vary, depending on the organisms monitored. Most monitoring of invertebrates can be conducted in late summer to observe the widest array of organisms in the invertebrate community, and sampling should span several years to capture natural variation. For juvenile fishes, monitoring must be conducted during seasons when the species of interest are present and which reflect conditions that juveniles have experienced during their residence (e.g., end of summer to detect influences of summer rearing habitat conditions on stream-rearing anadromous fish). Monitoring of egg incubation success obviously should be conducted when eggs are in the spawning gravel. Duration of monitoring for biological parameters typically is at least several years to account for interannual variation, but must also account for the lag times between treatments and habitat responses, as discussed previously. More information on sample sizes and duration of biological sampling efforts is discussed in Chapter 2.

Selecting Study Locations

There are three basic approaches to selecting study locations for effectiveness monitoring of road treatments: (1) random selection, (2) systematic selection, and (3) opportunistic or arbitrary selection. Random selection first requires identification of all sites included in the sample pool (e.g., all road segments treated to reduce hydrologic connectivity) and subsequent random selection of sites from the pool. Systematic selection chooses every nth site for sampling (e.g., every 10th culvert) and ensures a more even spatial distribution of study sites when sample size is relatively small. Opportunistic or arbitrary selection may be appropriate when the number of treatment sites is very small and when monitoring must take advantage of virtually all treatment sites to have sufficient sample size. For any of these site selection procedures, control or reference road segments should have similar characteristics to the treatment segments (e.g., hillslope location, road slope, number of crossings, etc.) and should be located as closely as possible to treatment roads. Where all roads are treated and reference segments are not available, monitoring before and after treatment substitutes pretreatment monitoring for reference segments. However, variation in storm magnitudes before and after treatment may preclude conclusions of cause and effect (i.e., differences may be due to environmental variation rather than the road treatment).

Effectiveness monitoring also can examine the degree to which road treatments reduce sediment production in an entire watershed by using the sediment budget as a monitoring framework. In this case, either single or paired watersheds can be examined (lower two rows in Figure 3), and selection of monitored watersheds usually will be opportunistic due to the limited number of treatment and control watersheds available. The sediment budget allows apportioning of sediment sources and can help determine whether the road-related component of the total sediment supply is reduced to near zero even if the remaining sources continue to fluctuate. For single watersheds, lack of replication precludes statistical analysis of the results. Use of a reference watershed provides some degree of statistical control and can show evidence that an apparent treatment effect is not also expressed in an untreated watershed.

Ultimately, validation monitoring can use the same three sampling strategies described above but only after narrowing the pool of potential study reaches by considering site characteristics, such as channel type and lag time between treatment and response. The first and perhaps most important consideration in selecting study reaches is to select reaches that are sensitive to the types of changes expected as a result of road treatment actions (Table 4). In general, channels with slope greater than 0.04 will be poor reaches for monitoring most of the sediment indicators we discuss in this chapter, and channels with slope less than 0.01 or 0.02, will be the most sensitive reaches for monitoring the majority of physical indicators listed here (Montgomery and Buffington 1997). Sensitivity of the response reach also will be affected by the proximity of the reach to sediment sources, because sediment routing in a channel network diffuses much of the sediment supply signal as the contributing area of the channel becomes larger (e.g., Naiman et al. 1992; Benda and Dunne 1997b). In other words, small low-gradient channels may exhibit pronounced changes in monitoring parameters because they are close to a small number of sediment sources, whereas the sediment supply signal may be dampened and difficult to detect in larger channels. This dampening results from a number of factors, including increased temporal distribution of supply events (i.e., a large drainage will likely have some landslides every year, whereas a small drainage may have many years with no landslides; Benda and Dunne 1997a), particle attrition during bed-load transport (i.e., abrasion of bed-load particles into finer grains that then travel in suspension; Collins and Dunne 1980; Dietrich et al. 2001), and the dispersion of bed-load pulses (Benda and Dunne 1997b; Lisle et al. 1997; Lisle et al. 2001). In general, study reaches for detecting changes in coarse sediment supply will be most useful if they have slopes less than 0.04, are near the road treatments, and have limited influence from other potential sediment sources (Figure 4).

Selection of study locations for hydrologic connectivity and suspended sediment should focus more on the proximity of sites to treatments than on channel types (which have a relatively small effect on suitability of sampling locations; Table 4). The most important considerations for selecting study locations for these param-

Table 4.
Likely responses of selected physical parameters to a moderate increase in sediment supply in different channel types (based, in part, on MacDonald et al. 1991, Montgomery and Buffington 1997, Montgomery and MacDonald 2002). Parameters rated possible (p) or unlikely (u) indicate measurements that are poor monitoring choices. Parameters that are likely to increase (I) or decrease (D) as a function of increased sediment supply are most likely to exhibit measurable responses, and those in bold generally are more repeatable among observers or more precise (based in part on Bauer and Ralph 1999 and Kaufmann et al. 1999).

	Channel type				
	Response			Transport	
	Dune–ripple	Pool–riffle	Plane-bed	Step-pool	Cascade
Remote-sensing indicators of coarse-sediment change in channel					
Channel width	p	**I**	**I**	u	u
Channel-stored sediment	**I**	**I**	**I**	p	u
Field indicators for coarse-sediment change in channel					
Width–depth ratio	**I**	**I**	**I**	**I**	u
Residual pool depth	p	**D**	**D**	**D**	u
Scour depth	p	I	I	u	u
D*	p	I	I	p	u
Q*	p	I	I	p	u
Field indicators for fine-sediment change in channel					
Fines in subsurface	u	I	I	u	u
Fines on surface	u	I	I	u	u
Water column	**I**	**I**	**I**	**I**	**I**

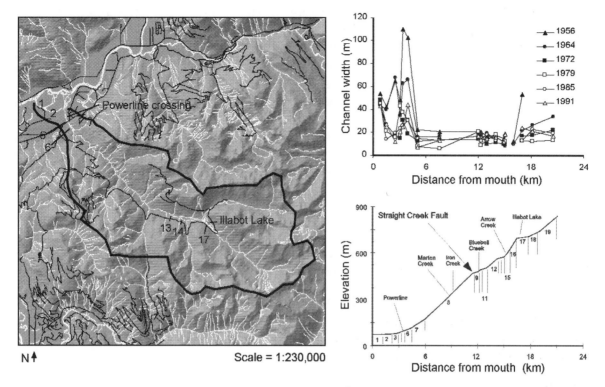

Figure 4.
Study reaches selected for monitoring channel changes due to change in sediment supply from mass-wasting in Illabot Creek, northwestern Washington State. Map shows streams as white lines, roads as thin black lines, and the watershed boundary as a heavy black line. All of the road segments within the watershed were either obliterated or storm-proofed. Numbered reaches on map and in longitudinal profile (lower right panel) are response reaches. Changes in channel width over time (mainly in reaches 2 through 6) indicate sensitivity to changes in sediment supply or peak flows (upper right panel). Reaches 13 and 14 are reaches where effects of road treatments are most likely to be observed because they are nearest the road treatment and most isolated from natural sediment supply influences upstream of the roads (sediment from the upper basin is trapped in Illabot Lake, Reach 17). Reaches 1–6 receive sediment from more of the road length, but also more nonroad sediment sources.

eters are proximity to the road treatment and limited influence from other sediment sources. Other, more pragmatic considerations for selecting sample locations include ease of access (because parameters must be sampled during a wide range of flows on short notice), ease of installing sampling equipment, such as staff gauges, and stability of the channel geometry (to develop consistent stage-discharge relationships).

Study reaches for biological monitoring should correspond to locations of channel or habitat monitoring to improve chances of identifying causal links between road treatments and biological responses. Within those reaches, sample locations are dependent on the types of organisms monitored, as well as the specific parameters to be assessed (see Chapter 6 for more details on sample locations for biological parameters).

Monitoring Parameters and Techniques

In this subsection, we describe selection of appropriate monitoring parameters and review techniques for monitoring sediment sources, hydrologic changes, and channel or habitat changes. We only briefly review techniques for biological monitoring because they are discussed in detail in other chapters (Chapters 6, 8, and 9). We focus on monitoring sediment supply from mass wasting and surface erosion but also discuss parameters for detecting hydrologic changes. For each process, we briefly discuss measurement techniques, limitations of methods, and data analyses that may be conducted.

Selecting Parameters

Effectiveness monitoring of road treatments can include measuring sediment supply, stream discharge, or proportion of roads hydrologically connected to streams, as well as direct observations of how specific installations or techniques function during storms. Quantification of sediment supply and stream discharge indicate whether road treatments accomplish their environmental objective (e.g., reduced sediment delivery or peak flows). Field observations of how specific techniques function during storms help determine whether the various techniques accomplish their design objectives (e.g., disconnecting a road ditch from a stream). Both should be considered part of a comprehensive effectiveness monitoring program, as it is important not only to understand where restoration actions have failed to accomplish their objectives but also why they might have failed.

Monitoring changes in sediment supply from forest roads focuses on the rate at which sediment is supplied to streams by various processes, including both erosion rates and the proportion of eroded sediment delivered to streams (Table 5). The level of detail desired in the assessment (e.g., the number and types of erosion processes assessed) is, in part, determined by the objectives of the project (e.g., Bauer and Ralph 1999) but also by other factors such as cost, repeatability of measures, and sensitivity of the monitoring parameter (see also MacDonald et al. 1991). Depending on the level of detail desired, various size fractions of the sediment load may be monitored separately (e.g., Reid et al. 1981), or the project may simply monitor total sediment supply without differentiating among particle sizes. Monitoring road treatments to reduce hydrologic connectivity focuses on the proportion of road ditches connected directly to streams during storms, new rills or gullies connecting roads to streams, and the proportion of connected road that can be disconnected from streams by various techniques (Furniss et al. 2000). Region 5 of the U.S. Forest Service has developed a system for monitoring performance of individual techniques, and more details can be found in its user's guide (USFS 2000). Monitoring hydrologic changes focuses on detecting changes in peak flows associated with road rehabilitation actions designed to decrease hydrologic connectivity.

Validation monitoring can include a wide range of parameters that indicate responses to changes in sediment supply or hydrology, which can be grouped into three main categories to help organize selection of parameters (Table 5):
1. Detecting channel changes caused by altered coarse sediment supply
2. Detecting channel changes caused by altered fine sediment supply
3. Biological responses and other measures

The most pronounced effects of increased coarse sediment supply are channel aggradation and widening. These effects often are so large that they can be detected through remote-sensing methods. For example, the riparian aerial photographic inventory of disturbance (RAPID) technique (Grant 1988; Harvey 1991; Ryan and Grant 1991) detects changes in channel widening based on analysis of sequential aerial photographs. A more detailed approach measures changes in channel-stored sediment from aerial photographs and may include field measurement of depth of sediment storage reservoirs such as gravel bars (Madej 1992). Both techniques indicate obvious channel changes that may be related to changes in sediment supply. However, recovery in semiarid or arid regions may extend to decades or even centuries if drought prohibits vegetation recovery on the channel margins (Wolman and Gerson 1978). Therefore, channel width may be an unreliable indicator of reduced sediment supply from roads in semiarid and arid regions. In addition, other events (e.g., large floods) can significantly alter channel widths or sediment storage, even without changes in sediment supply, and one should not conclude that changes in channel width or channel-stored sediment indicate a change in sediment supply unless sediment supply information supports that conclusion.

Potential field measures of physical responses to altered coarse-sediment supply include repeated measurements of cross sections (e.g., Bergstrom 1982; Harvey 1991; Lisle and Madej 1992), longitudinal profiles (e.g., Madej and Ozaki 1996), and residual pool depths (e.g., Lisle 1982). Residual pool-depth and channel-geometry measurements are independent of the flows at which measurements are taken, exhibit relatively predictable responses to altered supply, and are relatively repeatable and precise (Bauer and Ralph 1999; Kauffman et al. 1999). However, both methods have some restrictions on their use, owing to spatial and temporal variability in measurements (Olson-Rutz and Marlow 1992; Paige and Hickin 2000; Keim and Skaugset 2002). In terms of sampling effort, measurement of residual pool depths over time is relatively rapid and inexpensive, whereas repeated longitudinal profiles or cross sections are more time consuming and costly. Scour depth monitoring is perhaps the most expensive option, given the effort required to install and monitor scour depth indicators and the high degree of spatial variation within channels.

Table 5.

Examples of parameters for effectiveness and validation monitoring of road rehabilitation actions. Effectiveness monitoring parameters typically are measured at the scale of road segments or watersheds. Validation monitoring parameters typically are measured at the reach scale.

Parameter	Purpose
Indicators of change in sediment supply[a]	
Road landslide rate	Detect change in number of landslides (no. landslides·km^{-1}·year^{-1})
Road landslide sediment volume	Detect change in landslide total volume (m^3·km^{-1}·year^{-1})
Sediment volume from erosion around culverts	Detect changes in erosion volume from erosion of culvert fills or at culvert outfalls (m^3·km^{-1}·year^{-1})
Surface erosion volume (includes sheetwash, rills, gullies, etc.)	Detect changes in coarse or fine sediment volume (m^3·km^{-1}·year^{-1})
Indicators of hydrologic change[a]	
Stream discharge	Detect change in peak flows
Proportion of road hydrologically connected to streams	Detect change in proportion of roads delivering water or suspended sediment to streams
Indicators of coarse sediment change in channel[b]	
Bank-full channel width	Detect large changes in channel width (m)
Channel stored sediment	Detect changes in channel-stored sediment (m^2 if remote sensing only; m^3 if combined with field-measured depths of storage reservoirs)
Channel cross sections	Detect bed aggradation or degradation (m), as well as channel widening (m) or changes in width/depth ratio (dimensionless: m/m)
Longitudinal bed profile	Detect zones of aggradation and degradation resulting from wave-like movements of bed-load sediment (m)
Residual pool depth	Detect decreased pool depths (m)
Scour depth	Detect changes in depth of bed scour (m)
Q*	Detect changes in the proportion supply of sediment relative to transport capacity (dimensionless)
Indicators of fine sediment change in channel[b]	
Fines fraction in subsurface	Detect changes in fine sediment, particularly in spawning gravels (% by volume or weight)
Surface fines (pebble count)	Detect changes in fine sediment on the bed surface (% by frequency)
Surface fines (embeddedness)	Detect changes in filling of interstices by fine sediment (% by area)
V*	Detect changes in residual pool volume from fine sediment (dimensionless: m^3/m^3)
Turbidity	Detect changes in suspended-sediment concentrations (mg/liter)
Biological indicators and other measures[b]	
Bed scour and fill	Detect changes in scour depth that may be related to changes in either sediment supply or hydrology
Invertebrate indicators	Detect changes in invertebrate communities
Fish	Detect changes in fish abundance, survival, or community structure

[a]Parameters in these categories are part of effectiveness monitoring.
[b]Parameters in these categories are part of validation monitoring.

Potential field indicators of a change in fine-sediment supply include the proportion of fine sediments in the surface or subsurface layers of the bed material, the amount of fine sediments filling pools, and turbidity. In cases of extreme increases in fine-sediment supply, the most visible effect on habitats is the filling of pools with fine sediment, which can be measured as the proportion of residual pool volume filled with fine sediment (V*; Lisle and Hilton 1992; Hilton and Lisle 1993). The size composition of sediments measured by V* must be much smaller than that of the underlying bed and must be penetrable by a metal probing rod. Large increases in the supply of fine sediment also may be obvious in the bed-surface material, which can be evaluated by surface pebble counts or a measure of embeddedness (e.g., Potyondy 1989; Schnackenberg and MacDonald 1998; Buffington and Montgomery 1999a). More subtle changes in fine-sediment delivery to channels may be monitored by changes in the subsurface material, which may not be obvious on the bed surface (e.g., Young et al. 1991; Clarke and Scruton 1997). Finally, changes in turbidity or suspended-sediment concentrations can be used to detect changes in the supply of very fine suspended sediments to streams (e.g., MacDonald et al. 1991).

For both coarse- and fine-sediment-supply monitoring, floods and wood abundance are two of the most important factors that may confound results of the monitoring program. Therefore, it is important to understand their potential influences and to monitor them to assure that changes in the selected monitoring parameters are due to changes in sediment supply. Floods may increase channel widths by reactivating sediment stored in the floodplain (Madej 1992). Therefore, changes in channel morphology and sediment texture may manifest in a response reach, even if there have been no changes in sediment supply from hillslopes or roads. In most cases, nearby stream gauges and weather stations provide the data needed to detect significant storms and floods, and data collection and analysis from existing sources are relatively rapid and inexpensive. Wood debris can decrease the size of bed sediments (Buffington and Montgomery 1999b) or increase abundance and depths of pools (e.g., Bilby and Ward 1989; Montgomery et al. 1995; Abbe and Montgomery 1996; Beechie and Sibley 1997). Therefore, changes in abundance or size of wood can alter pool depths or surface texture of the streambed and confound channel responses caused by changes in sediment supply.

Biological responses can be monitored by using a wide array of measures of primary productivity, invertebrates, or fishes (see Chapters 6, 8, and 9 for more detail on biotic measures). However, clearly identifying causal links between road-treatment actions and biological responses will be extremely difficult because biological responses are regulated not only by the road-treatment effects on watershed processes but also by other factors, such as nutrient availability, trophic interactions, species interactions, and habitat conditions outside the monitoring area (e.g., ocean conditions for anadromous fishes). Establishing appropriate controls on these other factors may be next to impossible, and many of these measures require several decades of monitoring to detect changes.

Techniques for Monitoring Sediment Supply and Hydrology (Effectiveness Monitoring)

In this subsection, we first discuss monitoring of sediment supply by using the sediment budget as a basic framework for analysis. Hydrology is discussed more briefly, focusing on measuring the amount of hydrologically connected road as the most informative parameter to measure.

Sediment supply

The conceptual framework for monitoring changes in sediment supply from various sources is the sediment budget (Reid et al. 1981; Dietrich et al. 1982; Swanson and Fredrickson 1982; Reid and Dunne 1996). The full sediment budget for streams can be expressed simply as

$$\Delta S = I - O$$

where ΔS is change in storage of sediment in a channel, I is input of sediment, and O is output of sediment. Monitoring of sediment from forest roads typically focuses only on the input component of the budget (referred to as a partial sediment budget). Measuring quantities of all sources of sediment (e.g., road-related landslides, natural landslides, landslides in clearcuts, gullies, road surface erosion) provides a more complete context for interpreting the effectiveness of road-sediment reduction projects and helps evaluate the quantity of road-related sediment supplies relative to nonroad sediment sources (Table 6). Use of probability sampling methods (e.g., stratified random sampling) in constructing sediment budgets can help partition the uncertainty associated with various types of erosion measurements (Lewis 2002). A more thorough discussion of important concepts in constructing sediment budgets can be found in Reid and Dunne (1996).

There are two basic approaches to monitoring supply of sediment: (1) remote-sensing methods such as landslide inventories and measurement of landslide areas from aerial photographs and (2) field measurements of

Table 6.
Example of partial sediment budgets, showing impact of roads on sediment production from landslides. (adapted from Sidle et al. 1985.)

Region	Erosion rate ($m^3 \cdot ha^{-1} \cdot year^{-1}$)		
	Forest	Clear-cut	Road
New Zealand (North Westland)	1.0	11.8–40.4	267
Coastal British Columbia	0.1	0.3	2.8
Oregon Cascade range (H. J. Andrews)	0.9	2.5	26.2
Oregon Cascade range (Alder Creek)	0.5	1.2	155.7
Oregon Cascade range (Blue River)	0.4	3.2	16.3
Oregon coast ranges (Mapleton Area)	0.3	0.6	15.9
Western Washington (Olympic Peninsula)	0.7	0	117.8
Idaho Batholith	0.1	1.4	13.2

erosion volumes by repeated surveys or runoff sampling. Remote-sensing methods are suitable for monitoring volumes of sediment produced by road-related landsliding but not for monitoring of surface erosion from roads (including erosion around culverts). Quantification of mass wasting sediment is composed of inventory and measurement of landslide surface areas from aerial photographs, combined with field methods that estimate volumes of a subset of landslides and debris-flow erosion tracks (Benda and Dunne 1987; Reid and Dunne 1996). A regression of field-measured sediment volumes against landslide area measurements then is used to estimate sediment volumes for all landslides in the aerial photograph inventory, and field-measured debris flow volumes per meter of travel length are used to estimate total volumes of debris flows measured on aerial photographs. However, many small landslides are obscured by forest vegetation (Hovius et al. 1997; Paulson 1997), and landslide rates in forests typically are underestimated more than landslide rates in roads and clearcuts (Robison et al. 1999). Use of minimum effective mapping areas as minimum size criteria for aerial photograph inventories may help alleviate bias, but it also may eliminate the majority of landslides from the inventory (Robison et al. 1999). Field measures of gully erosion and smaller landslide volumes also may be necessary to fully account for sediment produced from roads treated for landslide hazard reduction (e.g., Madej 2001).

There are a number of methods available for direct measurement of sediment yield from road surfaces and gullying at road drainage outfalls (Reid et al. 1981; Kochenderfer and Helvey 1987; Sasich 1998; Madej 2001). Sediment from surface erosion can be captured, along with road runoff, as it is carried in suspension from the roadway, using either grab samples or an automated water sampler. Alternatively, passive sediment-collection devices such as catch basins or silt fences can accumulate eroded material over longer time periods. Each method can be used easily to verify site-scale erosion rates, but using direct measurement approaches to quantify sediment inputs at a watershed or road network scale requires considerably more effort. These larger scale estimates depend on site-scale values for a variety of road conditions (i.e., various traffic rates, soil types, and cover conditions) over a range of climatic conditions and generally have been made only in the context of research efforts (e.g., Reid and Dunne 1984; Burroughs and King 1989; Table 7). Total coarse and fine sediments eroded by gullying are estimated from field measurements of gully dimensions (Madej 2001).

An alternative to field measurements is the estimation of road-surface erosion rates based on road conditions and relationships derived from published sediment production measurements (e.g., WFPB 1997; Ketcheson et al. 1999). These methods are particularly useful for estimating the magnitude of sediment yield changes that have resulted (or may result) from various road prescriptions that combine multiple treatments, such as enhancing soil cover or reducing the proportion of hydrologically connected roads. Despite their relative ease of use, these simulation approaches do not substitute for measured sediment rates to determine effectiveness of road treatments. However, they may be useful for integrating site-specific effectiveness measurements to estimate the aggregate effectiveness of multiple treatments in a road improvement strategy.

Table 7.
Sediment yields from three types of road surface in a West Virginia experiment (from Kochenderfer and Helvey 1987). Each treatment was applied to three replicate sites and monitored over 4 years.

Treatment	Mean sediment yield (metric tons/ha)			
	1980	**1981**	**1982**	**1983**
Ungraveled	84.1	117.7	114.1	107.8
1-in crusher-run gravel	13.4	38.8	18.2	20.0
3-in clean gravel	8.7	15.2	12.6	14.3

Hydrology

To monitor changes in water (or fine sediment) delivery to channels from roads, the simplest parameter to monitor is the proportion of the road network that is hydrologically connected to streams. Field observations should be made during storms, and all portions of the road system that are connected to streams via surface-flow paths (ditches, cross drains, gullies, rills, and overland flow) should be considered hydrologically connected (Furniss et al. 2000). Observations of rilling, sediment delivery to channels, scouring at cross drains, and similar features during nonstorm periods also are useful in this form of effectiveness monitoring (USFS 2000). Stream discharge also may be monitored by using stream gauges, but temporal variability in discharge measurements makes it difficult to detect changes due to road rehabilitation. Stream gauging methods are discussed in Chapter 6.

Techniques for Monitoring Channel, Habitat, and Biological Responses (Validation Monitoring)

In this subsection, we describe specific techniques for monitoring channel and habitat responses to sediment supply. We discuss techniques for measuring size composition of bed sediments, suspended sediments, channel geometry and morphology, scour depth, and biota. As stated earlier, we do not discuss monitoring of sediment transport rates, which is extensively treated in Bunte and MacDonald (1999).

Size composition of bed sediments

Detecting channel responses to changes in the supply of coarse sediment to streams can involve monitoring changes in sediment texture (e.g., the proportion of fines in the bed or on the surface), channel geometry (e.g., bed aggradation or channel widening), or channel morphology (e.g., pool frequency or depth). Where sediment supply changes are expected to be large, monitoring might focus on sediment texture by using the ratio of surface particle size to subsurface particle size (D^*; Lisle and Madej 1992) or the ratio of sediment supply to transport capacity (Q^*; Dietrich et al. 1989). Where sediment supply is much less than the transport capacity of the stream, the bed will be armored (i.e., D^* will be high and Q^* will be low). As sediment supply increases, the surface of the bed becomes finer and the median grain size of the surface approaches that of the subsurface (i.e., D^* decreases and Q^* increases). Both measures can indicate whether sediment supply has increased to the point that the stream is incapable of efficient bed-load transport, but spatial variation within reaches typically is high, and treatment effects may be difficult to detect without large sample sizes.

To account for the high degree of spatial variation in both D^* and Q^* in channels (Dietrich et al. 1989; Lisle and Madej 1992), samples should be taken in consistent locations from site to site and from year to year. Selection of a well-defined location (e.g., halfway between the bar apex and upper end of the bar) can partly control for within-reach variation in particle sizes and increase repeatability among observers. By contrast, exercising careful judgment in the field may help assure that sites are more uniform with respect to depositional environment (Church and Kellerhals 1978) but at the expense of decreased consistency among samplers. With consistent sampling locations and sufficient sample size, analysis of temporal changes in D^* or Q^* can be a simple comparison of changes in average values of the parameters over time. However, it should be noted that pooling of samples from multiple reaches is problematic and that it may be difficult to achieve sufficient sample size, even if all suitable sites within a reach are sampled (Church and Kellerhals 1978).

Fine sediments can be monitored either within the streambed or on the surface of the bed. In general, monitoring fine-sediment accumulation on the surface or within the streambed is appropriate in situations where a restoration project is expected to reduce delivery of silt to small gravels (0.004–4.0 mm) to response reaches. However, high spatial variability in sediment texture in gravel-bed rivers severely inhibits the detection of all but the most extreme changes in bed-sediment texture. Thus, the methods described here may yield little useful information where changes are expected to be slight or moderate (i.e., many road-treatment applications).

Two approaches are available to sample subsurface fine sediments—bulk sampling and fine sediment trapping. Bulk sampling involves extracting samples of streambed material from areas of suitable spawning habitat. If the bed-grain size distribution is relatively fine (e.g., medium gravel and smaller), bulk samples can be collected by using several methods, including coring with a McNeil cylinder (McNeil and Ahnell 1964; Grost et al. 1991), freezing bed materials to a metal probe filled with liquid nitrogen or $CO2$ (freeze coring), or excavating material with a shovel. The McNeil cylinder is less cumbersome and less biased than freeze coring or shovel techniques. However, freeze cores preserve the vertical stratification of bed materials, which is useful for some applications (Platts and Penton 1980). Samples should be collected once per year at the same time each year, typically at a stable, low discharge to avoid temporal variability associated with storm events (Adams and Beschta 1980), and sample weights must be large enough to avoid biasing the data (Church et al. 1987; Ferguson and Paola 1997). Since substrate composition varies both longitudinally (along the length of the stream channel) and laterally (across the channel width), potential spawning habitat should be inventoried throughout the reach with sampling points well distributed both longitudinally and laterally (Schuett-Hames et al. 1999).

The two most common monitoring parameters derived from bulk samples are (1) percent fine sediment, %F (%F = the fraction of particles smaller than a specified particle size), and (2) the geometric mean particle size, Dg (Dg characterizes the overall particle size distribution). Both %F and Dg have been correlated with survival to emergence (STE) and changes in substrate composition resulting from forest management (Shirazi et al. 1980; Chapman and McLeod 1987; Young et al. 1991; Peterson et al. 1992), although the relationships have varied between studies because a single metric does not represent the suite of factors influencing STE (Chapman and McLeod 1987). Bulk sample data have been used widely to characterize changes in spawning habitat due to increased fine sediments associated with forest management activities (McNeil and Ahnell 1964; Hall and Lantz 1969; Cederholm and Salo 1979; Tripp and Poulin 1986b; Platts et al. 1989; Scrivener and Brownlee 1989).

Fine-sediment trapping is an alternative method that involves placement of containers filled with clean gravel at or below the surface of the bed to collect fine sediment intruding into the streambed (Lisle 1989). Containers must allow free movement of fine sediment in and out, and must be strong enough to survive in the streambed. Plastic Whitlock-Vibert incubation boxes with slots to allow circulation of water and fine sediment are widely used (Wesche et al. 1989). The devices are installed before the spawning season for the species of concern and remain in the gravel during the incubation period to collect intruded sediment. At the end of the incubation period, the containers are removed from the gravel, and the contents are sorted and processed to estimate the percentage of fine sediment, as described for bulk samples. This technique more directly characterizes effects within the egg pocket (Chapman 1988) and has been used to detect increases in fine-sediment accumulation associated with forest road construction (Clarke and Scruton 1997). Salmonid eggs are sometimes placed in the containers with the gravel, which allows a direct measurement of egg survival (McHenry et al. 1994).

Several approaches and parameters are available to document changes in deposition of fine sediment on the streambed surface. The volume of fine sediment deposited in pools as a percentage of the total residual pool volume (V*) has been correlated with relative basin sediment production and also is sensitive to local increases in sediment production associated with land-use activity (Lisle and Hilton 1992; Hilton and Lisle 1993). Shifts in the particle-size distribution of surface materials estimated by pebble counts or visual estimation techniques have been used to document the effects of sediment delivery from forest road construction (Schnackenberg and MacDonald 1998), wildfires and dam failure (Potyondy and Hardy 1994), and sediment reduction after road restoration (Platts et al. 1989). Cobble embeddedness, a measure of the amount of fine sediment deposited around larger particles on the surface of the streambed, has been used in the northern Rockies as an indicator of juvenile salmonid rearing-habitat quality. However, Potyondy (1989) concluded that measures of cobble embeddedness were highly variable and that the sampling technique was unsuitable for streams less than 20 ft wide, which limits its use for many streams found in close proximity to road restoration activities.

Where changes in bed-sediment composition are expected to be large, the pebble count technique can be used to monitor changes in size of particles on the bed (Wolman 1954; Kondolf and Li 1992; Potyondy and Hardy 1994). However, training of personnel in pebble measurement techniques, unbiased selection of particles, and adequate sample size are critical (Marcus et al. 1995), and the method is biased against finer particles (Fripp and Diplas 1993). There is no single standardized procedure for pebble count sampling because the technique has been used for a wide variety of purposes. A systematic sampling approach to monitor changes in sediment texture involves collecting data along cross-sectional transects placed at intervals along survey reaches at least 20 times the mean channel width in length, similar to the system described by Platts et al. (1983) and Harrelson et al. (1994). Details on methods, including unbiased pebble selection, measurement of pebble diameter, and minimum sample size can be found in Wolman (1954), Wolcott and Church (1991), Reid and Dunne (1996), Rice and Church (1996), and Bunte and Abt (2001).

Suspended sediments

Suspended sediment monitoring has been used to estimate changes in sediment load from forest roads and timber harvest (Fredriksen 1970; Beschta 1978; Rice et al. 1979; Kochenderfer and Helvey 1987), and to evaluate whether forest practices are meeting state water-quality criteria (Lynch and Corbett 1990). Suspended sediments are monitored by collection of depth-integrated water samples throughout high discharge events to obtain a sediment rating curve (e.g., Dunne and Leopold 1978). Details on sampling methods can be found in Thomas (1985). Analysis of samples can yield several parameters, including total suspended solids, total suspended organic and mineral material, total suspended mineral material, suspended sediment, and turbidity (the amount of light absorbed or diffracted by particles suspended in the water; MacDonald et al. 1991).

Developing an effective sampling strategy to monitor management-related changes to suspended fine sediment concentrations is challenging, due to the highly variable nature of suspended sediment transport and the numerous factors that can influence suspended-sediment concentrations (MacDonald 1993). Sediment concentrations are highly dependent on discharge, and much of the suspended-sediment load transported in mountain streams can occur during a few peak-flow events (Beschta 1978). For a given discharge, suspended-sediment concentrations often are higher on the rising limbs of storm hydrographs (Sidle and Campbell 1985) and during events early in the storm season (before the largest peak flow). Therefore, moderate-sized storm events early in the season may be most useful for comparison purposes (Sidle and Campbell 1985), and comparison of pre- and posttreatment sediment rating curves (i.e., sediment concentration plotted against discharge) among treatment and reference sites improves the likelihood of detecting treatment effects (Rice et al. 1979; Thomas 1985).

Channel geometry and morphology

Changes in channel geometry currently are difficult to measure by using remote-sensing methods due to relatively low vertical accuracy (e.g., Brasington et al. 2000). However, channel widths measured from sequential aerial photographs can detect time trends in channel-width responses (e.g., Kelsey 1982b; Harvey 1991), spatial patterns in stream-channel responses, or the cumulative effect of multiple road treatments (e.g., Ryan and Grant 1991). Several channel widths should be measured within each response reach to accurately represent the average change in channel width, and field measurements should be compared with a subset of aerial photograph measurements to evaluate the effect of overhanging vegetation (Figure 5).

Surface areas of sediment stored in bars and in the active channel can be measured by digitizing storage areas from orthorectified aerial photographs, whereas monitoring changes in volume of stored sediment requires field measurement of depths of various storage features (Madej 1992). Increases in bar storage may indicate increased sediment delivery to channels from roads but also may indicate from bank erosion of floodplain sediments. Therefore, monitoring changes in channel width or sediment storage alone should not be considered

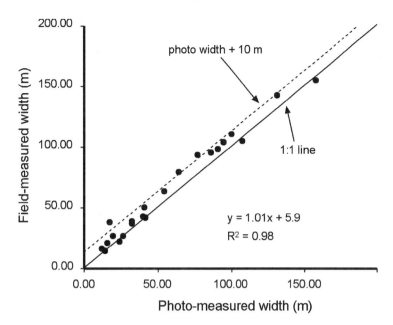

Figure 5.
Relationship of channel width measured from aerial photographs and bank-full channel width measured in the field (L. Holsinger, Northwest Fisheries Science Center, unpublished data). Regression indicates an average underestimate of channel width of approximately 6 m when measured from aerial photographs, due to overhanging trees.

sufficient to indicate changes in sediment supply from roads. Rather, they should be considered components of a broader monitoring plan that includes monitoring of sediment sources (including supply from roads).

Changes in channel geometry are surveyed with either an autolevel or total station and consist of repeated surveys of monitored cross sections (e.g., Olson-Rutz and Marlow 1992; Paige and Hickin 2000) or of the thalweg profile (e.g., Madej 1999). Surveys can detect changes on the order of 0.01 m and can be used to quantify changes in sediment storage (Madej 1992) or cross-sectional area and width–depth ratio (Olson-Rutz and Marlow 1992). Repeated surveys of thalweg profiles can indicate changes in bed-elevation variability, filling or clearing of pools, and the proportion of channel length in riffles (Madej 1999).

Measuring changes in channel morphology (e.g., number of pools or residual pool depth) is, perhaps, more efficient than other techniques in that it can be conducted rapidly and does not require detailed topographic or cross-sectional surveys. The number of pools in selected response reaches can be monitored as long as the pools can be reliably identified through standardized criteria. Residual depth is defined as the depth of the pool measured when discharge goes to zero and is, therefore, independent of stream flow (Lisle 1987). Residual pool depth is calculated by measuring water depth at the deepest part of the pool, then subtracting water depth at the deepest portion of the downstream riffle crest (Lisle 1987). Where pool locations are relatively constant, monitoring depths of individual pools allows paired sample testing of the depth data. Where pool locations change frequently, one can measure residual depths of all pools within a reach and plot their frequency distributions to compare distributions of residual depths over time (Figure 6).

Bed scour

Scour depth can be measured by using one of several types of scour-depth indicators, including link chains, stacked ping pong balls, nylon cord, artificial fish eggs, tracer stones, and different versions of movable indicators that slide along a line or cable. Plastic practice golf balls strung on a thin wire cable have proven to be particularly reliable and practical devices in gravel-bed streams (Klassen and Northcote 1986; Tripp and Poulin 1986b; Schuett-Hames et al. 1996; DeVries 2000). All devices are installed vertically within the streambed, and maximum depth of streambed disturbance is indicated by the depth to the undisturbed portion of each device. As a general rule, more monitors can be installed per unit time by using impact devices than with vibration devices or excavation (Haschenburger 1996).

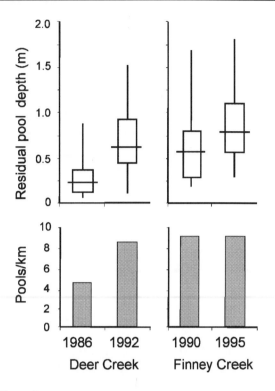

Figure 6.

Examples of monitored changes in number of pools (lower panels) and residual pool depths (median and interquartile range; upper panels) after decline in sediment input in two Washington streams (Deer Creek data from Collins et al. 1994; Finney Creek data from Beechie, unpublished data). The bulk of Deer Creek landsliding occurred between 1983 and 1986 upstream of the 13-km-long sampling reach, filling most pools (left panels). Export of channel-stored sediment between 1986 and 1992 approximately doubled the number of units classified as pools, and significantly increased pool depths (one-sided Wilcoxon rank sum test, $p < 0.001$). Finney Creek landslide cluster occurred in 1987 approximately 1 km upstream of the 3-km-long sampling reach. Pools were not completely filled by sediment from the landslide cluster, so export of channel-stored sediment did not increase number of pools but significantly increased pool depths (one-sided Wilcoxon rank sum test, $p = 0.02$) (right panels).

Scour depth varies spatially within a homogeneous patch of streambed, even under similar shear-stress conditions (DeVries 2000; Rennie and Millar 2000). Hence, it is important to install more than one or two scour monitors to characterize the central tendency and variance of scour depth in a patch. If the goal is to characterize scour on a reach scale, it is important to stratify the sample across patches with different grain-size distributions, analogous to sediment sampling (Wolcott and Church 1991). Sample-size requirements for evaluating scour at the reach scale will vary, depending on anticipated variability in the study stream, desired level of precision, and target scour depth (e.g., Schuett-Hames et al. 1996; DeVries 2000).

Because scour depth scales with particle size, grain-size distribution measurements should be representative of the patch in which scour depth is measured. A pebble count is recommended over bulk sampling. Pebble counts are methodologically biased with respect to determining fine sediment fractions (Fripp and Diplas 1993) but provide a reasonably accurate estimate of the higher percentiles (e.g., D_{90}) and are more practical than bulk samples in coarser substrates where sample weight statistical requirements become more stringent (Church et al. 1987; Ferguson and Paola 1997). Topographic surveying should be done before and after transport events to determine changes in bed elevation. Surveys can be performed across scour-monitor transects by using an auto level, or over the reach by using a total station. In either case, fixing a 127-mm (5 in) diameter base to the bottom of the stadia rod or prism ensures spatially and temporally consistent bed-elevation surveys that are not influenced by bed microtopography (DeVries and Goold 1999).

Biota and other instream measurements

A variety of water-quality and biological parameters can be measured to detect the effects of changes in sediment supply or hydrology on the aquatic ecosystem. These include water temperature, primary production, macroinvertebrates, and vertebrates (e.g., fishes). However, each of these parameters is another step removed from road rehabilitation actions, and attributing changes in these parameters to road improvement actions is exceedingly difficult. Sampling procedures for water quality and biota are discussed in more detail in subsequent chapters (Chapter 6, 8, and 9).

Summary

Monitoring effects of road treatments on aquatic systems is made difficult by a sequence of complex linkages among road treatments, watershed processes, channel changes, and biological responses. Each individual linkage (i.e., that roads alter sediment supply and hydrology, that changes in sediment supply or hydrology affect channel conditions, or that changes in channel conditions affect biota) is documented in the scientific literature. In aggregate, these studies indicate that roads affect aquatic biota. However, each linkage is fraught with uncertainties, and lag times of decades or more between road treatments and channel responses inhibit our ability to attribute channel and biological changes to road treatments.

Organizing the monitoring problem into the common structure of effectiveness monitoring and validation monitoring helps distinguish the various monitoring tasks. Effectiveness monitoring of road treatments answers two basic questions: (1) are the road treatments functioning as intended and (2) are they having the desired effect on watershed processes? Validation monitoring answers additional questions intended to confirm that channels and biota respond as anticipated: (3) do channels and habitat respond to the altered watershed processes as expected and (4) do biological communities respond to the channel changes as expected? Effectiveness monitoring is relatively straightforward and cost effective, because there are shorter lag times between treatment and response, and fewer confounding factors to consider. Validation monitoring must account for decadal lag times between treatment and response, and must consider numerous confounding factors that may obscure the treatment effect. In general, effectiveness monitoring can be implemented by a relatively broad spectrum of organizations that undertake monitoring efforts, whereas validation monitoring should be conducted in a research context.

There is no single monitoring protocol that is applicable to all settings or management scenarios, so each monitoring effort requires thoughtful planning to realize useful results. Design of both effectiveness and validation monitoring programs should begin with clear hypotheses of treatment outcomes (Table 2). These hypotheses guide the monitoring effort throughout, indicating parameters to be measured, sample-site selection, and frequency and duration of sampling. In general, parameter selection first considers which measures most strongly respond to the expected treatment outcome, and final selection considers such factors as cost and repeatability of measurements. Sample-site selection is guided first by the overall study design, then by the availability of treatment and reference sites. Sampling frequency and duration is determined based on the estimated lag time between treatment and response, anticipated duration of the effect, and sample size required to detect treatment effects.

Our brief review of monitoring techniques in this chapter is certainly not exhaustive and only briefly describes each procedure discussed. We have attempted to provide key references that will allow readers to assess the suitability of each technique for their own purposes. Before embarking on any monitoring program, readers should critically evaluate each potential monitoring parameter or technique for its sensitivity to the changes expected, repeatability of measurements, and cost-effectiveness. Ultimately, the success of any monitoring program will depend on clearly stated hypotheses, thoughtful study design, and careful selection of monitoring parameters and sampling protocols.

As with any scientific study, monitoring results for road treatments must be interpreted with appropriate cautions. Interpretation of effectiveness-monitoring results should be straightforward in most cases. That is, treatment effects such as reduced surface erosion should be relatively easy to demonstrate with appropriate monitoring designs (e.g., use of a BACI design and sediment rating curves), and there are relatively few factors that might confound interpretation of the results. By contrast, most validation-monitoring results can be confounded by lag times between treatment and response, as well as numerous other physical or biological processes affecting the response parameters. Therefore, attributing monitoring results to road treatments is problematic, and the use of multiple diagnostics is necessary to support cause-and-effect linkages. Rigorous study designs that include good controls and sufficient resources to monitor over decadal time frames are critical to successful validation monitoring.

Acknowledgments

We appreciate critical reviews of the manuscript by Michael J. Furniss, Aimee Fullerton, and one anonymous reviewer. We also thank Martin Liermann and Dave Jensen for insightful discussions of various study designs and their application to the problem of monitoring road treatments.

References

Abbe, T. B., and D. R. Montgomery. 1996. Large woody debris jams, channel hydraulics and habitat formation in large rivers. Regulated Rivers: Research and Management 12:201–221.

Adams, J. N., and R. L. Beschta. 1980. Gravel bed composition in Oregon coastal streams. Canadian Journal of Fisheries and Aquatic Sciences 37:1514–1521.

Angradi, T. R. 1999. Fine sediment and macroinvertebrate assemblages in Appalachian streams: a field experiment with biomonitoring applications. Journal of the North American Benthological Society 18:49–66.

Bauer, S. B., and S. C. Ralph. 1999. Aquatic habitat indicators and their application to water quality objectives within the clean water act. U.S. Environmental Protection Agency, Region 10, Report #EPA-910-R-99-014, Seattle.

Beamer, E. M., and G. R. Pess. 1999. Effects of peak flows on chinook (Oncorhynchus tshawytscha) spawning success in two Puget Sound river basins. Pages 67–70 in R. Sakrison and P. Sturtevant, editors. Watershed management to protect declining species. American Water Resources Association, Middleburg, Virginia.

Beechie, T. J. 2001. Empirical predictors of annual bed load travel distance, and implications for salmonid habitat restoration and protection. Earth Surface Processes and Landforms 26:1025–1034.

Beechie, T., and S. Bolton. 1999. An approach to restoring salmonid habitat-forming processes in Pacific Northwest watersheds. Fisheries 24(4):6–15.

Beechie, T., G. Pess, E. Beamer, G. Lucchetti, and R. E. Bilby. 2003. Role of watershed assessments in salmon recovery planning. Pages 194–225 in D. R. Montgomery, S. Bolton, D. Booth, and L. Wall, editors. Restoration of Puget Sound rivers. University of Washington Press, Seattle.

Beechie, T. J., and T. H. Sibley. 1997. Relationships between channel characteristics, woody debris, and fish habitat in northwestern Washington streams. Transactions of the American Fisheries Society 126:217–229.

Benda, L., and T. Dunne. 1987. Sediment routing by debris flow. Pages 213–223 in R. L. Beschta, T. Blinn, G. E. Grant, G. G. Ice, and F. J. Swanson, editors. Erosion and sedimentation in the Pacific Rim. International Association of Hydrologic Sciences (IAHS), Publication 165, Wallingford, UK.

Benda, L., and T. Dunne. 1997a. Stochastic forcing of sediment supply to channel networks from landsliding and debris flow. Water Resources Research 33:2865–2880.

Benda, L., and T. Dunne. 1997b. Stochastic forcing of sediment routing and storage in channel networks. Water Resources Research 33:2849–2863.

Bergstrom, F. W. 1982. Episodic behavior in badlands: its effects on channel morphology and sediment yields. Pages 59–66 in F. J. Swanson, E. J. Janda, T. Dunne, and D. N. Swanson, editors. Sediment budgets and routing in forested drainage basins. U.S. Forest Service General Technical Report PNW-141, Portland, Oregon.

Beschta, R. L. 1978. Long-term patterns of sediment production following road construction and logging in the Oregon Coast Range. Water Resources Research 14:1011–1016.

Beschta, R. L. 1987. Sediment transport in gravel-bed rivers. Pages 387–408 in C. R. Thorne, J. C. Bathurst, and R. D. Hey, editors. Sediment transport in gravel-bed rivers. Wiley, London.

Beschta, R. L., and W. L. Jackson. 1979. The intrusion of fine sediments into a stable gravel bed. Journal of the Fisheries Research Board of Canada 36:204–210.

Beschta, R. L., M. R. Pyles, A. E. Skaugset, and C. G. Surfleet. 2000. Peakflow response to forest practices in the western Cascades of Oregon, U.S.A. Journal of Hydrology 233:102–120.

Bilby, R. E., K. Sullivan, and S. H. Duncan. 1989. The generation and fate of road-surface sediment in forested watersheds of southwestern Washington. Forest Science 35:453–468.

Bilby, R. E., and J. W. Ward. 1989. Changes in characteristics and function of woody debris with increasing size of streams in western Washington. Transactions of the American Fisheries Society 118:368–378.

Brasington, J., B. T. Rumsby, and R. A. McVey. 2000. Monitoring and modeling morphological change in a braided gravel-bed river using high resolution GPS-based survey. Earth Surface Processes and Landforms 25:973–990.

Buffington, J. M., and D. R. Montgomery. 1999a. Effects of sediment supply on surface textures of gravel-bed rivers. Water Resources Research 35:3523–3530.

Buffington, J. M., and D. R. Montgomery. 1999b. Effects of hydraulic roughness on surface texture of gravel-bed rivers. Water Resources Research 35:3507–3521.

Bunte, K., and S. R. Abt. 2001. Sampling surface and subsurface particle-size distributions in wadeable gravel- and cobble-bed streams for analyses in sediment transport, hydraulics, and streambed monitoring. U.S. Forest Service General Technical Report GTR-74, Fort Collins, Colorado.

Bunte, K., and L. H. MacDonald. 1999. Scale considerations and the detectability of sedimentary cumulative watershed effects. National Council for Air and Stream Improvement, Technical Bulletin No. 776, Research Triangle Park, North Carolina.

Burroughs, E. R., Jr., and J. G. King. 1989. Reduction of soil erosion on forest roads. U.S. Forest Service Research Paper INT-264, Ogden, Utah.

Cederholm, C. J., L. M. Reid, B. G. Edie, and E. O. Salo. 1982. Effects of forest road erosion on salmonid spawning gravel composition and populations of the Clearwater River, Washington. Pages 1–17 in K. A. Hashagen, editor. Habitat disturbance and recovery: proceedings of a symposium. California Trout, Inc., San Francisco.

Cederholm, C. J., and E. O. Salo. 1979. The effects of logging road landslide siltation on the salmon and trout spawning gravels of Stequaleho Creek and the Clearwater River Basin, Jefferson County, Washington, 1972–1978. Fisheries Research Institute, University of Washington, Final Report Part III, FRI-UW-7915, Seattle.

Chapman, D. W. 1988. Critical review of variables used to define effects of fines in redds of large salmonids. Transactions of the American Fisheries Society 117:1–21.

Chapman, D. W., and K. P. McLeod. 1987. Development of criteria for fine sediment in the Northern Rockies ecosystem. U.S. Environmental Protection Agency, Water Division, EPA 910/9-87-162, Seattle.

Chatwin, S. C., D. E. Howes, J. W. Schwab, and D. N. Swanston. 1994. A guide for management of landslide-prone terrain in the Pacific Northwest. 2nd edition. British Columbia Ministry of Forests Land Management Handbook, ISSN 0229-1622; No. 18. Victoria.

Church, M. 1983. Pattern of instability in a wandering gravel bed channel. Special Publications of the International Association of Sedimentologists 6:169-180.

Church, M., and R. Kellerhals. 1978. On the statistics of grain size variation along a gravel river. Canadian Journal of Earth Sciences 15:1151-1160.

Church, M. A., D. G. McLean, and J. F. Wolcott. 1987. River bed gravels: Sampling and analysis. Pages 43-79 in Thorne, C. R., J. C. Bathurst, and R. D. Hey, editors. Sediment transport in gravel-bed rivers. Wiley, New York.

Clarke, K. D., and D. A. Scruton. 1997. Use of the Wesche method to evaluate fine-sediment dynamics in small boreal forest headwater streams. North American Journal of Fisheries Management 17:188-193.

Collins, B., T. Beechie, L. Benda, P. Kennard, C. Veldhuisen, V. Anderson, and D. Berg. 1994. Watershed assessment and salmonid habitat restoration strategy for Deer Creek, North Cascades of Washington. Report to Stillaguamish Tribe of Indians and Washington Department of Ecology, Olympia.

Collins, B. D., and T. Dunne. 1980. Gravel transport, gravel harvesting, and channel-bed degradation in rivers draining the southern Olympic Mountains, Washington, USA. Environmental Geology and Water Sciences 13:213-224.

Croke, J., and S. Mockler. 2001. Gully initiation and road-to-stream linkage in a forested catchment, southeastern Australia. Earth Surface Processes and Landforms 26:205-217.

DeVries, P. E. 2000. Scour in low gradient gravel bed rivers: patterns, processes, and implications for the survival of salmonid embryos. University of Washington, Department of Civil and Environmental Engineering, Water Resources Series Technical Report No. 160, University of Washington, Seattle.

DeVries, P. E., and D. J. Goold. 1999. Leveling rod base required for surveying gravel river bed surface elevations. Water Resources Research 35:2877-2879.

Dietrich, W. E., Y. Cui, G. Parker, and A. Moi. 2001. The damping of large sediment signals due to attrition, channel morphologic change, and storage: the Fly River watershed, Papua New Guinea. Abstract H51F-10, Eos Transactions AGU 82, fall meeting supplement, American Geophysical Union, Washington, D.C.

Dietrich, W. E., T. Dunne, N. F. Humphrey, and L. M. Reid. 1982. Construction of sediment budgets for drainage basins. Pages 5-23 in F. J. Swanson, E. J. Janda, T. Dunne, and D. N. Swanson, editors. Sediment budgets and routing in forested drainage basins. U.S. Forest Service General Technical Report PNW-141, Portland, Oregon.

Dietrich, W. E., J. W. Kirchner, H. Ikeda, and F. Iseya. 1989. Sediment supply and the development of the coarse surface layer in gravel-bedded rivers. Nature (London) 340:215-217.

Dunne, T., and L. B. Leopold. 1978. Water in environmental planning. Freeman, San Francisco.

Dyrness, C. T. 1967. Mass soil movements in the H. J. Andrews Experimental Forest. U.S. Forest Service Research Paper PNW-42, Portland, Oregon.

Eschner, A. R., and J. H. Patric. 1982. Debris avalanches in eastern upland forests. Journal of Forestry 80:342-347.

Ferguson, R. I., and C. Paola. 1997. Bias and precision of percentiles of bulk grain size distributions. Earth Surface Processes and Landforms 22:1061-1077.

Flanagan, S. A., M. J. Furniss, T. S. Ledwith, S. Theisen, M. Love, K. Moore, and J. Ory. 2000. Methods for inventory and environmental risk assessment of road drainage crossings. U.S. Forest Service, San Dimas Technology and Development Center, San Dimas, California.

Fransen, P. J. B., C. J. Phillips, and B. D. Fahey. 2001. Forest road erosion in New Zealand: overview. Earth Surface Processes and Landforms 26:165-174.

Fredriksen, R. L. 1970. Erosion and sedimentation following road construction and timber harvest on unstable soils in three small western Oregon watersheds. U.S. Forest Service Research Paper PNW-104, Portland, Oregon.

Fripp, J. B., and P. Diplas. 1993. Surface sampling in gravel streams. Journal of Hydraulic Engineering 119:473-490.

Furniss, M. J., S. Flanagan, and B. McFadin. 2000. Hydrologically-connected roads: an indicator of the influence of roads on chronic sedimentation, surface water hydrology and exposure to toxic chemicals. Stream Notes, July 2000. Online at http://www.stream.fs.fed.us/streamnt/jul00/jul00_2.htm [Accessed 23 March 2003].

Furniss, M. J., T. D. Roelofs, and C. S. Yee. 1991. Road construction and maintenance. Pages 297-324 in W. R. Meehan, editor. Influences of forest and rangeland management on salmonid fishes and their habitats. American Fisheries Society, Special Publication 19, Bethesda, Maryland.

Grant, G. E. 1988. The RAPID Technique: a new method for evaluating downstream effects of forest practices on riparian zones. U.S. Forest Service General Technical Report PNW-220, Portland, Oregon.

Grost, R. T., W. A. Hubert, and T. A. Wesche. 1991. Field comparison of three devices used to sample substrate in small streams. North American Journal of Fisheries Management 11:347-351.

Gucinski, H., M. J. Furniss, R. R. Zeimer, and M. H. Brookes, editors. 2000. Forest roads: a synthesis of scientific information. U.S. Forest Service, Corvallis, Oregon.

Hall, J. D., and R. L. Lantz. 1969. Effects of logging on the habitat of coho salmon and cutthroat trout in coastal streams. Pages 355-375 in T. G. Northcote, editor. Symposium on salmon and trout in streams. H. R. MacMillan Lectures in Fisheries. University of British Columbia, Vancouver.

Harr, R. D., W. C. Harper, J. T. Krygier, and F. S. Hsieh. 1975. Changes in storm hydrographs after road building and clear-cutting in the Oregon Coast Range. Water Resources Research 11:436–444.

Harr, R. D., and R. A. Nichols. 1993. Stabilizing forest roads to help restore fish habitats: a northwest Washington example. Fisheries 18(4):18–22.

Harrelson, C. C., C. L. Rawlins, and J. P. Potyondy. 1994. Stream channel reference sites: an illustrated guide to field technique. U.S. Forest Service General Technical Report RM-245, Fort Collins, Colorado.

Harvey, A. M. 1991. The influence of sediment supply on the channel morphology of upland streams: Howgill Fells, northwest England. Earth Surface Processes & Landforms 16:675–684.

Harvey, M. D. 1987. Sediment supply to upland streams: influence on channel adjustment. Pages 121–150 in C. R. Thorne, J. C. Bathurst, and R. D. Hey, editors. Sediment transport in gravel-bed rivers. Wiley, London.

Haschenburger, J. K. 1996. Scour and fill in a gravel-bed channel: observations and stochastic models. Doctoral dissertation. University of British Columbia, Vancouver.

Hicks, B. J., J. D. Hall, P. A. Bisson, and J. R. Sedell. 1991. Responses of salmonids to habitat changes. Pages 483–518 in W. R. Meehan, editor. Influences of forest and rangeland management on salmonid fishes and their habitats. American Fisheries Society, Special Publication 19, Bethesda, Maryland.

Hilton, S., and T. E. Lisle. 1993. Measuring the fraction of pool volume with fine sediment. U.S. Forest Service, Research Note PSW-RN-414, Berkeley, California.

Hovius, N., C. P. Stark, and P. A. Allen. 1997. Sediment flux from a mountain belt derived by landslide mapping. Geology 25:231–234.

Jacobsen, R. B., and K. B. Gran. 1999. Gravel sediment routing from widespread, low-intensity landscape disturbance, Current River basin, Missouri. Earth Surface Processes and Landforms 24:897–917.

Jones, J. A., and G. E. Grant. 1996. Peakflow responses to clear-cutting and roads in small and large basins, western Cascades, Oregon. Water Resources Research 32:959–974.

Kauffman, P. R., P. Levine, E. G. Robison, C. Seeliger, and D. V. Peck. 1999. Quantifying physical habitat in wadeable streams. U.S. Environmental Protection Agency, EPA/620/R-99/003, Corvallis, Oregon.

Keim, R. F., and A. E. Skaugset. 2002. Physical aquatic habitat I. Errors associated with measurement and estimation of residual pool volumes. North American Journal of Fisheries Management 22:145–150.

Kelsey, H. M. 1982a. Influence of magnitude, frequency, and persistence of various types of disturbance on geomorphic form and process. Pages 150–153 in F. J. Swanson, E. J. Janda, T. Dunne, and D. N. Swanson, editors. Sediment budgets and routing in forested drainage basins. U.S. Forest Service General Technical Report PNW-141, Portland, Oregon.

Kelsey, H. M. 1982b. Hillslope evolution and sediment movement in a forested headwater basin, Van Duzen River, north coastal California. Pages 86–96 in F. J. Swanson, E. J. Janda, T. Dunne, and D. N. Swanson, editors. Sediment budgets and routing in forested drainage basins. U.S. Forest Service General Technical Report PNW-141, Portland, Oregon.

Ketcheson, G. L., W. F. Megahan, and J. G. King. 1999. "R1-R4" and "BOISED" sediment prediction model tests using forest roads in granitics. Journal of the American Water Resources Association 35:83–98.

King, J. G., and L. C. Tennyson. 1984. Alteration of streamflow characteristics following road construction in North Central Idaho. Water Resources Research 20:1159–1163.

Klassen, H. D., and T. G. Northcote. 1986. Stream bed configuration and stability following gabion weir placement to enhance salmonid production in a logged watershed subject to debris torrents. Canadian Journal of Forest Research 16:197–203.

Knighton, D. 1998. Fluvial forms and processes. Wiley, New York.

Kochenderfer, J. N., and J. D. Helvey. 1987. Using gravel to reduce soil losses from minimum-standard forest roads. Journal of Soil and Water Conservation 42:46–50.

Kondolf, G. M., and S. Li. 1992. The pebble count technique for quantifying surface bed material size in instream flow studies. Rivers 3:80–87.

LaMarche, J. L., and D. P. Lettenmaier. 2001. Effects of forest roads on flood flows in the Deschutes River, Washington. Earth Surface Processes and Landforms 26:115–134.

Lewis, J. 2002. Quantifying recent erosion and sediment delivery using probability sampling: a case study. Earth Surface Processes and Landforms 27:559–572.

Lisle, T. E. 1982. Effects of aggradation and degradation on riffle-pool morphology in natural gravel channels, northwestern California. Water Resources Research 18:1643–1651.

Lisle, T. E. 1987. Using "residual depths" to monitoring pool depths independently of discharge. U.S. Forest Service Research Note PSW-394, Albany, California.

Lisle, T. E. 1989. Sediment transport and resulting deposition in spawning gravels, north coastal California. Water Resources Research 25:1303–1319.

Lisle, T. E., Y. Cui, G. Parker, J. E. Pizzuto, and A. M. Dodd. 2001. The dominance of dispersion in the evolution of bed material waves in gravel-bed rivers. Earth Surface Processes and Landforms 26:1409–1420.

Lisle, T. E., and S. Hilton. 1992. The volume of fine sediment in pools: an index of sediment supply in gravel-bed streams. Water Resources Bulletin 28:371–383.

Lisle, T. E., and S. Hilton. 1999. Fine bed material in pools of natural gravel bed channels. Water Resources Research 35:1291–1304.

Lisle, T. E., and M. A. Madej. 1992. Spatial variation in armoring in a channel with high sediment supply. Pages 277–293 in P. Billi, R. D. Hey, C. R. Thorne, and P. Tacconi, editors. Dynamics of gravel-bed rivers. Wiley, Ltd., New York.

Lisle, T. E., J. E. Pizzuto, H. Ikeda, F. Iseya, and Y. Kodama. 1997. Evolution of a sediment wave in an experimental channel. Water Resources Research 33:1971–1981.

Luce, C. H., and T. A. Black. 1999. Sediment production from forest roads in western Oregon. Water Resources Research 35:2561–2570.

Luce, C. H., B. E. Rieman, J. B. Dunham, J. L. Clayton, J. G. King, and T. A. Black. 2001. Incorporating aquatic ecology into decisions on prioritization of road decommissioning. Water Resources Impact 3(3):8–14.

Lynch, J. A., and E. S. Corbett. 1990. Evaluation of best management practices for controlling nonpoint pollution from silvicultural operations. Water Resources Bulletin 26:41–52.

MacDonald, L. H. 1993. Sediment monitoring: reality and hope. Pages 81–87 in Proceedings: technical workshop on sediments. U.S. Environmental Protection Agency, Corvallis, Oregon.

MacDonald, L. H., R. W. Sampson, and D. M Anderson. 2001. Runoff and road erosion at the plot and road segment scales, St. John, U.S. Virgin Islands. Earth Surface Processes and Landforms 26:251–272.

MacDonald, L. H., A. W. Smart, and R. C. Wissmar. 1991. Monitoring guidelines to evaluate effects of forestry activities on streams in the Pacific Northwest and Alaska. U.S. Environmental Protection Agency Region 10, EPA 910/9-91-001, Seattle.

Madej, M. A. 1982. Sediment transport and channel changes in an aggrading stream in the Puget Lowland, Washington. Pages 97–108 in F. J. Swanson, E. J. Janda, T. Dunne, and D. N. Swanson, editors. Sediment budgets and routing in forested drainage basins. U.S. Forest Service General Technical Report PNW-141, Portland, Oregon.

Madej, M. A. 1987. Residence times of channel-stored sediment in Redwood Creek, northwestern California. Pages 429–438 in R. L. Beschta, T. Blinn, G. E. Grant, G. G. Ice, and F. J. Swanson, editors. Erosion and sedimentation in the Pacific Rim. International Association of Hydrologic Sciences (IAHS), Publication 165, Wallingford, UK.

Madej, M. A. 1992. Changes in channel-stored sediment, Redwood Creek, northwestern California, 1947 to 1980. U.S. Geological Survey Open-file Report 92-34, Denver.

Madej, M. A. 1999. Temporal and spatial variability in thalweg profiles of a gravel-bed river. Earth Surface Processes and Landforms 24:1153–1169.

Madej, M. A. 2001. Erosion and sediment delivery following removal of forest roads. Earth Surface Processes and Landforms 26:175–190.

Madej, M. A., and V. Ozaki. 1996. Channel response to sediment wave propagation and movement, Redwood Creek, California, USA. Earth Surface Processes and Landforms 21:911–927.

Marcus, W. A., S. C. Ladd, J. A. Stoughton, and J. W. Stock. 1995. Pebble counts and the role of user-dependent bias in documenting sediment size distributions. Water Resources Research 31:2625–2631.

McHenry, M. L., D. C. Morrill, and E. Currence. 1994. Spawning gravel quality, watershed characteristics and early life history survival of coho salmon and steelhead in five north Olympic Peninsula watersheds. Lower Elwha S'Klallam Tribe, Port Angeles, Washington.

McNeil, W. J., and W. H. Ahnell. 1964. Success of pink salmon spawning relative to size of spawning bed materials. U.S. Fish and Wildlife Service, Special Report Fisheries No. 469, Washington, D.C.

Megahan, W. F. 1972. Subsurface flow interception by a logging road in mountains of central Idaho. Pages 350–356 in National Symposium on Watersheds in Transition. American Water Resources Association, Proceedings No. 14, Middleburg, Virginia.

Megahan, W. F., and W. J. Kidd. 1972. Effects of logging and logging roads on erosion and sediment deposition from steep terrain. Journal of Forestry 70:136–141.

Megahan, W. F., M. Wilson, and S. B. Monsen. 2001. Sediment production from granitic cutslopes on forest roads in Idaho, USA. Earth Surface Processes and Landforms 26:153–163.

Miller, D. J., and L. E. Benda. 2000. Effects of punctuated sediment supply on valley-floor landforms and sediment transport. Geological Society of America Bulletin 112:1814–1824.

Montgomery, D. R. 1994. Road surface drainage, channel initiation, and slope instability. Water Resources Research 30:1925–1932.

Montgomery, D. R., and J. M. Buffington. 1997. Channel-reach morphology in mountain drainage basins. Geological Society of America Bulletin 109:596–611.

Montgomery, D. R., J. M. Buffington, R. D. Smith, K. M. Schmidt, and G. Pess. 1995. Pool spacing in forest channels. Water Resources Research 31:1097–1105.

Montgomery, D. R., and L. H. MacDonald. 2002. Diagnostic approach to stream channel assessment and monitoring. Journal of the American Water Resources Association 38:1–16.

Naiman, R. J., T. J. Beechie, L. E. Benda, D. R. Berg, P. A. Bisson, L. H. MacDonald, M. D. O'Connor, P. L. Olson, and E. A. Steel. 1992. Fundamental elements of ecologically healthy watersheds in the Pacific Northwest coastal ecoregion. Pages 127–188 in R. J. Naiman, editor. 1992. Watershed management: balancing sustainability and environmental change. Springer-Verlag, New York.

Nicholas, A. P., P. J. Ashworth, M. J. Kirkby, M. G. Mackin, and T. Murray. 1995. Sediment slugs: large-scale fluctuations in fluvial sediment transport rates and storage volumes. Progress in Physical Geography 19:500–519.

Nyssan, J., J. Poesen, J. Moeyersons, E. Luyten, M. Veyret-Picot, J. Deckers, M. Haile, G. Grovers. 2002. Impact of road building on gully erosion risk: a case study from the Northern Ethiopian Highlands. Earth Surface Processes and Landforms 27:1267–1283.

O'Loughlin, C. 1974. The effect of timber removal on the stability of forest soils. Journal of Hydrology (New Zealand) 13:121–134.

Olson-Rutz, K. M., and C. B. Marlow. 1992. Analysis and interpretation of stream channel cross-sectional data. North American Journal of Fisheries Management 12:55–61.

Packer, P. E. 1967. Criteria for designing and locating logging roads to control sediment. Forest Science 13:2–18.

Paige, A. D., and E. J. Hickin. 2000. Annual bed elevation regime in the alluvial channel of the Squamish River, southwestern British Columbia, Canada. Earth Surface Processes and Landforms 25:991–1009.

Paulson, K. 1997. Estimating changes in sediment supply due to forest practices: a sediment budget approach applied to the Skagit River basin, Washington. Master's thesis. College of Forest Resources, University of Washington, Seattle.

Peterson, N. P., A. Hendry, and T. P. Quinn. 1992. Assessment of cumulative effects on salmonid habitat: some suggested parameters and target conditions. Washington Department of Natural Resources, Forest Practices Division, TFW-F3-92-001, Olympia.

Pickup, G., R. J. Higgins, and I. Grant. 1983. Modeling sediment transport as a moving wave—the transfer and deposition of mining waste. Journal of Hydrology 60:281–301.

Pitlick, J. C., and C. R. Thorne. 1987. Sediment supply, movement, and storage in an unstable gravel-bed river. Pages 121–150 in C. R. Thorne, J. C. Bathurst, and R. D. Hey, editors. Sediment transport in gravel-bed rivers. Wiley, London.

Platts, W. S., W. F. Megahan, and G. W. Minshall. 1983. Methods for evaluating stream, riparian and biotic conditions. U.S. Forest Service General Technical Report INT-138, Ogden, Utah.

Platts, W. S., and V. E. Penton. 1980. A new freezing technique for sampling salmonid redds. U. S. Forest Service General Technical Report INT-148, Ogden, Utah.

Platts, W. S., R. J. Torquemada, M. L. McHenry, and C. K. Graham. 1989. Changes in salmon spawning and rearing habitat from increased delivery of fine sediment to the South Fork Salmon River, Idaho. Transactions of the American Fisheries Society 118:274–283.

Potyondy, J. P. 1989. Cobble embeddedness as an effectiveness monitoring tool. Pages 91–98 in U. S. Forest Service, editor. Proceedings of the national soil and water monitoring workshop. U. S. Forest Service, Watershed and Air Management, Washington, D.C.

Potyondy, J. P., and T. Hardy. 1994. Use of pebble counts to evaluate fine sediment increase in stream channels. Water Resources Bulletin 30:509–520.

Reeves, G., F. Everest, and T. Nickelson. 1989. Identification of physical habitats limiting the production of coho salmon in western Oregon and Washington. U.S. Forest Service General Technical Report PNW-GTR-245, Portland, Oregon.

Reid, L. M. 1998. Calculation of average landslide frequency using climatic records. Water Resources Research 34:869–877.

Reid, L. M. 2001. The epidemiology of monitoring. Journal of the American Water Resources Association 37:815–820.

Reid, L. M., and T. Dunne. 1984. Sediment production from forest road surfaces. Water Resources Research 20:1753–1761.

Reid, L. M. and T. Dunne. 1996. Rapid evaluation of sediment budgets. Catena Verlag, Reiskirchen, Germany.

Reid, L. M., T. Dunne, and C. J. Cederholm. 1981. Application of sediment budget studies to the evaluation of logging road impact. Journal of Hydrology (New Zealand) 20:49–62.

Rennie, C. D., and R. G. Millar. 2000. Spatial variability of stream bed scour and fill: a comparison of scour depth in chum salmon (Oncorhynchus keta) redds and adjacent bed. Canadian Journal of Fisheries and Aquatic Sciences 57:928–938.

Rennison, W. 1998. Risky business. U.S. Forest Service Engineering Field Notes 30:7–20.

Rice, R. A. 1982. Sedimentation in the chaparral: how do you handle unusual events? Pages 39–49 in F. J. Swanson, E. J. Janda, T. Dunne, and D. N. Swanson, editors. Sediment budgets and routing in forested drainage basins. U.S. Forest Service General Technical Report PNW-141, Portland, Oregon.

Rice, R. M., F. B. Tilley, and P. A. Datzman. 1979. A watershed's response to logging and roads: south fork of Caspar Creek, 1967–76. U.S. Forest Service, Research Paper PSW-146, Berkeley, California.

Rice, S., and M. Church. 1996. Sampling surficial fluvial gravels: the precision of size distribution percentile estimates. Journal of Sedimentary Research 66:654–665.

Richards, K. 1982. Rivers: form and process in alluvial channels. Methuen, London.

Roberts, R. G., and M. Church. 1986. The sediment budget in severely disturbed watersheds, Queen Charlotte ranges, British Columbia. Canadian Journal of Forest Research 16:1092–1106.

Robison, G. R., K. A. Mills, J. Paul, L. Dent, and A. Skaugset. 1999. Oregon Department of Forestry storm impacts and landslides of 1996: final report. Oregon Department of Forestry, Forest Practices Technical Report 4, Salem.

Ryan, S. E., and G. E. Grant. 1991. Downstream effects of timber harvesting on channel morphology in the Elk River basin, Oregon. Journal of Environmental Quality 20:60–72.

Sasich, J. 1998. Monitoring effectiveness of forest practices and management systems—surface erosion: study design guidelines, procedures, and methods. TFW Effectiveness Monitoring and Evaluation Program, Washington Department of Natural Resources, Olympia.

Schnackenberg, E. S., and L. H. MacDonald. 1998. Detecting cumulative effects on headwater streams in the Routt National Forest, Colorado. Journal of the American Water Resources Association 34:1163–1177.

Schuett-Hames, D., B. Conrad, A. Pleus, and K. Lautz. 1996. Literature review and monitoring recommendations for salmonid spawning gravel scour. Washington Department of Natural Resources, TFW-AM-9-96-001, Olympia.

Schuett-Hames, D. E., R. Conrad, R. A. Pleus, and M. McHenry. 1999. TFW monitoring program manual for the salmonid spawning gravel composition survey. Washington Department of Natural Resources, TFW-AM9-99-006, Olympia.

Schuett-Hames, D. E., N. P. Peterson, R. Conrad, and T. P. Quinn. 2000. Patterns of gravel scour and fill after spawning by chum salmon in a western Washington stream. North American Journal of Fisheries Management 20:610–617.

Scrivener, J. C., and M. J. Brownlee. 1989. Effects of forest harvesting on spawning gravel and incubation survival of chum (Oncorhynchus keta) and coho salmon (O. kisutch) in Carnation Creek, British Columbia. Canadian Journal of Fisheries and Aquatic Sciences 46:681–696.

Shirazi, M. A., W. K. Seim, and D. H. Lewis. 1980. Characterization of spawning gravel and stream system evaluation. U.S. Environmental Protection Agency, EPA-600/3-79-109, Corvallis, Oregon.

Sidle, R. C., and A. J. Campbell. 1985. Patterns of suspended sediment transport in a coastal Alaska stream. Water Resources Bulletin 31:909–917.

Sidle, R. C., A. J. Pierce, and C. L. O'Loughlin. 1985. Hillslope stability and land use. American Geophysical Union, Water Resources Monograph Series Volume 11, Washington, D.C.

Spina, A. J. 2001. Incubation discharge and aspects of brown trout population dynamics. Transactions of the American Fisheries Society 130:322–327.

Swanson, F. J., and R. L. Fredrickson. 1982. Sediment routing and budgets: implications for judging impacts of forestry practices. Pages 129–137 in F. J. Swanson, E. J. Janda, T. Dunne, and D. N. Swanson, editors. Sediment budgets and routing in forested drainage basins. U.S. Forest Service General Technical Report PNW-141, Portland, Oregon.

Thomas, R. B. 1985. Measuring suspended sediment in small mountain streams. U.S. Forest Service. Pacific Southwest Forest and Range Experiment Station, Berkeley, California.

Thomas, R. B., and W. F. Megahan. 1998. Peak flow responses to clear-cutting and roads in small and large basins, western Cascades, Oregon: a second opinion. Water Resources Research 34:3393–3403.

Tripp, D. B., and V. A. Poulin. 1986a. The effects of logging and mass wasting on juvenile fish habitats in streams on the Queen Charlotte Islands. British Columbia Ministry of Forests and Lands, Land Management Report 45, Victoria.

Tripp, D. B., and V. A. Poulin. 1986b. The effects of logging and mass wasting on salmonid spawning habitat in streams on the Queen Charlotte Islands. British Columbia Ministry of Forests and Lands, Land Management Report 50, Victoria.

USFS and BLM (U.S. Forest Service and Bureau of Land Management). 1994. Record of decision for amendments to Forest Service and Bureau of Land Management planning documents within the Range of the Northern Spotted Owl. U.S. Forest Service, Washington, D.C.

USFS (U.S. Forest Service). 1995. Ecosystem analysis at the watershed scale, federal guide for watershed analysis. U.S. Forest Service, Regional Ecosystem Office, Portland, Oregon.

USFS (U.S. Forest Service). 2000. Region 5 best management practices evaluation procedure user's guide. U.S. Forest Service, Region 5, San Francisco.

WFPB (Washington Forest Practices Board). 1997. Standard methodology for conducting watershed analysis, Appendix B—Surface erosion module. Washington Department of Natural Resources, Olympia.

Waters, T. F. 1995. Sediment in streams: sources, biological effects, and control. American Fisheries Society, Monograph 7, Bethesda, Maryland.

Wemple, B. C., J. A. Jones, and G. E. Grant. 1996. Channel network extension by logging roads in two basins, western Cascades, Oregon. Water Resources Bulletin, 32:1195–1207.

Wemple, B. C., F. J. Swanson, and J. A. Jones. 2001. Forest roads and geomorphic process interactions, Cascade Range, Oregon. Earth Surface Processes and Landforms 26:191–204.

Wesche, T. A., D. W. Reiser, V. R. Hasfurther, W. A. Hubert, and Q. D. Skinner. 1989. A new technique for measuring fine sediment in streams. North American Journal of Fisheries Management 9:234–238.

Wolcott, J., and M. Church. 1991. Strategies for sampling spatially heterogeneous phenomena: the example of river gravels. Journal of Sedimentary Petrology 61:534–543.

Wolman, M. G. 1954. A method of sampling coarse river-bed material. Transactions of the American Geophysical Union 35:951–956.

Wolman, M. G., and R. Gerson. 1978. Relative scales of time and effectiveness of climate in watershed geomorphology. Earth Surface Processes and Landforms 3:189–208.

Wood, P. J., and P. D. Armitage. 1997. Biological effects of fine sediment in the lotic environment. Environmental Management 21:203–217.

Wright, K. A., K. H., Sendek, R. M. Rice, and R. B. Thomas. 1990. Logging effects on streamflow: storm runoff at Caspar Creek in Northwestern California. Water Resources Research 26:1657–1667.

Young, M. K., W. A. Hubert, and T. A. Wesche. 1991. Selection of measures of substrate composition to estimate survival to emergence of salmonids and to detect changes in stream substrates. North American Journal of Fisheries Management 11:339–346.

Zielger, A. D., R. A. Sutherland, and T. W. Gaimbelluca. 2001. Interstorm surface preparation and sediment detachment by vehicle traffic on unpaved mountain roads. Earth Surface Processes and Landforms 26:235–250.

Chapter 4
Monitoring Restoration
of Riparian Forests

Michael M. Pollock, Timothy J. Beechie
Northwest Fisheries Science Center, National Marine Fisheries Service
2725 Montlake Boulevard East, Seattle, Washington 98112, USA
michael.pollock@noaa.gov, tim.beechie@noaa.gov

Samuel S. Chan
Oregon State University, Extension Sea Grant, 200 Warner-Milne Road
Oregon City, Oregon 97045 USA
samuel.chan@oregonstate.edu

Richard Bigley
Washington State Department of Natural Resources, Post Office Box 47014
Olympia, Washington 98504, USA
richard.bigley@wadnr.gov

Introduction

Riparian forests are among the most biologically diverse portions of the terrestrial landscape and provide numerous benefits to instream habitat (Salo and Cundy 1987; Naiman et al. 1993; Nilsson et al. 1994; Pollock et al. 1998). Among these important benefits are the transport of large wood, fine organic material, nutrients, sediment, water, and thermal energy to the stream network, such that a natural aquatic environment is maintained. Alterations to riparian vegetation can alter or disrupt these watershed processes, which affect instream parameters such as stream productivity and the abundance of desirable fishes (Swanson and Lienkaemper 1978; Bisson et al. 1987; Lienkaemper and Swanson 1987). Riparian forest conditions largely determine instream conditions. Riparian areas also are a necessary habitat component for many wildlife species (Kondolf et al. 1987; Raedeke 1988). The loss of riparian habitat throughout much of North America and elsewhere is extensive, but the number of successful efforts to restore these systems is growing (Boldt et al. 1979; GAO 1988; Mutz 1989; BLM 1991; NRC 1992; Kattelman and Embury 1996; Wissmar and Beschta 1998). Riparian restoration describes a suite of restorative management techniques that can alter forest development in riparian areas for the purpose of improving instream and riparian habitat conditions (Oliver and Hinckley 1987; Berg 1990, 1995; Kohm and Franklin 1997).

Monitoring the effectiveness of these restoration actions requires measuring the response of vegetation in the riparian areas, as well as measuring the physical responses (e.g., stream channels, fish habitat, temperature) and biological responses (e.g., primary production, macroinvertebrates, fishes). Several guidelines for determining what and how to monitor specific instream parameters have been published (MacDonald et al. 1991; Bauer and Ralph 1999; Kaufmann et al. 1999), but aspects of monitoring design for restoration of riparian areas have not been well developed, and consistent criteria for determining the success of riparian restoration efforts are lacking. In particular, there has been little analysis of riparian silvicultural treatments on forest conditions and how those changes affect instream habitat (Beechie et al. 2000). For monitoring fencing and grazing projects (another form of riparian restoration), see Chapter 5.

In this chapter, we first provide a background on natural successional processes in riparian forests and an overview of typical practices for restoring riparian areas or accelerating successional trajectories. We then discuss design of effectiveness monitoring programs for riparian restoration, including goals, hypothesis, monitoring design, controls and length of monitoring, and parameters to monitor. Finally, we provide a case study to elucidate the concepts we discuss and the challenges of monitoring riparian restoration projects. Our focus is primarily on effectiveness monitoring (see Chapter 1 for a review of monitoring types), though we briefly discuss the importance of implementation or compliance monitoring, as well as monitoring of instream parameters such as nutrients, temperatures, and physical or biological responses (validation monitoring). Further discussion of instream parameters is provided at length elsewhere in this volume.

Background

In spite of their importance to streams, riparian systems have a long history of being degraded by land-use activities such as logging, grazing, agriculture, road building, and urbanization. This is, in large part, because riparian areas, and especially floodplains, usually are the most productive portions of a landscape and offer relatively easy access. Because of their gentle slopes, river valleys have almost always been preferred as routes of travel relative to mountainous or hilly terrain; so roads and railways often have been built in or near riparian areas. Thus, the numerous economic opportunities riparian areas provide relative to uplands have made them a preferred piece of real estate, which, combined with an historic lack of knowledge about how to properly manage them, has made their degradation all but inevitable.

Riparian Processes and Functions

Successional processes in riparian areas are different from those in adjacent uplands, primarily because riparian areas have a different disturbance regime and often are more productive than uplands (Malanson 1993; Naiman et al. 1993). Additionally, soil water levels often are near the surface, which alters the species composition relative to uplands and creates a patchy or heterogeneous environment at small spatial scales (Pollock et al. 1998). Riparian forests are unique in that they are periodically disturbed by floods and, in larger rivers, by channel migration (Nanson and Beach 1977; Walker et al. 1986; Kalliola and Puhakka 1988; Tabacchi et al. 1998). In small, low-order streams, unique disturbances, such as debris flows and slope failures, also influence riparian forests (Benda and Dunne 1987; Benda 1990; Benda and Dunne 1997). In moist, low-lying floodplains, fire frequencies tend to be lower than in surrounding uplands, while fires can funnel up steeper headwater streams, making riparian areas burn more severely than surrounding uplands (Agee 1988, 1993). Such disturbances create heterogeneous site conditions in riparian areas. As a result, riparian forests tend to be patchy in terms of age and species composition (Nanson and Beach 1977; Walker et al. 1986; Johnson 1994; Fetherston et al. 1995). They also tend to be more biologically diverse (Gregory et al. 1991; Naiman et al. 1993; Pollock et al. 1998).

Fetherston et al. (1995) hypothesized a process of riparian succession along large, unconstrained rivers, whereby sediment deposition followed wood accumulation, which then was followed by plant colonization of the sediment. This process produces patches of vegetation that expand in an area as sediment collects and provides additional germination sites. This patch of vegetation ultimately coalesces with the adjacent riparian forest. The product is a mosaic of riparian forest patches of various ages and species compositions.

If left undisturbed, riparian forests follow typical successional processes, whereby, stands go through four phases: (1) stand initiation, when a site is colonized by trees after a stand-replacing disturbance; (2) stem exclusion, when tree densities become so high that no more trees can become established and the dense canopy eliminates understory vegetation; (3) understory reinitiation, when some of the dominant trees begin to die off, creating gaps in the canopy, allowing for understory vegetation to become reestablished; and, finally, (4) old-growth stages, when a multilayered canopy develops as the dominant trees continue to die, opening up more gaps, and understory trees begin to develop one or more additional canopy layers (O'Hara and Latham 1996; Oliver and Larson 1996). In riparian areas, however, the high rate of disturbance and site heterogeneity generally prevents such a standard successional sequence from occurring. Riparian stands often develop in a much more open structure, such that stem exclusion is much less common and understory vegetation usually is present throughout the development of a forest. Parts of a riparian area may be wet enough that tree growth is slowed, creating openings for understory plants adapted to saturated soil conditions and disturbance. Floods or avulsions may reduce the size of undisturbed patches so light can get in from the sides of such a patch and an understory is maintained (Oliver and Hinckley 1987; Malanson 1993; Pollock 1995).

Riparian disturbances create successional processes that are highly patchy over small spatial scales. O'Hara and Latham (1996) outline a hypothetical riparian successional sequence and describe how it differs from those found in uplands (Figure 1). The hypotheses of both Fetherston et al. (1995) and O'Hara and Latham (1996) suggest that multiple processes driving riparian succession depend on channel size and form, disturbance history, climate, geology, and the availability of large wood. Designing riparian restoration projects that restore natural conditions presents a unique challenge. Silviculture techniques that create the diverse nature of natural riparian areas are important to consider. These and other techniques and models that acknowledge successional processes can assist us in designing restoration activities by helping us understand and mimic the complex natural patterns of riparian succession.

The Need for Restoration and Monitoring

Monitoring restored riparian areas also is challenging because often, riparian forests are restored to meet different management objectives (NRC 1992; FEMAT 1993). Typically, riparian silviculture and other treat-

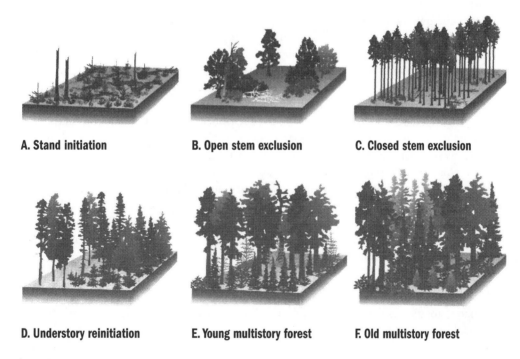

A. Stand initiation   **B. Open stem exclusion**   **C. Closed stem exclusion**

D. Understory reinitiation   **E. Young multistory forest**   **F. Old multistory forest**

Figure 1.
Schematic representation of proposed stand structure classes in riparian areas. (A) Stand initiation: growing space is reoccupied after a stand-replacing disturbance such as a severe flood or fire; one canopy stratum (may be broken or continuous); one cohort of seedlings or saplings; graminoids, herbs, and shrubs may be present. (B) Open stem exclusion: underground competition or saturated soil limits establishment of new individuals; one broken canopy stratum that includes smaller trees; graminoids, shrubs, or forbs also may be present. (C) Closed stem exclusion: new individuals are excluded through light or underground competition; continuous closed canopy, usually one cohort; small or medium trees present; suppressed trees, graminoids, shrubs, and forbs may be absent in some cover types. (D) Understory reinitiation: initiation of new cohort as older cohort occupies less than full growing space; broken overstory canopy with formation of understory stratum; two or more cohorts; overstory consists of larger trees; understory of seedlings, saplings, graminoids, forbs, or shrubs. (E) Young multistory forest: two or more cohorts present through establishment after periodic disturbances, including harvest events; multiaged stand with assortment of tree sizes and canopy strata present but very large trees absent; graminoids, forbs, and shrubs may be present. (F) Old multistory forest: two or more cohorts and strata present, including large, old trees; multi-aged stand with assortment of tree sizes and canopy strata present, including large, old trees; graminoids, forbs, and shrubs may be present. (Adapted from Oliver and Larson 1996 and O'Hara and Latham 1996.)

ments are used to improve riparian forest and instream habitat or to improve commercial harvest opportunities. Riparian restoration projects designed to improve stream habitat usually are concerned with goals such as increasing the amount of wood, leaves, and shade to the stream; improving bank stability; or minimizing erosion. Restoration projects designed to improve riparian habitat usually are concerned with goals such as increasing downed wood on the forest floor, increasing snag habitat, and developing a structurally complex forest canopy (e.g., multiple canopy layers, patchy species distributions, variable live crown depths, and diverse understory vegetation; Berg et al. 1996). Conversely, commercial silviculture usually is concerned with maximizing the growth, yield, and quality of commercially important tree species. In the past, this often has meant growing monocultures of densely packed trees, usually conifers that are harvested before they grow beyond the stem exclusion stage, meaning that little of the forest wood is used for stream habitat or riparian habitat purposes (Oliver and Hinckley 1987; Franklin 1989; Burkhart et al. 1993; Curtis et al. 1998).

Riparian management is slowly shifting toward multiresource management, particularly on public lands, and restoration projects are more and more frequently designed for multiple functions (Sedell et al. 1993; WDNR 1997; Curtis et al. 1998; WFPB 2000). For monitoring, this means that success may not always be measured solely by improvements in stream habitat but also by whether habitat for forest-dependent creatures, such as birds or amphibians, is developing at the expected rate or whether commercial harvest can occur.

Restoring riparian habitat to benefit both aquatic and upland species is increasingly necessary because riparian areas are often the only part of forested landscapes receiving substantial protection from human disturbance, and thus they must contain adequate habitat for multiple species (Sedell et al. 1993). Whether more upland species can persist in landscapes where only riparian areas are protected remains to be seen, and, for many federal forests, monitoring of riparian areas and restored riparian areas includes extensive monitoring for upland wildlife species (USFS and BLM 1994; Hemstrom et al. 1998; Mulder et al. 1999). Generally speaking, the need to manage for multiple resource goals in riparian areas has meant viewing riparian areas from an ecosystem perspective, and many researchers consider the definition of riparian restoration to be those actions that restore natural processes typical of riparian systems, such that they no longer need to be managed (NRC 1992). However, many projects called restoration activities might more properly be called riparian improvement or enhancement projects, since their objective is not to restore the system but to provide improvements to an existing degraded environment. Such activities might include bank stabilization projects or planting cottonwood stakes in a riparian zone on a regulated river because they can no longer establish themselves naturally. Whatever the management objective, to implement a meaningful monitoring program, the management goals need to be specified, and the monitoring effort needs to be designed around determining whether those goals are being met.

Overview of Riparian Restoration Techniques

We define riparian restoration as the process whereby conditions in a riparian area are altered to achieve a desired outcome that would otherwise not occur or would occur over a longer time frame than in the absence of such alterations. As with all types of restoration, monitoring is an integral part of the restoration design. Obtaining meaningful data are much more difficult if monitoring plans are developed after a restoration activity has taken place rather than during the restoration design. A variety of treatments are used to alter riparian conditions and to set the system on a restorative path. In broad terms, this includes some traditional silviculture techniques, such as the planting and removal of trees or removal of competing understory vegetation, as well as the removal of a disturbance suppressing vegetation or the alteration of physical conditions (e.g., flood regimes or sediment supply), such that desired vegetation becomes established or undesirable vegetation dies (Smith 1986; Verry et al. 1999; Stromberg 2001).

The details of silviculture often involve how and where trees are removed or planted, which species are removed or planted, how the soil surface is treated, and how the site is otherwise altered to encourage vegetative removal or establishment. Traditional silvicultural techniques generally have been applied in the arena of commercial forestry, where the goal is to plant commercially valuable species to maximize timber production and quality (e.g., minimize knotwood). Thus, much of the silvicultural literature focuses on techniques to grow tall, straight, densely packed, commercially important trees, often as monocultures, rather than focusing on creating a diverse and functional ecosystem (Smith 1986; Burkhart et al. 1993; Curtis et al. 1998).

Monitoring of riparian restoration requires assessing whether the silvicultural techniques or other treatments applied to a certain area resulted in changed conditions and the desired outcome. Determining the appropriate techniques for a site and developing a monitoring plan require understanding the common riparian restoration silvicultural techniques. Riparian silviculture has not yet evolved into its own subdiscipline. Silvicultural techniques applied to riparian areas are mostly derived from upland silvicultural practices (Berg 1995; Curtis et al. 1998). Many of the basic principles of silviculture do not change in riparian areas. The traditional techniques are described in the context of riparian silviculture in the following subsections and are summarized in Table 1. We also describe other restoration techniques that are unconventional silvicultural practices generally unique to riparian areas, such as simulating natural flow regimes downstream of dams, restoring natural flow regimes through dam removal, bank stabilization by using vegetation, and managing invasive exotics common to riparian areas.

Table 1.
Common silvicultural techniques used in riparian restoration. Pruning and harvesting also are used occasionally to improve or restore riparian functions.

Technique	Definition	Objectives or comments
Thinning or harvesting	Cutting or killing of trees in a stand, usually the smaller, less vigorous trees.	Increases the growth rate of remaining trees. Trees can be left on site to provide organic matter or large woody debris (LWD) to forest floor. Harvest differs from thinning in that larger, commercially valuable trees are taken. Harvest, if done carefully, can minimize damage to riparian functions and, in some cases, even enhance them.
Girdling	Killing trees by removing the cambial layer.	Same as thinning, but trees are left standing to create snag habitat and (eventually) LWD.
Competitive release	Killing vegetation that is competing with desired species (e.g., hardwoods or shrubs competing with conifers).	Increases the growth rate of remaining trees. Can be labor intensive and need to be repeated in riparian areas where growth rates are robust.
Pruning	Removal of limbs from live trees.	Reduces fire hazards or windthrow and allows increased growth of desired species.
Seeding	Planting of seeds of desired species.	Establishes desired vegetation. Often unreliable, depending on species and weather.
Coppicing	Regeneration from vegetative sprouts (stumps, limbs).	Easily establishes vegetation from stumps or limbs (usually certain deciduous trees).
Staking	Vertical insertion of live stems or branches partially into the ground to then take root.	Used to quickly establish trees or bushes. In riparian settings, commonly used to establish willows and cottonwoods.
Layering	Complete or partial horizontal burial of live stems that then take root.	Useful for bank stabilization or other projects where rapid root growth is need. Also used to propagate some conifers that grow slowly.
Planting	Placing live plants of target species into the ground.	Standard technique for establishing plants. Cost of planting largely depends on size of plants.
Site preparation	Alteration of site conditions before the application of regeneration techniques.	Done to improve physical conditions so that regeneration, survival rates, and growth rates increase. Burning, discing, draining, fertilizing, and irrigating are common techniques.

Removing Vegetation

Thinning and harvesting

Thinning involves the cutting of live and dead trees from an existing stand. In commercial silviculture, it is done when stands are so dense that they significantly slow the growth rate of the trees. If there is little or no value to the thinned trees, it is referred to as a precommercial thinning, and the trees normally are felled and left on site. If the trees are large enough to have commercial value and are removed from the site, it is still a thinning operation if some trees are left standing, but, this is more commonly known as harvesting. For riparian restoration that is not tied to commercial harvesting, thinning often is done to open up the overstory and allow more light to understory trees or to create a more diverse canopy structure.

Harvesting of riparian timber for commercial purposes usually is not considered a silvicultural activity for restoration purposes, but it is a frequent occurrence where riparian timber is valuable. Riparian stands can benefit from the removal of commercially valuable (usually large diameter) timber but may also be degraded. Harvesting removes trees that might die and be left as snags or that are felled to add large wood and other organic material to the stream and riparian forest floor. Conversely, removal of trees allows the remaining trees to grow faster and reduces the time it takes for the forest to attain certain aspects of late-successional characteristics, such as low densities of overstory trees, a multilayered canopy, and abundant and varied understory vegetation. Such characteristics often are common management objectives for riparian forests (FEMAT 1993; Berg et al. 1996; Curtis et al. 1998; WFPB 2000). Thus, removal of large trees from riparian areas can accelerate the formation of certain desirable late-successional characteristics, while retarding the development of other desirable characteristics, such as higher densities of large snags and large downed wood.

Forestry on private lands is moving toward the management of riparian areas for commercial timber harvest that also enhances certain habitat features (e.g., WFPB 2000). Multiresource riparian management is a new, evolving discipline, and silvicultural techniques for achieving both of these objectives are constantly being refined (BCMF 2001). There is not a long track record for many of the harvest methods that seem most appropriate for multipurpose riparian management. Many of these activities will need monitoring to see if the harvest actually increases the rate of attainment of desired habitat features. Although commercial harvest of timber in riparian areas is not done for the sole purpose of restoration, it can be done in such a way as to improve some habitat conditions. Thus, we consider it a restorative action if done properly, under the right conditions, with advance agreement on habitat objectives.

Commercial harvest methods most suitable for experimentation in riparian areas include many New Forestry concepts (Kohm and Franklin 1997), such as variation in harvest patterns in the degree of both aggregation and dispersion of trees. (Figure 2). Both aggregated retention and dispersed retention provide habitat benefits and drawbacks, and commercial benefits and drawbacks. The decision of which method to use and at what level of retention will always be a negotiated compromise between competing management objectives.

Girdling

Girdling is a form of thinning in which the dead trees are left standing. The trees are killed by removing a layer of bark and cambium around the entire circumference of the tree (Figure 3). Girdling is used to more closely mimic natural processes such as density-dependent mortality, fire, or insect outbreak, where trees die standing and fall in a stochastic temporal pattern rather than all at once, as is the case with thinning. Girdling can be used to create snag habitat or to reduce the abundance of undesirable species. As a restoration technique, it can be used on large trees as well as small ones.

Competitive release

Competitive release is a commercial forestry term that refers to the release of commercially important species from competition with other species. In commercial silviculture, such activities include application of herbicides to kill undesirable species, usually shrubs and hardwoods, and the manual removal of such species with hand tools, such as chainsaws and pruning shears. Riparian restoration efforts generally have not included application of herbicides but have used the techniques of mulching and grubbing (see McDonald and Fiddler 1994), whereby the roots of competing vegetation, usually shrubs, are dug out of the ground in a circle around

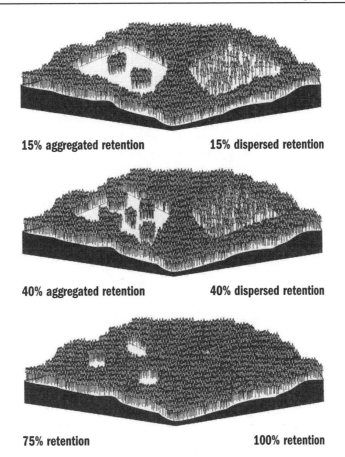

15% aggregated retention   15% dispersed retention

40% aggregated retention   40% dispersed retention

75% retention   100% retention

Figure 2.
Examples of aggregation and dispersion cutting patterns with 15%, 40%, 75%, and 100% retention. (Adapted from Kohm and Franklin 1997.)

each site where the target species (usually a tree) is to be planted, and an artificial or natural mulch is placed around the tree to keep competing vegetation down. In cases where competition is intense, grubbing and mulching may have to occur repeatedly in the years after the target species has been planted (see Emmingham et al. 2000).

Thinning also can be used to open up dense canopies to ensure more light reaches desirable shade-tolerant understory trees, thus accelerating natural successional processes. However, such thinning does not necessarily help understory trees, since the understory shrub layer also responds to the thinning and can outcompete the small trees for light (Wishnie and McClintick 1999).

Pruning
Pruning is a technique that generally has been used in commercial applications to eliminate the limbs that create knotwood in lumber, thereby increasing the value of the timber. Pruning also is useful as a restoration tool to reduce windthrow and fire hazards in riparian buffers (BCMF 2001).

Figure 3.
Forester Bill Emmingham examines a patch of girdled red alder trees. Girdling keeps dead trees standing, providing valuable snag habitat. (Photograph by Sam Chan.)

Planting and Regeneration

Many riparian restoration projects involve planting trees or other vegetation. There are a number of techniques for establishing trees in riparian areas. These include direct seeding, natural seeding, coppicing, staking, layering, and planting of seedlings (Rose et al. 1998). Initial site preparation is a part of many of these restorative techniques. Site preparation is a generic term to describe alteration of site conditions before the application of techniques to increase success. Site preparation often is needed when site conditions are unfavorable to target species or when they are more favorable to nontarget species likely to colonize the site. Site preparation for commercial purposes can involve removal of harvest slash and other organic material, draining, fertilizing, irrigating, removal of competing vegetation, exposing mineral soil on the forest floor, typically by burning or mechanically scarifying, and mounding (Smith 1986; Sutton 1993). There are advantages and disadvantages to each of these techniques. Determining whether to engage in site preparation and what techniques are appropriate for a particular site are an important part of the restoration process and will vary considerably, depending on existing site conditions and management objectives. For riparian restoration, all these techniques have their place, since if used in the appropriate situation, they greatly increase initial tree growth and survival.

Seeding

Restoration of riparian forests from seed can be successful if site conditions are right. Seeding is a natural process and the primary means by which many riparian species colonize new areas. Successful seeding involves understanding the site conditions under which a target species is likely to become successfully established. To germinate, seeds may require mineral soil, organic soil, burned soil, porous gravel, saturated soil, fluctuating water tables, sun, shade, certain soil fungi, a lack of certain soil fungi, rainfall at certain times, and various combinations of these conditions. For many commercially unimportant species, the site conditions needed for successful germination in the wild are not well studied, even if nursery techniques are known. Even when site conditions leading to the successful establishment of a species are known, gramnivory (seed eating) from birds and small mammals can be a problem. Additionally, successful seeding requires viable seeds from a genotype native to and suitable for the target riparian area. All this does not mean riparian restoration from seeds cannot be successful. Appropriate site conditions for the establishment of many species from seed are known. However, direct seeding generally does require more knowledge and technical skill than simpler regeneration techniques such as planting of seedlings. If seeding is considered, examine whether natural seeding will occur when the site is properly prepared. That is, will direct seeding increase the rate of forest development over the natural rate? A final potential drawback is that direct seeding delays the restoration process relative to planting of seedlings, because of the time needed for seeds to germinate and grow.

Coppicing

Coppicing is the term used to describe forest regeneration from vegetative sprouts. Many hardwoods, such as those from the genera maples *Acer*, cottonwoods *Populus*, and willows *Salix*, and a few conifers, most notably coast redwoods *Sequoia sempervirens*, sprout from stumps (Smith 1986; Burns and Honkala 1990a, 1990b). Some species such as cottonwoods and certain maples also sprout from branches or exposed roots. Coppicing can be a relatively passive restoration technique, although work can be done to clear away competing vegetation. Knowing which species coppice can help to determine the appropriate course of action when designing a riparian restoration plan where stumps are present.

Staking and layering

The use of cuttings in layering and staking is a common technique to reforest riparian areas in the immediate nearstream areas where moisture is abundant. These techniques generally use species that readily sprout from branches, such as willows and cottonwoods. Layering involves burying branches approximately horizontal to the ground, often completely covered, while staking involves inserting branches into the ground vertically, usually with some of the branch exposed. Natural layering involves the partial burial of live branches of standing trees so that the branches develop adventitious roots. This has been used to regenerate black spruce *Picea mariana* and northern white-cedar *Thuja occidentalis* in bogs (Johnston 1977). Rose (1998) is a good reference on the propagation of woody plants from cuttings.

Planting

Direct planting of seedlings is perhaps the most common form of riparian restoration. Seedlings are either planted underneath an existing canopy (understory planting) or where there are no trees (open canopy planting). For most species, growth occurs more quickly in an open canopy, but some species require shade, at least when they are young, to survive. Understory planting often occurs when the existing riparian trees are providing some ecological function, such as shade that would be lost if the trees were removed. Understory planting can be used to change the species composition of a riparian forest canopy over time. In the western United States, shade-tolerant western red cedar *Thuja plicata*, Sitka spruce *Picea sitchensis*, and western hemlock *Tsuga heterophylla* often are planted under red alder *Alnus rubra* dominated riparian canopies to hasten succession to a conifer dominated system (Hibbs and Giordano 1996). This technique commonly is called conifer conversion. Understory planting often is done after a thinning operation designed to let in additional sunlight to the understory. However, such thinning also can increase the growth of understory shrubs, thus requiring application of competitive release techniques if the restoration is to be successful.

Seedlings, though more robust than seeds, are still vulnerable to damage from herbivores, competing plants, and disease (Wishnie and McClintick 1999; Emmingham et al. 2000). Techniques for reducing animal damage to planted vegetation include fencing, plastic mesh cages, netting, and chemical sprays (Black 1992). Competition from other plants is reduced through cutting and grubbing. Diseases are minimized by planting the right species and genotype or strain in the appropriate sites.

Any restoration activity that involves planting and monitoring vegetation should recognize that herbivores such as deer *Odocoileus* sp., elk *Cervus* sp., and beaver *Castor canadensis* can undermine restoration efforts (Emmingham et al. 2000; Figure 4). Techniques for reducing animal damage to planted vegetation include fencing, plastic mesh cages, netting, and chemical sprays (Black 1992). An important part of any monitoring effort should be an assessment of the effectiveness of antiherbivory techniques.

Removal of Invasive Exotic Species

Because of their natural high rates of disturbance, which create unoccupied patches, riparian areas are relatively susceptible to colonization by exotic species, and, in some river systems, the number of exotics is quite high (Nilsson 1986; deWaal et al. 1995). As such, the problem of controlling exotic species in riparian areas is global in nature (Dudgeon 1992; Rowlinson et al. 1999; Tickner et al. 2001). However, most of these species do not significantly alter ecosystem functions or outcompete native species and, thus, are not considered invasive or noxious. In contrast, invasive species are aggressive and often form monocultures or become the dominant species if left unchecked. In some instances, riparian areas are dominated by nonnative species, and restoration involves removing such species. In the temperate United States, problematic riparian invasive species include but are not limited to Japanese knotweed *Fallopia japonica*, tamarisk or salt cedar *Tamarix ramosissima* and *T. chinoensis*, reed canary grass *Phalaris arundinacea*, giant reed *Arundo donax*, and leafy spurge *Euphorbia esula*.

Figure 4.
Damage caused by beaver after a tree reached "free to grow" stage. Monitoring for potential damage from animals is essential for successful establishment of trees in riparian areas. (Photograph by Sam Chan)

In the case of tamarisk, monitoring efforts often focus on success of removal efforts and success of recolonization by native species (usually cottonwoods and willows). Tamarisk has light seeds, enabling it to disperse easily, and readily occupies recently disturbed riparian areas (Sudbrock 1993). Its rapid growth, high evapotranspiration demands, and rapid production of dry litter all contribute to its success and the subsequent exclusion of native species. It has caused considerable degradation of riparian habitat throughout Texas, New Mexico, Arizona, Colorado, and Utah (Zavaleta 2000). Taylor and McDaniel (1998), Roelle and Gladwin (1999), Sprenger et al. (2002), and others have monitored and examined the success of various chemical, burning, mechanical, and hydrological treatments in removing tamarisk and the subsequent recolonization of native species. Application of a combination of these techniques, in addition to cottonwood and willow plantings and timed irrigations, have produced diverse riparian habitat (Taylor and McDaniel 1998), while Roelle and Gladwin (1999) were able to prevent the establishment of tamarisk seedlings at a restoration site by regular, controlled fall flooding.

For other invasive species such as Japanese knotweed (Beerling 1991), which is known to disrupt riparian habitat throughout Europe and North America, there has been little in the way of monitoring to determine at what rate riparian habitat is being lost to the species. Knotweed is a large rhizomatous perennial that develops into dense monospecific stands with bamboo-like stems up to 3 m tall (deWaal et al. 1995). It is thought to impact riparian areas because it grows out onto sand and gravel bars, where its dense root system stabilizes the substrate, thus reducing sediment transport.

Reed canary grass, another invasive exotic, is common to wetlands and wet meadows throughout temperate North America. Where low-energy streams flow through wet meadows, the density of reed canary grass can be such that it grows across the entire stream and blocks the movement of salmonids. In Chimicum Creek, a small salmon-bearing stream in western Washington, passage of fish was blocked so extensively by reed canary grass that removal with dynamite was used to create an open waterway for fish passage (M. Pollock, personal observation). The only apparent long-term control of this invasive exotic is to shade it out by creating a dense canopy of trees, because that reduces both germination of seeds and the vigor of established plants (Lindig and Zedler 2002).

Flood Simulations Downstream of Dams

The timed release of waters downstream of dams to mimic natural flows at certain times is becoming recognized as a valuable restoration technique (Rood and Mahoney 1993). Many riparian species (e.g., cottonwood) become established under specific flow conditions, such as floods (Fenner et al. 1985; Auble and Scott 1998). When floods are eliminated, the natural establishment of such species becomes problematic. Additionally, species that would not become established because of the scouring of floods appear in places they are not regularly seen. For example, along the Colorado River in the Glen Marble and Grand Canyon reaches, forests and marshlands have become established in areas that were formerly scoured by floods (Stromberg 2001).

Recently, restoration activities that simulate floods have resulted in changes to the colonization of riparian areas that more closely mimic natural colonization patterns and have reduced nearshore woody vegetation that artificially established as a result of flood control (Rood and Mahoney 1990; Ellis et al. 2001; Stevens et al. 2001). As an example, Stevens et al. (2001) monitored the effects of flood simulations downstream of Glen Canyon Dam on the Colorado River. The floods effectively restored sandbar habitat and inundated patches of woody vegetation with as much as 1 m of sand. However, the woody vegetation was not completely eliminated, and backwater marshlands that had established after dam construction also remained. Similarly, Hill and Platts (1998) monitored the effect of altered flows in the form of flood simulations and increased base flows in the Owens River, California. They found that riparian vegetation rapidly recovered after the changed flow regime and that instream habitat and fish abundance dramatically improved concurrent with the changes in vegetation.

Riparian Restoration after Dam Removal

More than 400 dams have been removed in American rivers, and trends suggest that the rate of dam removal is increasing (Pohl 2002). As dam removal becomes more common, assessments of how to restore downstream areas and monitor such recovery are being considered (Bushaw-Newton et al. 2002; Nislow et al. 2002; Pohl 2002). Changes in flow regimes and sediment supplies associated with dam removal can be expected to have significant effects on both instream and riparian biota (Bushaw-Newton et al. 2002; Nislow et al. 2002; Shafroth et al. 2002). Dam removal usually increases both downstream sediment supplies and flooding. This suggests that the riparian environment will change dramatically as floods remove vegetation and create habitat suitable for more flood-tolerant species. Increases in sediment generally can be expected to raise bed elevation and to increase lateral movement where there is room within the floodplain (Pizzuto 2002; Shafroth et al. 2002). Such changes should result in more depositional bars and other newly created landforms that would favor early successional riparian species.

Bank Protection

Riparian restoration activities concerned with using living materials such as trees and shrubs for bank protection and other forms of fluvial geomorphic control often are termed bioengineering (Schiechtl and Stern 1997). Often the purpose of such activities is to rapidly increase both above-ground and below-ground biomass, such that the erosion of the underlying substrate is minimized during floods. Bioengineering frequently involves the use of both living and nonliving materials to create a desired feature. Thus crib walls, gabions, groins, and sills are planted with living material, such as live cuttings of willow, to restore certain riparian functions. The numerous bioengineering techniques that can be applied toward bank protection are described in detail elsewhere (Gray and Sotir 1996; Schiechtl and Stern 1996, 1997).

Passive Restoration Techniques

Although it involves little effort, letting natural processes take their course also is a restoration technique. This is known as passive restoration to differentiate it from the previously described restoration techniques, which involve active intervention by humans to change existing successional trajectories. Sometimes natural recovery rates are sufficient, such that hands-on restoration is not necessary and, potentially, could be counterproductive. For example, Briggs (1996) describes the recovery of Arivaipa Creek, Arizona, after a 500-year flood destroyed most of the riparian vegetation. A massive recovery effort was implemented to accelerate recovery, which included planting of thousands of cottonwood stakes. However, just 8 years after the flood, the riparian areas had recovered so robustly with natural vegetation that the artificial plantings could not even be found. In this case, the restoration effort was not needed. The question of what, if any, improvement a restoration effort might have over natural processes should always be answered.

Designing a Monitoring Program

Defining the Goals, Objectives, and Hypotheses

Recognizing and describing the goals and objectives of a proposed restorative action is the first step in developing a monitoring program. If the project only has general goals, specific objectives will need to be generated. Objectives can be transformed into testable hypotheses. Typically, the first questions to ask are: What riparian functions are degraded, and which ones will a proposed activity restore? These questions, focused on the restoration effort, also guide the structure of the monitoring program. Monitoring determines if the desired riparian functions are, in fact, being restored over time and at the projected rate.

Generating hypotheses is a necessary step in the restoration monitoring process, because it provides a context within which to analyze trends in monitoring data. Whether they are put in writing or not, all riparian restoration projects have working hypotheses. When a project is initiated, it is based on the general assumption that the restoration action is going to lead to an improvement in habitat conditions. Thinking out the how, when, and why of this assumption leads to developing formal hypotheses. This allows specific predictions to be made about how habitat will improve in response to the restorative action. Such predictions also guide the development of what aspects of the habitat should be monitored (see examples in Table 2).

Riparian requirements for instream species (e.g., fishes), riparian species, and timber harvest often are at odds with each other, leading to numerous and often conflicting goals of riparian restoration projects (Curtis et al. 1998). Generating specific objectives and hypotheses up front has the advantage of clearly specifying what the purpose of the restoration project is and helps to guide the restoration design to achieve the goals. For example, riparian restoration may be planned to accelerate the development of late-successional forests for the benefit of riparian wildlife species or to accelerate the development of large trees that will fall into streams and form pool habitat for fishes (Berg et al. 1996; Beechie et al. 2000). These objectives are not entirely exclusive, but restorative actions designed to meet both objectives may take longer and require more careful planning and monitoring. Managing for both resource extraction and fish or wildlife habitat is even more problematic, since removing large, commercially valuable trees often delays the formation of snags and large woody debris (LWD) on the forest floor that are typical of late-successional habitat, as well as delaying the opportunity for trees to die, fall into streams, and create fish habitat. Understanding the trade-offs needed to achieve multiple goals and objectives, particularly the time delays in achieving certain objectives, is a key to developing a workable restoration strategy and an effective monitoring strategy that will determine if the agreed to goals are being achieved.

Table 2.
Selected examples of monitoring hypotheses and potential monitoring parameters for riparian restoration actions.

Hypothesis	Potential monitoring parameters
Planting willow stakes at a density of 2,000 stakes/ha in a 10-m-wide zone adjacent to a 3-m-wide stream will result in complete canopy closure over the treated stream reach within 10 years.	Monitoring may include stem density and canopy closure measured over at least the 10-year period indicated in the hypothesis.
Planting willow stakes at a density of 2,000 stakes/ha in a 10-m-wide zone adjacent to a 3-m-wide stream will reduce stream temperature to background levels within 10 years.	Low-cost temperature loggers can be used to evaluate project success in terms of stream temperature (compared to a reference site) measured over time.
Thinning a riparian Douglas-fir stand with a quadratic mean diameter breast height (DBH_q) of 23 cm and an initial density of 1,000 trees/ha to a density of 500 trees/ha along a 20-m-wide channel will increase functional wood delivery to the stream within 80 years relative to an unthinned stand.	Monitoring should include (1) marking location of the site where thinning will occur, (2) measuring DBH of all trees in the stand, (3) recording number of pieces of large woody debris and whether or not they are functioning to form habitat in the stream. Practically speaking, it makes sense to map and tag all of the trees in the initial monitoring effort so that they can be relocated over long periods of time. A control site where no thinning will occur needs to be similarly monitored.
Implementation of Washington's new forest practice regulations will result in a 10-fold increase in riparian canopy cover within 15 years at the watershed-level scale (WFPB 2000).	Monitoring this hypothesis will require the use of aerial photography or satellite imagery combined with geographic information system stream and riparian areas to assess long-term landscape-level changes. Digital imagery allows for the use of algorithms to automatically detect changes in spectral characteristics of riparian areas reflective of changes in cover type.
(1) Planting high densities of willows and cottonwood next to a small low-gradient stream will create a riparian forest of these species and encourage colonization by beaver *Castor canadensis*, (2) beaver will use this material as food and to dam the stream, (3) creating pool habitat that will be used by juvenile coho salmon *Oncorhynchus kisutch*.	This is a complex, cascading hypothesis, the success of which is beyond the control of the initial restorative action. Monitoring will include repeated measures of (1) stem density and size, (2) number and size of beaver dams and impoundments, and (3) changes in fish abundance or community structure.

Models are a useful tool for hypothesizing the long-term effects of restoration activities. Silvicultural growth and yield models such as the Forest Vegetation Simulator (FVS; Wykoff et al. 1982) or the Oregon Growth Analysis and Projection (Hann et al. 1995), riparian function models such as Riparian in a Box (RIAB; Kennard et al. 1998; Beechie et al. 2000), and combined models such as the Riparian Aquatic Interactions Simulator (Welty et al. 2002) can predict how silvicultural actions might affect long-term forest and stream conditions. Such models can help generate quantitative monitoring hypotheses for long-term programs. The FVS is a general model that has been adapted to every ecoregion of the United States, such that there is a family of FVS models. These models take initial stand data and project how the stand will develop over time. The models also allow silvicultural treatments such as thinning and planting to take place at specific times, thus providing a means of generating how a forest might respond to a particular restorative action over long periods of time. However, these models were not developed specifically for riparian areas, and they do not take into account how stochastic disturbances common to riparian areas might affect stand development. They primarily were developed to provide guidance on how silvicultural activities can increase forest growth and yield for commercial harvest. Nonetheless, until riparian-specific models are developed, they are among the best publicly available models for predicting long-term consequences of riparian silvicultural activities.

The FVS model, in combination with RIAB, also has been used to estimate how different silvicultural activities will affect long-term LWD delivery to streams, an important consideration in managing fish habitat. For example, Beechie et al. (2000), by using FVS and RIAB, ran a series of simulations for riparian forests to determine under what conditions harvest of riparian trees would accelerate the delivery of large woody debris to streams at a rate that was large enough to form pool habitat. (Figure 5).

For a Douglas fir riparian forest with a quadratic mean diameter breast height (DBH_q) of 23 cm next to a 10-m-wide stream, they found that thinning tree densities from about 1,000 trees/ha down to about 500 trees/ha results in a loss of pool-forming LWD delivery to streams beginning about 20 years after thinning. The term pool-forming refers to LWD that is large enough to form pool habitat, based on an empirical relationship of

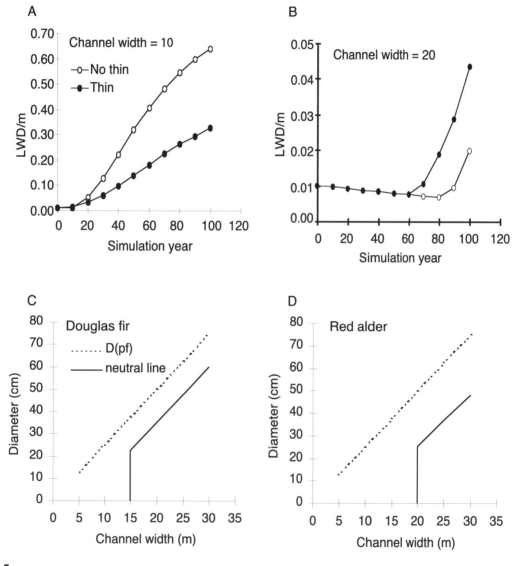

Figure 5.
Graphs A and B are examples of predicted large woody debris (LWD) abundance over time for thinning of Douglas-fir with initial quadratic mean diameter breast height (DBH_q) = 23 cm for channels 10 m wide and 20 m wide. The "No thin" stand has no thinning treatment; the "Thin" stand was thinned to 495 trees per hectare. Note different y-axis scales. Graphs C and D model prediction of DBH_q and channel width combinations, where thinning enhances LWD recruitment for the Douglas-fir and red alder pathways. Dashed line (D_{pf}) is the minimum diameter of pool-forming LWD by channel width. Solid line represents the predicted DBH_q at which LWD recruitment after a thinning treatment is not significantly different from LWD recruitment for the unthinned case. Combinations of stand diameter and channel width that plot below and to the right of the solid line represent cases where thinning should enhance recovery of LWD recruitment; those that plot above and to the left of the solid line represent cases where thinning will inhibit recovery of LWD recruitment.

stream size to size of wood needed to form pools. In contrast, the same thinning operation on a similar stand along a 20-m-wide stream helps to create larger trees (and larger LWD) faster than if no thinning had occurred. Because this larger stream needs larger pieces of wood to form pool habitat, the thinning operation helps to accelerate the rate of functional LWD delivery to the stream. These model results suggest that for larger streams, silvicultural treatments that increase the growth rates of riparian trees will provide functional LWD sooner than without such a treatment and that some timber harvest is compatible with the goal of improving instream habitat. Conversely for smaller streams, removing timber delays functional LWD delivery to streams because trees are being removed that are large enough to form pool habitat in the near future, should they die.

The model also provides an estimate of the time lag between thinning and when the impact to the stream will occur. Because these time lags are on the order of many decades, it suggests that for many situations, measuring the direct effects of riparian restoration activities on instream LWD levels and physical conditions will probably not yield meaningful results within a short time period. Determining the short-term success of such a project will require monitoring of more responsive parameters, such as tree growth rates or possibly changes in shade levels or stream temperature. Thus, using such a model helps to develop quantitative testable hypotheses that can be answered within the desired time frame. In the example above, using the model, specific quantitative hypotheses can be generated concerning how the abundance of instream LWD is expected to change over time relative to a control site.

Study Design

Once the goals of the restoration plan are determined and the hypothesis is generated, the restoration treatment needs to be implemented in such a way that the hypothesis can be tested. This probably is the most difficult part of the process, but a poorly designed treatment will make it difficult to interpret the results of any monitoring effort. The key point is that plans for monitoring need to be integrated into the restoration design early in the process. Monitoring of reference sites, as well as treatment sites (either paired or unpaired), allows statistical comparisons between treated and untreated sites. Without replication, statistical inferences are applicable only to the single site and cannot be generalized to other riparian sites. Where both treatment and reference sites are replicated in space (extensive before–after or posttreatment designs, see Chapter 2), statistical inferences can be generalized to other similar sites. The number of sites (spatial replication) and the length of monitoring (temporal replication) also are critical factors to consider in designing the study or monitoring program. Spatial and temporal replication will affect the ability of a monitoring program to detect significant change after riparian restoration. Chapter 2 provides detailed descriptions of various study designs, considerations for selecting controls, estimating sample sizes, and strengths and weaknesses of common study and monitoring designs. In general, the ideal design would include replication across many sites or watersheds and long-term monitoring before and after treatment. Unfortunately, this may not be possible for many restoration activities, including riparian restoration, due to a variety of constraints that make it both financially and logistically difficult to monitor multiple projects at multiple scales.

Parameters for Monitoring Riparian Restoration

Deciding what to monitor is a key step in the monitoring process. There are potentially more things to monitor than there are resources, and there are trade-offs between the cost of acquiring additional information and of using resources for other activities. A good monitoring effort recognizes this and prioritizes data collection efforts based on the goal of the restoration plan. At the very least, a good monitoring plan will ensure that enough data can be collected to determine if the primary objective or objectives of the restoration effort were met (examples of simple hypotheses and the parameters needed to test them are provided in Table 2). Additional data can be collected if resources are available to answer questions of secondary or tertiary importance. General categories of parameters monitored for riparian restoration projects include groundwater levels, vegetative growth and survival, tree planting, understory response, shade and stream temperature, and instream habitat. Information about parameters typically monitored as part of riparian restoration projects and references directing the reader where to find more information are provided in Table 3.

The selection of monitoring parameters can be influenced by a variety of factors, including study design, costs, and logistics. In addition, the number and intensity of sampling will depend on the scale of the project. More detailed information typically is collected when examining a single reach-scale project, while examining many

Table 3.
Potential parameters to measure when monitoring riparian restoration projects along with references to find additional information on methodologies. Information on instream parameters such as temperature, instream large woody debris (LWD), channel morphology, habitat units, biota, and primary productivity can be found elsewhere in this volume.

Parameter	Examples of measure	References
Basic site information	Slope, stream gradient, elevation	Wenger 1984; Harrelson et al. 1994
Mapping	Site map	Wolf and Brinker 1994
Soil conditions	Depth of organic layer, soil composition	USFS 1987; NRCS 1999
Groundwater levels	Water elevation	Freeze and Cherry 1979; Nielsen 1991
Disturbance history	Fire, logging and land use, landslides, etc.	Agee 1993; Benda et al. 1998
Shade (stream and riparian)	Canopy closure, light penetration	Steinblums 1984; MacDonald et al. 1991; Brosofske et al. 1997; OPSW 2000
Tree survival and growth		
—General data	Location, size, species; method of tree removal; site preparation (burning, mounding, slash removal); method of brush control (cutting, grubbing, tying back); method of herbivore control; source of plants	Wenger 1984
—Basic stand characteristics	Basal area, density, height	Wiant 1979; Wenger 1984; USFS 1987; BCMF 2001
—LWD (stream and riparian)	Diameter, length, species, decay class (riparian , only) location relative to stream	Hitchcock and Cronquist 1973; Maser et al. 1988; MacDonald et al. 1991; Maser and Sedell 1994; Ralph et al. 1994; Smith 1998; Schuett-Hames et al. 1999
—Tree biomass (riparian)	mean diameter breast height (DBH), height, canopy depth	Crow 1971; Baskerville 1972; Koerper and Richardson 1980; Crow 1983; Crow and Schlaegel 1988; Bormann 1989; Smith 1998
—Snags (removed/retained)	Species, height, DBH, decay class	Wiant 1979; Maser et al. 1988; Maser and Sedell 1994; Smith 1998
—Spatial patterns of trees	Aggregation, dispersion	Kohm and Franklin 1997; Dale 1999; BCMF 2001
Understory survival and growth		
—Biomass accumulation (riparian)	Percent cover, stem diameter (smaller trees and shrubs)	Alaback 1986, 1987; Pollock 1995
—Biodiversity (species richness and evenness)	Presence/absence, biomass, frequency	Magurran 1988; Pollock 1998

projects throughout a watershed or region might require less intensive sampling efforts across more sites. Clearly defining hypotheses will greatly simplify selection of parameters. In this subsection, first we discuss information needed for project implementation (e.g., baseline maps, project maps). This data will be useful for understanding project effectiveness and factors that should respond directly to riparian treatments (soils, groundwater, vegetation, shade) or provide indications of riparian treatment effectiveness. Then, we discuss those instream parameters that respond indirectly to changes in riparian vegetation (e.g., temperature, channel morphology, biota). These three categories are roughly identical to what is often thought of as implementation monitoring, effectiveness monitoring, and validation monitoring (MacDonald et al. 1991; see also Chapter 2). While our focus is on monitoring project effectiveness, information on project implementation or compliance is needed to assist in understanding why a riparian treatment was or was not effective.

The purposes of effectiveness monitoring and validation monitoring typically are to determine if the site is moving along the expected recovery trajectory and the ultimate success of the project. For riparian silviculture, success generally is determined by measuring the attributes of the vegetation, usually trees, such as survival, growth, abundance, percent blowdown. For tree mortality, the cause of death could be noted if known. Done properly, effectiveness monitoring for riparian restoration usually is an undertaking that will last decades. Many of the current forest management plans require long-term monitoring efforts, sometimes essentially in perpetuity. There are already a number of long-term forest monitoring efforts in the network of the National Science Foundation's Long Term Ecological Research sites and elsewhere that have provided interesting insights into long-term monitoring challenges.

The parameters monitored for various types of riparian restoration will depend on the projects goals, objectives, and hypotheses, as well as a variety of funding and logistic factors. Thus, it is difficult to identify or recommend which parameters should be monitored for each type of restoration. In spite of this, there are a number of things that typically would be collected for various project types. For example, background information that might be measured for a restoration project involving killing or removing trees might include data on trees removed or killed (number, size, species, location), method of killing and removal, trees retained (number, size, species, location), snags cut or retained (number, size, species, decay class, location), LWD removed or LWD retained (number, size, species, decay class), date of harvest, harvest damage to trees, and understory (Table 3).

Also important to consider before selecting monitoring parameters is the history of a site's human and natural disturbances, which can help predict how a site will respond with or without restoration. Historical aerial photographs and the records of the landowner often are the best sources of such information. Disturbances that may affect the outcome of the restoration project include changes in upstream sediment supplies (such as might occur if there were a dam upstream or if there has been recent mass wasting), fire, logging, urbanization in the watershed (e.g., altered hydrology as a result of an increase in impervious surfaces), diking, agricultural clearing, dredging, water diversions, recent insect outbreaks, and historic channel migrations. Determining the complete disturbance history of the watershed upstream of the restoration site clearly can be a daunting challenge, but having some idea of how the watershed has been altered by natural and human actions is helpful in planning a restoration project, in determining what to monitor, and in having realistic expectations regarding the likelihood for success. For example, if an analysis of the disturbance history indicates that large fluctuations of sediment move through a stream system, then species will have to be planted that can withstand burial, excavation, and highly variable water tables. Because high sediment loads also can lead to increased channel meandering, it is possible that entire riparian restoration projects can be destroyed by channel migration.

General Descriptive Field Data

As an initial part of the monitoring effort, regardless of what is monitored over the long term, basic site information generally needs gathering for a context within which to interpret the monitoring data. Obvious exceptions to this are coarse-scale monitoring efforts where data are gathered remotely. Without basic site information, it is difficult to interpret trends in monitoring data or to understand unexpected results. Much of this site information also is needed as part of any well-executed riparian restoration. Side slope, stream gradient, stream width, and relative site elevation are descriptive data that can easily be obtained with a clinometer or laser range finder. Many riparian monitoring efforts require an initial map of the site before the restoration effort. The relative affordability of laser range finders, global positioning satellites, and other mapping equipment has simplified the initial monitoring phase of mapping the treatment and control sites. Basic information is mapped, such as the location and corners of the restoration area, species DBH (diameter breast height), and height of all major trees within the restoration area. If it is a large area, random or systematic subsampling may be necessary. Forest plots are easily mapped by using a polar coordinate system, whereby the distance and angle of all objects are measured from a fixed point, but other techniques are suitable as well. Outside of the restoration site, the location of the stream, nearby roads, or other major objects are mapped as locator objects. Global positioning satellites often are used to locate restoration sites as well, though, under canopy and in narrow valleys, this can be difficult.

Descriptive information for monitoring plans may, in some instances, include a determination of the soil conditions at each microsite where vegetation is planted. Much of the variation in growth or survival of vegetation is a result of soil conditions. Interpretation of postrestoration monitoring results may be greatly enhanced if soil conditions are known. The degree of soil saturation, permeability, porosity, percent organic matter, and other factors (see Table 3) will determine which species of plants will thrive in a given area. In riparian areas, soil conditions can be quite variable, especially the degree of saturation, and a knowledge of which plants do well under which microsite conditions can substantially increase the success of the project. For example, plants such as cottonwoods, which are adapted to porous, gravelly soils, generally do not do well when planted in heavy clay soils. Even if some plants survive in a particular soil site, if they are not well adapted to site conditions, they will eventually be outcompeted by species that are better adapted to the site, and the goals of the restoration project will not be achieved (although perhaps a more natural outcome will occur).

Basic Parameters

Groundwater levels

For many areas, monitoring groundwater levels yields general information essential to the success of any riparian restoration project. This is particularly true in arid regions where ignoring groundwater levels or depth to saturation and how this fluctuates over time can lead to regeneration failure. It also is important where water flows have been altered or have been restored as part of the restoration effort. Predicting how the riparian vegetation itself will affect groundwater levels also is something to consider. Not recognizing areas where groundwater levels are high for much of the year can lead to regeneration failure if flood-tolerant species are not planted. Whether groundwater monitoring should occur depends on whether changes are expected based on the activities undertaken. For example, it might be particularly important for assessing causes for plant mortality where flow regimes have been altered, either through the removal of dams or changes in flow releases from dams. Monitoring the success of the "natural" establishment of riparian species when floods are simulated downstream of dams generally uses techniques for measuring vegetation establishment discussed below coupled with the rate the water table drops, because it appears to affect the survival of certain species such as cottonwood (Rood and Mahoney 1990). Groundwater levels typically are measured by using groundwater monitoring wells (Figure 6; see also Chapter 6). Additional information on monitoring groundwater can be found in Nielsen (1991).

Vegetation composition, growth, and survival

One of the major factors to monitor for any riparian restoration project is vegetation growth, survival, and community composition. How this is monitored depends on the species of interest. Examples of techniques for measuring plant growth, survival, and changes in community composition typically involve monitoring changes in biomass, as described in Alaback (1987) and Alaback and Herman (1988). Changes in tree biomass usually are determined by measuring changes in tree diameter and tree height, which then are incorporated into species-specific regional regression equations that predict biomass based on these parameters (e.g., Crow and Schlaegel 1988). When a restoration action requires the killing or removal of trees and there is interest in determining the response of the remaining trees to the treatment, location, species, DBH, and height of all major trees within the restoration area should be mapped, and trees should be tagged with unique identifier numbers. If it is a large area or if tree densities are high, subsampling may need to occur. Location, size, species, and decay class of snags and logs also should be noted if time allows, since these are important habitat features. Tree height, live crown or canopy depth, snag decay class, canopy closure, as well as understory condition (percent cover of forbs and shrubs, biomass of forbs and shrubs, height of understory shrubs), and herbivore browse levels also could be measured if relevant to monitoring hypotheses. Location, species, and size of any understory trees also should be included if relevant to the monitoring question (e.g., what are the species-specific changes in growth rates as a result of the treatment). If there is extensive understory tree regeneration, then marking the location of all trees typically is not practical, and general descriptions (e.g., percent area covered or average height) of regeneration are used instead. Tagging both overstory and understory trees

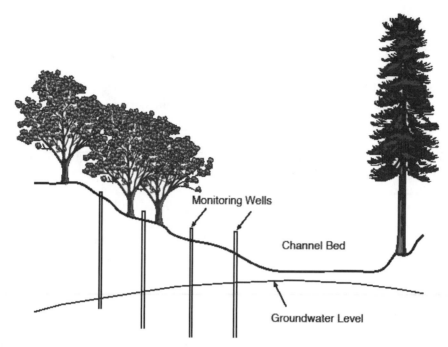

Figure 6.
Location of monitoring wells across an idealized stream channel.

makes mapping easier and allows future monitoring crews to locate themselves spatially within a site. More importantly, tagging each tree with a unique identification number ensures that over time the same measures are attributed to the same tree. If subsampling of the plot is to occur by using permanent subplots, then the location of each subsample needs to be monumented. Radial plots with a monumented center are common and usually the simplest. Parameters to consider monitoring when tree removal occurs are in Table 3.

Many restoration efforts involve the planting of trees, either where there is no forest or in the understory of an existing forest. For monitoring purposes, it is especially important that the location of the planted trees be mapped and that each tree be tagged. Many young trees do not survive, and when a tree is missing, it can be difficult to verify that fact if the location is not known, particularly if the site has become overgrown. Sites may experience some natural regeneration, which will lead to artificially high estimates of survival if the planted trees are not mapped and tagged.

A good monitoring program will document where and what planting techniques were used and will include many details of the operation, so there is a reasonable chance of understanding why a technique is successful or unsuccessful. If possible and if restoration crews have adequate training, describing microsite conditions at each place that a tree is planted is very useful. Information such as depth to water table, soil saturation, soil substrate, canopy closure, and surrounding vegetation provide insight into survival patterns. Other information that is important to note include the size and species of each seedling and whether and how it is protected against herbivores. Often, brush will need to be controlled by cutting or grubbing. The length of the radius of clearing around each planting site and any other relevant information should be noted so as to relate future patterns of survival to site conditions. General data that should be gathered if a restoration plan involves planting trees include trees or stakes planted (number, size, species, location, microsite conditions), site preparation (burning, mounding, slash removal), method of brush control (cutting, grubbing, tying back), date of planting, method of herbivore control, planting crew, and origin of plants. All this data may be useful later to understand why a project succeeded or failed.

Understory or herbaceous layers may need to be monitored, depending on the nature of the restoration activity and the hypotheses. For example, on the Pacific Coast, riparian red alder forests that have been thinned to allow newly planted trees (usually conifers) to grow often end up with a dense understory of salmonberry *Rubus spectabilis* that competes with the new tree growth. This has led to understory removal experiments to reduce shrub growth (through pruning and grubbing) long enough for the conifers to rise above the salmonberry, which may be several meters high. An early increase in survivorship and improved growth has been observed where such shrub competition has been reduced (Wishnie and McClintick 1999). How much this improves the growth of the target species over the long term remains to be determined. Other understory riparian monitoring efforts, though not always associated with restoration activities, include monitoring of herbaceous vegetation and bryophytes (Pollock 1995; Pollock et al. 1998). Whether or not such detailed monitoring efforts should occur depends on the nature of the restoration objectives. In portions of the arid West, increasing availability of forage in riparian areas is often an explicit restoration objective (see Chapter 5), and thus the understory response to silvicultural treatments (e.g., reforestation) becomes very important.

Measuring the response of understory vegetation to silvicultural treatments is not done routinely because it can be quite time consuming and expensive. But it can yield useful information that may be pertinent to management questions, particularly when improved wildlife habitat or increased biodiversity are management objectives. Understory monitoring often is concerned with biomass accumulation, species diversity, or the effects of shrub competition on understory trees. Biomass usually is determined by measuring plant parameters, such as stem diameter, frond length, or percent cover, then relating it to biomass by using local, species-specific regression equations. Species diversity is determined by measuring both the number and the relative abundance of species, where abundance is measured as either frequency of individuals, biomass, or percent cover. Accurately estimating understory biomass is a time-consuming affair that usually involves estimating percent cover of the various species of herbs and forbs and measuring the basal diameter of shrubs (Pollock 1995). These measures then are converted to biomass by using regression equations. Biodiversity estimates are easier, especially if only species richness is measured and the relative abundance of each species are not a concern. However, plant identification requires specialized knowledge, particularly for granimoids (grasses, sedges, and rushes), which are common in riparian areas. Detailed descriptions of protocols for measuring understory can be found in Alaback (1986), Magurran (1988), Buech and Rugg (1989), Pollock (1995), and Elzinga et al. (1998).

Broad-scale assessment of riparian condition

The previously mentioned methods for monitoring riparian vegetation have focused on reach-scale projects and direct measures of tree or plant. However, monitoring riparian conditions at coarser scales—for example, to assess overall changes in watershed riparian conditions or across multiple stream reaches—is important. Broad-scale evaluations of riparian conditions usually involve remote sensing, either satellite imagery or aerial photography. Examples of types of remote-sensing options, along with the character of the data they provide, are presented in Table 4. Until recently, aerial photography was the primary means by which watershed vegetation was assessed, but this approach is time consuming and expensive. Landsat Thematic Mapper satellite data provides another means to assess vegetative conditions, but Thematic Mapper spatial resolution limits its utility for detecting relatively narrow objects such as riparian buffers. Ikonos satellite imagery, at a nominal spatial resolution of 4 m, provides a capability for mapping riparian forest buffers of 12 m or wider. Incorporating 1 m Ikonos imagery could reduce the detectable minimum buffer width to just a few meters, while Quickbird satellite imagery from Earthwatch offers submeter resolution. Some of the drawbacks to higher-resolution mapping include increased data processing requirements, associated computing and data storage capabilities, a host of image preprocessing considerations required to ensure consistent mapping across a range of conditions, and cost. However, the drawback to low-resolution imagery is a decrease in accuracy and the ability to differentiate riparian condition from that of the adjacent uplands.

Multispectral imagery from aircraft also provide additional remote-sensing tools useful for assessing riparian conditions that, in some instances, are superior to the more traditional black and white or color photographs. For example, airborne visible infrared imaging spectrometer (AVIRIS) imagery was used to estimate the amount of infestation of a perennial weed *Euphorbia esula* into riparian areas of Wyoming (Williams and Hunt 2002). Similarly, DiPetrio (2002) used AVIRIS hyperspectral data to map Californian riparian vegetation communities being invaded by the giant reed *Arundo donax*, while Everitt and Deloach (1990) used a similar technique to detect the spread of the invasive Chinese tamarisk *Tamarix chinensis* in the American Southwest. Aspinall (2002) used hyperspectral data from aerial photography, by using a Probe 1 (Earth Search Systems Inc.) sensor with 1-m resolution to differentiate between three different types of riparian cottonwood species,

Table 4.

Examples of advanced remote-sensing technologies for detecting vegetation changes (from U.S. Forest Service, Rocky Mountain Region, unpublished data). NA = not available, N/A = not applicable.

Remote-sensing technologies	Spectral band	Maximum resolution —pixel (m)	Maximum resolution —feature (m)	Scene width (km)
Low-resolution, broad-swath satellite data				
AVHRR	4	1,100	3,300	NA
OrbView-2 SeaWiFs	8	1,100	3,300	2,800
SPOT4 vegetation sensor	4	1,000	3,000	2,000
MODIS	27	1,000	3,000	1,150
Moderate resolution	7	500	1,500	1,150
Imaging spectrometer	2	250	750	1,150
Medium-resolution, medium-swath satellite data				
Landsat7	Thermal	60	180	185
Landsat7	6	30	90	185
Landsat7	Panchromatic	15	45	185
SPOT 4	4	20	60	60
SPOT 4	Panchromatic	10	30	60
SOVINFORM-SPUTNIK, Spin-2	Panchromatic	NA	10	200
High-resolution, narrow-swath satellite data				
SOVINFORM-SPUTNIK, Spin-2	Panchromatic	NA	2	40
Space Imaging EOSAT	4	4	12	11
Ikonos 1	Panchromatic	1	3	11
Earthwatch-Earlybird	3	15	15	30
Earthwatch-Earlybird	Panchromatic	3	9	6
Earthwatch-Quickbird	4	4	12	NA
Earthwatch-Quickbird	Panchromatic	1	3	NA
OrbView-3	4	8	24	8
OrbView-3	Panchromatic	2	6	4
OrbView-3	3	1	3	4
Aerial photography				
Large format 1:40,000	3	N/A	1	10
Small format 35-mm 1:30,000	3	N/A	1	1
Small format 70-mm 1:15,000	3	N/A	0.5	1
Large format 1:4,000 to 1:12,000	3	N/A	0.3	2
Helicopter 70-mm 1:2,000	3	N/A	0.05	0.1

as well as to identify the location of LWD, indicating the versatility of remote sensing when there is adequate resolution. For another example, Hawkins et al. (1997) used airborne multispectral videography to monitor the loss of riparian vegetation along the San Luis Rey River of California after a major flood.

The use of Landsat satellite data to evaluate changes in riparian condition has met with mixed success due to the large pixel size; but, in some cases, it can be useful (Narumalani et al. 1997; Chehbouni et al. 2000; Apan et al. 2002; Congalton et al. 2002). Of the available satellite data, Landsat data has probably been the most commonly used, in spite of its poor resolution, primarily because of the length of time it has been available and its low cost.

Aerial photography is still currently far more useful in accurately assessing changes in riparian conditions over time relative to satellite imagery simply because of its high resolution relative to cost and its ease of use. Although somewhat time consuming, a skilled operator can assess, with reasonable accuracy, riparian width, canopy density, and vegetative height, and can differentiate between conifer and deciduous species, at a minimum, for typical aerial photographs with a scale in the range of 1:12,000.

Remote sensing can be used to assess riparian condition along a stream, an entire watershed, or even a entire province. For example, aerial photography and satellite imagery are being used to assist in examining changes in riparian, as well as watershed condition, as a result of the Northwest Forest Plan, a policy covering most of the federal forest lands in northwest California and western Washington and Oregon. It also can be used to monitor the spread or control of exotic clonal species such as reed canary grass.

Shade and Stream Temperature

Where shade and stream water temperature are a concern, canopy closure or shade and water temperature are other common monitoring parameters (Kaufmann et al. 1999). There are a number techniques for measuring canopy closure, each of which provides trade-offs between speed, accuracy, and cost. Typical methods include spherical densiometer, angular canopy density, light meters, and aerial photography. Discussions of the pros and cons of each technique are provided in Kaufmann et al. (1999). All methods, except light meters, are limited in that they do not differentiate how dense the canopy is above the sample point. Since canopy density controls how much light passes through the canopy, such methods are not a very good measure of light penetration to the forest floor or to the stream. However, what these measures lack in accuracy or relevance, they make up for in their low cost relative to light meters. While the data are not the best, given the size of many monitoring budgets, they often are the only data that can be obtained. Continuous records of instream temperatures can be obtained easily by deploying readily available and inexpensive temperature data loggers (e.g., Onset Tidbit loggers) and returning to the field periodically to download the data. Typically, the data loggers are set to record temperatures every 15–60 min, and comparisons are made between sites (e.g., control vs. experimental) by using statistical parameters such as the average daily maximum, the average daily range of temperatures, or the number of times temperatures exceeded a certain threshold relevant to the survival of important instream species such as salmonids (Figure 7). If temperature within the riparian zone itself is to be monitored, a similar approach is taken.

Instream Habitat

Monitoring parameters for physical habitat changes in streams might include wood abundance and size (e.g., Bilby and Ward 1991; Montgomery et al. 1995; Beechie and Sibley 1997); pool frequency, areas, or residual pool depths (Montgomery et al. 1995; Beechie and Sibley 1997); or sediment texture and storage volumes (Bilby and Ward 1989; Buffington and Montgomery 1999). For additional physical parameters that might be monitored, also see Chapters 3 and 8. Nutrient and biological responses might be monitored by using a wider variety of parameters, including water chemistry measures, primary productivity, invertebrate assemblages, and fish abundance or community structure (see also Chapters 6, 8, and 9). Instream variables will respond indirectly to riparian restoration, and linking instream or in-channel responses to changes in riparian vegetation can be difficult. Therefore, the selection, measurement, and interpretation of these variables for evaluating effectiveness of riparian restoration should be done cautiously.

Analyzing Monitoring Data, Comparison of Projected to Actual Trends

When effectiveness-monitoring measurements have been made consistently and repeatedly over a sufficient time period, usually years, data can be analyzed for trends or patterns. Such trends might include, for example, change in shade, instream wood, basal area, seedling or tree survival, height or biomass, species diversity, understory biomass. Examination of these trends allows a determination as to whether the restorative activity is on target toward achieving its desired outcome. If precise hypotheses have been generated about the shape of these trends over specific time periods, then the data can be compared to the hypothesized trends and the hypotheses thus tested. As a simple example, Figure 8 illustrates the hypothesized (modeled) increase in height over time for the riparian tree red alder (Worthington et al. 1960). By measuring the height of planted red alder over time as part of the monitoring program, the hypothesis can be tested.

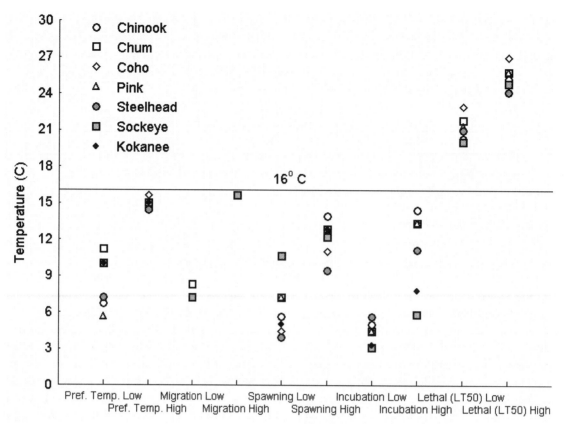

Figure 7.

Temperature preferences for Pacific Coast salmonids, showing that 16.0°C is the upper end of preferred temperatures for these species for various life history stages. For this reason, monitoring the frequency that the 16.0°C threshold is exceeded can be a good means of determining if a restored site is recovering adequately. (Data from Brett 1952; Bell 1973; Hicks 1999)

Determination of whether a monitored recovery trajectory is sufficiently close to the hypothesized trajectory is why quantitative performance standards need to be established. Quantitative standards might include the number of surviving seedlings, the total basal area after a specific number of years, or some other quantifiable criteria. Where recovery trajectories have been projected by using models, statistical methods can be used to compare the actual versus the projected trends. One should make an a priori decision on what level of statistical significance will be required for a recovery trend to be considered close enough to the projected trend to be declared a success. Statistical techniques for making such comparisons are discussed briefly in Chapter 2 and in detail in statistical texts such as Zar (1999).

Case Study: Oregon Department of Forestry Studies on Wood Recruitment and Shade

Few published examples of quantitative monitoring and evaluation of riparian planting and restoration are available. The following Pacific Northwest case study elucidates the principles we discussed in previous subsections. The Oregon Department of Forest (ODF) Practices Monitoring Program is responsible for monitoring the implementation and effectiveness of the forest practice rules and for reporting those findings and recommendations to the Oregon Board of Forestry on an annual basis. The Oregon Board of Forestry considers the findings and recommendations and adapts regulatory policies accordingly. Recent studies have been designed to answer questions regarding the effectiveness of the forest practice rules in protecting riparian function. The specific focus has been on potential large wood recruitment and shade.

Wood Recruitment Study

The ODF monitored 25 harvest sites adjacent to streams throughout the state of Oregon (Dent 2001). The objective of the study was to test the hypothesis that forest practice riparian rules are effective at retaining large wood recruitment and stream cover after timber harvest. Data were collected preharvest and 1 year after harvest in 500-ft-long by 100-ft-wide strips along the stream within the 25 harvest sites. Measurements included

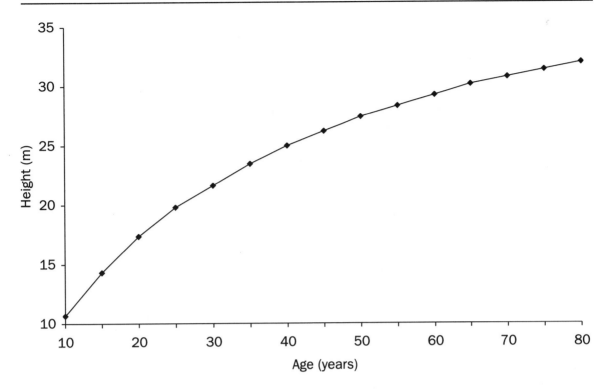

Figure 8.
Expected height increase with age for a typical riparian red alder stand. (Based on Worthington et al. 1960.)

diameter, height, and species of trees, and distance of these trees from the stream. Stream cover was measured with a spherical densiometer every 100 ft along the stream.

Initial results suggest that both shade and large wood recruitment potential after harvest are reduced on very small fish-bearing streams as compared to preharvest conditions (Table 5). No difference was seen in mean diameter of trees pre- and posttreatment, though results of longer-term monitoring may produce different results. This study also indicated that stand characteristics of riparian forests vary greatly across the landscape, making a single regulatory target or goal problematic. However, it appears that the current rules have underestimated the prevalence of conifer trees within the first 20 ft of very small and medium streams, thereby underestimating the amount of coniferous basal area that is available on these streams. Recommendations for increasing requirements for numbers of trees left along small and medium streams were made to the forest practices advisory committee. Dent (2001) provides a detailed description of the results of this study.

Shade Study

The ODF also monitored 42 harvested and 19 unharvested sites adjacent to streams in northeast and northwest Oregon (Allen and Dent 2001). The objective of this study was to evaluate the range of stream shade conditions provided under current forest practice rules, how shade conditions compare between harvested and unharvested stands, and how shade conditions relate to riparian stand structure. Data were collected in 500–1,000-ft-long by 100-ft-wide strips adjacent to streams within the study sites. Measurements included tree species, distance from stream, diameter, height, and live crown ratio. Stream cover was calculated with a densiometer. Stream shade was calculated from hemispherical photographs with a fish-eye lens (Figure 9).

Results suggest that overall stand structure influences stream shade and that combinations of basal area, stand density (trees/acre), species composition, average stand diameter, and live crown ratios may have a greater influence on shading than any single variable. Furthermore, the interaction between stand structure and aspect are clearly important when predicting shade. In this study, results show that the average shade was lower on harvested sites compared to unharvested sites. However, maximizing shade over streams by promoting stands in the stem-exclusion stage may not meet other long-term goals such as recruiting large woody material to act as stable key pieces in the stream. Managers must consider carefully what their objectives are for stream shad-

Table 5.
Monitoring of the effects of riparian thinning along small (S), medium (M), and large (L) streams by the Oregon Department of Forestry. Thinning produced no significant change in average tree diameter, and percent cover (over the stream) was significantly reduced only for the small streams. However, wood recruitment potential was greatly reduced, by 18–59%, depending on stream size. Differences in pre- and postharvest cover and tree diameters were determined by using a two-sample t-test. Data are from Dent (2001).

	Percent cover		
	S*	M	L
Preharvest	91.0	88.0	83.8
Postharvest	78.3	81.0	82.5
n	9	7	8
	Average tree diameter (cm)		
	S	M	L
Preharvest	41.6	37.8	37.1
Postharvest	42.9	39.1	40.6
n	180	463	339
	Large wood debris recruitment potential (% reduction)		
	S	M	L
Preharvest	0%	0%	0%
Postharvest	–59%	–32%	–18%
n	10	7	7

* = statistically significant difference at the 0.05 level.

ing in relation to stand structure and the myriad of other "goods" produced by a riparian stand. Allen and Dent (2001) provide detailed information on the results of this study.

The ODF has initiated a new study of riparian areas and stream temperature on state and private forestlands in northwest Oregon. This study is designed to evaluate effectiveness of riparian protection measures by using a before–after control–treatment design. Additional information on these and other riparian studies can be found by contacting the ODF.

Figure 9.
Examples of hemispherical (fish-eye) photographs taken at a site in the Oregon Coast Range (left) and at a site in eastern Oregon (right).

Summary

This chapter has focused on discussing common techniques for restoring riparian systems and the methods for monitoring these activities to determine if the restoration activity met its desired goal. The steps involved in setting up a monitoring program for riparian restoration projects are similar to other restoration projects and include (1) determining the desired outcome or objectives of the restoration activity; (2) generating formal hypotheses for testing whether the desired outcome was achieved in the desired time frame; (3) identifying a control site and collecting prerestoration activity data, if possible; (4) developing a study or restoration design that will ensure that the restoration activity is carried out as planned; (5) collecting the appropriate data; and (6) analyzing the data to test the hypotheses and to determine if the restoration activity resulted in the desired outcome. This information then can be used in the context of adaptive management.

We emphasized that a restoration project should be designed with the monitoring component in mind to ensure that the monitoring effort is successful. Setting up a monitoring program requires development of hypotheses about the expected outcome, then development of a monitoring design that will enable that hypothesis to be tested. The physical measurements needed to be taken for measuring changes in riparian (or any) vegetation over time are fairly straightforward, and the equipment needed for field measurements is relatively inexpensive. Measuring instream physical and biological parameters is more difficult, because these parameters do not respond directly to changes in riparian vegetation. A major challenge in monitoring riparian restoration is developing a monitoring design that measures the rates of change of selected parameters over time but also stays within budget for monitoring efforts.

Monitoring riparian restoration projects often requires a considerable amount of patience because tangible improvements to habitat, particularly instream habitat, often are not observed for years to decades. For this reason, short-term monitoring of riparian restoration projects often requires indirect measures of habitat quality, such as the growth rates or survival rates of trees, and the use of predictive models to determine long-term consequences of restoration. Moreover, information on management history, site conditions, and project implementation are needed to understand why a project may or may not have achieved the desired objectives.

A tremendous amount of time and money has gone toward restoring degraded riparian areas, mostly by planting trees in deforested areas. Unfortunately, there has been little monitoring of such efforts or formal assessment of which restoration designs are successful and why. Widespread monitoring and documentation of the successes and failures of riparian restoration efforts can help formalize our collective knowledge base and ensure that future restoration projects have a higher probability of success. Neither monitoring without an understanding of the restoration design nor restoration without a monitoring design will provide any real insights into how to improve our efforts. Through explicitly stating the expected outcome of a restoration project and the reasons for that outcome, and then monitoring the results, we will learn.

References

Agee, J. K. 1988. Successional dynamics in riparian forests. Pages 31–43 in K. J. Raedke, editor. Streamside management: riparian wildlife and forestry interactions. University of Washington, College of Forest Resources, Contribution No. 59, Seattle.

Agee, J. K. 1993. Fire ecology of Pacific Northwest forests. Island Press, Washington, D.C.

Alaback, P. B. 1986. Biomass regression equations for understory plants in coastal Alaska: effects of species and sampling design on estimates. Northwest Science 60:90–103.

Alaback, P. B. 1987. Biomass-dimension relationships of understory vegetation in relation to site and stand age. Pages 141–148 in Eric H. Wharton and Tiberius Cunia, editors. Estimating tree biomass regressions and their error. Proceedings of the workshop, May 26–30, 1986, Syracuse, NY. U.S. Forest Service, General Technical Report NE-GTR-117, Broomall, Pennsylvania.

Alaback, P. B., and F. R. Herman. 1988. Long-term response of understory vegetation to stand density in Picea-Tsuga forests. Canadian Journal of Forest Research 12:1522–1530.

Allen, M., and L. Dent. 2001. Shade conditions over forested streams in the Blue Mountain and coast range georegions of Oregon. Oregon Department of Forestry Technical Report 13, Salem.

Apan, A. A., S. R. Raine, and M. S. Paterson. 2002. Mapping and analysis of changes in the riparian landscape structure of the Lockyer Valley catchment, Queensland, Australia. Landscape and Urban Planning 59:43–57.

Aspinall, R. J. 2002. Use of logistic regression for validation of maps of the spatial distribution of vegetation species derived from high spatial resolution hyperspectral remotely sensed data. Ecological Modeling 157:301–312.

Auble, G. T., and M. L. Scott. 1998. Fluvial disturbance patches and cottonwood recruitment along the upper Missouri River, Montana. Wetlands 18:546–556.

Baskerville, G. L. 1972. Use of logarithmic regression in the estimation of plant biomass. Canadian Journal of Forest Research 2:49–53.

Bauer, S. B., and S. C. Ralph. 1999. Aquatic habitat indicators and their application to water quality objectives within the Clean Water Act. U.S. Environmental Protection Agency, EPA 910-R-99-014, Seattle.

BCMF (British Columbia Ministry of Forests). 2001. Silvicultural systems handbook for British Columbia. British Columbia Ministry of Forests, Forest Practices Branch, Victoria.

Beechie, T. J., G. Pess, P. Kennard, R. E. Bilby, and S. Bolton. 2000. Modeling rates and pathways of recovery of woody debris recruitment in northwestern Washington streams. North American Journal of Fisheries Management 20:436–452.

Beechie, T., and T. H. Sibley. 1997. Relationships between channel characteristics, woody debris and fish habitat in northwestern Washington streams. Transactions of the American Fisheries Society 126:217–229.

Beerling, D. J. 1991. The effect of riparian land use on the occurrence and abundance of Japanese knotweed *Reynoutria japonica* on selected rivers in South Wales. Biological Conservation 55:329–337.

Bell, M. C. 1973. Fisheries handbook of engineering requirements and biological criteria. U.S. Army Corps of Engineers, Portland, Oregon.

Benda, L. 1990. The influence of debris flows on channels and valley floors in the Oregon coast range, U.S.A. Earth Surface Processes and Landforms 15:457–466.

Benda, L., and T. Dunne. 1987. Sediment routing by debris flow. Pages 213–223 *in* R. L. Beschta, T. Blinn, G. E. Grant, G. G. Ice, and F. J. Swanson, editors. Erosion and sedimentation in the Pacific Rim. Oregon State University, International Association of Hydrological Sciences Publication No. 65, Corvallis.

Benda, L., and T. Dunne. 1997. Stochastic forcing of sediment routing and storage in channel networks. Water Resources Research 33:2865–2880.

Benda, L. E., D. J. Miller, T. Dunne, G. H. Reeves, and J. K. Agee. 1998. Dynamic landscape systems. Pages 261–288 *in* R. J. Naiman and R. E. Bilby, editors. River ecology and management: lessons from the Pacific coastal ecoregion. Springer-Verlag, New York.

Berg, D. R. 1990. Active management of streamside forests. Master's thesis. University of Washington, Seattle.

Berg, D. R. 1995. Riparian silvicultural system design and assessment in the Pacific Northwest Cascade Mountains, USA. Ecological Applications 5:87–96.

Berg, D. R., T. K. Brown, and B. Blessing. 1996. Silvicultural systems design with emphasis on the forest canopy. Northwest Science 70:31–36.

Bilby, R. E., and J. W. Ward. 1989. Changes in characteristics and function of woody debris with increasing size of streams in western Washington. Transactions of the American Fisheries Society 118:368–378.

Bilby, R. E., and J. W. Ward. 1991. Characteristics and function of large woody debris in streams draining old-growth, clear-cut, and second-growth forests in southwestern Washington. Canadian Journal of Fisheries and Aquatic Sciences 48:2499–2508.

Bisson, P. A., R. E. Bilby, M. D. Bryant, C. A. Dolloff, G. B. Grette, R. A. House, M. L. Murphy, K. V. Koski, and J. R. Sedell. 1987. Large woody debris in forested streams in the Pacific Northwest: past, present, and future. Pages 143–190 *in* E. O. Salo and T. W. Cundy, editors. Streamside management: forestry and fishery interactions. University of Washington, College of Forest Resources, Seattle.

Black, H. C. 1992. Silvicultural approaches to animal damage management in Pacific Northwest forests. U.S. Forest Service, PNW-GTR-287, Portland, Oregon.

BLM (Bureau of Land Management). 1991. Riparian-wetland initiative for the 1990s. U.S. Department of the Interior, Bureau of Land Management, Washington, D.C.

Boldt, C. E., D. W. Uresk, and K. E. Severson. 1979. Riparian woodlands in jeopardy on northern High Plains. U.S. Forest Service, WO-GTR-12, Washington, D.C.

Bormann, B. T. 1989. Diameter based biomass regression models ignore large sapwood-related variation in Sitka spruce. Canadian Journal of Forest Research 20:1098–1104.

Brett, J. R. 1952. Temperature tolerance in young Pacific salmon, genus *Oncorhynchus*. Journal of the Fisheries Research Board of Canada 9:265–323.

Briggs, M. K. 1996. Riparian ecosystem recovery in arid lands: strategies and references. University of Arizona Press, Tucson.

Brosofske, K. D., J. Chen, R. J. Naiman, and J. F. Franklin. 1997. Harvesting effects on microclimatic gradients from small streams to uplands in western Washington. Ecological Applications 7:1188–1200.

Buech, R. R., and D. J. Rugg. 1989. Biomass relations of shrub components and their generality. Forest Ecology and Management. 26:257–264.

Buffington, J. M., and D. R. Montgomery. 1999. A procedure for classifying textural facies in gravel-bed rivers. Water Resources Research 35:1903–1914.

Burkhart, H. E., T. G. Gregoire, and J. L. Smith, editors. 1993. Modeling stand response to silvicultural practices. Virginia Polytechnic Institute and State University, Blacksburg.

Burns, R. M., and B. H. Honkala. 1990a. Silvics of North America, Volume 1, Conifers. U.S. Forest Service, Washington, D.C.

Burns, R. M., and B. H. Honkala. 1990b. Silvics of North America, Volume 2, Hardwoods. U. S. Forest Service, Washington, D.C.

Bushaw-Newton, K. L., D. D. Hart, J. E. Pizzuto, J. R. Thomson, J. Egan, J. T. Ashley, T. E. Johnson, R. J. Horwitz, M. Keeley, J. Lawrence, D. Charles, C. Gatenby, D. A. Kreeger, T. Nightengale, R. L. Thomas, and D. J. Velinsky. 2002. An integrative approach towards understanding ecological responses to dam removal. Journal of the American Water Resources Association 38:1581–1600.

Chehbouni, A., D. C. Goodrich, M. S. Moran, C. J. Watts, Y. H. Kerr, G. Dedieu, W. G. Kepner, W. J. Shuttleworth, and S. Sorooshian. 2000. A preliminary synthesis of major scientific results during the SALSA program. Agricultural and Forest Meteorology 105:311–323.

Congalton, R. G., K. Birch, R. Jones, and J. Schriever. 2002. Evaluating remotely sensed techniques for mapping riparian vegetation. Computers and Electronics in Agriculture 37:113–126.

Crow, T. R. 1971. Estimation of biomass in an even-aged stand-regression and "mean tree" techniques. Maine Agricultural Experimental Station Miscellaneous Reports 132:35–48.

Crow, T. R. 1983. Comparing biomass regressions by site and stand age for red maple. Canadian Journal of Forest Research 13:283–288.

Crow, T. R., and B. E. Schlaegel. 1988. A guide to using regression equations for estimating tree biomass. North Journal of Applied Forestry 5:15–22.

Curtis, R. O., D. S. DeBell, C. A. Harrington, D. P. Lavender, J. B. St. Clair, J. C. Tappeiner, and J. D. Walstad. 1998. Silviculture for multiple objectives in the Douglas-fir region. U.S. Forest Service, Pacific Northwest Station General Technical Report 435, Portland, Oregon.

Dale, M. R. T. 1999. Spatial pattern analysis in plant ecology. Cambridge University Press, Cambridge, UK.

Dent, L. 2001. Harvest effects on riparian function and structure under current Oregon forest practice rules. Oregon Department of Forestry, Technical Report 12, Salem.

deWaal, L. C., L. E. Child, and M. Wade. 1995. The management of three alien invasive riparian plants: *Impatiens glandulifera* (Himalyan balsam), *Heracleum mantegazzianum* (giant hogweed) and *Fallopia japonica* (Japanese knotweed). Pages 315–321 *in* D. M. Harper and A. J. D. Ferguson, editors. The ecological basis for river management. Wiley, New York.

DiPetrio, D. Y. 2002. Mapping the invasive plant *Arundo donax* and associated riparian vegetation using hyperspectral remote sensing. Master's thesis. University of California, Davis.

Dudgeon, D. 1992. Endangered ecosystems: a review of the conservation status of tropical Asian rivers. Hydrobiologia 248:167–191.

Ellis, L. M., C. S. Crawford, and M. C. Molles, Jr. 2001. Influence of annual flooding on terrestrial arthropod assemblages of a Rio Grande riparian forest. Regulated Rivers: Research and Management 17:1–20.

Elzinga, C. L., D. W. Salzer, and J. W. Willoughby. 1998. Measuring and monitoring plant populations. U.S. Bureau of Land Management Technical Reference 1730–1, Denver.

Emmingham, B., S. Chan, D. Mikowski, P. Owston, and B. Bishaw. 2000. Silviculture practices for riparian forests in the Oregon coast range. Oregon State University, College of Forestry, Research Contribution 24, Corvallis.

Everitt, J. H., and C. J. Deloach. 1990. Remote sensing of Chinese tamarisk (*Tamarix chinensis*) and associated vegetation. Weed Science 38:273–278.

FEMAT (Forest Ecosystem Management Assessment Team). 1993. Forest ecosystem management: an ecological, economic, and social assessment, report of the Forest Management Assessment Team. U.S. Forest Service, Washington, D.C.

Fenner, P., W. W. Brady, and D. R. Patton. 1985. Effects of regulated water flows on regeneration of Fremont cottonwood. Journal of Range Management 38:135–138.

Fetherston, K. L., J. Naiman Robert, and R. Bilby. 1995. Large woody debris, physical process, and riparian forest development in montane river networks. Geomorphology 13:133–144.

Franklin, J. F. 1989. Toward a new forestry. American Forests 95(11–12):37–44.

Freeze, R. A., and J. A. Cherry. 1979. Groundwater. Prentice Hall, Englewood Cliffs, New Jersey.

GAO (General Accounting Office). 1988. Public rangelands: some riparian areas restored but widespread improvement will be slow. Report to congressional requesters. General Accounting Office, Washington, D.C.

Gray, D. H., and R. B. Sotir. 1996. Biotechnical and soil bioengineering slope stabilization: a practical guide for erosion control. Wiley, New York.

Gregory, S. V., F. J. Swanson, W. A. McKee, and K. W. Cummins. 1991. An ecosystem perspective of riparian zones. Bioscience 41:540–551.

Hann, D. W., A. S. Hester, and C. L. Olsen. 1995. ORGANON user's manual: edition 5.0. Oregon State University, Department of Forest Resources, Corvallis.

Harrelson, C. C., C. L. Rawlins, and J. P. Potyondy. 1994. Stream channel reference sites: an illustrated guide to field technique. U.S. Forest Service, General Technical Report RM-245, Fort Collins, Colorado.

Hawkins, C. P., K. L. Bartz, and C. M. U. Neale. 1997. Vulnerability of riparian vegetation to catastrophic flooding: implications for riparian restoration. Restoration Ecology 5:75–84.

Hemstrom, M. A., T. A. Spies, C. J. Palmer, R. Kiester, J. Teply, P. McDonald, and R. Warbington. 1998. Late-successional and old-growth forest effectiveness monitoring plan for the Northwest Forest Plan. U.S. Forest Service, General Technical Report PNW-438, Corvallis, Oregon.

Hibbs, D. E., and P. A. Giordano. 1996. Vegetative characteristics of alder-dominated riparian buffer strips in the Oregon coast range. Northwest Science 70:213–222.

Hicks, M. 1999. Evaluating criteria for the protection of aquatic life in Washington's surface water quality standards. Washington State Department of Ecology, Olympia, Washington.

Hill, M. T., and W. S. Platts. 1998. Ecosystem restoration: a case study in the Owens River gorge, California. Fisheries 23:18–27.

Hitchcock, C. L., and A. Cronquist. 1973. Flora of the Pacific Northwest. University of Washington Press, Seattle.

Johnson, W. C. 1994. Woodland expansion in the Platte River, Nebraska: patterns and causes. Ecological Monographs 64:45–84.

Johnston, W. F. 1977. Manager's handbook for black spruce in the North Central States. U.S. Forest Service, North Central Forest Experiment Station, General Technical Report NC-34, St. Paul, Minnesota.

Kalliola, R., and M. Puhakka. 1988. River dynamics and vegetation mosaicism: a case study of the River Kamajohka, northernmost Finland. Journal of Biogeography 15:703–719.

Kattelman, R., and M. Embury. 1996. Riparian areas and wetlands. Pages 201–273 *in* Sierra Nevada Ecosystem Project: final report to Congress, volume III. University of California, Davis.

Kaufmann, P. R., P. Levine, E. G. Robison, C. Seeliger, and D. V. Peck. 1999. Quantifying physical habitat in wadeable streams. U.S. Environmental Protection Agency, EPA/620/R-99/003, Corvallis, Oregon.

Kennard, P., R. Pess George, T. Beechie, R. Bilby, and D. Berg. 1998. Riparian-in-a-box: a manager's tool to predict the impacts of riparian management of fish habitat. Pages 483–490 in Forest-fish Conference: land management practices affecting aquatic ecosystems. Proceedings of the Forest-Fish Conference. May 1–4, 1996, Calgary, Alberta. Natural Resources Canada, Edmondton, Alberta.

Koerper, G. J., and C. J. Richardson. 1980. Biomass and net annual primary production regressions for Populus grandis on three sites in northern lower Michigan. Canadian Journal of Forest Research 10:92–101.

Kohm, K. A., and J. F. Franklin, editors. 1997. Creating a forestry for the 21st century. Island Press, Washington, D.C.

Kondolf, G. M., J. W. Webb, M. J. Sale, and T. Felando. 1987. Basic hydrologic studies for assessing impacts of flow diversions on riparian vegetation: examples from streams of the eastern Sierra Nevada, California, USA. Environmental Management 11:757–769.

Lienkaemper, G. W., and F. J. Swanson. 1987. Dynamics of large woody debris in streams in old-growth Douglas-fir forests. Canadian Journal of Forest Research 17:150–156.

Lindig, C. R., and J. I. Zedler. 2002. Relationships between canopy complexity and germination microsites for Phalaris arundinacea L. Oecologia 133:159–167.

MacDonald, L. H., A. W. Smart, and R. C. Wissmar. 1991. Monitoring guidelines to evaluate effects of forestry activities on streams in the Pacific Northwest and Alaska. U.S. Environmental Protection Agency, Region 10, EPA/910/9-91/001, Seattle.

Magurran, A. E. 1988. Ecological diversity and its measurement. Princeton University Press, Princeton, New Jersey.

Malanson, G. P. 1993. Riparian landscapes. Cambridge University Press, Cambridge, UK.

Maser, C., and J. R. Sedell. 1994. From the forest to the sea: the ecology of wood in streams, rivers, estuaries, and oceans. St. Lucie Press, Delray Beach, Florida.

Maser, C., R. F. Tarrant, J. M. Trappe, and J. F. Franklin. 1988. From the forest to the sea: a story of fallen trees. U.S. Forest Service, General Technical Report PNW-160, Portland, Oregon.

McDonald, P. M., and G. O. Fiddler. 1994. Mulching and grubbing techniques in forest vegetation management: a research synthesis. Pages 92–98 in T. B. Harrington and L. A. Parendes, editors. Forest vegetation management without herbicides, proceedings of a workshop, February 18–19, 1992. Oregon State University, Corvallis.

Montgomery, D. R., J. M. Buffington, R. D. Smith, K. M. Schmidt, and G. Pess. 1995. Pool spacing in forest channels. Water Resources Research 31:1097–1105.

Mulder, B. S., B. Noon, T. A. Spies, M. G. Raphael, C. J. Palmer, A. R. Olsen, G. H. Reeves, and H. H. Welsh. 1999. The strategy and design of the effectiveness monitoring program for the Northwest Forest Plan. U.S. Forest Service, General Technical Report PNW-437, Portland, Oregon.

Mutz, K. M. 1989. Restoration, creation and management of wetland and riparian ecosystems in the American West: a symposium of the Rocky Mountain Chapter of the Society of Wetland Scientists, November 14–16, 1988, Denver, Colorado. PIC Technologies, Denver.

Naiman, R. J., H. Decamps, and M. Pollock. 1993. The role of riparian corridors in maintaining regional biodiversity. Ecological Applications 3:209–212.

Nanson, G. C., and H. F. Beach. 1977. Forest succession and sedimentation on a meandering river floodplain, northeast British Columbia, Canada. Journal of Biogeography 4:229–251.

Narumalani, S., Y. Zhou, and R. Jensen John. 1997. Application of remote sensing and geographic information systems to the delineation and analysis of riparian buffer zones. Aquatic Botany 59:393–409.

Nielsen, D. M. 1991. Practical handbook of ground-water monitoring. Lewis Publishers, Inc., Chelsea, Michigan.

Nilsson, C. 1986. Change in riparian plant community composition along two rivers in northern Sweden. Canadian Journal of Botany 64:589–592.

Nilsson, C., A. Ekblad, M. Dynesius, S. Backe, M. Gardfjell, B. Carlberg, S. Hellqvist, and R. Jansson. 1994. A comparison of species richness and traits of riparian plants between a main river channel and its tributaries. Journal of Ecology 82:281–295.

Nislow, K. H., F. J. Magilligan, H. Fassnacht, D. Bechtel, and A. Ruesink. 2002. Effects of dam impoundment on the flood regime of natural floodplain communities in the upper Connecticut River. Journal of the American Water Resources Association 38:1533–1548.

NRC (National Research Council). 1992. Restoration of aquatic ecosystems. National Academy Press, Washington, D.C.

NRCS (Natural Resources Conservation Survey). 1999. Soil taxonomy: a basic system of soil classification for making and interpreting soil surveys. USDA Natural Resources Conservation Survey, Washington, D.C.

O'Hara, K. L., and P. A. Latham. 1996. A structural classification for inland northwest forest vegetation. Western Journal of Applied Forestry 11:97–102.

Oliver, C. D., and T. M. Hinckley. 1987. Species, stand structures, and silvicultural manipulation patterns for the streamside zone. Pages 259–276 in E. O. Salo and T. W. Cundy, editors. Streamside management: forestry and fishery interactions. University of Washington, College of Forest Resources, Seattle.

Oliver, C. D., and B. C. Larson. 1996. Forest stand dynamics. Wiley, New York.

OPSW (Oregon Plan for Salmon and Watersheds). 2000. Water quality monitoring guidebook. Oregon Plan for Salmon and Watersheds, Governor's Natural Resource Office, Salem.

Pizzuto, J. 2002. Effects of dam removal on river form and processes. Bioscience 52:683–691.

Pohl, M. M. 2002. Bringing down our dams: trends in American dam removal. Journal of the American Water Resources Association 38:1511–1520.

Pollock, M. M. 1995. Patterns of plant species richness in emergent and forested wetlands of southeast Alaska. Doctoral dissertation. University of Washington, Seattle.

Pollock, M. M. 1998. Biodiversity. Pages 430–452 in R. E. Bilby and R. J. Naiman, editors. Ecology and management of streams and rivers in the Pacific Northwest coastal ecoregion. Springer-Verlag, New York.

Pollock, M. M., R. J. Naiman, and T. A. Hanley. 1998. Predicting plant species richness in forested and emergent wetlands—a test of biodiversity theory. Ecology 79:94–105.

Raedeke, K. J. 1988. Introduction. Pages xiii–xvi in K. J. Raedeke, editor. Streamside management: riparian wildlife and forestry interactions. University of Washington, Institute of Forest Resources, Seattle.

Ralph, S. C., G. C. Poole, L. L. Conquest, and R. J. Naiman. 1994. Stream channel morphology and woody debris in logged and unlogged basins of western Washington. Canadian Journal of Fisheries and Aquatic Sciences 51:37–51.

Roelle, J. E., and D. N. Gladwin. 1999. Establishment of woody riparian species from natural seedfall at a former gravel pit. Restoration Ecology 7:183–192.

Rood, S. B., and J. M. Mahoney. 1990. Collapse of riparian poplar forests downstream from dams in western prairies: probable causes and prospects for mitigation. Environmental Management 14:451–464.

Rood, S. B., and J. M. Mahoney. 1993. River damming and riparian cottonwoods: management opportunities and problems. U.S. Forest Service, General Technical Report RM-226, Fort Collins, Colorado.

Rose, R., C. E. C. Chachulski, and D. L. Haase, editors. 1998. Propagation of Pacific Northwest native plants. Oregon State University Press, Corvallis.

Rowlinson, L. C., M. Summerton, and F. Ahmed. 1999. Comparison of remote sensing data sources and techniques for identifying and classifying alien invasive vegetation in riparian zones. Water SA 25:497–500.

Salo, E. O., and T. W. Cundy, editors. 1987. Streamside management: forestry and fishery interactions. University of Washington, College of Forest Resources, Seattle.

Schiechtl, H. M., and R. Stern. 1996. Ground bioengineering techniques for slope protection and erosion control. Blackwell Scientific Publications, London.

Schiechtl, H. M., and R. Stern. 1997. Water bioengineering techniques for watercourse, bank and shoreline protection. Blackwell Scientific Publications, London.

Schuett-Hames, D., A. E. Pleus, J. Ward, M. Fox, and J. Light. 1999. TFW Monitoring Program method manual for the large woody debris survey. Department of Natural Resources, TFW-AM9-99-004, DNR #106, Olympia, Washington.

Sedell, J. R., G. H. Reeves, K. Burnett, L. Brown, M. Furniss, E. Gaar, G. Grant, B. McCannon, T. Robertson, F. Swanson, C. Berman, J. Cannell, D. Harr, B. House, D. Montgomery, C. Novak, L. Reid, C. Ricks, P. Teensma, F. Weimann, J. Williams, and R. Ziemer. 1993. Aquatic ecosystem assessment. Pages V-1 to V-95 in J. W. Thomas, editor. Forest ecosystem management: an ecological, economic, and social assessment. Report of the Forest Ecosystem Management Assessment Team. U.S. Forest Service, National Marine Fisheries Service, Bureau of Land Management, U.S. Fish and Wildlife Service, National Park Service, and Environmental Protection Agency, Washington, D.C.

Shafroth, P. B., J. M. Friedman, G. T. Auble, M. L. Scott, and J. H. Braatne. 2002. Potential responses of riparian vegetation to dam removal. Bioscience 52:703–712.

Smith, D. 1998. TFW Effectiveness Monitoring and Evaluation Program. Riparian stand survey-final draft. Washington Department of Natural Resources, Olympia.

Smith, D. M. 1986. The practice of silviculture. Wiley, New York.

Sprenger, M. D., L. M. Smith, and J. P. Taylor. 2002. Restoration of riparian habitat using experimental flooding. Wetlands 22:49–57.

Steinblums, I. J. 1984. Designing stable buffer strips for stream protection. Journal of Forestry 82:49–52.

Stevens, L. E., T. J. Ayers, J. B. Bennett, K. Christensen, M. J. C. Kearsley, V. J. Meretsky, A. M. Phillips, III, R. A. Parnell, J. Spence, M. K. Sogge, A. E. Springer, and D. L. Wegner. 2001. Planned flooding and Colorado River riparian trade-offs downstream from Glen Canyon Dam, Arizona. Ecological Applications 11:701–710.

Stromberg, J. C. 2001. Restoration of riparian vegetation in the south-western United States: importance of flow regimes and fluvial dynamism. Journal of Arid Environments 49(1):17–34.

Sudbrock, A. 1993. Tamarisk control. I. Fighting back An overview of the invasion, and a low-impact way of fighting it Restoration and Management Notes 11:31–34.

Sutton, R. F. 1993. Mounding site preparation: a review of European and North American experience. Northern Forestry 7:151–192.

Swanson, F. J., and G. W. Lienkaemper. 1978. Physical consequences of large organic debris in Pacific Northwest streams. U.S. Forest Service, General Technical Report PNW-69, Portland, Oregon.

Tabacchi, E., D. L. Correll, R. Hauer, G. Pinay, A. M. Planty Tabacchi, and R. C. Wissmar. 1998. Development, maintenance and role of riparian vegetation in the river landscape. Freshwater Biology 40:497–516.

Taylor, J. P., and K. C. McDaniel. 1998. Restoration of salt cedar (Tamarix sp.)-infested floodplains on the Bosque del Apache National Wildlife Refuge. Integrated systems for noxious weed management on rangelands. Weed Technology 12:345–352.

Tickner, D. P., P. G. Angold, A. M. Gurnell, and J. O. Mountford. 2001. Riparian plant invasions: hydrogeomorphological control and ecological impacts. Progress in Physical Geography 25:22–52.

USFS and BLM (U. S. Forest Service and Bureau of Land Management). 1994. Record of decision for amendments of Forest Service and Bureau of Land Management planning documents within the range of the northern spotted owl. Standards and guidelines of habitat for late-successional and old-growth forest related species within the range of the northern spotted owl. U.S. Government Printing Office, USGPO 1994-589-111/00001, Washington, D.C.

USFS (U. S. Forest Service). 1987. Forester's field handbook. U.S. Forest Service, Pacific Northwest Region, Portland, Oregon.

Verry, E. S., J. W. Hornbeck, and C. A. Dolloff, editors. 1999. Riparian management in forests of the continental eastern United States. Lewis Publishers, New York.

Walker, L. R., J. C. Zasada, and F. S. Chapin. 1986. The role of life history processes in primary succession on an Alaskan floodplain. Ecology 67:1508-1523.

WFPB (Washington Forest Practices Board). 2000. Washington forest practices. Washington Department of Natural Resources, Olympia.

WDNR (Washington Department of Natural Resources). 1997. Final habitat conservation plan. Washington Department of Natural Resources, Olympia.

Welty, J., T. Beechie, K. Sullivan, D. M. Hyink, R. E. Bilby, C. Andrus, and G. Pess. 2002. Riparian Aquatic Interactions Simulator (RAIS): a model of riparian forest dynamics for the generation of large woody debris and shade. Forest Ecology and Management 162:299-318.

Wenger, K. F. 1984. Forestry handbook. Wiley, New York.

Wiant, H. V. 1979. Elementary timber measurements. Vandalia Press, Morgantown, West Virginia.

Williams, A. P., and E. R. Hunt. 2002. Estimation of leafy spurge cover from hyperspectral imagery using mixture tuned matched filtering. Remote Sensing of the Environment 82:446-456.

Wishnie, M., and N. L. McClintick. 1999. Lummi natural resources riparian zone restoration project. Preliminary report on seedling growth and survival. Lummi Indian Nation, Lummi Natural Resources, Bellingham, Washington.

Wissmar, R. C., and R. L. Beschta. 1998. Restoration and management of riparian ecosystems: a catchment perspective. Freshwater Biology 40:571-585.

Wolf, P. R., and R. C. Brinker. 1994. Elementary surveying. Harper Collins, New York.

Worthington, N. P., F. A. Johnson, G. R. Staebler, and W. J. Lloyd. 1960. Normal yield tables for red alder. U.S. Forest Service, Pacific Northwest Station Research Paper 36, Portland, Oregon.

Wykoff, W. R., N. L. Crookston, and A. R. Stage. 1982. User's guide to the Stand Prognosis Model. U.S. Forest Service, General Technical Report INT-133, Ogden, Utah.

Zar, J. H. 1999. Biostatistical analysis. Prentice-Hall, Englewood Cliffs, New Jersey.

Zavaleta, E. 2000. The economic value of controlling an invasive shrub. Ambio 29:462-467.

Chapter 5
Riparian Restoration through Grazing Management: Considerations for Monitoring Project Effectiveness

Alvin L. Medina, John N. Rinne

U.S. Department of Agriculture, Forest Service, Rocky Mountain Research Station
2500 South Pine Knoll Drive, Flagstaff, Arizona 86001, USA
almedina@fs.fed.us, jrinne@fs.fed.us

Philip Roni

Northwest Fisheries Science Center, National Marine Fisheries Service
2725 Montlake Boulevard East, Seattle, Washington 98112, USA
phil.roni@noaa.gov

Introduction

Many riparian areas throughout the United States were altered by the European settlement and the westward migration. Riparian areas currently comprise 1–5% of the landscape in the conterminous United States (Swift 1984; Knopf 1988), depending on the region. Their use is disproportionate to their relative extent and resource value. Swift (1984) estimated about 67 million riparian acres existed before European settlement. These areas were obligate settlement locations because of the presence of water. By the early twentieth century, the demand for surface water initiated a period of water resource development for irrigation, hydropower, and flood control. These early impacts were followed, midcentury, by mining (extraction) of subsurface waters to provide for rapidly developing metropolitan areas. Rivers and streams were dammed or diverted, and wetlands were drained, resulting in a drastic reduction in riparian habitats.

The settlement of rural areas included livestock grazing in riparian areas. The demand for beef increased as the population grew and as urban centers expanded in the late 1800s and early 1900s. Wild ungulates (e.g., bison *Bison bison*, elk *Cervus elaphus*, deer *Odocoileus* spp.) were a limited and unreliable food source for a developing nation; hence, livestock were extensively substituted. In the late 1800s, livestock in the West numbered in the millions and, coupled with drought, depleted vegetative resources across the landscape, including water-rich wetlands (Hendrickson and Minckley 1984) and riparian areas (Young 1998). Although the U.S. Forest Service recognized the need to control livestock numbers on public lands, not until the 1934 Taylor Grazing Act was livestock grazing management affected on public lands.

The grazing of public lands by livestock has been a highly contentious issue since the enactment of the National Environmental Policy Act of 1969. In the 1970s, a series of acts, including the Endangered Species Act and Public Rangelands Improvement Acts, further affected livestock management and reduced herd numbers across the West (Rinne and Medina 1996). Livestock numbers on western rangelands have been reduced by about half since the early part of the twentieth century (Medina and Rinne 1999), and considerable reductions were witnessed recently in response to drought and litigation over critical habitat issues. However, the relative decline in livestock numbers on rangelands has been replaced by an expansion of elk populations throughout western U.S. rangelands and Canada. Successful elk reintroductions in many western states have resulted in large herds with similar grazing effects of cattle. Elk ranching has even replaced cattle ranching in parts of the Rocky Mountain regions of North America. This change may satisfy political needs but does little for restoration of riparian habitats. Ungulate grazing issues will remain contentious for some time to come.

Although impacts to riparian and aquatic systems resulting from overgrazing are not limited to western North America, much research has focused on this region, primarily because of its large tracts of public and private rangelands used for grazing livestock (Belsky et al. 1999). Yet grazing in watersheds and riparian areas is an important issue throughout the world. Impacts of grazing on aquatic systems have been studied and reported in the eastern and midwestern United States (Wohl and Carline 1996; Weigel et al. 2000; Meals and Hopkins 2003), Europe (Diaz et al. 1996; Humphrey and Patterson 2000; O'Grady 2002), and Australia (Robertson and Rowling 2000; Jansen and Robertson 2001). Impacts to aquatic systems undoubtedly occur in other areas where humans use and manage livestock or ungulate populations. Impacts of grazing of riparian areas and uplands have been well documented (see Platts 1991 and Belsky et al. 1999 for thorough reviews). Grazing can alter natural riparian and channel processes (e.g., upland and streambank erosion, channel sedimentation and widening), increase stream temperatures, decrease water quality, change the water table and hydrologic regime, and, ultimately, affect aquatic biota (Elmore and Beschta 1987; Armour et al. 1991; Platts 1991; Belsky et al. 1999). Impacts on fishes and other biota are apparent but are more difficult to measure and are less well documented than physical changes (Platts 1991; Rinne 1999a).

Resource managers faced with the challenge of monitoring and mitigating grazing effects have devised many assessment models, such as the General Aquatic Wildlife Survey (GAWS) and the COWFISH habitat model used by the U.S. Forest Service (Lloyd 1985; USFS 1998), or the Rapid Bioassessment Habitat Evaluation Protocols or RBP (Plafkin et al. 1989) used by the Environmental Protection Agency (EPA). The RBPs and the qualitative habitat assessment approaches were developed as inexpensive screening tools for determining whether a stream is supporting a designated aquatic life use (Plafkin et al. 1989; Barbour and Stribling 1991, 1994; Rankin 1991, 1995). Barbour and Stribling (1991, 1994) modified the habitat assessment approach originally developed for the RBPs to include additional assessment parameters for high-gradient streams and a more appropriate parameter set for low-gradient streams. Habitat Evaluation Procedures (HEP) can be used to document the quality and the quantity of available habitat (USFWS 1980). Habitat Evaluation Procedures provide information for general instream and riparian habitat comparisons of the relative value of different areas at the same or future points in time. By combining the two types of comparisons, the impact of proposed or anticipated land- and water-use changes on instream and riparian habitat is quantified.

However, to date, there are no comprehensive models or methods for the assessment of ungulate grazing effects on fish habitats that have been validated across various ecosystems. For example, Contor and Platts (1991) evaluated COWFISH (Lloyd 1985) and determined that its capabilities were limited to qualitative estimations of stream or riparian health and, more importantly, that the model is based on vital assumptions of fish–terrestrial habitat linkages (Platts 1990). Deficiencies in habitat assessment methods have lead resource managers to develop and deploy many methodologies, most often with little validation but with honorable intentions, to meet monitoring requirements. The fundamental problem lies in establishing the direct linkages between fish and other aquatic biota health factors and the complex interactions of ungulates and many environmental variables (e.g., vegetation, hydrology, geomorphology, geology, climate). Many studies report negative interactions between fish and ungulates (Kauffman and Krueger 1984; Platts 1991; Fleischner 1994; Belsky et al. 1999; Rinne 1999a), but none have established direct linkages of cause and effect. This is not to deny that livestock impair various riparian functions when habitats are overused, but we emphasize that grazing is a function that can occur even in the absence of livestock, such as by various herbivores (e.g., elk, deer). While the assessment of direct effects often is difficult, it should be performed with objectivity and validated methods. For example, Medina and Steed (2002) found that elk have impacts similar to cattle on vegetation and stream channels. The impacts of grazing vary within and among ecoregions, depending on a suite of factors (e.g., geology, channel type, vegetation, ungulate species, elevation, hydrology). Some riparian areas can sustain little to no ungulate grazing, while others (e.g., Nebraska sedge *Carex nebraskensis* sites) can sustain very high use. However, a divergence from ecosystem science occurs when "ungulate" grazing is selectively applied to livestock, especially where habitats are managed for fisheries with critical habitat designations for threatened or endangered populations (Rinne 2003a). These fisheries and their associated riparian habitat may require some form of protection from grazing of all ungulates (e.g., elk, deer, cattle), as well as recreation, or other land uses for vegetation and channel recovery on selected reaches.

Numerous strategies to restore or to improve riparian areas and aquatic habitats impacted by grazing have been developed and implemented throughout North America and other parts of the world. Platts (1991) listed several innovative management strategies for addressing and corroborating livestock grazing impacts in riparian areas. While numerous and sometimes complex, all grazing strategies include control of livestock numbers, distribution, duration, timing of grazing, control of forage use, or some combination of these factors (Platts 1991). Strategies such as rest–rotation and seasonal use often require active management to periodically move livestock, reduce their numbers, or prevent them from grazing riparian areas. Fencing and complete grazing removal are the most common and potentially successful "grazing strategies" used to provide short- and long-term exclusion of ungulates and allow for riparian recovery. To ensure success, all grazing strategies should be approached in a context similar to a U.S. Forest Service multiple-use paradigm and in a multidisciplinary (e.g., fisheries, hydrology, botany, geology) frame of reference. We try to adhere to these frames of reference as we discuss and suggest monitoring needs and approaches.

Clearly, the success of various grazing strategies depends on thorough monitoring and evaluation to determine the effectiveness of different grazing reduction and removal strategies. In this chapter, we provide the reader with practical information on issues of monitoring riparian areas, with emphasis on fisheries. First, we provide an overview of considerations in designing a monitoring and evaluation program (e.g., questions and hypotheses, study design, and duration) and selecting useful monitoring parameters. Next, we present three grazing case studies wherein we describe the purpose of the study, problems and issues, methods, and what was measured and what was learned (results). Lastly, we synthesize general principles from the case studies that should apply for any monitoring program when addressing grazing and fencing in riparian areas. While several types of monitoring exist (status, compliance, effectiveness, validation, etc.), our discussion focuses on effectiveness monitoring and validation monitoring: determining whether the fencing or grazing strategy had the desired physical and biological effects.

Design Considerations for Monitoring Grazing Strategies

The development of a monitoring program to evaluate a grazing or a fencing strategy to restore or to improve stream and riparian conditions—similar to other types of habitat restoration and improvement—should follow several logical steps. These include determining project objectives and hypotheses, appropriate experimental design (e.g., scale, duration, replication), selecting appropriate parameters and sampling protocols and strategies, and implementing the monitoring program. Chapter 2 discusses these steps, as well as statistical considerations, in detail. Rather than reiterate those here, we briefly describe unique study design and parameter selection considerations for grazing and fencing projects.

Defining Project Objectives and Monitoring Hypotheses

One of the initial steps in developing any monitoring and evaluation program is to clearly articulate the specific objectives of the project (i.e., to allow for the recovery of herbaceous and woody riparian vegetation through the removal of grazing) and specific hypotheses. Without overarching goals and specific objectives, it will be difficult to determine key questions and phrase these as testable hypotheses the monitoring program will answer. Examples of key questions might be:
- What is the effect of removal of grazing on riparian vegetation species and growth over time?
- What is the effect of grazing removal on physical habitat (e.g., bank stability, fine sediment, channel type)?
- What is the effect of grazing removal on aquatic biota (e.g., fishes, macroinvertebrates)?

Articulating the project objectives and testable hypotheses sets the stage for subsequent steps in designing a monitoring program.

Study Design and Spatial and Temporal Considerations

Selecting an appropriate study design for monitoring a grazing strategy depends upon a number of factors, including the scale (reach or watershed) of the project or projects, duration, and replication. Many evaluations of grazing strategies have attempted to use a before–after (BA) or before–after control–impact (BACI) study design. Indeed, because grazing and fencing are treatments that can be relatively easily manipulated (i.e., fencing or changing livestock numbers), monitoring and evaluation of grazing and fencing projects lend themselves to BA and BACI designs. However, most studies that have used this design included little pretreatment monitoring, whereas conducting a thorough BA study requires considerable preproject planning and commitment of resources (Platts 1991; Rinne 1999a). Thus posttreatment designs with paired treatment and reference (control) reaches or watersheds with sampling immediately after treatment (implementation of new grazing strategy) are particularly common (e.g., Myers 1989; Wohl and Carline 1996; Clary 1999). However, finding sites with similar grazing strategies and physical features to serve as replicates and controls can be very difficult. Harrelson et al. (1994) and Downes et al. (2002) provide good criteria in selecting control reaches or streams. These typically include finding stream reaches with similar geology, channel type, substrate, vegetation, and more. Establishment of short- or long-term control over a study reach by using fencing or by excluding ungulates requires not only knowledge of technical aspects of a monitoring plan but also specific knowledge of other wildlife needs (Kie et al. 1994; Acorn 1997; Huedepohl 2000), livestock (Worley and Heusner 2000), fencing designs, costs and materials (BLM 1985; Craven and Hygnstrom 1996; De Calesta and Witmer 1996; Mayer 1999; Bekaert 2002), and environmental conditions (Hygnstrom et al. 1996). Retrospective or posttreatment studies can provide useful comparisons of physical and biological conditions in treated and untreated areas but typically require extensive replication to detect changes in fish abundance due to grazing or removal of grazing.

The spatial scale of the project also will help determine the type of study design. If a grazing project occurs along a short stream reach and changes are expected to be localized, a reach-scale approach may be needed. A grazing or fencing project that occurs along multiple reaches or in upland areas may require monitoring the entire watershed or subwatershed. In the absence of extensive preproject data, a reference or control reach or watershed is needed to account for variability not associated with the treatment (grazing or reduced grazing). As with evaluations of other types of restoration projects, one of the pitfalls of studies evaluating the effects of grazing strategies on instream conditions is ignoring watershed-scale effect (Kondolf 1993; Rinne 1999a). For example, both Myers and Swanson (1995) and Kondolf (1993) demonstrated that while riparian vegetation conditions improved along fenced treatment areas, channel width and sediment levels did not change due to upstream and upslope roads and grazing, which contributed sediment and altered hydrology in treatment reaches.

Measurements usually are made at sites, within reaches, along a stream course, or positioned within a watershed or catchment basin. A very basic consideration is the mobility of a response variable across these scales within the riparian corridor. Plants, streambanks, and channels are stationary at a site within a reach of a riparian-stream corridor. By contrast, fishes, invertebrates, substrates, and chemical factors are very dynamic and move through these spatial scales. That is, response variables transcend controls and treatments frequently positioned linearly within riparian corridors (Rinne 1999a, 2000). Based on these functions and processes, monitoring protocols, analyses, and interpretations must be markedly different for these two response groups. Fences preclude grazing impacts on the stationary response variables (e.g., vegetation and streambanks) within an exclosure (i.e., a site or a reach of stream). Outside exclosures, the effects on static (stationary) variables are directly linked and relatively easily measured and interpreted. In stark contrast, the mobile response variables (e.g. sediment, biota) are indirectly and independently linked to potential grazing impacts. Accordingly, their measurement, analyses, and interpretations are more complex and often are subject to misinterpretation. All study design and interpretations of results of study must be made within the context of the stream continuum (Vannote et al. 1980). To do otherwise may fail to obtain viable, defendable monitoring information that could benefit land managers.

Placing controls and treatments linearly upon a stream can lead to pseudoreplication (Hurlbert 1984). Scientific controls are difficult to achieve in the natural world because of habitat complexity and our inadequate knowledge of interactions (Likens 1984). Rinne (1999a) reported that a third of the grazing studies he examined in the literature had no controls and most of the remaining two-thirds were positioned linearly upon the same stream that contained treated (grazed) reaches. Using "control" reaches interspersed with treatments on the same stream to satisfy the lack of pretreatment data for the entire stream is problematic: streams are continuums, and treated areas can influence conditions in interposed control areas. Some of the studies reviewed by Rinne (1999a) were inconclusive because they did not consider channel type. Considering both the channel type and the positioning of treatments and controls is crucial when designing riparian monitoring.

Replication of study areas in time is another common problem with evaluation of fencing riparian areas for restoration (Rinne 1988, 1999a). Only half of studies examined in the literature reviewed by Rinne (1999a) were replicated in time. Temporal, pretreatment information in the target area to be restored is desirable, but usually lacking (Rinne 1999a, 2000). When possible, a minimum of 2–3 years of information and preferably 5–7 years is desirable before rehabilitative treatment (Rinne 1999a). The duration of monitoring realistically should extend to twice the minimum period of time (i.e., 4–6 years) or longer (e.g., 10 years) in an attempt to address natural variability. Studies on juvenile salmonids and other fishes suggest that more than 10 years (>5 before and 5 after) are needed to detect significant changes in fish abundance after habitat changes unless the magnitude of change in fish abundance is large (>threefold) or the treatments and controls are extensively replicated (Bisson et al. 1997; Roni et al. 2003). Decades of before or after monitoring may be needed to detect significant responses of anadromous salmonids (Bisson et al. 1997), likely because other factors, such as ocean conditions and migration, are affecting their survival and are increasing interannual variability. Estimating the duration of monitoring needed to detect statistical significance can be done if estimates of the variability of the parameter of interest are available (see Chapter 2 for examples and statistical texts such as Zar 1999 for details). Finally, the frequency of monitoring a response variable should be determined based on the ecology of biological entities and seasonal and climatic considerations for physical and chemical variables.

Selecting Monitoring Parameters

The potential parameters to monitor the response of riparian restoration through grazing management fall into three general categories: physical, chemical, and biological (Table 1). Livestock grazing has been suggested to affect changes in all three areas (Kauffman and Krueger 1984; Platts 1991; Rinne 1999a). However, too frequently, monetary and human resources will limit the feasibility of measuring all variables within the three general response areas. Selection of appropriate parameters to monitor in these three categories will depend upon the objectives and hypotheses of the grazing strategy and the monitoring program. For example, if the project objective is to restore riparian vegetation by fencing to exclude cattle and the hypothesis is that riparian vegetation will recover in x number of years after fencing, then one of the most obvious categories of parameters to monitor will be riparian vegetation. The vegetation component of riparian resources is linked most directly to the herbivory response variable. Accordingly, specific monitoring parameters for herbaceous and woody vegetation should become a priority. On the other hand, if the stream is the water supply for domestic use in a downstream municipality and the key questions or hypotheses relate to water quality, then the chemical responses, including concentrations of pollutants (e.g., *Escherichia coli*) and nutrients that potentially affect water quality, should be monitored. Finally, if threatened or endangered fishes occupy the stream and if the hypotheses regarding the effects of grazing management on fish are part of the monitoring program, then fish and fish habitat parameters should be part of the primary study focus of monitoring.

Unfortunately, selecting a single response variable normally results in more questions asked than answered at the completion of the monitoring activity. Notwithstanding that, one must begin with the key questions and hypotheses and must select response variables that can test these hypotheses. These variables should be the highest priority for monitoring. It also is important to consider whether variables will respond directly or indirectly to grazing management. For example, vegetation growth typically responds directly to grazing management, but stream shade and stream physical characteristics and biota respond indirectly (i.e., they depend on vegetation growth). Thus, indirect response variables need to be selected and linked (Rinne 1999a) to the primary response variable for greater definition and reliability of conclusions of monitoring. As we shall see, detecting changes in indirect response variables, which often are the objective of riparian restoration, can be difficult. Below, we discuss the major physical and biological parameters that often are monitored to determine the response of riparian and aquatic systems to fencing and other grazing strategies and provide some examples of their use (see also Table 1). We briefly discuss chemical parameters to monitor in the "other parameters" subsection. They are discussed in more detail in Chapter 9.

Physical Parameters

There are several key categories of parameters of physical instream and riparian variables that may respond to changes in grazing, including channel morphology, channel stability, sediment (fine and coarse), bank stability, stream flow, and water temperature.

Table 1.

Major categories and potential variables (parameters) to monitor to determine effectiveness of riparian grazing or fencing project. Which parameters are appropriate will depend on objectives of project and questions and hypotheses determined before initiating project and monitoring. Not all parameters are appropriate for every fencing or grazing project.

General categories	Common parameters monitored	References with protocols
Physical parameters		
Channel morphology	Channel type, longitudinal and cross sections, channel maps, aerial photographs, channel migration	Rosgen 1996; Montgomery and Buffington 1997
Bank stability	Rooting depth, vegetation cover, soil types, slope angles, soil moisture, bank erosion	Pfankuch 1975, Platts et al. 1987, Myers 1989, Bauer and Burton 1993, Schuett-Hames et al. 1994, FISRWG 1998; Newton et al. 1998; Casagli et al. 1999, Rinaldi and Casagli 1999, Simon et al. 1999; Burton and Cowley 2002; Simon and Collison 2002
Channel stability	Channel substrates	Rosgen 1996, 2001b; Montgomery and Buffington 1997
Hydrology	Flow, velocity	Dunne and Leopold 1978; Gordon et al. 1992; Harrelson et al. 1994
Substrates	Embeddedness, fine sediment levels, particle size, subsurface analysis	Gangmark and Bakkala 1958; Schuett-Hames et al. 1994; Bevenger and King 1995; Waters 1995; Bunte and Abt 2001; Sylte and Fischenich 2002; see also Chapter 3
Temperature	Daily continuous, maximum and minimum	Newton et al. 1998
Chemical parameters		
Nutrients	Cations (Ca, Fe, Mg, Mn), Nutrients (NO_2, e.g., NO_3, PO_4), pollutants (e.g. sulfates)	NRCS 1996, 1999; Newton et al. 1998; Clesceri et al. 1999; see also Chapter 9
Water quality	Dissolved oxygen, pH, alkalinity, conductivity, hardness, salinity	Newton et al. 1998; Clersceri et al. 1999; NRCS 1999
Biological parameters		
Vegetation	Cover, frequency, density, composition, production, utilization	Elzinga et al. 1998; BLM 1999a, 1999b; Clary and Leininger 2000
Fish	Abundance, survival; species, length, age composition	Platts et al. 1983; Murphy and Willis 1996; Barbour et al. 1999; Moulton et al. 2002; see also Chapter 8
Macroinvertebrates	Abundance, diversity functional feeding groups, various metrics and indices of integrity	Platts et al. 1983; Rosenburg and Resh 1993; Barbour et al. 1999; Karr and Chu 1999; Moulton et al. 2002
Other biota	Primary productivity (periphyton, algae, etc.), aquatic plants	Barbour et al. 1999; Moulton et al. 2002; see also Chapters 6 and 9

Channel morphology and complexity

Channel type, geometry, width, sinuosity, movement, and channel units (i.e., pools and riffles) frequently are monitored to demonstrate changes due to various riparian and grazing strategies. For example, channels may narrow after removal of grazing, growth of vegetation, and stabilization of banks; several studies have demonstrated this by measuring cross sections or stream widths (Platts 1991; Clary 1999; Myers and Swanson 1995).

However, other factors, such as sediment supply and streamflow, have a greater potential to affect channel morphology and complexity (see sediment subsection below and the case studies for further discussion). Habitat units or reaches of a stream with a similar nature (i.e., gradient, sinuosity, substrate) should be used cautiously when evaluating the effectiveness of grazing management strategies. We concur with Poole et al. (1997) that instream habitat unit classifications (i.e., pools, riffles, glides) should not be used to quantify and monitor aquatic habitat and channel morphology response to grazing management or riparian restoration, owing to subjectivity, lack of validation, and statistical limitations. As indicted previously, considering or stratifying reaches by channel type is a critical component of selecting study reaches. Details on methods for monitoring channel morphology are provided in Chapters 3 and 8.

Sediment

Grazing generally is thought to increase levels of fine sediments and to decrease the size of bed materials in stream channels (Platts 1991). The ecology of aquatic biota such as fishes are intimately linked to substrates they occupy for breeding, feeding, and cover (Rinne and Stefferud 1996; Rinne and Deason 2000; Rinne 2001a, 2001b). Sediment most often is considered synonymous with "fines" or materials of less than a millimeter or two in size. Parent geology, location within a watershed, and hydrology are major factors influencing fine sediment and substrate size within a stream reach. A number of methods exist for measuring substrate size. The zigzag transect method of Bevenger and King (1995) provides an efficient, reliable method of assessing change in the surface nature of bedload composition, because it responds to impacts on a watershed or within the riparian area proper. More detailed methodologies are available for examining surface and subsurface sediments or substrates (Everest et al. 1987; Chapman 1988). Typically, in these types of studies, the focus is on the levels of fine sediment in redds and the levels potential effects on salmonid egg development and survival. For example, Rinne (1988) used a standpipe (Gangmark and Bakkala 1958) driven into the substrate to determine substrate permeability in one montane stream subjected to grazing removal. However, aside from salmonids, most cypriniforms, and many other species, are nest builders or surficial substrate spawners or broadcast spawners. The pebble count methodology of Bevenger and King (1995) or a similar method can assess changes in substrates that would, in turn, affect these spawning behaviors. Given that a stream is a continuum, sediment impacts from a grazed area above an ungrazed area could affect the substrate composition bedload through the ungrazed area. Additional details on sampling fine and coarse sediment is provided in Chapter 3.

Major off-site disturbances may cause excessive sedimentation changes within the channel, such as to increase substrate embeddedness. Various techniques for measuring substrate embeddedness have been developed (Platts et al. 1987; Bain and Stevenson 1999). Sylte and Fischenich (2002) provide an in-depth review of seven methods, definitions, and various rating systems, and of the significance of embeddedness to fisheries. Despite many methods, there are fundamental problems with them, including wide disparity in methodologies, fundamental defects, and poor guidance criteria (Sylte and Fischenich 2002). The use of existing embeddedness measures is not recommended for monitoring grazing impacts on streams, because the results are unreliable.

As indicated previously, subsurface analysis methods sometimes are used to determine the composition of spawning substrates, especially where fine sediments are of concern. The McNeil sampler (McNeil and Ahnell 1964) is an instrument commonly used in salmonid monitoring studies in Washington State (Schuett-Hames et al. 1994). The "shovel method" also has been used with some success (Grost et al. 1991). A comprehensive review of particle-size analysis and sampling is provided by Bunte and Abt (2001) and also is discussed in Chapter 3 and will not be covered here.

Channel and bank stability

Bed and channel stability generally is a prerequisite to streambank stability (FISRWG 1998). The complex hydrological interactions of streamflow, erosion, and sediment can act upon the channel to cause instability (Rosgen 2001c), though channel movement and migration are natural stream processes and occur at higher rates in some channels types and geologies than others. Channel instability can lead to major shifts in lateral migration of the channel but is a natural phenomenon that can occur gradually, as in the erosion of meander bends of low-gradient meadow streams. While channel avulsions occur during bank-full events, their scouring effects can be magnified by flood flows, excessive sedimentation, debris jams, or mass wasting (Keller and Swanson 1979). Stream types with wide valley floors and low entrenchment ratios typical of Rosgen (1996) types E and C would be most susceptible.

Streambank integrity and stability are principal concerns of riparian monitoring for grazing impacts, because the streambank is the zone where ungulates can exert their greatest physical impact. Since the early 1970s, several methods were devised to estimate the relative stability of streambanks (Pfankuch 1975; Platts et al. 1987; Myers 1989; Bauer and Burton 1993; Schuett-Hames et al. 1994; FISRWG 1998; Burton and Cowley 2002). The basis for most methods is founded on the premise that streambank integrity is a direct factor affecting fish populations through sequential alteration of streambanks, channel stability, and riparian habitat. The term "integrity" connotes the use of a measure that integrates, at a minimum, specific types of herbaceous and woody vegetation, the soil type, the hydrologic regime, and geomorphic conditions. However, because of the complex interactions between physical and biological factors, to date, there is no one single approach that accurately provides a measure of streambank stability. Qualitative approaches rely on visual estimates of cover of aboveground biomass, root density and rooting depth, and relative bank erosion rates to estimate stability. Quantitative approaches apply physical laws (e.g., force and resistance) to estimate bank instability (FISRWG 1998). Hybrid models may incorporate both qualitative and quantitative aspects of biological and physical factors. Most streambank stability assessment methods apply to low-gradient meadow habitats, where ungulates tend to congregate, because higher-gradient habitats generally are stabilized by rock–boulder substrates. The type of vegetation that occupies the streambank is linked to elements for measuring bank stability (Rosgen 1996; Clary 1999). Many stream types are morphologically dependent on herbaceous vegetation (e.g., sedges; Medina 1995), deeply rooted woody species (e.g., willows), or large and coarse woody debris (Rosgen 1996; Montgomery and Buffington 1997).

Newton et al. (1998) provide a typical example of a qualitative streambank stability rating protocol (Table 2). Four categories of condition are delineated based on bank height, percent of exposed bank actively eroding, roots, and stability of overhanging woody vegetation. Platts et al. (1983) suggested rating streambank erosion and vegetative stability separately. Examples of modifications to previous models or hybrid models are Johnson et al. (1998), Rosgen (1996), and others. For example, Rosgen (1996) developed a hybrid model that derives an erodibility hazard index for streambank assessment that incorporates bank heights, angles, materials, presence of layers, rooting depth and density, and percent bank protection. The index, coupled with calculated near-bank stresses, is used to develop a quantitative prediction model of streambank erosion rates

Table 2.
Descriptions of qualitative bank stability criteria and ratings (modified from Newton et al. 1998). Numeric values at bottom row indicate rating on a scale of 1–10 that fit the narrative descriptions. Intermediate numeric scores would be given to bank stability that falls between the qualitative verbal descriptions.

Banks are stable	Moderately stable	Moderately unstable	Unstable
Banks are low (at elevation of active floodplain); 33% or more of eroding surface area of banks in outside bends is protected by roots that extend to the base-flow elevation.	Banks are low (at elevation of active floodplain); less than 33% of eroding surface area of banks in outside bends is protected by roots that extend to the base-flow elevation.	Banks may be low but typically are high (flooding occurs 1 year out of 5 or less frequently); outside bends are actively eroding (overhanging vegetation at top of bank, some mature trees falling into steam annually, some slope failures apparent).	Banks may be low but typically are high; some straight reaches and inside edges of bends are actively eroding, as well as outside bends (overhanging vegetation at top of bare bank, numerous mature trees falling into stream annually, numerous slope failures apparent).
10	7	3	1

(Rosgen 2001a). Platts et al. (1983, 1987) presented hybrid approaches in which various attributes of the streambank (e.g., soil alteration, vegetative stability, streambank undercut, and channel-bank angle) were rated and measured to obtain estimates of bank stability. Intensive stream stability assessment methods such as those developed by Rosgen (2001b, 2001c), or other similar intensive approaches, are very useful for monitoring riparian management but require hydrological expertise. Examples of quantitative estimations of bank stability include those of Casagli et al. (1999), Rinaldi and Casagli (1999), Simon et al. (1999), and Simon and Collison (2002). These models examine the mechanics of soil and water interactions that result in the failure of streambanks. Simon and Collison (2002) have developed an interactive software model that examines bank geometry material, root strength, pore pressure, and other factors to assist in the quantitative monitoring of streambank stability. Refinements to traditional streambank monitoring protocols to increase consistency and reliability are described by Burton and Cowley (2002) and have shown promising results for monitoring streambank alteration. Their protocol strives for objectivity and consistency, with warnings that appropriate training to understand and identify streambank alteration processes is essential.

Stream flow

The hydrologic regime of a stream has a direct impact on riparian areas, stream channels, and the biota that inhabit them. Differences in flow regimes may have marked effects on fish assemblages and their sustainability (Rinne 2002). For example, in the Southwest, many of the native, mostly threatened and endangered, fishes depend upon elevated flow or flood events (Minckley and Meffe 1987; Rinne and Stefferud 1997; Rinne 2002). The antithesis of elevated flow is base or sustained surface flow (Neary and Rinne 1997). The removal of water from streams and aquifers can effectively and completely override any grazing reduction or other riparian restoration efforts (Neary and Rinne 2001; Rinne 2002).

Monitoring flow is essential to evaluation of grazing activities and of a stream restoration. At a fine scale, characteristics of the water column, such as width, depth, the ratio of the two, and velocity, can be monitored (Platts et al. 1983, 1987). Because of characteristic habitat use or selection by aquatic biota (Rinne and Stefferud 1996), changes in these flow attributes may result from riparian restoration and may explain presence, absence, or abundance of respective species. Changes in ratios of pool to riffle habitat can markedly affect reduction in numbers or complete disappearance of some species. Changes in water column characteristics and dynamics ultimately may change fish assemblages (Rinne et al. 1998; Rinne 1999b).

Common measures for quantifying flow include staff gauges, stream gauges, and flowmeters, described in Chapter 6. In larger rivers, U.S. Geological Survey stream gauging stations are available and provide invaluable resources to define base and peak flows and variability of the system. Unfortunately, only a small portion of streams have stream gauging stations.

Temperature

Water temperature of streams varies seasonally and diurnally. In rivers and streams in the Southwest, water temperatures can vary 10°C in a 24-h period (Rinne et al. 2002). Measurement of water temperature is relatively straightforward, given the availability of relatively inexpensive data loggers that can be placed throughout the stream network and programmed to record temperatures at desired time intervals (daily, hourly, etc.) and for several months at a time. Stream water temperatures are affected by climate, ambient air temperatures, subsurface flow, springs, topography, and exposure. The variability of stream temperature and the multiple factors that can affect stream temperature make this parameter problematic for monitoring changes in grazing. In the context of grazing management and riparian restoration, stream exposure to solar radiation is most often of concern. Water temperature, indeed, can be affected by streamside vegetation or channel morphology that affects the surface area of the water. However, because of the complicating factors listed above, it is difficult to delimit with precision the relative effects of either stream shading by vegetation or relative stream surface-area exposure as related to stream channel morphology. Some researchers argue for streamside vegetation (Betscha 1997) as a controlling factor of water temperature. Others (Larson and Larson 1996) suggest that temperatures in streams are influenced by ambient temperatures and surface exposure as affected by channel morphology. Clearly, water temperature is affected by a suite of factors, including water sources (i.e., groundwater, snowmelt, surface runoff) stream size, channel morphology, geology (alluvial versus bedrock), vegetation type, and riparian canopy. Whether this parameter responds to reduction or removal of grazing in a particular stream or stream reach may not be as straightforward as many researchers contend.

The thermal limits of aquatic biota also should be considered when measuring water temperature. Cold versus cool or warmwater species will respond differently to changes in temperature and may help explain changes in the fish community associated with removal or change in grazing management. Rinne et al. (2002) demonstrated that several species of cypriniforms in one Southwest desert river sustain markedly elevated heart rates with increasing water temperatures. Two points that monitoring programs need to embrace are that (1) most often, specific information on thermal tolerances of fishes is not available; and (2) because of seasonal, diel, and diurnal variations of water temperatures in rivers and streams, a wide range of temperature tolerances by species should be expected. These ranges may be broader than those achievable by streamside vegetation restoration and its effect on water temperatures. Further, the common sectioning or partitioning of stream reaches by fencing and varying the grazing strategies characteristic of many studies (Rinne 1999a) results in temperature sinks and sources in the stream continuum, one potentially canceling the influence of the other.

In summary, water temperature can be an important parameter to monitor, but the results need to be interpreted with caution because a number of factors outside the study area may influence temperature. This emphasizes the need for temperature monitoring beyond a reach scale to tease out effects of grazing and fencing activities from other factors that may have a substantial influence on stream temperatures. Linking changes in temperature resulting from grazing management to changes in fish populations is, indeed, more problematic. The continual mixing of water, the array of factors influencing temperatures within a reach or habitat, the frequent lack of thermal data for fishes, and their probable wide range of tolerances of different fish species can confound linking changes in temperature to changes in vegetation and, ultimately, in grazing.

Biological Parameters

Many biological parameters are used to monitor direct and indirect changes in terrestrial and aquatic habitats in response to ungulate grazing, including herbaceous and woody vegetation, fishes, macroinvertebrates, periphyton, and other benthos components.

Vegetation

Streambank vegetation is the most common parameter used in monitoring of ungulate grazing. It is expected that presence, reduction or absence of ungulate foraging, or trampling of streamside habitats will invoke a change in the vegetation community, and such changes can be quantified by monitoring various attributes of the vegetation. Quantitative, semiquantitative, and qualitative approaches can be used, depending on project constraints. Several vegetation attributes should be measured to provide a better estimation of grazing effects on streambanks, but six principal attributes are cover, frequency, density, composition, structure, and production or utilization.

Many quantitative methods are available for measuring changes in vegetation attributes, including frequency, dry weight rank, Daubenmire, line intercept, step-point, point-intercept, cover board, density, double-weight, harvest, comparative yield, visual obstruction (robel pole), and other methods. The applicability and description of quantitative methods that measure these attributes are described in detail in BLM (1999a, 1999b). Additional information on general vegetation monitoring can be found in Kent and Coker (1994) and Elzinga et al. (1998). A quantitative method used to specifically monitor changes in streamside habitats, commonly known as the greenline method, is described in Winward (2000). This method measures the first perennial vegetation that forms a lineal grouping of community types on or near the waters' edge (i.e., the "greenline") typically slightly below bank-full stage, an important area for determining effects of grazing activities on streambank stability. Winward (2000) also describes methods for measuring vegetation cross-section composition and woody species generation. Similarly, the U.S. Forest Service is developing a quantitative methodology for detecting ungulate effects on streambank vegetation (Medina, unpublished). The protocol differs from the greenline method in that (1) aquatic and terrestrial plant- and ground-cover attributes are measured at the land–water interface, (2) vegetation transects follow the contour of the water interface, and (3) it yields repeatable quantitative estimates of plant and ground cover. The method also yields information on species frequency and composition. Many aquatic plants function as colonizers of the streambank interface zone and, as such, are important indicators of trend and condition (Medina 1995). The method is flexible to accommodate other parameters of interest (e.g., trampling, geomorphology) that can be used in combination to estimate ungulate impacts, as well as to provide measures of aquatic plant attributes. Quantitative methods are recommended where endangered species or litigative issues are present.

Similarly, semiquantitative and qualitative methods commonly are used in habitat assessments and generally are built into habitat assessment models (e.g., GAWS, COWFISH). For example, Platts et al. (1987) described a qualitative method to assess stream cover and habitat conditions by using a ranking approach. These qualitative approaches often are favored because they require considerably less field time and no technical botanical expertise. They may be adequate as diagnostic tools to identify potential problems and trends but typically are not good indicators for long-term monitoring.

The measurement of any single vegetation attribute (e.g., vegetative cover) is insufficient to estimate grazing effects, despite the fact that vegetative cover has been linked to salmonid abundance in many studies (Platts 1991). The type of plant cover, whether herbaceous, woody, or aquatic, yields important information about the habitat type and its functional state. For example, herbaceous cover provided by dense sedge stands is functionally different from woody plant cover for the same range site. In the latter case, the woody component may be indicative of a disturbed habitat condition versus a stable high-successional stage. However, the woody condition may provide better cover to ameliorate water temperatures. Frequency and density attributes are used to describe relative abundance of plant species or groups. Species composition provides a description of the individual plants that comprise the site. All these measures collectively provide evidence of ungulate effects. The interpretation of these attributes into causal effects requires technical knowledge of individual plant and community functions. For example, plant cover may remain constant, but plant composition may change from a sedge type to mesic species (e.g., Kentucky bluegrass *Poa pratensis*), a condition indicative of a general loss in soil moisture through the soil profile, which may be in response to a hydrological change exclusive of ungulates, or a combination thereof. The combination of vegetation attributes also can aid in interpretations of successional dynamics, functionality, trend, and disturbance regime, or to quantify and describe riparian habitat types. Additional information about the habitat type may be derived from vegetation attributes that measure plant community structure (i.e., diameter, height). Platts et al. (1983) and others have suggested that fish productivity can be determined from the type and diversity of habitat types of a given stream.

Various methods are available for measuring the production and utilization of biomass (e.g., browse removal, stubble height, residue measuring, herbaceous removal, landscape appearance) on riparian areas (BLM 1999a) and are used in conjunction with other vegetation attributes to assess grazing impacts. The assessment of production or utilization can require extensive time and effort, especially if causal factors are sought. There are several considerations (e.g., seasonal and annual effects, differences due to methods and observers) that should be weighed prior to selecting a specific method (Krueger 1998). The stubble height method has been advocated for use in riparian areas by Clary and Leininger (2000), who recommend a streamside stubble height of 10 cm as near optimal in many situations. They further suggest that the recommended height be adjusted to meet site conditions, such as increasing the height to 15–20 cm where willow browsing is of concern. The criterion is suggested primarily for small streams or sensitive streambanks, not for dry meadows or other similar sites. Users are cautioned not to emphasize the method as the management goal; rather, the resource manager should have a clear picture of the ecological structure and function of the area before settling on a specific height.

In summary, the use of vegetation attributes to assess grazing impacts on riparian areas requires measurement of several attributes and careful interpretation of the results. Vegetation changes may result from a variety of intrinsic (e.g., community dynamics) and extrinsic factors (e.g., ungulates, floods, drought, disease). As such, it is important to at least control for habitat or vegetation type, channel type, seasonal influences on vegetative production, ungulate class, and methodology.

Fishes

Like many restoration and habitat improvement techniques, the objective of grazing and fencing projects often are to increase fish abundance and survival. Monitoring of fish often includes examining fish size, age, abundance, and survival at various life stages, as well as species composition and diversity. Monitoring riparian-stream restoration projects for fish response must be based on the ecology and basic biology of the species. Most of the information on effects of grazing and for restoration activities, in general, is based on studies of salmonid fishes (Rinne 1988; Medina and Rinne 1999; Roni et al. 2002). In regions other than the Pacific Northwest and northern Rockies, salmon and trout are not the dominant species taxonomically, politically, or economically. For example, in the Southwest, there are about 40 native species of fishes, only 3 of which are salmonids. Although some general principles may apply to fishes as a group, the biology and ecology of most of the cypriniform species in the Southwest, and we suggest elsewhere in North America, is highly specialized and differs significantly from that of salmonids. To adopt a "one size fits all" approach may be expedient for managers, but it has a high probability of being detrimental to sustainability of many native cypriniform species. In a context of restoration of riparian-stream areas, the antithesis, namely destruction, extirpation, and possible extinction of a native species of fish or their assemblages, may be the end result because alien fish species are favored by vegetation changes (see case studies below). Many of the cypriniform species in the West (Minckley and Deacon 1991; Rinne and Minckley 1991; Rinne 1999a) and elsewhere throughout the United States (Williams et al. 1989) are threatened, endangered, or of special concern. Others are candidate and sensitive species (Rinne 2003a). Therefore, it is necessary to design monitoring protocols relative to the biology and ecology of the species of interest.

An equally important consideration to the salmonid versus nonsalmonid issue is that of native versus nonnative (alien) fish species. Introduction of nonnative species of fishes is cosmopolitan, with more than 500 nonindigenous species documented throughout inland waters of the United States (Fuller et al. 1999). For example, more than 100 species have been introduced into the waters of Arizona since 1890 (Rinne 1995; in press), and almost half have become established, self-sustaining populations. Through mechanisms of competition, displacement, and direct predation by nonnatives, native fish species have declined markedly. In restoration projects, the impact of nonnative fish species on natives may be more direct and negative than the positive influences of riparian restoration. Further, changes affected by restoration (e.g., instream vegetation increase and streambank changes) may favor nonnative fishes over natives (Rinne and Neary 1997).

Finally, one may approach fish monitoring in restoration projects from the "guild" or fish assemblage context. For example, in the Southwest, there are native "cryptic species," such as roundtail chub *Gila robusta*, Colorado pikeminnow *Ptychocheilus lucius*, Apache trout *Oncorhynchus apache*, Gila trout *O. gilae*, and Rio Grande cutthroat trout *O. clarki virginalis*, which are predators and feed in open waters but spend much of their life in deep pools or under banks and woody debris. There are "pelagic water" species, such as spikedace *Meda fulgida*, Little Colorado spinedace *Lepidomeda vitatta*, longfin dace *Agosia chrysogaster*, pupfishes *Cyprinodon* spp., and topminnow *Poeciliopsis* spp., that are normally in the open water column. Then there are "demersal species" such as loach minnow *Rhinichthys cobitis*, speckled dace *R. osculus*, and several sucker species *Catostomus* spp. that spend almost their entire existence on the bottom, within and upon stream substrates. A shortcoming of the guild approach is that, as noted above, each fish species has specific habitat requirements (Rinne 1992; Rinne and Stefferud 1996). Monitoring must address these specific, diverse habitat requirements. Further, in areas with naturally low diversity of fishes, such as the Pacific Northwest or Alaska or higher elevation streams in the West, examining diversity of fishes or fish guilds is difficult when only a handful or few species may be present.

The techniques or gear for monitoring fishes in response to riparian and grazing projects are similar to those for other habitat restoration techniques, including electrofishing, visual observation (snorkeling), seining, trapping, and more. The techniques and gear vary in their effectiveness in different stream habitats and stream types. For example, snorkeling has been used widely in the larger, less turbid montane streams of the Pacific Northwest and northern Rockies inhabited by salmonid fishes (Hankins and Reeves 1988). If snorkeling is selected as a sampling approach, snorkel estimates should be calibrated with a more accurate technique, such as electrofishing, to estimate the precision of snorkel estimates and to provide defendable monitoring of restoration efforts (Thompson 2003). Many streams of lower elevations in the West and Southwest have very meager flows (<0.01 m3/s) and depths (<10 cm), which render them less conducive to snorkel sampling. Methods for enumerating fish and their limitations are discussed in more detail in Chapter 8.

Aquatic macroinvertebrates

Macroinvertebrates are highly sensitive indicators of habitat change and may be useful for examining the effects of changes in grazing on stream health and biota (Merritt and Cummins 1996; Karr and Chu 1999). In addition to individual species or genus information, species richness, indexes of biotic integrity (i.e., Karr and Chu 1999), or presence and density of Ephemeroptera, Plecoptera, and Trichoptera (EPT index) may be useful indicators of changes in habitat associated with changes in grazing management. Similar to other biota, one must determine how often and where to sample macroinvertebrates. Increase in fine sediments often is offered as a negative impact of livestock grazing. Assessing or sampling of the fine (<2 mm) component of these same stream substrates is an important response factor to relate to any change in density and diversity of invertebrates. Sampling of more diverse substrates (i.e., pebble, gravel, and cobble) may be desirable to detect a change in diversity of macroinvertebrate communities. Sampling should be timed to get the maximum diversity of invertebrates; this generally is in the spring or fall, depending on the region. Temporally, sampling quarterly should be adequate to define seasonal variability and yet detect changes resulting from restoration. Equipment and protocols for sampling aquatic macroinvertebrates are readily available (Platts et al. 1987; Merritt and Cummins 1996). Invertebrate analyses are time and money consuming, and managers should consider contracting to entities that specialize in this field. Additional information on macroinvertebrate sampling can be found in Chapters 6, 8, and 9, as well as in texts on identification and sampling of macroinvertebrates, such as Rosenburg and Resh (1993) and Merritt and Cummins (1996).

Other Parameters

Other biotic and abiotic parameters also may be of interest in examining biological responses to grazing and fencing activities, depending upon project objectives. These may include algal (primary productivity) and other aquatic plants, sediment, nutrients, pollutants, potentially harmful bacteria, and vertebrates (e.g., amphibians). Algal and bacteria production may respond quickly to changes in light, nutrients, and sediment, and may be useful in assessing in-channel effects of the reduction in grazing. Methods for sampling algae and bacteria are fairly straightforward; two common measures include ash-free dry mass and chlorophyll a (see Steinman and Lamberti 1996). Additional information on methods for sampling algae and primary productivity are provided in Chapter 9.

Pollutants are important when the stream restoration has the object of improving water for domestic consumption and recreation, as well as fish and fisheries. With ever-increasing human use of riparian-stream areas, there is always a degree of organic or bacterial contamination or pollution in rivers and streams throughout the United States. Pollution, in general, comes from sources such as mining, industrial activities, irrigational return waters, municipal waste water systems, and sand and gravel operations within riparian areas.

Efforts in monitoring and estimating nutrient levels, contaminants, and major cations and anions in the waters of streams and rivers should be based on careful considerations. State departments of environmental quality and the EPA must be considered as sources of information on general water-quality parameters. Not all pollution or other parameters will be useful for a project. As with our general thesis in this chapter and book, always first determine the project objectives and hypotheses, and then determine if specific parameters can test the hypotheses or help link a change in grazing management to physical or biological factors of interest.

Case Studies in the Southwest

Below, we present three case studies of monitoring riparian-stream restoration by grazing removal in two montane and one lower-elevation aquatic ecosystem in the southwestern United States. The case studies emphasize pitfalls and confounding factors that may, potentially, strongly affect valid, defendable monitoring of riparian-stream areas that are restored through alteration of grazing strategy. Temporal-spatial problems, fish species considerations, fisheries management in restored streams, and natural impacts, such as flood and drought, can quickly and effectively alter a well-designed study and greatly reduce its value for land managers in their attempts to restore riparian-stream areas. We submit that objectivity is foremost in defining the scope of the resource problem and developing a monitoring plan that meets legal, statistical, and biological requirements. We recognize legal and regulatory mandates upon resource managers to monitor management actions. However, as we illustrate in these case studies, monitoring to meet legal mandates is different from monitoring to discover the underlying relationships, thresholds, and linkages between fish and their habitats. The former assumes that the relationships and linkages are well established and, hopefully, uses a valid methodology; the latter takes into account the spectrum of ecological facts, recognizes that cause and effect linkages may be weakly defined or lacking, and proceeds to develop an understanding of relationships, with validation of methods and results.

Case Study One: Long-Term Monitoring of the Rio de Las Vacas Exclosures

Project overview

The Rio de Las Vacas, located on the Santa Fe National Forest, New Mexico, was fenced to improve riparian habitat during the early to late 1970s. Two stream reaches, approximately 1 km long and 50 m wide, were fenced in 1972 and in 1975 to exclude livestock. These exclosures were separated by private lands from a downstream grazed study area. The objective of the research and monitoring was to determine if livestock exclusion benefited the riparian ecosystem (habitat and fishes). The stream supported three fish species native to upper elevation tributaries to the Rio Grande: Rio Grande sucker *Catostomus plebeius*, Rio Grande chub *Gila pandora*, and Rio Grande cutthroat trout (Rinne 1985, 1988; Calamusso and Rinne 1995). In addition, two nonnative trouts, brown trout *Salmo trutta* and rainbow trout *Oncorhynchus mykiss*, were present in the stream.

Monitoring approach

Six sample units (50-m sections) were studied in both grazed and ungrazed reaches of a stream (Rinne 1985, 1988). To estimate fish populations, 50-m, blocked-netted sections of the stream were sampled, from 1982 to 1985, with electrofishing gear. Initially, the grazed sample units were separated from the ungrazed units by about 4 km of stream on private lands that originally were not available for sampling. Ultimately, permission was received to sample these private holdings in 1985. In addition, the water quality, substrate permeability, and streambank stability and vegetation were measured.

Results

Fish population densities were highly variable within and among reaches and years in 50-m study reaches (21–181 and 33–545 fish/50 m reach in grazed and ungrazed reaches, respectively) and not significantly different between grazed and ungrazed reaches of stream throughout the 4 years of study. After 10 years of streambank protection from grazing, streambank stability was 100% in exclosures, but 64% were unstable in grazed areas, and both percentages of streambank (8% versus 1%) and overhanging vegetation (17.2% versus 0%) were greater in grazed compared to ungrazed reaches of stream. Substrate permeability of streambed generally was lower in ungrazed areas, and intergravel flow was slightly higher in ungrazed areas, but the differences were not significant (Rinne 1988). There was no difference in the basic nutrients NO_3, PO_4, and SO_4 in waters among the grazed and ungrazed reaches of stream. Conclusions from this case study of an upper-elevation montane stream removed from grazing for about a decade were that three major design problems were inherent: (1) absence of pretreatment data on fishes, vegetation, bank stability, or water quality; (2) spatial–temporal design of the study confounded results; and (3) fisheries management actions (e.g., stocking, fishing regulations) induced additional variation into the study.

The lack of pretreatment data, as seen in the Rio de Las Vacas study, has been a common flaw in monitoring physical and biological responses to grazing and other habitat protection and restoration activities. Rinne (1999a) reported that only 1 in 10 studies of grazing effects on riparian habitats and fishes across the West included adequate prestudy information. Often, the necessity and importance of such data are ignored. As was the case with the Rio de Las Vacas study, researchers most often adapt their study design to fit the situation that presents itself, with all its inherent shortcomings.

In the Rio de Las Vacas, grazed and ungrazed study reaches were separated by several kilometers because of the interpositioning of private land that was not originally available for study. Since completion of the study, it has been confirmed that stream-channel type (Rosgen 1996) had changed in that distance. The lower, grazed study reaches were within a C-type meadow reach, with less streamside vegetation and a different substrate composition. Based on intragravel flow rates, substrates characterized by a greater fine component also were present in the lower gradient, C-type channel. In the upstream, grazed, higher gradient, B-type channel, less fines and greater intragravel flow were present. These changes in riparian habitat cannot only affect fish abundance (Rinne and Stefferud 1996; Rinne and Neary 1997; Rinne 2001b) but also fish species distribution linearly in a channel. Higher densities in the ungrazed, lower gradient, C-type meadow reaches of the Rio de Las Vacas could be attributed, in part, to the gradient (Rinne 1988). Without information on channel and habitat preferences of various species, one could obviously, alternatively, and erroneously explain the increase of this species to degradation of habitat caused by livestock grazing.

Another major consideration in conducting studies on the effects of livestock exclosure concerns fish species, their interactions, and their management. Studies need to consider salmonids, as well as nonsalmonid species; their interactions and their habitat requirements and ecology are very different. Further, most studies never consider the widespread, common practice of "put and take" fisheries for salmonid species in the West (Platts and Nelson 1988). In one given year in the Rio de Las Vacas study, more than 9,000 catchable rainbow trout and 800 catchable brown trout were stocked. These introductions increased the density estimates of brown trout the following year. Thus, fisheries management actions, such as stocking or access for fishing, need to be carefully controlled or they make detecting a fish response to grazing activities even more difficult.

Case Study Two: The West Fork Grazing Allotment Riparian Grazing Study

Project overview

Ungulate grazing studies were initiated in 1993 on the West Fork Grazing Allotment of the Apache Sitgreaves National Forest (Medina and Steed 2002). The problem defined by the U.S. Fish and Wildlife Service and the Arizona Game and Fish Department was overgrazing of riparian habitats by cattle, with negative effects on Apache trout habitat and populations. The Forest Service contended that various factors, including cattle grazing, were causing changes in riparian and stream channels (Figure 1; top photograph). Ranchers argued that elk were responsible for limited forage resources. Environmental activists cited studies from other regions, noting cattle as the culprit. The species at issue was the threatened Apache trout, which reportedly occupied three streams on the allotment: Wildcat, Boggy, and Centerfire. The project objectives were to improve habitat for trout and to improve riparian conditions. The principal objectives included determining the relative effects of ungulate grazing on riparian habitats and Apache trout, assessing the utility of GAWS as a monitoring protocol, and developing grazing prescriptions for livestock. Resource managers agreed to resolve the highly contentious issue by soliciting the U.S. Forest Service Rocky Mountain Research Station to monitor riparian conditions, cattle grazing, and Apache trout for 6 years, and they agreed to incorporate newfound knowledge into allotment management plans.

Monitoring approach

The streams were variously fenced to impose three grazing treatments: no grazing (elk exclosures), elk use only (standard 5-strand barb wire), and both elk and cattle grazing. Monitoring parameters included streambank vegetation, water quality, channel geomorphology, ungulate trampling (crossings), assessment of Habitat Condition Indices used in GAWS (USFS 1998), production and utilization of herbaceous vegetation, and fish. Sampling of riparian vegetation, streambanks, channel morphology and fish habitat, and fish abundance occurred within permanent 40-m stream reaches dispersed among the streams and treatments. Sampling stations were established within Boggy and Centerfire Creeks on alder and nonalder sites, whereas, in Wildcat Creek, transects were established based on flow conditions (perennial and intermittent streams), since there were no alder stands. Study progress was reviewed annually, with frequent field sessions to discuss current findings

Results

Changes in riparian conditions varied relative to the hydrogeomorphic condition of the excluded stream reaches. Herbaceous vegetation (i.e., biomass, production) responded favorably across all treatments and controls, including the common use areas (Figures 1 and 2). Pretreatment baseline monitoring occurred in 1993–1994, with grazing reduction treatments occurring in 1995. Sedges generally increased in vigor and abundance in the grazing exclosures (Figure 1; middle photograph) and slightly in the common use areas. General increases in herbaceous biomass production across the study period were noted but were offset by an increase in relative utilization (spring >85%; mean annual >45%) by elk. Trampling of streambanks was most common in stream crossings, though relatively minor changes (<6 cm²/channel profile/year) in channel geomorphology were noted across all streams. In 4 of the 6 years of the study, various sections of the three streams

Figure 1.
Photographs of Boggy Creek, showing effects of cattle use before initiation of study and removal cattle in May 1991 (top photograph); 5 years after cattle exclusion in August 1996 (middle photograph); and same reach after completion of study in May 2000, showing heavy elk damage (bottom photograph).

dried in the lower meadow reaches. Rodents (i.e., voles, shrews, and mice) were largely responsible for sedimentation effects and the collapse of overhanging streambanks (Figure 3). Freezing and thawing also promoted bank instability, and the fine soil material became available for transport during the next flow event. Cattle were thought to be the principal agent, but these studies illustrate that many other interactions also are likely factors affecting riparian condition. Despite habitat condition indices (HCI) meeting a 70% criterion set by managers, Apache trout did not respond positively. The natural die-off of alder stands left the channel

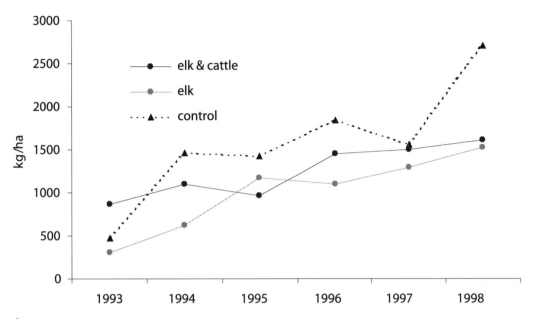

Figure 2.
Increase in mean standing biomass (dry weight) of vegetation at grazing treatments and controls on Boggy Creek between 1993 and 1998. Similar results were found on sites at Centerfire and Wildcat Creek study sites.

exposed to higher solar irradiation and water temperature fluctuations (Figure 4; top photograph). The presence of woody plants is a major constituent of the HCI methodology, resulting in higher index values compared with herbaceous streambanks. Additionally, woody debris from the alders caused debris jams to form, which eroded the streambanks or caused braiding (Figure 4; bottom photograph). Continued observations between 1998 and 2003 indicated similar trends, despite continued improvement in vegetative conditions. However, despite the fact that cattle have not grazed the allotment since 1998, streambank conditions on many reaches are similar to pre-1993 conditions, owing to heavy grazing by elk after cattle removal (Figure 1; bottom photograph).

After 4 years of treatment, fishes did not respond to grazing treatments. Trout density per kilometer successively decreased in two of the streams (Table 3), and various external factors, such as stream intermittency and drying (climatic), limited fish sampling, underlying geology, soils, and hydrology, appear to limit our ability to detect changes in fish production in the study streams. Additional assessments of channel habitats and contrasts with reference streams suggest that these streams are marginal at best for sustaining an Apache trout fish-

Figure 3.
Rodent burrowing (right bank) at an grazing exclusion site, causing increased bank instability.

Figure 4.
Multiple alder debris jams causing braiding of channel (top photograph) and debris jam redirecting streamflow and causing bank erosion on Centerfire Creek, April 1998.

ery (Medina and Steed 2002). Ongoing research suggests that parent geology and resulting substrate composition of streams are far more important factors defining Apache trout habitats and their populations. The West Fork streams are positioned upon basaltic soils, which naturally have high amounts of fines and do not provide optimal salmonid spawning habitat (16–64-mm gravels) compared to glaciated, alluvial soils in the White Mountains that typify salmonid reference streams. Finally, data suggest that the GAWS and HCI are inappropriate methods for monitoring and evaluating grazing effects in the Southwest. Stream reaches in common use by both cattle and elk improved (e.g., streambank stability, vegetation density, and composition) outside the exclosures. We conclude that optimal, high-quality fish habitat is primarily defined by the inherent hydrogeomorphological structure of the stream. The extent of grazing influences seems minor comparatively but, nonetheless, important on sensitive riparian habitats. In short, various other factors, both intrinsic (e.g., nonnative fishes, limited substrate availability) and extrinsic (e.g., drought, floods, vegetation–animal interactions, wildlife), may exert a greater influence on fishery habitats and populations than a grazing strategy and must be a primary consideration when monitoring fish-grazing relationships.

In this study, the combined interactions of animals, vegetation, climate, and natural attributes among study areas partially masked detection of ungulate grazing effects on streambanks. Complex interactions are a common confounding factor in grazing studies but often are ignored. The relative utilization of key riparian species was easily observed throughout most of the year, except during the latter phase of the growing season, when herbaceous species (e.g., sedges, rushes) grew faster than they were consumed. Biomass production and

Table 3.

Mean number of trout per kilometer in three West Fork allotment streams, autumn, 1993–1996. Common use treatment included grazing by elk and cattle, cattle exclusion = excluded cattle but not elk (elk use only), and the elk exclusion = excluded all ungulates. NA = not applicable (not collected).

Treatment	Stream		
Year/type	Centerfire	Boggy	Wildcat
1993			
Common use	240	330	12.5
Cattle exclusion	7	4	0
Elk exclusion	0	0	NA
1994			
Common use	160	180	30
Cattle exclusion	40	4	30
Elk exclusion	20	0	NA
1995			
Common use	38	60	25
Cattle exclusion	129	5	0
Elk exclusion	33	0	NA
1996			
Common use	NA	19	NA
Cattle exclusion	6	4	NA
Elk exclusion	0	0	NA

utilization steadily increased over the study period, probably in response to the initial release from cattle grazing for 3 years and the cattle grazing treatments, which limited cattle use to near the end of the growing season. Species differences were observed, such as with beaked sedge *Carex rostrata*, which produced minimal biomass in response to spring use by elk. Conversely, Nebraska sedge was grazed extensively yearlong by elk and exhibited overcompensation. These responses to grazing at the species level may account for the presence of a grazing effect or may account for a different response at the community level (species–species interactions). Secondly, climate was a major factor controlling the hydrological (i.e., flow, water quality) and biological (i.e., vegetation, fish) variables, which exhibited a chaotic response to drought and floods. Grazing effects are most evident and lasting during drought and are minimized during wet periods. Unusually high precipitation during study years may explain why vegetation growth increased in both grazed and ungrazed sites. The conclusions differed with each additional year of study. Hence, monitoring should encompass a period that adequately spans a period of time to account for climatic influences and carryover effects.

Case Study Three: The Verde River Threatened and Sensitive Fish and Riparian Studies

Project overview

The upper Verde River study area lies below the Mogollon Rim of central Arizona, at an elevation of 1,000 m, and encompasses about 50 km of river principally within the pinyon–juniper woodland type. The contentious question of cattle grazing effects on warmwater fishes was the impetus for this study, similar to the West Fork case, except that litigation over livestock grazing of riparian areas on a regional basis invoked a greater need for information of potential grazing effects on fish. Many biologists indicated that riverine conditions were impaired because of livestock grazing on the river and the watershed. A principal theory was that "the river was sediment enriched." In response to endangered fishes and critical habitat designations, including the riparian corridor of the study area, and to improve the riparian area, all livestock on public lands within the watershed were removed in 1998. Strategic fencing and rough terrain were used to exclude livestock, which had grazed the river bottom with varying strategies for over a century. Trespassing animals were monitored for and removed upon discovery. Exclusion of livestock grazing continues to the present, but elk have moved in and replaced cattle. The objectives of the monitoring study were multifold, including inventory of the fish populations, assessment of fish and riparian habitats, inventory and classification of vegetation and channel types, assessment of sediment influences, and water quality.

Monitoring approach

Riparian studies were initiated in 1996 and included monitoring at different scales. A complete inventory of upper Verde River channel conditions ensued to classify the channel types (Rosgen 1996; Neary et al. 2001). Permanent riparian vegetation transects (n = 48) were established across various habitat types and were superimposed on channel sample sites. Streambanks were intensively sampled by using a modified green line approach developed specifically for monitoring ungulate–streambank influences (Medina and Steed 2002). Vegetation and channel measurements were taken each year to provide an estimate of type and rate of change. Water-quality studies were initiated in 2000 to assess potential sedimentation and turbidity problems. Automated water samplers were used to collect water samples for sediment analyses. Pebble count transects (Bevenger and King 1995) were established in all major tributaries to detect changes in substrate composition and to identify potential sources of fine sediments. In 2001, macroinvertebrate sampling was initiated to provide an additional measure of aquatic habitat quality. Samples were taken across seasons and habitat types. To address questions of channel stability, annual aerial flights of the riverine corridor were used to detect changes in channel position across the entire 50-km reach. In 2000, a long-term river change detection study was initiated to quantify changes in channel position over the past 70+ years for which aerial imagery was available.

Fisheries studies were initiated in 1994 after elevated levels of flooding in the winter of 1992–1993 (Stefferud and Rinne 1995). Additional elevated flow events occurred in spring 1995; however, the upper 60 km of river has sustained low flow drought conditions since that time. Seven permanent sites 300–500 m long were established in the upper Verde and were sampled, with seines and electrofishing gear, annually for fishes. The relative proportions of native versus nonnative fish species were used as an indicator of fish responses to flooding. Six native species were common in spring 1994 (Stefferud and Rinne 1995; Rinne and Stefferud 1997; Table 4). In addition, several nonnative fishes were present but not abundant.

Results

The series of diagnostic studies did not identify any physical, biological, or chemical parameter to suggest an impairment of water quality or riparian functions. All parameters (i.e., dissolved oxygen, temperature, conductivity, pH, total suspended sediments) measured for water quality were within established standards for warmwater fisheries (Medina 2001). Vegetation cover, density, and composition increased across grazed and ungrazed sites (Medina 2001; Figure 5). Increased plant cover and species diversity were attributed to post-

Table 4.
Changes in fish assemblages in the upper Verde River, 1994–2002.

Species	1994	1995	1996	1997	1998	1999	2000	2001	2002	2003
Longfin dace	1319	12	282	21	13	2	1	2	1	1
Spikedace	428	72	141	0	0	0	0	0	0	0
Speckled dace	172	25	68	1	12	2	7	0	0	0
Desert sucker *Catostomus clarki*	2644	328	471	231	126	167	137	376	148	128
Sonora sucker *C. insignis*	1810	322	654	240	128	118	197	163	90	75
Roundtail chub	776	341	259	50	64	25	20	43	20	4
Smallmouth bass	14	10	32	35	66	104	48	163	211	193
Red shiner	1473	97	275	2238	1047	545	1594	1608	276	632
Green sunfish	4	29	6	8	21	49	95	192	53	139

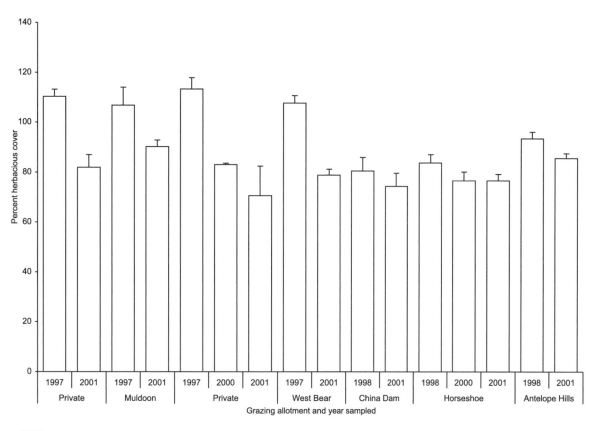

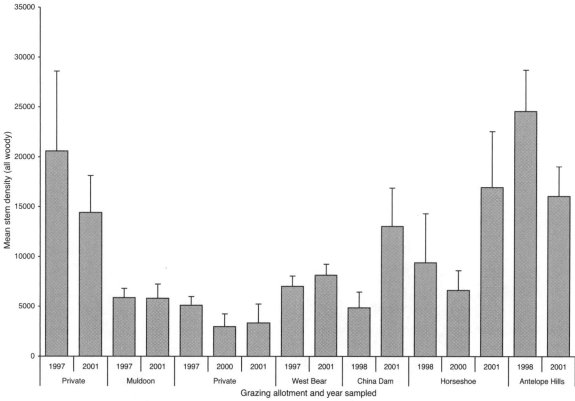

Figure 5.

Comparisons of mean percent cover of total herbaceous vegetation and mean stem density or woody vegetation at six allotments on the Verde River (51 transects) repeatedly sampled between 1997 and 2001. Grazed lands included only private lands, and ungrazed lands included all other U.S. Forest Service allotments (Muldoon, West Bear, China Dam, Horseshoe, and Antelope Hills). Sites are in order from upstream to downstream (left to right). Error bars represent standard error.

flood disturbance dynamics that masked effects of livestock removal. Invasive and exotic species also increased in both grazed and ungrazed reaches. The distribution of channel types, substrates, and associated geomorphological attributes were consistent with reference reaches for alluvial desert rivers (Medina et al. 1997; Neary et al. 2001). A preliminary analysis of aerial imagery indicates that the main channel has remained relatively static since 1947. However, since 1979, the channel has incised 1–5 m and has become dominated by woody vegetation (Figure 6). Channel degradation was attributed to a sediment imbalance caused by dams upstream, a common phenomenon observed elsewhere (Collier et al. 2000). Encroachment of woody vegetation was attributed to a 1993 historic flood and ongoing channel degradation associated with sediment impoundment by the dams. Reaches where sedges and bulrushes prevailed on grazed sites remained relatively stable in channel form and vegetation communities.

Immediately after the floods (1994), native fishes dominated the fish community (Table 4). Native species comprised over 80% of the total fishes sampled each spring from 1994 to 1996. In 1997, the relative composition of native fishes dropped dramatically to 19% and has remained below 30% since that time. The three small-sized, short-lived species—longfin dace, speckled dace, and spikedace—have declined to zero or near zero. The last species is listed as threatened under the U.S. Endangered Species Act. The longfin dace was very abundant in 1994, averaging almost 200 individuals per sample section. In the past 4 years of sampling, only six of this threatened species have been collected during sampling at all seven established sample sites. Although the three longer-lived, larger-sized species have survived, even these species may become extirpated. Presently, primarily adults of each species have been captured and are represented in samples. These remaining native species have been reduced 20- to 30-fold in total numbers from spring samples of 1994. By contrast, introduced red shiner *Cyprinella lutrensis*, green sunfish *Lepomis cyanellus*, and smallmouth bass *Micropterus dolomieu* have steadily increased. The increase in nonnative species abundance has been attributed to a general increase in nearstream and instream aquatic herbaceous vegetation (Medina and Rinne 1999). Bass and sunfish are cover inhabitants in aquatic systems (Pflieger 1975) and have responded very favorably to the changes in habitat conditions. By contrast, the native species are either absent from samples or are rapidly being extirpated from the Verde River system.

This study suggests that improved conditions in vegetative and channel conditions have not benefited native fishes (Rinne 1999a, 2003a, 2003b). On the other hand, nonnatives species have benefited from the changes. The results of a recently initiated predator removal study (i.e., nonnative species from reaches of a stream; Rinne 2001a) suggest that direct predation by nonnative species may be the primary cause for the dramatic reduction of native fishes. As with both the Rio Las Vacas and West Fork studies, fish species interactions and

Figure 6.
Verde River Bear Siding site before (left) and in 2002, 4 years after removal of grazing (right slide), demonstrating recovery of vegetation. It was not possible to take right photograph from exactly the same location because vegetation recovery and channel incision created a deep pool where earlier photograph had been taken.

fishery management are major contributors to the outcome of monitoring studies of grazing exclusion. Habitat change with grazing removal obviously has an influence on fishes (Rinne and Neary 1997); however, it is an unintended response. That is, the increase in habitat complexity had unintended positive benefits for nonnative fish species that prey upon native fishes. The absence of recent (post-1993) flood events also has benefited the nonnative species and harmed the native species (Rinne and Stefferud 1997).

Synthesis of Case Studies: Confounding Factors in Monitoring Effects Grazing on Fishes

These three case studies point out some inherent problems that must be addressed in the design and monitoring of effectiveness of grazing and riparian restoration projects on fishes. Several factors apparent in these case studies can confound interpretation of data, including (1) species interactions, (2) management practices, (3) spatial–temporal factors (replication and spacing of treatments and controls), (4) geology and geomorphology, and (5) climate and hydrology. We suggest these same factors are applicable to all studies evaluating grazing and riparian restoration. Some additions, explanations, and interpretations of these factors are appropriate and offered here.

Species interactions

First, native and exotic species and their interactions have to be taken into consideration for study design, monitoring, and interpretation of the effects of grazing management (Rinne 2002), for example, in the Verde River, the positive influence of grazing removal on nonnative compared to the negative influence on native fish species. One has to go a step further and examine the interactive influence of predation by the nonnative species, such as red shiner, smallmouth bass, and green sunfish. Based on our data (Rinne 1995, 2001a, 2003a, 2003b; Rinne and Alexander 1995) and that of others (Minckley 1983; Minckley and Deacon 1991), predation is one of the primary negative impacts of nonnative species on the native species. The change in cover habitat in the upper Verde has strongly and positively influenced the nonnative predators, which, in turn, have negatively impacted all native species, perhaps to the point of extirpation of smaller-sized, short-lived species (i.e., longfin dace, speckled dace, and spikedace, Rinne 1999b). Similarly, on the Rio de Las Vacas, regular stocking of rainbow trout and brown trout has negatively impacted native Rio Grande cutthroat and two native cyprinids through hybridization and predation, respectively. Changes in native and nonnative vegetation also influenced the vegetation and bank stability, both of which may influence instream factors such as fishes. These examples emphasize the need to examine species interactions for both vegetation and aquatic biota when conducting studies on riparian restoration.

Management practices

A second consideration involves interactions of both historic and contemporary management activities. Grazing management in the form of livestock removal from the Verde River corridor was assumed beneficial for the riparian habitat and native fish species. Fisheries management in the form of stocking nonnative species (Rinne et al. 1998; Rinne, in press) was initiated 50 years ago, and grazing, another half century earlier. So, while grazing and fish stocking occurred together for at least a half century, native fish species persisted. One possible explanation for their persistence is the repression of vegetative growth in this period, which benefited the native species. In the same line of reasoning, native species in this region appear to be adapted to natural disturbances such as floods (Rinne 2003a, 2003b) and also can withstand a certain level of anthropogenic disturbances (e.g., grazing). More recently, catch limits have been removed for nonnative sport species in the Verde River by the Arizona Game and Fish Department. However, the U.S. Forest Service, as the manager of the river habitat, has closed road access to formerly easily accessed areas of the river, making removal of nonnative predators by fishermen unlikely. Similarly, the removal of cattle grazing in the case studies often was followed by an increase in grazing of native ungulates (elk). Here again, we see one management activity counteract another. All three case studies demonstrate the importance of examining the influence and the interactions of current and past management practices on multiyear studies.

Spatial and temporal factors

Spatially fencing is problematic, because, by design, it is linear and it fragments the riparian habitat. Both the Rio de Las Vacas and West Fork Case studies had this inherent design flaw. The only alternative to such an intrastream approach is to design interstream comparison of data. However, variation (as suggested above for fishes) is present in all physical and biological factors of respective streams, rendering such comparisons suspect or invalid. Change in stream type (see habitat influences below) was present on both the Rio de Las Vacas and the West Fork and private lands in the former affected the initial study design. These results indicate that one should control for additional factors, including stream type, geology, and, especially, habitat and channel type, when selecting study sites. To reemphasize, perhaps, the most important spatial consideration to remember is that the stream is a continuum (Vannote et al. 1980). Sectioning by fences to exclude grazing and to improve riparian-stream habitat, although it segregates the riparian area, will induce recovery within the treated areas but probably will not affect upstream and downstream processes that operate on large scales.

Temporal influences often are intricately linked to these spatial influences. Large interannual variation (>50%) in wild fish populations is the norm rather than the exception. This was noted over several years on all three case study areas and has been documented elsewhere (Platts and McHenry 1988; Platts and Nelson 1988). For example, after year one on the Rio de Las Vacas, it appeared that the conventional knowledge of that time (i.e., grazing removal enhanced trout populations) was corroborated. However, additional years of data suggest no effect of grazing removal on fishes. As with instream restoration and other long-term monitoring, it is necessary to adequately quantify interannual variation in fish populations before drawing conclusions on the effectiveness of riparian restoration projects on fish or habitat.

Geology and geomorphology

Understanding the underlying geology and changes in geomorphology and habitat resulting from grazing are critical to valid interpretation of riparian restoration. For example, the longitudinal change in channel type along the stream continuum is a basic tenet of stream morphology: streams change from one channel type to another in montane areas as they flow through higher gradient reaches and meadow reaches. Both the Rio de Las Vacas and the West Fork study designs were influenced by stream type. Although the Verde is primarily composed of C-type channels, Rinne and Neary (1997) demonstrated that with a change in channel type, a change in fish assemblage occurred. The respective biology of native fish species in the Verde and their habitat preferences are very specific (Rinne and Stefferud 1996). Accordingly, even slight changes in habitat, whether natural or by artificial, anthropogenic activities, such as grazing (or its removal), can dramatically affect fish distribution and abundance. Substrate composition is largely dictated by parent geology and is very strongly and directly influenced by stream gradient, which dictates water velocity. Velocity and substrate are strong influences of native fish presence and abundance (Heede and Rinne 1990; Rinne 1992, 2001b, 2001c; Rinne and Deason 2000). This relationship between channel type, velocity, and substrate, and fish distribution has been well documented in other areas (e.g., Montgomery et al. 1999; Weigel and Sorensen 2001). Thus, geology, geomorphology, and channel type are important factors to control for when designing a monitoring program.

Climate and hydrology

Finally, the results of these studies must be interpreted in the context of natural hydrologic patterns and climate (Platts 1991; Rinne 2003a, 2003b). Hydrology has been a major controlling factor on both the West Fork and the Verde case studies. In the former, drought in most of the years of the study affected fish populations more than did grazing treatment. In the Southwest (Rinne, in press) and throughout many areas of the West (Platts et al. 1985), cycles of flood and drought are the norm. The Verde study, for example, was initiated during a period of high flow (1993–1995); however, most monitoring (1996–2002) was under drought conditions. Floods in the Verde (Rinne and Stefferud 1997) and elsewhere in the Southwest (Minckley and Meffe 1987) have been demonstrated to have a marked positive influence on native fishes. By contrast, drought or low and more stabilized flows, which occur below dams in the West, often favor nonnative fishes. Indeed, a portion of the changes in fish community structure in the Verde can be attributed to changes in hydrology. Similarly, changes in vegetation growth (or lack thereof) between grazed and ungrazed sites appear to be related to changes in climate (rainfall). Differences between vegetation attributes in treatment and controls are most pronounced during drought years but are absent during wet years. Thus, it is important to consider changes in hydrology and climate when interpreting the results of grazing studies. This emphasizes the need for long-term monitoring to completely understand the effects of changes in grazing management on riparian recovery.

Summary

As with most restoration actions, determining the objectives and hypotheses of both the grazing and fencing project and the monitoring program are critical steps. The monitoring design is equally important, and many grazing studies have been limited by not considering the location of control and treatments or by not adequately replicating them in space or time. Many parameters typically monitored for grazing project, such as temperature, bank stability, and fishes, while important, can be confounded by complex interactions of many factors, including species of fishes and other biota, fishery management practices (e.g., stocking, fishing pressure and regulations, and exotics), spatial and temporal scale and replication, channel and habitat type, hydrology and climate, and others. Vegetation and bank stability typically respond directly to changes in grazing intensity, but they also may be confounded by factors such as hydrology, climate, and grazing by wild ungulates. Interpreting the results of riparian restoration should be done cautiously, particularly for instream variables (e.g., fish, sediment, temperature), which may respond secondarily to improvement in vegetation after grazing (a direct response). That is not to say that monitoring the response of instream parameters is not valuable; but, as we have demonstrated in the case studies, many other factors (e.g., fish species and management, habitat influence, hydrology) can confound interpretation of results in the absence of adequate spatial, temporal replication, and other monitoring design considerations. One must not jump to quick conclusions without considering at least the influencing and controlling factors discussed in this chapter. Only by addressing the issue, resource, or questions to be answered and by carefully arriving at conclusions and coming up with, and continually refining, new models, will riparian-stream areas be properly understood, managed, and restored.

References

Acorn, R. C. 1997. Using electric fences to protect stored hay from elk and deer. Alberta Agriculture, Food, and Rural Development Bulletin, Agdex 684–17. Alberta Queen's Printer, Edmonton, Alberta.

Armour, C. L., D. A. Duff, and W. Elmore. 1991. The effects of livestock grazing on riparian and stream ecosystems. Fisheries 16(1):7–11.

Bain, M. B., and N. J. Stevenson. 1999. Aquatic habitat assessment: common methods. American Fisheries Society, Bethesda, Maryland.

Barbour, M. T., and J. B. Stribling. 1991. Use of habitat assessment in evaluating the biological integrity of stream communities. Pages 25–39 in Environmental Protection Agency, editor. Biological criteria: research and regulation, 1991. U.S. Environmental Protection Agency, Office of Water, EPA-440/5-91-005, Washington, D.C.

Barbour, M. T., and J. B. Stribling. 1994. A technique for assessing stream habitat structure. Pages 156–178 in National Association of Conservation Districts, editor. Proceedings of the conference on riparian ecosystems of the humid U.S.: management, functions, and values. National Association of Conservation Districts, Washington, D.C.

Barbour, M., J. Gerritsen, B. D. Snyder, and J. B. Stribling. 1999. Rapid bioassessment protocols for use in streams and wadeable rivers: periphyton, benthic macroinvertebrates, and fish. 2nd edition. U.S. Environmental Protection Agency, Office of Water, EPA-841-B-99-002, Washington, D.C.

Bauer, S. B., and T. Burton. 1993. Monitoring protocols to evaluate water quality effects of grazing management on western rangeland streams. U.S. Environmental Protection Agency, Washington, D.C.

Bekaert. 2002. Tightlock™ game fence: high tensile fencing. Bekaert Corporation, Akron, Ohio.

Belsky, A. J., A. Matzke, and S. Uselman. 1999. Survey of livestock influences on stream and riparian ecosystems in the western United States. Journal of Soil and Water Conservation 54(1):419–431.

Betscha, R. L. 1997. Riparian shade and stream temperatures: an alternative view. Rangelands 19(2):25–28.

Bevenger, G. S., and R. M. King. 1995. A pebble count procedure for assessing watershed cumulative effects. U.S. Forest Service, GTR-RM-RP-319, Fort Collins, Colorado.

Bisson, P. A., G. H. Reeves, R. E. Bilby, and R. J. Naiman. 1997. Watershed management and Pacific salmon: desired future conditions. Pages 447–474 in D. J. Stouder, P. A. Bisson, and R. J. Naiman. Pacific salmon and their ecosystems. Chapman and Hall, New York.

BLM (Bureau of Land Management). 1985. Fencing. U.S. Bureau of Land Management Handbook H-1741-1, Denver.

BLM (Bureau of Land Management). 1999a. Utilization studies and residual measurements: interagency technical reference. Bureau of Land Management Technical Reference 1734-3, Denver.

BLM (Bureau of Land Management). 1999b. Sampling vegetation attributes: interagency technical reference. Bureau of Land Management Technical Reference 1734-4, Denver.

Bunte, K., and S. R. Abt. 2001. Sampling surface and subsurface particle-size distributions in wadeble gravel-and cobble-bed streams for analyses in sediment transport, hydraulics, and streambed monitoring. U.S. Forest Service, Rocky Mountain Research Station, General Technical Report RMRS-GTR-74, Fort Collins, Colorado.

Burton, T., and E. R. Cowley. 2002. Monitoring streambank stability. Bureau of Land Management, Idaho State Office Report, Boise, Idaho.

Calamusso, B., and J. N. Rinne. 1995. Distribution of Rio Grande cutthroat trout Oncorhynchus clarki virginalis and its co-occurrence with Rio Grande sucker Catostomus plebeius, and Rio Grande chub, Gila pandora, on the Carson and Santa Fe National Forests. Pages

157–167 *in* D. W. Shaw, and D. M. Finch, editors. Proceedings of the symposium of desired future conditions for southwestern riparian ecosystems: bringing interests and concerns together. U.S. Forest Service General Technical Report RM-272, Fort Collins, Colorado.

Casagli, N., M. Rinaldi, A. Gargini, and A. Curini. 1999. Pore water pressure and streambank stability: results from a monitoring site on the Sieve River, Italy. Earth Surface Processes and Landforms 24:1095–1114.

Chapman, D. W. 1988. Critical review of variables used to define effects of fines in redds of large salmonids. Transactions of the American Fisheries Society 117:1–21.

Clary, W. P. 1999. Stream channel and vegetation responses to late spring cattle grazing. Journal Range Management 52(3):218–227.

Clary, W. P., and W. C. Leininger. 2000. Stubble height as a tool for management of riparian areas. Journal of Range Management 53:562–573.

Clesceri, L. S., A. E. Greenburg, and A. D. Eaton, editors. 1999. Standard methods for the examination of water and wastewater. 20th edition. American Public Health Association, American Water Works Association, and Water Environment Federation, Washington, D.C.

Collier, M., R. H. Webb, and J. C. Schnidt. 2000. Dams and rivers: a primer on the downstream effects of dams. U.S. Geological Survey Circular 1126, Reston, Virginia.

Contor, C. R. and W. S. Platts. 1991. Assessment of COWFISH for predicting trout populations in grazed watersheds of the intermountain west. U.S. Forest Service, Intermountain Research Station General Technical Report INT-278, Ogden, Utah.

Craven, S. R., and S. E. Hygnstrom. 1996. Deer: damage prevention and control methods. Pages D25–D40 *in* S. E. Hygnstrom, R. M. Trimm, and G. E. Larson, editors. Prevention and control of wildlife damage. Diane Publishing Company, Collingdale, Pennsylvania.

De Calesta, D. S., and G. W. Witmer. 1996. Elk: damage prevention and control methods. Pages D-41-D50 *in* S. E. Hygnstrom, R. M. Trimm, and G. E. Larson, editors. Prevention and control of wildlife damage. Diane Publishing Company, Collingdale, Pennsylvania.

Diaz, M. E., Gonzalez, R. Munoz-Pulido, and M. A. Naveso. 1996. Habitat selection patterns of common cranes *Grus grus* wintering in holm oak *Quercus ilex dehesas* of central Spain: Effects of human management. Biological Conservation 75(2):119–123.

Downes, B. J., L. A. Barmuta, P. G. Fairweather, D. P. Faith, M. J. Keough, P. S. Lake, B. D. Mapstone, and G. P. Quinn. 2002. Monitoring ecological impacts: concepts and practice in flowing waters. Cambridge University Press, Cambridge, UK.

Dunne, T., and L. Leopold. 1978. Water in environmental planning. Freeman, New York.

Elmore, W., and R. L. Beschta. 1987. Riparian areas: Perceptions in management. Rangelands 9:260–265.

Elzinga, C. L., D. W. Salzer, and J. W. Willoughby. 1998. Measuring and monitoring plant populations. U.S. Bureau of Land Management Technical Reference 1730-1, Denver.

Everest, F. H., R. L. Betscha, J. C. Scrivener, K. V. Koski, J. R. Sedell, and C. J. Cederholm. 1987. Fire sediment and salmonid fish production—a paradox. Pages 98–142 *in* E. Salo and T. Cundy, editors. Streamside management and forestry and fishery interactions. University of Washington, College of Forest Resources, Contribution 57, Seattle.

FISRWG (Federal Interagency Stream Restoration Working Group). 1998. Stream corridor restoration: principles, processes, and practices. Federal Interagency Stream Restoration Working Group, GPO Item No. 0120-A; SuDocs No. A 57.6/2:EN 3/PT. 653, Washington, D.C.

Fleischner, T. L. 1994. Ecological costs of livestock grazing in western North America. Conservation Biology 8:629–644.

Fuller, P. L., L. G. Nico, and J. D. Williams, editors. 1999. Nonindigenous fishes introduced into inland waters of the United States. American Fisheries Society, Bethesda, Maryland.

Gangmark, A. A., and R. G. Bakkala. 1958. Plastic standpipe for sampling streambed environment of salmon spawning. U.S. Fish and Wildlife Service, Special Scientific Report on Fisheries 1, Washington, D.C.

Gordon, N. D., T. A. McMahon, and B. L. Finlayson. 1992. Stream hydrology: an introduction for ecologists. Wiley, Chichester, England.

Grost, R. T., W. A. Hubert, and T. A. Wesche. 1991. Field comparison of three devices used to sample substrate in small streams. North American Journal of Fisheries Management 11:347–351.

Hankin, D. G., and G. H. Reeves. 1998. Estimating total fish abundance and total habitat area in small streams based on visual estimation methods. Canadian Journal of Fisheries and Aquatic Sciences 45:834–844.

Harrelson, C. C., Rawlins, C. L., and J. P. Potyondy. 1994. Stream channel reference sites: an illustrated guide to field technique. U.S. Forest Service, Rocky Mountain Forest and Range Experiment Station General Technical Report RM-245, Fort Collins, Colorado.

Heede, B. H., and J. N. Rinne. 1990. Hydrodynamics and fluvial morphologic processes: implications for fisheries management and research. North American Journal of Fisheries Management 10:249–268.

Hendrickson, D. L., and W. L. Minckley. 1984. Cienegas—vanishing climax communities of the American Southwest. Desert Plants 6:131–175.

Huedepohl, C. 2000. The deer and elk procedures manual. Alberta Agriculture, Food, and Rural Development. Alberta Queen's Printer, Edmonton, Alberta.

Humphrey, J. W., and G. S. Patterson. 2000. Effects of late summer cattle grazing on the diversity of riparian pasture vegetation in an upland conifer forest. Journal of Applied Ecology 37:986–996.

Hurlbert, S. H. 1984. Pseudoreplication and the design of ecological field experiments. Ecological Monographs 54:187–211.

Hygnstrom, S. E., R. M. Trimm, and G. E. Larson. 1996. Prevention and control of wildlife damage. Diane Publishing Company, Collingdale, Pennsylvania.

Jansen, A., and A. I. Robertson. 2001. Relationships between livestock management and the ecological condition of riparian habitats along an Australian river floodplain. Journal of Applied Ecology 38:63–75.

Johnson, C. F., P. Jones, and S. Spencer. 1998. A guide to classifying selected fish habitat parameters in lotic systems of west central Alberta. Alberta Conservation Association, Foothills Model Forest, Hinton, Alberta.

Karr, J. R., and E. W. Chu. 1999. Restoring life in running waters: better biological monitoring. Island Press, Washington, D.C.

Kauffman, J. B., and W. C. Krueger. 1984. Livestock impacts on riparian ecosystems and streamside management implications—a review. Journal of Range Management 37(5):430–438.

Keller, E. A., and Swanson, F. J. 1979. Effects of large organic debris on channel form and fluvial processes. Earth Surface Processes 4:361–380.

Kent, M., and P. Coker. 1994. Vegetation description and analysis: a practical approach. Wiley, Chichester, England.

Kie, J. G., V. C. Bleich, A. L. Medina, J. D. Yoakum, and J. W. Thomas. 1994. Managing rangelands for wildlife. Pages 663–688 in T. A. Bookout, editor. Research and management techniques for wildlife and habitats. The Wildlife Society, Bethesda, Maryland.

Knopf, F. L. 1988. Riparian wildlife habitats: more, worth less, and under invasion. Pages 20–22 in K. M. Mutz, D. J. Cooper, M. L. Scott, and L. K. Miller, editors. Restoration, creation and management of wetland and riparian ecosystems in the American West. PIC Technologies, Denver.

Kondolf, G. M. 1993. Lag in stream channel adjustment to livestock exclosure, White Mountains, California. Restoration Ecology 1:226–230.

Krueger, W. C. 1998. Integrating utilization measurements into monitoring programs. Pages 71–72 in Oregon State University, Agriculture Experiment Station, editor. Stubble heights and utilization measurements: uses and misuses. Oregon State University, Station Bulletin 682, Corvallis.

Larson, L. L., and S. L. Larson. 1996. Riparian shade and stream temperature: a perspective. Rangelands 18(4):149–152.

Likens, G. E. 1984. Beyond the shoreline: a watershed-ecosystem approach. Internationale Vereinigung fur theoretische und angewandte Limnologie Verhandlungen 22:1–22.

Lloyd, J. 1985. COWFISH: habitat capability model. U.S. Forest Service, Northern Regional Office, Missoula, Montana.

Mayer, R. 1999. Estimated costs for livestock fencing. Iowa State University, Extension Circular FM 1855, Ames, Iowa.

McNeil, W. F., and W. H. Ahnell. 1964. Success of pink salmon spawning relative to size of spawning bed materials. U.S. Fish and Wildlife Service Special Scientific Report-Fisheries No. 469, Washington, D.C.

Meals, D. W., and R. B. Hopkins. 2003. Phosphorus reductions following riparian restoration in two agricultural watersheds in Vermont, USA. Water Science and Technology 45(9):51–60.

Medina A. L. 1995. Native aquatic plants and ecological condition of southwestern wetlands and riparian areas. Pages 329–335 in D. W. Shaw, D. M. Finch, editors. Proceedings of the symposium of desired future conditions for southwestern riparian ecosystems: bringing interests and concerns together. U.S. Forest Service General Technical Report RM-272, Fort Collins, Colorado.

Medina, A. L., and J. N. Rinne. 1999. Ungulate/fishery interactions in southwestern riparian ecosystems: pretensions and realities. Proceedings of the North American Wildlife and Natural Resources Conference 62:307–322.

Medina, A. L. 2001. A preliminary view of water quality conditions of the upper Verde River. Pages 25–33 in C. Decarlo, C. Schlinger, and A. Springer, editors. Verde Watershed Symposium: state of the watershed in 2001. Cliff Castle Lodge and Conference Center, Camp Verde, AZ. May 17–19, 2001. Northern Arizona University, Flagstaff.

Medina, A. L., and J. E. Steed. 2002. West Fork Allotment riparian monitoring study: 1993–1999. U.S. Forest Service, Rocky Mountain Research Station Final Project Report, Volume I, Flagstaff, Arizona.

Medina, A. L., M. B. Baker, Jr., and J. R. Turner. 1997. Channel types and geomorphology of the upper Verde River. Journal of the American Water Resources Association 33(4):465–473.

Merritt, R. W., and K. W. Cummins. 1996. An introduction to the aquatic insects of North America. 3rd edition. Kendall and Hunt Publishing Company, Dubuque, Iowa.

Minckley, W. L. 1983. Status of razorback sucker, Xyrauchen texanus, in the lower Colorado River basin The Southwestern Naturalist 28:165–187.

Minckley, W. L., and G. K. Meffe. 1987. Differential selection by flooding in stream fish communities of the arid American Southwest. Pages 93–104 in W. J. Matthews and D. C. Heins, editors. Community and evolutionary ecology of North American stream fishes. University of Oklahoma Press, Norman.

Minckley, W. L., and J. E. Deacon. 1991. Battle against extinction: native fish management in the American West. University of Arizona Press, Tucson.

Montgomery, D. R., and J. M. Buffington. 1997. Channel-reach morphology in mountain drainage basins. Geological Society America Bulletin 109(5):596–611.

Montgomery, D. R., E. M. Beamer, G. R. Pess, and T. P. Quinn. 1999. Channel type and salmonid spawning distribution and abundance. Canadian Journal of Fisheries and Aquatic Sciences 56:377–387.

Moulton, S. R. II, J. G. Kennen, R. M. Goldstein, and J. A. Hambrook. 2002. Revised protocols for sampling algal, invertebrate and fish communities as part of the National Water-Quality Assessment Program. U.S. Department of Interior, U.S. Geological Service, Open File Report 02-150, Reston, Virginia.

Murphy, B. R., and D. W. Willis. 1996. Fisheries techniques, 2nd edition. American Fisheries Society, Bethesda, Maryland.

Myers, L. H. 1989. Grazing and riparian management in southwestern Montana. Pages 117–120 in R. E. Gresswell, B. A. Barton, and J. Kershner, editors. Practical approaches to riparian resource management: an education workshop. U.S. Bureau of Land Management, Billings, Montana.

Myers, T. J., and S. Swanson. 1995. Impact of deferred rotation grazing on stream characteristics in central Nevada: a case study. North American Journal of Fisheries Management 15:428–439.

NRCS (Natural Resources Conservation Service) 1996. National handbook of water quality monitoring: Part 600. U.S. Department of Agriculture, Natural Resources Conservation Service, National Water and Climate Center, Portland, Oregon.

NRCS (Natural Resources Conservation Service). 1999. A procedure to estimate the response of aquatic systems to changes in phosphorus and nitrogen inputs. U.S. Department of Agriculture, Natural Resources Conservation Service, Washington, D.C.

Neary, D. G., A. L. Medina, and M. B. Baker, Jr. 2001. Geomorphic conditions of the riparian zone, Upper Verde River. Pages 45–52 in C. Decarlo, C. Schlinger, and A. Springer, editors. Proceedings, Verde Watershed Symposium: state of the watershed in 2001. Cliff Castle Lodge and Conference Center, Camp Verde, AZ. May 17–19, 2001. Northern Arizona University, Flagstaff.

Neary, D. G., and J. N. Rinne. 1997. Baseflow trends in the upper Verde River relative to Fish Habitat Requirements. Hydrology and Water Resources in Arizona and the Southwest 27:57–63.

Neary, D. G., and J. N. Rinne. 2001. Baseflow trends in the Verde River revisited. Hydrology and Water Resources of the Southwest 31:37–44.

Newton, B., C. Pringle, and R. Bjorkland. 1998. Stream visual assessment protocol. U.S. Natural Resources Conservation Service, National Water and Climate Center, Technical Note 991, Washington, D.C.

O'Grady, M. 2002. Proceedings of the 13th international salmonid habitat enhancement workshop. Central Fisheries Board, Dublin.

Pflieger, W. L. 1975. The Fishes of Missouri. Missouri Department of Conservation, Columbia.

Pfankuch, D. J. 1975. Stream reach inventory and channel stability evaluation. U.S. Forest Service, Northern Region, Missoula, Montana.

Plafkin, J. L., M. T. Barbour, K. D. Porter, S. K. Gross and R. M. Hughes. 1989. Rapid bioassessment protocols for use in streams and rivers: benthic macroinvertebrates and fish. U.S. Environmental Protection Agency, EPA/444/4-89-001, Washington, D.C.

Platts, W. S. 1990. Managing fisheries and wildlife on rangelands grazed by livestock: a guidance and reference document for biologists. Nevada Department of Wildlife, Reno.

Platts, W. S. 1991. Livestock grazing. Pages 389–423 in W. R. Meehan, editor. Influences of forest and rangeland management on salmonid fishes and their habitats. American Fisheries Society, Special Publication 19, Bethesda, Maryland.

Platts, W. S., C. Armor, B. D. Booth, M. Bryant, J. L. Bufford, P. Cuplin, S. Jensen, G. W. Leinkaemper, G. W. Minshall, S. B. Monsen, R. L. Nelson, J. R. Sedell, and J. S. Tuhy. 1987. Methods for evaluating riparian habitats with applications to management. U.S. Forest Service, Intermountain Forest and Range Experiment Station, General Technical Report INT-221, Ogden, Utah.

Platts, W. S., K. A. Gebhardt, and W. L. Jackson. 1985. The effects of large storm events on basin-range riparian stream habitats. Pages 30–34 in R. R. Johnson, C. D. Ziebel, D. R. Patton, P. F. Ffolliott, and R. H. Hamre, editors. Proceedings of the first North American riparian conference. Riparian ecosystems and their management: reconciling and conflicting uses. U.S. Forest Service General Technical Report RM-120, Fort Collins, Colorado.

Platts, W. S., and M. L. McHenry. 1988. Density and biomass of trout and char in western streams. U. S. Forest Service, Intermountain Research Station, GTR-INT-241, Ogden, Utah.

Platts, W. S., W. F. Megahan, and G. W. Minshall. 1983. Methods for evaluating stream riparian, and aquatic conditions. U.S. Forest Service, Intermountain Forest and Range Experiment Station General Technical Report INT-138, Ogden, Utah.

Platts, W. S., and R. L. Nelson. 1988. Fluctuations in trout populations and their implications for land-use evaluation. North American Journal of Fisheries Management 8:333–345.

Poole, G. C., C. A. Frissell, and S. C. Ralph. 1997. In-stream habitat unit classification: inadequacies for monitoring and some consequences for management. Journal of the American Water Resources Association 33(4):879–896.

Rankin, E. T. 1991. The use of the qualitative habitat evaluation index for use attainability studies in streams and rivers in Ohio. Page 25–38 in G. Gibson, editor. Biological criteria: research and regulation. U.S. Environmental Protection Agency, Office of Water, EPA 440/5-91-005, Washington, D.C.

Rankin, E. T. 1995. Habitat indices in water resource quality assessments. Pages 181–208 in W. S. Davis and T. P Simon, editors. Biological assessment and criteria: Tools for water resource planning and decision making. Lewis Publishers, Boca Raton, Florida.

Rinaldi, M., and Casagli, N. 1999. Stability of streambanks formed in partially saturated soils and effects of negative pore water pressures: the Sieve River (Italy). Geomorphology 26(4):253–277.

Rinne J. N. 1985. Livestock grazing effects on southwestern streams: A complex research problem. Pages 295–299 in R. R. Johnson, C. D. Ziebel, D. R. Patton, P. F. Ffolliot, and R. H. Hamre, editors. Proceedings of the first North American riparian conference. Riparian ecosystems and their management: reconciling and conflicting uses. U.S. Forest Service General Technical Report RM-120, Fort Collins, Colorado.

Rinne, J. N. 1988. Grazing effects on stream habitat and fishes: research design considerations. North American Journal of Fisheries Management 8:240–247.

Rinne, J. N. 1992. Physical habitat utilization of fishes in a Sonoran Desert stream, Arizona, southwestern United States. Ecology of Freshwater Fish 1992:35–41.

Rinne, J. N. 1995. Interactions of predation and hydrology on native southwestern fishes: Little Colorado spinedace in Nutrioso Creek, Arizona. Hydrology and Water Resources in Arizona and the Southwest. 22/ 25:33–38.

Rinne, J. N. 1999a. Fish and grazing relationships: the facts and some pleas. Fisheries 24(8):12–21.

Rinne, J. N. 1999b. The status of spikedace, *Meda fulgida*, in the Verde River, 1999. Implications for research and management Hydrology and Water Resources in Arizona and the Southwest 29:57–64.

Rinne J. N. 2000. Fish and grazing relationships in southwestern United States. Pages 329–371 in R. Jamison, and C. Raish, editors. Ecological and socioeconomic aspects of livestock management in the Southwest. Elsevier, Amsterdam.

Rinne, J. N. 2001a. Nonnative, predatory fish removal and native fish response: Verde River, Arizona, 1999–2000. Hydrology and Water Resources of the Southwest 31:29–36.

Rinne, J. N. 2001b. Effects of substrate composition on Apache trout *Oncorhynchus apache*. Journal of Freshwater Ecology 16(3):355–365.

Rinne, J. N. 2001c. Relationship of fine sediment and two native southwestern fish species Hydrology and Water Resources of the Southwest 31:67–70.

Rinne, J. N. 2002. Hydrology, geomorphology and management: implications for sustainability of native southwestern fishes. Hydrology and Water Resources of the Southwest 32:45–50.

Rinne, J. N. 2003a. Native and introduced fishes: their status, threat, and conservation. Pages 193 to 213 in P. F. Ffolliott, M. B. Baker, L. F. DeBano, and D. G. Neary, editors. Ecology, hydrology and management of riparian areas in the southwestern United States. CRC Press, Boca Raton, Florida.

Rinne, J. N. 2003b. Fish habitats: conservation and management implications. Pages 277 to 297 in P. F. Ffolliott, M. B. Baker, L. F. DeBano, and D. G. Neary, editors. Ecology, hydrology and management of riparian areas in the southwestern United States. CRC Press, Boca Raton, Florida.

Rinne, J. N. In press. Riparian restoration: grazing management considerations for monitoring project effectiveness. In J. Rinne, R. Hughes, and R. Calamusso, editors. Changes in large river fish assemblages in North America: implications for management and sustainability of native species. American Fisheries Society, Bethesda, Maryland.

Rinne, J. N., and M. A. Alexander. 1995. Nonnative salmonid predation on two threatened native species: preliminary results of field and laboratory studies. Proceedings of the Desert Fishes Council 26:114–116.

Rinne, J. N. and W. L. Minckley. 1991. Native fishes in arid lands: A dwindling natural resource of the desert Southwest. U.S. Forest Service Rocky Mountain Forest and Range Experiment Station, General Technical Report 206, Fort Collins, Colorado.

Rinne, J. N., and A. L. Medina. 1996. Implication of multiple use management strategies on southwestern (USA) native fishes. Pages 110–123 in R. M. Meyer, editor. Fisheries resource utilization and policy, proceedings of the World Fisheries Congress, Theme 2. Oxford and IBH Publishing Company, New Deli.

Rinne, J. N., and D. G. Neary. 1997. Stream channel and fish relationships: preliminary observations, Verde River, Arizona. Pages 475–482 in J. J. Warwick, editor. Proceedings of the American Water Resources Agency Symposium, water resources education, training, and practice: opportunities for the next century. American Water Resources Agency, Las Vegas, Nevada, June 29–July 3. American Water Resources Association, Herndon, Virginia.

Rinne, J. N., and J. A. Stefferud. 1996. Relationships of native fishes and aquatic macrohabitats in the Verde River, Arizona. Hydrology and Water Resources in Arizona and the Southwest 26:13–22.

Rinne, J. N., and J. A. Stefferud. 1997. Factors contributing to collapse yet maintenance of a native fish community in the desert Southwest (USA). Pages 157–162 in D. A. Hancock, D. C. Smith, A. Grant, and J. P. Beaumer, editors. Developing and sustaining world fisheries resources: the state of science and management. Second World Fisheries Congress, Brisbane, Australia.

Rinne, J. N., and B. P. Deason. 2000. Habitat availability and utilization by two native, threatened fish species in two southwestern rivers. Hydrology and Water Resources in the Southwest 30:43–52.

Rinne, J. N., J. A. Stefferud, A. Clark, and P. Sponholtz. 1998. Fish community structure in the Verde River, Arizona, 1975–1997. Hydrology and Water Resources in Arizona and the Southwest 28:75–80.

Rinne, J. N., B. Holland, and G. Sundnes. 2002. Comparative study of heart rates in fishes from cold and temperate sea water and warm (hot) desert rivers. Pages 13–26 in K. Gamperl, T. Farrel, and D. McKinlay, editors. Proceedings of the Symposium on Cardiovascular physiology of fish. 5th International Congress on Biology of Fishes. Vancouver, BC.

Robertson, A. I., and R. W. Rowling. 2000. Effects of livestock on riparian zone vegetation in an Australian dryland river. Regulated Rivers: Research and Management 16:527–541.

Roni, P., T. J. Beechie, R. E. Bilby, F. E. Leonetti, M. M. Pollock, and G. R. Pess. 2002. A review of stream restoration techniques and a hierarchical strategy for prioritizing restoration in Pacific Northwest watersheds. North American Journal of Fisheries Management 22:1–20.

Roni, P., M. Liermann, and A. Steel. 2003. Monitoring and evaluating responses of salmonids and other fishes to in-stream restoration. Pages 318–339 in D. R. Montgomery, S. Bolton, D. B. Booth, and L. Wall, editors. Restoration of Puget Sound rivers. University of Washington Press, Seattle.

Rosenburg, D. M., and V. H. Resh. 1993. Freshwater biomonitoring and benthic macroinvertebrates. Chapman Hall, New York.

Rosgen, D. L. 1996. Applied river morphology. Wildland Hydrology, Pagosa Springs, Colorado.

Rosgen, D. L. 2001a. A practical method of computing streambank erosion rate. Pages 9–17 in Interagency Advisory Committee on Water Quality, editors. Proceedings of the 7th Federal Interagency Sedimentation Conference, March 25–29, Reno, Nevada. Volume II. Interagency Advisory Committee on Water Quality, Reston, Virginia.

Rosgen, D. L. 2001b. A stream channel stability assessment methodology. Pages 18–26 in Interagency Advisory Committee on Water Quality, editors. Proceedings of the 7th Federal Interagency Sedimentation Conference, March 25–29, Reno, Nevada. Volume II. Interagency Advisory Committee on Water Quality, Reston, Virginia.

Rosgen, D. L. 2001c. A hierarchical river stability/watershed based sediment assessment technology. Pages 97–106 in Interagency Advisory Committee on Water Quality, editors. Proceedings of the 7th Federal Interagency Sedimentation Conference, March 25–29, Reno, Nevada. Volume II. Interagency Advisory Committee on Water Quality, Reston, Virginia.

Schuett-Hames, D., A. Pleus, L. Bullchild, and S. Hall. 1994. Timber-Fish-Wildlife ambient monitoring manual. Northwest Indian Fisheries Commission, TFW-AM9-94-001, Olympia, Washington.

Simon, A., A. Curini, S. E. Darby, and E. J. Langendoen. 1999. Streambank mechanics and the role of bank and near-bank processes in incised channels. Pages 123–152 in S. E. Darby, and A. Simon, editors. Incised river channels: processes, forms, engineering and management. Wiley, Chichester, England.

Simon, A., and A. J. C. Collison. 2002. Quantifying the mechanical and hydrologic effects of riparian vegetation on streambank stability. Earth Surface Processes and Landforms 27(5):527–546.

Stefferud, J. A., and J. N. Rinne. 1995. Preliminary observations on the sustainability of fishes in a desert river: the roles of streamflow and introduced fishes. Hydrology and Water Resources in Arizona and the Southwest 22/25:26–32.

Steinman, A. D., and G. A. Lamberti. 1996. Biomass and pigments of benthic algae. Pages 295–314 in F. R. Hauer and G. A. Lamberti, editors. Methods in stream ecology. Academic Press, San Diego, California.

Swift, B. L. 1984. Status of riparian ecosystems in the United States. Water Resources Bulletin 20(2):223–228.

Sylte, T. L., and J. C. Fischenich. 2002. Techniques for measuring substrate embeddedness. U. S. Army Engineer Research and Development Center, EMRRP Technical Notes Collection, ERDC TN-EMRRP-SR-36, Vicksburg, Maryland.

Thompson, W. L. 2003. Hankin and Reeves' approach to estimating fish abundance in small streams: limitations and alternatives. Transaction of the American Fisheries Society 132:69–75.

USFS (U. S. Forest Service). 1998. General aquatic wildlife surveys-manual. U.S. Forest Service Region 3, Albuquerque, New Mexico.

USFWS (U. S. Fish and Wildlife Service). 1980. Habitat evaluation procedures (HEP). U.S. Fish and Wildlife Service, Division of Ecological Services, Manual ESM 02, Washington, D.C.

Vannote, R. L., G. W. Minshall, K. W. Cummins, J. R. Sedell, and C. E. Cushing. 1980. The river continuum concept. Canadian Journal of Fisheries and Aquatic Sciences 37:130–137.

Waters, T. F. 1995. Sediment in streams: sources, biological effects, and control. American Fisheries Society, Monograph 7, Bethesda, Maryland.

Weigel, B. M., J. Lyons, L. K. Paine, S. I. Dodson, and D. J. Undersander. 2000. Using stream macroinvertebrates to compare riparian land use practices on cattle farms in southwestern Wisconsin. Journal of Freshwater Ecology 15:93–106.

Weigel, D. E., and P. W. Sorensen. 2001. The influence of habitat characteristics on the longitudinal distribution of brook, brown, and rainbow trout in a small Midwestern stream. Journal of Freshwater Ecology 16:599–614.

Williams, J. E., J. E. Johnson, D. A., Hendrickson, S. Contreras-Balderas, J. D. Williams, M. Navarro-Mendoza, D. E., McAllister, and J. E. Deacon. 1989. Fishes of North America endangered, threatened, and of special concern: 1989. Fisheries 14(6):2–21.

Winward, A. H. 2000. Monitoring the vegetation resources in riparian areas. U.S. Forest Service, Rocky Mountain Research Station General Technical Report RMRS-GTR-47, Ogden, Utah.

Wohl, N. E., and R. F. Carline. 1996. Relations among riparian grazing, sediment loads, macroinvertebrates, and fishes in three central Pennsylvania streams. Canadian Journal of Fisheries and Aquatic Sciences 53:260–266.

Worley, J. W., and G. Heusner. 2000. Fences for horses. University of Georgia, Cooperative Extension Service Bulletin 1192, Augusta.

Young, D. W. 1998. The history of cattle grazing in Arizona. Hydrology and Water Resources in Arizona and the Southwest 28:13–17.

Zar, J. H. 1999. Biostatistical analysis. Prentice Hall, Upper Saddle River, New Jersey.

Chapter 6
Monitoring Floodplain Restoration

George R. Pess, Sarah A. Morley
Northwest Fisheries Science Center, National Marine Fisheries Service
2725 Montlake Boulevard East, Seattle, Washington 98112, USA
george.pess@noaa.gov

Julie L. Hall, Raymond K. Timm
University of Washington, School of Fishery and Aquatic Sciences
Box 355020, Seattle, Washington 98195, USA
jlhall6@msn.com

Introduction

River corridors are naturally dynamic and ecologically complex components of a watershed and often contain a disproportionately high amount of the total regional biodiversity (Naiman et al. 1993; Ward et al. 2001). Unaltered river corridors have heterogeneous landscape features, dominated by dynamic conditions, and exhibit scale-dependent biophysical patterns and processes (Ward et al. 2001). A prominent feature within river corridors is the floodplain (Figure 1). Geomorphologists traditionally define a floodplain as a flat, depositional feature of the river valley adjoining the river channel, formed under the present climate and hydrologic regime and during times of high discharge (Leopold et al. 1964; Dunne and Leopold 1978; Leopold 1994). Hydrologists and engineers view the floodplain either as land subject to periodic flooding or the area flooded by the 100-year flood event (Dunne and Leopold 1978). Ecologists have defined the floodplain and accompanying habitats as areas that are periodically inundated by the lateral overflow of river or lakes, or direct precipitation or groundwater; the resulting physiochemical environment causes the biota to respond by morphological, anatomical, physiological, phonological, or ethnological adaptations, and produce community structures (Junk et al. 1989).

Some of the most common features and terms associated with the definition of floodplains regardless of discipline include main channels; oxbow lakes; point bars; meander bends; meander scrolls; floodplain channels, such as sloughs, beaver ponds, surface and groundwater-fed tributaries, natural levees, or raised berms above the floodplain; wetland areas created by finer sediment overbank deposits; coarser sand deposits called sand splays; accumulations of wood deposits, such as logjams; mid-channel islands created by obstructions, such as wood deposits; and unique vegetation patterns determined by flows, obstructions within the floodplain, and small changes in elevation (Figure 2; Table 1; Leopold et al. 1964; Dunne and Leopold 1978; Wohl 2000). These floodplain-associated features are unique and are needed to help maintain river dynamics, watershed processes, and community structure and function (Ward et al. 2001).

The objective of our chapter is to describe how to monitor the effectiveness of floodplain-associated projects that attempt to reconnect isolated habitats. First, we identify and briefly review common effects of anthropogenic disturbance to floodplains and restoration techniques used to reconnect floodplain habitats isolated by anthropogenic disturbance. Next, we discuss how developing a monitoring plan based upon clear restoration goals and objectives can be used to help guide the monitoring of individual or multiple floodplain reconnection projects. Then, we discuss the selection of physical and biological study parameters and sampling protocols that can be applied to different types of restoration approaches. Finally, we provide recommendations for applying these monitoring techniques to temperate rivers.

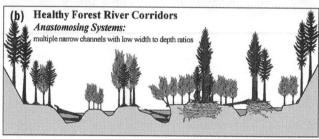

Figure 1.
The Taiya River, southeast Alaska, an example of an anthropomorphically undisturbed floodplain: (a) oblique view, and (b) schematics of how this anastomosing channel appears in cross section. (Photograph and schematic courtesy of Tim Abbe.)

Common Effects of Anthropogenic Disturbances to River–Floodplain Systems

Anthropogenic disturbances such as dams, levees, and the development of floodplains for agricultural, industrial, and residential use have disrupted the natural connection of many large rivers from their floodplains, reducing the interaction between lotic, lentic, riparian, and groundwater systems (Petts 1990; Ward and Stanford 1995). Hydrologic flow regulation by dams disrupts the downstream river system's natural disturbance regime (Ward and Stanford 1995). Such disruptions reduce and alter the frequency, extent, and duration of floodplain inundation, and truncate the input of sediments, nutrients, and wood into and out of the floodplain (Junk et al. 1989; Leopold 1994; Sparks 1995; Ward and Stanford 1995; Collins et al. 2002). This can disrupt the natural connection between rivers and their floodplain habitats (Bednarek 2001). For example, flood-control dams have changed the McKenzie River in Oregon from a multichannel river–floodplain system with midchannel bars and forested islands to a single-threaded channel (Ligon et al. 1995). Ligon et al. (1995) attribute the loss of these features to the reduction of peak flows that historically accessed the floodplain and cut new channels, recruiting the necessary sediment from local sources such as streambanks and terraces, which then deposited downstream and diverted flow. There also is evidence that such midchannel bars and islands were formed primarily from the recruitment of wood from local and upstream sources (Abbe and Montgomery 1996; Abbe 2000). Similar changes have occurred throughout watersheds in North America (Lowery 1968; Harvey et al. 1988).

Another common form of anthropogenic disturbance to the connection between main channels and their floodplains is the construction of levees. Levees are artificial embankments, normally higher than the river terrace banks, built close to the edges of riverbanks (Bolton and Shellberg 2001). Levees increase the flow capacity of a channel and contain floodwaters within an area narrower than the natural floodplain (Hey 1994). Reasons for constructing levees and modifying a river–floodplain system include flood control, increasing the speed of water conveyance during high flows, drainage of adjacent lands, navigation, and protection of roads and highways (Brookes 1988; Bolton and Shellberg 2001). While there are numerous effects from the construction and maintenance of levees, one of the most dramatic effects is the isolation of parts of the floodplain from its main channel (Brookes 1988).

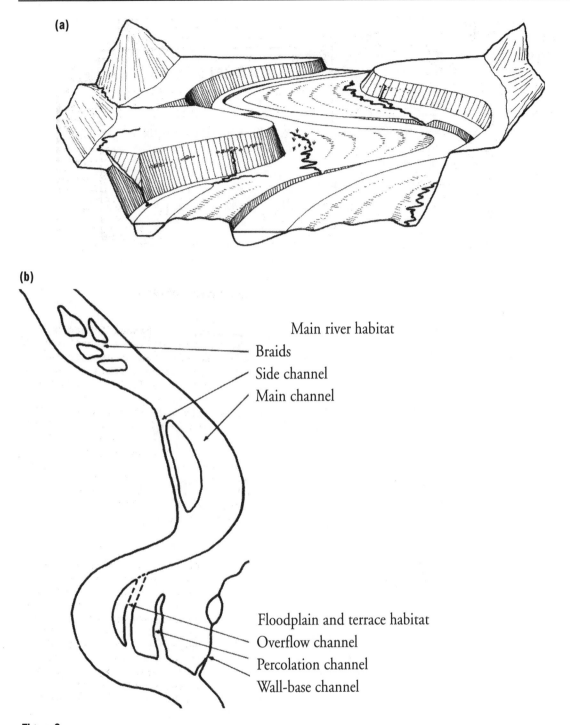

Figure 2.
Up-valley oblique view of meandering river and wall-based channels (a), and examples of associated habitat types in and along main rivers (b). (Reprinted with permission from Peterson and Reid 1984.)

One major consequence of floodplain alteration is the loss of habitats for fishes and other aquatic fauna (Beechie et al. 1994, 2001; Collins et al. 2002). For example, floodplain habitat isolation in several western Washington river basins has resulted in the virtual eradication of certain habitat types, such as large freshwater wetland and forest floodplain habitats in the lower portion of river basins (Beechie et al. 1994, 2001; Collins et al. 2002). Historically, most of the salmonid habitat (e.g., blind-tidal channels, side-channel sloughs, and beaver ponds) in two of these basins, the Skagit and Stillaguamish, were located in the floodplains and deltas (Beechie et al. 2001). These habitats have been reduced to less than 20% of their historic occurrence (Beechie et al. 1994, 2001). The disconnection of the floodplain not only disconnects habitat for fishes such as salmonids

Table 1.
Descriptions of floodplain features. Note that categories are not mutually exclusive (e.g., wall-based channel is one type of side channel). Definitions modified from Allaby and Allaby (1999), with additional references noted below.

Feature	Description
Floodplain	A flat, depositional feature of the river valley adjoining the river channel formed under the present climate and hydrologic regime and during times of high discharge (Leopold et al. 1964)
Alluvial rivers	Channels formed in and by river-transported sediment under its current hydrologic and climatic regime (Leopold et al. 1964). An alluvial channel is self-forming in that its form reflects the load and discharge of the river rather than the constraints of bedrock.
Meandering channels	Channels that have a main flow (the thalweg) that oscillates from one side of the channel to the other. Features such as bars and pools become more fixed as the magnitude of the meander becomes greater (Leopold et al. 1964).
Straight channels	Channels with a thalweg that is situated in the same location and concentrates flows, bars, and pool formation. Naturally straight channels are relatively uncommon, and straight channel reaches rarely exceed lengths of 10 channel widths (Dunne and Leopold 1978).
Braided channels	Channel with transient bars dividing flow between multiple channels (Dunne and Leopold 1978). Sediment frequently is transported, and a mix of sizes, banks easily erode, and discharge changes rapidly (Reid and Dunne 1996).
Anastomosing channels	Channels that branch and depart from the main channel, sometimes running parallel for several kilometers before rejoining (Collins and Montgomery 2002). Geomorphic features between channels are more stable (e.g., islands) than those between braided channels
Anabranching channels	A distributary channel that departs from the main channel, sometimes running parallel for several kilometers before rejoining the main stem. The anabranching channel differs from an anastomosing channel in remaining undivided.
Mid-channel islands	A body of land located within the river channel and completely surrounded by water.
River delta	A fan-shaped area of sediment deposited at the mouth of a river, where it enters a lake or the sea. Usually the river divides and subdivides into many smaller channels (distributaries), sometimes depositing bars and building up levees.
Distributary channels	Channels that branch from the main channel, which they may or may not rejoin before flowing into the estuary (Beechie et al. 1994). These typically occur in river deltas.
Side channels	Subsidiary channel located within the active exposed lower floodplain; percentage of flow relative to main channel is minute. These typically are abandoned river channels or overflow channels (Beechie et al. 1994).
Sloughs	Areas of dead water formed both in meander-scroll depressions and along valley walls as flood flows move down valley (Leopold et al. 1964). Side channels with more than 90% of their area consisting of pools (Beechie et al. 1994).
Wall-based channels	A side channel formed on floodplains or terrace surfaces by the channeling of runoff through swales created by the migration of the main-stem river near the base of valley walls (Peterson and Reid 1984).
Swales	A depression otherwise at ground level. Swales may be connected to the river channel through groundwater flow paths.
Terraces	Abandoned floodplains rarely, if ever, inundated by floods in the current hydrologic regime (Leopold 1994; Reid and Dunne 1996). Most terraces form when a river's erosional capacity increases such that it cuts down through its floodplain.

Table 1. continued

Feature	Description
Levees (natural)	Raised berms above the floodplain surface and adjacent to the channel, most frequently at the concave banks. Levees usually contain coarser materials deposited as rivers flood over the top of the channel banks (Leopold et al. 1964).
Meanders	A sinuous curve in a river. Flow velocity is highest on the outside of the meander bend with deposition occurring on the inside of the bend. The meander will become increasingly looped until the river eventually breaks through its narrow neck creating an oxbow lake.
Meander scrolls	Low, curved ridges of relatively coarse material deposited by the river and lying parallel to the main channel. These depressions and rises form on the convex side of bends as the channel migrates laterally down valley and toward the concave bank (Leopold et al. 1964).
Oxbow lakes	A crescent-shaped lake formed when a meander of a slow-flowing river is cut off from the main channel after the river in flood crosses the neck of land between two bends. Most oxbow lakes eventually silt up.
Backwater pools	A pool along the channel margin formed by an eddy downstream from obstructions (such as bars, rootwads, or boulders) or back flooding upstream from an obstruction (Bisson et al. 1982; Nickelson et al. 1992).
Off-channel ponds	A small body of standing water that is not part of an active channel but connects to the main river by a short access channel. Occurs in old flood terraces and near the base of valley walls (Peterson and Reid 1984).
Dammed ponds	A pond impounded upstream from a complete or nearly complete channel blockage (such as a beaver dam or logjam); most common on side channels and floodplain tributaries (Bisson et al. 1982; Nickelson et al. 1992)
Logjams	Large accumulations of wood frequently occurring along channel margins but sometimes spanning the entire width of the channel. These jams increase channel roughness, store sediment, provide cover for fish and substrate for invertebrates, and enhance flow diversity (Wohl 2000).
Sand splays	Deposits of flood debris, usually of coarser sand particles in the form of splays or scattered debris (Leopold et al. 1964).
Point bars	Accumulations of fluvial sediment at the relatively gentle slope on the inside of a meander.
Hyporheic zone	The saturated interstitial areas below the channel and floodplain containing a percentage of river water (White 1993). The size of the hyporheic zone will vary with channel type, valley form, and the hydraulic conductivity of alluvium (Wohl 2000).

but also alters the exchange of water, sediment, and nutrients between the floodplain and the main channel (Ward and Stanford 1995). In river–floodplain systems without levees, there normally is a net import of inorganic compounds and a net export of particulate organic matter, including live biomass from the floodplain (Ward and Stanford 1995). Exports include wood, benthos, plankton, and fishes (Welcomme 1985).

The natural disturbance regime of floods, channel migration, and wood recruitment is a main determinant in structuring alluvial forest succession, whether it is a tropical or temperate setting (Ward and Stanford 1995; Collins et al. 2002). Collins et al. (2002) found that an unleveed system and a forested floodplain with dams and flow regulation had significantly less alteration to the floodplain habitats than leveed systems with no forested floodplain and without dams, highlighting the importance of local wood recruitment processes in maintaining habitat structure. A reduction in flow, channel migration, and wood recruitment can both lower water table levels due to less floodplain inundation and increase main channel incision, allowing for dieback of floodplain forests and the establishment of upland species (Steiger et al. 1998).

Another effect that has not been extensively studied is the impact of levees on the hyporheic zone, which is the saturated interstitial area below the streambed and the streambanks that contains a percentage of channel water or that has been chemically altered by channel water (White 1993). The size of the hyporheic zone varies according to river size, discharge, sediment porosity and volume, and vertical and lateral exchange rates between the surface flow (Edwards 1998). The zone can range in size from a few meters deep and 100 m wide to 10 m deep and 3 km wide (Stanford and Ward 1988). Regardless of its extent, the hyporheic zone is critical to the function of river–floodplain systems, including retaining and storing of water, reducing peak flows and sustaining summer base flows, regulating stream temperature that results in a cooling of water in the summer and a warming in the winter, and creating downwelling zones that promote salmonid spawning and upwelling zones that enrich waters with nutrients for stream organisms (Edwards 1998; Bolton and Shellberg 2001). Changing any or all of these functions would lead to disconnection between the river and its floodplain and would have effects on floodplain habitats and the biota that use such habitats.

One of the most permanent effects to river–floodplain systems is the conversion of natural floodplain vegetation such as forests to agriculture, residential, or industrial use. This is particularly prevalent along the mouth and lower reaches of many large rivers, where land frequently is converted to industrial and agricultural uses and rivers become isolated from their floodplains (Beechie et al. 2001). Along with many of the deleterious effects associated with agricultural uses along waterways (e.g., runoff of pesticides and herbicides and potential grazing impacts), loss of riparian forests hydrologically and geologically disconnects the river and its floodplain at multiple dimensions. The most severe disconnection often derives from the generally permanent infrastructure accompanying urbanization along rivers and floodplains. As roads, rooftops, shopping malls, and other impervious surfaces replace native vegetation and soils, the delivery of water, sediment, and organic material to the channel is drastically altered (Booth and Jackson 1997). With the urban river penned into an artificially narrow channel, habitat heterogeneity is lost—particularly the shallow side margins and slow backwater areas characteristic of unaltered alluvial river–floodplain systems (Dunne and Leopold 1978). Not only is lateral connectivity gone but also vertical interchange of surface and groundwater is restricted, with impervious surfaces now covering river margins. Without room to expand and contract, temporal fluctuation of surface and groundwater levels and their interaction is also severely limited.

Review of Restoration Techniques Used to Reconnect River–Floodplain Systems

Over the last decade, the restoration of large rivers, and the reconnection of isolated floodplains and their associated habitats in particular, has become a critical component of river ecosystem restoration (Holmes and Nielsen 1998; Sear et al. 1998; Florsheim and Mount 2000). Techniques used to reconnect river–floodplain systems are at the early stage of development and often more theoretical than actual (Cowx and Welcomme 1998). Many of the river systems where such restoration efforts have taken or will take place are heavily engineered systems that rely on human intervention to be maintained in a specified state (Cowx and Welcomme 1998). Thus, many projects and subsequent techniques have been and will be a compromise between allowing natural processes to function and engineering solutions (Cowx and Welcomme 1998). Some of the most common restoration techniques used to reconnect isolated main-stem and floodplain habitats include dam removal, levee removal or setback, direct reconnection of floodplain channels, the creation of "new" floodplain channels, and culvert replacement or removal (Table 2; Figures 3 and 4).

Dam removal is a large-scale river restoration technique that is gaining greater acceptance within and outside the United States (Stanley and Doyle 2003). In the last 20 years, more than 500 dams have been removed in the United States, most of which have been smaller dams less than 20 m in height with a storage area of less than 100 acre-ft (123,000 m3; Hart and Poff 2002; The Heinz Center 2002; Stanley and Doyle 2003). Dam removal affects three areas—upstream of a dam reservoir, within a reservoir or impoundment area, and below a dam. Biotic exchange between a river system below and above a dam increases after dam removal, as does the role of aquatic migratory species (e.g., salmonids) that may have been blocked due to a dam (Hart and Poff 2002). For example, dam removal on the Clearwater River in Idaho in 1963 reconnected the main stem, increasing both habitat quality and chinook salmon *Oncorhynchus tshawytscha* runs (Shuman 1995). Reservoir areas or impoundments are dramatically affected by dam removal because reservoirs convert to river, riparian, and floodplain habitats (Stanley and Doyle 2003). This physical change reduces the residence time of water in a former reservoir reach and, subsequently, reduces the amount of sediment and other materials stored with-

Table 2.
Descriptions of common floodplain restoration techniques.

Restoration technique	Restoration location	Physical effects	Biological effects	Constraints
Dam removal	Main-stem channels	Change reservoir to riverine environment; increase downstream flux of sediment, wood, water, and energy	Change from lentic to lotic system; increase biotic exchange in up- and downstream directions	Infrastructure within the main stem and floodplain may not allow for complete reconnection
Levee removal or setback	Main-stem channels	Increase channel migration; allow for flow, sediment, and nutrient pulses	Increase in habitat types, potential for habitat formation, biological productivity, and diversity	Setback does not allow full floodplain function for entire floodplain
Reconnection of floodplain	Main-stem channels	Flow connection to main-stem	Create rearing environment for fish	Elevation differences, water quality degradation due to land use practices features (e.g., channels, ponds)
Aggrading main-stem channels (e.g., submersible dams, logjams)	Main-stem channels	Increase channel migration, allow for flow, sediment, and nutrient pulses	Increase in habitat types, potential for habitat formation, biological productivity, and diversity	Works best if floodplain has survived intact
Creation of floodplain habitats	Surface channel	Flow connection to main stem	Create spawning and rearing habitat for fish	Sedimentation problems; does not allow for full floodplain function; In some cases, includes bank armoring
	Groundwater channel	Flow connection to main stem	Create spawning and rearing habitat for fish	Does not allow for full floodplain function; in some cases, includes bank armoring
	Off-channel ponds from land use (e.g., gravel pits) or alcove ponds	Flow connection to main stem	Creates spawning and rearing habitat for fish	Risk of avulsion, adequate prey resources, cover, and water quality
Culvert replacement or removal	All channel types	Increase downstream flux of sediment, wood, water, and energy	Increase biotic exchange in upstream and downstream direction	Infrastructure within the main-stem and flood-plain may not allow for complete reconnection

in a reach. This, in turn, shifts the biota from a lentic to a lotic system (Hart and Poff 2002). For example, fish and macroinvertebrates adapted to a high sediment supply reservoir environment gave way to riverine fish and macroinvertebrates within a year of two separate dam removal projects in Wisconsin (Stanley et al. 2002; Stanley and Doyle 2003). Below a dam, several major changes occur, the most obvious being a change in channel form due to a change in sediment flux. Other changes include a return to a more natural temperature regime, plant colonization, and a greater exchange of nutrients and organic matter with upstream portions of a watershed. Downstream effects from dam removal on ecological attributes ultimately depend upon how reservoir-derived deposits move into and through downstream reaches (Stanley and Doyle 2003).

Figure 3.
Two common floodplain restoration techniques: (a) dam removal (photograph courtesy of Emily Stanley) and (b) levee removal or setback (photograph courtesy of Tim Beechie).

A levee setback project, whether full or partial, allows a river to migrate and, subsequently, to create and maintain different floodplain channel types, thereby increasing the habitat diversity of a floodplain. The relative extent of such restoration actions often is limited by land constraints, and, thus, many such projects are a combination of full and partial levee removal. One technique is a "beaded approach" to floodplains, where small sectors of the full floodplain width (e.g., 6–8 km long) are allowed to function, alternating with leveed sections of the river. In these full floodplain-width sections, several habitat features are included, such as floodplain channels and wetlands. This "family" of habitat will allow the river to function properly and possibly create sediment, flow, and nutrient pulses (Sparks 1995). This technique allows portions of the floodplain to be inun-

Figure 4.
Two common floodplain restoration techniques: (a) reconnection of floodplain habitats (photograph courtesy of Dan Cromwell) and (b) creation of new habitats.

dated and encourages scour, erosion, and deposition in those areas. Such a technique can be used in areas where natural channel migration is normally high, such as the confluence with tributary junctions. Restoration of portions of the floodplain could significantly improve the diversity, health, and productivity of fish and aquatic communities (Cowx and Welcomme 1998). For example, intentional levee breaches at two locations on the Cosumnes River, in northern California in the late 1990s resulted in the development of sand deposition, greater erosion patterns, wood recruitment, and an increase in topographic variation (Florsheim and Mount 2000). Sixteen juvenile and adult fish species were found to be using the shallow-water floodplain habitats associated with the levee breach areas after flows inundated the floodplain (Whitener and Kennedy 1998).

Removing a weir or a levee to reconnect a relic channel or larger floodplain water bodies, such as a pond or a lake to the main stem, is another technique. Notched dikes, culverts, submersible dikes, and controllable flow gates can be used to reconnect existing relic channels in areas where flow needs to be regulated (Cowx and Welcomme 1998). This is a technique that has been used to reconnect a section of a cutoff meander or channel and often results in a backwater environment for rearing fish. Two common problems that occur with such projects are (1) elevation differences between the main-stem and the relic channels due to main-stem channel incision from the time of floodplain channel disconnection and (2) water-quality degradation in the floodplain. For example, rehabilitation opportunities identified in the Stillaguamish River in Washington State include the reconnection of two former meander bends that are now floodplain sloughs (Pess et al. 1999). However, channel-bed surveys in the Stillaguamish River in the vicinity of these bends proposed for reconnection show that the river downcut by 1–2 m between the period when the bends where cut off in 1929 and 1991 (Collins et al. 2003). Restoring flow into these sloughs also will be difficult because both are filled by overbank deposits of fine sediment (Collins et al. 2003). Thus, rivers with a dynamic channel behavior and a higher sediment supply, similar to the Stillaguamish, may be more difficult to reconnect.

Submersible check dams are a technique used to raise rivers with incised main-stem channels. For example, in the Danube River in Slovakia, check dams in lateral artificial channels have been used to aggrade the river to the point where older channels are now reconnected, improving the retention time of water in the reach (Cowx and Welcomme 1998). On the Kissimmee River in Florida, channel filling has been used to reconnect old meanders and floodplains (Toth et al. 1993). The main channel has been filled from levee material at points in the river where the meander crosses the main channel. This only works if the floodplain has survived intact (Cowx and Welcomme 1998).

The creation of new floodplain habitats is a form of habitat enhancement that involves active construction of new floodplain channels. These projects often are designed for a specific species or species life stage. For instance, streams with constructed floodplain channel habitats in western Oregon had greater summer populations of juvenile coho salmon *Oncorhynchus kisutch* and higher numbers of coho salmon, cutthroat trout *O. clarki*, and steelhead *O. mykiss* smolts than streams without such habitats (Solazzi et al. 2000). Solazzi et al. (2000) and others concluded that creation of slow-water floodplain channel habitats increased overwinter survival for coho salmon, cutthroat trout, and steelhead. Creation of new habitats can be an important form of enhancement, replacing natural floodplain channels that have been lost due to flood control activities and other floodplain-isolating actions (Beechie et al. 2001). Floodplain habitat creation projects offer an alternative to main-stem restoration projects, which can be difficult to construct and maintain due to unstable flow and channel-bed conditions (Lister and Finnigan 1997). There are two major habitat types that typically are created in river floodplains: side channels (surface and groundwater fed) and off-channel ponds (e.g., gravel pits, mill ponds, mine dredge ponds, and alcove ponds).

Creation of surface water-fed side channels primarily provide spawning habitat for specific salmonids species such as chum *Oncorhynchus keta*, pink *O. gorbuscha*, and sockeye salmon *O. nerka* (Sheng et al. 1990). These channels also can offer rearing habitat for juvenile salmonid species such as coho salmon, chinook trout, and steelhead trout (Lister and Finnigan 1997). They typically are connected at both the upstream and the downstream ends to the main river channel, with an intake structure on the upstream end. Due to the surface water source, there is flexibility in choosing a project location. However, along with this water source comes sedimentation problems. Because of siltation concerns, this type of channel may be unsuitable for systems with high suspended sediment loads. Also, the location of the channel intake is critical for controlling sediment and organic introduction into the channel. Typically, a surface-fed side channel requires a dike or control structure and bank armoring at the upstream end to protect the channel from river flooding and bank erosion (Lister and Finnigan 1997).

A large number of groundwater-fed channels have been excavated to support spawning by many salmon species, including chum, coho, pink, and sockeye (Bonnell 1991; Cowan 1991; Hall et al. 2000). Similar to surface-fed side channels, groundwater-fed channels also provide rearing habitat for juvenile fishes, particularly coho salmon (Bonnell 1991). Groundwater-fed channels offer stable year-round water flows with little sediment, clean substrates, and stable water temperatures (Sheng et al. 1990; Bonnell 1991). Groundwater channels are excavated parallel to the main river channel, often along an existing intermittent stream or relic channel. The channel is protected from flooding by a dike at the upstream end, and another dike sometimes is placed between the side channel and the river (Cowan 1991; Lister and Finnigan 1997). As with surface-fed channels, the banks usually are armored (Bonnell 1991; Lister and Finnigan 1997).

Off-channel ponds provide valuable overwintering habitat for juvenile coho salmon and other fishes that prefer lentic habitats (Peterson 1980, 1982a, 1982b; Peterson and Reid 1984; Swales et al. 1986, 1988; Swales and Levings 1989). Overwintering and rearing in pond habitat is attractive due to low water velocities, abundant cover, more favorable water temperatures than the main river, abundant food supplies, and, in some cases, less predation (Swales et al. 1986). Ponds can be created through several excavation or construction methods. One method is to construct a dam or a dike and flood an existing wetland or abandoned river channel (Lister and Finnigan 1997). A second method is to blast holes into the channel of an existing side or wall-base channel that supports intermittent flow. In the blasting method, either one or a series of ponds can be created through exploding charges into the mud layer of the channel (Cederholm et al. 1988; Cederholm and Scarlett 1991). These ponds then are connected with each other and the river through the existing intermittent channel or an excavated downstream channel. Care should be taken to ensure that sufficient stream flow occurs in the spring to allow juvenile coho salmon and other species to migrate from the ponds into the river (Cederholm et al. 1988; Cederholm and Scarlett 1991).

Floodplain mining and other floodplain excavation activities have resulted in the creation of gravel pits, mill ponds, and mine-dredge ponds along river channels (Norman 1998). The connection of these ponds with the river channel provides opportunities for additional off-channel habitat. As with other off-channel ponds, these areas can provide rearing habitat for juvenile coho and chinook salmon and cutthroat trout and, in some instances, provide spawning habitat, though in some areas they are thought to provide refuge from predators and exotic species (Bryant 1988; Swales and Levings 1989; Richards et al. 1992; Norman 1998; Hall et al. 2000). The successful conversion of gravel pits and mill ponds depends on several factors, including good access for fish to migrate into and out of the pond area, low risk of river avulsion, and adequate prey resources, cover, and water quality (Norman 1998). Small, shallow ponds with complex shapes provide the best opportunities for successful use by juvenile salmon, because large and deep ponds will provide less prey, as well as substantially higher risk of avulsion (Peterson 1982a; Norman 1998). The design of these sorts of projects has included connection of one pond with the river, as well as connection of many ponds with each other in the floodplain before connection to the river (Bryant 1988; Richards et al. 1992; Norman 1998). These studies found that there were higher fish densities in the channels connecting ponds to one another or to the river than in the ponds themselves (Bryant 1988; Richards et al. 1992).

Alcoves are small ponds directly connected to the river. These ponds provide rearing opportunities for coho salmon and cutthroat and steelhead trout, particularly as overwintering habitat (Solazzi et al. 2000). Alcoves have been constructed through excavation of a pond directly adjacent to the river channel. Spanning logs may be placed immediately downstream of the entrance to the alcove to ensure that flooding occurs. Locations should be chosen based upon association with natural seeps, springs, or temporary streams, which help prevent sedimentation and blocking of the alcove entrance, although some maintenance may be required (Solazzi et al. 2000).

Culvert replacement or removal is another common channel and floodplain restoration practice. Fish passage through structures such as culverts and other stream crossings is critical to maintaining connectivity among floodplain habitats (Roni et al. 2002). Culverts can block access of migratory fishes such as salmonids and other aquatic fauna, and can result in large amounts of aquatic habitats being biologically "disconnected" from a river system. Such structures also can alter the downstream movement of materials such as sediment, wood, and organics. Thus, removal or improvement of fish passage and reestablishing connectivity among habitats often is an important part of floodplain restoration efforts. Additional information on culvert replacements and reconnection of isolated habitat can be found in Chapter 10, which covers this topic in detail.

This brief review suggests that floodplain channel reconnection and creation projects by using various techniques are being implemented in a variety of river systems throughout North America and Europe. A thoughtful monitoring and evaluation program that is based on clear hypotheses and a statistically valid monitoring design should be implemented with such projects. Guidance on monitoring and evaluating such projects is, thus, needed to help the restoration community gain a better understanding of the overall success of reconnecting isolated floodplain habitats.

Developing a Monitoring Plan

The first and most important step in developing a monitoring plan for assessing floodplain restoration is clearly identifying the overall goals and specific objectives of the project(s). Determining what specific restoration techniques to apply and when and where to focus subsequent monitoring will follow. Restoration objectives, therefore, should be as unambiguous as possible and not so broadly expressed as to be unfeasible to implement or impossible to monitor. Methods unrelated to project objectives should not be applied simply because the money or technology is available. The second step in developing a monitoring plan is developing clear hypotheses of project outcomes. Hypotheses are statements of prediction that describe, in concrete terms, the specific effects expected to result from restoration activities. To test these hypotheses, the third and fourth steps in developing a monitoring plan are formulating study design and selecting appropriate study parameters and sampling protocols.

It is on these last two steps that the remainder of this chapter focuses. Although extremely important, the first two steps are largely project specific and likely to be highly subjective. Depending on who has implemented the project and who is conducting the effectiveness monitoring and the validation monitoring, restoration objectives and hypotheses can often be very different (Chapter 2). Hypothesis testing requires us to determine the how, what, where, and when of monitoring. In many ways, the overall development of a complete monitoring plan is circular, with no absolute starting and ending point. Although we have placed study design before selection of study parameters and sampling protocols, recognize that many of the decisions to be made in study design (e.g., location and timing of sampling) will, in turn, be based on the study parameters themselves. Below, we discuss experimental, spatial, and temporal considerations in the design of floodplain monitoring studies. An example of how this framework can be applied in practice is given in Table 3.

Study Design

Experimental design

Floodplain restoration is very much an emerging science, with each new project an experiment from which we have much to learn. In designing effective monitoring programs, two important considerations are replication and the use of reference (control) sites. Replication can occur in space (e.g., monitoring multiple independent restoration projects) and in time (e.g., monitoring one restoration project over multiple independent sampling periods) and allows us to draw statistical inference beyond a single project at one point in time. Reference sites, the closest one can come to an experimental "control" in field studies (Conquest and Ralph 1998), help to distinguish if changes observed at a treatment site are due to restoration or other confounding factors (e.g., unrelated human or natural disturbances). Two basic experimental designs that incorporate the concepts of replication and reference condition are before–after and posttreatment studies. Various permutations on these two approaches are discussed in greater detail by other authors (Conquest and Ralph 1998; see also Chapter 2). We examine both approaches as they relate to floodplain monitoring and discuss the challenges inherent in applying traditional standards of experimental design to such large-scale field studies.

Collecting similar data before and after restoration treatment greatly enhances our abilities to interpret the physical and biological responses of specific restoration actions. Establishing a baseline condition through preproject monitoring is particularly critical when comparable references reaches are not available (such as is often the case in highly developed regions). Two examples of monitoring plans that have greatly benefited from multidisciplinary studies initiated before extensive floodplain restoration are on the Kissimmee River in Florida

Table 3.
Recommended steps in developing a floodplain restoration monitoring plan, with specific examples given for construction of groundwater channels in the floodplain.

Step	Example for constructed groundwater channels
Identify project objectives	Increase floodplain complexity by increasing habitat heterogeneity, by improving hydrologic connectivity, and by creating new off-channel spawning and rearing habitats for fishes.
Develop project hypotheses	Habitat heterogeneity will increase within study reaches as more off-channel habitats are made available, hydrologic connectivity between the floodplain and main stem will increase via groundwater channels, and fish will successfully use new habitats for spawning and rearing.
Formulate experimental design	Before–after design to evaluate changes in relative abundance of floodplain habitats and hydrologic connectivity between floodplain and main stem. Posttreatment paired-site design to compare habitat quality and fish use between constructed channels and naturally occurring reference channels.
Select physical monitoring parameters	Measure exchange rates of wood, sediments, and nutrients between floodplain and main-stem habitats, vertical and horizontal movement of water, and relative abundance of floodplain habitats before and after construction. Measure habitat heterogeneity, wood abundance, and temperature regime in constructed and reference channels.
Select biological monitoring parameters	Measure invertebrate and fish density, community composition, and diversity in constructed and reference channels.
Select appropriate spatial scales at which to monitor	At local scale, evaluate physical and biological differences between constructed and reference channels. At reach scale, evaluate changes in relative abundance of floodplain habitats and associated fish use. At basin scale, track changes in total smolt production and nutrient availability.
Determine monitoring frequency and duration	Sample over multiple seasons to capture seasonality of fish use (e.g., juvenile overwintering vs. late summer spawning) and changes in habitat availability during high and low water periods. Monitor parameters at least twice annually after construction to identify potential design problems, then semiannually for at least 10 years to allow for response lag time.
Analyze and report	Where appropriate, use paired t-tests to evaluate differences in means between before–after and between constructed–reference monitoring parameters. Consult a quantitative ecologist for additional statistical guidance. Report results at regional and national conferences, postproject updates at relevant Web sites, publish final results in peer-reviewed journal.

(Koebel 1995) and on the Danube River in Austria (Schiemer et al. 1999). In many cases, monitoring programs are designed to evaluate projects that have been in place for some time. Even when no explicit pretreatment monitoring has occurred, relevant data often can be drawn from historical data sources (e.g., aerial photographs, long-term gauging stations, related field studies, etc.). In examples drawn from California case studies, Kondolf (1998) illustrates how historic aerial photographs depicting temporal heterogeneity in channel width can serve to inform subsequent monitoring efforts. Use of other historical data sources is discussed further in the "when to monitor" subsection below. When limited or no pretreatment data are available, a space for time substitution can be applied with the posttreatment design (e.g., Gørtz 1998; Florsheim and Mount 2000).

Posttreatment studies rely heavily on the careful selection of appropriate references sites. Depending on the scale of the project (see "where to monitor" subsection below), a reference "site" can refer to an individual habitat unit, a river reach, or a neighboring drainage basin. As with a pre- and post-study design, similar data should be gathered for treatment and reference sites. Treatment and reference sites should be as similar as possible geomorphically, chemically, and biologically. Where appropriate, taking a paired study approach can increase statistical power substantially, thus improving our ability to detect treatment effects (Zar 1999). Various classification strategies that organize natural sources of variation in rivers are often a useful place to begin when pairing reference and treatment sites. Some common classification strategies include ecoregion designations (McMahon et al. 2001), degree of hydrologic connectivity to the main channel (Ward and Stanford 1995), and geomorphic characteristics (Rosgen 1994). Physically speaking, channel type, channel migration pattern, gradient, and valley confinement should be similar between reference and treatment sites. It also often is relevant to pair sites based on biological information (Hughes 1995). For example, the numbers and type of fish species in a reach will vary by river size and location (Fausch et al. 1984).

Ideally, a monitoring program will collect similar data both before and after treatment and at reference and treatment sites over a long enough time period to detect potential restoration effects (Figure 5). Although there are several examples of riverine restoration studies that have applied this before–after control–impact (BACI) approach (e.g., Biggs et al. 1998; Kelly and Bracken 1998; Stanley et al. 2002), more typically, the large-scale, high costs, and complexity typically associated with floodplain restoration projects make true replication in space and time challenging. For example, independent spatial replicates for large dam removal projects generally are not available. Temporally, another constraint is the potentially very long lag time between restoration treatment and physical and biological response due to natural variability in climate (and subsequently, in flow conditions) and the life cycles of floodplain species. Although carefully designed monitoring studies that are replicated in space and time are invaluable, floodplain restoration projects should not be judged by statistical significance alone. There is much to be learned from even a single case study, through simple graphical analyses and professional judgment (Conquest and Ralph 1998; see also Chapter 2).

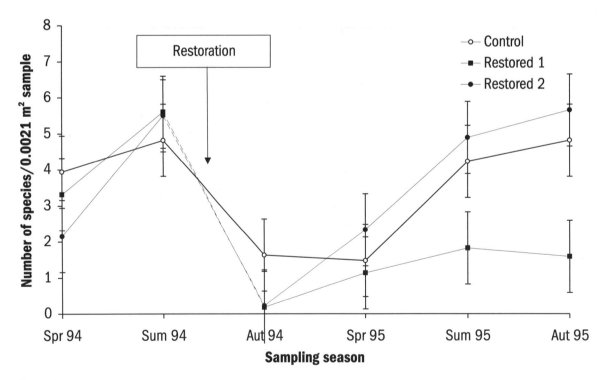

Figure 5.
A before–after control–impact study design applied to a floodplain restoration monitoring on the River Cole, England. Reprinted with permission from Biggs et al. (1998). These researchers evaluated biological response to channel remeandering by sampling benthic macroinvertebrates before and after restoration occurred and at treatment (impacted) and control reaches. While invertebrate taxa richness decreased dramatically at treatment reaches immediately after construction (Autumn 1994), a relatively quick recovery time was seen in subsequent sampling trips. Further long-term monitoring will be required to determine if a net positive benefit occurred as a result of restoration work undertaken.

Where to monitor

Given the geographic magnitude, spatial complexity, and habitat diversity represented by river floodplains, determining where to focus monitoring efforts can be a daunting task. Along with well-defined hypotheses, identifying appropriate sampling strategies for particular biological and physical parameters of interest will help direct where to sample within the floodplain. If an objective of a floodplain reconnection project is to increase sediment storage capacity, this often is estimated by comparing sediment discharge at points above, within, and below the treatment reach. If the focus is improving overwinter survival for juvenile coho salmon, then sampling that encompasses tributaries, off-channel habitats, and other slow-water areas will likely be most informative. Although restoration actions may be focused on a specific river reach, projects often have larger ranging effects across the basin or may have unintended effects either upstream or downstream from where restoration actions occurred. Physical processes occur over various spatial and temporal scales, and processes operating over the entire basin will likely influence the success of localized projects (Boon 1999). Because diverse species inhabit different microhabitats within the floodplain, focusing on only one habitat type risks missing important biological signals. Three important factors to consider when deciding where monitoring will occur are (1) spatial scale(s) of sampling, (2) habitat diversity within project reaches, and (3) upstream and downstream effects of restoration.

Rivers are hierarchical systems, highly connected longitudinally, laterally, and vertically to the landscapes they drain (Ward 1989; Ward et al. 1999) and, as such, their geomorphic and biochemical attributes also operate across multiple spatial scales (Frissell et al. 1986). Particular restoration strategies fit into this spatial hierarchy quite differently: dam breaching will likely have hydrologic effects felt throughout the basin, the impacts from partial levee breaching may be most prominent in reaches immediately adjacent and downstream, and the construction of a small alcove pond often has the greatest effect locally by providing a greater diversity of flow and depth conditions for resident biota. While there are many spatial scales that can be considered, we discuss restoration monitoring in the context of three: habitat, reach, and basin.

The habitat scale refers to the very local scale at which biological monitoring often occurs (e.g., individual pools, riffles, logjams, etc.). Invertebrate sampling often is done within discrete riffles, and periphyton samples are taken from individual rocks. The reach scale, which is often the scale at which restoration projects are undertaken, generally consists of a length of river at least 5–10 times the average bank-full width of the channel (Leopold et al. 1964). River reaches usually contain a variety of different habitat types (main stem, side channels, off-channel ponds, point bars, etc.) and are the scale at which much physical monitoring occurs. For example, when monitoring for restoration techniques, such as levee removal or setback, which allow large rivers to migrate more freely, changes in channel patterns should be documented at the reach scale. Channel pattern is the appearance of the channel and its floodplain in map view and occurs at the scale of hundreds of meters to kilometers. Channel patterns will change once a main stem is allowed to interact to a greater extent with its floodplain environments, subsequently changing where, and to a lesser extent how, the floodplain is connected to a main stem.

The basin scale refers to the entire drainage area of a given watershed. In many ways, restoration at this scale is the most meaningful—though most difficult to both implement and monitor (Frissell and Ralph 1998; Schiemer et al. 1999). Although restoration projects may be focused on very specific reaches, the hope often is that these actions will cumulatively translate to improved conditions over the larger basin scale. This does not mean that for every site-specific restoration project, monitoring should be done across the entire floodplain complex, but some effort should be made to put an individual project or multiple projects into a larger context (Table 4). For example, to determine how much a single constructed groundwater channel may be contributing to overall floodplain complexity, it would be pertinent to evaluate the relative abundance, distribution, and quality of off-channel habitats present throughout the basin.

Sampling at multiple spatial scales is very helpful in evaluating how isolated projects or multiple projects fit into this larger picture. This can be accomplished in many ways: (1) with the physical location of sampling (e.g., sampling juvenile salmonids at different habitat types within a treated river side channel, trapping outmigrants at the confluence of the side channel with the main stem, and sampling at the river's mouth to monitor trends in basin-wide smolt abundance), (2) with the choice of sampling parameters (e.g., fish are often

Table 4.
Monitoring at multiple spatial scales for common floodplain restoration techniques. Examples of physical and biological parameters are given for each category. Additional information on culvert replacement and reconnection of isolated habitats can be found in Chapter 10.

Technique	Local scale	Reach scale	Basin scale
Dam removal	Physical habitat formation (e.g., gravel bars, side channels, sloughs, forested wetlands, etc.)	Rate and type of channel migration, sediment delivery and storage, wood recruitment rates	Magnitude of associated sediment and nutrient pulses
	Diversity and biomass of periphyton and aquatic macrophytes within newly formed habitats	Composition and age structure of riparian vegetation, diversity of fish and invertebrate life history stages	Total basin productivity measured by fish, smolt, or invertebrate production
Levee removal or setback	Physical habitat formation (e.g., gravel bars, side channels, sloughs, forested wetlands, etc.)	Rate and type of channel migration, sediment delivery and storage, wood recruitment rates	Frequency, extent, and duration of floodplain inundation; magnitude of associated sediment and nutrient pulses
	Diversity and biomass of periphyton and aquatic macrophytes within newly formed habitats	Composition and age structure of riparian vegetation, diversity of fish and invertebrate life history stages	Total basin productivity measured by riverine smolt production or hyporheic invertebrate production
Reconnection of floodplain features	Flow connection to main-stem, local elevational differences, sedimentation rates at access point	Distribution and relative abundance of off-channel habitats within study reach, sediment storage and discharge	Basin hydrologic retentiveness; nutrient, sediment, and wood delivery rates across basin
	Fish passage at access point; establishment of periphyton, macrophyte, and invertebrate assemblages	Juvenile fish overwinter growth and survival, spawning density of adults; invertebrate taxa diversity	Degree of genetic diversity amongst previously isolated populations
Installation of grade control structures	Local elevational differences in riverbed, changes in channel geometry	Reconnection of floodplain habitats; floodplain channel length, width, and density	Amount, location, and travel distance of wood; retention of water, sediment, and nutrients within basin
	Periphyton growth on structures, invertebrate colonization, use by juvenile and adult fishes	Spatial distribution of fish within study reach, taxonomic composition of aquatic macrophytes	Composition and spatial pattern of riparian vegetation across basin (particularly from multiple projects)
Creation of floodplain habitats (e.g., side channels or off-channel ponds)	Quality of physical habitat (e.g., substrate distribution); flow connection to main stem	Relative abundance of reach-scale spawning and rearing habitats for fish, sedimentation rates within study reach	Hydrologic retention; habitat diversity across basin (particularly from multiple projects)
	Colonization by periphyton, aquatic macrophytes, fishes, and invertebrates	Spawner recruitment rates to study reach; growth, survival, and densities of juvenile fishes within reach	Total basin fish diversity and production
Culvert replacement		See Chapter 10	

good integrators of larger spatial scale effects, whereas periphyton sampling may reveal more information about local site conditions), and (3) with the choice of sampling protocols (e.g., for a revegetation project, riparian characteristics could be measured at the habitat scale within small plots, at the reach scale with transect surveys, and at the basin scale with remote-sensing technologies to monitor vegetation patterns over a larger portion of the landscape).

Within a floodplain reach, species use different microhabitats that are likely to be differentially affected by restoration. Even when the primary focus of restoration work is on a single species, this organism likely inhabits different environments throughout its life cycle and feeds on species that use other floodplain habitats. Thus, it is important not to focus sampling too narrowly on only one habitat type (Figure 6). For example, Ward et al. (1999) detected significant differences in benthic invertebrate taxa richness between floodplain habitats of impounded and free-flowing reaches of the Danube River, differences that were not observed by sampling only in the main stem. In a related study, Tockner et al. (1999) found that maximum diversity for different biological assemblages peaked in distinct channel types. By sampling across such a diversity of habitats, these researchers were able to investigate the spatial distribution of species within a floodplain complex, to examine how various habitats were being used at different life stages, and to predict how these patterns potentially change as a result of floodplain reconnection.

In addition to sampling at the project location itself, we also recommend monitoring physical and biological features at reaches both upstream and downstream of restoration treatment. Upstream reaches serve as potential references but, in some cases, also may be influenced by restoration work themselves, either by physical changes in channel morphology (e.g., avulsion) or in the upstream movement of biota (Pringle 1997). For these reasons, and the unfortunate reality that river reaches completely unaltered by human activities rarely exist today, upstream reaches generally are not true controls in the strictest sense of the word. They can, however, serve as reference reaches and help to distinguish whether changes observed in treatment reaches over time are due to restoration activities or other factors operating across the basin (e.g., human encroachment, climatic conditions, etc.). In some cases, the effects of specific restoration activities will be seen most prominently downstream of the actual restoration treatment.

Reaches downstream of levee breaching and dam removal generally benefit from a more natural hydrograph and greater delivery of wood and other organic materials (Bednarek 2001). On a shorter time scale, a number of studies report disturbance from construction both at the immediate site and downstream via increased delivery of sediment and nutrients (Biggs et al. 1998). To determine how floodplain restoration affects upstream and downstream control reaches, it is important to sample over multiple reaches. Working on a recently restored lowland river in England, Sear et al. (1998) used channel dimension information to document how restoration measures increasing the number of meander bends and reconnecting the floodplain with its main channel resulted in substantial morphological changes in both treatment and downstream reaches. In the treatment reach, both the amount of sediment stored and bank erosion increased, causing this reach to widen. Upstream, the control reach aggraded and increased in morphological diversity. Specific adjustments to both the treatment and control reaches were due to the availability and type of channel substrate, the stream power available to transport substrate, and the nature of the restored channel morphology (Sear et al. 1998).

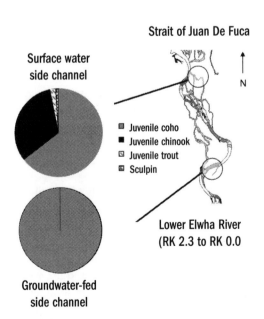

Figure 6.
Relative abundance of salmonid species by side-channel type. Data were collected by snorkel surveys conducted on the Elwha River, Washington State.

When to monitor

Knowing when to monitor strengthens the ability to detect and interpret restoration response. Baseline data collected before any restoration work gets underway not only aids in setting appropriate goals and design criteria but also is invaluable for interpreting results of postrestoration monitoring. Monitoring over a long enough period is also key, both to encompass the life cycles of many riverine organisms and to allow the reconfigured channel opportunity to interact with its floodplain. The timing and interval of monitoring also should reflect the temporal heterogeneity of flow conditions and the seasonality inherent in biological systems. Three basic guidelines for when to sample are (1) before restoration work begins, (2) within a period of temporal and seasonal variability, and (3) over the long term.

Successful floodplain restoration programs are based on preproject knowledge of the geomorphic and ecological context of a river past and present. This helps answer the questions: what did the river–floodplain complex look like predisturbance, in what ways has this system been modified, and what is its current condition and apparent trajectory? After centuries of human abuse, rivers may change in unforeseen ways, making restoration response unpredictable. For example, invasive species likely inhabit at least a portion of the floodplain (Baltz and Moyle 1993), and, by reconnecting areas, we may inadvertently put at risk species we are trying to protect. Physically, if dramatic postdevelopment changes in sediment and water budgets are not taken into consideration in restoration designs, well-meaning "enhancement" efforts can actually be detrimental (Kondolf 1998). The placement of a structure or the remeandering of a river will cause dramatic changes in "pre-" and "post-" channel variables such as channel slope, width, depth, and substrate size. Having before and after information on physical and biological study parameters will allow for the documentation of how the channel and resident biota respond to a restoration action.

Information on river conditions past and present can be drawn from historical data sources and preproject inventories and assessments. Historical data sources such as early field studies, maps, or photographs (Figure 7) provide insight into what the river and its floodplain once looked like (Boon 1999). Other sources for this type of information include less disturbed reference reaches (Hughes 1995) or paleoecological and paleohydrologic data (Hughes et al. 2000; Brown 2002). Preproject inventories and assessments aid in understanding the causes and subsequent symptoms of degradation and are crucial in predicting how rivers will respond to restoration activities (Kondolf 1998; Boon 1999). Examples include analysis of flood frequency rates, evaluation of sediment and wood budgets, inventory of floodplain blockages, taxa distribution studies, and biological assessment of river health at points throughout the basin.

Flow events, along with other natural disturbances such as debris flows, fire, or disease (Ward et al. 2002), will be a major influence on how the river responds to restoration. Rather than sampling at only one point in time, we recommend monitoring under a range of these conditions to capture temporal and seasonal heterogeneity. How does postrestoration channel morphology respond to a major sediment input from an upstream debris flow? How does the river operate in a low-water year when many floodplain habitats may be dewatered? Not only does flow shape channel geomorphology, but it greatly influences habitat availability for instream biota and successional patterns of riparian vegetation (Ward et al. 2002). While evaluating a constructed riverine–wetland project on the upper Mississippi River, Theiling et al. (1999) observed a fourfold increase in fish taxa richness in their study area after major flooding. Natural disturbance events are seasonal in nature, and biota have adapted accordingly. For example, during high-water months in the fall and winter, juvenile coho salmon often migrate into protected off-channel habitats to overwinter (Peterson 1982a, 1982b).

Determining what time of the year to conduct biological sampling should be informed by knowledge of the life cycle of study organisms and the seasonality in migration patterns. With the juvenile coho salmon example given above, sampling in summer only would overlook the importance of these backwater areas in overwinter survival. Seasonality also can affect the diurnal timing of sampling. During winter months or below certain temperatures, juvenile salmonids in freshwater become nocturnal, thus, winter sampling generally is done at night (Roni and Fayram 2000). The optimal sampling period will vary by assemblage and life stage. With aquatic invertebrates, the general index period for sampling in the Pacific Northwest is late summer to early fall, when flow generally is most stable and taxa richness is high (Hayslip 2003). If the goal is to quantify invertebrate drift, then the best time to sample generally is near or during sundown (Smock 1996). With vegetative sampling, knowledge of the growing and flowering period of floodplain species will assist in determining the best seasons in which to sample (USEPA 2002). If at all possible, we recommend sampling over multiple seasons, because seasonal life history requirements are not always well understood for many species.

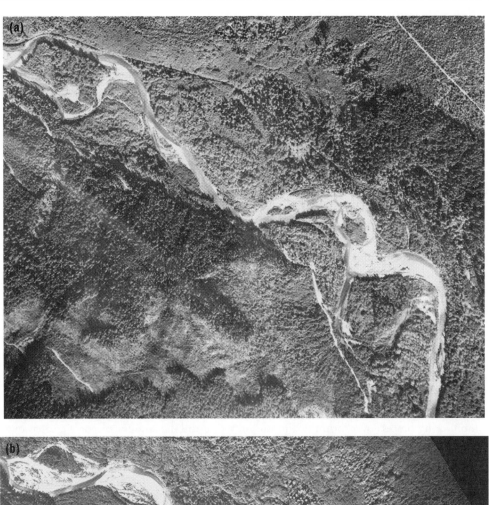

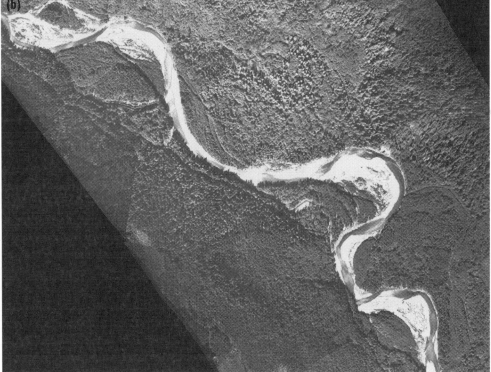

Figure 7.
Two aerial photographs of the Sauk River in Washington State depicting migration of the main stem across the valley floor and the formation of multiple side channels between (a) 1949 and (b) 1996. (Photographs courtesy of Ali Senauer and Tim Beechie.)

Because the river needs time to interact within the reconnected floodplain, and the biota need sufficient time to both recover from construction activities and respond to changes in physical habitat, we highly recommend that some degree of long-term monitoring occur. Levee setbacks, partial removals, and side-channel reconnections are all types of restoration actions that require evaluating how main stem–floodplain connections change over time. Unfortunately, most restoration monitoring, if it occurs at all, is done in the short term (Frissell and Ralph 1998). In terms of the response of biota, this may take centuries for some groups (e.g., in riparian forests), while the response of macrophytes, invertebrates, algae, and other groups with shorter life cycles and quick recolonization rates will likely be much more rapid. The amount of time necessary to document changes in physical characteristics may take one season or several years, because this is primarily a function of the number of larger flow events that allow the main stem–floodplain connection to recur (Junk et al. 1989). Monitoring changes to channel pattern over the period of years to decades will capture larger-scale trends and allows for the development of (1) channel migration rates and (2) identification of type of channel migration pre- and postrestoration action. Identifying the type of channel migration that occurs is important, because it is a main determinant in identifying what physical processes and inputs are forcing change and will be a guide for the type of change that may occur in the future.

What to Monitor: Selecting Study Parameters and Sampling Protocols

Determining what tools and techniques to apply in monitoring specific floodplain restoration projects involves identification of appropriate end-response variables and selection of suitable sampling protocols. Most importantly, these steps should be guided by the original objectives and hypotheses developed for the restoration program in question. At minimum, inclusion of both biological and physical measures is a critical element of any monitoring program. For example, we might measure the relative proportion of different habitat types within a river reach after restoration, but this information is incomplete without direct biological monitoring to determine how the biota are using these areas. Our focus on physical sampling techniques is to emphasize monitoring process over form (i.e., do not only measure the amount of pools created by a particular restoration action but also the flow regime, and sediment and wood delivery rates that contribute to pool formation). In designing a biological monitoring program, we caution against focusing only on abundance of single-species indicators and instead emphasize the value of taking a multiple-species and even multiple-assemblage approach that integrates a variety of different measurements. Explicitly linking biological and physical data collection, rather than having discrete monitoring programs, greatly enhances data interpretation. Chemical monitoring, treated in Chapter 9, also is important but not the focus of this chapter.

Because of the diversity of habitats present in river floodplains, sampling protocols developed for streams, rivers, wetlands, and forests are all applicable to monitoring floodplain restoration. Attempting to determine fish density in swift-water main-stem habitats will present very different challenges than forested backwater sloughs. For many of these backwater areas, sampling strategies developed for wetlands (Adamus et al. 2001; Rader et al. 2001) will be more applicable, whereas protocols developed for wadeable streams may be appropriate for braided portions of the river, side channels, and floodplain tributaries. There are entire texts dedicated solely to the topics of how to measure fish (e.g., Murphy and Willis 1996), the classification of wetland habitats based on vegetative and hydrologic characteristics (e.g., Cowardin et al. 1995), and the evaluation of sediment budgets (e.g., Reid and Dunne 1996). Rather than attempt to review these and related subjects in exhaustive detail, we present an overview of diverse tools and techniques applicable to monitoring floodplain habitats and discuss the various components involved with floodplain monitoring (e.g., selecting parameters, conducting fieldwork, analyzing data, and checking results). Additional references for more detailed descriptions of specific study parameters, sampling methodologies, and techniques for data analysis are in Tables 5 and 6.

Physical monitoring

Our discussion of physical monitoring focuses on alluvial channels, because many of the world's large rivers and associated floodplain channels are alluvial. Alluvial channels are formed in and by river-transported sediment under its current hydrologic and climatic regime (Leopold et al. 1964). There are several types of channel patterns that are common for alluvial channels: meandering, straight, braided, and anastomosing (Table 1). A change in channel pattern from one state to another can result in a change in the type and the occurrence of connected floodplain channels (Dunne and Leopold 1978). For example, a change in channel pattern from straight or braided to meandering or anastomosing normally indicates (1) an increased ability of the channel to migrate

Table 5.
Measures of physical response variables to floodplain restoration.

Category	Parameter	Technique	References
Channel morphology	Change in channel pattern	Historic vs. current comparison	Leopold et al. 1964 Dunne and Leopold 1978 Reid and Dunne 1996, Smelser and Schmidt 1998
	Rate and type of channel migration	Historic vs. current channel position —Photographs, maps, notes, fieldwork —Identify causes of change	Leopold et al. 1964 Dunne and Leopold 1978 Reid and Dunne 1996 Smelser and Schmidt 1998 Collins and Montgomery 2001
	Channel geometry	Cross sections	Leopold et al. 1964 Dunne and Leopold 1978
		Longitudinal profiles Characterize substrate distribution	Olson-Rutz and Marlow 1992 Harrelson et al. 1994 Reid and Dunne 1996 Madej 1999
Sediment storage	Channel sediment storage	Change in sediment storage and discharge	Madej 1992 Reid and Dunne 1996 Kronvang et al. 1998
Wood storage	Wood storage	Change in amount, location, and travel distance of wood	Martin and Benda 2001 Abbe et al. 2003 Abbe and White 2000
Floodplain morphology	Floodplain channel length, width, and density	See channel morphology	See channel morphology Bowen and Waltermire 2002
	Flows that inundate floodplain channels	See channel morphology	Steiger et al. 1998 Kronvang et al. 1998 Devries 2000
Flows	Surface flows	Staff gage	Dunne and Leopold 1978
Subsurface flows	Subsurface flows	Piezometer	Edwards 1998 Geist et al. 1998
Riparian vegetation	Vegetation composition and spatial patterns	Remote sensing	Bowen and Waltermire 2002

across its floodplain, thereby increasing floodplain inundation, channel sinuosity, and the number of floodplain channels (Abbe et al. 2003); and (2) that a vertical change in elevation has occurred, also greatly affecting the degree of main stem–floodplain connection. A priori knowledge of channel form and pattern at restoration reaches is, therefore, an essential foundation upon which any subsequent physical monitoring occurs.

Determining what specific physical parameters to evaluate in a given restoration monitoring program should be guided by hypotheses developed in the early stages of the monitoring plan. These hypotheses will help to focus selection of physical parameters on indicators of physical processes (e.g., channel morphology, sediment supply, flow regime, and wood delivery) that capture the appropriate scale of physical response. Four steps then can be used to answer the questions for any indicator: (1) acquiring background information; (2) subdividing area based upon general channel characteristics; (3) performing data collection (office and field), interpretation, and analysis; and (4) checking the results.

Table 6.
Sampling techniques for five river floodplain assemblages. This table is by no means exhaustive; consult references for additional detail on sampling protocols developed for specific taxonomic groups.

Assemblage	Sampling techniques	Selected references
Fishes	Population estimation: removal or mark-recapture Visual estimation: snorkel, videography Age analyses: scale and otolith samples Diet analyses: stomach contents via gastral lavage Genetic analyses: blood and tissues samples	Hocutt and Stauffer 1980; Li and Li 1996; Murphy and Willis 1996; Hughes et al. 1998; Simon 1998; Roni et al. 2003
Aquatic invertebrates	Hyporheos: wells, peizometers, benthic corer Soft bottom: corer, Ekman grab, suction sampler Rocky bottom: Surber or Hess sampler, kick-net Water column: plankton net, drift net Water surface: emergence traps, neuston nets	Rosenberg and Resh 1993; Hauer and Resh 1996; Merritt et al. 1996; Smock 1996; Scarsbrook and Halliday 2002; Hayslip 2003
Periphyton	Individual substrate samples (e.g., stones, wood) Colonization plates Removal by suction over a known area Chlorophyll analyses: spectrophotometry Biomass estimation: ash-free dry mass	Rott 1991; Bahls 1993; Lowe and LaLiberte 1996; Steinman and Lamberti 1996; Stevenson and Pan 1999; Hill et al. 2000; Fore and Grafe 2002
Aquatic macrophytes	Removal by hand collection Quadrat plots Transect surveys Remote sensing: aerial photographs, Landsat	Wright et al. 1981; Fox 1992; Sliger et al. 1990; Adamus et al. 2001; U.S. EPA 2002
Riparian vegetation	(see methods above for aquatic macrophytes) Remote sensing: aerial photographs, Landsat, LIDAR Canopy density: light meters and densiometers Age analysis: bore samples Leaf litter composition and biomass: leaf traps	Myers 1989; Leonard et al. 1992; Murphy et al. 1994; Innis et al. 2000; Lefsky et al. 2001; Bowen and Waltermire 2002

Although a great variety of physical measurements can be collected, we have organized our discussion of physical monitoring around five major topic areas: channel morphology, floodplain characteristics, sediment storage, wood storage, and flow regime (Table 5). These five broad categories are not an exhaustive inventory of every type of parameter applicable to physical monitoring, but they are the characteristics most often included in procedures to document physical response to aquatic restoration and most applicable to floodplain restoration.

Channel morphology, the first of the five categories, is defined as the form a channel takes resulting from inputs of water, sediment, and wood. This form can be expressed by channel slope, width, depth, sinuosity (ratio of channel length to a straight line down the valley distance), distribution of specific in-channel features such as bars and pools, and the degree of connection between a main stem and floodplain. Changes in channel morphology reflect the rate and the rate of change in the erosion, transport, and deposition of sediment and wood (Reid and Dunne 1996). These changes also help determine the degree of channel stability by characterizing past channel behavior and help predict the range of future channel response (Reid and Dunne 1996). A change in channel inputs (e.g., water, sediment) or dimensions will alter the connection between a main stem and floodplain by changing the rate of lateral channel movement (e.g., channel migration rate) or vertical channel change (e.g., channel aggradation or incision); thus, it is critical to understand how a main stem–floodplain connection is created and maintained over time.

Channel slope, width, depth, and substrate particle size are all required variables for determining sediment transport and flow calculations. These parameters determine the frequency and the magnitude of floodplain channel inundation and, thus, changes in connection between the floodplain and main stem (Reid and Dunne 1996). Such channel geometry measurements allow for the development of (1) empirical relationships between channel dimensions and response to changes in flow, sediment, and wood; (2) predictor models that allow restoration hypotheses to be quantified; and (3) more quantitative documentation of specific responses to changes in channel dimensions from restoration actions (Sear et al. 1998). Because low-gradient large river channels with floodplains are naturally dynamic and difficult to predict, such data collection is critical for trend and pattern analysis. Channel dimension information is particularly significant if it is done over a broad enough area, such as a reach or multiple reaches, where it can be used to identify how a treatment reach affects upstream and downstream control reaches.

Techniques for constructing channel position maps and interpreting channel patterns at the reach scale include a combination of remote sensing and field methods (Table 5). A basic understanding of the channel pattern can be gained by acquiring background information on the project area via such sources as historic and current aerial photographs (Figure 7), topographic maps, field notes from related studies, and anecdotal evidence from local field staff and residents (Reid and Dunne 1996; Collins and Montgomery 2001).

Historic and current aerial photographs are an invaluable source of information for mapping the channel position in larger river systems (Figure 7). The date of the flight, the type of aerial photograph (e.g., orthophotograph versus photograph), the scale, and the source of the photograph should all be identified to know how comparable photographs are to each other (Reid and Dunne 1996). Maps and field notes should also be identified in a similar fashion (Collins and Montgomery 2001). Key sources of information for photographs, maps, and field notes include (1) federal agencies such as the U.S. Army Corps of Engineer, the U.S. Forest Service, the U.S. Geologic Survey, and U.S. General Land Office (defunct); (2) state (provincial) and county land divisions; (3) individual project records on flood studies; and (4) maps and field records associated with levee construction.

To accurately quantify changes in channel morphology that occur over time, select aerial photograph dates that capture events that altered channel position (e.g., floods, the placement of levees, bank armoring, or the recruitment of large amounts of wood), as well as consistent channel definitions to demark areas such as thalweg, low flow, and active flow. Photograph and map rectification, stereoplotters, and geographic information system software can help with this step. Much of the information gleaned from aerial photographs, maps, and field notes can be used to compare and subdivide areas based upon geomorphic differences such as channel type, channel migration pattern, gradient break, and differences in valley confinement. Where possible, control and treatment reaches also should take into account differences in geomorphology and geomorphic responses before the restoration action.

Field data collection at the reach scale can include information on the following: bank materials, levees and revetments, bank height and composition, vegetation type and age, eroding banks, floodplain channels, floodplain edges, depositional zones, sediment size, longitudinal profiles, channel curvature, and channel migration rates (calculated on a reach scale by examining the distance moved at defined points within the reach over an arbitrary time period). This information will be useful for determining trends over time and allows for the development of empirical predictors or models (Sear et al. 1998). Channel pattern change, however, will not capture some of the changes that occur at the site-specific scale (e.g., meters to tens of meters; Leopold et al. 1964). Thus, it is important to couple channel pattern monitoring with site-specific channel dimension information.

In comparison to reach-scale measurements of channel morphology that rely heavily on the use of remote-sensing data, site-specific data collection has a greater focus on fieldwork. The types of information that can be collected include measuring permanent channel cross sections, identifying floodplain and bank-full width indicators, surveying longitudinal profiles, measuring discharge, characterizing bed and bank material, and installing stream and staff gauges (Table 5). An excellent reference on field techniques for these and other parameters is Harrelson et al. (1994). Analysis and interpretation of stream channel cross-sectional data can indicate changes in channel-bed elevation and bank erosion (Olson-Rutz and Marlow 1992), while changes in longitudinal profiles and sediment size can help interpret site-specific change in stream power and sediment transport (Leopold et al. 1964; Dunne and Leopold 1978; Reid and Dunne 1996; Madej 1999; Beechie 2001). Chapter 3 provides detail on reach and site-scale sampling of sediment.

Floodplain characteristics is the second major category for physical monitoring. Floodplain reconnection projects should extend identification of channel pattern and channel geometry measurements beyond the main channel and should include the floodplain and its channels. Accurately mapping the location of floodplain channels is a very important monitoring exercise, particularly when increasing floodplain channels is a restoration objective. Maps of floodplain channels should include information on channel type, location, length, width, habitat types, water source, bank material, and riparian vegetation type for each floodplain channel within treatment and control reaches. Because floodplain channels are smaller and more difficult to identify with aerial photographs (particularly in forested floodplains), channel mapping frequently requires more fieldwork than working only in the main channel. To increase fieldwork efficiency, begin with aerial photographs, maps, and other forms of historic information that allow development of preliminary base maps.

A change in the amount, location, and degree of connection between floodplain channels and a main channel will be an important indicator of the success of a floodplain reconnection project. Remote sensing and fieldwork to document change in floodplain characteristics use similar techniques to those identified in the discussion of channel morphology but with a few important differences. Reach-scale maps in control and treatment reaches should include documentation of vegetative conditions (see also Chapter 4), and cross sections should include the entire floodplain bottom where possible. These valley cross sections should be tied to the channel cross sections on a main channel and on floodplain channels. A cross section of the entire valley bottom allows a more thorough analysis of water discharge and sediment transport and identifies potential floodplain channels that may see new activity in terms of flow and sediment movement and storage.

Aerial photographs and some of the traditional photogrammetric techniques identified in the channel morphology subsection also can be used to identify floodplain channels and their dimensions; however, this can prove to be an unreliable method if the floodplain is forested. Furthermore, elevational differences, a critical component to monitoring changes in the floodplain and floodplain channels, cannot be determined by using such a technique, due to the amount of error involved with each measurement. Another relatively new technique that is substantially more accurate (range of 15–20 cm for elevations) is light detection and ranging (LIDAR), the use of a fast-firing laser mounted in a small aircraft to measure distances to the surface of the earth (Bowen and Waltermire 2002). This technique is more cost effective and accurate than traditional techniques and should be considered for larger scale reconnection projects.

Monitoring change to sediment storage, the third major physical category, is particularly important if a restoration objective is to increase the sediment storage capacity of a treatment reach to reduce the downstream rate of sediment inputs. Many floodplain reconnection projects affect where and how inputs of sediment, water, and wood are stored in main-stem and floodplain channels, because increased connection allows for more interaction between the two areas. Larger, low-gradient reaches that currently or historically had well-developed floodplain sediment deposits provide more opportunity for sediment storage and consequently are more sensitive to changes in sediment input or flow characteristics (Reid and Dunne 1996).

Techniques to monitor changes in sediment stored in main channels and floodplains are similar to those outlined for changes in channel morphology and floodplain characteristics (See alsoChapter 3). Aerial photographs, field measurements, historic and current discharge records at gauge stations, and measurements of sediment discharge are the types of information needed to identify changes in channel-stored sediment (Madej 1992).

Sediment-discharge measurements can either be calculated directly by measuring suspended load and bedload or estimated with sediment transport equations. Suspended sediment data can be collected when water-discharge data are collected, with water samples retained and filtered by using a variety of standard procedures (Dunne and Leopold 1978). Bedload transport measurements are more difficult to make and require specialized equipment and several years of data collection (Dunne and Leopold 1978). Reid and Dunne (1996) provide a comprehensive discussion of sediment transport equations appropriate to different channel types and bed conditions. Chapter 3 also provides a discussion of sediment transport measurements. Regardless of which equations are used, there are basic types of information that are needed to make such estimates, including bed-material grain-size distribution, discharge, hydraulic slope, relation between flow depth and discharge, and a record of continuous discharge measurements. Accurately measuring and estimating sediment discharge is a very difficult task, and estimates should be used as an indicator for overall trends within each reach (Vanoni 1975). The potential for aggradation or degradation can be identified with such trend data (Reid and Dunne 1996).

One method that can be used to estimate the change in sediment due to the change in sediment storage capacity is by comparing measured sediment discharge at several points above, within, and below the treatment reach. Such an approach was used on a 13-km reach of the River Culm in England to demonstrate that 28% of the suspended sediment entering the reach was deposited within the main channel and floodplain (Walling et al. 1986). In-channel measurements of sediment discharge, combined with valley cross sections and the use of sediment traps, can identify changes in floodplain characteristics, sediment storage, and sediment transport. For example, sedimentation on the River Brede was measured with cylindrical sediment traps along transects in upstream, treated, and downstream reaches to quantify the change in newly deposited sediments (Kronvang et al. 1998). Suspended sediment also was measured at permanent cross sections within each reach. Results extrapolated to the entire floodplain treatment reach from this effort showed that after five overbank flood events, approximately 9% of the suspended sediment that historically moved through this reach as suspended sediment had accumulated on the floodplain (Kronvang et al. 1998). Another example of monitoring changes in the type and quantity of channel-stored sediment is the Kissimmee River in Florida, where measurements of channel cross sections and accumulated sediment were made to evaluate the reintroduction of flow into remnant floodplain channels (Toth et al. 1993).

Another method that can be used is the categorical mapping of sediment storage areas (e.g., gravel bars, vegetated floodplain) based on how frequently the sediment is moved (Reid and Dunne 1996). Main-stem and floodplain channel related sediment storage locations can conveniently be divided into categories based on how frequently the sediment is moved (Reid and Dunne 1996). Two basic categories include channel sediment and floodplain sediment (Kelsey et al. 1987). Channel sediment can be further subdivided into two categories: active and semiactive. Active sediment accumulates in the active channel and unvegetated portions of bars and is moved at least once every several years, while semiactive sediment accumulates in portions of bars that are susceptible to revegetation (Madej 1992). Semiactive areas have sediment that moves only with large magnitude flow events such as the 5–20 year recurrence interval. Floodplain sediment can be further subdivided into three categories: inactive, stable alluvial deposits, and new deposits. Inactive sediment is stored in well-vegetated areas within the floodplain and only is moved during extreme flow events, while stable alluvial deposits are sediment accumulations that occurred during another climate regime but may be susceptible to channel erosion from a main-stem or floodplain channel (Madej 1992). Newly deposited sediments are deposited on the floodplain immediately after large flow events that inundate the floodplain. They typically are finer sediment material (e.g., sand, silt, mud, and clay) and include an organic component. These deposits typically form on top of the inactive deposits. The storage types can be discerned by vegetation age and location with respect to the main channel. Active main-stem and, to a lesser degree, floodplain channels will store larger material, while the finer sediment usually is stored as overbank deposits on floodplains (Wohl 2000).

A change in the amount and distribution of storage elements due to changes in erosion and sedimentation patterns is an indicator of change in the way a channel responds to sediment input and flow. For example, recent levee breaches on the Cosumnes River in northern California resulted in the creation of sand deposits and induced cottonwood and willow vegetation establishment in certain areas of the floodplain, while other areas of the floodplain were scoured and formed new channels through older deposits (Florsheim and Mount 2000). The reestablishment of erosional and depositional processes in the floodplain is, thus, changing the amount and distribution of sediment storage. To gain a better understanding of how physical processes interact with restoration actions, however, it is important to attempt to discern whether changes in sediment storage are due to restoration actions or other factors such as large flow events or wood accumulations.

Wood storage is the fourth major category of physical monitoring. Instream restoration projects, whether small stream, floodplain, or main-stem oriented projects, typically include the placement of wood (Chapter

8, for more detail). Wood is a critical component of channel structure (Bilby and Bisson 1998) and can have a large-scale effect upon channel pattern (Collins and Montgomery 2002). Wood accumulations have dramatic effects on erosion and deposition patterns and the type and duration of sediment storage before and after a restoration action. For example, wood jams have been identified as an integral part of creating and maintaining multiple main-stem and floodplain channels, flow in floodplain channels, and diverse habitats in floodplains (Abbe and Montgomery 1996; Beechie et al. 2001; Collins and Montgomery 2002).

Monitoring trends in wood amount should be a typical component of any floodplain reconnection project. Traditional wood survey techniques and methods enumerate the number and volume of wood pieces above a minimum size in control and treatment reaches as an indicator of changes in wood amount. This is primarily a field exercise and incorporates the use of many of the wood surveys techniques, as discussed in Chapter 8. However, such techniques often fall short of identifying how wood function is influenced by basic physical processes such as upstream inputs and bank erosion that create and maintain floodplain–main-stem reconnections.

Quantifying wood residence time and function, in addition to total wood amounts and volumes, in either a control–treatment reach or a before and after setting is a better indicator of how physical processes maintain and create floodplain–main-stem connections. Wood debris in main-stem channels, floodplain channels, and floodplains has definable inputs, outputs, and residence times, and, therefore, its mass budget can be analyzed in an orderly and quantitative fashion (Martin and Benda 2001). Once a floodplain reconnection project is implemented, a wood budget can be used to monitor how and where wood accumulates, in what quantity, and with what function.

A mass balance of wood can be calculated for treatment and control reaches by using the basic tenets of budgeting, such as input, output, and decay (Martin and Benda 2001). The general budget can be stated in equation form:

$$\Delta S = I - O$$

Where, ΔS is change in storage, I is input, and O is output. In essence, S is the stream condition for any parameter (e.g., the amount of wood or sediment), and quantifying changes in inputs or outputs indicate how the residence time of these inputs has been altered as a function of restoration, changes in watershed condition, or natural variation (Beechie et al. 2001). Each portion of the equation is over an arbitrary time period (e.g., seasonal, annually, etc.). Martin and Benda (2001) identified several general categories for a wood budget that need to be incorporated into the input variable, including bank erosion, stand mortality, toppling of trees, and upstream sources. Output can include fluvial transport out of a reach, overbank deposition onto the floodplain and floodplain channels, and abandonment of wood and burial in the main channel within the reach. Additional information that needs to be collected to categorize wood includes (1) mobility (mobile, new recruit, and embedded), (2) recruitment origin (bank erosion, landslide, mortality), (3) decay class (green leaves present, twigs present, secondary branches present, primary branches present, no branches, and log covered with growth), and (4) age (Martin and Benda 2001). Age is determined from a representative sample of increment bores that are dried and sanded to improve the accuracy of the ring count. Martin and Benda (2001) provide a detailed methodology for calculating wood budgets.

If a wood budget is to be done over multiple years, then tracking individual logs becomes important. One method that has been used is the tagging and cataloging of wood to (1) document changes in travel distance of wood through a treatment and control reach and (2) identify channel changes as a result of change in wood amount and residence time (Abbe et al. 2003). Logs can be tagged with aluminum or plastic, or can be painted, for identification, with different tags used during each field collection period to track new recruitment (Abbe and White 2000). Each log is measured, given a unique number, and mapped either with a global positioning satellite or with field mapping techniques. Other types of wood surveys that also may be useful in documenting changes to wood storage and its function in instream and floodplain reconnection projects are outlined in Chapter 8.

Flow regime is the fifth and final major category of physical monitoring we discuss. Reconnecting floodplain and main-stem channels can have dramatic effects on flow patterns, due to changes in hydraulic geometry. Lowering the bank level (through levee removal, setback, or reconnection of a specific floodplain channel) and increasing sinuosity of a main channel reduces the bank-full depth of a main channel, reduces channel slope, increases bed level, and increases the inundation of a floodplain and its accompanying channels. While the flow capacity of a main channel is reduced, the overall flow and water storage capacity of the floodplain reach can be increased with such actions. Floodplain reconnection and a reduction in channel incision also can reverse the unidirectional flow that occurs once a channel is disconnected from its floodplain and can allow greater exchange between surface flows and the hyporheic zone (Keller and Kondolf 1990). Greater exchange between surface and subsurface flows increases the retention and storage of water, thereby (1) reducing peak flows and sustaining summer baseflows, (2) regulating stream temperature (greater cooling in the summer and warming in the winter), and (3) enriching waters with nutrients for stream organisms (Edwards 1998; Bolton and Shellberg 2001).

Documenting changes to flow patterns requires some basic measurements of flow in the main channel and the reconnected floodplain. Dunne and Leopold (1978) provide a detailed explanation of the types of devices (stream gauges, staff gauges, and individual discharge measurements) that can be used to monitor surface flow. Stream gauges are preferred because they are permanent and continuous but require a higher degree of maintenance. A staff gauge is used when continuous readings are not needed and is measured with each field visit. Staff gauges that have Velcro attached to them (allowing sediment and organics to stick to the gauge) can be put in the floodplain to determine maximum flow height on the floodplain (Devries 2000). Individual discharge measurements also can be taken during field visits but may vary with location. All three methods can be used to monitor both instantaneous and continuous discharge, with a stream gauge being placed on a main channel and staff gauges and individual discharge measurement being taken in smaller, floodplain channels. Stream gauge locations also are proper places for the measurement of some of the preceding parameters, such as sediment discharge and hydraulic geometry.

Floodplain inundation is another parameter that can be measured for such situations and gives an indication of change in overall flood storage capacity and flood duration before and after restoration actions, as well as within control and treatment reaches (Kronvang et al. 1998; Steiger et al. 1998). A simple floodplain inundation index is

$$\text{Inundated floodplain area (length}^2)/\text{channel length (Steiger et al. 1998).}$$

This can be used to quantify the change in inundated floodplain area before and after restoration actions, as well as within control and treatment reaches, and will vary according to the magnitude of flooding. This type of approach was recently used on Brede, Cole, and Skerne River restoration projects in Europe, where they found that remeandering each of these rivers and connecting them to their respective floodplain resulted in a 41% to 67% decrease in main channel bank-full capacity. In the River Cole, the decrease in main channel bank-full capacity was coupled with a 70% increase in floodplain storage capacity and an increase of 40% in floodwater duration on the floodplain (Kronvang et al. 1998).

Mapping the vertical and horizontal movement of water in reconnected floodplain areas can help identify the degree of interchange that occurs between the surface and subsurface waters. Measuring hydraulic head, defined as water elevation and water pressure, and developing contour maps of floodplain areas are methods that can be used to monitor such interactions. Piezometers can be used to measure hydraulic head and to detect potential or actual vertical water movements (Figure 8; Edwards 1998). A detailed explanation of the placement of piezometers can be found in Geist et al. (1998). Head contour maps can suggest horizontal flow patterns, but the actual flow varies with the hydraulic conductivity of the sediments, which is a function of the sediments' porosity (Edwards 1998). The installation of piezometers in main-stem and floodplain channels also can help identify the source of water through the measurement of electric conductivity (Geist et al. 1998). Water source is another important determinant in the amount of surface–subsurface interaction that occurs between a main-stem and floodplain area.

Biological monitoring

Selecting appropriate biological response variables that are based in explicit monitoring objectives involves deciding (1) on which assemblage, species, or life stage to focus data collection efforts; and (2) what

Figure 8.
A piezometer installed on the Queets River in Washington State (photograph). This device (an open tube with one end buried in the sediment and the other end open to the atmosphere; Edwards 1998) can be used to measure hydraulic head, to sample invertebrates residing in the hyporheos, and to collect water samples for analysis of nutrient availability and primary productivity (Coe 2001). (Photograph and schematic courtesy of Holly Coe.)

taxonomic, ecological, or genetic attributes to measure. There are thousands of different species inhabiting the floodplain at varying life stages. We discuss the advantages and disadvantages, sampling strategies, and assessment protocols for five major groups: fish, aquatic invertebrates, periphyton, aquatic macrophytes, and riparian vegetation (Table 6). These are by no means the only assemblages relevant to floodplain monitoring, but they are the ones we found most commonly included in assessment protocols and referenced in the restoration literature. Although sampling methodologies are often assemblage specific, the myriad of ways in which these data can be analyzed generally are not. We discuss the multiple components of biodiversity and give specific examples of types of taxonomic, ecological, and genetic measures that may be used to monitor biological response to restoration—regardless of what specific biota are the focus of collection efforts. Because we advocate incorporating multiple measures within each of these categories, we conclude this section by reviewing the state of integrative bioassessment protocols as they apply to restoration monitoring for the river and its floodplain.

The first assemblage is fish. Comprising nearly half of the endangered vertebrate species in the United States (Warren and Burr 1994), fish are frequently the biological impetus for floodplain restoration. In general, fish are also very well-studied organisms: good taxonomic keys exist for most regions and much is known about geographic range, life history requirements, ecological niches, and disturbance tolerances (Lee 1980; Mayden 1992; Simon 1998). As indicator species for river conditions, the migratory nature of fish is both an advantage and a disadvantage. They integrate conditions over a large spatial scale but, because of this, are not always the best indicators of local site condition. Anadromous fish such as salmonids are particularly tricky as they reflect not only riverine conditions but also factors such as overfishing, pollution, oceanic conditions, and downstream migration blockages occurring in the larger salmon landscape.

Sampling strategies for fish vary greatly, depending on the habitat preferences and life history stage of specific species. Measurements of abundance generally are made by removal or mark–recapture methods such as by trapping or electrofishing (Table 6). Sampling can be fairly time intensive, but, depending on the type of information collected, subsequent laboratory time may not be required. Visual estimation such as snorkeling or videography (Hankin and Reeves 1988; Hatch et al. 1994) is another increasingly common method and may be preferable (or even required) when working with threatened or endangered species (Nielsen 1998). Regardless of the sampling strategy used, most fish monitoring can be done on live specimens, with fish subsequently released back into the habitats from which they were captured. Types of data commonly recorded include species identification, length and weight, and incidence of disease or other anomalies. Scale samples and stomach contents also can be collected from live specimens to determine age and diet, respectively. Specific strategies for sampling fish are discussed in greater detail in Chapter 8, as well as in Murphy and Willis (1996). For greater discussion of metrics applicable to analysis of fish community data, see Simon (1998).

The second biological assemblage is aquatic invertebrates. These invertebrates, such as insects, crustaceans, and mollusks, are ubiquitous and diverse, occupying nearly all microhabitats of the river from the roots of aquatic macrophytes to rock interstices deep within the hyporheic zone. As such, they exhibit a wide range in life history adaptations and tolerance to different forms of disturbance. In some cases, invertebrates are the specific motivation for restoration work. For example, conservation efforts directed toward endangered freshwater mussels in the eastern United States (Mignogno 1996). Whether or not invertebrates are the primary motivating force behind restoration, they are a key component of the aquatic food web—not only as a direct food source for fish, amphibians, and other predators but also as nutrient recyclers facilitating the breakdown of fungi, algae, and leaf litter. As adults, aquatic insects rely on riparian vegetation for pupation, emergence, feeding, and mating, thus, reflecting ecological conditions across both the terrestrial and aquatic zone. As with fish, much is already known about invertebrate life history requirements (Merit and Cummins 1996), and these organisms frequently are classified according to functional feeding group, voltinism (the number of life cycles repeated annually), habitat preference, and disturbance tolerance (Barber et al. 1999).

Invertebrates have been used in bioassessment strategies for decades, and well-developed sampling and assessment protocols exist throughout the world (Rosenberg and Resh 1993). For a review of invertebrate sampling protocols in place across the United States, see Barbour et al. (1999). One potential advantage of including invertebrates in restoration monitoring is their relatively quick response time: many species of invertebrates complete multiple generations within a year and are able to rapidly recolonize areas after disturbance (Figure 5; Biggs et al. 1998). Not all invertebrates are short lived, however, and those species that require multiple years to complete a life cycle reflect riverine conditions over a longer temporal scale. A variety of devices exist for sampling invertebrates in various habitats, from leaf packs to logjams (Table 6), and sampling is fairly straightforward. The time commitment comes in the laboratory, and a potential disadvantage in monitoring invertebrates is that it may be time consuming and costly to process many samples. Merritt et al. (1996) summarizes a variety of different sampling strategies for aquatic insects by habitat type and provides an extensive reference list for further reading.

The third assemblage is periphyton, the layer of biofilm growing on the submerged substrata, which includes species of bacteria, fungi, protozoans, and algae (Weitzel 1979). These attached microcommunitites contribute greatly to carbon cycling and to the accumulation and the retention of dissolved nutrients (Reynolds 1992). As a key producer in the riverine system, periphyton is an essential food source to invertebrates and fish. Growth, distribution, and community composition of periphyton are particularly sensitive to changes in turbidity, substrate, flow, and nutrient availability (Reynolds 1992; Kiffney and Bull 2000). Of the various assemblages that compose periphyton, diatomaceous algae are, perhaps, the most ubiquitous, well-studied, and frequently used indicators of water quality (Stevenson and Pan 1999). As a group, the diatoms are both species rich and relatively easily distinguished, and much is known about their natural history (Fore and Grafe 2002).

Although measures of periphyton assemblages have been used in European riverine monitoring programs for decades (Rott 1991), this group has only more recently been incorporated into river bioassessment protocols in the United States (Bahls 1993; Hill et al. 2000; Fore and Grafe 2002). With their rapid reproduction rates and short life cycles, periphyton respond rapidly to change and, thus, are particularly well suited to evaluating short-term impacts (Lowe and LaLiberte 1996). Analysis of diatom remains in floodplain sediments also may be very useful for drawing comparisons to historic conditions (Amoros and Van Urk 1989). Periphyton is easy and inexpensive to sample and is frequently collected by sampling substratum from within a known area, along transects, or by placement of artificial substrates such as colonization tiles (Figure 9; Lowe and LaLiberte 1996; Steinman and Lamberti 1996; Barbour et al. 1999). Commonly collected parameters include measures of total periphyton biomass, taxa composition, metabolic rates, chemical ratios, and structural and functional characteristics (Weitzel 1979; Steinman and Lamberti 1996; Stevenson and Pan 1999). Tolerance values for organic enrichment, metal contamination, or sedimentation also can be incorporated into periphyton indices for additional diagnostic information (Stevenson and Pan 1999; Fore and Grafe 2002).

The fourth assemblage is aquatic macrophytes. These photosynthetic plants, visible to the naked eye, are permanently or seasonally submerged in or floating on freshwater. This group can be further classified according to growth habitat: emergent, floating, leaved, free floating, and submerged (Fox 1992). In terms of ecological significance, macrophytes provide substrate for colonization by periphyton and habitat for fish and invertebrates, enhance nutrient interchange with substrate, and stabilize riverbeds and banks with their roots (Fox 1992). The

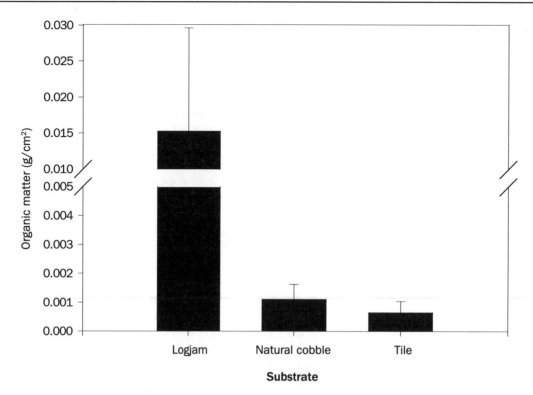

Figure 9.
Ash-free dry mass (AFDM) for total organic material collected from various natural and artificial substrate types within the Elwha River, Washington State. This data are being collected both to evaluate the productivity of constructed logjams relative to natural substrates and to provide baseline data prior to dam removal on the upper Elwha River. By evaluating the relationship between chlorophyll concentrations and total AFDM, researchers are able to quantify algal biomass available to invertebrate grazers. (Unpublished data courtesy of Holly Coe.)

presence of aquatic macrophytes also increases channel roughness, thereby attenuating high flows, enhancing sediment deposition, and increasing the diversity of flow conditions in the floodplain (Biggs et al. 1998). Through their influence on water flow and the distribution of flooding, aquatic macrophytes also have indirect effects on habitat availability and nutrient cycling in adjacent areas. In slower-moving backwater areas of the river floodplain (such as oxbow lakes), dense patches of emergent and floating macrophytes may dominate.

While aquatic macrophytes have not traditionally been a component of stream or river assessment protocols in North America, they are important constituents of wetland assessments (Adamus et al. 2001; Rader et al. 2001). In Europe, a number of studies examining large-scale floodplain restoration projects have evaluated the composition and distribution of macrophytes as indicators of hydrologic connectivity (Biggs et al. 1998; Tockner et al. 1999). Because macrophyte species exhibit varying tolerances to nutrient enrichment, flooding and flow regulation, and increased sediment loading and turbidity, this group is a useful indicator for monitoring floodplain conditions (USEPA 2002). Sampling strategies for macrophytes include traditional vegetation survey methods such as the quadrat method, transect sampling, and remote sensing (Table 6). Although good taxonomic field guides exist for most regions, identification to species may be difficult for some groups (e.g., grasses and sedges) or limited to a specific growing period. Bioassessment modules developed by the Wetlands Division of the U.S. Environmental Protection Agency contain a review of vegetative sampling methods and recommendations for successful metrics (USEPA 2002).

Riparian vegetation, the fifth and final biological assemblage we discuss, includes terrestrial and semiaquatic plant species growing in and adjacent to the floodplain. These plants greatly influence the degree of lateral connectivity between a river and its floodplain—through input of wood and other organic materials, bank stabilization, shading, evapotranspiration, and a variety of other functions (Gregory et al. 1991). By serving as migration corridors for plants and animals, riparian zones link aquatic and terrestrial zones. They also play a key role in regulating the vertical connectivity of floodplains by influencing the movement of water through soils. The relationship between a river and adjacent riparian vegetation is by no means unidirectional. Species composition and successional patterns of riparian vegetation reflect frequency, depth, and duration of flooding (Naiman et al. 1998). As rivers are channelized and flood pulses dulled by dams and other hydromodifications, riparian vegetation generally becomes more homogenous, with fewer seral stages and a higher proportion of terrestrial and invasive species (Ward and Stanford 1995). One advantage to monitoring response of riparian vegetation is its sessile nature; unlike fish and other more mobile organisms, riparian vegetation is unable to escape disturbance. A potential disadvantage is the long recovery period often required before restoration response is detected (Roni et al. 2002).

Because floodplain restoration frequently occurs within the riparian zone (e.g., levee removal, reforestation projects, etc.), it often is particularly relevant to monitor riparian vegetation. Sampling strategies for riparian vegetation may be very similar to those applied for aquatic macrophytes (e.g., quadrat plots, transect surveys, etc.; Table 6). When covering large areas of the floodplain, remote sensing with aerial photographs, satellite, and LIDAR imagery may be particularly useful for tracking change over time (Lefsky et al. 2001). Metrics frequently calculated to describe riparian vegetation include stand age, taxa richness, plant biomass, basal density, canopy heights, and various indices of canopy structure. Riparian vegetation can be further classified as to life history strategy (e.g., invader versus avoider), reproductive strategy (e.g., mode of seed dispersal), and a variety of other morphological adaptations riparian plants have devised to survive in the floodplain (Naiman et al. 1998). For a more detailed review of indicator and assessment methods for riparian zones, see Innis et al. (2000). This subject also is covered in greater detail in Chapter 4.

Different components of the biota reflect unique information about ecosystem structure and degree of floodplain connectivity (Tockner et al. 1999), and are sensitive to diverse forms of disturbance at varying spatial and temporal scales (Hughes et al. 2000). Therefore, we recommend that biological monitoring programs for floodplain restoration evaluate multiple assemblages. Although much current legislation focuses on species as the unit for conservation (e.g., the U.S. Endangered Species Act [ESA]), this may not always be the most biologically meaningful scale for monitoring ecosystem health or restoration success (Meffe 1994; Karr and Chu 1999). Even when a single species group is the incentive for restoration work, a multiassemblage approach to assessment holds many advantages. The assumption in monitoring only one indicator species is that other elements of the biota are responding similarly to restoration. Given the different habitat requirements and diversity of ecological niches occupied by various species (Noss 1994), this is often not the case. In the case of threatened and endangered salmon in the Pacific Northwest, invertebrates, amphibians, diatoms, and other stream organisms are integral parts of the aquatic food web upon which these imperiled fish depend.

After selecting biological assemblages on which to focus monitoring efforts, the next step is determining what types of data to collect about those species or groups. Biological information (attributes) can be organized in a multiplicity of ways, ranging from the level of the individual to the landscape (Table 7). Selected attributes should be (1) based on project objectives and monitoring hypotheses, (2) ecologically meaningful, and (3) linked to concurrent physical or chemical monitoring. We have organized our discussion of potential attributes around three major categories of biodiversity: taxonomic, ecological, and genetic. For the most part, all of the potential attributes discussed below can be applied to analysis of any assemblage, be it fish, invertebrates, periphyton, macrophytes, riparian vegetation, or another element of the biota. Because we recommend selecting attributes from multiple categories, we conclude with a discussion of bioassessment protocols that integrate diverse measures (Table 7).

Taxonomic information, the hierarchical classification of organisms based on phenotypic and genotypic characteristics, can be collected at various levels (Table 7). Taxonomic richness commonly is expressed as the number of unique taxa present—such as within a specific assemblage (e.g., how many different species of diatoms occur in a specific river reach) or perhaps the number of taxa present across multiple assemblages within a particular floodplain complex. Taxonomic diversity is a weighted average of taxa richness that accounts for the relative abundance of different taxa. Determining the appropriate taxonomic and spatial level at which to focus monitoring efforts will be guided by project hypotheses. For example, a subset of taxa richness measurements could focus on threatened populations of native species. The population of a given species also can be described in terms of information collected at the individual level for attributes such as age, growth, fitness, diet, or disease (Karr and Chu 1999).

Table 7.
Four categories of biological attributes to analyze which are applicable to floodplain monitoring.

Category	Level or type	Selected attributes
Taxonomic	Community	Number of assemblages, taxonomic composition, spatial distribution
	Assemblage	Total number and relative abundance of taxa, presence of indicator taxa, dominance
	Population	Total abundance, density, biomass, age or size structure, prevalence of disease or other anomalies
	Individual	Fitness, length, growth, disease, survival, age
Ecological	Trophic structure	Fish feeding guilds, functional feeding group for invertebrates, etc.
	Disturbance tolerance	Tolerance to gradients of temperature, salinity, oxygen, sedimentation, light, nutrient enrichment, inundation, etc.
	Invasive species	Proportion of native and exotic taxa, extent of upland plant species within the riparian zone
	Mode of existence	Epilithic vs. epiphytic (algae), emergent vs. free-floating (macrophytes), clingers vs. swimmers (invertebrates)
	Reproductive strategy	Complete vs. incomplete metamorphosis (invertebrates), sexual vs. asexual reproduction (plants)
Genetic	Within individuals	Heterozygosity (proportion of gene loci in an individual that contains alternative forms of alleles), mutation
	Within populations	Heterozygosity of individuals within a population, types and frequencies of alleles present, mutation rate
	Among populations	Mean genetic differences among geographic locations, gene flow
Assessment models	Multimetric	Index of Biological Integrity (Karr and Chu 1999), Rapid Bioassessment Protocols (Barbour et al. 1999)
	Multivariate	River Invertebrate Prediction and Classification System (Wright et al. 2000; Reynoldson et al. 2001)

In addition to taxonomic designations, organisms can be classified in various ecological ways. Some examples include feeding guilds for fish, reproductive strategies of invertebrates, light requirements of aquatic macrophytes, drought tolerance of riparian vegetation, and organic enrichment tolerance of periphyton (Table 7). Associating this type of ecological information with taxa distribution patterns greatly enhances our ability to interpret biological monitoring data. For example, the proportion of multivoltine (completing multiple life cycles within one year) to semivoltine (requiring more than two years) invertebrates may reveal information about the frequency and distribution of disturbance events such as floods or debris flows, a high proportion of drought-tolerant plant species within the floodplain may indicate a lack of hydrologic connection with the main channel, and high numbers of invasive warmwater species of fishes often signal a profound shift in temperature regime. These are but a few examples of the types of ecological attributes potentially useful for evaluating floodplain restoration.

In addition to the great ecological diversity found among various assemblages and species, large amounts of genetic variation also occurs within each species. The level of genetic diversity found within a species is a function of variation within individuals, among individuals within a population, and among populations (Meffe 1994). This genetic diversity is lost when habitat destruction, migration blockages, and other anthropomorphic activities in the floodplain isolate populations (Meffe 1994). Hatchery operations and selective harvesting of fish also may lead to loss of heterozygosity (genetic diversity within a population) and potentially may decrease population viability (Wang et al. 2002). In terms of restoration monitoring, genetic analysis can help identify populations in particular need of protection and aid in distinguishing between species that may be very similar morphologically. Two examples of genetic analysis from the Pacific Northwest are the evolutionary significant unit approach currently applied to protection of endangered populations of Pacific salmon under ESA (Waples 1991) and the hybridization between bull trout *Salvelinus confluentus* (a threatened species under the ESA) and Dolly Varden *S. malma* (Taylor et al. 2001). Orians et al. (1990) provides an overview on the conservation of genetic diversity for a variety of species, while Echelle (1991) and Ryman and Utter (1987) discuss genetic diversity in fishes.

In addition to looking at various aspects of diversity individually, assessment tools developed over the last two decades provide a means of integrating biological information from different categories. The two most common approaches currently used today are multivariate models (Wright et al. 2000; Reynoldson et al. 2001) and multimetric indexes (Davis and Simon 1995; Karr and Chu 1999). These models generally include measures of taxa richness and composition, disturbance tolerance, trophic structure, individual health, and population attributes (Barbour et al. 1999). In the multivariate approach, a predictive model is developed based on a large data set of reference (minimally disturbed) sites (Reynoldson et al. 2001). The level of impairment at a given sample site then is determined by comparison to the appropriate reference group. Multimetric indexes, such as an index of biological integrity (IBI), integrate empirically tested attributes (metrics) to provide a numeric synthesis of the biological dimensions of site condition (Karr and Chu 1999). As with multivariate models, IBIs and other multimetric indexes are regionally calibrated based on ecoregion designations and local reference conditions. Barbour et al. (1999) provides an overview of both methods.

Summary

Just as there is no cookbook to follow for restoring heterogeneous floodplains habitats (Kondolf 1998), there are no easy-to-follow recipes directing exactly how to monitor those diverse efforts. As Frissell and Ralph (1998) state in their review of stream and watershed restoration in the Pacific Coastal ecoregion, "no standard checklist, blueprint, or catalog exists for monitoring and evaluation that can be applied to all river and stream restoration programs and projects." Restoration ecology is an emerging science, with floodplain restoration one of the youngest. Even if there were enough existing data on successful floodplain monitoring studies for us to recommend specific sampling protocols, we do not advocate trying to fit all monitoring programs into the same model, although some common metrics between projects are likely. Instead, build a monitoring plan from a solid foundation of clearly defined restoration objectives that are linked to testable hypotheses. We will learn far more from monitoring efforts designed as experiments because researchers devise novel ways of answering new and different questions. Similar questions and results will be the outcome of monitoring efforts that occur in many places over a long enough time period.

Designing an effective floodplain-monitoring program is no easy task, and what we provided with this chapter is a toolbox. Along with a brief background on what biophysical elements constitute a floodplain, the ways in which these systems have been modified, and some current approaches to restoring floodplain processes, we have discussed a number of different physical and biological parameters that may be of interest in floodplain monitoring (Tables 5 and 6) and presented different approaches to analyzing these data (Table 7). Within the confines of a single chapter, we have only introduced the basics on each of these topics, and we strongly encourage readers to consult more detailed references on specific topics of interest. For any floodplain restoration monitoring plan we recommend the following:

1. Identify goals and objectives for the project(s).
2. Develop hypotheses for project outcomes. Formulate a study design that includes, where possible, replication and use of reference sites, and use appropriate statistical methods to test hypotheses.
3. Select study parameters and sampling protocols that help answer the hypotheses, and allow the use of a study design that includes replication and reference sites.
4. Choose the appropriate scales to monitor based on the hypotheses, study design, study parameters, and sampling protocols. In many cases, this will include multiple scales.
5. Make timing of when to monitor a function of the temporal heterogeneity and seasonality of the study parameters. Make sure natural variability is quantified.
6. Include both physical and biological metrics.

7. Make physical monitoring focus on process, such as rates of change in water, sediment, wood, and nutrients, rather than just amount.

8. Make biological monitoring focus on a multispecies or a multiassemblage approach that integrates a variety of different measurements.

9. Link the physical and biological metrics, where possible, to enhance data interpretation.

10. Take an integrated approach by addressing both physical processes and ecological outcomes and evaluating projects within a watershed context.

Regardless of how well designed a particular monitoring study may be, it is relatively pointless if results are not communicated beyond the immediate project participants. The whole point of the exercise is to determine whether these various restoration schemes are having any positive or negative effects. The field of restoration ecology, in general, is in need of such information. Project engineers and designers, scientists conducting evaluations, resource managers allocating restoration funds, and the public voting on conservation measures all need such information to make better informed decisions. Even when the results of a particular monitoring study are inconclusive, this is instructive in and of itself in guiding the design of future studies. Within the scientific community, the most accepted method of communicating results is through the peer-reviewed literature. In addition to formal publications in the scientific literature, we recommend that monitoring results also be communicated through other media such as community forums, Web-based publications, and technical reports.

Acknowledgments

We would like to thank Steve Ralph, Tim Beechie, Eric Iwamoto, Phil Roni, and Ed Quimby for their thoughtful comments. We also would like to thank Tim Abbe, Phil Petersen, Leslie Reid, Emily Stanley, Dan Cromwell, Ali Senaur, Tim Beechie, J. Biggs, and Holly Coe for use of their photographs, schematics, and figures.

References

Abbe, T. B. 2000. Patterns, mechanics, and geomorphic effects of wood debris accumulations in a forest river system. Doctoral dissertation. University of Washington, Seattle.

Abbe, T. B., and D. R. Montgomery. 1996. Large woody debris jams, channel hydraulics, and habitat formation in large rivers. Regulated Rivers: Research and Management 12:201–221.

Abbe, T. B., G. R. Pess, D. R. Montgomery, and K. L. Fetherston. 2003. Integrating log jam technology into river rehabilitation. Pages 443–482 in S. Bolton, D. R. Montgomery, and D. Booth, editors. Restoration of Puget Sound rivers. University of Washington Press, Seattle.

Abbe, T. B., and M. L. White. 2000. Wood debris tracking and ELJ performance report, North Fork Stillaguamish habitat enhancement project 1998-1999. Prepared for U.S. Army Corps of Engineers, Seattle District. Washington Trout, Duvall, Washington.

Adamus, P., T. J. Danielson, and A. Gonyaw. 2001. Indicators for monitoring biological integrity of inland, freshwater wetlands: a survey of North American technical literature (1990-2000). U.S. Environmental Protection Agency, Office of Water, EPA 843-R-01 Washington, D.C. Online at http://www.epa.gov/owow/ wetlands/bawwg/monidicators.pdf [Accessed 12 May 2003].

Allaby, A., and M. Allaby, editors. 1999. A dictionary of earth sciences. Oxford University Press, United Kingdom. Online at http://www.xrefer.com [Accessed 12 May 2003].

Amoros, C., and G. Van Urk. 1989. Paleoecological analyses of large rivers: some principles and methods. Pages 143–165 in G. E. Petts, H. Möller, and A. L. Roux, editors. Historical change of large alluvial rivers: Western Europe. Wiley, Chichester, UK.

Bahls, L. L. 1993. Periphyton bioassessment methods for Montana streams. Montana Water Quality Bureau, Department of Health and Environmental Science, Helena.

Baltz, D. M., and P. B. Moyle. 1993. Invasion resistance to introduced species by a native assemblage of California stream fishes. Ecological Applications 3:246–255.

Barbour, M. T., J. Gerritsen, B. D. Snyder, and J. B. Stribling. 1999. Rapid bioassessment protocols for use in streams and wadeable rivers: periphyton, benthic macroinvertebrates and fish, 2nd edition. U.S. Environmental Protection Agency, Office of Water, EPA 841-B-99-002. Washington, D.C. Available online at http://www.epa.gov/owowwtr1/ monitoring/rbp/index. html [Accessed 12 May 2003].

Bednarek, A. T. 2001. Undamming rivers: a review of the ecological impacts of dam removal. Environmental Management 27:803–814.

Beechie, T. J. 2001. Empirical predictions of annual bed load travel distance, and implications for salmonid habitat restoration and protection. Earth Surface Processes and Landforms 26:1025–1034.

Beechie, T., E. Beamer, and L. Wasserman. 1994. Estimating coho salmon rearing habitat and smolt production losses in a large river basin, and implications for habitat restoration. North American Journal of Fisheries Management 14:797–811.

Beechie, T. J., B. D. Collins, and G. R. Pess. 2001. Holocene and recent geomorphic processes, land use, and salmonid habitat in two north Puget Sound river basins. Pages 37–54 in J. B. Dorava, D. R. Montgomery, F. Fitzpatrick, and B. Palcsak, editors. Geomorphic processes and riverine habitat—water science and application, volume 4. American Geophysical Union, Washington D.C.

Biggs, J., A. Corfield, P. Grøn, H. O. Hansen, D. Walker, M. Whitfield, and P. Williams. 1998. Restoration of the rivers Brede, Cole, and Skerne: a joint Danish and British EU-LIFE demonstration project, V—short-term impacts on the conservation value of aquatic macroinvertebrate and macrophyte assemblages. Aquatic Conservation: Marine and Freshwater Ecosystems 8:241–255.

Bilby, R. E., and P. A. Bisson. 1998. Function and distribution of large woody debris. Pages 324–346 in R. J. Naiman and R. E. Bilby, editors. River ecology and management: lessons from the Pacific Coast ecoregion. Springer, New York.

Bisson, P. A., J. L. Nielsen, R. A. Palmason, and L. E. Grove. 1982. A system of naming habitat types in small streams, with examples of habitat utilization by salmonids during low stream flows. Pages 62–73 in N. B. Armantrout, editor. Acquisition and utilization of aquatic habitat inventory information. American Fisheries Society, Bethesda, Maryland.

Bolton, S., and J. Shellberg. 2001. White Paper: ecological issues in floodplains and river corridors. Prepared for the Washington Department of Fish and Wildlife, Washington Department of Ecology, and Washington Department of Transportation. Center for Streamside Studies, University of Washington, Seattle.

Bonnell, R. G. 1991. Construction, operation, and evaluation of groundwater-fed side channels for chum salmon in British Columbia. Pages 109–124 in J. Colt and R. J. White, editors. Fisheries Bioengineering Symposium. American Fisheries Society, Symposium 10, Bethesda, Maryland.

Boon, P. J. 1999. River restoration in five dimensions. Aquatic Conservation: Marine and Freshwater Ecosystems 8:257–264.

Booth, D. B., and C. R. Jackson. 1997. Urbanization of aquatic systems: degradation thresholds, stormwater detention, and the limits of mitigation. Journal of the American Water Resources Association 22:1–19.

Bowen, Z. H., and R. G. Waltermire. 2002. Evaluation of light detection and ranging (LIDAR) for measuring river corridor topography. Journal of the American Water Resources Association 38:33–41.

Brookes, A. 1988. Channelized rivers: perspectives for environmental management. Wiley, Chichester, UK.

Brown, A. G. 2002. Learning from the past: paleohydrology and paleoecology. Freshwater Biology 47:817–829.

Bryant, M. D. 1988. Gravel pit ponds as habitat enhancement for juvenile coho salmon. U.S. Forest Service, Pacific Northwest Research Station, General Technical Report PNW-GTR-212, Portland, Oregon.

Cederholm, C. J., and W. J. Scarlett. 1991. The beaded channel: a low-cost technique for enhancing winter habitat of coho salmon. Pages 104–108 in J. Colt and R. J. White, editors. Fisheries Bioengineering Symposium. American Fisheries Society, Symposium 10, Bethesda, Maryland.

Cederholm, C. J., W. J. Scarlett, and N. P. Peterson. 1988. Low-cost enhancement technique for winter habitat of juvenile coho salmon. North American Journal of Fisheries Management 8:438–441.

Coe, H. J. 2001. Distribution patterns of hyporheic fauna in a riparian floodplain terrace, Queets River, Washington. Master's thesis. University of Washington, Seattle.

Collins, B. D., and D. R. Montgomery. 2001. Importance of archival and process studies to characterizing pre-settlement riverine geomorphic processes and habitat in the Puget Lowland. Pages 227–243 in J. M. Dorava, D. R. Montgomery, B. B. Palcsak, and F. A. Fitzpatrick, editors. Geomorphic processes and riverine habitat: water and science application 4. American Geophysical Union, Washington, D.C.

Collins, B. D., and D. R. Montgomery. 2002. Forest development, wood jams, and restoration of floodplain rivers in the Puget Lowland, Washington. Restoration Ecology 11:237–247.

Collins, B. D., D. R. Montgomery, and A. D. Haas. 2002. Historical changes in the distribution and functions of large wood in Puget Lowland rivers. Canadian Journal of Fisheries and Aquatic Sciences 59:66–76.

Collins, B. D., D. R. Montgomery, and A. J. Sheikh. 2003. Reconstructing the historic riverine landscape of the Puget Lowland. Pages 79–128 in S. Bolton, D. R. Montgomery, and D. Booth, editors. Restoration of Puget Sound rivers. University of Washington Press, Seattle.

Conquest, L. L., and S. C. Ralph. 1998. Statistical design and analysis for monitoring and assessment. Pages 455–465 in R. J. Naiman and R. E. Bilby, editors. River ecology and management: lessons from the Pacific coastal ecoregion. Springer, New York.

Cowan, L. 1991. Physical characteristics and intragravel survival of chum salmon in developed and natural groundwater channels in Washington. Pages 125–131 in J. Colt and R. J. White, editors. Fisheries Bioengineering Symposium. American Fisheries Society, Symposium 10, Bethesda, Maryland.

Cowardin, L. M., V. Carter, F. C. Golet, and E. T. LaRoe. 1995. Classification of wetlands and deepwater habitats of the United States. U.S. Department of Interior, U.S. Fish and Wildlife Service, FWS/OBS-79/31, Washington, D.C.

Cowx, I. G., and R. L. Welcomme, editors. 1998. Rehabilitation of rivers for fish. Food and Agriculture Organization of the United Nations. Fishing News Books, Oxford, UK.

Davis, W. S., and T. P. Simon, editors. 1995. Biological assessment and criteria: tools for water resource planning and decision making. Lewis, Boca Raton, Florida.

Devries, P. 2000. Scour in low gradient gravel bed stream: patterns, processes, and implications for the survival of salmonid embryos. Doctoral dissertation. Water resource series technical report no. 160. Department of Civil Engineering, University of Washington, Seattle.

Dunne, T., and L. Leopold. 1978. Water in environmental planning. Freeman, New York.

Echelle, A. A. 1991. Conservation genetics and genetic diversity in freshwater fishes of western North America. Pages 141–153 in W. L. Minckley and J. E. Deacon, editors. Battle against extinction: native fish management in the American West. University of Arizona Press, Tucson.

Edwards, R. T. 1998. The hyporheic zone. Pages 399–429 in R. J. Naiman and R. E. Bilby, editors. River ecology and management. Springer, New York.

Fausch, K. D., J. R. Karr, and P. R. Yant. 1984. Regional application of an index of biotic integrity based on stream fish communities. Transactions of the American Fisheries Society 113:39–55.

Florsheim, J. L., and J. F. Mount. 2000. Intentional levee breaching as a floodplain restoration tool: monitoring floodplain topography, Cosumnes River, California. American Geophysical Union, Spring Meeting, Boston.

Fore, L. S., and C. S. Grafe. 2002. River diatom index. Pages 5-1 to 5-30 in C. S. Grafe, editor. Idaho river ecological assessment framework: an integrated approach. Idaho Department of Environmental Quality, Boise. (Also available from http://www.deq.state.id.us/water/surface_water/wbag/ Assessment-River-Complete.pdf [Accessed 12 May 2003]).

Fox, A. M. 1992. Macrophytes. Pages 216-233 in P. Calow and G. E. Petts, editors. The rivers handbook: volume 1. Blackwell Scientific Publications, Cambridge, Massachusetts.

Frissell, C. A., W. L. Liss, C. E. Warren, and M. D. Hurley. 1986. A hierarchical framework for stream habitat classification: viewing streams in a watershed context. Environmental Management 10:199-214.

Frissell, C. A., and S. C. Ralph. 1998. Stream and watershed restoration. Pages 599-624 in R. J. Naiman and R. E. Bilby, editors. River ecology and management. Springer, New York.

Geist, D. R., M. C. Joy, D. R. Lee, and T. Gonser. 1998. A method for installing piezometers in large cobble bed rivers. Groundwater Management and Remediation Winter:78-82.

Gørtz, P. 1998. Effects of stream restoration on the macroinvertebrate community in the River Esrom, Denmark. Aquatic Conservation: Marine and Freshwater Ecosystems 8:115-130.

Gregory, S. B., F. J. Swanson, W. A. McKee, and K. W. Cummins. 1991. An ecosystem perspective of riparian zones. Bioscience 41:540-551.

Hall, J. L., R. K. Timm, and R. C. Wissmar. 2000. Physical and biotic factors affecting use of riparian ponds by sockeye salmon (Oncorhynchus nerka). Pages 89-94 in P. J. Wigington and R. L. Beschta, editors. Proceedings of the American Water Resources Association International Conference on Riparian Ecology and Management in Multi-Land Use Watersheds, August 27-30, 2000, Portland, Oregon. American Water Resources Association, Herndon, Virginia.

Hankin, D. G., and G. H. Reeves. 1988. Estimating total fish abundance and total habitat area in small streams based on visual estimation methods. Canadian Journal of Fisheries and Aquatic Sciences 45:834-844.

Harrelson, C. C., C. L. Rawlins, and J. P. Potyondy. 1994. Stream channel reference sites: an illustrated guide to field technique. U.S. Forest Service, General Technical Report RM-245, Fort Collins, Colorado.

Hart, D. D., and N. L. Poff. 2002. A special section on dam removal and river restoration. Bioscience 52:653-655.

Harvey, M. D., D. S. Biedenharm, and P. Combs. 1988. Adjustments of Red River following removal of the Great Raft in 1873. EOS (Transactions of the American Geophysical Union) 69(18):567.

Hatch, D. R., M. Schwartzberg, and P. R. Mundy. 1994. Estimation of Pacific salmon escapement with a time-lapse video recording technique. North American Journal of Fisheries Management 14:626-635.

Hauer, F. R., and V. H. Resh. 1996. Benthic macroinvertebrates. Pages 339-369 in F. R. Hauer and G. A. Lamberti, editors. Methods in stream ecology. Academic Press, San Diego, California.

Hayslip, G. 2003. Biological assessment using benthic macroinvertebrates for wadeable streams in the Pacific Northwest. U.S. Environmental Protection Agency, Region 10, Office of Environmental Assessment, Seattle.

Hey, R. D. 1994. Environmentally sensitive river engineering. Pages 337-362 in P. Calow and G. E. Petts, editors. The rivers handbook: hydrological and ecological principles; volume two. Blackwell Scientific Publications, Oxford, UK.

Hill, B. H., A. T. Herlihy, P. R. Kaufmann, R. J. Stevenson, F. H. McCormick, and C. B. Johnson. 2000. Use of periphyton assemblage data as an index of biotic integrity. Journal of the North American Benthological Society 19:50-67.

Hocutt, C. H., and J. R. Stauffer, Jr. 1980. Biological monitoring of fish: proceedings of the American Fisheries Society symposium on biomonitoring. Lexington Books, Lexington, Massachusetts.

Holmes, N. T. H., and M. B. Nielsen. 1998. Restoration of the rivers Brede, Cole, and Skerne: a joint Danish and British EU-LIFE demonstration project, I-setting up and delivery of the project. Aquatic Conservation: Marine and Freshwater Ecosystems 8:185-196.

Hughes, R. M. 1995. Defining acceptable biological status by comparing with reference conditions. Pages 31-47 in W. S. Davis and T. P. Simon, editors. Biological assessment and criteria: tools for water resource planning and decision making. Lewis Publishers, Boca Raton, Florida.

Hughes, R. M., P. R. Kaufmann, A. T. Herlihy, T. M. Kincaid, L. Reynolds, and D. P. Larsen. 1998. A process for developing and evaluating indices of fish assemblage integrity. Canadian Journal of Fisheries and Aquatic Sciences 55:1618-1631.

Hughes, R. M., S. G. Paulsen, and J. L. Stoddard. 2000. EMAP-surface waters: a multisasemblage, probability survey of ecological integrity in the U. S. A. Hydrobiologia 422:429-443.

Innis, S. A., R. J. Naiman, and S. R. Elliott. 2000. Indicators and assessment methods for measuring the ecological integrity of semi-aquatic terrestrial environments. Hydrobiologia 422:111-131.

Junk, W. J., P. B. Bayley, and R. E. Sparks. 1989. The flood pulse concept in river-floodplain systems. Pages 110-127 in D. P. Dodge, editor. Proceedings of the International Large River Symposium. Canadian Special Publications of Fisheries and Aquatic Sciences 106.

Karr, J. R., and E. W. Chu. 1999. Restoring life in running waters: better biological monitoring. Island Press, Washington, D.C.

Keller, E. A., and G. M. Kondolf. 1990. Groundwater and fluvial processes: selected observations. Geological Society of America Special Paper 252:319-340.

Kelly, F. L., and J. J. Bracken. 1998. Fisheries enhancement of the Rye Water, a lowland river in Ireland. Aquatic Conservation: Marine and Freshwater Ecosystems 8:131-143.

Kelsey, H. M., R. Lamberson, and M. A. Madej. 1987. Stochastic model for the long-term transport of stored sediment in a river channel. Water Resources Research 23:1738-1750.

Kiffney, P. M., and J. B. Bull. 2000. Factors controlling periphyton accrual during summer in headwater streams of southwestern British Columbia, Canada. Journal of Freshwater Ecology 15:339–353.

Koebel, J. W., Jr. 1995. An historical perspective on the Kissimmee River Restoration Project. Restoration Ecology 3:149–159.

Kondolf, G. M. 1998. Lessons learned from river restoration projects in California. Aquatic Conservation: Marine and Freshwater Ecosystems 8:39–52.

Kronvang, B., L. M. Svendsen, A. Brookes, K. Fisher, B. Moller, O. Ottosen, M. Neson, and D. Sear. 1998. Restoration of the rivers Brede, Cole, and Skerne: a joint Danish and British EU-LIFE demonstration project, III-Channel morphology, hydrodynamics, and transport of sediment and nutrients. Aquatic Conservation: Marine and Freshwater Ecosystems 8:209–222.

Lee, D. S. 1980. Atlas of North American freshwater fishes. North Carolina Museum of Natural History, Raleigh, North Carolina.

Lefsky, M. A., W. B. Cohen, T. A. Spies. 2001. An evaluation of alternate remote sensing products for forest inventory, monitoring, and mapping of Douglas-fir forests in western Oregon. Canadian Journal of Forest Research 31:78–87.

Leonard, S., G. Staidl, J. Fogg, K. Gebhardt, W. Hagenbuck, and D. Pritchard. 1992. Riparian area management: procedures for ecological site inventory–with special reference to riparian-wetland sites. U.S. Department of the Interior, Bureau of Land Management, Denver.

Leopold, L. B. 1994. A view of the river. Harvard University Press, Cambridge, Massachusetts.

Leopold, L. B., M. G. Wolman, and J. P. Miller. 1964. Fluvial processes in geomorphology. Dover Publications, Inc., New York.

Li, H. W., and J. L. Li. 1996. Fish community composition. Pages 391–406 in F. R. Hauer and G. A. Lamberti, editors. Methods in stream ecology. Academic Press, San Diego, California.

Ligon, F. K., W. E. Dietrich, and W. J. Trush. 1995. Downstream ecological effects of dams: a geomorphic perspective. Bioscience 45:183–192.

Lister, D. B., and R. J. Finnigan. 1997. Rehabilitating off-channel habitat. Pages 7–1 to 7–29 in P. A. Slaney and D. Zaldokas, editors. Fish habitat rehabilitation procedures. Watershed Restoration Technical Circular No. 9, Watershed Restoration Program, Ministry of Environment, Lands and Parks and Ministry of Forests, Victoria, BC.

Lowe, R. L., and G. D. LaLiberte. 1996. Benthic stream algae: distribution and structure. Pages 269–293 in F. R. Hauer and G. A. Lamberti, editors. Methods in stream ecology. Academic Press, San Diego, California.

Lowery, W. M. 1968. The Red. Pages 53–73 in E. A. Davis, editor. The rivers and bayous of Louisiana. Louisiana Education Research Association, Baton Rouge.

Madej, M. A. 1992. Changes in channel-stored sediment, Redwood Creek, CA, 1947 to 1980. U.S. Geological Survey, Open-file Report 92–34, Denver.

Madej, M. A. 1999. Temporal and spatial variability in thalweg profiles of a gravel-bed river. Earth Surface Processes and Landforms 24:1153–1169.

Martin, D. J., and L. E. Benda. 2001. Patterns of instream wood recruitment and transport at the watershed scale. Transactions of the American Fisheries Society 130:940–958.

Mayden, R. G., editor. 1992. Systematics, historical ecology, and North American freshwater fishes. Stanford University Press, Palo Alto, California.

McMahon, G., S. M. Gregonis, S. W. Waltman, J. M. Omernik, T. D. Thorson, J. A. Freeouf, A. H. Rorick, and J. E. Keys. 2001. Developing a spatial framework of common ecological regions for the conterminous United States. Environmental Management 28:293–316.

Meffe, G. K. 1994. Principles of conservation biology. Sinauer Associates, Sunderland, Massachusetts.

Merritt, R. W., and K. W. Cummins, editors. 1996. An introduction to the aquatic insects of North America. Kendall Hunt Publishing Company, Dubuque, Iowa.

Merritt, R. W., V. H. Resh, and K. W. Cummins. 1996. Design of aquatic insect studies: collecting, sampling and rearing procedures. Pages 12–28 in R. W. Merritt and K. W. Cummins, editors. An introduction to the aquatic insects of North America. Kendall Hunt Publishing Company, Dubuque, Iowa.

Mignogno, D. C. 1996. Freshwater mussel conservation and the Endangered Species Act. Journal of Shellfish Research 15:486.

Murphy, B. R., and D. W. Willis, editors. 1996. Fisheries techniques. 2nd edition. American Fisheries Society, Bethesda, Maryland.

Murphy, K. J., E. Castella, B. Clément, J. M. Hills, P. Obradlik, I. D. Pulford, E. Schneider, and M. C. D. Speight. 1994. Biotic indicators of riverine wetland ecosystem functioning. Pages 659–682 in W. J. Mitsch, editor. Global wetlands: old world and new. Elsevier, New York.

Myers, L. H. 1989. Riparian area management: inventory and monitoring riparian areas. Publication TR-1737-3. U.S. Department of the Interior, Bureau of Land Management, Denver.

Naiman, R. J., H. Decamps, and M. M. Pollock. 1993. The role of riparian corridors in maintaining regional biodiversity. Ecological Applications 3:209–212.

Naiman, R. J., K. L. Fetherston, S. J. McKary, and J. Chen. 1998. Riparian forests. Pages 289–323 in R. J. Naiman and R. E. Bilby, editors. River ecology and management. Springer, New York.

Nickelson, T. E., J. D. Rodgers, S. L. Johnson, and M. F. Solazzi. 1992. Seasonal changes in habitat use by juvenile coho salmon (Oncorhynchus kisutch) in Oregon coastal streams. Canadian Journal of Fisheries and Aquatic Sciences 49:783–789.

Nielsen, J. L. 1998. Electrofishing California's endangered fish populations. Fisheries 23:6–12.

Norman, D. K. 1998. Reclamation of flood-plain sand and gravel pits as off-channel salmon habitat. Washington Geology 26(2/3):21–28.

Noss, R. F. 1994. Hierarchical indicators for monitoring changes in biodiversity. Pages 79–80 in G. K. Meffe, editors. Principles of conservation biology. Sinauer Associates, Sunderland, Massachusetts.

Olson-Rutz, K. M., and C. B. Marlow. 1992. Analysis and interpretation of stream channel cross-section data. North American Journal of Fisheries Management 12:55–61.

Orians, G. H., G. M. Brown, W. E. Kunin, and J. E. Swierzbinski, editors. 1990. The preservation and valuation of biological resources. University of Washington Press, Seattle.

Pess, G. R., B. D. Collins, M. Pollock, T. J. Beechie, A. Haas, and S. Grigsby. 1999. Historic and current factors that limit coho salmon production in the Stillaguamish River basin, Washington State: implications for salmonid habitat protection and restoration. Tulalip Tribes, Marysville, Washington.

Peterson, N. P. 1980. The role of spring ponds in the winter ecology and natural production of coho salmon (*Oncorhynchus nerka*) on the Olympic peninsula, Washington. Master's thesis. University of Washington, Seattle.

Peterson, N. P. 1982a. Population characteristics of juvenile coho salmon (*Oncorhynchus kisutch*) overwintering in riverine ponds. Canadian Journal of Fisheries and Aquatic Sciences 39:1303–1308.

Peterson, N. P. 1982b. Immigration of juvenile coho salmon (*Oncorhynchus kisutch*) into riverine ponds. Canadian Journal of Fisheries and Aquatic Sciences 39:1308–1310.

Peterson, N. P., and L. M. Reid. 1984. Wall-base channels: their evolution, distribution, and use by juvenile coho salmon in the Clearwater River, Washington. Pages 215–225 *in* J. M. Walton and D. B. Houston, editors. Proceedings of the Olympic Wild Fish Conference, March 23–25, 1983, Port Angeles, Washington. Fisheries Technology Program, Peninsula College, Port Angeles, Washington.

Petts, G. E. 1990. Forested river corridors: a lost resource. Pages 12–34 *in* D. E. Cosgrove and G. E. Petts, editors. Water, engineering and landscape. Belhaven, London.

Pringle, C. M. 1997. Exploring how disturbance is transmitted upstream: going against the flow. Journal of the North American Benthological Society 16:425–438.

Rader, R. B., D. P. Batzer, and S. A. Wissinger, editors. 2001. Bioassessment and management of North American freshwater wetlands. Wiley, New York.

Reid, L. M., and T. Dunne. 1996. Rapid evaluation of sediment budgets. Catena Verlag, Reiskirchen, Germany.

Reynolds, C. S. 1992. Algae. Pages 195–215 *in* P. Calow and G. E. Petts, editors. The rivers handbook: volume 1. Blackwell Scientific Publications, Cambridge, Massachusetts.

Reynoldson, T. B., D. M. Rosenberg, and V. H. Resh. 2001. A comparison of models predicting invertebrate assemblages for biomonitoring in the Fraser River catchment, British Columbia. Canadian Journal of Fisheries and Aquatic Sciences 58:1395–1410.

Richards, C., P. J. Cernera, M. P. Ramey, and D. W. Reiser. 1992. Development of off-channel habitats for use by juvenile chinook salmon. North American Journal of Fisheries Management 12:721–727.

Roni, P., T. J. Beechie, R. E. Bilby, F. E. Leonetti, M. M. Pollock, and G. P. Pess. 2002. A review of stream restoration techniques and a hierarchical strategy for prioritizing restoration in Pacific Northwest watersheds. North American Journal of Fisheries Management 22:1–20.

Roni, P., and A. Fayram. 2000. Estimating winter salmonid abundance in small western Washington streams: a comparison of three techniques. North American Journal of Fisheries Management 20:683–692.

Rosenberg, D. M., and V. H. Resh, editors. 1993. Freshwater biomonitoring and benthic macroinvertebrates. Chapman and Hall, New York.

Rosgen, D. L. 1994. A classification of natural rivers. Catena 22:169–199.

Rott, E. 1991. Methodological aspects and perspectives in the use of periphyton for monitoring and protecting rivers. Pages 9–16 *in* B. A. Whitton, E. Rott, and G. Friedrich, editors. Use of algae for monitoring rivers. Institut für Botanik, Universität Innsbruck, Austria.

Ryman, N., and F. Utter, editors. 1987. Population genetics and fishery management. University of Washington Press, Seattle.

Scarsbrook, M. R., and J. Halliday. 2002. Detecting patterns in hyporheic community structure: does sampling method alter the story? New Zealand Journal of Marine and Freshwater Research 36:443–453.

Schiemer, F., C. Baumgartner, K. Tockner, and J. B. Layzer. 1999. Restoration of floodplain rivers: the 'Danuabe restoration project.' Regulated Rivers: Research and Management 15:231–244.

Sear, D. A., A. Briggs, and A. Brookes. 1998. A preliminary analysis of the morphological adjustment within and downstream of a lowland river subject to river restoration. Aquatic Conservation: Marine and Freshwater Ecosystems 8:167–183.

Sheng, M. D., M. Foy, and A. Y. Fedorenko. 1990. Coho salmon enhancement in British Columbia using improved groundwater-fed side channels. Department of Fisheries and Oceans, Canadian Manuscript Report of Fisheries and Aquatic Sciences No. 2071, Vancouver, BC.

Shuman, J. R. 1995. Environmental considerations for assessing dam removal alternatives for river restoration. Regulated Rivers: Research and Management 11:249–261.

Simon, T. P., editor. 1998. Assessing the sustainability and biological integrity of water resources using fish communities. Lewis Publishers, Boca Raton, Florida.

Sliger, W. A., J. W. Henson, and R. C. Shadden. 1990. A quantitative sampler for biomass estimates of aquatic macrophytes. Journal of Aquatic Plant Management 28:100–102.

Smelser, M. G., and J. C. Schmidt. 1998. An assessment methodology for determining historical change in mountain streams. U.S. Forest Service General Technical Report-GTR-6, Fort Collins, Colorado.

Smock, L. A. 1996. Macroinvertebrate movements: drift, colonization, and emergence. Pages 371–390 *in* F. R. Hauer and G. A. Lamberti, editors. Methods in stream ecology. Academic Press, San Diego, California.

Solazzi, M. F., T. E. Nichelson, S. L. Johnson, and J. D. Rodgers. 2000. Effects of increasing winter rearing habitat of salmonids in two coastal Oregon streams. Canadian Journal of Fisheries and Aquatic Sciences 51:906–914.

Sparks, R. E. 1995. Need for ecosystem management of large rivers and their floodplains. Bioscience 45:168–182.

Stanford, J. A., and J. V. Ward. 1988. The hyporheic habitat of river ecosystems. Nature(London) 335:64–66.

Stanley, E. H., and M. W. Doyle. 2003. Trading off: the ecological effects of dam removal. Frontiers in Ecology and the Environment 1:15–22.

Stanley, E. H., M. A. Luebke, M. W. Doyle, and D. W. Marshall. 2002. Short-term changes in channel form and macro invertebrate communities following low-head dam removal. Journal of the North American Benthological Society 21:172–187.

Steiger, J., M. James, and F. Gazelle. 1998. Channelization and consequences on floodplain system functioning on the Garonne River, southwest France. Regulated Rivers: Research and Management 14:13–23.

Steinman, A. D., and G. A. Lamberti. 1996. Biomass and pigments of benthic algae. Pages 295–313 in F. R. Hauer and G. A. Lamberti, editors. Methods in stream ecology. Academic Press, San Diego, California.

Stevenson, R. J., and Y. Pan. 1999. Assessing environmental conditions in rivers and streams with diatoms. Pages 11–40 in E. F. Stoermer and J. P. Smol, editors. The diatoms: applications for the environmental and earth sciences. Cambridge University Press, Cambridge, UK.

Swales, S., F. Caron, J. R. Irvine, and C. D. Levings. 1988. Population characteristics of coho salmon (Oncorhynchus kisutch) and other juvenile salmonids overwintering in lake, tributary stream and main river habitats in the Keogh River system, Vancouver Island, British Columbia. Canadian Journal of Zoology 66:254–261.

Swales, S., R. B. Lauzier, and C. D. Levings. 1986. Winter habitat preferences of juvenile salmonids in two interior rivers in British Columbia. Canadian Journal of Zoology 64:1506–1514.

Swales, S., and C. D. Levings. 1989. Role of off-channel ponds in the life cycle of coho salmon (Oncorhynchus kisutch) and other juvenile salmonids in the Coldwater River, British Columbia. Canadian Journal of Fisheries and Aquatic Sciences 46:232–242.

Taylor, E. B., Z. Redenbach, A. B. Costello, S. M. Pollard, and C. J. Pacas. 2001. Nested analysis of genetic diversity in northwestern North American char, Dolly Varden (Salvelinus malma) and bull trout (Salvelinus confluentus). Canadian Journal of Fisheries and Aquatic Sciences 58:406–420.

The Heinz Center. 2002. Dam removal: science and decision making. Washington, D.C.

Theiling, C. H., J. K. Tucker, and F. A. Cronin. 1999. Flooding and fish diversity in a reclaimed river-wetland. Journal of Freshwater Ecology 14:469–475.

Tockner, K., F. Schiemer, C. Baumgartner, G. Kum, E. Wegand, I. Zweimüller, and J. V. Ward. 1999. The Danube Restoration Project: species diversity patterns across connectivity gradients in the floodplain system. Regulated Rivers: Research and Management 15:245–258.

Toth, L. A., J. T. B. Obeysekera, W. A. Perkins, and M. K. Loftin. 1993. Flow regulation and restoration of Florida's Kissimmee River. Regulated Rivers and Management 8:155–166.

USEPA (U. S. Environmental Protection Agency). 2002. Methods for evaluating wetland condition: no. 10, using vegetation to assess environmental conditions in wetlands. Office of Water, U.S. EPA, EPA-822-R-02-020. Washington, D.C. Online at http://www.epa.gov/waterscience/criteria/wetlands/10Vegetation.pdf [Accessed 12 May 2003].

Vanoni V. A., editor. 1975. Sedimentation engineering. American Society of Civil Engineers, New York.

Walling D. E., S. B. Bradley, and C. P. Lambert. 1986. Conveyance losses of suspended sediment within a floodplain system. Pages 119–131 in R. F. Hadley, editor. Drainage basin sediment delivery. International Association of Hydrological Sciences Publication 159, Oxfordshire, UK.

Wang, S. Z., J. J. Hard, and F. Utter. 2002. Genetic variation and fitness in salmonids. Conservation Genetics 3:321–333.

Waples, R. S. 1991. Definition of "species" under the Endangered Species Act: application to Pacific Salmon. National Marine Fisheries Service, NOAA Technical Memorandum NMFS F/NWC-194, Seattle.

Ward, J. V. 1989. The four dimensional nature of lotic ecosystems. Journal of the North American Benthological Society 8:2–8.

Ward, J. V., and J. A. Stanford. 1995. Ecological connectivity in alluvial river ecosystems and its disruption by flow regulation. Regulated Rivers: Research and Management 11:105–119.

Ward, J. V., K. Tockner, D. B. Arscott, and C. Claret. 2002. Riverine landscape diversity. Freshwater Biology 47:517–539.

Ward, J. V., K. Tockner, and F. Schiemer. 1999. Biodiversity of floodplain river ecosystems: ecotones and connectivity. Regulated Rivers: Research and Management 15:125–139.

Ward, J. V., K. Tockner, U. Uehlinger, and F. Malard. 2001. Understanding natural patterns and processes in river corridors as the basis for effective river restoration. Regulated Rivers: Research and Management 17:311–323.

Warren, M. L., Jr., and B. M. Burr. 1994. Status of freshwater fishes of the US: overview of an imperiled fauna. Fisheries 19:6–18.

Weitzel, R. L., editor. 1979. Methods and measurements of periphyton communities: a review. American Society for Testing and Materials, Special Technical Publication 690, Philadelphia.

Welcomme, R. L. 1985. River fisheries. Food and Agriculture Organization, Technical Paper 262, Rome.

White, D. S. 1993. Perspectives on defining and delineating hyporheic zones. Journal of the North American Benthological Society 12:61–69.

Whitener, K., and T. Kennedy. 1998. Evaluation of fisheries relating to floodplain restoration on the Cosumnes River Preserve, CA. Report to the fishery foundation of California and The Nature Conservancy. The Nature Conservancy, Sacramento.

Wohl, E. 2000. Mountain rivers. American Geophysical Union, Water Resources Monograph 14, Washington, D.C.

Wright, J. F., P. D. Hiley, S. F. Hamm, and A. D. Berrie. 1981. Comparison of three mapping procedures developed for river macrophytes. Freshwater Biology 11:369–379.

Wright, J. F., D. W. Sutcliffe, and M. T. Furse, editors. 2000. Assessing the biological quality of fresh waters: RIVPACS and other techniques. Freshwater Biological Association, Ambleside, UK.

Zar, J. H. 1999. Biostatistical analysis. Prentice Hall, Upper Saddle River, New Jersey.

Chapter 7
Monitoring Rehabilitation in Temperate North American Estuaries

Casimir A. Rice

Northwest Fisheries Science Center, National Marine Fisheries Service
2725 Montlake Boulevard East, Seattle, Washington 98112, USA
casimir.rice@noaa.gov

W. Gregory Hood

Skagit River System Cooperative, Post Office Box 368, LaConner, Washington 98257, USA
ghood@skagitcoop.org

Lucinda M. Tear

Parametrix, Inc. , 411 108th Avenue NE, Suite 1800, Bellevue, Washington 98004, USA
ltear@parametrix.com

Charles A. Simenstad

School of Aquatic and Fishery Sciences, 324A Fishery Sciences, 1122 NE Boat Street, Box 35502
University of Washington, Seattle, Washington 98195-5020, USA
simenstd@u.washington.edu

Gregory D. Williams

Battelle Marine Sciences Laboratory, 1529 West Sequim Bay Road, Sequim, Washington 98382, USA
gregory.williams@pnl.gov

Lyndal L. Johnson, Blake E. Feist, Philip Roni

Northwest Fisheries Science Center, National Marine Fisheries Service
2725 Montlake Boulevard East, Seattle, Washington 98112, USA
lyndal.l.johnson@noaa.gov, blake.feist@noaa.gov, phil.roni@noaa.gov

Introduction

At the seaward end of the watershed continuum, estuaries are rich and highly productive ecosystems, critically important to many living aquatic resources (Day et al. 1989; Knox 2001), yet are also among the environments most heavily altered by human activity (NOAA 1990; Tibbet 2002; POC 2003; USCOP 2004). Because of human population growth and continued decline in estuarine ecosystem abundance and quality, the pressure on estuarine resources continues to increase. Consequently, estuaries are a growing focus of habitat rehabilitation through restoration, enhancement, and creation (Thayer 1992; Restore America's Estuaries 2002; Thayer et al. 2003). Unfortunately, these projects are rarely evaluated effectively (NRC 1990, 1992, 2001; Wilbur et al. 2000). In this chapter, we propose that monitoring rehabilitation in estuarine ecosystems requires quantifying relationships between dynamic estuarine processes and sensitive indicators of ecosystem function. While we discuss temperate systems in general, we emphasize anadromous salmon (*Oncorhynchus* spp.) habitats in the Pacific Northwest because anadromous fishes are a major focus of rehabilitation efforts and present some of the greater challenges in linking functions of one segment of their life history to conditions in a specific habitat. We begin with a review of human impacts on estuaries, the estuarine environment, salmonid use of estuaries, and common estuarine rehabilitation techniques. Next, we discuss considerations in designing monitoring and evaluation programs for estuarine rehabilitation projects, including conceptual models, key questions, scale, study design, sampling strategies, reference materials, and timing and duration. We then discuss selection and measurement of physical, biological, and chemical parameters. Finally, we summarize the key considerations, challenges of estuarine monitoring, and additional information and research needs.

Estuaries and Human Society

Throughout human history, estuaries have been a major center of society, in large part because of their direct, protected links to the sea and the resulting hubs of transportation. Consequently, estuaries have been disproportionately affected by population density, commercial and industrial development, shipping and transportation traffic, recreational activity, and fisheries harvest (Beach 2002; Tibbet 2002). Globally, 14 of the 17 megacities (cities with greater than 10 million people) are located in coastal areas (Tibbet 2002). Five of the 10 largest metropolitan areas in the United States are centered around major estuaries (NOAA 1998). This intensive use of coastal areas has had severe effects on estuaries. Less than half of the estuarine wetland area present in the United States at the time of European settlement remains, and although the rate of loss has declined in recent decades, destruction and degradation continue (Dahl 2000). In more intensively altered estuaries, loss of historical estuarine wetland area approaches 100%. The primary causes of these changes are agricultural, industrial, and commercial development. In Puget Sound, for example, more than 70% of historical estuarine wetland area has been lost in the agriculturally dominated Skagit River system (Figure 1; Collins and Montgomery 2001; Collins et al. 2003), and more than 95% has been lost in the major urban estuaries of the Puyallup (city of Tacoma) and Duwamish (city of Seattle) river systems (Figure 2; Bortleson et al. 1980). This conversion to agriculture, industry, and urbanization is just one measure of the massive disturbance that has occurred in estuaries as a result of human activity. Another is the degree to which physical and biological connections at the land–water interface have been disrupted by hardening of the shoreline, primarily for erosion control, by concrete, stone, and wood bulkheads.

Anthropogenic changes in watersheds are the source of major degradation of estuaries that may otherwise be relatively unimpacted. For example, hydrologic alteration in the form of water diversion and impoundment, deforestation, and increased area of impervious surface have important effects on estuarine structure and function, changing the magnitude and timing of the delivery of water, sediment, nutrients, and other materials to estuaries, thereby altering geomorphology, water circulation, salinity and temperature regimes, nutrient dynamics, etc. (Simenstad et al. 1992; Valiela et al. 1992; Hopkinson and Vallino 1995).

Because estuaries are centers of population and industry, anthropogenic chemical contamination is often widespread in estuarine areas (NOAA 1990; USEPA 2001; Tibbet 2002). Although some of the most common toxic contaminants at urban sites (e.g., polychlorinated biphenyls, DDTs) are no longer being manufactured and inputs are generally declining, these contaminants remain a concern because their environmental persistence due to their chemical properties and tendency to be sequestered in sediment and biota. Additionally, concentrations of other contaminants, particularly from nonpoint sources, may be increasing due to population growth and urbanization. This is true of a number of pharmaceutical products whose effects on aquatic life have barely been studied (Daughton and Ternes 1999), as well as familiar contaminants such as polycyclic aromatic hydrocarbons (PAH), which are released directly into the environment as industrial waste, and as components of urban runoff that includes spilled oils, gasoline, automobile exhaust, soot, and breakdown products from tires and asphalt (Avakian et al. 2002).

The Estuarine Environment

Understanding the broad ecological patterns of the system under study is fundamentally important to the successful development and application of monitoring programs. In making this point about streams and rivers,

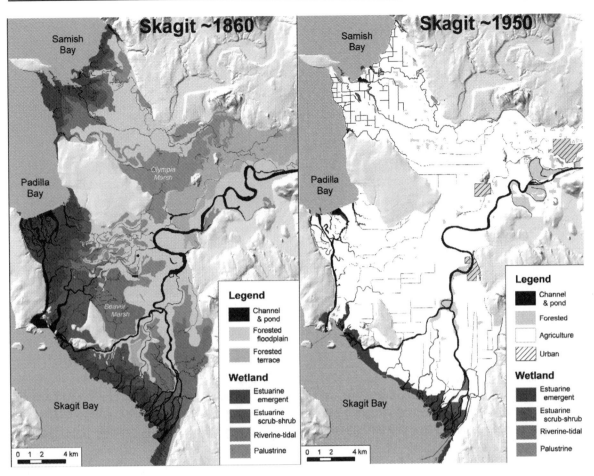

Figure 1.
Loss of estuarine habitats in an agriculturally dominated estuary of Puget Sound; comparison of historic delta conditions in the Skagit River basin (ca. 1860) and more recent conditions (ca. 1950; Collins et al. 2003). Historical loss of estuarine wetland in this agriculturally dominated system is over 70%. (Reprinted with permission from University of Washington Press.)

Downes et al. (2002a) note that "the functioning of flowing water ecosystems is strongly dependent on the operation of longitudinal and predominantly unidirectional linkages (upstream–downstream), and on lateral linkages (channel–floodplain). In contrast, estuarine ecosystems are highly multidirectional in nature, with major forcing from both ocean and watershed environments. As the sole marine contribution in this volume on a topic where the vast majority of work has been done in freshwater systems, we caution that few simple analogs from freshwater restoration and monitoring exist, and offer the following overview as an estuarine primer to highlight the more important differences.

Estuaries are typically defined as semienclosed coastal bodies of water freely connected to the open sea and measurably diluted by freshwater derived from surrounding watersheds (Pritchard 1967a). In addition to this conventional definition, estuaries should be considered more broadly as composed of three basic parts: the tidal freshwater zone, the mixing zone (the usual limit of the estuary), and the nearshore turbid zone or "plume." The boundaries of these zones vary with tides, freshwater inflow, and ocean conditions (Fairbridge 1980; Day et al. 1989). The tidal freshwater zone should be included because changing water levels and current reversals caused by the tides interacting with river flow are dominant hydrologic features that account for emerging estuarine processes above salinity intrusion, such as settling of suspended sediments, concentrations of planktonic organisms, and a gradient in flooding regime. This results in unique temporal and spatial habitat mosaics and, consequently, unique biota. The plume should be included because it too is a unique, dynamic coastal environment where water masses and materials from the adjacent watershed form a sharp surface interface with ocean waters. Under some circumstances, freshwater environments with cycling water level changes, such as in the North American Great Lakes, are grouped with estuaries for management purposes. However, we restrict our discussion to estuaries influenced by salt.

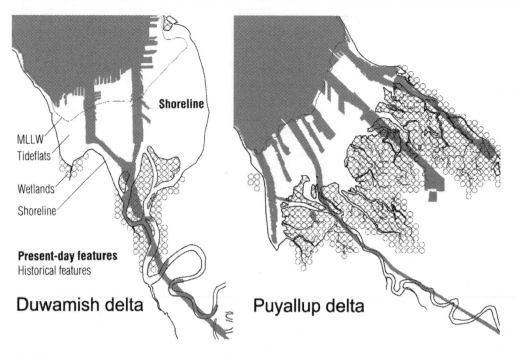

Figure 2.
Loss of estuarine habitats in two urban estuaries of Puget Sound (modified from Downing 1983, based on data from Bortleson et al. 1980). Solid gray areas represent current water bodies, open white areas represent historical tide flats and river channels, and circles represent historical wetlands. Historical loss of estuarine wetlands in these urban systems exceeds 95%. MLLW = mean lower low water. (Reprinted with permission from Washington Sea Grant Program, University of Washington.)

Estuaries are dominated by the physical forces characteristic of land–water and freshwater–marine interfaces (Day et al. 1989; Geyer et al. 2000; Knox 2001). Dominant environmental gradients in estuaries are salinity, elevation, substrate, temperature, and wave exposure (Day et al. 1989; Rafaelli and Hawkins 1996; Knox 2001). Erosion and deposition, tectonics, glaciation, tides and currents, wind and wave exposure, and weather patterns determine the geophysical setting, which in turn drives the biology. Abundant nutrients and organic matter are supplied from surrounding watersheds and upwelling marine waters, tidal action and freshwater inflow interact to circulate and exchange water and distribute organisms, and shores within the photic zone provide substrate for emergent and submergent vegetation. Estuaries are structured to a large degree by their geological legacy (and to some degree more recent sea-level rise), and they function within the geomorphic template as a result of the higher frequency events mentioned above. This is important because it explains why fjords, for example, with the same nutrients, organic matter, tidal action, and so forth, behave much differently from other kinds of estuaries such as drowned river valleys.

The great variety of geomorphic, hydrologic, climatic, and biological settings possible in estuaries results in an enormous diversity of estuarine types; indeed, estuaries are the most diverse of all marine environments (Jay et al. 2000). Classification of estuaries based on geomorphology places them into four major groups: coastal plain (e.g., drowned river valley), fjord, lagoon, and tectonic (Dyer 1973; Day 1989; Knox 2001). Hydrodynamic classification systems for estuaries are primarily based on salinity distributions and circulation patterns resulting from interaction between tides and river inflow. These include Stommel and Farmer's (1952) division of estuaries into mixed, partially mixed, fjord-like, and salt-wedge (types 1 through 4) estuaries, and later refinements (Hansen and Rattray 1966; Pritchard 1967b). Jay et al. (2000) propose a classification system that expands a hierarchical method from freshwater fluvial geomorphology (Montgomery and Buffington 1998) to accommodate the vastly more complex estuarine systems. Their process-based scheme attempts to combine and extend geomorphology and hydrodynamics to include ecosystem processes. Enumeration and characterization of habitat types (albeit without explicit consideration of underlying physical forcing) is another common way to "classify" estuaries (Cowardin et al. 1979; Dethier 1990), but this is more accurately considered characterization or delineation of estuarine components. Though critically important for effective management of estuarine ecosystems, estuarine classification schemes are limited by extensive gaps in our understanding of physical–ecological relationships, particularly at the landscape level (Geyer et al. 2000; Simenstad et al. 2000a).

Estuarine ecosystems are productive and diverse, supporting critical ecological functions such as foraging, nesting, breeding, refuge, rearing, and migration for various life stages of many fish and wildlife species (including all anadromous salmon) and making major contributions to recreational and commercial fisheries (Day et al. 1989; Valiela 1995; Weinstein and Kreeger 2000; Beck et al. 2001). For representative regional reviews of the geomorphology, oceanography, ecology, and human alteration of temperate North American estuaries, see Roman et al. (2000), Dame et al. (2000), and Emmett et al. (2000).

Salmon and the Estuary

Anadromous fishes are a major focus of aquatic habitat restoration activities, especially in western North America where the recovery and the enhancement of salmon and trout populations is the single most common restoration goal. To varying degrees, all anadromous salmonids are estuary dependent, relying on the estuary for migration, transition (both physiological and ecological), rearing, and refuge (Healey 1982; Simenstad et al. 1982; Thorpe 1994; Aitkin 1998). In particular, juvenile ocean-type chinook salmon *Oncorhynchus tshawytscha* and chum salmon *O. keta* use the estuary for extended periods as rearing habitat. Although there is little empirical, mechanistic evidence documenting estuary dependence of salmonids, patterns of spatiotemporal distribution, abundance, residence time, growth, and survival of juveniles in estuaries suggest that estuarine habitats contribute significantly to survival and fitness (Reimers 1973; Healey 1982; Levings et al. 1986, 1989).

Perhaps the most common misconception regarding anadromous salmonids and estuaries is that estuaries are simple bottlenecks, mere conduits where out-migrant juvenile salmon accumulate in major mortality sinks waiting to pass to the sea. To the contrary, for individual fish moving downstream, intact estuaries broaden their ecosystem in size, dynamics, and biota. Instead of a backlogging, it is more a process of diffusion into a wide range of habitats—rich and productive staging areas for the expression of the diverse life histories that are essential to the resilience and productivity of salmon populations.

Anadromous salmonids have thrived and persisted in a dynamic and broad habitat array because they possess a diverse suite of life history types that makes their populations robust to changing conditions. Thus, it is essential that the full spectrum, historical and extant, of estuarine habitats, species, and life history types be considered in determining not just restoration goals (Bottom et al. 2001) but monitoring strategies as well. For example, historical abundance patterns of juvenile chinook salmon migrating through and rearing in the Columbia River estuary indicate much higher life history diversity and a broader temporal distribution in historical than contemporary populations (Figure 3; Burke and Jones 2001). The implications for monitoring are that (1) population structure should be an important consideration of monitoring plans, (2) sampling may need to occur broadly in time and space, and (3) evaluation of a given restoration project or monitoring plan should not be based solely on detection of peak abundances of existing hatchery and remnant wild populations. A monitoring program that only samples out-migrating juvenile salmon between May and July because that is when "most of the fish" are present, for example, fails to recognize that "most" of the target fish for restoration (i.e., individuals with a relatively high probability of survival to adulthood [Reimers 1973] or rare or unique species or life history types) may in fact enter or remain in the system outside the limited sampling period and may show very different habitat-use patterns.

Estuarine Rehabilitation

The biological significance of estuaries and the pressure society places on them make effective coastal and estuarine management critically important, and conservation and rehabilitation of estuarine ecosystems have become fundamental components of both regulatory and nonregulatory responses to this need. As discussed in Chapter 1, there is considerable debate over restoration terminology. Because few estuarine projects are true restoration (returning the estuary to predisturbance conditions) and most are enhancement or creation projects, we will refer to them collectively as rehabilitation projects. Regardless of terminology, the need remains to rigorously evaluate the performance of all approaches to ecosystem recovery.

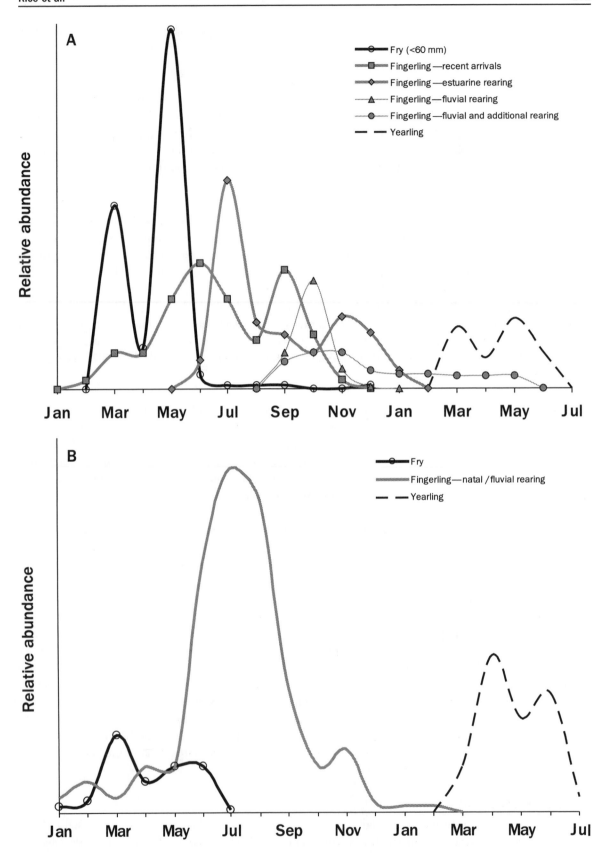

Figure 3.
Historical (A) and contemporary (B) relative abundances for 1-brood-year chinook salmon of various life history types in the Columbia River estuary (based on data from Rich 1920 and Dawley et al. 1985). Compared to contemporary populations, historical populations possessed more complex population structure and showed a broader temporal distribution in the estuary. (Source: Jennifer Burke, School of Aquatic and Fishery Sciences, University of Washington.)

Rehabilitation of estuarine and coastal marine habitats are reviewed in Thayer (1992), Kusler and Kentula (1990), and Zedler (2001), among many recent sources. In part because of the initial focus specifically on fish and wildlife habitats in temperate North America, discrete estuarine habitats such as salt marshes and seagrass meadows tended to be the rehabilitation target of choice, even though the lost wetlands involved other ecosystems or were mosaics of diverse systems (e.g., marshes with mudflats adjoining scrub–shrub and forested wetlands). Large, canopy-forming macroalgae (kelp) systems also became the focus of rehabilitation beginning in the late 1950s and early 1960s, when rehabilitation of these ecosystems was often conducted to replace or to enhance commercially valuable kelp plants for harvest and was supported and conducted in part by commercial interests.

Estuarine rehabilitation in the United States has primarily come from compensatory mitigation requirements beginning in the late 1950s to replace coastal wetlands lost to development, typically under the auspices of the Section 404, Clean Water Act (Public Law 92–500), and true restoration represents one of the most effective means of compensation for coastal wetland loss in an otherwise ineffective regulatory program (NRC 2001). Requirements for compensation for loss of coastal wetlands coincided with increasing appreciation of estuarine ecosystems by scientists, resource agencies, and the public (e.g., Odum 1961; Teal and Teal 1969). Historically, the field of estuarine rehabilitation has evolved from only site-scale mitigation, to implementation of multiple projects in support of "no net loss" policies, to consideration of whole estuary restoration (Kusler and Kentula 1990; Freeman 1999). Legislative mandates in support of estuarine rehabilitation are many (Kennish 2000; Restore America's Estuaries 2002), including the Clean Water Act; the Endangered Species Act; and the Comprehensive Environmental Response, Compensation, and Liability Act. Most recently at the federal level, the Estuary Restoration Act of 2000 aims to restore 1 million acres by 2010, allocating $275 million in federal matching funds over the first 5 years covered by the act.

The most common estuarine rehabilitation activity is returning tidal inundation by either breach or removal of barriers, such as dikes and levees, or excavation of fill (see special dedicated issue of *Restoration Ecology* 10(3), September 2002). Hydrologic control devices such as tide gates have also been used, despite substantial evidence that use of such structures may not be advisable (French and Stoddard 1992; Sanzone and McElroy 1998). Other common activities are the planting of native vegetation such as marsh plants and seagrasses; the addition of substrate materials such as sand, gravel, soil amendments, and fertilizer; the placement of structural elements such as large woody debris; control of grazers; and, particularly in urban or industrial environments, removal or containment of chemical contaminants. Examples of estuarine rehabilitation activities by ecosystem type are listed in Table 1.

Table 1.
Examples of estuarine rehabilitation activities by ecosystem type. The most common technique in estuarine rehabilitation is the return or the introduction of tidal inundation.

Ecosystem	Actions
Tidal marsh	Dike or levy breach or removal, excavation, substrate addition, transplantation, fertilization, hydrologic control (tidegates, etc.), grazer control, competitor control, large woody debris placement, wastewater and sediment discharge control, chemical contaminant removal or containment.
Seagrass	Transplantation, fertilization, excavation, substrate addition, wastewater and sediment discharge control, chemical contaminant removal or containment
Kelp	Transplantation, substrate addition, grazer control, competitor control, wastewater and sediment discharge control
Mudflat	Dike or levy breach or removal, excavation, substrate addition, chemical contaminant removal or containment
Sand/gravel beach	Substrate addition, excavation

Urban estuaries are particularly challenging for rehabilitation because of the typically small size and limited distribution of available sites, constraints on what physical and chemical processes can be improved or restored given irreversible alteration of the landscape, isolation from intact habitats that could serve as sources of colonizing biota, relatively high inputs of nutrients and chemical contaminants, and different rehabilitation goals and resources of local management jurisdictions (Shreffler and Thom 1993; Ehrenfeld 2000).

Although estuarine wetlands include a variety of vegetated, nonvegetated, hard substrate, and soft substrate types, vegetated, soft substrate habitats such as salt marsh and seagrass have been the focus of the vast majority of estuarine rehabilitation activity. Detailed overviews of rehabilitation techniques are available for tidal marshes (Zedler 2001) and seagrass beds (Fonseca et al. 1998). The typical approach is to return favorable hydrodynamic and physical and chemical conditions for the desired biotic community and to accelerate succession from a relatively immature ecological condition to a more mature state, often via planting of desirable native species and removal of unwanted or exotic species.

In vegetated tidal wetlands such as salt marsh, vegetation performance depends on careful design that considers the following major physical processes: tidal dynamics, salinity regime, sedimentation, subsidence (historical and future), freshwater inputs and drainage (including flood events), and relative sea-level change (Zedler 2001; Williams and Orr 2002; Williams et al. 2002). Regional examples with longer-term monitoring data (e.g., >5 years) and published results are the Sweetwater Marsh and Tijuana estuaries (Zedler 2001), the San Francisco estuary in Southern California (Williams and Orr 2002), the Salmon River in Oregon (Frenkel and Morlan 1991; Gray et al. 2002), the Gog-Li-Hi-Te created wetland in Washington (Simenstad and Thom 1996), the Campbell River in British Columbia (Dawe et al. 2000), Long Island Sound in New England (Warren et al. 2002), and coastal North Carolina in the Southeast Atlantic (Craft et al. 1999; Craft et al. 2002). Experience in these and other systems shows that extensive and productive marsh vegetation can be established within a few years (sometimes without plantings) but that restored marshes may not develop the same plant species composition, soil and sediment characteristics, or channel complexity as natural marshes for several decades, if ever. In addition, developmental trajectories of ecosystem components moved in variable and often unpredictable directions and rates, requiring monitoring periods of at least 5 years to multiple decades to characterize them.

Seagrass habitat rehabilitation performance depends on many of the same physical processes as in tidal marshes, but there is generally less intensive site manipulation. Primary methods are the identification of unvegetated but otherwise suitable sites for seagrass growth, followed by transplantation (Fonseca et al. 1998). Kelp rehabilitation is primarily accomplished through transplantation, substrate addition, and grazer control (Schiel and Foster 1992).

Faunal use of restored estuarine habitats can also occur relatively quickly, particularly by relatively large, motile species such as birds and fishes (Brown-Peterson et al. 1993; Montagna 1993; Simenstad and Thom 1996; Able et al. 2000; Roman et al. 2002). However, assemblage structure may be relatively simple in terms of species richness and trophic composition immediately after rehabilitation and may take a decade or more to approach more natural systems (Simenstad and Thom 1996; Warren et al. 2002). In some cases, assemblage development may peak soon after rehabilitation, then decline through time as sediment and hydrologic processes of a site change and stabilize (Williams and Desmond 2001). Fish species in rehabilitated habitats have shown residence times and growth rates similar to those in reference systems (Shreffler et al. 1990; Miller and Simenstad 1997; Miller and Able 2002). However, while successful foraging has been shown in rehabilitated habitats (e.g., Shreffler et al. 1992), diet composition can be quite different from that at reference sites. For example, juvenile out-migrant salmonids occupying rehabilitation sites in Puget Sound (Cordell et al. 2001) and in southwest Washington (Miller and Simenstad 1997) showed diet composition different from what might be expected in natural reference systems. The significance of such dietary differences on functional performance (e.g., fish growth and survival) remains largely untested.

Simenstad and Bottom (2002) recommend the following principles, developed in the context of estuarine habitat restoration for salmon recovery for the lower Columbia River system, that are applicable to a wide variety of rehabilitation activities:

1. Protect first; restore second.
2. Do no harm.
3. Use natural processes to restore and maintain structure.
4. Restore rather than enhance or create.
5. Incorporate salmon life history.
6. Develop a comprehensive restoration plan using landscape ecology concepts to reestablish ecosystem connectivity and complexity.
7. Use history as a guide, but recognize irreversible change.
8. Establish performance criteria based on explicit objectives, and monitor performance both independently and comprehensively.
9. Take advantage of the best interdisciplinary science and technical knowledge and use a scientific peer-review process.

Implicit and explicit in these recommendations is the importance of monitoring. Monitoring is essential for assessing whether the action led to the hypothesized result and for providing managers and researchers with increasing knowledge about the feasibility of and approaches to rehabilitation. Such assessment can be used for several purposes, each of which requires a particular approach and design: (1) compliance ("implementation" monitoring)—to document whether a particular rehabilitation action has been implemented as designed; (2) status and trend—to determine whether the attributes of a rehabilitation action are developing as anticipated, at an acceptable rate, and are sustainable; (3) performance ("effectiveness" monitoring)—to evaluate whether a rehabilitation action is providing the ecosystem functions and services for which it was intended; and, (4) diagnostic ("validation" monitoring)—to assess the underlying processes that are responsible for the performance of the restored ecosystem and that can provide indicators useful for taking adaptive (contingency) actions in case the rehabilitation action is not performing as anticipated.

Development of a monitoring program should be considered a creative, problem-solving exercise that uses the scientific method as its model. The long history of inadequate monitoring of estuarine rehabilitation (NRC 1990, 1992, 2001; Thom and Wellman 1996; Thom 1997; Wilbur et al. 2000; Thayer et al. 2003) argues that monitoring should be based on some fundamental principles, including that monitoring (1) be a primary consideration at all project stages, including project design; (2) be based on a conceptual model of the system being restored; (3) include indicators of ecosystem processes rather than just structural attributes; (4) incorporate ecosystem and landscape perspectives; (5) use metrics that are biologically or physically meaningful and are tied to the goals of the rehabilitation; (6) be based on a design that is as statistically rigorous as possible and directly related to the goals of the project; (7) continue for a sufficient period of time to assess whether the goals have been met; and (8) be adaptive.

Unfortunately, these principles are seldom incorporated into rehabilitation actions. Inadequate planning, funding, or understanding of the system being rehabilitated, as well as lack of a clear analytic approach to defining goals, can interfere with the development and implementation of robust monitoring designs. Common weaknesses of estuarine monitoring programs include lack of temporal and spatial reference data, insufficient duration or frequency of monitoring, sampling at inappropriate scale(s), weak or absent biological components, single-species focus, and emphasis on structural attributes rather than ecosystem processes underlying functional trajectories. In the following subsections, we provide information to assist in avoiding such problems through sound monitoring design, including selection of appropriate methods for estuarine monitoring.

Developing a Monitoring Program for Estuarine Rehabilitation

Considerable background and guidance for studying estuarine and coastal marine environments is available from a number of sources (e.g., Simenstad et al. 1991; Schmitt and Osenberg 1996; Kingsford and Battershill 1998b; Gibson et al. 2000). General principles of monitoring designs for rehabilitation projects, including the importance of defining project objectives, establishing key questions and hypotheses, identifying appropriate scale, selecting an appropriate study design, and determining the number of sites and years that should be monitored were discussed in Chapter 2 (see Figure 1 in Chapter 2). Estuarine systems present some unique challenges compared to freshwaters systems (i.e., developing a conceptual model, difficulty in finding reference areas), and, in this section, we discuss the components of monitoring and design as they relate to estuarine rehabilitation.

Developing a Conceptual Model and Project Goals

One of the first steps in developing an estuarine rehabilitation project and an associated monitoring and evaluation program is the development of a conceptual model of the ecosystem being considered for rehabilitation. (Thom and Wellman 1996). This critical step helps refine the goals of the rehabilitation activity, the objectives of the monitoring program, and the sampling methods and designs that can be implemented; helps determine the sampling resources needed by the monitoring program; and provides support for adaptive management (Thom 1997, 2000). The main purpose of a conceptual model should be to facilitate understanding of how the rehabilitation activity fits into the system in which it is being implemented. The spatial and temporal extent of the action and its predicted consequences should be highlighted in the model with large- and small-scale components identified and developed as needed.

When developing a conceptual model, it is helpful to start with a simple form and then to expand upon components of the simple form in a methodical manner to show how elements of the system affect one another. Thom and Wellman (1996) describe a basic conceptual model that can serve as the simple form for almost any project. Their basic model of controlling factors that affect or create structure that produces biological and ecological function can be represented as

$$\text{Controlling Factors} \leftrightarrow \text{Structure} \leftrightarrow \text{Function}$$

Examples of physical, biological, and chemical controlling factors and structural and functional attributes for use in estuarine rehabilitation monitoring are listed in Table 2.

The degree to which a conceptual model is developed and how it is structured will depend on the goals of the rehabilitation and on the extent of the effects of the rehabilitation activity. The conceptual model that is developed for a site-specific rehabilitation activity at a small site in an estuary that has been highly modified may be different than the conceptual model for a similarly sized site in a system where watershed and estuarine processes are still relatively intact.

The conceptual framework developed by Simenstad and Cordell (2000) for rehabilitation of Pacific Northwest salmonid habitats suggests goals of rehabilitation that include increasing the "opportunity" (access of fish to the system) or the "capacity" (quality of the habitat). Increases in opportunity and capacity should improve some "realized function" (also termed performance) such as the growth, survival, or fitness of fish. Increasing both opportunity (e.g., breaching a dike to renew tidal inundation) and capacity (e.g., promoting the reintroduction of salmon prey) can be goals of rehabilitation activities (Figure 4). Because the particular components of capacity and opportunity that benefit salmonids depend on their life history stage and species, it is important to consider how species specific and life history stage specific the rehabilitation goals are.

Key Questions and Hypotheses

Based on the conceptual model, the goals of the rehabilitation action, and the objectives of the monitoring program, specific questions and hypotheses need to be defined. In addition to asking whether certain structural elements (e.g., tidal prism, percent coverage by emergent vegetation) are in place, key questions and hypotheses should also address functional performance (e.g., fish residence time and growth) whenever possible (Simenstad and Cordell 2000; Wilbur et al. 2000; Neckles et al. 2002). When available, descriptions of functional trajectories of rehabilitation performance can determine if a site is progressing toward the rehabilitation goal or whether midcourse corrections are required (Simenstad and Thom 1996; Zedler and Callaway 1999; Zedler and Lindig-Cisneros 2000; Morgan and Short 2002). Understanding whether and why a site is on a trajectory that will end up at a level of acceptable performance requires monitoring process variables that affect the course a site will take and that will help explain its "behavior" over time.

It should be possible to develop monitoring designs that use a limited number of performance criteria and involve equating species abundances and relative abundances, for example, at reference and rehabilitation sites, and a larger set of process or research questions. The questions could involve comparing measurements that describe process, creating mechanistic models, or creating statistical models for which the hypotheses test the significance of a model coefficient rather than of a difference between means. After key questions and

Table 2.
Examples of physical, chemical, and biological variables for controlling factors, and structural and functional attributes that could be considered as potential metrics in estuarine rehabilitation monitoring. This is not meant to be an exhaustive list. Regional protocols, background information, and expertise should be consulted to determine the most desirable metrics for specific rehabilitation actions. Birds are included in this table but are not discussed in this volume.

Category	Controlling factors	Structural attributes	Functional attributes
Physical			
Hydrology	Geomorphology, freshwater inflow, tidal regime	Tidal range, tidal prism, hydroperiod, residence time	Fish presence/absence (access to habitat)
Geomorphology/ topography	Geology, tidal regime, sedimentation	Elevation, connectivity, channel complexity	Fish presence/absence (access to habitat)
Water characteristics	Freshwater inflow, tidal regime, nutrient concentrations, biochemical oxygen demand, residence time	Temperature, salinity, dissolved oxygen (DO), current stratification	Fish prey production (capacity of habitat)
Soil/sediment	Geology, tidal regime, sediment supply	Grain size, organic carbon content, nutrient concentrations, salinity, redox potential	Sedimentation, organic carbon accumulation, nutrient accumulation
Chemical			
Nutrients and organic matter	Freshwater runoff, point and nonpoint sources, marine upwelling, sedimentation	Nutrient concentrations, organic carbon content	Primary production, invertebrate community structure and production
Contaminants	Point and nonpoint sources, organic carbon, hydrology	Chemical concentrations in sediment, water, and biota	Altered organism growth, reduced immune function
Biological			
Emergent vegetation	Elevation, tidal regime, salinity, soil composition, pore water salinity, competition, grazers	Area, percent coverage, shoot density, biomass, height, species richness, relative abundance	Primary production, faunal utilization
Submergent vegetation	Elevation, substrate, light, temperature, salinity, nutrients, flow	Area, percent coverage, shoot density, biomass,	Primary production, faunal utilization
Benthic invertebrates	Substrate, elevation, temperature, salinity, DO, chemical contaminants	Abundance, species richness, relative abundance, dominance	Biomass, presence in predator diet
Fishes	Temperature, salinity, DO, access, flow, food availability, predation, competition, harvest	Abundance, species richness, relative abundance, dominance	Growth, fecundity, residence time, movement patterns, survival, population structure, population growth
Birds	Access, food availability, nesting site availability, predation, competition	Abundance, species richness, dominance	Growth, fecundity, residence time, survival, behavior, population structure, population growth
Phytoplankton	Light, temperature, salinity, nutrients, stratification	Abundance, species richness, dominance	Primary production
Zooplankton	Temperature, salinity, DO, flow, phytoplankton	Abundance, species richness, dominance	Density, biomass, presence in predator diets

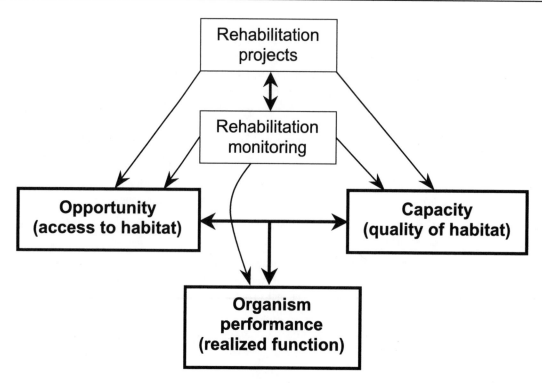

Figure 4.
Relationships among capacity, opportunity, and performance characteristics (bold boxes), and rehabilitation and monitoring. Bold arrows indicate interactive relationships. Rehabilitation actions can directly influence opportunity and capacity. Ideally, such influences result in improved performance (realized function), and monitoring should include opportunity, capacity, and performance metrics. (Based on Simenstad and Cordell 2000.)

hypotheses have been identified for the monitoring program, choices must be made about the basic study design (including scale), parameters to measure, and the appropriate timing, frequency, duration, and location of data collection. In making these choices, both ecological and statistical principles must be considered.

Scale and Estuarine Monitoring

Spatiotemporal scale, a critical issue when monitoring estuaries, involves consideration of both resolution (grain) and extent (Weins 1989). Sampling resolution determines the smallest sampling unit that can be described. Extent (the space or time over which sampling is conducted) determines the largest population about which inference can be drawn. Resolution, extent, and how units are summarized will determine the components of natural variability and pattern that are observed. Moreover, the scale of observation versus the scale over which the processes of interest occur can alter our perception of what we think we are measuring (Levin 1992; Legendre et al. 1997).

Choices about variables, sampling methods, and sampling design become intertwined with issues of scale during the process of making trade-offs between information needs, costs of sampling with different resolutions over different extents, and the associated variance that will be encountered. In some cases, the question asked will require sampling at more than one resolution over the extent of the population of interest. For example, vegetation structure can be delineated by using remote sensing, such as aerial photography; however, gathering ground-truthing data for identification of the delineated vegetation polygons will always involve subsampling, typically at a spatial resolution of meters to tens of meters. In the case of fish, those occupying breached dike sites can be sampled by blocking them off into dendritic tidal channels during a high tide, then collecting them in traps on the subsequent ebbing tide (e.g., Cordell et al. 2001; Cornu and Sadro 2002; Gray et al. 2002). With estimates of capture efficiency, the total abundance of fish occupying a site at one time can be estimated. However, sampling of other variables that would relate and potentially explain performance of fish at the site, such as prey availability or even water temperature, would still require sampling at a much finer resolution, since no low-resolution sampling methods exist. During data analysis, relating the fish population estimates to other explanatory variables would require pairing the two data sets in statistically and ecologically sound ways that consider both the scale and the independence of individual sampling units.

Determining the interaction among variables that operate at such different scales requires a sampling strategy that scales logically over space and time, even if the variables cannot be overlapped and synchronized. This is especially important, for example, when relating the presence of organisms with fluctuating behavior patterns (or processes that are not easily predicted) to other less variable processes such as tidal cycling. For instance, some prey organisms of fishes are highly evasive or have diel behaviors that affect their relative vulnerability to predation by the fish, so assumptions about their contribution to the fish diet depend upon sampling where prey and predator overlap in space and time. In complicated cases such as these, although it may require more effort and expertise, letting the fish conduct the "sampling" of prey composition and abundance at a reference site and, through stomach contents analysis, comparing the results to the diets of similar fish at a reference site may be more informative (Bowen 1996; Simenstad and Cordell 2000). Interpretation of the fishes' dietary sampling of the rehabilitation site can also provide insights into the validity of a prey resource sampling design. Similar approaches may be applied to other integrative variables, such as the behavior of birds occupying a site, the flux of pelagic organisms during a tidal cycle, and other mass balance approaches to nutrient, organic matter, and sediment cycling.

Study Design

As with other environments, most estuarine rehabilitation monitoring or study designs typically fall into two broad categories: posttreatment and before–after (see Chapter 2). Posttreatment designs (e.g., "space-for-time" substitution) are by far the most common in estuarine rehabilitation (Gray et al. 2002; Morgan and Short 2002; Warren et al. 2002). True before–after control–impact (BACI) studies (e.g., Roman et al. 2002) are relatively rare in the estuarine environment, especially with the replication desirable for such designs (Kingsford and Battershill 1998a).

If it is necessary to monitor for addressing performance criteria that involve comparison to a reference or control condition, factorial study designs (BACI and its variations) may be required to provide the foundation for statistical hypothesis testing. A simple factorial design and BACI analysis could be used to test whether the means of a selected parameter are different at reference and rehabilitation sites, if the means of parameters of the sites are different across all sampling times, and if an interaction exists between site and time (i.e., if the changes over time in the site means occur at unequal rates or with the opposite sign). More complicated designs with factorial and BACI analyses allow the incorporation of additional categorical factors besides site and time, continuous covariates, and complex analysis of the nature of the interaction effects.

The results of simple BACI analyses can be difficult to interpret if explanatory variables and a landscape perspective are not included in the analyses. Complex BACI analyses can be difficult to untangle (see Chapter 2 and Downes et al. 2002b). To assure adequate power to detect biologically meaningful effects, factorial designs can require intensive and extensive sampling unless low-variance measurements are selected.

While carefully designed studies with before data, appropriate references and replication, and efficient measurements are the ideal, ecological and practical realities often preclude them. That does not mean that no useful assessment and monitoring can be done in their absence. To the contrary, some of the most important estuarine rehabilitation case studies (e.g., Simenstad and Thom 1996) are collections of various components, opportunistically but thoughtfully managed and interpreted, some of which allow little in terms of formal statistical analysis. As noted in previous chapters, there is often much to be learned from even a single case study through simple graphical analysis and expert opinion (see Chapter 2 for a detailed discussion). Rigorous statistical analysis should be practiced when possible, but biological significance, not statistical significance, should be the primary emphasis in interpreting and reporting monitoring results (Yoccoz 1991; Karr and Chu 1999).

Complex Monitoring Designs

Variations on the basic designs mentioned earlier include modular and rotational designs (rotation of sampling, parameters, and sites in space or time) can be useful in estuarine systems (Urquhart and Kincaid 1999; Larsen et al. 2001; Chapter 2). Monitoring multiple parameters and endpoints (the variable, the sampling unit, and the statistic together comprise the endpoint), especially if the parameters have different types of spatial and temporal distributions, may require developing a monitoring design that includes two or more design modules. Modular designs can be useful, because not all variables will necessarily need to be monitored at the same temporal and spatial resolution and extent, as long as independent variables can be effectively related to dependent variables. For example, if no major changes in controlling factors have occurred, changes in landscape forms such as channel density, perimeter to area ratios, or areas covered by static or slowly changing vegetation assemblages may be adequately monitored at 3- to 5-year intervals by using remote-sensing methods, while more rapidly changing benthic invertebrates may need to be monitored annually to correlate to information on fish diet composition. Modular designs allow a monitoring program to develop separate designs for subsets of parameters and endpoints, to collect information about biases in the components of the design, to collect occasional data about smaller scale spatial or temporal (e.g., seasonal or weekly) variance, and, in general, to increase flexibility in how a monitoring program is implemented. Modular designs that incorporate scientific experiments and staggered or rotating sampling schedules will support collection of data about multiple variables so that effects of rehabilitation are not evaluated on the basis of only a few performance criteria and will optimize how sampling resources are allocated over space and time.

In situations where subsampling of a heterogeneous landscape presents challenges to establishing a representational picture of changes in monitoring variables, rotational designs that monitor status and trends can be especially useful to help increase the total area that can be sampled over time, to help reduce the variance of estimates of change over time, to separate spatial and temporal variability, and to develop time series of long-term trends that represent the entire site (Rao and Graham 1964; Urquhart et al. 1993; Tear 1995). Rotational designs preserve inferences about the full extent of a population by continually including new samples and reduce the variance of estimates of change if there is correlation over time in repeatedly sampled units. Rotational designs are quite flexible and can be developed for any scale of question. For example, within a site, the location of sampled quadrats or transects can be rotated. Sites, sections of a shoreline, and estuaries can be sampled on a rotational pattern. Whether or not correlation exists and variance in estimates of change is reduced, rotational designs will still help broaden the representation of different parts of the site and will allow for certain areas to be resampled simply because they are of special interest (Skalski 1995).

Pilot Studies

The role of pilot studies and other short-term, one-time scientific experiments should also be considered as important elements in developing estuarine and other monitoring programs. These can be used to estimate bias and precision of different sampling methods, to improve the overall monitoring design, and to describe smaller-scale spatial or temporal distributions of individual variables or processes or relationships between variables. In a true adaptive management mode (Holling 1978; Walters 1986; Walters and Holling 1990), these types of studies can provide complementary information to help interpret monitoring results and can provide the information needed to recommend midcourse corrections in methods, design, or site management (Thom 1997, 2000). For example, to develop a monitoring strategy for monitoring fish prey at restoration sites in the Duwamish River, Washington, a pilot study compared the capture success and efficiencies of epibenthic pumps and benthic cores at several elevations in several locations (Cordell et al. 1994). The study revealed that the benthic cores yielded a less variable and more representative measure of invertebrate assemblages than the frequently used epibenthic pumps.

Reference Material in Estuarine Monitoring Programs

Assessing the performance of rehabilitation actions requires some understanding of the target systems we are trying to promote. In this respect, the role of reference material (sites, historical reconstructions, literature reviews) in monitoring the effectiveness of estuarine rehabilitation efforts is quite important. Historical reconstructions of area and distribution of habitat types (Collins and Montgomery 2001; Collins et al. 2003), literature reviews, and ecosystem assessments (Simenstad 2000) can provide invaluable context for developing rehabilitation action goals, identifying reference sites, and interpreting monitoring results at multiple temporal and spatial scales. In particular, parallel monitoring of comparable reference sites will provide data on the natural temporal and spatial variability that might be expected from the manipulated site and the means to distinguish the rehabilitation signal from natural noise.

It is important to be aware of a habitat rehabilitation action's location in the estuarine continuum so that appropriate reference sites can be chosen for the project. For example, a reference site might be characterized by various vegetation assemblages, a certain density of tidal channels and characteristic channel geometry, particular tidal and salinity regimes, and the presence of certain fish and bird assemblages. Rehabilitation generally seeks to replicate these reference site characteristics; thus, these reference characteristics are the goals of the rehabilitation, and they serve as standards against which a rehabilitation action is measured.

Locating valid reference sites can be a challenge in estuaries, especially in highly modified systems (Shreffler and Thom 1993; Ehrenfeld 2000). A broad geographic search may be required, and appropriate reference sites may not be available in many areas. Uncertainty about rehabilitation design and performance will be present if reference sites cannot be found or are geographically distant. Uncertainty might be reduced by modeling hydrology, sediment transport, and vegetation succession in the proposed rehabilitation site. Uncertainty also might be addressed by conducting more intensive, frequent, and lasting monitoring.

Timing, Duration, and Intensity of Monitoring

The timing of monitoring will depend on the spatial and temporal distribution of the populations and variables being monitored, as well as on factors that control those distributions. Biological variables should be measured over periods when the biota in question is present and, preferably, when their presence and magnitude can be related to causal factors. Understanding when they are present, however, and what causal factors determine their presence, will be affected by the monitoring design. For example, when and where juvenile salmon may be present in low densities will not be known unless sampling is adequate to detect them in those situations. If detecting an endpoint in low densities is important, as in understanding the life history diversity of salmon or detecting the presence of invasive species, sampling will need to be frequent enough to detect critical numbers. The determination of what is critical will be based on ecological knowledge; the determination of how frequently to sample to detect that critical level will be based on statistical principles.

As noted previously, experience in estuarine rehabilitation tells us that at least 2–5 years and often decades are required to detect meaningful results, especially with respect to functional biological performance (Simenstad and Thom 1996; Craft et al. 1999, 2002; Morgan and Short 2002). Ideally, it would continue indefinitely. If we think about monitoring trajectories of selected parameters and endpoints, how long to monitor will depend on the length of time that is required for an endpoint to stabilize (i.e., to vary more in response to factors that are not a result of the rehabilitation action than to the effects of the rehabilitation action). For some endpoints, it may be possible to determine at the beginning of the monitoring program approximately how long such stabilization will take. When data are not adequate to allow a priori determination of the required length of a monitoring program, the program should include decision nodes at, say, 3, 5, 10, and 20 years to evaluate the adequacy of the data that have been collected and determine whether a rehabilitation action has generated desired and sustainable effects. If the data are adequate, monitoring may be either discontinued or, preferably, continued at a lower frequency. If uncertainty about the results of the rehabilitation action still exists, monitoring should be continued and the design potentially altered to allow uncertainty to be resolved.

Selecting and Measuring Monitoring Parameters

Which variables are selected for a given monitoring program will depend on the key questions and hypotheses, and the resources available. The National Research Council (NRC 1992) recommends that at least three measures (or metrics) be tracked: one for controlling factors, one for structure, and one for function. Examples of such variables for estuaries are listed in Table 2. In a protocol developed for salt marshes in the Gulf of Maine, Neckles et al. (2002) recommend core structural variables that can be measured in any tidal rehabilitation project and additional functional variables for specific situations, and stress the importance of standardizing methodologies to ensure comparable data among projects at both local and regional scales. In the context of Pacific salmon, the Simenstad and Cordell (2000) approach mentioned earlier recommends metrics based on opportunity (access to habitat), capacity (quality of habitat), and performance (realized function in a target species or population) (Figure 4; Table 3). Variables that respond at more than one scale (e.g., vegetation abundance within assemblages, distribution of assemblages through a site) and represent responses from different components of the system (e.g., mobile and sedentary invertebrates, run timing, fish size, tidal

Table 3.
Categories and examples of attributes for use in assessment and monitoring of fish response to estuarine rehabilitation actions. (Based on recommendations by Simenstad and Cordell 2000 for Pacific salmonids.)

Category	Attributes
Opportunity (access to habitat)	Tidal elevation, tidal channel/slough density, fish presence/absence
Capacity (quality of habitat)	Density/biomass and availability of preferred invertebrate prey organisms, physicochemical conditions that promote these particular invertebrate communities, structural attributes that serve as refugia from predators
Performance (realized function)	Fish growth, residence time, survival

channel perimeter to edge ratios, carbon transport) can provide a weight of evidence approach to understanding the effects of rehabilitation and can allow the performance of rehabilitation projects to be evaluated in a more holistic way (Simenstad and Thom 1996; Wilbur et al. 2000).

Because the ultimate goals of most estuarine rehabilitation are usually biological, it follows that the most important indicator of performance is biological condition, measured directly whenever possible (Karr and Chu 1999). However, because biology is largely dependent on physicochemical processes to create and maintain habitat, monitoring of physical, chemical, and biological characteristics are all important. In this subsection, we provide an overview and guidance on selection and measurement of physical (hydrology, geomorphology, soil and sediment, water characteristics), biological (vegetation, fishes, invertebrates, food webs, nonindigenous species), and chemical (contaminants) parameters. Methods for estuarine and coastal marine assessment and monitoring are reviewed in detail in a number of other volumes (e.g., Simenstad et al. 1991; Fonseca et al. 1998; Kingsford and Battershill 1998b; Gibson et al. 2000; Callaway et al. 2001; Coyer et al. 2001; Thayer et al. 2003). Sampling strategies or schemes (e.g., random, stratified random, line transect) and power analysis are discussed in Chapter 2. Cochran (1977), Hicks (1982), and Thompson (2002) provide more detailed discussions of sampling and subsampling strategies. Whatever endpoints are selected, the sampling strategy must be selected to facilitate data collection and to provide low-variance estimates for selected measures. To whatever extent possible, samples should be located randomly through the entire stratum or site being sampled. Transect-based designs (Buckland et al. 1993, 2001; Thompson 2002), where samples are collected along one or more transects laid across a site, are often used to facilitate navigation through dense vegetation and to direct sampling across known gradients of salinity, elevation, exposure, and so forth. In general, transects should be used as a means to facilitate movement among random sampling locations; otherwise, the transect must be considered the sampling unit, and any samples taken along the transect are subsamples of that transect.

A critical perspective often missing from monitoring estuarine rehabilitation is the landscape setting and consequential role of a rehabilitation site (Forman 1995; Kentula 2000; Simenstad et al. 2000b). Monitoring within the landscape structure of large sites, as well as evaluating the role of any site within the larger estuarine landscape, should be an important factor in designing and implementing monitoring plans. Surveys of the literature (e.g., Shreffler et al. 1995) suggest that many if not most estuarine habitat rehabilitation sites are relatively small, that is, less than 25 ha, some are as small as 0.25 ha (Moy and Levin 1991). For such small projects, intensive sampling of vegetation (above- and below-ground biomass, stem density, etc.), sediments (grain-size, organic content, etc.), and other such parameters with 1-m² or smaller plots is feasible and, to a large degree, representative. However, for larger rehabilitation actions, this scale of sampling is not only problematic but also may be inappropriate. For example, in the South Fork delta of the Skagit River, Washington, a total of 235 ha of tidal wetlands are scheduled for restoration and will alter the flow pattern of delta distributary channels, tidal circulation patterns, sediment routing in the delta, and patterns of marsh progradation and erosion in areas that are up to 4 km downstream from the restoration sites (W. G. Hood, Skagit System Cooperative, unpublished data). Thus, the effects of the restoration action will extend off site, and monitoring and evaluation may be required beyond the project area. In general, the larger a rehabilitation action, the greater the likelihood that it will affect other areas in the landscape. For this reason, landscape-scale questions will generally be more relevant for large rehabilitation actions than for small ones. However, the landscape context for small sites is also important since they are certainly influenced by landscape-scale hydrologic and sediment transport processes. In addition, small rehabilitation actions may be arrayed in the landscape to play a comparable or even superior role to one large action.

Monitoring on the scale of 1-m^2 plots is not generally optimal for large rehabilitation actions, so remote sensing is a practical alternative (Lyon 2001; Feist and Box 2002). It also is relatively inexpensive and essential to answer landscape-scale questions. Infrared orthophotographs (flown at low tide) are commercially available with a pixel resolution of 15 cm. At this resolution, one can distinguish tidal channels only 0.5 m wide. One can also use the different infrared signatures (texture and color) coupled with ground-truth sampling to distinguish dominant species of vegetation. Exposed mudflats or sand flats are easily identifiable, as are shallow reefs of mud and sand in tidal channels and river distributaries. Thus, infrared orthophotographs can be used to design monitoring strata; to distribute monitoring points and transects in representative and landscape-significant positions; and to directly monitor changes in tidal channels and river distributaries, gross changes in vegetation distribution, and gross changes in sediment accumulation patterns. Tracking gross changes in vegetation or sedimentation patterns may provide as sufficient an indication of the trajectory of the rehabilitation action as higher-resolution monitoring. Several studies have shown that salt marsh communities are subject to high temporal variability, that is, noisy on a short time scale (Zedler 1988; Moy and Levin 1991; Allison 1992). It may not be necessary to resolve that noise with high-resolution monitoring when the larger scale signal of the change trajectory is of greater interest. For example, is it really important to be able to detect plant species that occur in low densities, or is it more important to know if species A is being replaced by species B and C? Other methods of remote sensing include multispectral and hyperspectral images for terrestrial and intertidal areas, and acoustical methods such as multibeam and side-scan sonar for subtidal areas (e.g., Garono et al. 2004). Additionally, geographical information system (GIS) software can be used to compare current photographs with historic ones, thereby allowing insight into historic, possibly preimpact conditions. In this manner, aerial photographs allow the temporal as well as the spatial scale of study to be broadened.

Remote sensing generally cannot resolve details of vegetation community composition, shoot density, epiphytic communities on submerged aquatic vegetation, depths of channel cross sections, depths of sediment accumulation or erosion, or other such monitoring parameters. In addition, some physical and biotic processes, including measures of fish habitat function, do not have site- or landscape-scale signatures. However, for these variables, remote sensing can be used to provide the context within which more focused sampling or ground-truthing is conducted. Remotely sensed images can be used to stratify a site, identify areas where rapid change or certain biota might be expected, and to understand the range of situations that need to be assessed to completely describe a physical or biological process or population. Because remote sensing can be used to monitor a variety of estuarine parameters and endpoints, additional examples of the uses of remote sensing are provided below in specific categories of parameters and endpoints. Chapter 4 provides additional discussion on the resolution of different types of remote sensing technologies.

Physical Parameters

Hydrology and geomorphology

Because hydrology is a primary determinant of estuarine rehabilitation performance, characterization of tidal regime and landform development are important monitoring components. Tidal inundation (Figure 5) can be measured with a variety of techniques, including electronic probes, data loggers, and graduated staffs placed at various locations to record water depth, and time and duration of inundation. Topographic changes are best measured by using a combination of techniques that characterize surface elevation, substrate composition, and channel morphology. In this subsection, we concentrate on tidal channel morphology; methods for evaluating surface elevation and substrate composition are discussed below in the Soils and Sediment subsection.

Estuarine rehabilitation is often focused on intertidal marshes dissected by dendritic tidal channels. This type of estuarine environment is very common in North America and has frequently been impacted by historical development. Dendritic tidal channels are central to the ecological structure and function of these marshes.

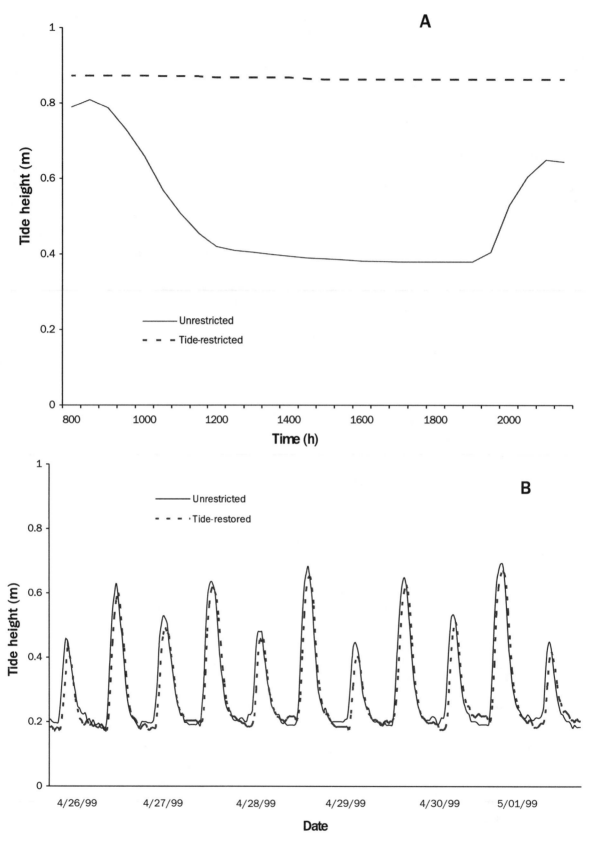

Figure 5.
Example of changes in tidal regime resulting from a rehabilitation action (replacement of a culvert that restricted flow) in a New England salt marsh. Water elevation in severely hydrologically restricted and less restricted marshes over one tidal cycle before rehabilitation (A), and in the same marshes over several tidal cycles after rehabilitation (B). Monitoring hydrology confirmed similar tidal regimes in reference and rehabilitated marshes as a result of culvert installation. (From Roman et al. 2002.)

While large fourth- or fifth-order tidal channels may be the most conspicuous and common focus of rehabilitation due to their size, development of small first- and second-order tidal channels in rehabilitated estuarine marshes is critical to their ecological function. Several studies indicate the upper reaches (first and second order) of tidal channels support higher densities of many species of fish and marine invertebrates than do the lower reaches (third to fifth order) of tidal channels (Hackney et al. 1976; Levy and Northcote 1982; Rozas and Odum 1987; Halpin 1997). Consequently, it is vital that rehabilitation and monitoring focus not only on changes in large-channel morphometry as tidal flow is restored to an area but also on the development of the critical low-order tidal channel network.

Tidal channels and river distributary channels are formed by flowing water. In the case of river distributaries, this flow is dominated by river discharge; in the case of dendritic tidal channels, channel-forming flow is dominated by bidirectional tidal discharge, which is related to tidal prism. Tidal prism is usually defined as the volume of water between mean higher high water and mean lower low water (MLLW). The relationship between riverine flow and channel form has traditionally been described by mathematical functions relating discharge to channel cross-sectional area, width, depth, and flow velocity; that is, fluvial hydraulic geometry (Leopold et al. 1964). The same approach has been applied to tidal channels, substituting tidal prism for river discharge (Coats et al. 1995).

Because tidal flows shape the geometry not only of a particular channel cross section but also of every possible cross section of a channel, integrating the power functions of hydraulic geometry equations over the length of a channel produces an allometric relationship between tidal channel volume and surface area, and, similarly, between tidal channel surface area and perimeter (Hood 2002). This modified approach to hydraulic geometry is useful because surface area and perimeter can be measured from aerial photographs and entered into the GIS, thus allowing the use of remote-sensing technology to monitor habitat rehabilitation. Furthermore, allometric relationships extend beyond tidal channels to the larger landscape (e.g., Woldenberg 1966; Church and Mark 1980). For example, marsh island area is allometrically related to the surface area of tidal channels draining the islands (Figure 6; Hood 2004). An allometric relationship like this one, developed in a reference marsh area, can be used to predict the amount of tidal channel that could be restored in a given area (i.e., tidal channel density). However, relationships like these are likely sensitive to estuary and habitat type, and location in the estuarine gradient. Marshes high in the estuarine gradient may have lower channel density than those low in the gradient, because tidal range will be lower and less tidal energy is available to cut dendritic tidal channels in the higher zone of the estuarine gradient than in the lower zone.

In addition to tidal channel density, another potentially useful monitoring metric is channel bifurcation ratio, or the number of first-order channels divided by the number of second-order channels, the number of second order divided by third order, and so on. Bifurcation ratios provide insight into the maturity of tidal channel development. Two modes of channel development have been theorized: one in which tidal channel networks develop fully and slowly extend headward (Mode 1) and one characterized by the rapid growth of long mainstem channels, with most tributary addition occurring later (Mode 2; Knighton et al. 1992). Under natural conditions, both modes may operate; but, under conditions of habitat rehabilitation, Mode 2 will likely predominate, because large remnant channels may still exist as drainage features on the site of the rehabilitation, while smaller channels are absent. If large channels do not exist, they may be more likely to be excavated as part of the rehabilitation action than are small channels. Thus, the development of large channels is likely to be more advanced than that of small channels, which would favor Mode 2 channel evolution. Consequently, bifurcation ratios of newly rehabilitated marsh or channel systems are likely to be very low initially, increase with time as smaller tributaries develop, and eventually approach the levels found in reference sites as channel network development matures. Network magnitude, which is simply a count of the number of first-order channels in a drainage network, is another metric that can be useful for monitoring tidal channel development.

Several factors are likely to affect the rate of channel development. Large tidal range will contribute to rapid development (Knighton et al. 1992), thick vegetation with dense root systems is likely to retard development (Garofalo 1980), and the presence of paleochannels or remnant channels will provide the principal routes for main channel extension and will concentrate much of the more vigorous tributary activity (Knighton et al. 1992; Cornu and Sadro 2002). Observed tidal channel headcut migration rates range from 5 to 7 m per year

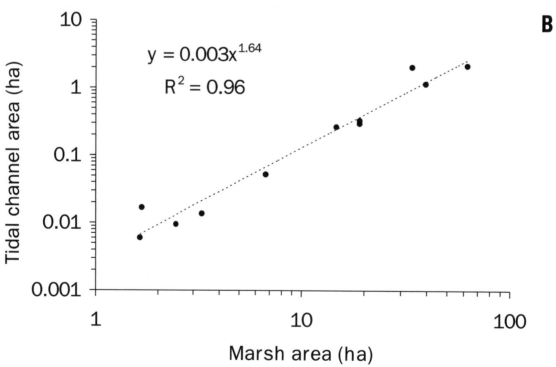

Figure 6.
Marsh island area delineations (A), and relationship between marsh island area and tidal channel area (B). Such relationships, developed from reference systems, can be used to estimate the amount of tidal channel that should be achieved and maintained by a given action, and to track its performance. (From G. Hood, Skagit River System Cooperative, LaConner, Washington, unpublished data.)

(Steers 1960) to 500 m per year (Knighton et al. 1992). The lower limit of the range is likely to be more common than the upper limit, so monitoring channel change will generally require a long-term commitment on the order of several decades. On the other hand, some aspects of channel morphometry may change very quickly. For example, 2 years after a disconnected delta distributary channel of the Skagit River in Washington was reconnected by dike removal, the channel widened from 3 to 12 m. In addition, sediment is accumulating at the channel outlet, possibly leading to marsh accretion and recovery. This example illustrates that rehabilitation can have off-site consequences, arguing that monitoring should not be limited to the immediate area of the rehabilitation action.

Soils and sediment

As noted previously, monitoring of substrate characteristics is important for evaluating hydrologic changes but also for assessing suitability for plants and invertebrates. Substrate characteristics include sediment movement (sedimentation and erosion), grain size, bulk density, and organic carbon and nutrient content. Sediment movements result from tidal flushing or riverine transport (especially during floods). A variety of built structures (dikes, jetties, causeways, tide gates, culverts, bridges, etc.) can have far-reaching effects on sediment transport, so it is sometimes difficult to predict sediment movements in estuarine environments that have a legacy of human modifications (sediment movement in streams is discussed in Chapter 3). Conversely, monitored patterns in sediment erosion or deposition (e.g., changes in elevation or horizontal area) can be indicators of the performance of returning natural tidal and riverine processes (Figure 7).

Marsh surface elevation change is influenced by several sediment processes: (1) vertical accretion, which can include the accumulation of inorganic or organic materials, (2) erosion, (3) decomposition of organic material, and (4) subsoil compression. Net elevation change can be measured by using arrays of sedimentation–erosion tables (SET; Boumans and Day 1993; Cahoon et al. 1995). A permanent pipe is driven into the marsh soil to the point of refusal to establish a benchmark pipe, and the SET is attached to the pipe during sampling to measure surface elevation (±0.001 m). The SET is a plane with a regular array of perforations and a bubble level. Uniform metal pins are lowered through the perforations of the leveled plane until they touch the marsh surface. The length of pin above the surface of the plane is used to calculate the distance of the marsh surface from the reference plane. Repeated measurements can be made by using the permanent benchmark pipe, so elevation change can be tracked over time. If SET pipes are driven into marsh soils without reaching

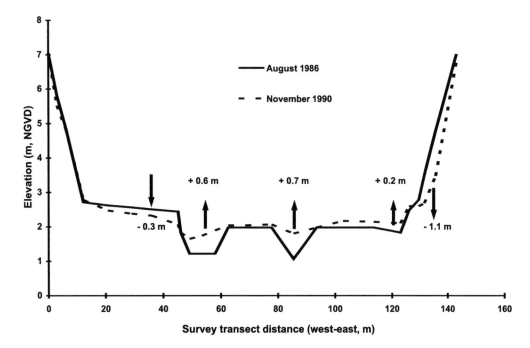

Figure 7.
Changes in vertical elevation along a cross-sectional profile of the Gog-Le-Hi-Te restored wetland in Tacoma, Washington, showing accretion and erosion on intertidal flats and tidal channels between 1986 and 1990. (From Simenstad and Thom 1996.)

resistance (bedrock, sand, or hard clay), the pipes should be periodically surveyed relative to a reliable benchmark to adjust for pipe subsidence. Sedimentation–erosion tables should be used in conjunction with artificial horizons to determine the relative contributions of vertical accretion and subsoil compression and expansion to elevation change (Figure 8). For example, if SET measurements indicate 2 cm of elevation gain and artificial horizons indicate 3 cm of sedimentation, then there must have been 1 cm of subsoil compression. Artificial horizons may consist of 100-cm² plots of plastic glitter flakes or feldspar. Sediments can be sampled for such markers periodically after installation with 15-cm-diameter corers, whose large diameter minimizes sediment core compression. The corers should be frozen, then the sediment cores extruded and subsampled at 0.5-cm increments and glitter flakes counted in each of the thawed core increments. Cryogenic cores may be necessary for very unconsolidated sediments where sample compression is a problem. Artificial horizons are not useful in areas where there are periods of erosion that can remove the horizon, nor are they useful in areas of high bioturbation, such as mudflats. In addition to elevation change, sediment grain size, organic content, and density can be measured concurrently to better ascertain the likely causes of elevation change.

In circumstances where dramatic changes in marsh elevation can be expected over a period of time, detailed topographic surveys using optical surveying methods, or, preferably, a survey-grade (±0.02 m horizontal and vertical) global positioning system (GPS) produce coarser vertical measurements but may allow easier collection of a greater density of data over large areas. Rehabilitation sites that have experienced significant subsidence before the action and where there are significant tidal or riverine sources of sediments are likely to experience significant accumulations of sediment that may be adequately monitored by using GPS.

Remote sensing also can be used to monitor gross topographic change. Light detection and ranging (LIDAR) uses a laser system coupled to an inertial guidance system and a high resolution GPS unit, mounted on an airplane or helicopter to measure ground elevation over very large areas, on the order of hundreds to thousands of square kilometers. Vertical accuracy for LIDAR is 15 cm, and horizontal accuracy is around 120 cm. Horizontal resolution is determined by the elevation of the aircraft and the sampling scheme selected by the investigators. Many surveys are commonly sampled at a 3-m resolution. The LIDAR acquires around 15,000 x, y, and z coordinates every second, so vast areas can be sampled in a short period of time. One of the shortcomings of LIDAR is that the laser has difficulty penetrating low, dense vegetation such as cattails, sedges, shrubs or forests. Consequently, LIDAR is most accurate when flown during the late autumn to early spring over bare agricultural fields or marsh areas where above-ground vegetation does not persist. When flown over persistent vegetation, LIDAR elevations must be ground-truthed with GPS surveying (2 cm horizontal and vertical precision) and linked to vegetation coverage. Another remote-sensing approach is simply to use GIS to compare historical photographs with current ones to estimate marsh progradation or erosion and tidal channel filling or erosion.

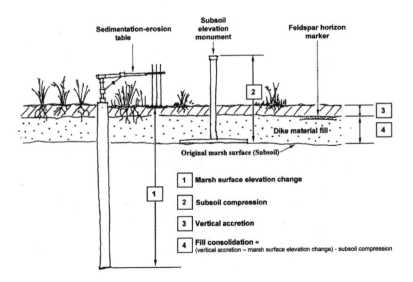

Figure 8.
Illustration (not to scale) of substrate profile measurements using sedimentation–erosion tables, artificial horizon markers, and elevation change monuments. (From Cornu and Sadro 2002 after Cahoon et al. 1995)

Sediment characteristics are also indicators of rehabilitation of physical and biochemical processes. Additionally, they affect ecological community structure and ecosystem function. Sediment grain size, for example, is an excellent indicator of hydraulic energy and is strongly correlated to community composition of benthic invertebrates. Areas exposed to high wave energy, tidal energy, or river flow will tend to have larger sediment grain size. Sheltered areas will consist of finer sediments and organic matter.

Sediment grain size can be determined by sorting through a series of sieves for coarse sediments (>63 microns) and through standard pipette techniques for fine sediments (Folk 1968; Plumb 1981). Sediment organic content is generally a reliable indicator of the accumulation of detritus in marsh sediments. Organic material is important for several reasons: (1) it is the foundation of the detrital food web; (2) the amount of sediment organic material affects nitrogen availability to plants (Langis et al. 1991); (3) accumulation of detritus in marsh sediments can be a significant means of marsh accretion (increase in surface elevation), sometimes accounting for the bulk of accretion (Anisfeld et al. 1999); and (4) organic carbon content of sediments affects the bioavailability of chemical contaminants (Baudo et al. 1990). There are usually significant differences between diked or drained wetlands and natural wetlands in sediment organic content. When wetlands are drained, soil organic material is oxidized (consumed by aerobic bacteria). Loss of sediment organic material contributes significantly to soil compaction and marsh subsidence (Anisfeld et al. 1999). Thus, high sediment bulk density indicates human impact from marsh diking and draining. Marsh recovery from this impact after rehabilitation is often reflected in a decrease in bulk density (Craft et al. 1999, 2002). Indeed, in some instances, an increase in sediment pore space may be the dominant source of vertical accretion after tidal influence is restored to previously isolated marshes (Anisfeld et al. 1999). Soil organic content can be determined by combustion of a sample and calculating the mass difference pre- and postcombustion (Plumb 1981).

Sediment characteristics are affected by several geophysical processes (e.g., river discharge, tidal flow, waves, sediment suspended load transport, and sediment bed load transport) and biological processes (e.g., vegetation growth, bioturbation, and oxidative decomposition of organic material) that are distributed differently in tidal channels than on marsh and mudflat surfaces. Rates of change in sediment characteristics are usually relatively slow, so long-term monitoring will usually be required to monitor sediment responses to rehabilitation of fundamental driving processes. However, such monitoring is important because sediment characteristics are of fundamental (indeed foundational) importance to biotic communities, directly influencing vegetation and benthic and epibenthic invertebrates, while indirectly influencing higher trophic groups.

Water characteristics

Basic water parameters to be measured as standard practice in estuarine rehabilitation monitoring are salinity, temperature, and dissolved oxygen (DO). While continuous recording of these and other parameters (e.g., turbidity, nutrient concentrations) is the generally preferred sampling approach, some parameters can be adequately characterized by strategic grab sampling.

Salinity affects estuarine organisms in diverse ways. Estuarine plant species generally have narrow salinity tolerances. Some species (e.g., *Salicornia virginica*) prefer euhaline zones, others (e.g., *Carex lyngbyei*) prefer oligohaline to mesohaline zones, and others (e.g., *Spartina alternaflora*, which can grow at salinities of up to 40 parts per thousand [ppt] but grows best at 10 ppt) have broad tolerances but growth optima in particular salinity zones (Linthurst 1980). Analogous salinity tolerances can be found in other groups such as zooplankton, fish, and wildlife (reviewed in Day et al. 1989). Many species of wildlife may use habitats of different salinities to satisfy different needs, and certain salinity conditions may be tightly associated with specific life history stages. Anadromous fish are a dramatic example, but the same is true for many bird species that winter in estuarine areas (Woodin 1994; Adair et al. 1996).

Typical marine salinities range from 32 to 35 ppt. Estuarine salinity can range from 0.5 ppt to more than 50 ppt in areas of high evaporation. The generally recognized halinity classes and preferred terminology of tidal fresh (<0.5 ppt), oligohaline (0.5–5 ppt), mesohaline (5–18 ppt), polyhaline (18–30 ppt), euhaline (30–40 ppt), and hyperhaline (>40 ppt) are most useful (Cowardin et al. 1979). The often-used term brackish corresponds to mixohaline or the very broad range of 0.5 to 30 ppt.

Water salinity should be characterized throughout a water column, and this is most easily done with an electronic salinity-conductivity meter. Soil pore water salinity can also be measured. Salinity refractometers are useful for characterizing soil pore water salinity, since very small volumes of water are sufficient for a refractometer; compressing a soil sample (e.g., with a syringe or garlic press) is often more than sufficient to obtain an adequate sample. In this case, samples should be taken from within the root zone or at the depth at which benthic organisms of interest reside.

Water temperature strongly affects the growth and the survival of aquatic organisms and varies between species and within the life cycle of a given species. Continuous temperature data loggers, the preferred means for monitoring water temperature, are typically set to record continuously at regular intervals (e.g., every 15–30 min) for weeks or even months.

Various factors influence DO concentrations, including water temperature, photosynthetic production of oxygen by aquatic plants, turbulent aeration of surface water with atmospheric oxygen, mixing of high and low salinity water masses, respiration by aquatic plants, and respiration by bacteria and other detritivores during decomposition of organic materials. Water-quality criteria have been developed for DO based on the life history requirements of aquatic species, particularly salmonids (DEQ 1994). The timing of sample collection should be standardized. Dissolved oxygen concentrations will vary throughout the day due to oxygen production by aquatic plants, respiration, changes in water temperature, and stratification of the water column. Low DO concentrations usually occur in the early morning because photosynthesis and oxygen production occur during the day. Dissolved oxygen concentrations usually peak in the afternoon, then decline as respiration exceeds photosynthesis (Ricklefs 1979). The timing of sample collection may also be influenced by other oxygen sinks and sources that occur at a specific time of day or season. For example, large inputs of organic material may result in a significant drop in oxygen concentration due to an increase in biochemical oxygen demand.

Biological Parameters

Vegetation

Emergent and submergent vegetation is commonly monitored as an indicator of estuarine rehabilitation site performance and ecosystem health. Comparisons of vegetation between restored and reference sites are often used to indicate the degree to which biogeochemical processes have been restored to a site. Estuarine vegetation plays important structural and functional roles in estuarine ecosystems. The spatial and temporal distribution of plant species, species composition, and biomass produced are determined by abiotic factors, such as solar incidence, soil pore water salinity and texture, elevation (frequency and extent of inundation), and soil redox potential (Ewing 1983), as well as biotic factors, such as herbivory (Gough and Grace 1999), competition, harvesting, deposition of wrack, and trampling (e.g., animal pathways and resting areas).

At small sites (<80 acres), or for focused sampling in a subarea of a larger rehabilitation site, quadrat or transect sampling methods as described in several sources (Fonseca et al. 1998; Elzinga et al. 2001; Roman et al. 2001; Zedler 2001) are used to quantify the relative abundance of individual species within assemblages. Different measures of abundance and different sizes of sampling units may be selected, depending on the degree to which quantification versus qualitative description of assemblages is required. Common measures of estuarine vegetation assemblages include frequency (presence/absence) and percent frequency (a/n where a = number of sampling units containing species and n = total sampling units sampled), percent cover, shoot density, and biomass.

Many measures of abundance were developed by terrestrial rangeland botanists for the purpose of quantifying small-scale species abundances, species interactions, and competition among species and may be too time consuming or destructive for consideration at large sites or where removal of vegetation is not desired. Measures of percent cover (whether measured by using visual estimation measures or point–quadrat measures) are especially common.

Infinitesimally small points where only the presence or absence of species is recorded are called percent frequency and are thought to be equated with percent cover (Goodall 1951; Grieg-Smith 1964). This equality may or may not be true and depends on the spatial distribution and morphology of the plant species. Working with sampling units (e.g., quadrats) greater than 1 m² can be very time consuming, subject to high measurement error, and include large sampling variance unless sampling is highly stratified. Quantification at this level may not be needed to determine rehabilitation performance. Measures of percent frequency (presence or absence) are generally more rapid, contain less measurement error, and make as much intuitive sense as estimates of cover. The size of the sampling unit can be adjusted to reflect the need to account for more species (larger quadrats will tend to encounter more species) or resolve differences between relative frequencies and cover of species (smaller quadrats will tend to encounter fewer species, so species that are either more frequent or have higher cover will be encountered more frequently). An example of the application of vegetation percent frequency measurements in estuarine rehabilitation is the experimental manipulation of marsh surface elevation in Coos Bay, Oregon (Figure 9; Cornu and Sadro 2002), which showed clear patterns of succession that differ by elevation.

Measures of plant fitness (seed production, flowering), growth (changes in shoot height, shoot density, biomass over time), and survival can also be useful in comparing vegetation assemblages between or among sites. Survival of plantings in small sites is often a monitoring requirement for mitigation projects. Other measures can be labor intensive but may become important indicators of community change as changes in species abundance and composition slow down. For example, it is possible that 100% cover of desired species may be achieved, but other attributes, such as canopy height, structural complexity, above- and below-ground biomass, nitrogen reserves, and soil organic matter content, might be well below the levels found in reference systems (reviewed in Callaway et al. 2001). Thus, more focused sampling of these detailed vegetation parameters may be incorporated into a monitoring program. Experimentation with multiple sampling methods may help develop surrogate measures of biomass using nondestructive measures such as plant height, stem density, and cover.

At larger sites, it will often not be feasible to sample the entire site by using methods and designs that might be appropriate for smaller sites. For larger sites, remote sensing and GIS should be used to map the distribution of vegetation patches. An image or GIS map of the site can be used to stratify the site and to develop ground-truthing data and sampling designs to identify and quantify (to the extent needed) species composition in the different patches. Aerial photography and other remote imagery (including infrared, orthorectified color photographs, multispectral and hyperspectral imagery) can be used for salt marsh vegetation and some intertidal vegetation. Multibeam (with backscatter), side-scan, and other acoustical measures that record backscatter can be used for eelgrass and certain other submerged aquatic species.

It should be noted that the relative abundance of species in different assemblages can vary with habitat and season, so the spatial and temporal intensity of sampling strategy and method selected should depend on the importance of vegetation to the rehabilitation and interest in seasonal changes. If community composition is of interest, methods that focus on presence or absence will be adequate and multivariate analytical methods can be used to evaluate change (Legendre and Legendre 1998). It can be useful to use different methods in different parts of a site or for different species, depending on the type of information needed. It is also helpful to include sampling for measures of factors that affect vegetation, such as soil pore water salinity, level of the water table, elevation, evidence of grazing or trampling, amount of organic matter, and so forth.

Fishes

Estuarine rehabilitation frequently aims to benefit certain fish species, particularly those of high commercial or recreational value that spend at least part of their life cycles in these ecosystems. Accordingly, it is necessary to demonstrate at a minimum that these fish are accessing target areas (Figure 10) and, preferably, that condition and survival are improved by these habitats. Fish are highly mobile animals that may use a matrix of habitats over a variety of time scales and correspondingly present a difficult sampling issue in terms of quantifying both the contribution of rehabilitation to their habitat requirements and sampling efficiency (Kneib 1997; Simenstad et al. 2000b). Consequently, most assessment and monitoring approaches involve simple metrics of fish use (species occurrence, abundance/density, diversity; Figure 10), which may fall short of actually establishing functionally relevant indicators of habitat suitability (growth, production, survival) or the underlying mechanisms (Simenstad and Cordell 2000; Williams and Desmond 2001). While estimates of fish growth or survival are more appropriate indicators of fish habitat quality, the difficulty, rigor, and labor involved is seldom within the scope of monitoring. This is particularly true for juvenile salmon, which occur

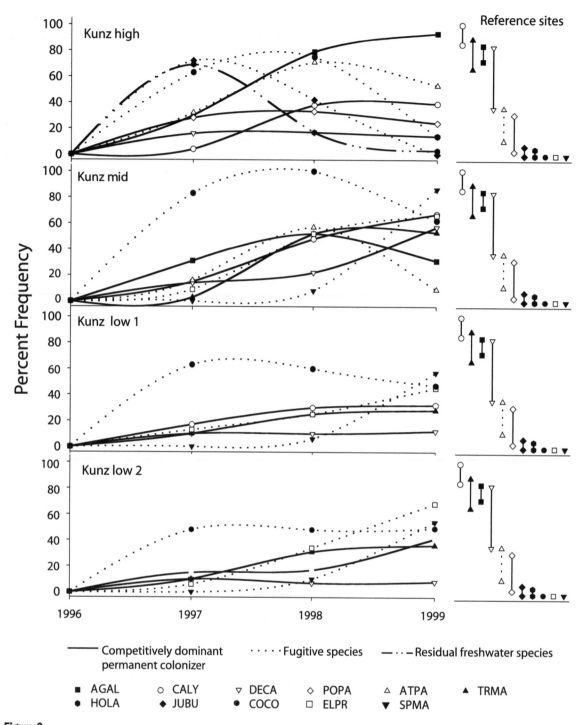

Figure 9.

Example of vegetation percent frequency monitoring in an experimental manipulation of Kunz Marsh and reference salt marshes in Coos Bay, Oregon, from 1996 to 1999. All elevations (high, middle, and low) show successional changes in selected vegetation as a result of the rehabilitation, with striking differences among elevations. Vegetation codes: AGAL, Agrostis alba; ATPA, Atriplex patula; CALY, Carex lyngbyei; COCO, Cotula coronopilfolia; DECA, Deschampsia caespitosa; ELPR, Eleocharis parvula; HOLA, Holcus lanatus; JUBA, Juncus balticus; POPA, Potentilla pacifica; SPMA, Spergularia marina; TRMA, Triglochin maritimum. (From Cornu and Sadro 2002.)

episodically in estuarine habitats and are influenced by a number of other factors before returning several years later as adults. As a result, mere presence or density may be a limited or unreliable indicator of estuarine habitat function for these species (Simenstad and Cordell 2000).

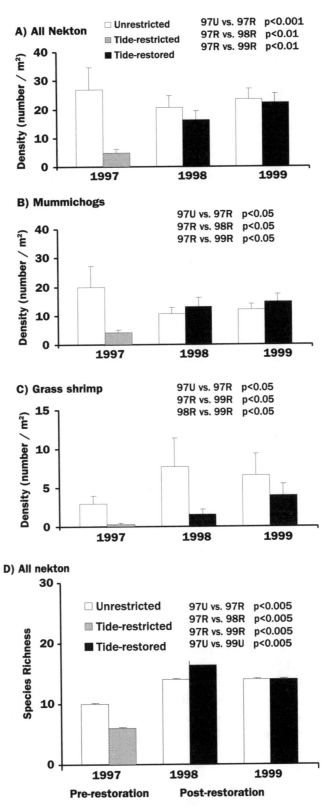

Figure 10.
Examples of simple fish and macroinvertebrate metrics used to evaluate biological response to rehabilitation actions. Density of all nekton (actively swimming animals) (A), density of dominant fish species (mummichogs Fundulus heteroclitus) (B), density of a dominant crustacean species (grass shrimp Palaemonetes pugio) (C), and species richness of all nekton (D) in reference (unrestricted) and treatment (tide-restricted before and tide unrestricted after restoration) marshes in New England before and after rehabilitation action (culvert replacement). All metrics show similar but not identical responses to the rehabilitation and temporal variation. (From Roman et al. 2002.)

As mentioned earlier, the three categories of assessment metrics (Table 3; Figure 4) proposed by Simenstad and Cordell (2000) are opportunity, capacity, and performance. These directly relate to the ecological and physiological responses of juvenile salmonids to rehabilitated estuarine habitats and, potentially, offer more tractable and appropriate assessment criteria. Opportunity metrics (e.g., tidal elevation, geomorphic features or edge, proximity to disturbance, refuge from predation, other cues) assess the capability of juvenile salmon to access and benefit from a habitat's capacity. Capacity refers to habitat attributes (e.g., availability and quantity of prey, physiological conditions that maintain prey, salinity and temperatures that promote high assimilation efficiencies, structural characteristics that provide protection from predators) that promote juvenile salmonid production. Performance (realized function) includes direct measures of physiological or behavioral response (e.g., survival, residence time, foraging success, and growth) attributed to habitat that promote fitness.

Obviously, the presence of a highly mobile indicator species within a restored habitat does provide evidence that fishes are capable of accessing the habitat and using its potential benefits. However, the presence of other, more common fishes (e.g., Figure 10) that are long-term residents of their estuarine habitats and that may have less variable populations, may actually be a less variable metric of opportunity. Inclusion of common estuarine resident fishes may also improve the robustness of the statistical comparisons of fish usage between the rehabilitation and the reference sites. Care must be taken to select fish species and assemblages whose habitat preferences are relevant to the rehabilitation goal and monitoring objectives.

Fish use of estuarine environments can be sampled with a variety of methods and gear. Fish are most commonly captured with nets, including beach seines, fyke traps, blocking nets, drop or throw nets, and trawls. Seines come in a variety of sizes and dimensions. A standard beach seine design used in Pacific Northwest estuaries is 37 m by 2 m, with a 0.6-cm mesh bag (Simenstad et al. 1991). Seines are often deployed parallel to and a set distance from shore (often at a standardized tide) from a small boat and are retrieved by pulling the two wings simultaneously to shore. Adherence to such standard protocols allows a reasonably reliable measure of effort in terms of area or volume of habitat sampled.

Small blocking nets are useful in conjunction with seines for sampling short reaches (small-scale habitat investigation) of shallow tidal channels (Nordby and Zedler 1991). Blocking nets are deployed to completely enclose one section of the channel, while a seine is used to sweep the channel between them. Fish are collected and counted with each sweep through the channel, until the catch approaches zero (depletion seining). Catches should show an exponential decay pattern with increasing sweep number, allowing estimation of fish densities in the blocked reach.

Fyke trap nets (with an attached live box) can be set at high tide, blocking a tidal channel at a strategic point (e.g., highest-order channel at a point above which the marsh channel system completely dewaters on a sampling tide), and sampled until low tide (Shreffler et al. 1990; Miller and Simenstad 1997; Gray et al. 2002). One basic design described in Levy and Northcote (1982) typically uses 3.2-mm (one-eighth-inch) knotless nylon mesh net with an attached fyke tunnel. In addition, screened fence panels can be installed upstream of the fyke net to deflect fish into the net (Conlin and Tutty 1979). These panels should extend from the shoreline to the net. It should be noted that even when tidal channels appear to drain completely at low tide, fish will usually remain in relict channel pools that never drain. An accurate estimate of fish abundance in these channels will require additional sampling of these residual fish, usually by pole seining or by dip netting the various pools, or mark–recapture. In channels that do not dewater at low tide, it is important to correct catch for gear efficiency (Figure 11).

Additional sampling techniques vary with the objectives or creativity of the investigator. For example, Moy and Levin (1991) used pit traps to catch young mummichogs *Fundulus heteroclitus* on marsh surfaces. They buried plastic tubs (34 × 30 × 10 cm) flush with the marsh surface to catch fish that seek refuge in marsh pools on the retreating tide. Rozas and Minello (1997) recommend enclosure-type samplers for estimating densities of small fishes and crustaceans in shallow estuarine habitats typical of the Gulf Coast.

While underwater videography and snorkel or dive surveys have been successfully applied in a variety of freshwater and marine environments (Kingsford and Battershill 1998b; see also Chapter 8), applications in estuaries

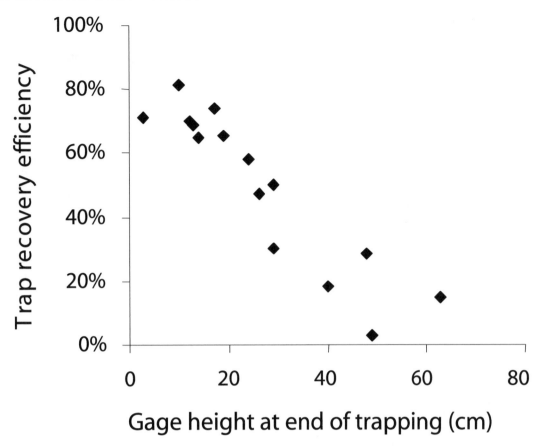

Figure 11.
Relationship between trap efficiency and tidal height in sampling juvenile chinook salmon from a tidal channel in the Skagit River Estuary, Washington. Failure to account for gear efficiency can lead to erroneous interpretation of catch data. (From E. Beamer, Skagit River System Cooperative, LaConner, Washington, unpublished data.)

have had limited application and mixed results (Haggarty 2001; Toft et al. 2003). A number of papers highlight the relative benefits of capture sampling techniques and provide more extensive descriptions of sampling protocols, designs, and gear characteristics (e.g., Simenstad et al. 1991; Rozas and Minello 1997; Callaway et al. 2001; Neckles et al. 2002). Sampling methods that produce quantitative density estimates (and minimize injury to fish) are recommended and may allow for habitat-based comparisons of standing stock or production (Beck et al. 2001). Likewise, length and wet-weight measurements of the collected fish (or a subsample) are recommended to provide additional information on individual condition and population structure, including life history stage and reproductive status. In many cases, it is often critical that an estimate of gear efficiency is calculated to correct abundance estimates; mark–recapture techniques are generally used to estimate gear efficiency.

As discussed earlier, the mere presence of fish does not indicate that they are benefiting from the attributes of a restored habitat or whether the capacity of the habitat promotes their survival and growth. Highly motile fish may not be feeding in the habitat in which they are caught due to the lack of appropriate prey, inhibition of foraging behavior due to predators, or physicochemical conditions (e.g., high current velocities, high temperatures, low salinities, noise and other disturbances). As a result, stomach content data, preferably correlated with estimates of prey availability and water characteristics information, provide more convincing evidence that fish are rearing in a rehabilitated habitat.

Diet analysis can be performed by a variety of methods, and the method chosen is strongly dependent on the study question (Bowen 1996). Traditionally, diets have been evaluated by dissecting preserved fish to examine stomach contents. Recently, stomach lavage (e.g., Hartleb and Moring 1995) has been used to minimize mortality of threatened or endangered fish. Anesthetized fish have their stomach contents flushed out with water through the use of a large syringe or pump device. Stomach contents should be sorted, identified to lowest taxonomic level, counted, and weighed (blotted wet weight). Stomach fullness can be estimated, for example, on a scale of 1 (empty) to 5 (completely full), and total stomach contents can be weighed collectively before sorting. If the prey items are sufficiently large (e.g., amphipods or neomysid shrimp) or abundant, dry weight may also be calculated for greater measurement precision (Terry 1977; Cailliet et al. 1986). Fish diet composition can be represented by an index of relative importance (IRI) (Pinkas et al. 1971) for each prey item, i, such that

$$\mathrm{IRI}_i = [\%\mathrm{FO}_i\,(\%\mathrm{NC}_i + \%\mathrm{GC}_i)]\,,$$

where %FO is the percent frequency of occurrence in all of the sampled fish (i.e., the proportion of fish that ate prey item i); %NC is the percent numerical composition (i.e., the number of prey i divided by total numbers of prey); and %GC is the percent gravimetric or volumetric composition (i.e., the weight or volume of prey i, divided by the total weight or volume of all prey items). Because the resulting numerical values for IRI greatly depend on sample size, IRI should be converted to the percent of the total IRI (i.e., %IRI for each prey item; Cailliet et al. 1986). It should be noted that the IRI is a relative measure that characterizes three important aspects of prey in fish diets (number, mass, and frequency of occurrence), thereby reducing the influence of extreme values in any category but potentially obscuring importance of individual elements. Blotted wet weights and lengths of each subsampled fish should also be measured in conjunction with the gut content data, because diets often depend on fish size.

Controlled studies that assess both the opportunity for fishes to access restored habitats and the capacity of these habitats to promote fish population resilience and production (as assayed by fish presence, abundance, population structure, gut fullness, or diet composition) provide a tractable approach for assessment (Simenstad and Cordell 2000; Gray et al. 2002). Furthermore, with corresponding temperature and other physicochemical measurements of the habitat during fish occupation, these data can be used in bioenergetics models to estimate growth of fishes under various conditions (Madon et al. 2001). However, this information cannot always substitute for unambiguous empirical studies that confirm the value of rehabilitated estuarine habitats in terms of realized survival and growth. Wherever possible, we recommend continued efforts at rigorously assessing residence times (Shreffler et al. 1990), growth (Figure 12) (Shreffler et al. 1992; Miller and Simenstad 1997; Miller and Able 2002), and survival (Levings et al. 1986) of fishes in rehabilitated habitats. Use of bioenergetics models (Madon et al. 2001), large-scale manipulative experiments (Zedler 2001; Cornu and Sadro 2002), innovative approaches to evaluating historic rehabilitation actions (Gray et al. 2002), and emerging methodologies that evaluate the physiological condition of organisms offer further opportunities to improve assessments of realized habitat functions to fishes.

Evaluation of fish assemblage structure can be a powerful tool in assessment and monitoring (Simon 1998). For example, multimetric indexes based on the original index of biological integrity (IBI) work with stream fishes by Karr (1981) have been successfully developed for a wide range of freshwater applications. Combining a wide spectrum of biological attributes (e.g., species richness, relative abundances of certain indicator taxa) that have known responses to environmental gradients (physical, biological, chemical) produces a multimetric index focused on biology, responsive to a variety of environmental changes, and relatively simple to measure and interpret (Karr and Chu 1999). While this approach does show some promise in estuaries (Deegan et al. 1997; Hughes et al. 2002), we found no applications of it in estuarine rehabilitation.

Invertebrates

Aquatic and terrestrial invertebrates are monitored in estuarine rehabilitation actions primarily because of their importance as food for fish and wildlife but also because they can play important roles in ecosystem processes such as sedimentation, bioturbation, and nutrient cycling. Many benthic and epibenthic organisms are dependent on physicochemical characteristics such as sediment grain size, sediment organic content, reducing conditions, and pore-water salinity. They may be slow to respond to rehabilitation actions, depending on the responses of sediment characteristics to newly restored physical and ecological conditions. In contrast, benthic and epibenthic invertebrates that are more dependent on detritus availability or microalgal productivity are likely to respond very quickly to changes in their food sources. Water quality (temperature, salinity, DO, dissolved nutrients, turbidity) will also constrain invertebrate community development. Thus, differences in invertebrate abundance between rehabilitation and reference sites may be the result of a variety of environmental factors. In this respect, benthic and epibenthic invertebrates serve as an index of overall habitat quality.

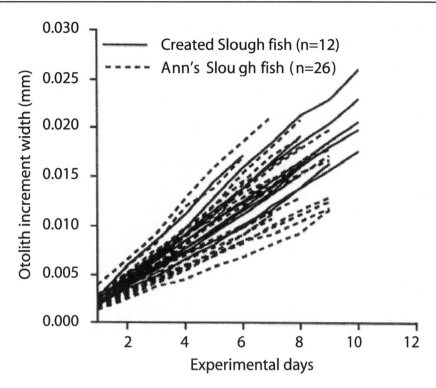

Figure 12.
Otolith increment width in juvenile coho salmon rearing in created and reference sloughs in the Chehalis River Estuary, Washington. Such experimental assessments of organism growth provide information on the functional performance of rehabilitation actions. (From Miller and Simenstad 1997.)

As previously noted, the diets of fishes are not necessarily indicative of on-site feeding, unless fish have occupied the capture location for a significant portion of their expected gastric evacuation time. Estimates of the available on-site prey resources, followed by an analysis of the overlap between fish diet composition and potential prey availability, can provide valuable corroborative evidence. If the goals of the rehabilitation and monitoring plan are specific to certain fish species, preliminary knowledge, or, preferably, fish stomach content data from both the rehabilitation and reference sites, can provide valuable guidance on the taxa of invertebrates that sampling should emphasize. However, this approach has two caveats: the sampled invertebrates may not be easily available to the fish, or it may not be possible to sample the prey (invertebrates) accurately. Hence, diet overlap analysis should be carefully interpreted.

Infauna are generally sampled by inserting a rigid polyvinyl chloride (PVC) or metal tube (corer) into the sediment and preserving the extracted core in 10% buffered formalin for later processing in the laboratory (Simenstad et al. 1991). If increasing the performance of fish is a major goal of the rehabilitation action, it is important that all benthic samples be taken to the same shallow sediment depth corresponding to the depth prey colonize or the fish access for feeding. In many studies of infauna, the diameter and depth of core sampling depends upon whether sampling is directed toward large mollusks (clams), which are poorly sampled by small diameter cores; some clams occur predominantly within 10 cm of the surface, but many taxa occur deeper than that. By definition, benthic macroinvertebrates are those that are retained on a 0.5-mm sieve; sampling for meiofauna, which may provide an important indication of prey of very small or juvenile fishes, requires further retention of the organisms that pass through the 0.5-mm sieve but are retained on an approximately 0.1-mm sieve.

Pelagic plankton are rarely sampled in estuarine rehabilitation, but there are many well-developed sampling techniques available (Harris et al. 2000), including fine-meshed nets of many configurations, acoustical and optical techniques, and even remote sensing. Neustonic organisms (those that occur at the very surface layer of the water column) can include adult and larval insects deposited on or emerged into the surface layer, as well as other aquatic insects and crustaceans that spend the majority of their time in the surface layer. Neuston are typically sampled with plankton nets adapted to float and skim the surface layer either by towing or by being held in current.

Terrestrial insects and invertebrates may also be an important parameter to monitor for some estuarine reha-bilitation efforts. A wide variety of methods exists for sampling terrestrial insects (see Merritt and Cummins 1996). Each has its biases and imperfectly samples the insect community. Fallout traps are recommended because they sample insects that are most directly available for consumption by fish (i.e., insects that have fall-en onto the water's surface). Fallout traps are simply large plastic trays or bins (e.g., 40 x 70 x 15 cm) that con-tain dilute soap or some other material that breaks water surface tension and, thus, serve to passively retain and preserve insects that fall into the trays or bins. Dilute ammonium is often used because it is not an attractant and it is easily disposed after use. The bins should be filled minimally, to about 4–5 cm depth. The bins can be designed to float on the rising and falling tide corralled by tall PVC or garden (e.g., bamboo) stakes inserted vertically into the sediments at each side of the fallout trap. If the ground surface on which the bins settle at low tide is uneven, a landing frame made from PVC pipes can be constructed to provide a level surface.

Food webs

Analysis of food webs can provide important insights in estuarine ecology, including understanding of troph-ic relationships, sources of organic matter and nutrients, and energy flow. Food webs are studied with several techniques, including observations of feeding behavior, stomach contents analysis, and stable isotope analysis (see also Chapter 9). Although a potentially powerful tool in estuarine rehabilitation monitoring, more thor-ough discussion of food webs is beyond the scope of this chapter. Additional information can be found in the following sources: Simenstad (1979), Cohen (1988), Paine (1988), Kwak and Zedler (1997), Page (1997).

Nonindigenous species

Invasions by nonindigenous species are a leading cause of global biodiversity loss (Pimm 1987; Gophen et al. 1995; Vitousek et al. 1997), and estuaries are considered particularly vulnerable to invasion (Carlton 2001). Hundreds, perhaps thousands of nonindigenous aquatic species have become established in U.S. estuaries, and the rate of invasion is apparently increasing (Cohen and Carlton 1998; Ruiz et al. 2000). Nonindigenous species can alter the physical environment of estuarine systems as well as the behavior, distribution, and troph-ic interactions of native species (Ruiz et al. 1997; Grosholz 2002). While the extent and severity of the prob-lem of nonindigenous species is generally recognized, relatively little is understood in detail about ecosystem and management responses to habitat invasion by nonindigenous species. Even less is known with respect to rehabilitation and management (D'Antonio and Meyerson 2002).

While a tremendous variety of nonindigenous species have invaded estuarine systems, ranging from viruses and bacteria to mammals, those thought to be of highest priority for monitoring are plants, mammals, fish, and macroalgae—based on their ease of collection, ease of identification, ability to be controlled, and man-agement concern (Wasson et al. 2002). Given that there are limited resources for rehabilitation in most cases, it would seem prudent to adopt some of the general strategies presented by D'Antonio and Meyerson (2002). If an exotic species of concern is relatively short lived and facilitates colonization by native species via succes-sion, then its eradication or control might not be a top priority. But if a long-lived exotic species is known to have dramatic impacts on successional patterns, then eradication or control is critical.

The methods for sampling nonindigenous species are generally the same as those for native taxa. Thus, we will only describe general monitoring issues and recommendations for monitoring of nonindigenous species (reviewed in Wasson et al. 2002) and defer to previous subsections on techniques for sampling vegetation, fish, and so forth. In general, monitoring for nonindigenous species should be part of a larger baseline monitoring program to detect long-term change, new invasions, and interactions of species distributions and abundance with sea level rise, climate change, disturbance (e.g., drought or flooding), construction development, water diversion, eutrophication, and more. These concerns are usually relevant to most estuarine monitoring pro-grams. Native and nonindigenous species should be monitored together; as a corollary, sites where there are not yet any invaders should be monitored, as well as sites containing nonindigenous species (see also Chapter 11). Such monitoring allows investigation of fundamental and unanswered questions about the ecology of invasion. The spatial distribution of monitoring effort typically should be stratified among habitat types, with extra focus on zonal borders, which may be sensitive to a variety of stresses, including climate change and inva-sion by nonindigenous species. Other potential hotspots of invasion meriting extra sampling effort could include areas subject to periodic disturbances such as floods.

Chemical Contaminants

While impacts of toxic chemicals have not been included elsewhere in this volume, we discuss them briefly here because of their particular relevance in estuaries as urban centers and as the downstream repositories for watershed inputs. Although chemical contaminants are not emphasized in many habitat remediation and rehabilitation actions (except those that are part of U.S. Environmental Protection Agency Superfund Program cleanup activities or Natural Resource Damage Assessment actions), evidence suggests that exposure to contaminants is having negative effects on a wide variety of species. In wild salmonids, for example, contaminant exposure has been linked to adverse effects on important life history processes such as survival, growth, homing behavior, and disease resistance (Scholz et al. 2000; Arkoosh et al. 2001). If such impacts are not addressed, the performance of physical habitat rehabilitation efforts may be limited, or such efforts might even attract organisms to habitats where they are at increased risk of exposure to environmental contaminants.

Monitoring of anthropogenic chemical contaminants in estuaries is relatively straightforward, at least in those cases where analytical techniques for the contaminants of concern have been developed, and can include measurements of chemical concentrations in water, sediment, and biota, as well as assessments of associated biological effects in both field and laboratory settings (Rand 1995). Environmental concentrations of chemicals are typically compared to various chemical criteria to determine the potential for effects. It is important to keep in mind the ecological context of such criteria in evaluating the biological significance of contaminants in the environment. For example, many criteria are derived from laboratory bioassays exposing single species to single toxicants through a single pathway and measuring acute lethality as the endpoint (e.g., 96 hour LC50, USEPA 1986; USEPA 2002). This approach fails to consider the potential for simultaneous exposure of multiple contaminants through multiple pathways (e.g., water, sediments, and diet) and is also likely to miss highly significant, sublethal biological effects (e. g., impaired growth, increased disease susceptibility, behavioral alterations). Additionally, concentrations that may not cause obvious adverse effects at one trophic level (in say, benthic, deposit- or filter-feeding invertebrates typical of bioassay organisms) may result in adverse effects at higher trophic levels through bioaccumulation and trophic transfer (Rice et al. 2000).

An alternative approach to chemical contaminant criteria development and use is based on evaluation of tissue concentrations in the species of concern or in representative species in the ecosystem (Johnson 2000; Meador 2000; Meador et al. 2002). For bioaccumulative contaminants (e.g., PAHs), such an approach would be more effective in accounting for exposure through multiple pathways, bioaccumulation, and biomagnification than the current regulatory framework, which addresses exposure via water and via sediments separately. Another approach to criteria development that may be more appropriate for contaminants that do not bioaccumulate in some taxa is to link field data on sublethal biological effects to sediment contaminant concentrations (e.g., Johnson 2000). An advantage of using field data for the analyses is that effect threshold estimates are based on health effects measured in a native organism collected from its natural environment. A disadvantage of the field-based approach is that it may not adequately differentiate between biological effects resulting from exposure to the contaminant of interest and effects due to other contaminants or contaminant mixtures. However, this can be mitigated to some extent by choosing parameters where the contaminant of interest is known to be a strong causative factor.

Summary

Because of the ecological significance of estuaries and their heavy alteration and use by humans, rehabilitation of estuarine ecosystems (typically involving the return of tidal inundation, substrate manipulation, and revegetation) is an increasingly common goal in the pursuit of natural resource conservation, recovery, and enhancement. Unfortunately, the performance of such efforts is rarely evaluated well, primarily because estuarine assessment and monitoring programs are either piecemeal or nonexistent, and also because estuarine programs are often confounded by several major sources of uncertainty, including ecosystem complexity, limited knowledge of historical conditions, inadequate data on specific biological responses to various environmental changes, inadequate data on specific habitat requirements for certain species and life history types, and poor or nonexistent models for habitat succession. Finally, estuarine assessment and monitoring programs often lack efficient metrics that relate directly to ecosystem processes or the survival and fitness of target resources.

Similar to monitoring rehabilitation in other environments, monitoring in estuaries requires a sound conceptual model of the ecosystem in question and the role of the rehabilitation action in it, clear objectives, well-defined hypotheses, appropriate study designs and sampling strategies, and the selection of appropriate parameters and methods. Monitoring should be conceived as a long-term investment in the sustainable performance of rehabilitation actions and should be a primary concern during all stages of rehabilitation actions, beginning with the design phase. Monitoring is the most effective means to learn from rehabilitation approaches and techniques.

Improved monitoring of estuarine rehabilitation actions depends on progress in a number of fields. Understanding biological change resulting from human activities and knowing the natural history and the habitat requirements of various species and life history types are extremely useful in defining rehabilitation goals and interpreting monitoring data, yet are sorely lacking in many temperate estuarine systems. Perhaps even more pressing is the scarcity of meaningful indicators of estuarine rehabilitation performance. Species- and habitat-specific indicators are relatively poor indicators of the role of a restoring ecosystem in estuarine landscapes. Landscape scale indicators are needed that capture internal attributes and the role of the site within a larger landscape setting (e.g., metrics of tidal channel geomorphology, matrix composition, corridors, core areas, etc.). These should be developed from reference systems and would serve estuarine rehabilitation design and planning, as well as monitoring. Finally, it is important to improve monitoring of process rather than just structure. Ecosystem structure may be diagnostic of performance, but it really does not provide any indication of the ecosystem processes that may or may not maintain that structure. Therefore, more synthetic ecosystem indicators are needed that better reflect the role and contribution of rehabilitation sites to ecosystem processes. Adaptive management of poorly functioning rehabilitation sites is considerably more difficult, if not impossible, without process data.

Perhaps the largest weakness in estuarine rehabilitation monitoring programs is the emphasis on short-term description of estuarine habitat attributes, rather than longer-term evaluation of the fundamental ecosystem processes that create and sustain restored conditions. We recommend long-term assessment and monitoring programs that (1) emphasize direct measures of the linkages between ecosystem processes and ecological condition, (2) are conceptually broad enough to consider landscape and ecosystem contexts, and (3) with respect to specific sites and biological components, explore relationships between criteria and metrics based on habitat opportunity, capacity, and resource (e.g., anadromous fish) performance. We also advocate systematic sampling and experiments that directly assay how habitat capacity and opportunity relate to performance and function of the rehabilitation.

Poor or nonexistent monitoring of estuarine rehabilitation in the future will not only result in our failure to detect changes in the condition of target resources and identify factors affecting them but also will impair the advancement of rehabilitation techniques, application, and science. Moreover, it will result in wasted resources and poor management, undermining social and political support for estuarine rehabilitation efforts.

Acknowledgments

We thank Martin Liermann, Ed Quimby, and Russell Bellmer of the National Oceanic and Atmospheric Administration (NOAA) for helpful comments on drafts of this chapter. We also gratefully acknowledge Eric Beamer of the Skagit River System Cooperative, Jennifer Burke of the School of Aquatic and Fishery Sciences, University of Washington, Dr. Charles Roman of the National Park Service, and Craig Cornu of the South Slough National Estuarine Reserve for contributing figures.

References

Able, K. W., D. M. Nemerson, P. R. Light, and R. O. Bush. 2000. Initial response of fishes to marsh restoration at a former salt hay farm bordering Delaware Bay. Pages 749–773 in M. P. Weinstein and D. A. Kreeger, editors. Concepts and controversies in tidal marsh ecology. Kluwer Academic Publishers, The Netherlands.

Adair, S. E., J. L. Moore, and W. H. Kiel. 1996. Wintering diving duck use of coastal ponds: an analysis of alternative hypotheses. Journal of Wildlife Management 60:83–93.

Aitkin, J. K. 1998. The importance of estuarine habitats to anadromous salmonids of the Pacific Northwest: a literature review. U.S. Fish and Wildlife Service, Lacey, Washington.

Allison, S. K. 1992. The influence of rainfall variability on the species composition of a northern California salt marsh plant assemblage. Vegetation 101:145–160.

Anisfeld, S. C., M. J. Tobin, and G. Benoit. 1999. Sedimentation rates in flow-restricted and restored salt marshes in Long Island Sound. Estuaries 22:231–244.

Arkoosh, M. A., E. Clemons, P. Huffman, A. N. Kagley, E. Casillas, N. Adams, H. R. Sanborn, T. K. Collier, and J. E. Stein. 2001. Increased susceptibility of juvenile chinook salmon to vibriosis after exposure to chlorinated and aromatic compounds found in contaminated urban estuaries. Journal of Aquatic Animal Health 13:257–268.

Avakian, M. D., B. Dellinger, H. Fiedler, B. Gullet, C. Koshland, S. Marklund, G. Oberdörster, S. Safe, A. Sarofim, K. R. Smith, D. Schwartz, and W. A. Suk. 2002. The origin, fate, and health effects of combustion by-products: a research framework. Environmental Health Perspectives 110:1155–1162.

Baudo, R., J. P. Geisy, and H. Muntau, editors. 1990. Sediments: chemistry and toxicity of in-place pollutants. Lewis Publishers, Ann Arbor, Michigan.

Beach, D. 2002. Coastal sprawl: the effects of urban design on aquatic ecosystems in the United States. Pew Oceans Commission, Arlington, Virginia.

Beck, M. W., K. L. Heck, K. W. Able, D. L. Childers, D. B. Eggleston, B. M. Gillanders, B. Halpern, C. G. Hays, K. Hoshino, T. J. Minello, R. J. Orth, P. F. Sheridan, and M. P. Weinstein. 2001. The identification, conservation, and management of estuarine and marine nurseries for fish and invertebrates. Bioscience 51:633–641.

Bortleson, G. C., M. J. Chrzastowski, and A. K. Helgerson. 1980. Historical changes of shoreline and wetland at eleven major deltas in the Puget Sound region, Washington. U.S. Geological Survey hydrological investigations atlas HA-617, Washington, D.C.

Bottom, D. L., C. A. Simenstad, A. M. Baptista, D. A. Jay, J. Burke, K. K. Jones, E. Casillas, and M. H. Schiewe, editors. 2001. Salmon at river's end: the role of the estuary in the decline and recovery of Columbia River salmon. Report to the U.S. Department of Energy, Bonneville Power Administration, Contract 98-AI06603, Portland, Oregon.

Boumans, R. M. J., and J. W. Day, Jr. 1993. High precision measurements of sediment elevation in shallow coastal areas using a sedimentation-erosion table. Estuaries 16:375–380.

Bowen, S. H. 1996. Quantitative description of the diet. Pages 513-522 in B. R. Murphy and D. W. Willis, editors. Fisheries techniques. American Fisheries Society, Bethesda, Maryland.

Brown-Peterson, N. J., M. S. Peterson, D. A. Rydene, and R. W. Eames. 1993. Fish assemblages in natural vs. well established recolonized seagrass meadows. Estuaries 16:177–189.

Buckland, S. T., D. R. Anderson, K. P. Burnham, J. L. Laake, D. L. Borchers, and L. Thomas. 1993. Introduction to distance sampling: estimating of biological problems. Chapman and Hall, London.

Buckland, S. T., D. R. Anderson, K. P. Burnham, J. L. Laake, D. L. Borchers, and L. Thomas. 2001. Introduction to distance sampling: estimating abundance of biological populations. Oxford University Press, Oxford, UK.

Burke, J., and K. K. Jones. 2001. Change in juvenile salmon life history, growth, and estuarine residence. Pages 164–217 in D. L. Bottom, C. A. Simenstad, A. M. Baptista, D. A. Jay, J. Burke, K. K. Jones, E. Casillas, and M. H. Schiewe, editors. Salmon at river's end: the role of the estuary in the decline and recovery of Columbia River salmon. Report to the U.S. Department of Energy, Bonneville Power Administration, Contract 98-AI06603, Portland, Oregon.

Cahoon, D. R., D. J. Reed, and J. W. Day, Jr. 1995. Estimating shallow subsidence in microtidal salt marshes of the southeastern United States: Kaye and Barghoorn revisited. Marine Geology 128:1–9.

Cailliet, G. M., M. S. Love, and A. W. Ebeling. 1986. Fishes: a field and laboratory manual on their structure, identification, and life history. Wadsworth Publishing Company, Belmont, California.

Callaway, J. C., G. Sullivan, J. S. Desmond, G. D. Williams, and J. B. Zedler. 2001. Assessment and monitoring. Pages 271–335 in J. B. Zedler, editor. Handbook for restoring tidal wetlands. CRC Press, Boca Raton, Florida.

Carlton, J. T. 2001. Introduced species in US coastal waters: environmental impacts and management priorities. Pew Oceans Commission, Arlington, Florida.

Church, M., and D. M. Mark. 1980. On size and scale in geomorphology. Progress in Physical Geography 4:342–390.

Coats, R. N., C. K. Cuffe, J. B. Zedler, D. Reed, S. M. Waltry, and J. S. Noller. 1995. Design guidelines for tidal channels in coastal wetlands. U.S. Army Corps of Engineers, Waterways Experiment Station, Vicksburg, Mississippi.

Cochran, W. G. 1977. Sampling techniques. Third edition. John Wiley & Sons, New York.

Cohen, A. N., and J. T. Carlton. 1998. Accelerating invasion rate in a highly invaded estuary. Science 279:555–558.

Cohen, J. E. 1988. Food webs and community structure. Pages 181–202 in J. Roughgarden, R. M. May, and S. A. Levin, editors. Perspectives in ecological theory. Princeton University Press, Princeton, New Jersey.

Collins, B. D., and D. R. Montgomery. 2001. Importance of archival and process studies to characterizing presettlement riverine geomorphic processes and habitat in the Puget Lowland. Pages 227–243 in J. M. Dorava, D. R. Montgomery, B. B. Palcsak, and F. A. Fitzpatrick, editors. Geomorphic processes and riverine habitat. Water science and application series. Volume 4. American Geophysical Union, Washington, D.C.

Collins, B. D., D. R. Montgomery, and A. J. Sheikh. 2003. Reconstructing the historic riverine landscape of the Puget Lowland. Pages 79–128 in S. Bolton, D. R. Montgomery, and D. Booth, editors. Restoration of Puget Sound rivers. University of Washington Press, Seattle.

Conlin, K., and B. D. Tutty. 1979. Juvenile salmonid field trapping manual. British Columbia Department of Fisheries and Oceans Resource Services Branch, Habitat Protection Division, Fisheries and Marine Service Manuscript Report #1530, Vancouver.

Cordell, J. R., L. M. Tear, and K. Jensen. 2001. Biological monitoring at Duwamish River coastal America restoration and reference sites: a seven-year retrospective. University of Washington, School of Aquatic and Fishery Sciences, SAFS-UW-0108, Seattle.

Cordell, J. R., L. M. Tear, C. A. Simenstad, S. M. Wenger, and W. G. Hood. 1994. Duwamish River coastal America restoration and reference sites: results and recommendations from year one pilot and monitoring studies. University of Washington, Fisheries Research Institute Technical Report FRI-UW-9416, Seattle.

Cornu, C. E., and S. Sadro. 2002. Physical and functional responses to experimental marsh surface elevation manipulation in Coos Bay's South Slough. Restoration Ecology 10:474–486.

Cowardin, L. M., V. Carter, F. C. Golet, and E. T. LaRoe. 1979. Classification of wetlands and deepwater habitats of the United States. U.S. Fish and Wildlife Service, FWS, OBS-79/31, Washington, D.C.

Coyer, J., D. Steller, and J. Witman. 2001. The underwater catalog: a guide to methods in underwater research. Second edition. Shoals Marine Laboratory, Cornell University, Ithaca, New York.

Craft, C., S. W. Broome, and C. Campbell. 2002. Fifteen years of vegetation and soil development after brackish-water marsh creation. Restoration Ecology 10:248–258.

Craft, C. B., J. Reader, J. Sacco, and S. W. Broome. 1999. Twenty-five years of ecosystem development of constructed *Spartina alterniflora* (Loisel) marshes. Ecological Applications 9:1405–1419.

D'Antonio, C., and L. A. Meyerson. 2002. Exotic plant species as problems and solutions in ecological restoration: a synthesis. Restoration Ecology 10:703–713.

Dahl, T. E. 2000. Status and trends of wetlands in the conterminous United States 1986 to 1987. U.S. Fish and Wildlife Service, Washington, D.C.

Dame, R., M. Alber, D. Allen, M. Mallin, C. Montague, A. Lewitus, A. Chalmers, R. Gardner, C. Gilman, B. Kjerfve, J. Pinckney, and N. Smith. 2000. Estuaries of the South Atlantic coast of North America: their geographical signature. Estuaries 23:793–819.

Daughton, C. G., and T. A. Ternes. 1999. Pharmaceutical and personal care products in the environment: agents of subtle change. Environmental Health Perspectives 107:907–938.

Dawe, N. K., G. E. Bradfield, W. S. Boyd, D. E. C. Trethewey, and A. N. Zolbrod. 2000. Marsh creation in a North Pacific Estuary: is thirteen years of monitoring vegetation dynamics enough? Conservation Ecology 4. Online at http://www.consecol.org/vol4/iss2/art12 [Accessed 30 May 2003].

Dawley, E. M., R. D. Ledgerwood, and A. L. Jensen. 1985. Beach and purse seine sampling of juvenile salmonids in the Columbia River Estuary and ocean plume, 1977–1983. Volumes I-II. U.S. Department of Commerce, NOAA Technical Memorandum NMFS, F/NWC-74, Seattle.

Day, J. W., C. A. S. Hall, W. M. Kemp, and A. Yanez-Arancibia. 1989. Estuarine ecology. John Wiley & Sons, New York.

Deegan, L. A., J. T. Finn, S. G. Ayvazian, C. A. Ryder-Kieffer, and J. Buonaccorsi. 1997. Development and validation of an estuarine biotic integrity index. Estuaries 20:601–617.

DEQ (Department of Environmental Quality). 1994. Dissolved oxygen: 1992–1994 water quality standards review. Report of the State of Oregon Technical Advisory Committee, Policy Advisory Committee, Dissolved Oxygen Subcommittee, Portland, Oregon.

Dethier, M. N. 1990. A marine and estuarine classification system for Washington State. Washington Natural Heritage Program, Washington Department of Natural Resources, Olympia.

Downes, B. J., L. A. Barmuta, P. G. Fairweather, D. P. Faith, M. J. Keough, P. S. Lake, B. D. Mapstone, and G. P. Quinn. 2002a. The ecological nature of flowing waters. Pages 14–27 *in* Monitoring ecological impacts: concepts and practice in flowing waters. Cambridge University Press, Cambridge, UK.

Downes, B. J., L. A. Barmuta, P. G. Fairweather, D. P. Faith, M. J. Keough, P. S. Lake, B. D. Mapstone, and G. P. Quinn. 2002b. Inferential uncertainty and multiple lines of evidence. Pages 249-288 *in* Monitoring ecological impacts: concepts and practice in flowing waters. Cambridge University Press, Cambridge, UK.

Downing, J. 1983. The coast of Puget Sound: its processes and development. Washington Sea Grant Program, University of Washington, Seattle.

Dyer, K. R. 1973. Estuaries, a physical introduction. Wiley-Interscience, New York.

Ehrenfeld, J. G. 2000. Evaluating wetlands within an urban context. Ecological Engineering 15:253–265.

Elzinga, C., D. Salzer, J. G. Willoughby, and J. Gibbs. 2001. Monitoring plant and animal populations. Blackwell, Malden, Massachusetts.

Emmett, R., R. Llanso, J. Newton, R. Thom, M. Hornberger, C. Morgan, C. Levings, A. Copping, and P. Fishman. 2000. Geographic signatures of west coast estuaries. Estuaries 23:765–792.

Ewing, K. 1983. Environmental controls in Pacific Northwest intertidal marsh plant communities. Canadian Journal of Botany 61:1105–1116.

Fairbridge, R. 1980. The estuary: its definition and geodynamic cycle. Pages 1-35 *in* E. Olausson and I. Cato, editors. Chemistry and biochemistry of estuaries. Wiley, New York.

Feist, B. E., and E. O. Box. 2002. Vegetation and ecosystem mapping. Pages 203–209 *in* Encyclopedia of science and technology, 9th edition, volume 19. McGraw-Hill Publishers, New York.

Folk, R. L. 1968. Petrology of sedimentary rocks. Hemphills, Austin, Texas.

Fonseca, M. S., W. J. Kenworthy, and G. W. Thayer. 1998. Guidelines for the conservation and restoration of seagrasses in the United States and adjacent waters. NOAA Coastal Ocean Program decision analysis series #12. NOAA, National Marine Fisheries Service, Southeast Fisheries Science Center, Beaufort Laboratory, Beaufort, North Carolina.

Forman, R. T. T. 1995. Land mosaics: the ecology of landscapes and regions. Cambridge University Press, Cambridge, UK.

Freeman, R. 1999. Restoring healthy riparian and wetland ecosystems: an interview with Phil Williams. Ecological Restoration 17:202–209.

French, J. R., and D. R. Stoddard. 1992. Hydrodynamics of salt marsh creek systems: implications for marsh morphological development and material exchange. Earth Surface Processes and Landforms 17:235-252.

Frenkel, R. E., and J. C. Morlan. 1991. Can we restore our salt marshes? Lessons from the Salmon River, Oregon. The Northwest Environmental Journal 7:119-135.

Garofalo, D. 1980. The influence of wetland vegetation on tidal stream channel migration and morphology. Estuaries 3:258-270.

Garono, R. J., C. A. Simenstad, R. Robinson, and H. Ripley. 2004. Using high spatial resolution hyperspectral imagery to map intertidal habitat structure in Hood Canal, Washington, U.S.A. Canadian Journal of Remote Sensing 30:54-63.

Geyer, W. R., J. T. Morris, F. G. Prahl, and D. A. Jay. 2000. Interaction between physical process and ecosystem structure: a comparative approach. Pages 177-206 in J. E. Hobbie, editor. Estuarine science: a synthetic approach to research and practice. Island Press, Washington, D.C.

Gibson, G. R., M. L. Bowman, J. Gerritsen, and B. D. Snyder. 2000. Estuarine and coastal marine waters: bioassessment and biocriteria technical guidance. U.S. Environmental Protection Agency, Office of Water, EPA 822-B-00-24, Washington, D.C.

Goodall, D.W. 1951. Some considerations in the use of point quadrats for the analysis of vegitation. Australian Journal of Science Research Service 5:1-4.

Gophen, M., P. B. O. Ochumba, and L. S. Kaufman. 1995. Some aspects of perturbation in the structure and biodiversity of Lake Victoria (East Africa). Aquatic Living Resources 8:27-41.

Gough, L., and J. B. Grace. 1999. Effects of environmental change on plant species density: comparing predictions with experiments. Ecology 80:882-890.

Gray, A., C. A. Simenstad, D. L. Bottom, and T. J. Cornwell. 2002. Contrasting functional performance of juvenile salmon habitat in recovering wetlands of the Salmon River Estuary, Oregon, U.S.A. Restoration Ecology 10:514-526.

Grieg-Smith, P. 1964. Quantitative plant ecology. 2nd edition Butterworths, London.

Grosholz, E. 2002. Ecological and evolutionary consequences of coastal invasions. Trends in Ecology and Evolution 17:22-27.

Hackney, C. T., W. D. Burbanck, and O. P. Hackney. 1976. Biological and physical dynamics of a Georgia tidal creek. Chesapeake Science 17:271-280.

Haggarty, D. 2001. An evaluation of fish habitat in Burrard Inlet, British Columbia. Master's thesis. University of British Columbia, Vancouver.

Halpin, P. M. 1997. Habitat use patterns of the mummichug, *Fundulus heteroclitus*, in New England. I. Intramarsh variation. Estuaries 20:618-625.

Hansen, D. V., and M. Rattray Jr. 1966. New dimensions in estuary classification. Limnology and Oceanraphy 11:319-325.

Harris, R. P., P. H. Wiebe, J. Lenz, H. R. Skjoldal, and M. Huntley, editors. 2000. ICES zooplankton methodology manual. Academic Press, San Diego, California.

Hartleb, C. F., and J. R. Moring. 1995. An improved gastric lavage device for removing stomach contents from live fish. Fisheries Research 24:261-265.

Healey, M. C. 1982. Juvenile Pacific salmon in estuaries: the life support system. Pages 315-341 in V. S. Kennedy, editor. Estuarine comparisons. Academic Press, New York.

Hicks, C. R. 1982. Fundamental concepts in the design of experiments. Holt, Reinhart and Winston, Inc., New York.

Holling, C. S., editor. 1978. Adaptive environmental assessment and management. John Wiley & Sons, New York.

Hood, W. G. 2002. Application of landscape allometry to restoration of tidal channels. Restoration Ecology 10:213-222.

Hood, W. G. 2004. Indirect environmental effects of dikes on estuarine tidal channels: thinking outside of the dike for habitat restoration and monitoring. Estuaries 27:273-282.

Hopkinson, C., and J. J. Vallino. 1995. The relationships among man's activities in watersheds and estuaries: a model of runoff effects on patterns of estuarine community metabolism. Estuaries 18:598-621.

Hughes, J. E., L. A. Deegan, M. J. Weaver, and J. E. Costa. 2002. Regional application of an index of estuarine biotic integrity based on fish communities. Estuaries 25:250-263.

Jay, D. A., W. R. Geyer, and D. R. Montgomery. 2000. An ecological perspective on estuarine classification. Pages 149-176 in J. E. Hobbie, editor. Estuarine science: a synthetic approach to science and practice. Island Press, Washington, D.C.

Johnson, L. L. 2000. An analysis in support of sediment quality thresholds for polycyclic aromatic hydrocarbons (PAHs) to protect estuarine fish. Northwest Fisheries Science Center, White Paper, Seattle.

Karr, J. R. 1981. Assessment of biotic integrity using fish communities. Fisheries 6:21-27.

Karr, J. R., and E. W. Chu. 1999. Restoring life in running waters: better biological monitoring. Island Press, Washington, D.C.

Kennish, M. J. 2000. Estuary restoration and maintenance. CRC Press, Boca Raton, Florida.

Kentula, M. E. 2000. Perspectives on setting success criteria for wetland restoration. Ecological Engineering 15:199-210.

Kingsford, M. J., and C. N. Battershill. 1998a. Procedures for establishing a study. Pages 29-48 in M. J. Kingsford and C. N. Battershill, editors. Studying temperate marine environments. A handbook for ecologists. Canterbury University Press, Christchurch, New Zealand.

Kingsford, M. J., and C. N. Battershill. 1998b. Studying temperate marine environments. A handbook for ecologists. Canterbury University Press, Christchurch, New Zealand.

Kneib, R. T. 1997. The role of tidal marshes in the ecology of estuarine nekton. Oceanography and Marine Biology: An Annual Review 35:163-220.

Knighton, A. D., C. D. Woodroffe, and K. Mills. 1992. The evolution of tidal creek networks, Mary River, Northern Australia. Earth Surface Processes and Landforms 17:167-190.

Knox, G. A. 2001. The ecology of seashores. CRC Press, Boca Raton, Florida.

Kusler, J. A., and M. E. Kentula, editors. 1990. Wetland creation and restoration: the status of the science. Island Press, Washington, D.C.

Kwak, T., and J. B. Zedler. 1997. Food web analysis of southern California coastal wetlands using multiple stable isotopes. Oecologia 110.

Langis, R., M. Zalejko, and J. B. Zedler. 1991. Nitrogen assessments in a constructed and a natural salt marsh of San Diego Bay, California. Ecological Applications 1:40–51.

Larsen, D. P., T. M. Kincaid, S. E. Jacobs, and N. S. Urquhart. 2001. Designs for evaluating local and regional scale trends. BioScience 51(12):1069–1078.

Legendre, P., and L. Legendre. 1998. Numerical ecology. Second English edition. Elsevier Science, B.V., Amsterdam.

Legendre, P., S. F. Thrush, V. J. Cummings, P. K. Dayton, J. Grant, J. E. Hewitt, A. H. Hines, and M. R. Wilkinson. 1997. Spatial structure of bivalves in a sandflat: scale and generating processes. Journal of Experimental Marine Biology and Ecology 216:99–128.

Leopold, L. B., M. G. Wolman, and J. P. Miller. 1964. Fluvial processes in geomorphology. W. H. Freeman, San Francisco.

Levin, S. A. 1992. The problem of pattern and scale in ecology. Ecology 73:1943–1967.

Levings, C. D., C. D. McAllister, and B. D. Cheng. 1986. Differential use of the Campbell River Estuary, British Columbia, by wild and hatchery-reared juvenile chinook salmon. Canadian Journal of Fisheries and Aquatic Sciences 43:1386–1397.

Levings, C. D., C. D. McAllister, J. S. MacDonald, T. J. Brown, M. S. Kotyk, and B. A. Kask. 1989. Chinook salmon (*Oncorhynchus tshawytscha*) and estuarine habitat: a transfer experiment can help evaluate estuary dependency. Pages 116–122 *in* C. D. Levings, L. B. Holtby, and M. A. Henderson, editors. Proceedings of the national workshop on effects of habitat alteration on salmonid stocks. Canadian Special Publications in Fisheries and Aquatic Sciences 105.

Levy, D. A., and T. G. Northcote. 1982. Juvenile salmon residency in a marsh area of the Fraser River Estuary. Canadian Journal of Fisheries and Aquatic Sciences 39:270–276.

Linthurst, R. 1980. An evaluation of aeration, nitrogen, pH and salinity as factors affecting Spartina alterniflora growth: a summary. Pages 235–247 *in* V. Kennedy, editor. Estuarine perspectives. Academic Press, New York.

Lyon, J. G. 2001. Wetland landscape characterization. Ann Arbor Press, Chelsea, Michigan.

Madon, S. P., G. D. Williams, J. M. West, and J. B. Zedler. 2001. The importance of marsh access to growth of the California killifish, *Fundulus parvipinnis*, evaluated through bioenergetics modeling. Ecological Modeling 136:149–165.

Meador, J. P. 2000. An analysis in support of a sediment quality threshold for tributyltin to protect prey species for juvenile salmonids listed by the Endangered Species Act. Northwest Fisheries Science Center, White Paper, Seattle.

Meador, J.P., T. K. Collier, and J. E. Stein. 2002. Use of tissue and sediment based threshold concentrations of polychlorinated biphenyls (PCBs) to protect juvenile salmonids listed under the Endangered Species Act. Aquatic Conservation: Marine and Freshwater Ecosystems 12:493–516.

Merritt, R. W., and K. W. Cummins. 1996. An introduction to the aquatic insects of North America. Third edition. Kendall and Hunt Publishing Company, Dubuque, Iowa.

Miller, J. A., and C. A. Simenstad. 1997. A comparative assessment of a natural and created estuarine slough as rearing habitat for juvenile chinook and coho salmon. Estuaries 20:792–806.

Miller, M. J., and K. W. Able. 2002. Movements and growth of tagged young-of-the-year Atlantic croaker (*Micropogonias undulatus* L.) in restored and reference marsh creeks in Delaware Bay, USA. Journal of Experimental Marine Biology and Ecology 267:15–33.

Montagna, P. A. 1993. Comparison of ecosystem structure and function of created and natural seagrass habitats in Laguna Madre, Texas. University of Texas Marine Science Institute, Technical Report Number TR/93-007, Port Aransas.

Montgomery, D. R., and J. M. Buffington. 1998. Channel processes, classification, and response potential. Pages 13–42 *in* R. J. Naiman and R. E. Bilby, editors. River ecology and management. Springer-Verlag, New York.

Morgan, P. A., and F. T. Short. 2002. Using functional trajectories to track constructed salt marsh development in the Great Bay Estuary, Maine/New Hampshire, U.S.A. Restoration Ecology 10:461–473.

Moy, L. D., and L. A. Levin. 1991. Are Spartina marshes a replaceable resource? A functional approach to evaluation of marsh creation efforts. Estuaries 14:1–16.

Neckles, H. A., M. Dionne, D. M. Burdick, C. T. Roman, R. Buchsbaum, and E. Hutchins. 2002. A monitoring protocol to assess tidal restoration of salt marshes on local and regional scales. Restoration Ecology 10:556–563.

NOAA (National Oceanic and Atmospheric Administration). 1990. Estuaries of the United States: vital statistics of a national resource. A special NOAA 20th anniversary report, National Ocean Service, National Oceanic and Atmospheric Administration, Rockville, Maryland.

NOAA (National Oceanic and Atmospheric Administration). 1998. Population: distribution, density and growth. Essay by Thomas J. Culliton *in* NOAA's state of the coast report. National Oceanic and Atmospheric Administration, Silver Spring, Maryland. Online at http://www.nos.noaa.gov/websites/ retiredsites/supp_sotc_retired.html [Accessed 30 June 03].

Nordby, C. S., and J. B. Zedler. 1991. Responses of fish and macrobenthic assemblages to hydrologic disturbances in Tijuana Estuary and Los Penasquitos Lagoon, California. Estuaries 14:80–93.

NRC (National Research Council). 1990. Managing troubled waters, the role of marine environmental monitoring. National Academy Press, Washington, D.C.

NRC (National Research Council). 1992. Restoration of aquatic ecosystems: science, technology, and public policy. National Academy Press, Washington, D.C.

NRC (National Research Council). 2001. Compensating for wetland losses under the Clean Water Act. Committee on Mitigating Wetland Losses, Board on Environmental Studies and Toxicology. National Academic Press, Washington, D.C.

Odum, E. P. 1961. The role of tidal marshes in estuarine production. New York State Conservationist 15:12–15.

Page, H. M. 1997. Importance of vascular plant and algal production to macro-invertebrate consumers in a southern California salt marsh. Estuarine, Coastal and Shelf Science 54:823–883.

Paine, R. T. 1988. Food webs: road maps of interactions or grist for theoretical development? Ecology 69:1648–1654.

Pimm, S. L. 1987. The snake that ate Guam. Trends in Ecology and Evolution 2:293–295.

Pinkas, L., M. S. Oliphant, and I. L. K. Iverson. 1971. Food habits of albacore, bluefin tuna, and bonito in California waters. Fisheries Bulletin of California 152:1–105.

Plumb, R. H. 1981. Procedures for handling and chemical analysis of sediment and water samples. U.S. Army Corps of Engineers, Technical Report EPA/CE-81-1, Vicksburg, Mississippi.

POC (Pew Oceans Commission). 2003. America's living oceans: charting a course for sea change. Summary report. Pew Oceans Commission, Arlington, Virginia.

Pritchard, D. W. 1967a. Observations of circulation in coastal plain estuaries. Pages 37–44 in G. Lauff, editor. Estuaries. American Association for the Advancement of Science, Publication number 83, Washington, D.C.

Pritchard, D. W. 1967b. What is an estuary: physical viewpoint. Pages 3–5 in G. Lauff, editor. Estuaries. American Association for the Advancement of Science, Publication number 83, Washington, D.C.

Rafaelli, D., and S. Hawkins. 1996. Intertidal ecology. Chapman and Hall, London.

Rand, G. M., editor. 1995. Fundamentals of aquatic toxicology: effects, environmental fate, and risk assessment. Second edition. Taylor and Francis, Washington, D.C.

Rao, J. N. K., and J. E. Graham. 1964. Rotation designs for sampling on repeated occasions. Journal of the American Statistical Association 59:492–509.

Reimers, P. E. 1973. The length of residence of juvenile fall chinook in the Sixes River. Research Briefs—Fish Commission of Oregon 4:1–43.

Restore America's Estuaries. 2002. A national strategy to restore coastal and estuarine habitat. Restore America's Estuaries. Online at http://restoration.nos.noaa.gov/pdfs/ entire.pdf [Accessed 30 June 03].

Rice, C. A., M. S. Myers, M. L. Willis, B. L. French, and E. Casillas. 2000. From sediment bioassay to fish biomarker—connecting the dots using simple trophic relationships. Marine Environmental Research 50:527–533.

Rich, W. H. 1920. Early history and seaward migration of chinook salmon in the Columbia and Sacramento Rivers. U.S. Bureau of Fisheries Bulletin 37:2–73.

Ricklefs, R. E. 1979. Ecology. 2nd edition Chiron Press, New York.

Roman, C. T., M. J. James-Pirri, and J. F. Heltsche. 2001. Monitoring salt marsh vegetation: a protocol for the long-term Coastal Ecosystem Monitoring Program at Cape Cod National Seashore. Cape Cod National Seashore, Wellfleet, Massachusetts.

Roman, C. T., N. Jaworski, F. T. Short, S. Findlay, and R. S. Warren. 2000. Estuaries of the northeastern United States: habitat and land use signatures. Estuaries 23:743–764.

Roman, C. T., K. B. Raposa, S. C. Adamowics, M. J. James-Pirri, and J. G. Catena. 2002. Quantifying vegetation and nekton response to tidal restoration of a New England salt marsh. Restoration Ecology 10:450–460.

Rozas, L. P., and T. J. Minello. 1997. Estimating densities of small fishes and decapod crustaceans in shallow estuarine habitats: a review of sampling design with focus on gear selection. Estuaries 20:199–213.

Rozas, L. P., and W. E. Odum. 1987. Use of tidal freshwater marshes by fishes and macrofaunal crustaceans along a marsh stream-order gradient. Estuaries 10:36–43.

Ruiz, G. M., J. T. Carlton, E. D. Grosholz, and A. H. Hines. 1997. Global invasions of marine and estuarine habitats by non-native species: mechanisms, extent, and consequences. American Zoologist 37:621–632.

Ruiz, G. M., P. W. Fofonoff, J. T. Carlton, M. J. Wonham, and A. H. Hines. 2000. Invasion of coastal marine communities in North America: apparent patterns, processes, and biases. Annual Review of Ecology and Systematics 31:481–531.

Sanzone, S., and A. McElroy, editors. 1998. Ecological impacts and evaluation criteria for the use of structures in marsh management. U.S. Environmental Protection Agency, Science Advisory Board, Washington, D.C.

Schiel, D. R., and M. S. Foster. 1992. Restoring kelp forests. Pages 279–342 in G. W. Thayer, editor. Restoring the nation's marine environment. Maryland Sea Grant College Publication UM-SG-TS-92-06, University System of Maryland, College Park.

Schmitt, R. J., and C. W. Osenberg, editors. 1996. Detecting ecological impacts: concepts and applications in coastal habitats. Academic Press, San Diego, California.

Scholz, N. L., N. K. Truelove, B. L. French, B. A. Berejikian, T. P. Quinn, E. Casillas, and T. K. Collier. 2000. Diazinon disrupts antipredator and homing behaviors in chinook salmon (Oncorhynchus tshawytscha). Canadian Journal of Fisheries and Aquatic Sciences 57:1911–1918.

Shreffler, D. K., C. A. Simenstad, and R. M. Thom. 1990. Temporary residence by juvenile salmon of a restored estuarine wetland. Canadian Journal of Fisheries and Aquatic Sciences 47:2079–2084.

Shreffler, D. K., C. A. Simenstad, and R. M. Thom. 1992. Juvenile salmon foraging in a restored estuarine wetland. Estuaries 15:204–213.

Shreffler, D. K., and R. M. Thom. 1993. Restoration of urban estuaries: new approaches for site location and design. Washington State Department of Natural Resources, Olympia.

Shreffler, D. K., R. M. Thom, M. J. Scott, K. F. Wellman, M. A. Walters, and M. Curran. 1995. National review of nonCorps environmental restoration projects. Institute of Water Resources, and Waterways Experimental Station, IWR Report 95-R-12, U.S. Army Corps of Engineers, Alexandria, Virginia, and Vicksburg, Mississippi.

Simenstad, C. A. 2000. Commencement Bay aquatic ecosystem assessment. Ecosystem-scale restoration for juvenile salmon recovery. University of Washington School of Fisheries, SOF-UW-2003, Seattle.

Simenstad, C. A., and D. L. Bottom. 2002. Guiding ecological principles for restoration of salmon habitat in the Columbia River Estuary. Online at http://www.fish.washington.edu/ research/WET/publications/ecol_principles.doc [Accessed 30 June 03].

Simenstad, C. A., S. B. Brandt, A. Chalmers, R. Dame, L. A. Deegan, R. Hodson, and E. D. Houde. 2000a. Habitat-biotic interactions. Pages 427–455 in J. E. Hobbie, editor. Estuarine science: a synthetic approach to research and practice. Island Press, Washington, D.C.

Simenstad, C. A., and J. R. Cordell. 2000. Ecological assessment criteria for restoring anadromous salmonid habitat in Pacific Northwest estuaries. Ecological Engineering 15:283–302.

Simenstad, C. A., K. L. Fresh, and E. O. Salo. 1982. The role of Puget Sound and Washington coastal estuaries in the life history of Pacific salmon: an unappreciated function. Pages 343–364 in V. S. Kennedy, editor. Estuarine comparisons. Academic Publishers, New York.

Simenstad, C. A., W. G. Hood, R. M. Thom, D. A. Levy, and D. L. Bottom. 2000b. Landscape structure and scale constraints on restoring estuarine wetlands for Pacific Coast juvenile fishes. Pages 597–630 in M. P. Weinstein and D. A. Kreeger, editors. Concepts and controversies in tidal marsh ecology. Kluwer Academic Publishing, Dordrecht, The Netherlands.

Simenstad, C. A., D. A. Jay, and C. R. Sherwood. 1992. Impacts of watershed management on land-margin ecosystems: the Columbia River Estuary as a case study. Pages 266–306 in R. Naiman, editor. Watershed management: balancing sustainability and environmental change. Springer-Verlag, New York.

Simenstad, C. A., B. S. Miller, C. F. Nyblade, K. Thornburgh, and L. J. Bledsoe. 1979. Food web relationships of northern Puget Sound and the Strait of Juan de Fuca. U.S. Environmental Protection Agency, Office of Engineering and Technology, Office of Research and Development, EPA 600/7-79-259, Washington, D.C.

Simenstad, C. A., C. D. Tanner, R. M. Thom, and L. L. Conquest. 1991. Estuarine habitat assessment protocol. Report to the U.S. Environmental Protection Agency, Region 10. University of Washington, Fisheries Research Institute, EPA 910/9-91-037, Seattle.

Simenstad, C. A., and R. M. Thom. 1996. Functional equivalency trajectories of the restored Gog-Le-Hi-Te estuarine wetland. Ecological Applications 6:38–56.

Simon, T. P., editor. 1998. Assessing the sustainability and biological integrity of water resources using fish communities. CRC, Boca Raton, Florida.

Skalski, J. R. 1995. Use of "bellwether" stations and rotational sampling designs to monitor Harlequin duck abundance. Report to Pete Zager, Idaho Department of Fish and Game, Boise.

Steers, J. A. 1960. Physiography and evolution. Pages 12–66 in J. A. Steers, editor. Scolt Head Island. W. Heffer, Cambridge, UK.

Stommel, H., and H. G. Farmer. 1952. On the nature of estuarine circulation. Reference notes 52-51, 52-63, and 52-88, Woods Hole Oceanographic Institution, Woods Hole, Massachusetts.

Teal, J., and M. Teal. 1969. Life and death of the salt marsh. Ballentine, New York.

Tear, L. M. 1995. Estimating species abundances in estuarine wetland plant assemblages: an examination of methods and designs. Master's thesis. University of Washington, Seattle.

Terry, C. 1977. Stomach analysis methodology: still lots of questions. Pages 87–92 in C. A. Simenstad and S. J. Lipovsky, editors. Proceedings of Fish Food Habits Studies: 1st Pacific Northwest Technical Workshop, October 13–15, 1976, Astoria, Oregon. Washington Sea Grant Program, WSG-WO 77-2, University of Washington, Seattle.

Thayer, G. W., editor. 1992. Restoring the nation's marine environment. Maryland Sea Grant College, University System of Maryland, College Park.

Thayer, G. W., T. A. McTigue, R. J. Bellmer, F. M. Burrows, D. H. Merkey, A. Nickens, S. Lozano, P. F. Gayaldo, P. J. Polmateer, and P. T. Pinit. 2003. Science-based restoration monitoring of coastal habitats, volume one: a framework for monitoring plans under the estuaries and Clean Waters Act of 2000 (Public Law 160-457). National Oceanic and Atmospheric Administration, National Centers for Coastal Ocean Science, NOAA Coastal Ocean Program Decision Analysis Series No. 23, Volume 1, Silver Spring, Maryland.

Thom, R. M. 1997. System-development matrix for adaptive management of coastal ecosystem restoration projects. Ecological Engineering 8:219–232.

Thom, R. M. 2000. Adaptive management of coastal ecosystem restoration projects. Ecological Engineering 15:365–372.

Thom, R. M., and K. F. Wellman. 1996. Planning aquatic ecosystem restoration monitoring programs. Institute of Water Resources, and Waterways Experimental Station, IWR Report 96-R-23, U.S. Army Corps of Engineers, Alexandria, Virginia, and Vicksburg, Mississippi.

Thompson, S. K. 2002. Sampling. 2nd edition John Wiley & Sons, Inc., New York.

Thorpe, J. E. 1994. Salmonid fishes and the estuarine environment. Estuaries 17:76–93.

Tibbet, J. 2002. Coastal cities: living on the edge. Environmental Health Perspectives 110:A674-A681.

Toft, J.D., C. A. Simenstad, J. R. Cordell, C. D. Young, and L. Stamatiou. 2003. Juvenile salmon usage of nearshore habitats along modified shorelines. Poster presentation abstract, 17th Biennial Conference of the Estuarine Research Federation, September 14–18, 2003, Seattle, Washington.

Urquhart, N. S., and T. M. Kincaid. 1999. Designs for detecting trend from repeated surveys of ecological resources. Journal of Agricultural, Biological, and Environmental Statistics 4:404–414.

Urquhart, N. S., W. S. Overton, and D. S. Birkes. 1993. Comparing sampling designs for monitoring ecological status and trends: impact of temporal patterns. Pages 71–85 in V. Barnett and K. F. Turkman, editors. Statistics for the environment. John Wiley and Sons, Ltd., New York.

USCOP (United States Commission on Ocean Policy). 2004. An ocean blueprint for the 21st century. Final report of the U.S. Commission on Ocean Policy, Washington, D.C.

USEPA (U.S. Environmental Protection Agency). 1986. Quality Criteria for Water. U.S. Environmental Protection Agency, Office of Water, Regulations and Standards, EPA 440/5-86-001, Washington, D.C.

USEPA (U.S. Environmental Protection Agency). 2001. National coastal condition report. U.S. Environmental Protection Agency, EPA620-R-01-005, Washington, D.C.

USEPA (U.S. Environmental Protection Agency). 2002. National Recommended Water Quality Criteria: 2002. U.S. Environmental Protection Agency, Office of Water, Office of Science and Technology, EPA-822-R-02-047, Washington, D.C.

Valiela, I. 1995. Marine ecological processes. 2nd edition. Springer-Verlag, New York.

Valiela, I., K. Foreman, M. LoMontagne, D. Hersh, J. Costa, P. Peckol, B. DeMeo-Anderson, C. D'Avanzo, M. Babione, C. H. Sham, J. Brawley, and K. Lajtha. 1992. Couplings of watersheds and coastal waters: sources and consequences of nutrient enrichment in Waquoit Bay, Massachusetts. Estuaries 15:443–457.

Vitousek, P. M., H. A. Mooney, J. Lubchenko, and J. M. Melillo. 1997. Human domination of earth's ecosystems. Science 277:494–499.

Walters, C. J. 1986. Adaptive management of renewable resources. Macmillan, New York.

Walters, C. J., and C. S. Holling. 1990. Large-scale management experiments and learning by doing. Ecology 71:2060–2068.

Warren, R. S., P. E. Fell, R. Rosza, A. H. Brawley, A. C. Orsted, E. T. Olson, V. Swamy, and W. A. Niering. 2002. Salt marsh restoration in Connecticut: 20 years of science and management. Restoration Ecology 10:497–513.

Wasson, K. D., Lohrer, M. Crawford, and S. Rumrill. 2002. Non-native species in our nation's estuaries: a framework for an invasion monitoring program. National Estuarine Research Reserve, Technical Report Series 2002:1, Online at http://www.ocrm.nos.noaa.gov/nerr/resource.html [Accessed 30 June 03].

Weins, J. A. 1989. Spatial scaling in ecology. Functional Ecology 3:385–397.

Weinstein, M. P., and D. A. Kreeger, editors. 2000. Concepts and controversies in tidal marsh ecology. Klewer Academic Publishers, Dordrecht, The Netherlands.

Wilbur, P., G. W. Thayer, M. Croom, and G. Mayer. 2000. Goal setting and success criteria for coastal habitat restoration. Ecological Engineering 15:165–395.

Williams, G. D., and J. S. Desmond. 2001. Restoring assemblages of invertebrates and fishes. Pages 235–269 in J. B. Zedler, editor. Handbook for restoring tidal wetlands. CRC Press, Boca Raton, Florida.

Williams, P. B., and M. K. Orr. 2002. Physical evolution of restored breached levee salt marshes in the San Francisco Bay Estuary. Restoration Ecology 10:527–542.

Williams, P. B., M. K. Orr, and N. J. Garrity. 2002. Hydraulic geometry: a geomorphic design tool for tidal marsh channel evolution in wetland restoration projects. Restoration Ecology 10:577–590.

Woldenberg, M. J. 1966. Horton's laws justified in terms of allometric growth and steady state in open systems. Geological Society of America Bulletin 77:431–434.

Woodin, M. C. 1994. Use of saltwater and freshwater habitats by wintering redheads in southern Texas. Hydrobiologia 279/280:279–287.

Yoccoz, N. G. 1991. Use, overuse, and misuse of significance tests in evolutionary biology and ecology. Bulletin of the Ecological Society of America 71:106–111.

Zedler, J. B. 1988. Salt marsh restoration: lessons from California. Pages 123–138 in J. Cairns, editor. Rehabilitating damaged ecosystems. Volume 1. CRC Press, Boca Raton, Florida.

Zedler, J. B., editor. 2001. Handbook for restoring tidal wetlands. CRC Press, Boca Raton, Florida.

Zedler, J. B., and J. C. Callaway. 1999. Tracking wetland restoration: do mitigation sites follow desired trajectories? Restoration Ecology 7:69–73.

Zedler, J. B., and R. Lindig-Cisneros. 2000. Functional equivalency of restored and natural salt marshes. Pages 565–582 in M. P. Weinstein and D. A. Kreeger, editors. Concepts and controversies in tidal marsh ecology. Klewer Academic Publishing, Dordrecht, The Netherlands.

Chapter 8
Monitoring and Evaluating Instream Habitat Enhancement

Philip Roni

Northwest Fisheries Science Center, National Marine Fisheries Service
2725 Montlake Boulevard East, Seattle, Washington 98112, USA
phil.roni@noaa.gov

Andrew H. Fayram, Michael A. Miller

Bureau of Fisheries Management and Habitat Protection, Wisconsin Department of Natural Resources
101 South Webster Street, Madison, Wisconsin 53707, USA
FayraA@mail01.dnr.state.wi.us, MilleMa@mail01.dnr.state.wi.us

Introduction

The placement of physical structures into lotic environments to create pools, to alter channel morphology, and to provide cover and habitat for fish and other aquatic organisms has a long history (White 1996, 2002). It was one of the first methods used to mitigate habitat degradation and to increase fish production in streams and rivers (Tarzwell 1934, 1937, 1938), and also is arguably one of the most common and widespread restoration methods in regular use throughout North America and Europe. Many different configurations of instream structures and methods have been used over the years to improve habitat (White and Brynildson 1967; Vetrano 1988; Hunt 1993; Riley and Fausch 1995), but they are all generally composed of rocks, boulders, trees, and brush bundles. They can be categorized by purpose (e.g., create pools, trap gravel) and material and can include such structures as boulder or log weirs, dams and deflectors, cover structures (particularly common in streams of the midwestern states), rootwads and brush bundles, spawning pads, gabions, and, more recently, the construction of logjams in larger rivers (Table 1; Figure 1). These techniques, generally referred to as instream restoration or enhancement, involve placement of materials into the active stream channel or actual manipulation of the active channel itself in an effort to improve fish habitat (Table 1). Because these activities seek to enhance habitat rather than restore a deficient process (e.g., riparian, hydrology) or return a stream to some predisturbance state, they are technically habitat enhancement, and we refer to them as such in this chapter.

Most instream enhancement techniques used today were developed in the 1930s in the relatively low-gradient streams of the upper Midwest (Hunt 1993; White 1996). They were designed to enhance trout habitat that had been simplified and degraded through agriculture, forestry, and other land use. The primary purpose of instream structures in midwestern streams was to narrow channels, to provide cover for trout and other game fish, and to reduce mortality due to predation (Tabor and Wurtsbaugh 1991; Gregory and Levings 1996). Instream enhancement techniques developed in the Midwest were later applied to streams in the western United States with varying degrees of success (Ehlers 1956; Armantrout 1991). They subsequently were modified for use in the higher energy mountainous streams common in western North America, where the objectives focus primarily on creating pools and on increasing habitat complexity, rather than providing cover (Reeves et al. 1991). Comparable instream enhancement efforts have been applied in Western Europe, which

Table 1.

Common types of instream enhancement and their purpose. Many of these actions are implemented in conjunction with other restoration actions described in other chapters.

Type of instream restoration	Definition	Typical purpose
Log structures (e.g., weirs, sills, deflectors, single logs, wing deflectors, k-dams)	Placement of logs or log structures into active channel	Create pools and cover for fish, trap gravel, confine channel, or create spawning habitat
Logjams (multiple log structures, engineered logjams)	Multiple logs placed in active channel to form a debris dam and trap gravel channel migration, restore floodplain	Create pools and holding and rearing areas for fish, trap sediment, prevent channel migration, restore floodplain and side channels
Cover structures (lunker structures, rock or log shelters)	Structures embedded in stream bank	Provide fish cover and prevent erosion
Boulders, boulder weirs, boulder clusters, boulder deflectors	Single or multiple boulders placed in wetted channel	Create pools and cover for fish, trap gravel, confine channel, or create spawning habitat
Gabions	Wire-mesh baskets filled with gravel and cobble	Trap gravel and create pools or spawning habitat
Brush bundles/rootwads	Placement of woody material in pools or slow water areas	Provide cover for juvenile and adult fish, refuge from high flows, substrate for macroinvertebrates
Gravel additions and spawning pads	Addition of gravels or creation of riffles	Provide spawning habitat for fishes
Sediment traps	Excavation of a depression or pond in active channel to trap fine sediment	Improve channel conditions and morphology, and increase grain size
Channel reconstruction and realignment	Alter channel morphology by excavating new channel to restore meander patterns or return to historic channel	Restore meander patterns, increase habitat complexity and pool:riffle ratio, reduce channel width

has experienced similar yet more intensive degradation of watersheds due to a longer history of land use (Iversen et al. 1993; O'Grady 1995; Cowx and Welcomme 1998; Gortz 1998; Laasonen et al. 1998).

Though instream habitat enhancement is popular and widespread, and has a lengthy history, most techniques have not been thoroughly evaluated. The need for rigorous monitoring and evaluation has been noted for many decades (Tarzwell 1937; Reeves et al. 1991) and is as important in the twenty-first century as it was in the early part of the twentieth century (Roni et al. 2002, 2003). Despite the call for a thorough evaluation of physical and biological responses to various instream enhancement techniques, the effectiveness of these techniques is unknown for many regions, channel types, and biota. Habitat enhancement projects, like many management actions, are, in essence, experiments with uncertain outcomes and should be implemented according to the standard rules for designing experiments (Caughley 1994). Because instream enhancement actions focus on fish and direct manipulations of habitat, they represent one of our best opportunities to test hypotheses and to conduct timely applied research regarding fish and habitat alterations.

There is considerable debate about the appropriateness of instream enhancement, because these techniques historically occurred without an assessment of what factors caused the lack of habitat complexity, what processes in the watershed might be disrupted and need to be corrected, and what factors might be limiting

Figure 1.
Three common instream habitat enhancement techniques or structures: rock weir (top), log weir (middle), and logjam or multiple log structure (bottom).

the physical and biological production of a system (Roni et al. 2002; White 2002). For example, the failure of instream wood and boulder structures to increase fish abundance in a stream reach may be related to delivery of large amounts of sediment from an upstream area or from high water temperatures due to a lack of riparian vegetation, caused, in turn, by heavy grazing. Thus, in some cases, if the underlying cause of the problem is not addressed, instream enhancement may represent only a short-term improvement in habitat. Nonetheless, habitat enhancement projects are not without merit. Short-term habitat improvements may be needed to protect rare fishes and biota or to provide short-term benefits where some watershed process cannot be restored (e.g., woody debris in urban streams). They are particularly relevant when coupled with habitat restoration techniques that restore natural processes, such as riparian restoration or road improvement. While we will not cover determining where, how, and whether to implement habitat enhancement projects, the reader should be aware that instream enhancement projects are not appropriate in all instances, and many larger factors can affect their success.

Our objective in this chapter is to describe considerations for monitoring and evaluating individual and multiple instream enhancement projects at multiple spatial scales (site, reach, watershed, region). First, we provide a brief review of the effectiveness of various techniques in different geographic regions. Next, we go through the steps for designing a monitoring strategy, including enhancement objectives, key questions, study design, selecting appropriate physical and biological parameters to measure, and special considerations. The vast majority of work on instream enhancement has been for salmonid fishes. We draw from these studies in our examples and illustrations. Detailed information on construction and implementation of instream enhancement techniques is beyond the scope of this chapter can be found in Wesche (1985), Vetrano (1988), Hunter (1991), Reeves et al. (1991), Hunt (1993), Cowx and Welcomme (1998), FISRWG (1998), and others.

Review of Previous Evaluations of Instream Enhancement

Most evaluations of restoration and improvement of aquatic ecosystems have focused on responses of physical habitat; instream enhancement is no exception. The majority of monitoring and evaluation efforts of instream projects have focused on the effects of the project on channel morphology and instream habitat (Hunt 1988; Reeves et al. 1991; Binns 1999; Roni et al. 2002). Early evaluations reported on the durability of instream structures, whether they created pools, and their longevity (Ehlers 1956; Gard 1972; Armantrout 1991; Frissell and Nawa 1992). Early failures in western North America often resulted from applying techniques developed for low-gradient (<1% slope) streams, such as weirs and deflectors, to high gradient and higher energy streams (Platts and Rinne 1985; White 2002). More recently, these techniques have been modified to mimic natural wood accumulations, and these newer methods have been demonstrated to be more durable and effective at producing changes in habitat than traditional structures (Cederholm et al. 1997; Thom 1997; Roni and Quinn 2001a). Many studies in the Pacific Northwest and Rocky Mountains have reported large (>50%) and significant increases in pool frequency, pool depth, woody debris, spawning gravel, and sediment retention after placement of instream structures (e.g., Crispin et al. 1993; Cederholm et al. 1997; Reeves et al. 1997; Binns 1999; Roni and Quinn 2001a). Studies in Europe and in the midwestern United States also have demonstrated physical habitat changes, including increased depth, cover, and narrower channels, as a result of instream enhancement projects (Hunt 1988; Jutila 1992; Kern 1992; O'Grady 1995, 2002; Gortz 1998).

Biological evaluations of different enhancement techniques have been less frequently conducted than physical evaluations and have produced inconsistent results, depending upon the technique, region, species, and life stage examined, as well as the duration of monitoring. The majority of these evaluations have focused on trout or juvenile anadromous salmonids, which are the focus of most instream enhancement efforts in North America. Monitoring of instream enhancement has been more intensive in the western United States. The results, however, have been variable, and there is still much debate in the scientific community about the biological effectiveness of instream enhancement in this region. In a synthesis of the effectiveness of such efforts for Pacific salmon Oncorhynchus spp., Roni et al. (2002, 2003) recently reviewed published evaluations of anadromous salmonid response to enhancement and found that while many reported positive responses of juvenile coho salmon O. kisutch, steelhead trout O. mykiss, and cutthroat trout O. clarki to instream enhancement, few of these responses were statistically significant. Their synthesis and previous reviews (Reeves et al. 1991; Beschta et al. 1994; Chapman 1996) emphasize the need for rigorous long-term evaluations of the responses of juvenile fishes to instream enhancement.

The response of adult and spawning anadromous or resident fishes to enhancement also has rarely been examined (Roni et al. 2002, 2003), though the restoration of spawning gravels and adult holding habitat have been an objective of many instream structures, including gravel placement. Where spawning gravels are in low abundance or are of low quality, habitat structures such as channel-spanning LWD, boulder clusters, or gabions may recruit and store gravel (House et al. 1989; House 1996). The evaluations of adult salmonid response to enhancement structures or gravel placement have been limited to a few short-term studies that demonstrated adult salmonid use of gravel accumulated at structures (Crispin et al. 1993; Avery 1996; House 1996; Gortz 1998) or observations of redds or adult spawning near enhancement sites (Anderson et al. 1984; Moreau 1984; House et al. 1989). This lack of rigorous evaluation of adult salmon and trout response to instream enhancement stems, in part, from the multiple generations and, thus, long time frame (>10 years) needed to detect an adult response to habitat alterations (Bisson et al. 1997; Korman and Higgins 1997). Nonetheless, evaluating adult response is critical for projects focusing on enhancement of spawning habitat.

Responses of resident trout to instream enhancement have been examined the most frequently. Early work examining the effectiveness of instream structures on resident trout suggested moderate increases of abundance, growth, condition, and survival of trout species associated with placement of structures (Tarzwell 1938; Gard 1961). More recent efforts have shown positive increases in both juvenile and adult trout abundance. Three compendiums on the response of trout to enhancement of Rocky Mountain and midwestern streams summarize much of this work (Hunt 1988; Binns 1999; Avery 2004). In a review of 71 different instream enhancement projects installed between 1953 and 1998 in Wyoming, Binns (1999) detected increases in trout abundance either after treatment or between treatment and reference reaches; however, few evaluations included more than a few years of data collection. Many projects Binns (1999) examined included other types of restoration, such as fencing and grazing removal, which made attributing response to specific techniques difficult.

Numerous techniques for improving habitat for trout, including brush bundles, current deflectors, bank cover, cut or cover logs, and large woody debris (LWD) placement, have been evaluated in Midwest streams. Hunt (1988) and Avery (2004) examined evaluations of instream habitat enhancement efforts in a total of 103 Wisconsin streams. Streambank debrushing and installation of brush bundles produced rather disappointing trout response in 11 different streams in Wisconsin (Hunt 1988; Avery 2004). Conversely, bank cover and current deflector structures demonstrated excellent results in increasing trout mean size and biomass, with 75% of the projects examined showing an increase in local abundance of 25% or more (Hunt 1988; Avery 2004). An early 2-year study found increases in the number and the biomass of brook trout *Salvelinus fontinalis*, brown trout *Salmo trutta*, and rainbow trout *Oncorhynchus mykiss* after addition of brush bundles, and a decrease after removal of overhanging brush in other stream reaches (Broussu 1954). The Midwest and Wyoming compendiums on instream enhancement demonstrate that overall instream enhancement efforts may increase local trout abundance and condition. However, multiple types of enhancement practices were implemented in many stream reaches, and few projects were monitored long term (>5 years), making determination of which method led to increased fish abundance unclear in many instances.

Even less information exists on the response of nonsalmonid fishes to habitat enhancement (Lonzarich and Quinn 1995; Bilby and Fransen 1996; Roni 2000). Roni (2000, 2003) examined the response of reticulate sculpin *Cottus perplexus*, torrent sculpin *C. rhotheus*, larval lamprey *Lampetra* spp., and Pacific giant salamanders *Dicamptodon ensatus* to LWD placement in the coastal Pacific Northwest and found higher densities of lamprey in treated stream reaches but little difference for other nonsalmonid species. A review of habitat enhancement projects in warmwater streams throughout the Midwest found that a wide variety of techniques were successful in altering stream morphology and in increasing stream cover, although rigorous physical and biological evaluation of individual projects generally was lacking (Lyons and Courtney 1990). Angermeier and Karr (1984) examined responses of 10 warmwater fishes to wood removal and placement in a small Illinois stream and found more and larger fish in stream sections with woody debris. Lonzarich and Quinn (1995) found no effect of woody debris cover and depth on threespine stickleback *Gasterosteus aculeatus* or coastrange sculpin *Cottus aleuticus* habitat use, growth, or survival in an artificial stream channel. The effects of habitat alteration and degradation in streams have been assessed successfully by using fish communities, particularly in the Midwest, which has a very diverse fish fauna (e.g., Gorman and Karr 1978; Schlosser 1982; Fausch and Bramblett 1991). Monitoring the response of the entire fish community is important in determining both project effectiveness and whether instream techniques are restoring fish communities, rather than just manipulating habitat for individual species.

Examination of changes in fish abundance at instream enhancement projects can be complicated by immigration and emigration of fishes from nearby habitats or watersheds, or by the effects of instream structures on fish movement. This is particularly evident for salmonid fishes. For example, Riley and Fausch (1995) demonstrated an increase in abundance and biomass of three species of trout associated with structure installation in Colorado streams; however, a subsequent analysis of the same projects demonstrated that increases in biomass and abundance were strongly influenced by movement of trout into treated stream reaches (Gowan and Fausch 1996). In contrast, Roni and Quinn (2001b) found little movement of juvenile salmonids between treatment and nearby reference reaches in a small western Washington stream. Rinne (1982) reported reduced movement of gila trout *Oncorhynchus gilae* after the placement of high (>0.5 m) log dam structures. The question of whether instream enhancement increases fish production or simply shifts fish distribution should be an important component of project evaluation (Gowan et al. 1994; Frissell and Ralph 1998; Roni and Quinn 2001b).

Equally important to monitoring responses of fishes to habitat enhancement is the need to examine the responses of aquatic macroinvertebrates, which are an important food source for fishes and which are highly sensitive to habitat alteration and disturbance (Merritt and Cummins 1996; Karr and Chu 1999). Because there is much to be learned regarding the response of macroinvertebrates to instream enhancement, several authors have considered the response of macroinvertebrates as a component of their monitoring strategy, if not focusing exclusively on them. Early investigations by Tarzwell (1938) and Gard (1961) demonstrated an increase in macroinvertebrates after instream enhancement. More recently, Gortz (1998) detected an increase in some species of macroinvertebrates after placement of instream structures, and Wallace et al. (1995) found changes in functional feeding groups only within habitats altered by wood placement. Conversely, Hilderbrand et al. (1997), Laasonen et al. (1998), Larson et al. (2001), Brooks et al. (2002), and Roni (unpublished data) detected no difference of macroinvertebrate density or diversity in enhanced and unenhanced stream reaches. These disparate results suggest that additional information is needed on macroinvertebrate responses to instream enhancement.

Our brief review suggests apparent physical and biological successes of instream enhancement projects and provides some support for their continued use. However, given the variability in results for various species, the limited number of statistically rigorous studies, the differential responses by different species or life stages, and the cost of instream enhancement projects, it is apparent that these projects should be undertaken with careful consideration and should be coupled with a rigorous monitoring program. A statistically valid, broadly based, and rigorous monitoring strategy is a critical component of any instream enhancement project. The lack of rigorous studies indicates that both adequate funds for monitoring and guidance on proper monitoring and evaluation of instream enhancement projects are needed.

Designing Monitoring of Instream Enhancement Projects

As noted earlier, instream enhancement projects and other manipulations represent unique opportunities to answer critical questions about habitat enhancement techniques and fish–habitat relationships. This information is particularly important for guiding future habitat enhancement efforts, because millions of dollars are being spent on techniques that we know little about with regard to their short- and long-term effectiveness. Developing an adequate and rigorous monitoring study of individual or multiple enhancement projects is challenging but critical to determining success and guiding future enhancement efforts. There are several logical steps to setting up any monitoring program, including determining project goals and objectives, key questions and hypotheses, study design and scale, replication (number of sites) and duration (years of monitoring), parameters (variables) to monitor, sampling schemes for parameters (e.g., random, stratified random, number of samples per site), monitoring implementation, and analysis and reporting of results (Table 2).

Project Goals

The first step in developing a monitoring plan is to determine the goals and objectives of the enhancement project. Clearly defining the goals and objectives of the project is critical to determining the key questions and

Table 2.
List of key steps in developing a monitoring program and an example for a single large woody debris (LWD) placement project on a kilometer-long stream reach.

Step	Example for LWD placement
Enhancement goal	Improve habitat for fish
Enhancement objective	Increase pool frequency, habitat complexity, and fish abundance in treatment reach
Key question (hypothesis)	What is the effect of LWD placement on pool area and local fish abundance within project reach?
Study design and scale	Reach-scale project, no adequate control exists, use a before–after design
Number of sites and years to monitor (spatial and temporal replication)	One study reach, previous analyses suggest that at least 10 years of monitoring are needed to detect change in fish abundance, monitor a minimum of 5 years before and 5 years after
Parameters to monitor	LWD, habitat survey (pools), fish abundance during late summer and mid winter
Sampling scheme	Habitat and LWD—complete census of 500 m study reach, Fish and macro-invertebrates—systematic random sample (every nth riffle unit)
Implement monitoring	Collect data annually or more frequently if funding allows
Analysis and reporting	Analyze data using t-tests to compare means before and after, write up results and recommend changes in enhancement techniques if appropriate

hypotheses to test the appropriate monitoring design. All subsequent steps depend on this first step. The overall goals of most habitat enhancement projects are to improve habitat complexity and quality in hopes of improving fish or biota numbers and diversity. The objectives are related to the project goals but are more specific and may vary by project type. For example, the common goal of both a channel realignment project and a wood placement project may be to improve habitat through addition of pools, but the objectives of the channel realignment may be to narrow the stream channel and to increase sinuosity by 100% and, ultimately, to increase adult trout numbers, while the objectives of the wood placement project may be to increase pools and to improve overwinter survival of a particular fish species. These differing objectives will, in turn, affect the key monitoring questions or testable hypotheses for each project. The more specific the objectives, the easier it will be to transform them into specific questions and testable hypotheses.

Key Questions and Hypotheses

Instream enhancement projects, like other restoration techniques, are management experiments and, as such, should have clear testable hypotheses defined before implementing the projects and monitoring program. The scale of the projects and the key questions will help determine the appropriate study design. Key questions regarding instream enhancement can be divided into two categories, based on scale: those that have local or reach-scale effects, and those that have effects on conditions throughout a watershed (Table 3; see also Chapter 2). The key questions presented in Table 3, with slight modification, cover most stream enhancement projects. Key questions then can be restated as testable hypotheses. Hypotheses also may be generated that examine changes within individual habitat units. For example, Wallace et al. (1995) tested hypotheses regarding macroinvertebrate responses in individual habitat units to log additions. Site specific and detailed questions and hypotheses should be defined for each given study or situation.

Study Design

Once these questions are defined, one can determine the appropriate study design (Table 2). Study designs, reviewed in Chapter 2, include the following four basic study designs: before–after (BA), before–after control–impact (BACI), extensive posttreatment (EPT), and intensive posttreatment. Intensive study designs typically involve detailed monitoring at one or a few sites, and extensive monitoring involves less detailed moni-

Table 3.

Key questions for instream enhancement projects at reach or watershed scales. In relation to biota, the terms reach and watershed are roughly equivalent to examining changes in local abundance (site or reach) and population-level responses (watershed). Project X represents instream enhancement action of interest such as large woody debris (LWD) placement, boulder additions, for example. The most appropriate study designs are in parentheses.

I. Site, reach, or local conditions or local abundance

    A. What is the effect of instream enhancement project X (e.g., LWD placement, instream structures, gravel addition) on local physical habitat (site or reach) and biota? (before–after [BA] or before–after control–impact [BACI])

    B. What is the effect of instream enhancement projects like X (e.g. LWD placement, instream structures, gravel addition) on physical habitat and biota at a reach scale? (EPT or replicated BA or BACI design)

II. Watershed or population scale

    A. What is the effect of an instream enhancement project X on physical habitat and biota at a watershed scale? (BA or BACI)

    B. What is the effect of all instream enhancement and restoration projects throughout a watershed on physical habitat and biota at a watershed scale? (BA or BACI)

toring at a number of sites. Many study designs exist, but they represent modifications of these four basic types. The most appropriate type will depend upon the project and monitoring goals, the project type, the scale of the project, the scale of the key questions or the hypotheses, and whether data can be collected before treatment. For example, if the goal of a LWD placement project is to increase local fish abundance within a stream reach through increasing habitat complexity, the key question is whether an individual project was successful at achieving this objective locally at a reach scale. The most appropriate study design is either an intensive BACI or BA study design (Table 2). In contrast, if the key question is whether a particular technique is effective within a basin or geographic province, some type of extensive study design, including either an EPT design or an extensive BA (multiple sites), would be appropriate. Below, we give examples of studies that generally have been set up to address the key questions described above.

Site or reach-scale designs

Most evaluations of stream enhancement are case studies that have occurred at a reach level on one stream (see Hunt 1988; Binns 1999; Roni et al. 2003). They usually examine changes in physical habitat (e.g., pools, channel width, cover, habitat complexity) and fish and macroinvertebrate abundance before and after treatment or in treatment and reference (control) reaches. For example, Hunt (1974) monitored brook trout before and after placement of instream structures (Figure 2). Individual projects such as these can be evaluated by using either a BA design or a BACI design (addition of a control site or reach to the BA).

Examining whether a particular technique has been effective across a region or a defined geographic area requires a different study design. Testing hypotheses about regional effectiveness has been examined by using two methods: (1) an extensive study design (multiple sites) such as in Riley and Fausch (1995; BA design) or in Roni and Quinn (2001a; EPT design), or (2) a compendium of all projects in a given region such as those conducted by Hunt (1988) and Avery (2004) in Wisconsin, Chapman (1996) for Snake River tributaries, and Binns (1999) for Wyoming. However, compendiums typically rely on previous evaluations that are of limited scope, do not examine biological response, and synthesize investigations with inconsistent or incompatible data or protocols. Therefore, it is often difficult to draw statistically significant conclusions. Gurevitch and Hedges (2001) discuss some of the limitations and statistical methods for combining data from independent studies.

A more rigorous experimental approach is an extensive study design where many sites are sampled simultaneously. These types of studies are rare, in part because they can require a large investment in time, planning, and financial resources. However, they can provide definitive results about the effectiveness of different techniques and, since multiple sites are sampled, can allow for correlation of physical and biological responses. Riley and Fausch (1995) examined the response of resident trout to log weirs in six small streams in the Col-

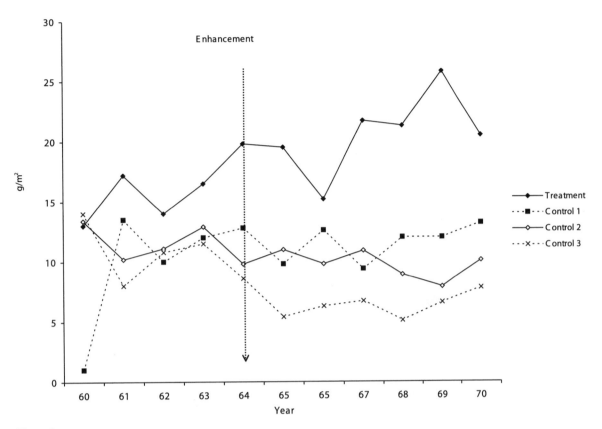

Figure 2.
Example of reach-level response of brook trout to instream restoration. Annual production (g/m²) of brook trout in four reaches of Lawrence Creek 1960–1970, before and after habitat enhancement (data from Hunt 1974). Dashed arrow indicates year habitat enhancement occurred.

orado Rocky Mountains by using an extensive BACI study design. Roni (2000) and Roni and Quinn (2001a) used an EPT design, sampling 30 streams with treatment and reference reaches after treatment, rather than before and after treatment, to examine the effects of LWD placement on fishes, salamanders, and macroinvertebrates in coastal streams of the Pacific Northwest (Figure 3A). Extensive study designs are particularly powerful in that adequate replication allows one to correlate biotic responses with physical variables, as well as to determine overall response (Figure 3B). While these type of studies require extensive coordination and multiple enhancement sites, the large habitat monitoring programs being initiated by many agencies for endangered species and land management plans, coupled with increased interest in habitat enhancement, will likely provide increased opportunity for extensive regional studies.

Watershed-scale designs

While most instream projects occur at a site or reach scale, these projects may produce responses or affect responses of physical habitat and fish production in downstream reaches, in adjacent habitats, or throughout a watershed. This has been a particular concern for highly migratory fishes such as salmonids (Northcote 1992) that typically have seasonal habitat preferences (Nickelson et al. 1992; Roni 2002). Thus, changes in one stream reach may affect salmonid abundance in adjacent stream reaches (Gowan and Fausch 1996; Kahler et al. 2001; Roni and Quinn 2001b). Assessing the biotic responses and the physical responses at a watershed scale is arguably more important (and more difficult) than examining reach-scale responses such as changes in local fish abundance. Both the costs and the difficulty in implementation have made examining the effect of individual or multiple projects on physical habitat, fish populations, and other biota at a watershed-scale relatively rare. Yet watershed-scale monitoring and evaluation is a particularly important perspective to consider.

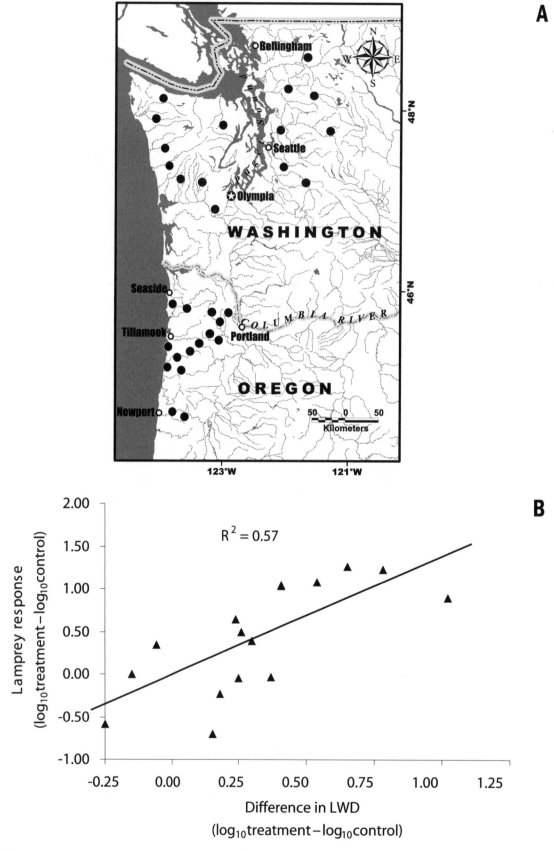

Figure 3.
Example of evaluation of overall technique effectiveness at a reach scale. Figure 3A represents instream enhancement projects sampled in Pacific Northwest. Figure 3B represents correlation between juvenile lamprey response to habitat enhancement (treatment-control) and increase in large woody debris (LWD) due to enhancement (treatment-control). (Modified from Roni 2000.)

We found no examples of studies where the effect of an individual project on fish populations or habitat were examined at a watershed scale; but, a handful of examples of watershed-scale assessments of multiple activities have been conducted. Reeves et al. (1997) and Solazzi et al. (2000) examined juvenile and smolt abundance before and after habitat enhancement in watersheds in Oregon (Figure 4). These studies produced different results, but they also included different study designs (BA in Reeves et al. 1997 versus BACI in Solazzi et al. 2000) and different levels of habitat modification. These two examples demonstrate the importance of monitoring before and after treatment, having an adequate control or reference watershed, and the importance of monitoring both physical and biological factors. However, these studies focused on a few salmonid fishes, and data on nonsalmonids were either not collected or not reported. Information on all species and life stages is important. In the examples provided, juvenile coho salmon are known to prefer pools, and habitat modifications were designed to increase pool frequency or quality. However, some activities designed to improve summer rearing habitat for one species may be detrimental to another (see Roni and Quinn 2001a). Examining watershed-scale effects is difficult, and examining the influence of an individual project on fish production

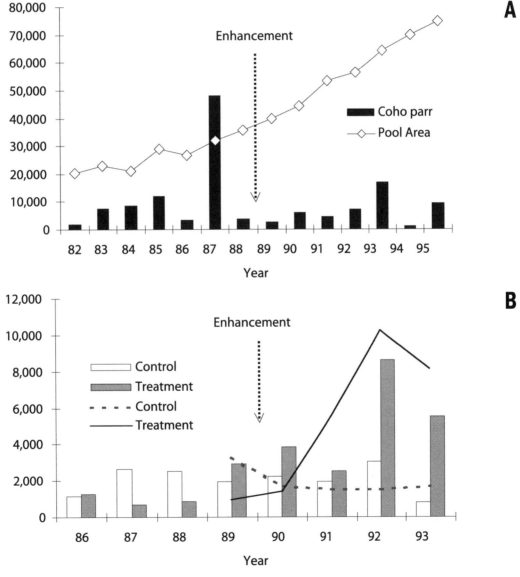

Figure 4.
Two examples of watershed scale evaluation of habitat enhancement activities. Pool area (m²; line) and juvenile coho salmon abundance (parr number) before and after completion of restoration activities in Fish Creek, Oregon (A; data from Reeves et al. 1997). Coho smolt production (bars) and pool area (m²) from treatment and control watersheds in the Alsea basin of Oregon, before and after treatment (B; data from Solazzi et al. 2000). Treatment consisted of placement of large woody debris and creation of overwinter habitat for coho salmon. Arrow indicates year habitat enhancement occurred.

within a watershed requires both evaluation of project-level changes in fish abundance and entire watershed monitoring. This would most likely be achieved through linking individual project monitoring with broad-scale status monitoring and trend monitoring throughout a watershed.

References, controls, and spatial and temporal replication

The importance of references or controls and replication in space and time cannot be understated (Downes et al. 2002), because most evaluations of monitoring programs have lacked adequate replication and have been of short duration (Roni et al. 2003). The simplest study design is a BA design without a control or a reference. Deciding whether to add a reference or a control; how many sites, reaches, or watersheds to sample (spatial replication); and how long to monitor (temporal replication) can be challenging. A reference or a control provides a basis of comparison between the restored area and the conditions before restoration and serves as a covariate to account for natural variability. A control typically is thought of as a reach or a watershed that is identical to the treated stream reach before treatment. A reference is often thought of as a reach that represents the conditions one is trying to achieve with the treatment. Monitoring controls along with treatments before and after habitat enhancement has a number of advantages, including helping account for background variability not associated with the treatment. However, selection of reference or control streams or reaches must be done carefully (Downes et al. 2002). If the parameters measured in the control reach do not follow a pattern similar to that in the treatment reach, this can lead to more noise in the data and can make it more difficult to detect a change in the absence of a control (Roni et al. 2003; see also Chapter 2). If examinations are done at a reach scale, pairing reaches within a stream reduces the variability more than choosing reaches in other streams; but, as indicated previously, adjacent stream reaches may not be totally independent (i.e., upstream–downstream effects, fish movement). Within a stream, control reaches generally should be located upstream from treatment reaches. Locating control reaches downstream from treatments may result in instream treatments such as wood structures moving downstream and influencing control reaches.

The duration of monitoring needed to detect a change is particularly important in any type of BA study design and will depend, in part, on the monitoring parameters selected. Most work on salmonids has suggested that more than 10 years (5 before and 5 after) are needed to detect significant changes in fish abundance, unless the magnitude of change is very large (>threefold; Bisson et al. 1997; Roni et al. 2003). Decades of before or after monitoring may be needed to detect significant responses of adult anadromous salmonids to enhancement because of high interannual variability in adult abundance (Bisson et al. 1997). These limitations can be overcome in part by replication, which is important in all study designs. This is particularly important for an EPT, which includes sampling many sites over a short period of time. Sample size and power calculations for fishes suggest that at least 20 streams with paired treatment and reference reaches would be needed to detect significant changes in fish abundance at a reach scale (see Chapter 2). Replication is typically absent in BA and BACI studies, generally due to costs and logistics; however, it is particularly critical for these studies to reduce variability and to make the findings more broadly applicable. Sample size and power estimates for both duration and replication (number of sites) can be made by using simple statistical techniques (Zar 1999) and should be estimated before finalizing the number of sites and temporal length of sampling. Discussions of power and sample size for various study designs also are discussed in detail in Chapter 2.

Selecting Monitoring Parameters

Physical habitat

After determining the key questions and hypotheses and study design, and after selecting study locations, the next step is to determine the appropriate physical and biological variables to monitor. This typically occurs simultaneously with determining spatial and temporal replication. The majority of stream enhancement evaluations have focused on physical monitoring (Reeves et al. 1991; Roni et al. 2002). Given that the goal of instream enhancement usually involves the manipulation of physical habitat and often results in a rapid change in physical habitat and channel morphology, a number of important parameters can be measured and monitored. These parameters will differ slightly among instream projects based on the objectives, the scale of the project, and the intensity of the study design. For example, the objectives of wood placement and spawning habitat enhancement generally are very different: enumeration of LWD would be important for a wood placement project but not necessarily for placement of spawning gravel. Monitoring parameters need to be selected judiciously, because many may appear to be useful but may not be sensitive to small changes (<25%) in the habitat (Poole et al. 1997; Kaufmann et al. 1999; Bauer and Ralph 2001). We discuss important physical parameter to consider when evaluating instream enhancement; but, the most appropriate parameters and the level of detail or intensity of sampling will depend upon the objectives, the key questions and hypotheses of the project, and the monitoring program.

Physical habitat parameters can be measured at three scales: habitat unit or site (i.e., pool or riffle units), stream reach, and watershed scale. The best protocol for a particular parameter will depend on the project goals and objectives, duration and intensity of monitoring, funding, and region. We provide an overview of important monitoring methods, but detailed information on protocols can be found in numerous texts and technical publications that cover regional monitoring protocols (e.g., Murphy and Willis 1996; Bain and Stevenson 1999; Johnson et al. 2001).

At a habitat unit or site scale, physical features to monitor include pool and riffle types (e.g., Bisson et al. 1982; Hawkins et al. 1993), number and size of LWD, and substrate size and composition (Table 4). A number of systems for classifying habitat units exist. For example, Bisson et al. (1982) defined habitat types based partly on channel slope and pool forming features. Hawkins et al. (1993) described a hierarchical system for classifying habitats in small streams (<15-m bank-full width), with the first tier being fast- or slow-water habitats. Habitat surveys often are subjective, particularly for distinguishing between pool types or pools and glides (Poole et al. 1997). Residual pool depth, which is the difference between maximum depth and depth at tailout of pool or habitat (Lisle 1987), can be used to make classification of pools more rigorous. Schuett-Hames et al. (1994) present a method for classifying pools based on residual depth and habitat size that is scaled by channel width. Surveying the gradient of habitat units also can help distinguish between riffles and cascades. Working in larger rivers can be more challenging, and methods for surveying habitats in rivers differ from those for wadable streams (Hawkins et al. 1993; see also Chapter 6). Detailed information for conducting habitat surveys vary by region, and numerous texts examine this in detail (e.g., Harrelson et al. 1994; Overton et al. 1997; Bain and Stevenson 1999; Pleus et al. 1999).

Table 4.
Common parameters for monitoring physical and biological effects of instream restoration. Scale: 1 = habitat unit, 2 = reach, 3 = watershed.

Parameter	Project types	Scale
Physical		
Habitat units	All	1, 2, 3
Large woody debris	Logs, log structures	1, 2, 3
Cover	Logs, cover structures, boulders, gabions	1
Substrate	Spawning habitat improvement, logs, instream structures, gravel additions	1, 2
Channel morphology/type	Logs, log structures, gabions, boulders, gravel additions, channel realignment or construction	1, 2
Cross sections or long profiles	All	1, 2
Biological		
Egg to fry survival	Spawning habitat improvement, gravel additions, sediment traps	2, 3
Juvenile fish	All	1, 2, 3
Smolts/outmigrants	All	2, 3
Adults	All	1, 2, 3
Macroinvertebrates	All	1, 2, 3
Primary productivity	All	1, 2

Recording other features during habitat surveys, such as primary pool forming features (Montgomery et al. 1995), number of structures, and amount of cover, also are important for monitoring placement of instream structures. Since many instream projects involve the placement of wood or logs to increase habitat complexity, and, because wood levels are reduced compared to historical levels in many streams (Harmon et al. 1986), enumerating woody debris is an important component of a monitoring program. Typically, LWD is defined as wood greater than 10 cm in diameter and 1 m in length, but this varies by geographic region (Bilby and Bisson 1998). Length, width, and location within the habitat unit and the stream channel should be recorded. Recording whether the LWD or the instream habitat structure is within the low-flow wetted channel, the bank-full channel width, or outside the channel also is important in determining its influence on the stream channel (Robison and Beschta 1990). In addition, recording the function of an individual piece of LWD or an instream structure, based on its influence on pool formation and channel scour, can be important. For example, Montgomery et al. (1995) classified LWD into one of three categories: (1) dominant—primary factor contributing to pool formation, (2) secondary—influences zone of channel scour but not responsible for pool formation, (3) negligible—may provide cover but not involved in scour. Quantifying the amount of cover within habitat units provided by structures, logs, or other material in or adjacent to the channel also is important, particularly for techniques designed to provide cover. This typically is estimated either visually or by measuring the surface area covered by LWD or structure (Bain and Stevenson 1999). If detailed LWD surveys are conducted, including the length and the width of each piece of LWD, then the volume of wood within the bank-full channel can be used as an indication of cover and habitat complexity.

Both instream structures and gravel additions may affect the substrate composition and sorting within and below treatment areas. Measuring the size, the composition, the percent fines, and the embeddedness of both surface and subsurface sediments can be an important part of project evaluation. Methods for estimating these parameters vary from visual estimation of dominant and subdominant particle size (Bain and Stevenson 1999) to more quantitative methods, such as Wolman (1954) pebble counts or freeze core samples. Methods for sampling substrate are detailed in Platts et al. (1983), Bunte and Abt (2001), Chapter 3, and elsewhere. The addition of gravel to create spawning habitat or to compensate for a reduction of gravel transport below dams or impoundments should include monitoring of substrate composition, area, and volume within individual habitats and stream reaches, as well as substrate movement and transport. Methods for measuring the scour and transport of gravel and substrate include scour monitors, addition of tracer or marker particles (typically painted or colored stones), and attachment of a tag or transmitter to selected particles (DeVries 2000; Chapter 3).

In addition to the habitat-unit-level physical measures outlined above, cross sections, longitudinal profiles, reach-level morphology, and mapping before and after can all be important components of monitoring and evaluating instream enhancement projects. A detailed survey of changes in bed elevation along the channel thalweg, commonly called a long or longitudinal profile, can be particularly effective at demonstrating changes in the streambed after placement of instream structures or gravel (Figure 5; Harrelson et al. 1994). Before planning an instream enhancement project, the channel or reach type should be identified or classified by using a method such as Rosgen (1996), Montgomery and Buffington (1997), or a similar channel classification system. These surveys also should be completed after project implementation, because instream manipulations often lead to dramatic changes in reach morphology, channel type, and long profile. Many of these habitat-unit parameters also can be measured at a reach or watershed scale. For example, Hankin and Reeves (1988) and Dolloff et al. (1997) outline a method for estimating habitat parameters at a reach and watershed scale by using a combination of low-intensity visual estimates and more precise measurements and surveys on a subset of habitats to calibrate visual estimates. Broad-scale aerial photos that show the entire channel and riparian zone can help demonstrate large changes in channel morphology (see Chapters 3 and 6). Finally, photographic points and site maps are useful for documenting changes in physical habitat and reach morphology before and after treatment.

Biological parameters

Biological monitoring can be placed into four categories: fishes, macroinvertebrates, other biota (e.g., primary production, vegetation), and community measures (e.g., species richness, indices of biotic integrity). We will focus our discussion on fishes and macroinvertebrates, the two most common biological parameters used to monitor and to evaluate instream restoration. Information on primary production, riparian vegetation, biot-

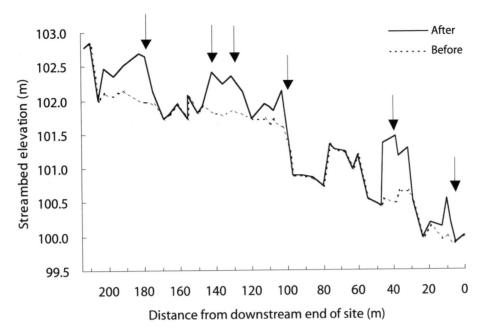

Figure 5.
Example of a longitudinal profile before and after placement of logs and boulders in a 200-m reach of Paradise Creek, Oregon. After data was collected during 2002 survey, while before data was estimated from bedrock below structures. Arrows indicate location of boulder weirs or placed log. Before and after profiles are rare for instream projects (we found no published examples) but provide important information on changes in channel profile, morphology, and project effectiveness.

ic integrity, and other biotic parameters are less frequently a part of instream enhancement monitoring but can provide important information regarding community structure and function. These topics are covered in more detail in other chapters in this volume.

Fishes

Monitoring responses of fishes to instream enhancement is particularly critical to evaluating project success when projects are designed specifically to increase fish numbers or condition. The fish sampling technique, as with other techniques, should be linked to the key questions and hypotheses. Methods for enumerating fish include direct capture techniques, such as electrofishing, seining, trapping, or visual counts, such as spawner surveys, snorkel surveys, or underwater videography (Table 5). These techniques vary in their ability to estimate different important population parameters such as abundance, species richness and distribution, population size, length and weight, and survival. Each of the common techniques, described below, has advantages and disadvantages. For example, electrofishing is particularly effective in small streams and allows for direct measurement and tagging of fish but may cause injury or unacceptable levels of mortality and can be quite time consuming (Roni and Fayram 2000).

The most commonly used techniques to estimate fish abundance within stream reaches or individual habitats are mark–recapture and multiple-removal methods (Murphy and Willis 1996). Mark–recapture, which involves the capture of fish, tagging, release, and subsequent recapture, can be a very accurate method for enumerating fishes (Peterson and Cederholm 1984; Zubik and Fraley 1988; Rodgers et al. 1992). Numerous techniques exist to mark fish, including fin clips, passive integrated transponder (PIT) tags, visible implant tags, injection of pigment into fins, and others. The appropriateness of marking techniques varies by species, size, and longevity of mark required. The advantages of mark–recapture techniques are that they can be applied in both large and small streams, and can provide accurate and robust estimates, assuming enough fish can be marked and recaptured (Peterson and Cederholm 1984; Rodgers et al. 1992). This technique, however, can be time consuming and depends on the efficiency of common techniques (electrofishing, seining, trapping), which may vary by species and physical stream conditions (flow, temperature, habitat complexity). Mark–recapture techniques commonly are applied at the habitat unit or reach level but, by using a two-stage sampling method (Hankin and Reeves 1988; Dolloff et al. 1997), can be expanded to an entire watershed.

Table 5.

Common methods for enumerating fish and the most appropriate scale and fish life stage. Multiple-removal and mark–recapture techniques may use a variety of capture techniques, including electrofishing, seining, trapping, and others. Growth and survival can be estimated with capture techniques if fish are marked and sampled more than once.

Technique	Appropriate scale	Life stage(s)	Parameter estimated	Concerns and limitations
Multiple removal	Habitat unit, reach[a]	Juveniles, resident adults	Abundance, size	Capture mortality (electrofishing in particular), capture efficiency may vary by species and habitat
Mark–recapture	Habitat unit, reach, watershed	All life stages	Abundance, size, survival	Tagging/marking mortality, difficulty in marking small fish
Migrant traps (smolt traps)	Reach or watershed (drainage upstream of trap)	Juveniles and smolts	Abundance, size, survival, population size	Trap efficiency, must calibrate to determine proportion of downstream migrants captured
Spawner surveys	Habitat, reach, or watershed	Adults	Abundance, distribution	Accuracy of counts, observer error
Upstream downstream weirs or traps (or traps at dam, falls or fish passage structure)	Watershed (drainage upstream of trap)	Any migrants (juveniles, smolts, adults)	Abundance, size, survival, population size	Trap efficiency, change in movements or migrations due to weir
Snorkel counts	Habitat unit and reach scale[a]	All	Abundance, size	No direct size measurements, observer error, counts vary with temperature, flow, visibility, species, difficult for benthic species
Underwater videography	Habitat unit	All	Abundance	Gaining popularity with availability of inexpensive equipment, but technique has not been rigorously evaluated in streams

[a]Two-stage sampling can be used to expand to a watershed scale (Dolloff et al. 1997)

The multiple-removal estimate is another common method for estimating fish abundance within a habitat, stream, or reach. This method originally was developed for mammals but has been used extensively for fish and requires sampling a habitat or area repeatedly, enumerating the animals in each pass, and retaining them until all removals are completed (Zippin 1958). For stream fishes, this most frequently involves the placing of nets to isolate a habitat or stream reach and the use of electrofishing to make two or more passes (removals) through the habitat or reach. The individual fish are identified and enumerated, and abundance estimates usually are made with a multiple removal estimator (e.g., Zippin 1958; Carle and Strub 1978) and computer software (White et al. 1982; Van Deventer and Platts 1989; and others). Studies have shown that three or more removals generally are needed to provide accurate estimates of fish abundance (Riley and Fausch 1992). Some authors have suggested that a 50% reduction from the second to third removal is needed; otherwise, additional passes are required (Roni and Fayram 2000). Other capture methods, such as trapping or seining, can be used in place of electrofishing for multiple removals.

Snorkeling and scuba diving are common, benign, direct observational techniques for enumerating fish in small and large streams and can provide accurate counts, assuming adequate visibility exists to observe and to identify fish. In small streams, this method usually involves one or two snorkelers moving upstream, either recording fish number, species, and size as they go or relaying the numbers to an individual on the bank. In larger streams, multiple snorkelers float downstream side by side and enumerate fish (Thurow 1994). Visual counts from the streambank often are used to enumerate adult anadromous fish, to count the number of redds, or, in some cases, to enumerate fry along streambanks or in very small channels. However, unless visual counts are repeated, the accuracy of a survey cannot be estimated, and, because fish are not handled, size and species must be estimated. Therefore, it is important that divers and snorkelers receive training in both snorkeling techniques and fish identification to assure that their estimates are comparable. Reiger and Robson (1967) and Hicks and Watson (1985) describe methods of repeated or bounded counts that can be used to calibrate the accuracy of both the observer and the snorkel surveys.

The nocturnal behavior of many salmonids during winter months or cold temperatures precludes the use of many other techniques for estimating fish abundance and habitat use. Night snorkel surveys have been used successfully during winter months in streams in the western North America to enumerate juvenile fishes and to evaluate stream enhancement projects (Roni and Fayram 2000; Roni and Quinn 2001a). Snorkeling is a relatively benign and cost-effective method for estimating fish abundance and for observing behavior; however, it has limited applicability in deep water and for benthic stream fishes, and the accuracy can be influenced by observer error and many physical factors (e.g., flow, temperature, turbidity; Thurow 1994; Roni and Fayram 2000).

Minnow traps, seining, and underwater videography are other techniques for enumerating stream fishes. They are less common than electrofishing, snorkeling, or other trapping techniques but may be useful in some situations. Minnow traps have been used successfully to capture and enumerate juvenile salmonids (Bloom 1976; Swales et al. 1986). Seining can be useful in areas where the habitat is simple (little LWD or boulders), the velocities are low, and the substrate is small and uniform—atypical conditions in many streams. Finally, the advent of small, relatively inexpensive underwater videocameras has led to an expansion of their use to enumerate fish in streams. Video techniques have been used widely for both marine fish and invertebrates surveys (Tracy 2000; Willis et al. 2000; Heithaus et al. 2001), but little published information exists on their effectiveness in streams other than at dams, weirs, or counting fences.

Enumerating the number of smolts or downstream migrants emigrating from a watershed or a stream reach is a critical parameter for many habitat enhancement projects for anadromous or migratory fishes. For example, Cederholm et al. (1997), Solazzi et al. (2000), and Reeves et al. (1997) used downstream migrant traps to estimate the number of smolts produced from stream reaches and watersheds receiving enhancement. On small streams, a weir or downstream traps can be constructed to estimate the number of migrating fish produced. Floating traps, such as incline-plane or screw (auger) traps, often are used in larger rivers (Thedinga et al. 1994). When coordinated with other fish sampling efforts, smolt and downstream migrant traps can be used to estimate growth, survival, and a suite of other life history characteristics. Smolt traps are particularly effective for estimating watershed-scale effects of habitat enhancement or other activities on anadromous fish production and survival (Kennen et al. 1994; Thedinga et al. 1994). They also can be used to evaluate fish production from stream reaches, but this requires multiple traps at the upstream and downstream end of each study reach. Cederholm et al. (1997) used multiple traps to estimate coho and steelhead smolts produced from treated and untreated stream reaches. Regardless of the type of trap or weir used, some method of marking and recapturing is needed to estimate trap efficiency (percent of downstream migrants actually being captured in the trap). Smolt and downstream migrant counts are a critical component of evaluating habitat enhancement projects for migratory fishes but can be costly, because they often need to be checked daily and run over the course of the out-migration period, which may be several months for some or multiple species. The efficiency of traps also may vary with flow and time of day, as well as fish size and species (Thedinga et al. 1994).

The goal of many instream enhancement projects for anadromous fishes is to increase returning adults numbers; thus, adult fish enumeration can be important. Adult anadromous salmonids generally are enumerated either by constructing a counting weir or a fence at an existing dam or fish passage facility, or through spawner or redd surveys. Spawner surveys often are done on foot but also can be done from a plane or a boat, through snorkel surveys, or with videography at a trap or a fish passage facility. Adult anadromous fish response to instream enhancement has rarely been recorded, in part, because detecting a statistically significant response requires monitoring many generations (Bisson et al. 1997; Korman and Higgins 1997). If direct adult counts are not available, then the number of redds often is used as an index of the use of sites by migratory fishes, though obtaining accurate redd counts can be difficult (Dunham et al. 2001).

Fish size, growth, age, condition, survival, and community structure also are important factors for evaluating the effects of restoration and enhancement activities that can be obtained by using most of the techniques described above. Habitat enhancement activities can lead to increased numbers but smaller size (Roni and Quinn 2001a), changes in age structure (Hunt 1988), or larger individuals. Survival has not received as much attention as abundance, because survival is difficult to estimate and it requires repeated sampling and information on fish habitat use, movement, and mortality. It is, however, an important parameter to measure, one of the key research needs for quantifying fish response to habitat enhancement, and potentially is more sensitive to changes in habitat than abundance (Paulsen and Fisher 2003). Moreover, given improvements in tagging and detection technology with PIT tags and radiotelemetry, survival is more easily quantifiable than a decade ago.

Fish community structure also is an important metric to evaluate instream enhancement activities, particularly in areas with diverse fish fauna (Karr 1981; Fausch et al. 1990; Simon 1999). The shortcoming of most early evaluations of stream enhancement and restoration is that they sampled and focused on one or two fish species (usually salmonid fishes; Reeves et al. 1991; Roni et al. 2002). This is problematic because non-salmonid species may be impacted by enhancement or restoration activities (Roni and Quinn 2001a) and may be more sensitive to habitat alteration than the economically important migratory species often monitored. Further, detecting changes in abundance often is more difficult than monitoring changes in community structure and diversity, and a single-species approach tells us nothing about whether we have restored the natural diversity of species and habitats. Therefore, monitoring the response of various species and the structure and diversity of the fish community can provide important information about the success of the project. Diversity, richness, species dominance, and other fish community measures usually can be estimated with standard fish sampling techniques, though species-specific differences in capture efficiency can affect estimates of these parameters, and consistent sampling methods should be used when comparing community measures among sites, streams, dates, or years.

In streams, there tends to be an increase in species diversity as one moves from headwaters to the estuary. This can affect the underlying diversity in different stream reaches throughout a watershed. Fish community structure within a stream also can be influenced by reach-scale characteristics, such as slope, channel confinement, complexity, and other factors (Reeves et al. 1998). Differences in diversity among streams and watersheds may be the result of restoration activities or inherent differences in reaches or in watersheds. These factors need to be considered when attributing changes in fish community structure among treatment and reference areas both within and among watersheds.

A criticism of instream enhancement is that projects may be attracting fish rather than increasing abundance. Artificial reefs and other similar structures in the marine environment are known to attract and concentrate fishes (Lindberg 1997), particularly very long-lived fishes (e.g., rockfishes; Matthews 1990a, 1990b). In streams, the attraction versus the abundance question is most relevant to resident fishes, because the larger and older individuals may be more than 3 years old and may vacate existing habitats for newly constructed habitats. For example, Riley and Fausch (1995) demonstrated that much of the increase in resident trout abundance they observed in restored reaches of Colorado streams was due to immigration from other stream reaches. This is less of a concern for juvenile anadromous fishes such as Pacific salmon, which usually spend 2 years or less in freshwater and produce a new cohort of fry to colonize habitats every year. Early work on juvenile and adult resident salmonids suggested that fish had small home ranges, typically less than a few hundred meters (Gowan et al. 1994). Similarly, work on juvenile anadromous salmonids suggested that they had small home ranges in summer or nonmigratory periods (Kahler et al. 2001; Rodriguez 2002) but may move long distances in the fall to overwintering areas (Peterson 1982) or in the spring while migrating to sea (Northcote 1992). However, work in the last decade has indicated that a small proportion of adult and juvenile salmonids, and possibly other stream fishes, may move long distances (Gowan et al. 1994). Thus, in some cases, short-term increases in fish abundance may be the result of immigration from adjacent stream reaches. However, higher numbers of fish in a treated (enhanced) stream reach indicate fish preference for artificially created or enhanced habitat. It may be important to monitor the movements of fishes to determine whether instream enhancement has lead to increased numbers of fish through increased survival rather than short-term redistribution or concentration. This can be done through fish marking and recapturing, radio or sonic tagging, or by monitoring their movement through weirs and traps. Stationary weirs, however, can affect fish movement and limit movement to and from a stream reach (Kahler 1999). Frissell and Ralph (1998) suggested a method for examining the redistribution versus the increased survival questions by examining changes in both age structure and abundance over time: an increase in abundance of multiple age-classes over time would suggest an increase in survival.

Even studies conducted at a watershed scale may be influenced by movement, because fish may move into or out of a watershed before enumeration. Thus, estimates for smolt production from an upstream watershed would exclude those fish that may have been produced (born) in the watershed but emigrated to overwinter elsewhere. Complete monitoring of fish response to instream enhancement would require estimates of fish abundance or population, size, condition, growth, age structure, and migrations among natural and artificial habitats and at a watershed scale. Projects that attract fish may be beneficial; assuming adequate spawners and reproduction in a watershed, fish will likely colonize the habitats made vacant by fish moving to a newly enhanced or accessible habitat. However, attracting or concentrating could make fish susceptible to predators that also prefer newly created habitats or susceptible to fishing or other forms of natural and human-induced mortality. Additional monitoring and research in this area will help address these important questions on fish movement and survival.

Macroinvertebrates

Macroinvertebrates are good indicators of habitat alteration, because they are highly sensitive to changes in physical habitat (e.g., depth, velocity, substrate size, and water quality), are vital components and indicators of the structure and function of aquatic systems, are food sources for vertebrates, and reproduce more rapidly than most fishes (Resh and Rosenburg 1984; Merritt and Cummins 1996; Karr and Chu 1999). The diversity and habitat-specific preferences of invertebrate taxa suggest that they have varying responses to different habitat manipulations produced by different instream enhancement techniques. Macroinvertebrate taxa show strong preferences for substrate size, with chironomids and burrowing ephemeropterans being most often associated with silts and sands, while the vast majority of plecopteran, ephemeropteran, and tricopteran taxa are associated with gravel and cobble substrates (Merritt and Cummins 1996). In general, macroinvertebrate abundance increases with substrate particle size (Resh and Rosenburg 1984; Gore 1985). Velocity and substrate size within a stream are correlated, and many species show preferences for both. Ephemeropteran, plecopteran, and tricopteran taxa tend to predominate in stream erosional areas and corresponding course substrate. Gastropods, amphipods, isopods, many coleopterans, and odonates commonly are found in lower velocity habitats with greater percent substrate embeddedness and organic richness, while annelids, chironomids, and burrowing ephemeroptera often inhabit slow-flowing depositional areas of streams (McCafferty 1981; Merritt and Cummins 1996).

Habitat enhancement can alter stream morphology, reach-scale habitat diversity (pools and riffles, deep and slow-water habitats), substrate composition, depth, and velocity—all factors that can affect aquatic macroinvertebrates. Some instream enhancement techniques, such as the addition of brush bundles, can provide direct habitat and potential food sources for macroinvertebrates (Anderson and Sedell 1979). The ability to detect changes in biotic communities due to habitat enhancement and the time required to do so are a function of the degree of change that is actually taking place (Peterman 1990; Kelly and Harwell 1990). As with fishes, inherent spatial and temporal variability of streams, upstream influences, dynamic watershed land use, and hydrologic and meteorologic events can act singly or in concert to alter, dampen, or mask potential macroinvertebrate community responses resulting from instream enhancement or other habitat alterations (Weigel et al. 2000). Streams where habitat is significantly manipulated over relatively long stream reaches are likely to have a stronger and quicker effect on the macroinvertebrate community than those with minor instream alterations or those that occur on short stream reaches.

Season, frequency, duration, sample size, type of sampling gear, and protocols necessary to examine macroinvertebrate response to habitat enhancement ultimately should be determined by the goals and the hypotheses of the study (Rosenburg and Resh 1993; Merritt et al. 1996). Understanding the various influences different instream enhancement efforts have on habitat will help determine sampling locations and the gear and the protocols that should be used. Emergent and drift samples, as well as hyporheic samples also can be collected, but we will focus our discussion on benthic sampling, because it has extensively used to examine habitat change (see Merritt and Cummins 1996; Rosenburg and Resh 1993; and others for drift samples).

In general, macroinvertebrate sampling is either qualitative or quantitative. Qualitative sampling often is done with a D-frame or kick net, whereby benthic organisms are dislodged by kicking or disturbing the area upstream from the net. The resulting qualitative samples can be used for various biotic indices, as well as richness, diversity, ratio, or dominance measures (Rosenberg and Resh 1993). These methods tend to be less labor intensive, both in terms of collecting and processing organisms than quantitative sampling. Quantitative samples usually are collected with Surber or Hess samplers or stovepipe (coring) devices, which sample a fixed area. Given the spatial (patchy distribution) and temporal variability (seasonal emergence of aquatic insects) of macroinvertebrates, quantitative sampling requires greater rigor in the consideration of seasonal effects, sampling locations and frequency, and number of sample replicates (Rosenburg and Resh 1993; Merritt and Cummins 1996). Other macroinvertebrate sampling methods include the placement of tiles, leaf packs, and other artificial substrates in the stream channel for a specified time period to allow macroinvertebrates to colonize a standard substrate among sites. The appropriate time of year to sample depends on the region and species of interest. For example, benthic macroinvertebrate samples generally are collected in late summer to early fall in the Pacific Northwest (Fore et al. 1996). The decision between taking quantitative and qualitative samples of macroinvertebrates depends upon the objectives of the project and the questions being asked in the monitoring program as well as costs. If the objective is primarily creating cover structures for fish, then less intensive qualitative sampling may be more appropriate.

Determining the number of macroinvertebrate samples to take within a reach or a habitat can be challenging. It often is influenced by logistics and by costs of both collecting and later processing samples in the laboratory, and the level of accuracy and precision needed to address the questions and the hypothesis of the monitoring program. Ideally, within treatment and reference areas or before and after treatment, one would stratify samples by habitat type (e.g., fast versus slow water, or pools versus riffles) and collect multiple samples within an individual habitat. This would allow calculation of variability within a habitat, among habitat types, and within a stream reach or a watershed. For example, collecting three samples within three randomly selected riffles and three randomly selected pools within treatment and reference reaches recently was used to evaluate instream LWD placement (P. Roni, unpublished data).

Once samples are collected, they either can be processed in the field (qualitative samples) or can be taken to the laboratory (quantitative samples) for detailed identification. Determining the appropriate taxonomic level to identify macroinvertebrates is a topic of considerable debate and is dependent upon the goals of the study. Often, the macroinvertebrates are identified to the lowest taxonomic level possible (typically genus), but this is less common for families such as Chironomidae or in samples identified in the field. Identification and analysis of macroinvertebrate samples are beyond the scope of this chapter, but several comprehensive texts and manuals cover these topics (McCafferty 1981; Resh and Rosenburg 1984; Klemm et al. 1990; Cuffney et al. 1993; Rosenburg and Resh 1993; Merritt and Cummins 1996; Barbour et al. 1999).

Numerous metrics can be used to evaluate the success or effects of instream enhancement efforts on macroinvertebrates (Table 6). These include but are not limited to abundance, diversity measures (Minshall et al. 1985; Magurran 1988), functional feeding groups (Wallace and Webster 1996), criteria derived from biotic indices (Washington 1984; Karr and Chu 1999), or expectation models (Novak and Bode 1992; Hawkins et al. 2000) based on data from streams of similar nature (e.g., catchment land cover, water temperature, elevation, gradient, stream order, etc.) compared to the stream being evaluated (Table 6, see also Chapter 6). As with identification and specific field sample collection protocols, there are a number of comprehensive guidance documents available (Resh and Rosenburg 1984; Klemm et al. 1990; Rosenburg and Resh 1993; Merritt and Cummins 1996; Barbour et al. 1999).

Assessing macroinvertebrate community responses to instream enhancement efforts should recognize the influence these practices have on benthic habitat, autochthonous and allochthonous energy sources, and other

Table 6.
Common metrics and indices for measuring macroinvertebrate response to habitat change.

Name or description	Taxonomic level	Reference
Taxa richness		
Total number of species	Genus, species	Barbour et al. 1999
Generic richness	Genus	Barbour et al. 1999
Ephemeroptera–plecoptera–tricoptera generic richness	Genus	Barbour et al. 1999
Diversity		
Margalef's diversity index	Genus	Margalef 1959
Shannon's index of diversity	Genus	Magurran 1988
Sequential comparison index	Mixed	Resh and Price 1984
Trophic functions		
Percent of total: scrapers, filterers, shredders, gatherers, or collectors	Individuals, genus	Cummins and Merritt 1996
Dominance		
Percent of total count represented by dominant genera, families, or species	Genus, families, or species	Plafkin 1989
Biotic indices		
Hilsenhoff's biotic index	Genus, species	Hilsenhoff 1987
Multimetric indices: combinations of various sample taxa attributes, such as pollution tolerance, trophic function, diversity, etc.	Mixed	Winget and Mangum 1979; Kerrans and Karr 1994; DeShon 1995; Fore et al. 1996; Karr and Chu 1999
Predictive models		
Comparisons of observed taxa to those expected to occur in the absence of human disturbance	Mixed	Barbour et al. 1999; Armitage et al. 1987; Wright 1995; Hawkins et al. 2000

environmental factors that affect macroinvertebrates. Alterations in stream flow and channel morphology can influence autotrophic production and food sources for macroinvertebrates, which, in turn, can affect fish growth, survival, and abundance (Newbury and Gaboury 1993). Channel narrowing along with increasing stream flow velocities reduces the surface area available for autotrophic production and potential habitat for benthic macroinvertebrates (Statzner et al. 1988). If stream channels are significantly narrowed or water depth is sufficiently increased, photosynthetic productivity can be reduced. Conversely, this increase in substrate coarseness may increase surface area and may provide additional habitat for macroinvertebrates. Thus, primary production and water chemistry are other factors that can be monitored in conjunction with macroinvertebrates and fishes to determine the effects of habitat enhancement on biota. Additional information on sampling to detect changes in primary productivity, water chemistry, and biotic community based measures can be found in a detailed discussion of monitoring nutrient enrichment techniques in Chapters 6 and 9.

Sampling Schemes or Strategies

Once parameters have been selected, or concurrent with selecting parameters, one needs to determine the sampling scheme for this parameter within the study sites (e.g., random, stratified random, multistage sampling). Different sampling schemes were briefly reviewed in Chapter 2 and are discussed at length in many statistical texts (Hunter 1992; Zar 1999). Similarly, quality control both in field data collection and in data entry are important aspects of monitoring that need to be well thought out before and refined during the life of a monitoring project.

Considerations for Unique Project Types

A few types of projects may require special considerations, and many other projects that are considered instream enhancement can be monitored by using similar techniques. For example, some consider the restoration or augmentation of instream flows to be a type of instream habitat enhancement. Monitoring changes in instream flows would require monitoring not only physical conditions (i.e., channel morphology, substrate size), fish, macroinvertebrates, and primary production but also changes in hydrology and riparian vegetation. Gravel placement would require monitoring of gravel scour, deposition, and movement (discussed in Chapter 3). Excavation of sediment traps, a common technique in parts of the Midwest to improve habitat and to create spawning habitat (Avery 1996), should include monitoring of fine sediment levels, channel width, depth, and morphology, and, ultimately, changes in survival of fish and other biota. Channel realignment, a common technique in urban and agricultural areas where streams have been straightened and highly channelized (i.e., see Figure 4A in Chapter 6), would require similar techniques as described above but should include more in-depth physical and hydrologic monitoring and monitoring of the riparian zone (e.g., Clayton 2002).

Summary

The monitoring of instream enhancement techniques has been more intensive than most other stream, watershed, or estuarine restoration and enhancement monitoring; yet efforts have been inadequate for evaluating most instream techniques. The general guidance we provide on monitoring instream enhancement allows for the evaluation of single or multiple projects, and can be tailored to the questions at hand and the scope of the project. A well-designed monitoring program will include objectives and explicit hypotheses; an appropriate study design, with spatial and temporal replication; and measurement of appropriate monitoring parameters to test the hypotheses. We have outlined numerous variables that can be monitored, knowing that, ideally, monitoring all these variables would be beneficial, though, realistically, prohibitively expensive in most cases. Thus, we provide a discussion essentially to illustrate a complete list that could be tailored for the goals, objectives, and hypotheses pertinent to specific project and monitoring needs.

Instream enhancement actions are experiments and each provides a unique opportunity to answer key questions and hypotheses. Rigorous monitoring of instream enhancement projects will help us allocate limited funds for restoration wisely and plan and refine future projects. Three key areas that have been largely overlooked in monitoring response of biota to instream enhancement projects include watershed-scale effects on abundance and habitat, fish movements, and effects of projects on fish survival. Recent advances in tagging and sampling techniques should allow future projects to estimate these and to determine the effectiveness of instream techniques on fish populations. As noted previously, most instream habitat enhancement monitoring has focused on individual projects. Broad-scale evaluations of multiple projects within a region or across a watershed are needed. This will require coordination and linking project-level monitoring with larger status monitoring and trend monitoring programs (if they exist) and integration of monitoring designs into other programs. Survival is the ultimate measure of whether habitat enhancement projects have truly resulted in an increase in fish numbers and population size.

The success of instream enhancement projects at improving physical habitat and at increasing abundance and survival of biota often depends on whether basic watershed processes (e.g., delivery of wood, water, and sediment; functioning riparian areas) are restored (Roni et al. 2002) and whether factors limiting biotic production have been identified and addressed. In some cases, other restoration activities should be initiated before instream enhancement techniques are used, and instream enhancement techniques are not appropriate in many situations (Minns et al. 1996; Beechie and Bolton 1999; Roni et al. 2002). Although instream enhancement techniques have their limitations, they are particularly useful when coupled with larger process-based restoration (e.g., reconnection of isolated habitats, road removal, riparian replanting, removal of grazing) or when short-term improvements in habitat are needed, such as for endangered species recovery or when it may be many years before watershed processes recover or land uses improve (Roni et al. 2002). Monitoring of instream enhancement activities is critical for adaptive management and testing key questions and hypotheses about biotic and physical responses to habitat enhancement. Without rigorous monitoring, we risk throwing good money after bad and never knowing which instream enhancement projects and techniques are truly effective.

Acknowledgments

We thank Steve Clayton, Fred Geotz, George Pess, and Ed Quimby for their helpful comments on earlier versions of this manuscript.

References

Anderson, J. W., R. A. Ruediger, and W. F. Hudson. 1984. Design, placement and fish use of instream structures in southwestern Oregon. Pages 165–180 in T. J. Hassler, editor. Proceedings: Pacific Northwest stream habitat management workshop. American Fisheries Society, Humboldt Chapter, Humboldt State University, Arcata, California.

Anderson, N. H., and J. R. Sedell. 1979. Detritus processing by macroinvertebrates in stream ecosystems. Annual Review of Entomology 24:351–377.

Angermeier, P. L., and J. R. Karr. 1984. Relationship between woody debris and fish habitat in a small warmwater stream. Transactions of the American Fisheries Society 113:716–726.

Armantrout, N. B. 1991. Restructuring streams for anadromous salmonids. Pages 136–149 in J. Colt and R. J. White, editors. Fisheries Bioengineering Symposium. American Fisheries Society, Symposium 10, Bethesda, Maryland.

Armitage, P. D., R. J. M. Gunn, M. T. Furse, J. F. Wright, and D. Moss. 1987. The use of prediction to assess macroinvertebrates in response to river regulation. Hydrobiologia 144:25–32.

Avery, E. L. 1996. Evaluations of sediment traps and artificial gravel riffles constructed to improve reproduction of trout in three Wisconsin streams. North American Journal of Fisheries Management 16:282–293.

Avery, E. L. 2004. A compendium of 58 trout stream habitat development evaluations in Wisconsin- 1985–2000. Wisconsin Department of Natural Resources, Research Report 187, Madison.

Bain, M. B., and N. J. Stevenson, editors. 1999. Aquatic habitat assessment: common methods. American Fisheries Society, Bethesda, Maryland.

Barbour, M. T., J. Gerritsen, B. D. Snyder, and J. B. Stribling. 1999. Rapid bioassessment protocols for use in streams and wadable rivers: periphyton, benthic macroinvertebrates, and fish (2nd edition): U. S. Environmental Protection Agency Report, EPA 841-B-99-002, Washington, D. C.

Bauer, S. B., and S. C. Ralph. 2001. Strengthening the use of aquatic habitat indicators in Clean Water Act programs. Fisheries 26(6):14–24.

Beechie, T. J., and S. Bolton. 1999. An approach to restoring salmonid habitat-forming processes in Pacific Northwest watersheds. Fisheries 24(4):6–15.

Beschta, R. L., W. S. Platts, J. B. Kauffman, and M. T. Hill. 1994. Artificial stream restoration—money well spent or expensive failure? Pages 76–104 in UCOWR, editor. Proceedings of environmental restoration, UCOWR 1994 annual meeting, Big Sky, Montana. University Council on Water Resources, University of Illinois, Carbondale.

Bilby, R. E., and P. A. Bisson. 1998. Function and distribution of large woody debris. Pages 324–326 in R. J. Naiman and R. E. Bilby, editors. River ecology and management. Springer-Verlag, New York.

Bilby, R. E., and B. R. Fransen. 1996. Effect of habitat enhancement and canopy removal on the fish community of a headwater stream. Northwest Science 66:137.

Binns, N. A. 1999. A compendium of trout stream habitat improvement projects done by the Wyoming Game and Fish Department, 1953–1998. Wyoming Game and Fish Department, Fish Division, Cheyenne.

Bisson, P. A., J. L. Nielsen, R. A. Palmason, and L. E. Grove. 1982. A system of naming habitat types in small streams, with examples of habitat utilization by salmonids during low stream flows. Pages 62–73 in N. B. Armantrout, editor. Acquisition and utilization of aquatic habitat inventory information. American Fisheries Society, Bethesda, Maryland.

Bisson, P. A., G. H. Reeves, R. E. Bilby, and R. J. Naiman. 1997. Watershed management and Pacific salmon: desired future conditions. Pages 447–474 in D. J. Stouder, P. A. Bisson, and R. J. Naiman. Pacific salmon and their ecosystems. Chapman and Hall, New York.

Bloom, A. M. 1976. Evaluation of minnow traps for estimating populations of juvenile coho salmon and Dolly Varden. Progressive Fish-Culturist 38:99–101.

Brooks, S. S., M. A. Palmer, B. J. Cardinale, C. M. Swan, and S. Ribblett. 2002. Assessing stream ecosystem rehabilitation: limitations of community structure data. Restoration Ecology 10:156–168.

Broussu, M. F. 1954. Relationship between trout populations and cover on a small stream. Journal of Wildlife Management 18(2):229–239.

Bunte, K., and R. Abt. 2001. Sampling surface and subsurface particle-size distributions in wadable gravel- and cobble-bed streams for analyses in sediment transport, hydraulics, and streambed monitoring. U.S. Forest Service, Rocky Mountain Research Station, General Technical Report RMRS-GTR-74, Fort Collins, Colorado.

Carle, F. L., and M. R. Strub. 1978. A new method for estimating population size from removal data. Biometrics 34:621–630.

Caughley, G. 1994. Directions in conservation biology. Journal of Animal Ecology 63:215–244.

Cederholm, C. J., R. E., Bilby, P. A. Bisson, T. W. Bumstead, B. R. Fransen, W. J. Scarlett, and J. W. Ward. 1997. Response of juvenile coho salmon and steelhead to placement of large woody debris in a coastal Washington stream. North American Journal of Fisheries Management 17:947–963.

Chapman, D. W. 1996. Efficacy of structural manipulations of instream habitat in the Columbia River Basin. Northwest Science 5(4):279–293.

Clayton, S. R. 2002. Quantitative evaluation of physical and biological responses to stream restoration. Doctoral dissertation. University of Idaho, Moscow.

Cowx, I. G., and R. L. Welcomme. 1998. Rehabilitation of rivers for fish. Fishing News Books, Oxford, England.

Crispin, V., R. House, and D. Roberts. 1993. Changes in instream habitat, large woody debris, and salmon habitat after the restructuring of a coastal Oregon stream. North American Journal of Fisheries Management 43:96–102.

Cuffney, T. F., M. E. Gurtz, and M. R. Meador. 1993. Methods for collecting benthic macroinvertebrate samples as part of the National Water-Quality Assessment Program: U.S. Geological Survey Open-File Report 93–046, Raleigh, North Carolina.

Cummins, K. W., and R. W. Merritt. 1996. Ecology and distribution of aquatic insects. Pages 74–86 in R. W. Merritt and K. W. Cummins, editors. An introduction to aquatic insects of North America. Kendall/Hunt Publishing Company, Dubuque, Iowa.

DeShon, J. E. 1995. Development and application of the Invertebrate Community Index (ICI). Pages 217–244 in W. S. Davis and T. P. Simons, editors. Biological assessment and criteria: tools for water resource planning and decision making. Lewis Publishers, London.

DeVries, P. 2000. Scour in low gradient gravel bed streams: patterns, processes, and implications for survival of salmonid embryos. University of Washington, Department of Civil Engineering Water Resources Series Technical Report No. 160, Seattle.

Dolloff, C. A., H. E. Jennings, and M. D. Owen. 1997. A comparison of basinwide and representative reach habitat survey techniques in three southern Appalachian watersheds. North American Journal of Fisheries Management 17:339–347.

Downes, B. J., L. A. Barmuta, P. G. Fairweather, D. P. Faith, M. J. Keough, P. S. Lake, B. D. Mapstone, and G. P. Quinn. 2002. Monitoring ecological impacts: concepts and practice in flowing waters. Cambridge University Press, Cambridge, UK.

Dunham, J., B. Rieman, and K. Davis. 2001. Sources and magnitude of sampling error in redd counts for bull trout. North American Journal of Fisheries Management 21:343–352.

Ehlers, R. 1956. An evaluation of stream improvement project devices constructed eighteen years ago. California Fish and Game 42:203–217.

Fausch, K. D., J. Lyons, J. R. Karr, and P. L. Angermeir. 1990. Fish communities as indicators of environmental degradation. Pages 123–144 in S. M. Adams, editor. Biological indicators of stress in fish. American Fisheries Society, Symposium 8, Bethesda, Maryland.

Fausch, K. D., and R. G. Bramblett. 1991. Disturbance and fish communities in intermittent tributaries of a western Great Plains river. Copeia 3:659–674.

FISRWG (Federal Interagency Stream Restoration Working Group). 1998. Stream Corridor Restoration: Principles, processes, and practices. United States Department of Agriculture, GPO Item No. 0120-A, Washington, D.C.

Fore, L. S., J. R. Karr, and R. W. Wisseman. 1996. Assessing invertebrate responses to human activities: evaluating alternative approaches. Journal of the North American Benthological Society 15:212–231.

Frissell, C. A., and R. K. Nawa. 1992. Incidence and causes of physical failure of artificial habitat structures in streams of western Oregon and Washington. North American Journal of Fisheries Management 12:182–187.

Frissell, C. A., and S. C. Ralph. 1998. Pages 599–624 in R. J. Naiman, and R. E. Bilby, editors. River ecology and management: lessons from the Pacific Coastal ecoregion. Springer-Verlag, New York.

Gard, R. 1961. Creation of trout habitat by constructing small dams. Journal of Wildlife Management 52:384–390.

Gard, R. 1972. Persistence of headwater check dams in a trout stream. Journal of Wildlife Management 36:1363–1367.

Gore, J. A. 1985. The restoration of rivers and streams: theories and experience. Butterworth Publishers, Boston.

Gorman, O. T., and J. R. Karr. 1978. Habitat structure and stream fish communities. Ecology 59:507–515.

Gortz, P. 1998. Effects of stream restoration on the macroinvertebrate community in the River Esrom, Denmark. Aquatic Conservation: Marine and Freshwater Ecosystems 8:115–130.

Gowan, C., and K. D. Fausch. 1996. Long-term demographic responses of trout population to habitat manipulation in six Colorado streams. Ecological Applications 6:931–946.

Gowan, C., M. K. Young, K. D. Fausch, and S. C. Riley. 1994. Restricted movement in resident stream salmonids: a paradigm lost? Canadian Journal of Fisheries Aquatic Sciences 51:2626–2637.

Gregory, R. S., and C. D. Levings. 1996. The effects of turbidity and vegetation on the risk of juvenile salmonids, Oncorhynchus spp., to predation by adult cutthroat trout, O. clarkii. Environmental Biology of Fishes 47(3):279–288.

Gurevitch, J., and L. V. Hedges. 2001. Meta-analysis: combining the results of independent experiments. Pages 347–370 in S. M Scheiner and J. Gurevitch, editors. Design and analysis of ecological experiments. Oxford University Press, New York.

Hankin, D. G., and G. H. Reeves. 1988. Estimating total fish abundance and total habitat area in small streams based on visual estimation methods. Canadian Journal of Fisheries and Aquatic Sciences 45:834–844.

Harmon, M. E., J. F. Franklin, F. J. Swanson, P. Sollins, S. V. Gregory, J. D. Lattin, N. H. Anderson, S. P. Cline, N. G. Aumen, J. R. Sedell, G. W. Lienkaemper, K. Cromack, and K. W. Cummins. 1986. Ecology of coarse woody debris in temperate ecosystems. Advances in Ecological Research 15:133–302.

Harrelson, C. C., C. L. Rawlins, and J. P. Potyondy. 1994. Stream channel reference sites: an illustrated guide to field technique. U. S. Forest Service, Rocky Mountain Forest and Range Experiment Station, General Technical Report RM-245, Fort Collins, Colorado.

Hawkins, P. C., J. L. Kershner, P. A. Bisson, M. D. Bryant, L. M. Decker, S. V. Gregory, D. A. McCullough, C. K. Overton, G. H. Reeves, R. J. Steedman, and M. K. Young. 1993. A hierarchical approach to classifying stream habitat features. Fisheries 18(6):3–11.

Hawkins, C. P., R. H. Norris, J. N. Hogue, and J. W. Feminella. 2000. Development and evaluation of predictive models for measuring the biological integrity of streams. Ecological Applications 10:1456–1477.

Heithaus, M. R., G. J. Marshall, B. M. Buhleier, and L. M. Dill. 2001. Employing Crittercam to study habitat use and behaviour of large sharks. Marine Ecology Progress Series 209:307–310.

Hicks, B. J., and N. R. N. Watson. 1985. Seasonal changes in the abundance of brown trout (*Salmo trutta*) and rainbow trout (*S. gairdnerii*) assessed by drift diving in the Rangitikei River, New Zealand. New Zealand Journal of Marine and Freshwater Research 19:1–10.

Hilderbrand, R. H., A. D. Lemly, C. A. Dolloff, and K. L. Harpster. 1997. Effects of large woody debris placement on stream channels and benthic macroinvertebrates. Canadian Journal of Fisheries and Aquatic Sciences 54:931–939.

Hilsenhoff, W. L. 1987. An improved biotic index of stream pollution. Great Lakes Entomologist 20:31–39.

House, R. 1996. An evaluation of stream restoration structures in a coastal Oregon stream 1981–1993. North American Journal of Fisheries Management 16:272–281.

House, R., V. Crispin, and R. Monthey. 1989. Evaluation of stream rehabilitation projects—Salem District (1981–1988). U.S. Department of Interior Bureau of Land Management, Technical Note T/N OR-6, Portland, Oregon.

Hunt, R. L. 1974. Annual production by brook trout in Lawrence Creek during eleven successive years. Wisconsin Department of Natural Resources, Technical Bulletin No. 82, Madison.

Hunt, R. L. 1988. A compendium of 45 trout stream habitat development evaluations in Wisconsin during 1953–1985. Wisconsin Department of Natural Resources, Technical Bulletin No. 162, Madison.

Hunt, R. L. 1993. Trout stream therapy. University of Wisconsin Press, Madison.

Hunter, C. J. 1991. Better trout habitat: a guide to stream restoration and management. Island Press, Washington, D.C.

Hunter, S. K. 1992. Sampling. Wiley. New York.

Iversen, T. M., B. Kronvang, B. L. Madsen, P. Markmann, and M. B. Nielsen. 1993. Re-establishment of Danish streams: restoration and maintenance measures. Aquatic Conservation: Marine and Freshwater Ecosystems 3:73–92.

Johnson, D. H., N. Pittman, E. Wilder, J. A. Silver, R. W. Plotnikoff, B. C. Mason, K. K. Jones, P. Roger, T. A. O'Neil, and C. Barrett. 2001. Inventory and monitoring of salmon habitat in the Pacific Northwest: directory and synthesis of protocols for management/research and volunteers in Washington, Oregon, Idaho, Montana, and British Columbia. Washington Department of Fish and Wildlife, Olympia.

Jutila, E. 1992. Restoration of salmonid rivers in Finland. Pages 353–362 *in* P. J. Boon, P. Calow, and G. E. Petts, editors. River conservation and management. Wiley, West Sussex, England.

Kahler, T. H. 1999. Summer movement and growth of individually marked juvenile salmonids in western Washington streams. Master's thesis. University of Washington, Seattle.

Kahler, T. H., P. Roni, and T. P. Quinn. 2001. Summer movement and growth of juvenile anadromous salmonids in small western Washington streams. Canadian Journal of Fisheries and Aquatic Sciences 58:1947–1956.

Karr, J. R. 1981. Assessment of biotic integrity using fish communities. Fisheries 6:21–27.

Karr, J. R., and E. W. Chu. 1999. Restoring life in running waters: better biological monitoring. Island Press, Washington, D.C.

Kaufmann, P. R., P. Levine, E. G. Robison, C. Seeliger, and D. V. Peck. 1999. Quantifying physical habitat in wadeable streams. U.S. Environmental Protection Agency, EPA/620/R-99/003, Washington, D.C.

Kelly, J. R., and M. A. Harwell. 1990. Indicators of ecosystem recovery. Environmental Management 14(5):527–545.

Kennen, J. G., S. J. Wisniewski, N. H. Ringler, and H. M. Hawkins. 1994. Application and modification of an auger trap to quantify emigrating fishes in Lake Ontario tributaries. North American Journal of Fisheries Management 14:828–836.

Kern, K. 1992. Rehabilitation of streams in south-west Germany. Pages 322–335 *in* P. J. Boon, P. Calow, and G. E. Petts, editors. River conservation and management. Wiley, West Sussex, England.

Kerrans, B. L., and J. R. Karr. 1994. A benthic index of biotic integrity (B-IBI) for rivers of the Tennessee Valley. Ecological Applications 4:768–785.

Klemm, D. J., P. A. Lewis, F. Fulk, and J. M. Lazorchak. 1990. Macroinvertebrate field and laboratory methods for evaluating the biological integrity of surface waters. U.S. Environmental Protection Agency EPA 600-4-90-030, Cincinnati, Ohio.

Korman, J., and P. S. Higgins. 1997. Utility of escapement time series data for monitoring the response of salmon populations to habitat alteration. Canadian Journal of Fisheries and Aquatic Sciences 54:2058–2067.

Laasonen, P., T. Muotka, and I. Kivijarvi. 1998. Recovery of macroinvertebrate communities from stream habitat restoration. Aquatic Conservation: Marine and Freshwater Ecosystems 8:101–113.

Larson, M. G., D. B. Booth, and S. A. Morley. 2001. Effectiveness of large woody debris in stream rehabilitation projects in urban basins. Ecological engineering 18:211–226.

Lindberg, W. J. 1997. Can science resolve the attraction-production issue. Fisheries 22:10–13.

Lisle, T. E. 1987. Using "residual depths" to monitor pool depths independently of discharge. U.S. Forest Service, Pacific Southwest Forest and Range Experimental Station, Research Note PSW-394, Berkeley, California.

Lonzarich, D. G., and T. P. Quinn. 1995. Experimental evidence for the effect of depth and structure on the distribution, growth, and survival of stream fishes. Canadian Journal of Zoology 73:2223–2230.

Lyons, J., and C. C. Courtney. 1990. A review of fisheries habitat improvement projects in warmwater streams, with recommendations for Wisconsin. Wisconsin Department of Natural Resources, Technical Bulletin No. 169, Madison.

Magurran, A. E. 1988. Ecological diversity and its measurement. Princeton University Press, Princeton, New Jersey.

Margalef, R. 1959. Information theory in ecology. General Systematics 3:36–71.

Matthews, K. R. 1990a. An experimental study of the habitat preferences and movement patterns of copper, quillback rockfishes (*Sabastes* spp.). Environmental Biology of Fishes 29:161–178.

Matthews, K. R. 1990b. A telemetric study of the home ranges and homing routes of copper and quillback rockfishes on shallow rocky reefs. Canadian Journal of Zoology 68:2243–2250.

McCafferty, W. P. 1981. Aquatic entomology: the fisherman's and ecologist's illustrated guide to insects and their relatives. Jones and Bartlett Publishers Inc., Boston.

Merritt, R. W., and K. W. Cummins. 1996. An introduction to the aquatic insects of North America. 3rd edition. Kendall and Hunt Publishing Company, Dubuque, Iowa.

Merritt, R. W., K. W. Cummins, and V. H. Resh. 1996. Design of aquatic insect studies: collecting, sampling, and rearing studies. Pages 12–28 in R. W. Merritt and K. W. Cummins, editors. An introduction to aquatic insects of North America. 3rd edition. Kendall and Hunt Publishing Company, Dubuque, Iowa.

Minns, C. K., J. R. M. Kelso, and R. G. Randall. 1996. Detecting the response of fish to habitat alterations in freshwater ecosystems. Canadian Journal of Fisheries and Aquatic Sciences 53:403–414.

Minshall, G. W., R. C. Petersen, and C. F. Nimz. 1985. Species richness in streams of different size from the same drainage basin. American Naturalist 125:16–38.

Montgomery, D. R., and Buffington, J. M. 1997. Channel-reach morphology in mountain drainage basins. Geological Society of America Bulletin 109:596–611.

Montgomery, D. R., J. M. Buffington, R. D. Smith, K. M. Schmidt, and G. Pess. 1995. Pool spacing in forest channels. Water Resources Research 31:1097–1105.

Moreau, J. K. 1984. Anadromous salmonid habitat enhancement by boulder placement in Hurdygurdy Creek, California. Pages 97–116 in T. J. Hassler, editor. Proceedings: Pacific Northwest Stream Habitat Management Workshop. American Fisheries Society, Humboldt Chapter, Humboldt State University, Arcata, California.

Murphy, B. R., and D. W. Willis, editors. 1996. Fisheries techniques, 2nd edition. American Fisheries Society, Bethesda, Maryland.

Newbury, F., and M. Gaboury. 1993. Exploration and rehabilitation of hydraulic habitats in streams using principles of fluvial behavior. Freshwater Biology 29:195–210.

Nickelson, T. E., J. D. Rodgers, S. L. Johnson, and M. F. Solazzi. 1992. Seasonal changes in habitat use by juvenile coho salmon (Oncorhynchus kisutch) in Oregon coastal streams. Canadian Journal of Fisheries and Aquatic Sciences 49:783–789.

Northcote, T. G. 1992. Migration and residency in stream salmonids—some ecological considerations and evolutionary consequences. Nordic Journal of Freshwater Research 67:5–17.

Novak, M. A., and R. W. Bode. 1992. Percent model affinity: a new measure of macroinvertebrate community composition. Journal of the North American Benthological Society 11(1):80–85.

O'Grady, M. 1995. The enhancement of salmonid rivers in the Republic of Ireland. Journal of the Chartered Institution of Waters and Environmental Management 9:164–172.

O'Grady, M. 2002. Proceedings of the 13th international salmonid habitat enhancement workshop. Central Fisheries Board, Dublin.

Overton, C. K., S. P. Wollrab, B. C. Roberts, and M. A. Radko. 1997. R1/R4 (Northern Intermountain Regions) fish and fish habitat standard inventory procedures handbook. U.S. Forest Service, General Technical Report INT-GTR-346, Ogden, Utah.

Paulsen, C. M., and T. R. Fisher. 2003. Detecting juvenile survival effects of habitat actions: power analysis applied to endangered Snake River spring-summer Chinook (Oncorhynchus tshawytscha). Canadian Journal of Fisheries and Aquatic Sciences 60:1–11.

Peterman, R. M. 1990. Statistical power analysis can improve fisheries research and management. Canadian Journal of Fisheries and Aquatic Sciences 47:2–15.

Peterson, N. P. 1982. Population characteristics of juvenile coho salmon (Oncorhynchus kisutch) overwintering in riverine ponds. Canadian Journal of Fisheries and Aquatic Sciences 39:1303–1307.

Peterson, N. P., and C. J. Cederholm. 1984. A comparison of the removal and mark-recapture methods of population estimation for juvenile coho salmon in a small stream. North American Journal of Fisheries Management 4:99–102.

Plafkin, J. L. 1989. Rapid bioassessment protocols for use in streams and rivers: benthic macroinvertebrates and fish. U.S. Environmental Protection Agency, Assessment and Watershed Protection Division, EPA/444/4-89-001, Washington, D.C.

Platts, W. S., W. F. Megahan, and G. W. Minshall. 1983. Methods for evaluating stream, riparian, and biotic conditions. U.S. Forest Service, General Technical Report INT-138, Ogden, Utah.

Platts, W. S., and J. N. Rinne. 1985. Riparian and stream enhancement management and research in the Rocky Mountains. North American Journal of Fisheries Management 5:115–225.

Pleus, A. E., D. Shuett-Hames, and L. Bullchild. 1999. Method manual for habit unit survey. Washington Department of Natural Resources, TFW-AM9-99-003 DNR 105, Olympia.

Poole, J. E., C. A. Frissell, and S. C. Ralph. 1997. In-stream habitat unit classification: inadequacies for monitoring and some consequences for management. Journal of the American Water Resources Association 33:879–896.

Reeves, G. H., P. A. Bisson, and J. M. Dambacher. 1998. Fish communities. Pages 200–234 in R. J. Naiman and R. E. Bilby, editors. River ecology and management. Springer-Verlag, New York.

Reeves, G. H., J. D. Hall, T. D. Roelofs, T. L. Hickman, and C. O. Baker. 1991. Rehabilitating and modifying stream habitats. Pages 519–557 in W. R. Meehan, editor. Influences of forest and rangeland management on salmonid fishes and their habitats. American Fisheries Society, Special Publication 19, Bethesda, Maryland.

Reeves, G. H., D. B. Hohler, B. E. Hansen, F. H. Everest, J. R. Sedell, T. L. Hickman, and D. Shively. 1997. Fish habitat restoration in the Pacific Northwest: Fish Creek of Oregon. Pages 335–359 in J. E. Williams, C. A. Wood, and M. P. Dombeck, editors. Watershed restoration: principles and practices. American Fisheries Society, Bethesda, Maryland.

Reiger, H. A., and D. S. Robson. 1967. Estimating population number and mortality rates. Pages 31–66 in S. D. Gerking, editor. The biological basis of freshwater fish production. Blackwell Scientific Publications Scientific, Oxford.

Resh, V. H., and D. G. Price. 1984. Sequential sampling: a cost-effective approach for monitoring benthic macroinvertebrates in environmental impact assessments. Environmental Management 8:75–80.

Resh, V. H., and D. M. Rosenburg. 1984. The ecology of aquatic insects. Praeger Publishers, New York.

Riley, C. S., and K. D. Fausch. 1992. Underestimation of trout population size by maximum-likelihood removal estimates in small streams. North American Journal of Fisheries Management 12:768–776.

Riley, S. C., and K. D. Fausch. 1995. Trout population response to habitat enhancement in six northern Colorado streams. Canadian Journal of Fisheries and Aquatic Sciences 52:34–53.

Rinne, J. N. 1982. Movement, home range, and growth of a rare southwestern trout in improved and unimproved habitats. North American Journal of Fisheries Management 2:150–157.

Robison, E. G., and R. L. Beschta. 1990. Coarse woody debris and channel morphology interactions for undisturbed streams in southeast Alaska, U.S.A. Earth Surface Processes Landforms 15:149–156.

Rodgers, J. D., M. F. Solazzi, S. L. Johnson, and M. A. Buckman. 1992. Comparison of three techniques to estimate juvenile coho salmon populations in small streams. North American Journal of Fisheries Management 12:79–86.

Rodriguez, M. A. 2002. Restricted movement in stream fish: the paradigm is incomplete, not lost. Ecology 83:1–13.

Roni, P. 2000. Responses of fishes and salamanders to instream restoration in western Oregon and Washington. Doctoral dissertation. University of Washington, Seattle.

Roni, P. 2003. Responses of benthic fishes and giant salamanders to placement of large woody debris in small Pacific Northwest streams. North American Journal of Fisheries Management 23:1087–1097.

Roni, P., and A. Fayram. 2000. Estimating winter salmonid abundance in small western Washington streams: a comparison of three techniques. North American Journal of Fisheries Management 20:683–692.

Roni, P. 2002. Habitat use by fishes and Pacific giant salamanders in small western Oregon and Washington streams. Transactions of the American Fisheries Society 131:743–761.

Roni, P., T. J. Beechie, R. E., Bilby, F. E. Leonetti, M. M. Pollock, and G. P. Pess. 2002. A review of stream restoration techniques and a hierarchical strategy for prioritizing restoration in Pacific Northwest watersheds. North American Journal of Fisheries Management 22:1–20.

Roni, P., M. Liermann, and A. Steel. 2003. Monitoring and evaluating responses of salmonids and other fishes to in-stream restoration. Pages 318–339 in D. R. Montgomery, S. Bolton, and D. B. Booth, editors. Restoration of Puget Sound rivers, University of Washington Press. Seattle.

Roni, P., and T. P. Quinn. 2001a. Density and size of juvenile salmonids in response to placement of large woody debris in western Washington and Oregon streams. Canadian Journal of Fisheries and Aquatic Sciences 58:282–292.

Roni, P., and T. P. Quinn. 2001b. Effects of wood placement on movements of trout and juvenile coho salmon in natural and artificial stream channels. Transactions of the American Fisheries Society 130:675–685.

Rosenberg, D. M., and V. H. Resh, editors. 1993. Freshwater biomonitoring and benthic macroinvertebrates. Chapman and Hall, New York.

Rosgen, D. L. 1996. Applied river morphology. Wildland Hydrology, Pagosa Springs, Colorado.

Schlosser, I. J. 1982. Trophic structure, reproductive success, and growth rate of fishes in a natural and modified headwater stream. Canadian Journal of Fisheries and Aquatic Sciences 39:968–978.

Schuett-Hames, D., A. Pleus, L. Bullchild, and S. Hall. 1994. Timber-Fish-Wildlife ambient monitoring program manual. Northwest Indian Fisheries Commission, TFW-AM9-94-001, Olympia, Washington.

Simon, T. P., editor. 1999. Assessing the sustainability and biological integrity of water resources using fish communities. CRC Press, Boca Raton, Florida.

Solazzi, M. F., T. E. Nickelson, S. L. Johnson, and J. D. Rodgers. 2000. Effects of increasing winter rearing habitat on abundance of salmonids in two coastal Oregon streams. Canadian Journal of Fisheries and Aquatic Sciences 57:906–914.

Statzner, B., J. A. Gores, and V. H. Resh. 1988. Hydraulic stream ecology: observed patterns and potential implications. Journal of the North American Benthological Association 7(4):307–360.

Swales, S., R. B. Lausier, and C. D. Levings. 1986. Winter habitat preferences of juvenile salmonids in two interior rivers in British Columbia. Canadian Journal of Zoology 64:1506–1514.

Tabor, R. A., and W. A. Wurtsbaugh. 1991. Predation risk and the importance of cover of juvenile rainbow trout in lentic systems. Transactions of the American Fisheries Society 120:728–738.

Tarzwell, C. M. 1934. Stream Improvement Methods. U.S. Bureau of Fisheries Division of Scientific Inquiry, Ogden, Utah.

Tarzwell, C. M. 1937. Experimental evidence on the value of trout stream improvement in Michigan. Transactions of the American Fisheries Society 66:177–187.

Tarzwell, C. M. 1938. An evaluation of the methods and results of stream improvement in the Southwest. Transactions of the 3rd North America Wildlife Conference 1938:339–364.

Thedinga, J. F., M. L. Murphy, S. W. Johnson, J. M. Lorenz, and K. V. Koski. 1994. Determination of salmonid smolt yield with rotary-screw traps in the Situk River, Alaska, to predict effects of glacial flooding. North American Journal of Fisheries Management 14:837–851.

Thom, B. 1997. The effects of woody debris additions on the physical habitat of salmonids: A case study on the Northern Oregon Coast. Master's thesis. University of Washington, Seattle.

Thurow, R. F. 1994. Underwater methods for study of salmonids in the Intermountain West. U.S. Forest Service, Intermountain Research Station, General Technical Report INT-GTR-307, Odgen, Utah.

Tracy, D. 2000. Application of underwater time-lapsed video technology to observe king and tanner crab behavior in and around commercial crab pots. Journal of Shellfish Research 19:667.

Van Deventer, J. S., and W. S. Platts. 1989. Microcomputer software system for generating population statistics from electrofishing data—user's guide for MicroFish 3.0. U.S. Forest Service, Intermountain Research Station, General Technical Report INT-254. Ogden, Utah.

Vetrano, D. M. 1988. Unit construction of trout habitat improvement structures for Wisconsin coulee streams. Wisconsin Department of Natural Resources Administrative Report No. 27, Madison.

Wallace, J. B., and J. R. Webster. 1996. The role of macroinvertebrates in stream ecosystem function. Annual Reviews in Entomology 41:115–139.

Wallace, J. B., J. R. Webster, and J. L. Meyer. 1995. Influence of log additions on physical and biotic characteristics of a mountain stream. Canadian Journal of Fisheries and Aquatic Sciences 52:2120–2137.

Washington, H. G. 1984. Diversity, biotic and similarity indices: a review with special relevance to aquatic ecosystems. Water Resources 18:653–694.

Weigel, B. M., J. Lyons, L. K. Paine, S. I. Dodson, and D. J. Undersander. 2000. Using stream macroinvertebrates to compare riparian land use practices on cattle farms in southwestern Wisconsin. Journal of Freshwater Ecology 15:93–106.

Wesche, T. A. 1985. Stream channel modifications and reclamation to enhance fish habitat. Pages 103–163 in J. A. Gore, editor. The restoration of rivers and streams: theories and experience. Butterworth Publishers, Boston.

White, G. C., D. R. Anderson, K. P. Burnham, and D. L. Otis. 1982. Capture-recapture and removal methods for sampling closed populations. Los Alamos National Laboratory, Report LA-8787-NERP, Los Alamos, New Mexico.

White, R. J. 1996. Growth and development of North American stream habitat management for fish. Canadian Journal of Fisheries and Aquatic Sciences 53(supplement 1):342–363.

White R. J. 2002. Restoring streams for salmonids: Where have we been? Where are we going? Pages 1–33 in M. O'Grady, editor. Proceedings of the 13th international salmonid habitat enhancement workshop, Westport, County Mayo, Ireland. Central Fisheries Board, Dublin.

White, R. J., and O. M. Brynildson. 1967. Guidelines for management of trout stream habitat in Wisconsin. Wisconsin Department of Natural Resources, Technical Bulletin No. 39, Madison.

Willis, T. J., R. B. Millar, and R. C. Babcock. 2000. Detection of spatial variability in relative density of fishes: comparison of visual census, angling, and baited underwater video. Marine Ecology Progress Series 198:249–260.

Winget, R. N., and R. A. Mangum. 1979. Biotic condition index: integrated biological, physical, and chemical stream parameters for management. U. S. Department of Agriculture, U.S. Government Printing Office 1980-0-677-133/7 (prepared under contract No. 40-84M8-8-524), Washington, D.C.

Wolman, M. G. 1954. A method of sampling coarse river-bed material. Transactions of the American Geophysical Union 35:951–956.

Wright, J. F. 1995. Development and use of a system for predicting the macroinvertebrate fauna in flowing waters. Australian Journal of Ecology 20:181–197.

Zar, J. H. 1999. Biostatistical analysis. Prentice Hall, Upper Saddle River, New Jersey.

Zippin, C. 1958. The removal method of population estimation. Journal of Wildlife Management 22:82–90.

Zubik, R. J., and J. J. Fraley. 1988. Comparison of snorkel and mark-recapture estimates for trout populations in large streams. North American Journal of Fisheries Management 8:58–62.

Chapter 9

Monitoring the Effects of Nutrient Enrichment on Freshwater Ecosystems

Peter M. Kiffney

Northwest Fisheries Science Center, National Marine Fisheries Service
Mukilteo Biological Field Station, 10 Park Avenue, Building B, Mukilteo, Washington 98275, USA
and Division of Ecosystem Sciences, University of Washington, Seattle, Washington 98195, USA
peter.kiffney@noaa.gov

Robert E. Bilby

Weyerhaeuser Company, Post Office Box 9777 - WTC 1A5, Federal Way, Washington 98063-9777, USA
bob.bilby@weyerhaeuser.com

Beth L. Sanderson

Northwest Fisheries Science Center, Environmental Conservation Division
2725 Montlake Boulevard East, Seattle, Washington 98112, USA
beth.sanderson@noaa.gov

Introduction

Nutrient enrichment projects are manipulations of the natural environment that aim to increase the productive capacity of an ecosystem. Like other aquatic enhancement projects, they provide an opportunity to test hypotheses regarding physical, chemical, and biological responses to different habitat-enhancement actions. Unfortunately, evaluation of how nutrient additions affect aquatic ecosystems is rare (Roni et al. 2002). The lack of attention to food-web productivity in restoration efforts is due, in part, to a misperception that manipulating the nutrient or the productive status of a stream, river, or lake is not possible.

The nutrient status of lakes, streams, and rivers can be affected by a variety of human activities. Agriculture and urbanization typically increase nutrient delivery to aquatic systems, often so much so that the capacity of these systems to support desirable species is damaged by eutrophication (Vitousek et al. 1997). Under some circumstances, nutrient inputs have been artificially reduced by human activities, leading to reductions in productivity of naturally oligotrophic systems (Stockner et al. 2000). For example, dams, fishing, and habitat degradation have contributed to declines in salmon stocks and other anadromous fish, thereby reducing subsidies of nutrients and organic matter returning to watersheds along the west and east coasts of North America and much of northern Europe and eastern Russia. These reductions in organic matter and nutrients likely have had major impacts on the growth and survival of juvenile fish, as well as other species, accentuating the decline in anadromous fish populations.

Over the last two decades, however, various methods of adding inorganic fertilizers to aquatic ecosystems have been designed and successfully implemented to increase trophic productivity (Johnston et al. 1990; Bradford et al. 2000). Inorganic nutrients have been added to lakes and streams in British Columbia for almost 30 years to increase the productive capacity of these systems, with the aim of boosting salmon stocks. In general, these studies have shown that concentration of surface water nutrients, primary and secondary productivity, and fish performance (e.g., growth) increased in response to fertilization. Recently, it was shown that adding salmon carcasses also can promote the productivity of aquatic food webs (Bilby et al. 1998; Wipfli et al. 1999), which has resulted in a number of watershed groups adding carcasses to streams in the Pacific Northwest (PNW) to increase the productivity of threatened salmon populations. This strategy may, in fact, benefit these fish and their food webs, especially in oligotrophic waters; however, there also are potential negative impacts, such as introducing pathogens or eutrophication that may result from carcass or inorganic nutrient additions. Assessing the physical, chemical, and biological attributes of the system of interest before any restoration or enhancement action is fundamental to understanding the potential impacts of these activities, such as nutrient enrichment on aquatic ecosystems. Moreover, rigorous evaluation of the ecological effects of nutrient enhancement on aquatic systems is essential, because the knowledge gained from these evaluations can be used to increase the likelihood that future enhancement efforts will be successful.

It may seem counterintuitive to add nutrients to streams, given that agricultural runoff and other human activities have raised nutrient levels in some streams. Nonetheless, many watersheds are nutrient deprived due to declines in anadromous fish populations (Nehlsen et al. 1991; Garman and Macko 1998; Gresh et al. 2000). This reduction has been linked to depression in the productivity of stream fishes (Bilby et al. 1998), riparian plants (Helfield and Naiman 2001), and terrestrial wildlife (Ben-David et al. 1998). Nutrient augmentation or the distribution of carcasses of hatchery-spawned fishes has been proposed as an approach to mitigate the lack of naturally spawning fish (Budy et al. 1998). Ultimately, the goal of this enhancement approach is to restore the natural process of adult anadromous fishes nourishing their progeny (Stockner and MacIsaac 1996).

In this chapter, we discuss nutrient supplementation as a tool to restore depressed fish populations, using Pacific salmon *Oncorhynchus* spp. as an example. We suggest, however, that concepts presented in this chapter should be applicable to any aquatic system used by threatened populations of migratory fishes that suffer high rates of postspawning mortality (e.g., Atlantic salmon *Salmo salar*, American shad *Alosa sapidissima*). We first provide a context for this restoration strategy by briefly discussing factors that limit productivity (defined here as the capacity of a system to generate biomass), the relative importance of salmon and anadromous fishes to aquatic ecosystems, common types of nutrient enhancement being applied in the PNW, and when nutrient enrichment might be appropriate. We describe elements critical to any monitoring plan aimed at evaluating the effectiveness of nutrient enrichment projects, including objectives and hypotheses, study design, and selection of monitoring parameters. Finally, we review and summarize several nutrient enrichment studies in British Columbia, Alaska, and Washington to elucidate the important monitoring principles we discuss. Our aim is to provide guidance on how to design a monitoring and evaluation program for nutrient enrichment projects.

Factors that Limit Productivity of Aquatic Ecosystems

Freshwater food webs are controlled by a variety of factors operating at multiple scales of time and space. The relative importance of proximate variables (i.e., variables directly controlling species composition and biomass, such as light) is constrained by large-scale habitat features, such as geomorphology, human land use, and vegetation (Biggs 1998). These features, in turn, are modified by climate and geology. The interactions of large-scale habitat features and geology, for example, dictate the general nature of plant communities that can exist in riparian areas in a given region. The riparian canopy composition and structure, in turn, provides proximate control over inputs of resources that limit food-web productivity, such as nutrients (e.g., Volk et al. 2003) and light (e.g., Hill et al. 1995).

Variability in these limiting resources is important, because food-web models predict (Ginzburg and Akçakaya 1992; Power 1992), and empirical studies have shown, that as limiting resources (light and nutrients) increase, so does the biomass of the top predator (Johnston et al. 1990; Wootton and Power 1993). Light primarily limits trophic productivity in small, heavily shaded streams and ponds, and in deep or turbid lakes. Light levels increase as the stream channel widens, and when light reaches levels that saturate photosynthesis, nutrients become the primary factor limiting primary productivity (Hill 1996). The major nutrients limiting primary productivity in freshwater ecosystems are nitrogen (N), phosphorus (P), and, in some cases, silica (Allan 1995; Borchardt 1996). The other major source of energy for streams is allochthonous organic matter, which is generated from terrestrial plants and animals or marine animals (Bisson and Bilby 1998). For example, Wallace et al. (1999) clearly demonstrated that reducing terrestrial leaf litter led to a collapse of the food web in a small mountain stream that depended on this material for energy.

Climatic variability is an important driver of ecosystem productivity. Over decadal time scales, atmospheric anomalies in the Pacific Ocean drive patterns in climate along the west coast of North America, which affect food-web productivity of oceans (Mantua et al. 1997) and streams (Kiffney et al. 2002). Interannual variability in climate, such as El Niño and La Niña events, drives patterns of precipitation and air temperature, and these, in turn, can control nutrient status and trophic productivity in a fairly predictable pattern (Kiffney et al. 2002). Within a year, seasonal highs in primary productivity generally occur in spring and summer in coastal streams of western North America, as scouring floods subside and light and water temperature increase (Stockner and Shortreed 1976; Kiffney et al. 2000).

Infrequent catastrophic disturbances, such as major floods or wildfire, also can affect ecosystem productivity over large spatial and long temporal scales, thereby fundamentally restructuring food webs (Lamberti et al. 1991). The immediate effect of a major disturbance event is a decrease in standing stocks of algae, invertebrates, and fish, due to direct mortality (Lamberti et al. 1991). However, food webs usually rebound very quickly, because disturbances often liberate stored nutrients and increase light levels by removing riparian vegetation (Bisson et al. 1997). For example, debris torrents in headwater streams can remove riparian vegetation, which leads to an increase in solar radiation and nutrient availability, promoting primary production (Lamberti et al. 1991). This increase in primary production can promote the production of aquatic insects that consume algae. The mayfly *Baetis* sp. was 4,350% more abundant after a debris flow in West Twin Creek, a headwater stream in Olympic National Park, Washington (Figure 1). This result was likely due to increases in solar radiation, reaching the stream surface after the debris flow removed riparian trees. Similar effects have been observed in streams affected by clear-cut logging (Murphy et al. 1981).

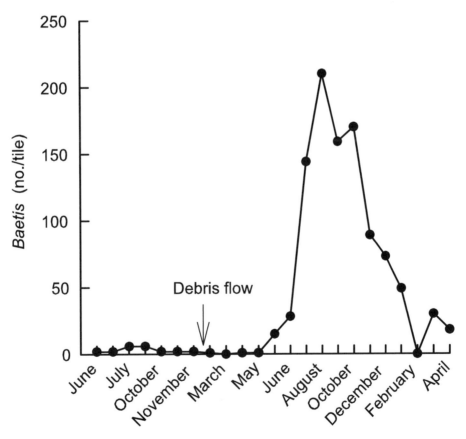

Figure 1.
Mean monthly abundance of *Baetis* mayflies before (June to November 2000) and after (February 2001 to March 2002) a debris flow in West Twin Creek, a stream draining old-growth forest in Olympic National Park, Washington. Arrow designates the approximate date for the debris flow.

Experimental studies also have shown that algal biomass and primary production increase as light (e.g., Wootton and Power 1993) or nutrients (e.g., Kiffney and Richardson 2001) increase. Increased primary production can lead to increased biomass, growth rate, or abundance of higher trophic levels (Wootton and Power 1993). These relationships suggest that increasing light or nutrient levels would increase the biomass or abundance of all trophic levels of unproductive systems (Figure 2). Others have shown that predation can affect how food webs respond to gradients of productivity (e.g., Power 1992). In a food chain of a given length, increasing productivity is expected to increase the abundance of populations at the top trophic level and at populations at alternate levels below it (Figure 2) but not intervening trophic levels, because the trophic level above crops surplus production of the trophic level below it. There is empirical support for both the top-down (e.g., Wootton and Power 1993) and bottom-up (e.g., Johnston et al. 1990) models, with a growing awareness among ecologists that both top-down and bottom-up forces are important in structuring communities (Hunter and Price 1992; Rosemond et al. 1993).

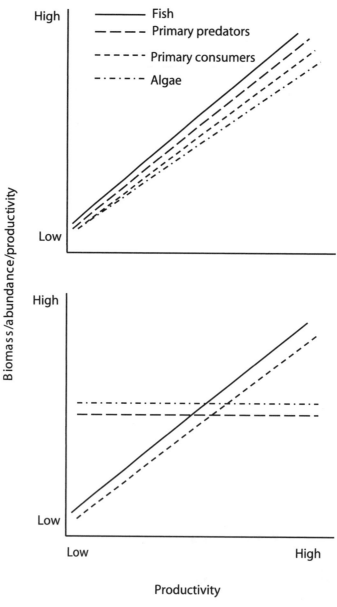

Figure 2.
Hypothesized patterns of accrual for different components of a freshwater food web along a gradient of environmental productivity (defined by light and nutrients). Top panel represents patterns in a bottom-up controlled food web, where primary producers, primary consumers (e.g., grazers), primary predators (insect predators and small fish), and adult fish increase as environmental productivity increases. Bottom panel represents a food web where patterns are driven by predation or top-down control.

Food-web productivity is a result of complex interactions among a suite of physical (e.g., channel gradient), chemical (e.g., nutrients), and biological (e.g., food-web composition) factors. Therefore, before conducting nutrient supplementation, it is critical to understand the relative importance of these factors and their interactions in determining food-web productivity. This knowledge can be used to identify areas that might benefit from nutrient enrichment and generate predictions of how these systems might respond to this approach.

Effects of Anadromous Fish on Aquatic Ecosystems

In some coastal regions of the world, one of the most important processes controlling ecosystem productivity is the spawning of anadromous fish, because they are a major source of organic matter and nutrients (Krokhin 1975; Durbin et al. 1979; Cederholm et al. 1999; Gresh et al. 2000) subsidizing these ecosystems (Polis et al. 1997). For example, Pacific salmon contribute significant amount of organic matter and nutrients to watersheds tributary to the North Pacific Ocean (Larkin and Slaney 1997; Gresh et al. 2000). Similar inputs are provided by clupeid *Alosa* spp. fishes on the Atlantic coast (Durbin et al. 1979; Garman and Macko 1998). Although adult anadromous fish can bring in large subsidies of organic matter, their offspring accumulate nutrients from nursery streams and lakes, and transfer these materials to the ocean when they migrate (Lyle and Elliott 1998). It is important to recognize that the nutrient dynamics in watersheds inhabited by anadromous fish are unique because of this two-way flux between oceans and freshwater ecosystems. Thus, management actions thought to conserve or restore populations, such as adding large numbers of hatchery juveniles to a stream or river, may actually contribute to population declines. This may occur because nutrient losses when smolts migrate from nursery habitats exceed nutrient subsidies provided by adults; adult returns may be low due to poor ocean survival, harvest, or mortality during river migration. Low adult returns, coupled with high smolt output may, accentuate nutrient declines of already oligotrophic systems, thereby leading to low food-web productivity and low juvenile salmon growth and survival.

The materials transported to freshwater by spawning fish are incorporated into the trophic system through two pathways: (1) direct consumption of carcass flesh and eggs (Bilby et al. 1996), and (2) chemical or biological uptake of dissolved materials released by fish metabolism and decomposing carcasses (Bilby et al. 1996; Naiman et al. 2002). Salmon eggs or carcass flesh often comprise the majority of the diet of stream-dwelling salmonids when these materials are available. More than 90% of the diet of Arctic char *Salvelinus alpinus* and Dolly Varden *S. malma* and rainbow trout *Oncorhynchus mykiss* consisted of salmon eggs and flesh in several small streams of the Wood River drainage in Alaska during the summer sockeye salmon *O. nerka* run (Eastman 1996). Coho salmon *O. kisutch* eggs and flesh provided 60 to 90% of the diet of juvenile steelhead *O. mykiss* and coho salmon in a southwest Washington stream (Bilby et al. 1998).

Aquatic invertebrates also consume carcass flesh and eggs (Wipfli et al. 1998); stoneflies of the families Pteronarcidae (Minakawa 1997) and Perlidae (Nicola 1968) and chironomids ingest carcass flesh or salmon eggs (Elliott and Bartoo 1981; Kline et al. 1997). Caddisfly larvae and mayfly nymphs also have been observed on salmon carcasses, often at high densities (Minakawa et al. 2002). These insects ingest both the flesh and the microbial growth covering the surface of the carcass (Minakawa 1997). Ingesting these materials can promote insect growth and standing stocks (Chaloner and Wipfli 2002; Minakawa et al. 2002). Growth rate of the caddisfly *Ecclisomyia conspera* was significantly higher when fed a diet of salmon carcasses (Figure 3).

Dissolved nutrients released from adult salmon can be captured and incorporated into the trophic system of aquatic ecosystems by several processes. Dissolved organic matter released as the carcasses decompose is used by heterotrophic organisms growing on the carcass (Kline et al. 1997) and on the streambed (Schuldt and Hershey 1995; Bilby et al. 1996). These organic molecules also can be chemically sorbed onto the biofilm encrusting streambed and hyporheic surfaces (Bilby et al. 1996). Inorganic nutrients released from adult fish are used by algae and vascular aquatic plants for growth and metabolism (Richey et al. 1975). Spawning pink salmon *Oncorhynchus gorbuscha* provided from 30 to 60% of the N in periphyton in a southeast Alaska stream (Kline et al. 1990). On average, periphyton chlorophyll a was twofold higher in a tributary to Lake Superior accessible to spawning chinook salmon *O. tshawytscha* compared to an upstream section, which was blocked to salmon (Figure 4).

Invertebrate production is stimulated by both direct consumption of carcasses and eggs, and by increased autotrophic production (Peterson et al. 1993; Perrin and Richardson 1997; Kiffney and Richardson 2001). This

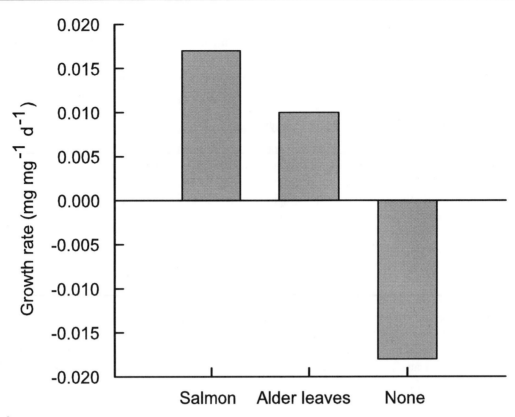

Figure 3.
Mean instantaneous growth rate of the caddisfly *Ecclisomyia conspersa* in containers with salmon, alder leaves, or no food source (data from Minakawa et al. 2002).

food subsidy can increase energy resources available for consumption by fish and other organisms. Ingestion of carcass flesh and eggs can produce dramatic increases in the growth rate of juvenile salmon and trout. Juvenile coho salmon growth in a small stream in southwestern Washington doubled after the addition of coho salmon carcasses (Bilby et al. 1998). Rapid increases in the proportion of salmon-derived N in muscle tissue of juvenile fish (as indicated by changes in the N stable isotope ratio) and the abundance of eggs and flesh in their stomachs at this site clearly indicated that material derived from carcasses was responsible for the accelerated growth rate (Figure 5). Higher growth rates in juvenile salmonids can significantly increase their survival. Larger juvenile coho salmon survive at higher rates while wintering in streams than do smaller fish (Hartman and Scrivener 1990; Quinn and Peterson 1996). Larger smolts of both coho salmon and steelhead enjoy a considerable advantage in survival once entering the ocean (Bilton et al. 1982; Ward and Slaney 1988; Holtby et al. 1990; Tipping 1997). Bradford et al. (2000) found that fertilization increased smolt size, which improved smolt-to-adult survival. The nutrients provided by higher adult returns may eventually promote the growth and the survival of future generations of fish, as well as terrestrial organisms (Hilderbrand et al. 1996; Hocking and Reimchen 2002).

The nutrient subsidy provided by spawning salmon also makes an important contribution to the productivity of sockeye salmon nursery lakes (Juday et al. 1932; Donaldson 1967; Mathisen et al. 1988; Bradford et al. 2000). Estimates of the annual nutrient contribution from salmon vary widely. Three percent of the P input to Redfish Lake, Idaho, a system with a very depressed sockeye salmon population, was from salmon (Gross et al. 1998). In systems with healthier populations, the contributions increase. Nitrogen input from salmon to Lake Iliamna, Alaska, ranged from 57 to 77% (Kline et al. 1997) and accounted for 90% of the N input to Karluk Lake, Alaska (Schmidt et al. 1998). Recent paleolimnological studies have not only quantified the contribution of salmon nutrients to sockeye nursery lakes in Alaska but also have documented shifts in food-web composition concurrent with changes in salmon abundance and harvest (Finney et al. 2000). This study showed that shifts in food-web composition were related to the nutrient status of the lakes, which was a reflection of the size of adult returns. The nutrient dynamics and trophic structure of these lakes, therefore, are intrinsically linked to the dynamics of anadromous salmonids.

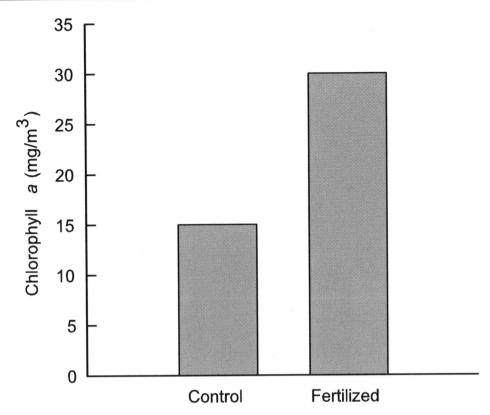

Figure 4.
Mean chlorophyll *a* measured on rocks from the Baptism River, Minnesota, a tributary to Lake Superior. Chinook salmon can access the lower 1.45 km of river, where a waterfall blocks anadromous fish passage. Chlorophyll *a* values from the "control" represent rocks collected from above the falls, with the "fertilized" representing algal biomass in the reach accessible to salmon (data from Schuldt and Hershey 1995).

The relative importance of the different mechanisms by which adult anadromous fish are incorporated into food webs will vary seasonally and will depend on characteristics of the watershed (Wipfli et al. 1999; Naiman et al. 2002). The size and timing of the run, nutrient storage capacity, water volume, limiting nutrient (i.e., N-versus P-limited system), canopy cover and water temperature, and trophic structure are but a few factors that will determine how and to what extent materials from fish carcasses are incorporated into the food web. Biological processes may dominate in unshaded ecosystems, which receive subsidies of adult fish during summer and early fall when water temperature is warm and light level is high. During summer, when sockeye salmon are present in the Stuart River, British Columbia, much of the incorporation of N from decomposing carcasses was attributed to algae (Johnston et al. 1997). In contrast, abiotic sorption by benthic biofilm was the primary uptake mechanism for dissolved organic matter from coho salmon carcasses in a western Washington stream during late fall (Bilby et al. 1996). Coho spawn at these sites in November and December when low water temperature and light, and high stream discharge likely limit biological uptake mechanisms. Background nutrient levels also will affect the relative importance of adult fish on ecosystem productivity. Spawning coho and chinook salmon were found to have little effect on soluble reactive P (SRP) availability or on primary production in a tributary to eastern Lake Ontario with high background levels of nutrients (Rand et al. 1992).

Salmon abundance in Washington, Oregon, California, Idaho (Nehlsen et al. 1991; Nickelson et al. 1992; WDF et al. 1993), and British Columbia (Slaney et al. 1996) has decreased dramatically over the last 150 years. The average number of Pacific salmon returning to river systems has declined to less than 2 million in recent years from approximately 45 million at the beginning of the twentieth century (Gresh et al. 2000). Salmon populations are considered to be stable or increasing in less than 20% of the systems currently inhabited, and they have been eliminated from about 40% of their historic range in these states (NRC 1996). Estimates of historic runs of Atlantic salmon range from 300,000–500,000 fish; only 1,450 fish returned to rivers of the eastern United States in 1999 (Colligan et al. 1999). Declines also have been documented for anadro-

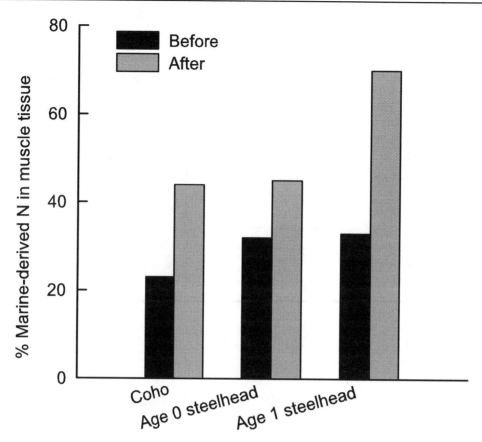

Figure 5.
Increase in the proportion of salmon-derived N in the dorsal muscle tissue of juvenile steelhead and salmon in stream A400 in southwestern Washington, to which salmon carcasses were added. The before values indicate the proportion before addition of carcasses and the after values represent the proportion after carcasses had fully decomposed (about 6 weeks after carcass addition). The proportion of salmon-derived N was estimated from N stable isotope ratios (data from Bilby et al. 1998).

mous clupeids along the Atlantic coast (Garman and Macko 1998). The potential carrying capacity of the James River, Virginia, for anadromous clupeids is estimated to be 3.6 × 10⁶ adults annually (Garman and Macko 1998). However, *Alosa* spp. abundance levels have declined by as much as 90% since the early 1970s, because of commercial exploitation, habitat alteration, and migration barriers.

Declines in anadromous fish populations have caused a corresponding decrease in the deposition of nutrients and organic matter to freshwater, terrestrial, and estuarine ecosystems throughout coastal North America, as well as northern Europe. Gresh et al. (2000) estimate nutrients transported by spawning salmon is currently about 7% of what historically was delivered to watersheds in California, Oregon, Idaho, and Washington (Table 1). The loss of these important subsidies is likely contributing to declines in the population growth rate of anadromous fishes, as well as aquatic and terrestrial food webs in watersheds where these fish spawned. The general acceptance of the important contribution salmon and other anadromous fishes make to watershed productivity, coupled with the dramatic decrease in the amount of material deposited by spawning salmon over the last 150 years (Gresh et al. 2000), has prompted management agencies to add carcasses or inorganic nutrients to streams in an attempt to stimulate productivity. In general, these enhancement actions were not treated as experiments (except see Stockner and MacIsaac 1996); therefore, we have learned little about how effective these actions were in restoring fish populations.

Types of Nutrient Enrichment

Numerous approaches have been used to enrich aquatic ecosystems, such as carbon (C) additions (Warren et al. 1964; Mundie et al. 1983), inorganic nutrients (Johnston et al. 1990; Stockner and MacIsaac 1996; Kiffney and Richardson 2001; Mazumder and Edmundson 2002), and carcasses (Bilby et al. 1998; Wipfli et

Table 1.

Estimated range in metric tons (mt) of N and P biomass delivered by spawning salmon to watersheds in California, Oregon, Idaho, and Washington historically and currently. Data are from Gresh et al. (2000).

	Historic (mt)	Current (mt)
Biomass	156,000–254,298	11,843–13,747
N	4,853–6,854	360–418
P	574–810	43–49

al. 1998, 1999; Figure 6). We speculate that adult salmon represent the most energetically profitable method of nutrient supplementation because they are incorporated into food webs via direct consumption and uptake of dissolved materials. Furthermore, organisms living within these watersheds were adapted to using resources from adult fish. Adult fish also benefit both aquatic and terrestrial food webs (Hilderbrand et al. 1996; Ben-David et al. 1997; Cederholm et al. 1999; Hocking and Reimchen 2002). There are, however, ecological and logistical concerns with adding carcasses to enrich freshwater ecosystems. Salmon are carriers of a number of pathogens, for example, infectious hematopoietic necrosis virus, that can be transferred to other fishes (Gustafason et al. 1997). One way to limit transmission of novel diseases is to use carcasses from within the same basin. Fish from the same basin should be exposed to the same suite of pathogens, and, thus, it is not likely that novel pathogens will be introduced when supplementing with these carcasses (J. Winton, U. S. Geological Survey, Seattle, personal communication). Recently, fish analogs have been developed (Bio-Oregon, Warrenton, Oregon) to simulate the input of organic nutrients delivered by fish carcasses. Because fish analogs are made from sterilized marine fish by-products, they potentially provide a disease-free source of marine-derived nutrients and organic matter. The effectiveness of these analogs in promoting growth of juvenile chinook salmon and steelhead is being evaluated in eastern Washington streams (T. Pearsons, Washington Department of Fish and Wildlife, Ellensburg, unpublished data).

Another consideration when fertilizing with carcasses is the number of fish needed to promote food-web productivity. Bilby et al. (2001) found that levels of marine-derived N in juvenile salmonids rearing in small,

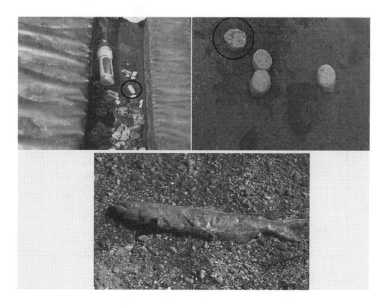

Figure 6.

Three types of nutrient enrichment used in aquatic ecosystems: top left panel shows inorganic fertilizers in an experimental stream; top right panel shows fish analogs in a natural stream (courtesy of T. Pearsons, Washington Department of Fish and Wildlife, Ellensburg, Washington); and bottom panel shows a chinook salmon carcass decomposing in a tributary of the Salmon River, Idaho. Circles surround one inorganic nutrient and fish analog pellet, respectively.

headwater streams reached an asymptote at approximately 200 fish/km (0.2 kg wet mass/m²). Periphyton biomass and total macroinvertebrate abundance increased up to a loading rate of 3.22 kg wet mass/m² in stream mesocosms (Figure 7). This loading rate represents the upper range for medium-sized rivers, where chum salmon *Oncorhynchus keta* and pink salmon spawn in southeast Alaska. Therefore, it would require many fish to promote primary and secondary productivity, which limits this approach to streams and lakes with road access. Additional evaluation of how adult returns affect trophic capacity is needed, because we may expect different relationships between returns and nutrient levels, primary and secondary productivity, juvenile density and growth rate, smolt size, and marine survival. It is important to note that there have been few experiments examining the response of freshwater food webs to carcass additions (except Bilby et al. 1998; Wipfli et al. 1998, 1999) or studies that examine long-term patterns of adult returns and food webs (except Finney et al. 2000). Furthermore, experiments have been conducted at relatively small scales and over short time periods (Bilby et al. 1996; Wipfli et al. 1999). Nevertheless, these short-term studies showed that lower trophic levels (algae and invertebrates) and fish responded positively to carcasses.

One way to alleviate problems (e.g., disease) associated with carcass augmentation is to use inorganic fertilizers either in the form of liquid or pellets. The use of inorganic fertilizers to enhance fish populations has a long history in British Columbia (Johnston et al. 1990; Stockner and MacIsaac 1996) and Alaska (e.g., Mazumder and Edmundson 2002). Not only is the approach biologically effective, it is relatively cost effective (Stockner and MacIsaac 1996; Maxwell 2000). In 1993, 30 km of the Salmon River, British Columbia, were fertilized for about 10–25% of the cost of habitat enhancement efforts (e.g., boulder placements) and resulted in a two- to threefold increase in mean standing crop of steelhead and rainbow trout compared with unfertilized reaches (Ashley and Slaney 1997). The cost of fertilization averaged about Can$160–180 per km per year. In addition, using inorganic fertilizers negates the issue of introducing novel diseases (Ashley and Slaney 1997). One of the main drawbacks of using inorganic fertilizer is that there is no direct consumption, and, thus, nutrients enter the aquatic

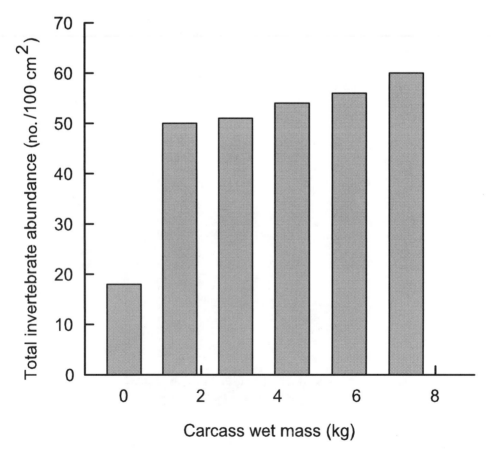

Figure 7.
Relationship between mean number of invertebrates/100 cm² in stream mesocosms averaged over time and salmon carcass loading levels (data from Wipfli et al. 1999).

food web via algal and bacterial production only. Similarly, terrestrial food webs would receive minimal benefits from fertilizer additions until adult returns increase. In addition, commercial fertilizers contain toxic metals (Garbarino et al. 1995), and these metals are known to negatively impact aquatic food webs (Kiffney and Clements 1996). Thus, it is important to have information on the composition of the fertilizer before it is added.

Carcasses and inorganic fertilizers present two reasonable and effective alternatives for enriching aquatic ecosystems. Fish analogs (i.e., artificial carcasses) offer a promising approach, but research is needed to evaluate their effectiveness. Future research also should evaluate the relative effectiveness of the three approaches in terms of ecological response, economic costs and benefits, as well as under what conditions (streams versus lakes, coastal versus interior, unshaded versus shaded). No matter what method is used, the restoration goal should be to increase fish population growth rate so that adult returns replenish and enrich their natal habitats, rather than relying on long-term nutrient augmentation.

When to Conduct Nutrient Enrichment

Adding nutrients to streams, rivers, and lakes may seem paradoxical when many local, state, and federal agencies regulate the release of nutrients into the environment due to the possibility of causing eutrophic conditions (Dodds et al. 1997, 1998; Biggs 2000; Dodds and Welch 2000). About 40% of U.S. streams and rivers are estimated to be impaired by high levels of N and P (Dodds and Welch 2000). To date, however, there are no established federal criteria for nutrient levels in freshwater ecosystems. To minimize growth of esthetically unpleasing blooms of algae (200 mg/m² chlorophyll a), total N and P should remain below 3 mg/L and 0.4 mg/L, respectively (Dodds and Welch 2000). High nutrient loading can negatively affect ecosystem structure and function (Vitousek et al. 1997; Dodds and Welch 2000). Species richness has been observed to decline with productivity because highly productive or eutrophic lakes are light limited and have low levels of dissolved oxygen at night (Dodson et al. 2000). In general, freshwater ecosystems where Pacific salmon live have low levels of nutrients, except in lowland rivers that course through land dominated by agriculture or urban areas (Welch et al. 1998). This pattern suggests that nutrient enrichment of freshwater ecosystems should be limited to upstream portions of the river network or relatively high-elevation habitats, which have low nutrient levels. If nutrients are added to a reach, it should be far enough away so that dilution or other processes (e.g., biological absorption) limit any negative impacts to downstream nutrient-rich areas.

Because of the potential impacts on water quality and biota, it is imperative to quantify the potential impacts before nutrient augmentation. Clearly, addition of inorganic nutrients or salmon carcasses may have little or no effect at sites with abundant nutrients (Rand et al. 1992) and may actually degrade biotic conditions. Care also must be taken not to fertilize reaches or subbasins that were naturally unproductive and historically did not support large fish populations. These sites may have been locations for high diversity of other taxa, such as stream invertebrates and amphibians, or unique salmon life history strategies. Therefore, we suggest that within and among watersheds, there may have been a high degree of variability in nutrient status and food-web productivity. This variability should be maintained.

Unfortunately, information on nutrient levels and food-web productivity is scarce or nonexistent for most watersheds. Habitat assessments have been developed over the last 20 years to evaluate quality and quantity of physical habitat (e.g., number and depth of stream pools; Bisson et al. 1982). These assessments are critical to formulating restoration plans, because they evaluate physical habitat; nutrient additions may have little or no impact if some element of physical habitat (e.g., large woody debris) is limiting. However, watershed assessments do not evaluate factors that correlate with food-web productivity, such as dissolved inorganic nutrients (Collins and Pess 1997). Ideally, information on nutrient concentrations in surface waters and trophic productivity (e.g., algal biomass) would be included with assessments of the physical attributes of watersheds. This information could be used to identify the nutrient status of a site (low to high nutrient levels) and, thus, the potential of these sites to benefit from nutrient enrichment. Sites with obvious nutrient deficiencies that correspond with areas of high-quality physical habitat would be expected to benefit most from fertilization in terms of fish population growth rate.

We suggest taking the following steps when evaluating the suitability of sites for nutrient supplementation: (1) assess status of fish stocks; (2) determine temporal trends in marine-derived nutrients (Gresh et al. 2000; Bilby et al. 2001); (3) analyze water samples for inorganic N and P to determine nutrient status (Wetzel 1983; Dodds and Welch 2000); (4) estimate potential impacts of added nutrients on recipient habitats, including uptake distances; (5) conduct small-scale nutrient-limitation studies to determine whether nutrients are indeed limiting and, if so, at what concentrations (Kiffney and Richardson 2001); (6) analyze food-web structure, because it can have a major impact on whether nutrients are efficiently transferred to fish (Wootton and Power 1993; Mazumder and Edmundson 2002); and (7) assess the quantity and quality of physical habitat at candidate sites (Roni et al. 2002). A similar set of criteria was used in the British Columbia lake fertilization program. Stockner and MacIsaac (1996) surveyed a number of lakes along the coast of British Columbia to determine candidates for a lake fertilization program by using the following criteria: (1) evidence for depressed fish stocks (estimates of catch + escapement), (2) low ambient total P concentrations (<3 µg/L) and chlorophyll (<3 µg/L), (3) depletion of nitrate-nitrogen in the epilimnion during the growing season, and (4) no evidence of physical limitation of phytoplankton (e.g., light limitation due to high levels of suspended sediment). Understanding what controls food-web productivity and the distribution and the range of productivities across a watershed is essential before nutrient augmentation, because there may be unintended consequences of adding nutrients to naturally oligotrophic streams, such as altering species diversity patterns (Dodson et al. 2000) or increasing nutrient levels to unacceptable levels (i.e., causing eutrophication; Dodds and Welch 2000).

Monitoring Design

Objectives and Hypotheses

After determining the feasibility of nutrient enrichment in promoting fish populations, development of a clear set of objectives and hypotheses predicting the outcome of the stated project objectives is needed. Hypotheses help in determining parameters to monitor, monitoring locations, and spatial and temporal extent of monitoring that is necessary to detect predicted effects (see also Chapter 2). Obvious research hypotheses are that adding nutrients will increase (1) concentrations of inorganic nutrients; (2) algal and bacterial productivity; (3) density, growth, and biomass of aquatic invertebrates; (4) growth and survival of juvenile salmonids and other fish; (5) ocean survival and adult returns of salmon; (6) populations of other fishes (e.g., sculpin *Cottus* spp.); and (7) populations of other wildlife and terrestrial plants. Not all parts of the food web, however, will respond to nutrient additions, because of food-web structure (e.g., Mazumder and Edmundson 2002; see below) or because there is no direct consumption of inorganic fertilizers (e.g., bears will eat carcasses but not fertilizers). We also must consider the hypothesis that nutrient enrichment will negatively impact freshwater or estuarine habitat.

Study Design

After hypotheses have been clearly formulated, a study design must be completed. Basic study designs such as before–after, before–after control–impact, posttreatment, and other experimental designs are discussed in detail in Chapter 2. Study or experimental design for nutrient enrichment should include details on the loading rate of inorganic nutrients or carcasses, parameters to measure and how to measure them, the selection of control and treatment reaches, selection of sample sites within experimental reaches, collection of data before enrichment, how many samples to collect within each reach and how many points through time, and how data will be analyzed. When planning a study to assess restoration actions, one must consider outside sources of variation so that variation in the dependent variable (e.g., fish growth rate) can be attributed to treatment (e.g., nutrient) effects. To do this, there are a number of statistical issues to consider, which are reviewed briefly in Chapter 2 and in more detail in statistical texts (e.g., Winer et al. 1991). We consider randomization, replication, and error reduction to be indispensable elements of any study design (Winer et al. 1991). Other important factors to consider in the study design phase include scale (temporal and spatial), food-web structure, and timing of enrichment, because they can affect how food webs respond to nutrient enrichment.

Randomization is an integral component of experimental design. Nature is characterized by variation (Winer et al. 1991), and this is certainly the case for streams and lakes. Not only is there considerable variability among ecosystems, there also is tremendous variation within a system. For example, streams are composed of a number of habitat types, such as pools and riffles, which have different physical, chemical, and biological attributes. It is not possible to control all factors that vary within and among streams and lakes, so decisions must be made about which attributes would be best controlled as independent variables, which can be controlled or measured as supplementary variables (e.g., covariates), and which can be neutralized by allowing them to vary at random (Winer et al. 1991). In our case, nutrient addition is the independent variable, stream gradient could be a covariate or a supplementary variable, and riffles could be our random variable. Randomization can occur at different points of the experiment. For example, to measure the effects of nutrient fertilization on periphyton biomass, we could randomly select control and treatment streams, riffles within streams, and rocks within riffles to measure periphyton biomass. The outcome of randomization is that over a large number of riffles, the unique characteristics of those riffles are distributed evenly over the treatment conditions, which removes bias from the estimates of treatment effects. Randomization also provides unbiased estimates of error variance and independence of errors (Winer et al. 1991).

Replication is another factor that increases control and, thereby, precision of estimating treatment effects. To replicate a study or an experiment is to repeat it under the same set of treatment conditions by using new subjects or streams. For example, we might randomly select six replicate riffles within a stream where we monitor the effects of carcass additions and compare these effects to six unmanipulated riffles. This approach limits inferences to the study stream, however, because there is not replication among streams. Therefore, to increase our inference to a population of streams, we would randomly select six streams from a population of streams and add carcasses to randomly selected riffles within each stream, while sampling riffles in six control or reference streams.

To estimate treatment effects with precision or to determine small treatment differences, reducing error associated with all uncontrolled sources of variation also is essential. Three general sources of error are (1) variability due to the large number of ways in which natural systems differ but which are not under experimental control, (2) variability due to differences in experimental conditions, and (3) variability due to choice of dependent variable (Winer et al. 1991). To minimize error associated with the choice of a dependent variable, one must select a response measure that has low variability but that also is ecologically relevant to nutrient enrichment. To minimize experimental conditions, one should select a time for nutrient enrichment that is relatively stable, such as summer base-flow conditions. Adding carcasses or inorganic nutrients to streams along the northeastern Pacific Coast during winter would increase the variability associated with environmental conditions, because of the dynamic precipitation and flow patterns during this time. To minimize variability among subjects, one uses supplementary variables to select subjects that are homogeneous with regard to that variable (Winer et al. 1991). For example, one would randomly select 12 streams from within a river basin that were as similar as possible in terms of land use, geology, gradient, riparian vegetation, and so forth. Another way to accomplish this is to block streams or subjects (e.g., riffles, reaches, or watersheds) based upon one or more supplementary variables or by the use of covariates (see Winer et al. 1991). For example, if one is interested in examining the effects of nutrient enrichment across a large river basin that has tributaries underlain by different geologies, they could block streams by geology. Control and treatment streams would be randomly selected within each block, and the blocking factor is examined in analysis of variance.

Consideration of scale (spatial and temporal) is another essential element when formulating a study design, because the importance of various processes on ecological properties can change as a function of experimental and observational scale (Peckarsky et al. 1997). Specifically, properties observed at small spatial scales (e.g., habitat unit) may not be apparent at larger scales (e.g., reach) and vice versa. Lack of treatment effects at larger spatial scales can be a result of many factors, for example, fish dispersal. Stream salmonids can move considerable distances (Gowan et al. 1994); fish may move from the control into the fertilized reach immediately before conducting fish surveys, thereby minimizing effects of nutrient additions on fish growth due to increased variance. Fertilization studies in streams primarily have been conducted at the reach scale (100s of meters, e.g., Peterson et al. 1993) or segment (1,000s of meters, e.g., Johnston et al. 1991), while large portions of, or entire, lakes have been fertilized (e.g., Bradford et al. 2001). Fertilizing whole watersheds is problematic, because it potentially is difficult to access all points within a watershed network and to determine the potential impacts to downstream areas. Nevertheless, there is a need to fertilize habitat units larger than stream reaches or segments because salmon and other fishes can range over large portions of the river network.

Spatial distribution of control and treatment reaches also may affect precision in detecting treatment effects. Control reaches typically are located upstream of treatment reaches; however, if control reaches are downstream of treatment reaches, they should be far enough apart so that nutrients are not affecting control sections. One way to assess downstream impacts of nutrient additions is to measure nutrient concentrations in water (see Water Chemistry under the subsection Selection of Parameters) at many points downstream of the treatment area. Other aspects of study design related to spatial scale include how multiple restoration projects within watersheds affect overall primary and secondary productivity and fish populations. For example, adding carcasses to multiple tributaries within a watershed may lead to nutrient levels exceeding a threshold, where they negatively alter water quality in downstream habitats, causing eutrophication. In contrast, adding nutrients may have no impact on fish populations if the treated reach contains no appropriate physical habitat.

Temporal dynamics also must also be factored into monitoring designs. Nutrient enrichment may not show any measurable effect on adult anadromous fish populations for a number of years because of the relatively long life cycle of many of these fishes. Moreover, large-scale atmospheric processes have a major impact on stream habitat (Kiffney et al. 2002) and fish populations (Mantua et al. 1997). These climatic anomalies, such as El Niño events or the Pacific Decadal Oscillation, last from one year to several decades (Mantua et al. 1997; Kiffney et al. 2002). If nutrient enrichment occurs during a period of poor ocean conditions, such as during an El Niño, there may be no measurable change in adult returns in systems enriched with nutrients until ocean conditions improve. Clearly, nutrient augmentation projects should factor into their study design processes that can influence fish populations over large areas and over many years. A project designed to follow the response of salmonids to nutrient enrichment, therefore, should last multiple generations and should integrate other sources of variability into the study design.

Trophic structure and community dynamics also may affect how food webs respond to nutrient additions. Surface-water nutrient concentrations may show no change to additions of inorganic fertilizers, because increased primary producers absorbed or adsorbed added nutrients (Kiffney and Richardson 2001). Peterson et al. (1993) found that algal biomass increased for the first two years after nutrient additions in an Alaskan river but not during years three and four. The lack of response by primary producers in these years was due to increased consumption of algae by stream grazers. Species composition and size structure of invertebrate communities may affect how food webs respond to nutrient enrichment. Additions of nutrients to Packers Lake, Alaska, led to significant increases in all trophic levels before manipulation of sockeye salmon fry densities via stocking (Mazumder and Edmundson 2002). After stocking fry, *Daphnia*, the main food item of sockeye fry, declined, as did the growth of juvenile sockeye salmon, even under continued fertilization. It was hypothesized that fertilization only produced large-sized sockeye smolts under high densities of large-sized (>1 mm) *Daphnia* and under low to moderate fry densities. These studies are only a few examples of how interactions among components of the food web can influence response to nutrients (Carpenter et al. 1996).

Another critical issue in the design of nutrient fertilization projects is timing. Anadromous fish runs that occur in summer and early fall may have immediate impacts on food webs because of high light and warm temperatures (spring and summer chinook salmon), which promote the production of food for fishes. Fish that spawn in their natal streams during late fall and winter (e.g., coho salmon), which are periods of relatively low primary and secondary productivity, may have less immediate or direct impacts on food-web productivity. Nutrient resources from these carcasses may enter the food chain via direct consumption, or more slowly as nutrients are released after storage in the hyporheic zone (Naiman et al. 2002).

Those are but a few of the statistical, ecological, and logistical factors that should be considered when designing a monitoring program to assess the effects of nutrient additions on aquatic ecosystems. By incorporating some or all of these issues into study designs, we may gain insight to the most ecologically and economically effective method of nutrient enrichment—when to add nutrients so as to provide the most benefit to the species of concern, and the physical, chemical, and biological characteristics that affect how food webs respond to added nutrients.

Selection of Parameters

In this subsection, we discuss the relative merits of different response variables used to assess the efficacy of nutrient enrichment on aquatic ecosystems. These parameters include (1) water chemistry, (2) primary productivity, (3) invertebrates, (4) fish, (5) stable isotopes, and (6) riparian vegetation. They differ in ease of collection, processing, analysis, and cost (Table 2). Selecting appropriate hypotheses and variables to assess the efficacy of nutrient supplementation is critical to successful monitoring designs. The scale of the project also should be considered when selecting parameters. If the project encompasses multiple stream reaches or lakes, logistics (e.g., costs) may preclude sampling fish across all study sites. Therefore, water chemistry or primary productivity might be selected as parameters to monitor across all sites, because they are less difficult and costly to collect, with a subset of sites sampled for fish. Similarly, if a whole tributary is fertilized, multiple water chemistry sites might be sampled, with a subset of these sampled for invertebrates or fish. The parameters included in a monitoring program will vary with the questions (hypotheses) being addressed. Ideally, the variables should be sensitive (minimal replication needed to detect statistical effects), ecologically important, relatively easy to collect and process, and inexpensive.

Water chemistry

Surface water nutrients are a simple, relatively inexpensive, and ecologically relevant measure because they generally are correlated with primary productivity and biomass of invertebrates and fish. In general, concentrations of N and P reflect ecosystem productivity (Brickell and Goering 1970; Bilby et al. 1996). Minakawa and Gara (1999) observed an increase in Kjeldahl-N, NH_4^+-N (ammonia), and SRP during spawning of chum salmon in Kennedy Creek, Washington. Schmidt et al. (1998) found that sockeye adults contributed 90% of the total P load to Karluk Lake, Alaska, which provided 45% of the total P for the following year. Bradford et al. (2000) showed that total P was approximately twofold higher after fertilization with inorganic fertilizers, compared to before (Figure 8). Adding carcasses or nutrients also can translate into higher production of primary producers and aquatic invertebrates, thereby providing additional energy for juvenile salmonids (Schmidt et al. 1998; Wipfli et al. 1998; Mazumder and Edmundson 2002). Long-term declines in sockeye populations in Karluk Lake correlated with reduced P availability, resulting in lower primary and secondary productivity (Schmidt et al. 1998).

Collecting water samples is relatively simple. Sample bottles must be thoroughly cleaned before collecting (Budy et al. 1998). In streams, samples should be collected from a well-mixed location within the central part of the channel, such as a riffle. Typically, samples are collected from multiple depths in lakes by using a water sampler (e.g., Budy et al. 1998). Samples should be kept cool until analysis (see APHA 1992 for further discussion of water sampling and analysis).

Table 2.
Summary of parameters that can be measured when assessing nutrient enrichment projects, and their relative variability, cost, and ease of sampling and processing.

Parameter	Variability	Cost	Difficulty in sampling/processing
Water chemistry	low	low	low
Algae			
Chlorophyll a	medium	high	medium
Periphyton biomass	medium	low	low
Primary production	medium	high	high
Invertebrates			
Community structure	high	high	high
Biomass	high	medium	medium
Fish			
Abundance	high	high	high
Growth rate	medium	medium	medium
Stable isotopes	low	medium	medium
Riparian vegetation	low	low	low

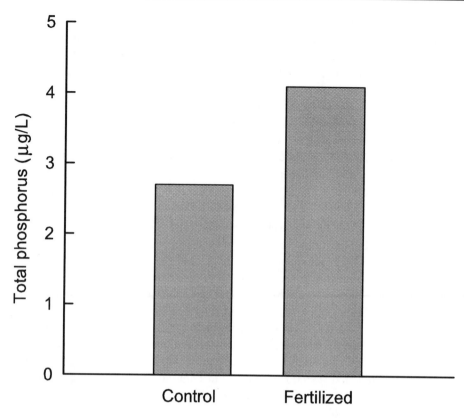

Figure 8.
Mean total P (μg/L) in Chilko Lake, British Columbia, during years when inorganic nutrients were ("fertilized") and were not added ("control") (data from Bradford et al. 2000).

Primary productivity

Increases in N and P concentrations suggest that nutrient augmentation will lead to increases in food-web productivity. In some cases, however, surface-water inorganic N and P levels are not affected by nutrient additions, because increased algal and bacterial production assimilates excess nutrients (Kiffney and Richardson 2001). As a result, algal or bacterial biomass may provide a more sensitive and ecologically relevant measure when assessing affects of nutrient augmentation on aquatic habitats. This is because nutrient supplementation can have an immediate and large affect on algal and bacterial communities. Stockner and MacIsaac (1996) suggested that bacterial communities are one of the most sensitive indicators of a lake's trophic status. Dissolved P levels were positively associated with periphyton biomass on rocks in oligotrophic streams of the Stanley River basin (Figure 9). Because of their small cell size and rapid nutrient uptake capabilities, bacterial populations typically exhibit strong and positive responses to nutrient applications (except see Carpenter et al. 1996).

Measures of algal biomass are the least difficult biological parameters to collect and analyze. Two common measures of periphyton or phytoplankton biomass are ash-free dry mass and chlorophyll a (see Steinman and Lamberti 1996). Ash-free dry mass is the simplest way of measuring periphyton or planktonic biomass; ash-free dry mass represents total organic matter (bacteria, fungi, particulate organic matter, and algae) that accumulates on a rock or is suspended in the water column. River algae that accumulates on inorganic surfaces typically is collected by using ceramic tiles (Kiffney and Bull 2000; Kiffney and Richardson 2001) or from rocks (e.g., Minakawa and Gara 1999), usually from fast-flowing habitats. Material on rocks or tiles is removed by scrubbing and rinsing, and this material is filtered onto a glass-fiber filter for measurement of biomass.

Chlorophyll *a* concentration also can be used to determine algal biomass. Filtered samples from lakes or streams are extracted in a solvent (e.g., acetone), and chlorophyll *a* is measured by using a fluorometer or spectrophotometer. An advantage to chlorophyll *a* is that it measures the abundance of living plant tissue. Chlorophyll *a*, however, may provide a less accurate or more variable estimate of true periphyton or planktonic bio-

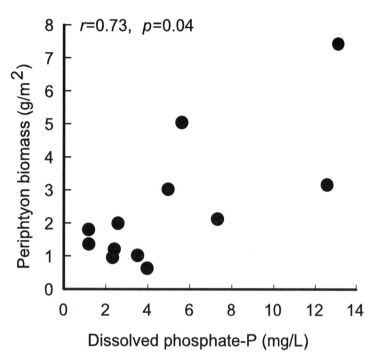

Figure 9.
Relationship between dissolved phosphate-P and periphyton biomass on rocks in 13 tributaries of the Salmon River basin, Idaho. Data points are based on mean values from 12 tributaries of the Salmon River basin. Linear regression showed that dissolved P explained a significant ($p < 0.05$) proportion of the variability in periphyton biomass.

mass than ash-free dry mass, because it can be too sensitive to other environmental factors (Feminella and Hawkins 1995). In addition, determining chlorophyll *a* in the laboratory requires chemical preparation (e.g., acetone extraction) and expensive equipment (e.g., fluorometer), whereas measuring total organic biomass requires relatively little laboratory preparation and equipment (drying and ashing oven, weighing balance), which are common to most laboratories. Measuring both variables simultaneously would improve interpretation of results from individual enrichment studies and would provide data for subsequent comparisons across locations (Feminella and Hawkins 1995).

Not only are these measures relatively easy to collect and process (Steinman and Lamberti 1996), they often are correlated with changes in primary consumers (invertebrates that eat periphyton) and top predators (fish) (Stockner and MacIsaac 1996). Nutrient addition does not always lead to increases in algal biomass, however, because of top-down control of algal abundance by herbivores (Rosemond et al. 1993; Peterson et al. 1993). Specifically, increased primary production resulting from nutrient additions is funneled into producing consumer biomass, causing no change in algal biomass. Periphyton biomass did not change with increases in light in the presence of snail grazers, whereas primary production was positively related to light (Hill et al. 1995). The same process can hold true for invertebrates, because fish predators can limit their population growth via increased predation rates (Wootton and Power 1993).

Measuring primary production and not biomass or chlorophyll *a* may provide a method for addressing the issue of top-down control of algal biomass. Primary production is the rate of production of new organic material, or fixation of energy, including that which is used and lost during that time interval (Wetzel 1983). Three methods are used to estimate primary production in aquatic systems: light- and dark-bottle oxygen technique, uptake of $^{14}CO_2$, and in situ diel changes in dissolved O_2 or particle matter over a 24-h period. Primary productivity can be measured by using rocks or artificial tiles collected from streams or lake water. All techniques rely on measuring the rate of uptake of carbon dioxide or the rate of production of oxygen (Bott 1996; Howarth and Michaels 2000). These measures also are sensitive to nutrient additions (e.g., Stockner and MacIsaac 1996), but they require relatively expensive equipment (dissolved oxygen meter), use of radioisotopes ($^{14}CO_2$), and can be technically difficult.

Invertebrates

Aquatic invertebrates provide another tool for monitoring changes in the environment resulting from nutrient supplementation. Monitoring invertebrates offers many advantages, some of which are intrinsic to the biology of the animals. They are ubiquitous, diverse, and exhibit a wide range of sensitivity to a variety of perturbations, including nutrient additions. Benthic invertebrates are sedentary in nature, which allows for effective spatial comparison of disturbance effects (e.g., comparing total invertebrate abundance upstream and downstream of a nutrient addition site). They are relatively long lived (some stoneflies have a 3-year larval stage), and, thus, temporal changes caused by perturbations can be examined (Rosenberg and Resh 1993). In addition, invertebrates can be sampled quantitatively in a wide variety of aquatic habitats (ponds, lakes, wetlands, streams), thus allowing statistical comparisons among locations. Typically, stream invertebrates are collected by using a Hess or Surber sampler (Merritt and Cummins 1996), whereas, lake invertebrates are collected by using an Eckman net (benthic habitat) or a plankton net (pelagic habitat; Wetzel and Likens 1990). Finally, nutrient fertilization potentially can affect invertebrate drift, which may be particularly important to drift-feeding fishes such as salmonids. Few studies have documented the effects of fertilization on drift (except see Deegan et al. 1997), but, if insect production increases in response to nutrients, so might drift. Insect drift from experimental channels with added inorganic nutrients was twofold higher than control channels (P. Kiffney, unpublished data). Drift is measured in streams by using nets set in the water for a specified length of time (see Smock 1996 for further details).

A number of studies have shown that invertebrate populations in streams (e.g., Johnston et al. 1990) and lakes (e.g., Stockner and MacIsaac 1996) increase because of nutrient enrichment, likely due to increased primary production. Kiffney and Richardson (2001) showed that Baetidae (mayfly) abundance was five times higher in nutrient-enriched channels compared to unenriched channels (Figure 10). Containers baited with salmon flesh had significantly higher total insect densities than unbaited containers (Minakawa and Gara 1999). Experiments in outdoor experimental channels showed that total macroinvertebrate densities were higher at the lowest loading rate of salmon carcasses (3.2 kg carcass wet mass/m^2) compared to controls, with no further increases at higher loading rates (Wipfli et al. 1999). Growth rates of some stream invertebrates also were higher in the presence of salmon carcasses (Chaloner and Wipfli 2002; Minakawa et al. 2002). Similar increases have been observed in lake fertilization programs. Fertilization of the metalimnon of Redfish Lake, Idaho, increased zooplankton biomass by 200% due to increased primary production (Budy et al. 1998). In general, these studies support the hypothesis that aquatic invertebrates increase in abundance due to increases of production of algae and bacteria, which respond to additions of nutrients and organic matter. There are exceptions to this pattern, however, pointing out the importance of understanding the trophic relationships within the system of interest. In some cases, fertilization will lead to little or no change in invertebrate abundance (e.g., Carpenter et al. 1996). Mazumder and Edmundson (2002) found that biomass and mean size of *Daphnia* increased immediately after fertilization of Packer Lake, Alaska, but declined after sockeye juveniles were stocked, even after continued fertilization.

There are statistical and logistical constraints with monitoring the response of aquatic invertebrates. Quantitative sampling of invertebrates is problematic, because the nonrandom distribution of these animals requires a high number of samples to achieve the desirable precision in estimating population abundance (Resh 1979). Therefore, insect responses to nutrients may be more variable than water chemistry parameters or algal biomass measures (Stockner and MacIsaac 1996). The resulting sample processing and identification also can be costly and time consuming.

Fish

Because they usually are the focal taxa in watershed restoration projects, fish are the most economically and socially important variable to measure in nutrient fertilization studies. However, fish populations are extremely variable in space and time (Bisson and Bilby 1998) and are difficult to sample with accuracy and precision. For example, many locations where Pacific salmon spawn and rear are remote, preventing deployment of fish enumeration fences and accurate assessment of returning adults to fertilized ecosystems (Hyatt and Stockner 1985). Typical measures of fish performance include size, density, growth rate, smolt yield, and adult returns. Methods for sampling fish populations are described in Chapter 8.

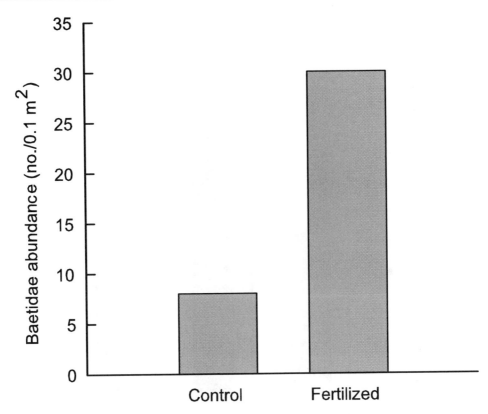

Figure 10.
Mean Baetidae abundance in control (*n* = 6) and fertilized (*n* = 6) channels averaged over time. Fertilized channels were enriched with pellets that released inorganic N and P (data from Kiffney and Richardson 2001).

Some studies have shown clear effects of nutrient supplementation on fish populations. Nutrient additions increased all trophic levels (bacteria to fish) in a number of sockeye salmon lakes in British Columbia (Stockner and MacIsaac 1996; Bradford et al. 2000; except see Mazumder and Edmundson 2002). A whole-river inorganic nutrient fertilization study resulted in increases in all trophic levels compared to reference reaches, including growth rate of coho salmon and steelhead juveniles and Dolly Varden (Figure 11). Other studies, however, did not detect statistical differences in fish performance in response to fertilization. Budy et al. (1998) found that zooplankton biomass increased by 250% in large enclosures in an oligotrophic lake, whereas growth of juvenile sockeye salmon increased by 12%. The increase in fish growth was not statistically different from controls. In one study, juvenile and adult Arctic grayling *Thymallus arcticus* grew faster and achieved a better condition in fertilized reaches of the Kuparuk River, Alaska, potentially in response to increases in insect size and abundance (Deegan and Peterson 1992). A follow-up study in the same system, however, found no difference in fish growth or condition factor between fertilized and control reaches (Deegan et al. 1997). Fish stocking also can affect how fish respond to nutrient enrichment. Stocking in conjunction with adding nutrients may not lead to increases in adult returns, because increased competition among juvenile fish limits accumulation of food resources necessary for metabolism and growth (Mazumder and Edmundson 2002). Moreover, stocking hatchery fish can create other problems that can affect wild stocks (Lichatowich 1999; Levin et al. 2002)

In addition to dealing with sampling and statistical issues associated with using fish in monitoring programs, it is increasingly difficult to receive permission from state and federal agencies to capture and handle these animals. This is especially true in the United States, because the number of fish stocks listed as threatened and endangered under the Endangered Species Act has increased with time. Theoretically, this act protects listed species from actions that may further hinder population viability. As a result, receiving a permit to handle listed species from agencies responsible for their protection and recovery is difficult. One way to monitor the response of fish to nutrient fertilization is to use a surrogate species that is not listed, such as resident trout or sculpins (Bilby et al. 1998). There are, however, obvious drawbacks to using surrogate species, such as that their response may show little correlation with the response of the species of interest.

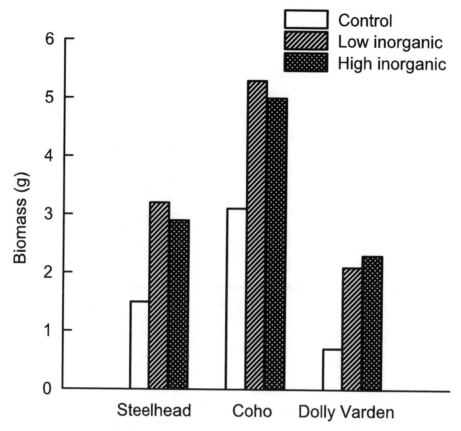

Figure 11.
Mean weights of salmonid fry from the Keogh River, British Columbia, in control and stream sections fertilized with inorganic nutrients (data from Johnston et al. 1990).

Stable isotopes

Quantifying isotopes of C and N is potentially one of the most effective methods of measuring the influence of carcasses on aquatic and terrestrial food webs. Nitrogen and C in spawning salmon contain higher proportions of the heavier isotopic form of both elements than N and C imported to freshwater and terrestrial systems from other sources (Bilby et al. 1996). Mixing models are used to determine the relative importance of marine-derived N for different components of the food web. For example, Phillips and Koch (2002) developed a concentration-corrected, two-end-member mixing model to determine the relative contribution of terrestrial versus instream primary production to secondary consumers. These isotopes, therefore, can be used to measure the contribution of marine-derived N and C to aquatic and terrestrial food webs. Collecting samples for stable isotopes is simple, and methods are described in other sources (Kline et al. 1990; Bilby et al. 1996; Chaloner and Wipfli 2002). Fish typically are collected by electroshocking or angling and then are sacrificed. Dorsal muscle tissue from this fish then is processed and analyzed on a mass spectrophotometer (Bilby et al. 1998). A recent study showed that it is possible to use fin clips of fish to measure the stable isotopes of C and N, which allows for nonlethal sampling (Finlay et al. 2002). In addition, tissue can be collected and processed from periphyton, insects, and riparian vegetation to track the movement of marine-derived N through the food web. Bilby et al. (1996) found that the proportion of N contributed from spawning salmon varied among trophic categories, ranging from 17% in some aquatic insects to 30% in juvenile coho salmon. Stable isotope studies also have documented the extent to which various species of wildlife rely on salmon (Hilderbrand et al. 1999) and the transport of salmon-derived nutrients into terrestrial ecosystems (Hocking and Reimchen 2002). By using stable isotopes, Helfield and Naiman (2001) found that trees and shrubs near spawning streams derived 22–24% of their foliar N from spawning salmon.

Inorganic fertilizer with very high levels of the heavier isotope of N are manufactured and have been used to evaluate N movement through stream and riparian ecosystems (Mulholland et al. 2000). However, this type of assessment has been done at very few sites. Processing samples for stable isotope analysis is time consuming, requires specialized equipment, and has high analytical costs (~U.S.\$8–30 per sample). More importantly, it requires sacrificing fish and other animals, which introduces a variety of ethical and legal issues that must be considered, especially for depressed populations. Although isotopes allow for tracking marine-derived nutrients through food webs, care should be taken when using this approach (Schindler et al. 2003). Stable isotopes measure trophic interactions integrated over time and reflect an individual's diet as well as its trophic position within the food web. In addition, environmental factors such as microbial processing can influence the cycling of N^{15} and thus the natural abundance of this isotope in freshwater food webs (Schindler et al. 2003). Nevertheless, the use of isotopes is a powerful way of tracking the contribution of marine-derived nutrients to aquatic and terrestrial food webs.

Riparian vegetation

Not only do carcasses enrich the aquatic environment, they provide critical limiting resources for terrestrial plants and animals, especially those near the stream. Stable isotope studies have shown that marine-derived nutrients are incorporated into foliage of terrestrial vegetation and animals (Bilby et al. 1996; Ben-David et al. 1998; Hilderbrand et al. 1999; Helfield and Naiman 2001). A recent study showed that these subsidies affect riparian plant growth: growth rates of Sitka spruce *Picea sithensis* were significantly higher near spawning streams compared to streams without spawning salmon (Helfield and Naiman 2001). These nutrient subsidies may impact other components of the riparian food web (Cederholm et al. 1989, 1999; Naiman et al. 2002). Terrestrial invertebrates were more enriched in marine-derived N in riparian areas along salmon streams compared to areas upstream of a barrier to fish passage (Hocking and Reimchen 2002). Brown bears *Ursus arctos* and black bears *Ursus americanus* depend heavily on salmon as a food source and serve as a vector for transport of salmon-derived N to riparian ecosystems (Hilderbrand et al. 1999; Reimchen 2000). More than 40 species of mammals and birds forage on salmon in freshwater habitats (Willson et al. 1998). Hunt et al. (1992) showed that the number of bald eagles *Haliaeetus leucocephalus* along the Skagit River was correlated with chum salmon escapement.

Similar to collecting tissue samples from stream food webs, one can collect and analyze riparian soils, plants, and organisms to determine the contribution of marine-derived N to the terrestrial food web (Helfield and Naiman 2001; Hocking and Reimchen 2002). For example, foliage can be collected from terrestrial plants near streams with and without salmon, and the needles and leaves from these plants are analyzed for N^{15} to estimate the proportion of N derived from salmon (Helfield and Naiman 2001). As mentioned previously, care must be taken when using stable isotopes to determine the relative importance of salmon-derived nutrients to the nutrient capitol of aquatic and terrestrial ecosystems, because other factors can affect N^{15} abundance besides salmon carcasses (Schindler et al. 2003). Differences in plant growth or biomass also can be used to determine the impacts of nutrients on riparian ecosystems (Helfield and Naiman 2001). A typical measure for tree biomass is to measure diameter at breast height (dbh), which is measured 1.37 m above the soil surface. Helfield and Naiman (2001) showed that tree size (dbh) was greater in riparian areas of a salmon stream than in streams without salmon.

Case Studies of Lake and Watershed Nutrient-Enrichment Projects

Here we summarize the results of important case studies to elucidate the process of designing and monitoring nutrient enrichment projects. The most extensive research on the effects of inorganic nutrient supplementation has occurred in the oligotrophic waters of British Columbia (Johnston et al. 1990; Stockner and MacIsaac 1996) and Alaska (Mazumder and Edmundson 2002). Recent studies also have shown that stream food webs respond to the additions of salmon carcasses (e.g., Wipfli et al. 1998). These projects were testing the hypothesis that fertilizing streams and lakes would promote the growth and production of Pacific salmon populations indirectly by increasing primary and secondary productivity of their food webs (inorganic nutrient additions) or by both indirect transfer and direct consumption of salmon carcasses (carcass additions).

Keogh River, British Columbia

In a before–after control–impact design, the effect of inorganic nutrients on the productivity of salmon populations has been evaluated in the Keogh River, Vancouver Island, British Columbia, since 1981 (Johnston et al. 1990; McCubbing and Ward 1997; McCubbing and Ward 2000). Nutrients were first added by dripping a concentrated solution into the stream. Nutrient levels in water, algal biomass, invertebrate communities, and fish populations were measured (Johnston et al. 1990). Addition of relatively small quantities of inorganic N and P to the Keogh River increased autotrophic production and the growth rate of juvenile salmonids (Johnston et al. 1990). Late summer weights of coho and steelhead fry in the Keogh River were 1.4–2.0 times greater, and smolt yield doubled during years when N and P were added to the river (Johnston et al. 1990; Ward 1996). Additional experiments have been carried out on the Keogh River since this initial study. Beginning in 1997, physical habitat structures have been added in conjunction with nutrient fertilization to examine the effects on coho and steelhead (McCubbing and Ward 1997). The early technique of adding liquid fertilizers required considerable maintenance to replenish the nutrient solution and to maintain the proper drip rate and was considered unfeasible for management applications. As a result, a slow-release fertilizer pellet was developed that releases nutrients into the water over a period of months, greatly simplifying the process (Ashley and Slaney 1997; Sterling et al. 2000). Results from these later studies also showed that juvenile salmonids were larger in fertilized reaches (McCubbing and Ward 2000).

Sockeye Nursery Lakes

Monitoring efforts to quantify the response of sockeye salmon populations and their food webs to nutrient additions have been included in many British Columbia and Alaska lake fertilization programs. The Department of Fisheries and Oceans Canada began enriching sockeye salmon nursery lakes with inorganic N and P in 1969 to increase their primary and secondary productivity and fry-rearing capacity (Stockner and MacIsaac 1996). Before embarking on this program, permits were required from the province of British Columbia. Prerequisite to obtaining these permits were assurances that additions of nutrients would maintain the oligotrophic nature of treated lakes and would not negatively alter water quality (e.g., reduced water transparency, excessive algae or macrophyte growth, potability of water). Pre- and posttreatment monitoring studies were also mandatory (Stockner and MacIsaac 1996).

Initially, an aqueous solution of inorganic N and P, prepared from dry pelleted, agricultural grade ammonium nitrate and ammonium phosphate fertilizers, was used to fertilize lakes. Since 1989, however, concentrated liquid fertilizers were used because they were easier and safer to store, handle, and mix. They also significantly reduced the cost of applying fertilizers, because of their high concentration compared with solutions prepared from dry fertilizers (Stockner and MacIsaac 1996). The N:P ratios of the fertilizer was high (20–30:1) to provide sufficient N to discourage growth of colonial nitrogen-fixing cyanobacteria and to promote the growth of algae that are within an edible size range (1–40 μm) for herbivorous zooplankton. Nutrients were added weekly, at higher loads in spring and reduced loads in late summer. This timing coincided with the seasonal peak in the abundance of copepods and other components of the zooplankton community, which are the dominant food items for sockeye salmon fry.

Increases at all trophic levels were observed in response to fertilization (see Stockner and MacIsaac 1996 and references therein for further details). Free-living bacteria, the most abundant heterotrophic organisms in the pelagic community of oligotrophic lakes, were 100% higher after fertilization. Primary production was approximately 146% greater after fertilization. Increases also were observed for zooplankton biomass (260%) and smolt weight (68%). An estimated 700,000–1,500,000 additional adult sockeye salmon returned to treated lakes. These extra salmon were attributed to increased fry production and survival in the treated lakes and to increased marine survival due to larger size of the smolts. In economic terms, it was estimated that the total landed value of adult returns to treated lakes exceeded Can$300 million over a 20-year period. The cost of nutrient application, research, and assessment totaled about $17 million since 1976. A cost-benefit analysis suggested that lake fertilization yielded one of the greatest production benefits for least cost of any salmonid enhancement technique (Guthrie and Peterman 1988). Fertilization of Chilko Lake, British Columbia, increased smolt size by 34% and produced a weak but positive correlation between smolt size and ocean survival. A cost-benefit analysis of fertilizing Chilko Lake also found a strong probability that lake fertilization increased the number of recruits per spawner and that this increase was sufficient to yield a large net economic benefit (Maxwell 2000).

Packers Lake, Alaska, is another sockeye salmon lake that has been fertilized and monitored for almost 20 years (Mazumder and Edmundson 2002). This study showed how nutrients and stocking of sockeye salmon fry interacted to affect productivity. After two years of baseline data collection, the lake was fertilized

(1983–1996) and stocked with sockeye fry (1987–1996). The lake was fertilized by plane and by boat, using applications of N fertilizer during spring and summer. Fry were added each year in spring at a density of about 50–150 fry/100 m², and nutrient chemistry, algal biomass (chlorophyll *a*), zooplankton abundance, composition, biomass, and juvenile sockeye and smolt abundance were monitored. Before stocking, all trophic levels responded positively to fertilization. Stocking of sockeye fry, however, produced declines in both biomass and mean length of *Daphnia* and size of smolts. The mechanism for the decline in smolt size was attributed to increased competition among sockeye juveniles for preferred food items (i.e., *Daphnia*); smolt length and weight were negatively correlated with fry density. Moreover, the largest smolts were produced when the lake was fertilized but not stocked.

Salmon Carcasses in Alaska and Washington

The case studies previously described provide compelling evidence that adding inorganic nutrients to oligotrophic streams and lakes can increase primary and secondary productivity and fish populations. There are fewer data on how additions of salmon carcasses may affect food-web productivity, but a few small-scale studies do suggest that carcasses can benefit stream food webs and juvenile fish (Schuldt and Hershey 1995; Bilby et al. 1998; Wipfli et al. 1998, 1999). In these Alaska and Washington State studies, salmon carcasses were added to experimental and to natural streams to test the hypothesis that carcasses increase food-web productivity. In the natural stream studies, carcasses were added to a treatment reach, with a upstream site used as a control or a reference reach. Depending on the study, inorganic nutrients, algal biomass, invertebrate communities, and fish populations were monitored to assess the ecological effects of carcass addition. Salmon carcasses can promote fish populations indirectly via the uptake of nutrients released from carcasses, which promote primary and secondary production, and directly via consumption of carcasses by invertebrates and fish. Periphyton biomass and macroinvertebrate density were higher in experimental channels and natural streams enriched with salmon carcasses compared to controls (Wipfli et al. 1998, 1999), as was insect growth rate (Chaloner and Wipfli 2002). Similar trends were observed in a carcass-enriched section of a nearby natural stream (Wipfli et al. 1999). Bilby et al. (1998) found that condition factor (Condition factor = 1,000 weight/length³), density, and growth of juvenile steelhead and coho salmon were higher in carcass-enriched stream sections compared to unenriched sections in western Washington. They attributed this increase in fish performance to direct consumption of carcasses by juvenile fishes, as indicated by stomach contents and changes in stable isotope values of the juvenile fish (Bilby et al. 1996). These short-term studies provide some evidence to suggest that carcasses can increase stream food-web productivity, but long-term (multiple generations of fish) and large-scale (reach to tributary) experiments are needed to assess the overall effectiveness of nutrient enrichment (both carcass and inorganic nutrients) on streams. Furthermore, studies are needed to evaluate whether continual fertilization is needed or whether initial fertilization efforts can start a positive feedback process in which increases in juvenile salmon survival translate to increased adult returns and, subsequently, more nutrients.

Summary

There is abundant evidence that the process of anadromous fish nourishing the freshwater and terrestrial ecosystems where they spawn and die has been severely compromised. The disruption of this linkage likely limits aquatic and terrestrial productivity and diversity, such as the growth and survival of juvenile and adult fishes and other wildlife. A logical extension of this observation is that supplementing oligotrophic ecosystems with nutrients may reverse these trends. Millions of dollars are spent annually on habitat restoration projects that generally do not consider freshwater productivity. These projects may have no measurable impact on fish populations, however, because factors that control the production of food for fish were not considered. Other wildlife also may benefit from nutrient-enrichment projects: adding carcasses to aquatic ecosystems may increase bear populations (Hilderbrand et al. 1999). Before we manipulate nutrient levels, however, we must examine how existing physical, chemical, and biological attributes (Wipfli et al. 1999) influence the effects of fertilization on aquatic ecosystems. We also need to evaluate the ecological and economic benefits of different nutrient-enrichment techniques, the relative importance of direct versus indirect pathways of nutrient enrichment, and when nutrient enrichment may cause negative impacts through eutrophication.

Considerable research also is needed to identify the natural variability in freshwater productivity both within and among watersheds. Typically, this information is not part of standard watershed assessments, but it is critical for identifying candidate areas for nutrient supplementation because not all reaches or tributaries can support high system productivity and some rivers already are nutrient rich. If this assessment suggests that nutrient enrichment is a viable option, specific hypotheses need to be formulated and appropriate response variables identified. Moreover, an experimental design must be formulated that considers replication, randomization, error reduction, and other essential factors. Are large-scale (whole tributary) enrichment projects more effective at increasing population growth rate than reach-scale projects that are scattered throughout the watershed? Large-scale and long-term processes, such as climate, must be incorporated into study designs, because ocean conditions are a major driver of salmon population cycles (Mantua et al. 1997). Timing of nutrient enrichment and food-web structure also must be considered, because both can influence how a food web responds to nutrients. Important parameters to monitor depend upon well-defined objectives and hypotheses and may include water chemistry, algae, macroinvertebrates, fishes and other vertebrates, stable isotopes, and riparian vegetation. Monitoring is critical because managers need to know how and when nutrient enrichment is effective in promoting food-web productivity and fish populations, as well as how and when it may have negative impacts.

The ultimate goal of habitat restoration is to restore the natural processes that initially created the tremendous diversity and productivity of watersheds used by anadromous fish. Nutrient enrichment, as well as other habitat restoration measures will not have their desired effect if other aspects that impact populations are not addressed. If increased fish production resulting from nutrient enrichment is harvested before adults can enrich their natal stream, there will be no benefits to future generations. Moreover, nutrient enrichment will need to continue indefinitely, and the natural processes governing ecosystem productivity will not be restored. If too many hatchery juveniles are released into the environment, there may be no effect of carcasses on wild fish populations, because of increased competition for invertebrate food resources. Nutrient enrichment also will not have the desired effect if other elements of the habitat, such as barriers or lack of habitat complexity, are not addressed. Effective river restoration will require an approach that evaluates the whole watershed, from the headwaters to the estuary, and the natural processes that form this watershed.

Acknowledgments

We would like to thank E. Quimby, P. Roni, M. Wipfli, and W. Reichert for valuable comments that improved the clarity of this chapter.

References

Allan, J. D. 1995. Stream ecology: structure and function of running waters. Kluwer Academic Publishers, Dordrecht, The Netherlands.

APHA (American Public Health Association). American Water Works Association and Pollution Control Federation. 1992. Standard methods for the examination of water and wastewater, 18th edition. American Public Health Association, Washington, D.C.

Ashley, K. I., and P. A. Slaney. 1997. Accelerating recovery of stream and pond productivity by low-level nutrient replacement. Chapter 13 in P. A. Slaney and D. Zaldokas, editors. Fish habitat restoration procedures for the Watershed Restoration Program. B. C. Ministry of the Environment, Lands and Parks and B.C. Ministry of Forest, Watershed Restoration Technical Circular 9, Vancouver.

Ben-David, M., M. Flynn, and D. M. Schell. 1997. Annual and seasonal changes in the diet of martens: evidence from stable isotope analysis. Oecologia 111:280–291.

Ben-David, M., T. A. Hanley, and D. M. Schell. 1998. Fertilization of terrestrial vegetation by spawning Pacific salmon: the role of flooding and predator activity. Oikos 83:47–55.

Biggs, B. J. E. 1998. Patterns in benthic algae in streams. Pages 31–56 in R. J. Stevenson, M. L. Bothwell, and R. L. Lowe, editors. Algal ecology: freshwater benthic ecosystems. Academic Press, San Diego, California.

Biggs, B. J. E. 2000. Eutrophication of streams and rivers: dissolved nutrient-chlorophyll relationships for benthic algae. Journal of the North American Benthological Society 19:17–31.

Bilby, R. E., B. R. Fransen, and P. A. Bisson. 1996. Incorporation of nitrogen and carbon from spawning coho salmon into the trophic system of small streams: evidence from stable isotopes. Canadian Journal of Fisheries and Aquatic Sciences 53:164–173.

Bilby, R. E., B. R. Fransen, P. A. Bisson, and J. K. Walter. 1998. Response of juvenile coho salmon (Oncorhynchus kisutch) and steelhead (O. mykiss) to the addition of salmon carcasses to two streams in southwestern Washington, U.S.A. Canadian Journal of Fisheries and Aquatic Sciences 55:1909–1918.

Bilby, R. E., B. R. Fransen, J. K. Walter, C. J. Cederholm, and W. J. Scarlett. 2001. Preliminary evaluation of the use of nitrogen stable isotope ratios to establish escapement levels for Pacific salmon. Fisheries 26:6–14.

Bilton, H. T., D. F. Alderdice, and J. T. Schnute. 1982. Influence of time and size at release of juvenile coho salmon (Oncorhynchus kisutch) on returns at maturity. Canadian Journal of Fisheries and Aquatic Sciences 39:426–447.

Bisson, P. A., and R. E. Bilby. 1998. Organic matter and trophic dynamics. Pages 373–398 in R. J. Naiman and R. E. Bilby, editors. River ecology and management: lessons from the Pacific coastal ecoregion. Springer-Verlag, New York.

Bisson, P. A., J. L. Nielson, R. A. Palmason, and L. E. Gore. 1982. A system for naming habitat types in small streams, with examples of habitat utilization of salmon during low flows. Pages 62–73 in N. B. Armantrout, editor. Acquisition and utilization of aquatic habitat information. American Fisheries Society, Portland, Oregon.

Borchardt, M. A. 1996. Nutrients. Pages 184–228 in R. J. Stevenson, M. L. Bothwell, and R. L. Lowe, editors. Algal ecology: freshwater benthic ecosystems. Academic Press, San Diego, California.

Bott, T. L. 1996. Primary productivity and community respiration. Pages 533–556 in F. R. Hauer and G. A. Lamberti, editors. Methods in stream ecology. Academic Press, San Diego, California.

Bradford, M. J., B. J. Pyper, and K. S. Shortreed. 2000. Biological responses of sockeye salmon to the fertilization of Chilko Lake, a large lake in the interior of British Columbia. North American Journal of Fisheries Management 20:661–671.

Brickell, D. C., and J. J. Goering. 1970. Chemical effects of salmon decomposition on aquatic ecosystems. Pages 125–138 in R. S. Murphy, editor. First International Symposium on Water Pollution in Cold Climates. U.S. Government Printing Office, Washington, D.C.

Budy, P., C. Luecke, and W. A. Wurtsbaugh. 1998. Adding nutrients to enhance the growth of endangered sockeye salmon: trophic transfer in an oligotrophic lake. Transactions of the American Fisheries Society 127:19–34.

Carpenter, S. R., J. F. Kitchell, K. L. Cottingham, D. E. Schindler, D. L. Chistensen, D. M. Post, and N. Voichick. 1996. Chlorophyll variability, nutrient input, and grazing: evidence from whole-lake experiments. Ecology 73:725–735.

Cederholm, C. J., D. B. Houston, D. L. Cole, and W. J. Scarlett. 1989. Fate of coho salmon (Oncorhynchus kisutch) carcasses in spawning streams. Canadian Journal of Fisheries and Aquatic Sciences 46:1347–1355.

Cederholm, C. J., M. D. Kunze, T. Murota, and A. Sibatani. 1999. Pacific salmon carcasses: essential contributions of nutrients and energy for aquatic and terrestrial systems. Fisheries 24(10):6–15.

Chaloner, D. T., and M. S. Wipfli. 2002. Influence of decomposing Pacific salmon carcasses on macroinvertebrate growth and standing stock in southeastern Alaska streams. Journal of the North American Benthological Society 21:430–442.

Colligan, M. A., J. F. Kocik, D. C. Kimball, G. Marancik, J. F. McKeon, and P. R. Nickerson. 1999. Status review for anadromous Atlantic salmon in the United States. National Marine Fisheries Service/U.S. Fish and Wildlife Service Joint Publication, Gloucester, Massachusetts.

Collins, B. D., and G. R. Pess. 1997. Critique of Washington's watershed analysis. Journal of the American Water Resources Association 33:997–1010.

Deegan, L. A., and B. J. Peterson. 1992. Whole-river fertilization stimulates fish production in an arctic tundra river. Canadian Journal of Fisheries and Aquatic Sciences 49:1890–1901.

Deegan, L. A., B. J. Peterson, H. Golden, C. C. McIvor, and M. C. Miller. 1997. Effects of fish density and river fertilization on algal standing stocks, invertebrate communities, and fish production in an arctic river. Canadian Journal of Fisheries and Aquatic Sciences 54:269–283.

Dodds, W. K., J. R. Jones, and E. B. Welch. 1998. Suggested criteria for stream trophic state: distributions of temperate stream types by chlorophyll, total nitrogen and phosphorus. Water Research 32:1455–1462.

Dodds, W. K., V. H. Smith, and B. Zander. 1997. Developing nutrient targets to control benthic chlorophyll levels in streams: a case study of the Clark Fork River. Water Research 31:1738–1750.

Dodds, W. K., and E. B. Welch. 2000. Establishing nutrient criteria in streams. Journal of the North American Benthological Society 19:186–196.

Dodson, S. I., S. E. Arnott, and K. L. Cottingham. 2000. The relationship in lake communities between primary productivity and species richness. Ecology 81:2662–2679.

Donaldson, J. R. 1967. The phosphorus budget of Illiamma Lake, Alaska, as related to the cyclic abundance of sockeye salmon. Doctoral dissertation. University of Washington, Seattle.

Durbin, A. G., S. W. Nixon, and C. A. Oviatt. 1979. Effects of spawning migrations of the alewife, Alosa pseudoharengus, on freshwater ecosystems. Ecology 60:8–17.

Eastman, D. E. 1996. Response of freshwater fish communities to spawning sockeye salmon (Oncorhynchus nerka). Master's thesis. University of Washington, Seattle.

Elliott, S. T., and R. Bartoo. 1981. Relation of larval Polypedilum (Diptera: Chironomidae) to pink salmon eggs and alevins in an Alaskan stream. Progressive Fish-Culturist 43:220–221.

Feminella, J. W., and C. P. Hawkins. 1995. Interactions between stream herbivores and periphyton: a quantitative analysis of past experiments. Journal of the North American Benthological Society 14:465–509.

Finlay, J. C., S. Khandwala, and M. E. Power. 2002. Spatial scales of carbon flow in a river food web. Ecology 83:1845–1859.

Finney, B. P., I. Gregory-Eaves, J. Sweetman, M. S. V. Douglas, and J. Smol. 2000. Impacts of climatic change and fishing on Pacific salmon abundance over the past 300 years. Science 290:795–799.

Garbarino, J. R., H. C. Hayes, D. A. Roth, R. C. Antweiler, T. I. Brinton, and H. E. Taylor. 1995. Contaminants in the Mississippi River. United States Geological Survey Circular 1133, Reston, Virginia.

Garman, G. C., and S. A. Macko. 1998. Contribution of marine-derived organic matter to an Atlantic coast, freshwater tidal stream by anadromous clupeid fishes. Journal of the North American Benthological Society 17:277–285.

Ginzburg, L. R., and H. R. Akçakaya. 1992. Consequences of ratio-dependent predation for steady-state properties of ecosystems. Ecology 73:1536–1543.

Gowan, C., M. K. Young, K. D. Fausch, and S. C. Riley. 1994. Restricted movement in resident stream salmonids: a paradigm lost? Canadian Journal of Fisheries and Aquatic Sciences 51:2626–2637.

Gresh, T., J. Lichatowich, and P. Schoonmaker. 2000. An estimation of historic and current levels of salmon production in the northeast Pacific ecosystem: evidence of a nutrient deficit in the freshwater systems of the Pacific Northwest. Fisheries 25:15–21.

Gross, H. P., W. A. Wurtsbaugh, and C. Luecke. 1998. The role of anadromous sockeye salmon in the nutrient loading and productivity of Redfish Lake, Idaho. Transactions of the American Fisheries Society 127:1–18.

Gustafason, R. G., T. C. Wainwright, G. A. Winans, F. W. Waknitz, L. T. Parker, and R. S. Waples. 1997. Status review of sockeye salmon from Washington and Oregon. U.S. Department of Commerce, NOAA Technical Memorandum, NMFS-NWFSC-33, Seattle.

Guthrie, I. C., and R. M. Peterman. 1988. Economic evaluation of lake enrichment strategies for British Columbia sockeye salmon. North American Journal of Fisheries Management 8:442–454.

Hartman, G. F., and J. C. Scrivener. 1990. Impacts of forestry practices on a coastal stream ecosystem, Carnation Creek, British Columbia. Canadian Bulletin of Fisheries and Aquatic Sciences 223.

Helfield, J. M., and R. J. Naiman. 2001. Effects of salmon-derived nitrogen on riparian forest growth and implications for stream productivity. Ecology 82:2403–2409.

Hilderbrand, G. V., S. D. Farley, C. T. Robbins, T. A. Hanley, K. Titus, and C. Servheen. 1996. Use of stable isotopes to determine diets of living and extinct bears. Canadian Journal of Zoology 74:2080–2088.

Hilderbrand, G. V., T. A. Hanley, C. T. Robbins, and C. C. Schwartz. 1999. Role of brown bears (*Ursus arctos*) in the flow of marine nitrogen into a terrestrial ecosystem. Oecologia 121:546–550.

Hill, W. R. 1996. Effects of light. Pages 121–149 *in* R. J. Stevenson, M. L. Bothwell, and R. L. Lowe, editors. Algal ecology: freshwater benthic ecosystems. Academic Press, San Diego, California.

Hill, W. R., M. G. Ryon, and E. M. Schilling. 1995. Light limitation in a stream ecosystem: responses by primary producers and consumers. Ecology 76:1297–1309.

Hocking, M. D., and T. E. Reimchen. 2002. Salmon-derived nitrogen in terrestrial invertebrates from coniferous forests of the Pacific Northwest. BMC Ecology 2:4 Online at http://www. biomedcentral.com/1472-6785/2/4 [Accessed 12 February 2003].

Holtby, L. B., B. C. Andersen, and R. K. Kadowaki. 1990. Importance of smolt size and early ocean growth to interannual variability in marine survival of coho salmon (*Oncorhynchus kisutch*). Canadian Journal of Fisheries and Aquatic Sciences 47:2181–2194.

Howarth, R. W., and A. F. Michaels. 2000. The measurement of primary production in aquatic ecosystems. Pages 72–85 *in* O. E. Sala, R. B. Jackson, H. A. Mooney, and R. W. Howarth, editors. Methods in ecosystem science. Springer-Verlag, New York.

Hunt, G. V., B. S. Johnson, and R. E. Jackman. 1992. Carrying capacity for bald eagles wintering along a northwestern river. Journal of Raptor Research 26:49–60.

Hunter, M. D., and P. W. Price. 1992. Playing chutes and ladders: bottom-up and top-down forces in natural communities. Ecology 73:724–732.

Hyatt, K. D., and J. G. Stockner. 1985. Response of sockeye salmon (Oncorhynchus nerka) to fertilization of British Columbia lakes. Canadian Journal of Fisheries and Aquatic Sciences 42:320–331.

Johnston, N. T., J. S., MacDonald, K. J. Hall, and P. J. Tschaplinski. 1997. A preliminary study of the role of sockeye salmon (*Oncorhynchus nerka*) carcasses as carbon and nitrogen sources for benthic insects and fishes in the "Early Stuart" stock spawning streams, 1050 km from the ocean. B.C. Ministry of Environment, Lands and Parks, Fisheries Project Report, RD55, Victoria.

Johnston, N. T., C. J. Perrin, P. A. Slaney, and B. R. Ward. 1990. Increased juvenile salmonid growth by whole-river fertilization. Canadian Journal of Fisheries and Aquatic Sciences 47:862–872.

Juday, C., W. H. Rich, G. I. Kemmerer, and A. Mean. 1932. Limnological studies of Karluk Lake, Alaska 1926–1930. U.S. Bureau of Fisheries Bulletin 47:407–436.

Kiffney, P. M., and J. P. Bull. 2000. Factors controlling periphyton during summer in headwater streams of southwestern British Columbia. Journal of Freshwater Ecology 15:339–353.

Kiffney, P. M., J. P. Bull, and M. C. Feller. 2002. Climatic and hydrologic variability in a coastal watershed of southwestern British Columbia. Journal of the American Water Resources Association 38:1437–1451.

Kiffney, P. M., and W. H. Clements. 1996. Effects of heavy metals on stream macroinvertebrate assemblages from different altitudes. Ecological Applications 6:472–481.

Kiffney, P. M., J. S. Richardson, and M. C. Feller. 2000. Fluvial and epilithic organic matter dynamics in headwater streams of southwestern British Columbia, Canada. Archives für Hydrobiologie 149:109–129.

Kiffney, P. M., and J. S. Richardson. 2001. Interactions among nutrients, periphyton, and invertebrate and vertebrate (*Ascaphus truei*) grazers in experimental channels. Copeia 2001:422–429.

Kline, T. C., Jr., J. J. Goering, O. A. Mathisen, P. H. Poe, and P. L. Parker. 1990. Recycling of elements transported upstream by runs of Pacific salmon: I. $\delta^{15}N$ and $\delta^{13}C$ evidence in Sashin Creek, southeastern Alaska. Canadian Journal of Fisheries and Aquatic Sciences 47:136–144.

Kline, T. C., Jr., J. J. Goering, and R. J. Piorkowski. 1997. The effect of salmon carcasses on Alaskan freshwaters. Pages 179–204 *in* A. M. Milner and M. W. Oswood, editors. Freshwaters of Alaska: ecological syntheses. Springer-Verlag, New York.

Krokhin, E. M. 1975. Transport of nutrients by salmon migrating from sea into lakes. Pages 153–166 *in* A. D. Hasler, editor. The coupling of land and water systems. Springer-Verlag, New York.

Kyle, G. B. 1994. Nutrient treatment of 3 coastal Alaskan lakes: trophic level responses and sockeye salmon production trends. Alaska Fishery Research Bulletin 1:153–167.

Lamberti, G. A., S. V. Gregory, L. R. Ashkenas, R. C. Wildman, and K. M. S. Moore. 1991. Stream ecosystem recovery following a catastrophic debris flow. Canadian Journal of Fisheries and Aquatic Sciences 48:196–208.

Larkin, G. A., and P. A. Slaney. 1997. Implications of trends in marine-derived nutrient influx to south coastal British Columbia production. Fisheries 22:16–24.

Levin, P. S., R. W. Zabel, and J. G. Williams. 2002. The road to extinction is paved with good intentions: negative association of fish hatcheries with threatened salmon. Proceedings of the Royal Society: Biological Sciences 268:1153–1158.

Lichatowich, J. 1999. Salmon without rivers: a history of the Pacific salmon crisis. Island Press, Washington, D.C.

Lyle, A. A., and J. M. Elliott. 1998. Migratory salmonids as vectors of carbon, nitrogen, and phosphorus between marine and freshwater environments in north-east England. The Science of the Total Environment 210:457–468.

Mantua, N. J., S. R. Hare, Y. Zhang, J. M. Wallace, and R. C. Francis. 1997. A Pacific-interdecadal climate oscillation with impacts on salmon production. Bulletin of the American Meteorological Society 78:1069–1079.

Mathisen, O. A., P. L. Parker, J. J. Goering, T. C. Kline, P. H. Poe, and R. S. Scalan. 1988. Recycling of marine elements transported into freshwater by anadromous salmon. Verhandlungen der Internationalen Vereinigung für Theoretische und Angewandte Limnologie 23:2249–2258.

Maxwell, M. R. 2000. A Bayesian benefit-cost analysis of an experimental fertilization project for sockeye salmon (Oncorhynchus nerka) in Chilko Lake, British Columbia. Master's thesis, Simon Fraser University, Burnaby, British Columbia.

Mazumder, A., and J. A. Edmundson. 2002. Impact of fertilization and stocking on trophic interactions and growth of juvenile sockeye salmon (Oncorhynchus nerka). Canadian Journal of Fisheries and Aquatic Sciences 59:1361–1373.

McCubbing, D. F. J., and B. R. Ward. 1997. The Keogh and Waukwaas rivers paired watershed study for B. C.'s watershed restoration program: juvenile salmonid enumeration and growth 1997. British Columbia Ministry of Environment, Lands, and Parks, and Ministry of Forests, Watershed Restoration Project Report Number 6, Victoria.

McCubbing, D. F. J., and B. R. Ward. 2000. Stream rehabilitation in British Columbia's watershed restoration program: juvenile salmonid response in the Keogh and Waukwaas Rivers, 1998. British Columbia Ministry of Environment, Lands, and Parks, and Ministry of Forests, Watershed Restoration Project Report Number 12, Victoria.

Merritt, R. W., and K. W. Cummins. 1996. An introduction to the aquatic insects of North America, 3rd edition. Kendall/Hunt, Dubuque, Iowa.

Minakawa, N. 1997. The dynamics of aquatic insects associated with salmon spawning. Doctoral thesis. University of Washington, Seattle.

Minakawa, N., and R. I. Gara. 1999. Ecological effects of chum salmon (Oncorhynchus keta) spawning run in a small stream of the Pacific Northwest. Journal of Freshwater Ecology 14:327–335.

Minakawa, N., R. I. Gara, and J. M. Honea. 2002. Increased individual growth rate and community biomass of stream insects associated with salmon carcasses. Journal of the North American Benthological Society 21:651–659.

Mulholland, P. J., J. L. Tank, D. M. Sanzone, W. M. Wollheim, B. J. Peterson, J. R. Webster, and J. L. Meyer. 2000. Nitrogen cycling in a forest stream determined by a ^{15}N tracer addition. Ecological Monographs 70:471–493.

Mundie, J. H., S. M. McKinnel, and R. E. Traber. 1983. Responses of stream zoobenthos to enrichment of gravel substrates with cereal grain and soybean. Canadian Journal of Fisheries and Aquatic Sciences 40:1702–1712.

Murphy, M. L., C. P. Hawkins, and N. H. Anderson. 1981. Effects of canopy modifications and accumulated sediment on stream communities. Transactions of the American Fisheries Society 110:469–478.

NRC (National Research Council). 1996. Upstream: salmon and society in the Pacific Northwest. National Academy Press, Washington, D.C.

Naiman, R. J., R. E. Bilby, D. E. Schindler, and J. M. Helfield. 2002. Pacific salmon, nutrients, and the dynamics of freshwater and riparian ecosystems. Ecosystems 5:399–417.

Nehlsen, W., J. E. Williams, and J. A. Lichatowich. 1991. Pacific salmon at the crossroads: stocks at risk from California, Oregon, Idaho and Washington. Fisheries 16:4–21.

Nickelson, T. E., J. W. Nicholas, A. M. McGie, R. B. Lindsay, D. L. Bottom, R. J. Kaiser, and S. E. Jacobs. 1992. Status of anadromous salmonids in Oregon coastal basins. Oregon Department of Fish and Wildlife, Corvallis.

Nicola, S. J. 1968. Scavenging by Alloperla (Plecoptera: Chloroperlidae) nymphs on dead pink (Oncorhynchus gorbuscha) and chum (O. keta) embryos. Canadian Journal of Zoology 46:787–796.

Peckarsky, B. L., S. D. Cooper, and A. W. McIntosh. 1997. Extrapolating from individual behavior: implications for interactions between stream organisms. Journal of the North American Benthological Society 16:375–390.

Perrin, C. J., and J. S. Richardson. 1997. N and P limitation of benthos abundance in the Nechako River, British Columbia. Canadian Journal of Fisheries and Aquatic Sciences 54:2574–2583.

Peterson, B. J., L. Deegan, J. Helfrich, J. E. Hobbie, M. Hullar, B. Moller, T. E. Ford, A Hershey, A Hiltner, G. Kipphut, M. A. Lock, D. M. Fiebig, V. McKinley, M. C. Miller, J. R. Vestel, R. Venutllo, and G. Volk. 1993. Biological responses of a tundra river to fertilization. Ecology 74:653–672.

Phillips, D. L., and P. L. Koch. 2002. Incorporating concentration dependence in stable isotope mixing models. Oecologia 130:114–125.

Polis, G. A., W. B. Anderson, and R. D. Holt. 1997. Toward an integration of landscape and food web ecology: the dynamics of spatially subsidized food webs. Annual Review of Ecology and Systematics 28:289–316.

Power, M. E. 1992. Top-down and bottom-up forces in food webs: do plants have primacy? Ecology 73:733–746.

Quinn, T. P., and N. P. Peterson. 1996. The influence of habitat complexity and fish size on over-winter survival and growth of individually marked juvenile coho salmon (Oncorhynchus kisutch) in Big Beef Creek, Washington. Canadian Journal of Fisheries and Aquatic Sciences 53:1555–1564.

Rand, P. S., C. A. S. Hall, W. H. McDowell, N. H. Ringler, and J. G. Kennen. 1992. Factors limiting primary productivity in Lake Ontario tributaries receiving salmon migrations. Canadian Journal of Fisheries and Aquatic Sciences 49:2377–2385.

Reimchen, T. E. 2000. Some ecological and evolutionary aspects of bear-salmon interactions in coastal British Columbia. Canadian Journal of Zoology 78:448–457.

Resh, V. H. 1979. Sampling variability and life history features: basic considerations in the design of aquatic insect studies. Canadian Journal of Fisheries and Aquatic Sciences 36:290–311.

Richey, J. E., M. A. Perkins, and C. R. Goldman. 1975. Effects of kokanee salmon (*Oncorhynchus nerka*) decomposition on the ecology of a subalpine stream. Journal of the Fisheries Research Board of Canada 32:817–820.

Roni, P., T. J. Beechie, R. E. Bilby, F. E. Leonetti, M. M. Pollock, and G. P. Pess. 2002. A review of stream restoration techniques and a hierarchical strategy for prioritizing restoration in Pacific Northwest watersheds. North American Journal of Fisheries Management 22:1–20.

Rosemond, A. D., P. J. Mulholland, and J. W. Elwood. 1993. Top-down and bottom-up control of stream periphyton: effects of nutrients and herbivores. Ecology 74:1264–1280.

Rosenberg, D. M., and V. H. Resh. 1993. Freshwater biomonitoring and benthic macroinvertebrates. Chapman and Hall, London.

Schindler, D. E., M. D. Scheuerell, J. W. Moore, S. M. Gende, T. B. Francis, and W. J. Palen. 2003. Pacific salmon and the ecology of coastal ecosystems. Frontiers in Ecology and the Environment 1:38–44.

Schmidt, D. C., S. R. Carlson, G. B. Kyle, and B. P. Finney. 1998. Influence of carcass-derived nutrients on sockeye salmon productivity in Karluk Lake, Alaska: importance in the assessment of an escapement goal. North American Journal of Fisheries Management 18:743–761.

Schuldt, J. A., and A. E. Hershey. 1995. Effect of salmon carcass decomposition on Lake Superior tributary streams. Journal of the North American Benthological Society 14:259–268.

Slaney, T. L., K. D. Hyatt, T. G. Northcote, and R. J. Fielder. 1996. Status of anadromous salmon and trout in British Columbia and Yukon. Fisheries 21(10):20–35.

Smock, L. A. 1996. Macroinvertebrate movement: drift, colonization, and emergence. Pages 371–390 *in* F. R. Hauer and G. A. Lamberti, editors. Methods in stream ecology. Academic Press, San Diego, California.

Steinman, A. D., and G. A. Lamberti. 1996. Biomass and pigments of benthic algae. Pages 295–314 *in* F. R. Hauer and G. A. Lamberti, editors. Methods in stream ecology. Academic Press, San Diego, California.

Sterling, M. S., K. I. Ashley, and A. B. Bautista. 2000. Slow-release fertilizing for rehabilitating oligotrophic streams: a physical characterization. Water Quality Research Journal of Canada 35:73–94.

Stockner, J. G., and E. A. MacIsaac. 1996. British Columbia lake enrichment programme: two decades of habitat enhancement for sockeye salmon. Regulated Rivers: Research and Management 12:547–561.

Stockner, J. G., E. Rydin, and P. Hyenstrand. 2000. Cultural oligotrophication: causes and consequences for fisheries resources. Fisheries 25:7–14.

Stockner, J. G., and K. R. S. Shortreed. 1976. Autotrophic production in Carnation Creek, a coastal rainforest stream on Vancouver Island, British Columbia. Journal of the Fisheries Research Board of Canada 33:1553–1563.

Tipping, J. M. 1997. Effect of smolt length at release on adult returns of hatchery reared steelhead. Progressive Fish-Culturist 59:310–311.

Vitousek, P. M., J. D. Aber, R. W. Howarth, G. E. Likens, P. A. Matson, D. W. Schindler, W. G. Schlesinger, and D. G. Tilman. 1997. Human alteration of the global nitrogen cycle: sources and consequences. Ecological Applications 7:737–750.

Volk, C. J., P. M. Kiffney, and R. L. Edmonds. 2003. Role of riparian red alder in the nutrient dynamics of coastal streams of the Olympic Peninsula, Washington, USA. Pages 213–225 *in* J. G. Stockner, editor. Nutrients in salmonid ecosystems: sustaining production and biodiversity. American Fisheries Society, Symposium 34, Bethesda, Maryland.

Wallace, J. B., S. L. Eggert, J. L. Meyer, and J. R. Webster. 1999. Effects of resource limitation on a detrital-based ecosystem. Ecological Monographs 69:409–442.

Ward, B. R. 1996. Population dynamics of steelhead in a coastal stream, the Keogh River, British Columbia. Pages 308–323 *in* I. Cowx, editor. Stock assessments in inland fisheries. Blackwell Scientific Publications, Oxford, England.

Ward, B. R., and P. A. Slaney. 1988. Life history and smolt-to-adult survival of Keogh River steelhead trout (*Salmo gairdneri*) and the relationship to smolt size. Canadian Journal of Fisheries and Aquatic Sciences 45:1110–1122.

Warren, C. E., J. H. Wales, G. E. Davis, and P. Doudoroff. 1964. Trout production in an experimental stream enriched with sucrose. Journal of Wildlife Management 28:617–661.

WDF (Washington Department of Fisheries, Washington Department of Wildlife, and Western Washington Treaty Indian Tribes). 1993. 1992 Washington state salmon and steelhead stock inventory. Washington Department of Fisheries Information and Education Division, Olympia.

Welch, E., J. Jacoby, and C. May. 1998. Stream quality. Pages 69–85 *in* R. Naiman and R. Bilby, editors. River ecology and management: lessons from the Pacific coastal ecoregion. Springer, New York.

Wetzel, R. G. 1983. Limnology. Sauders College Publishing, Fort Worth, Texas.

Wetzel, R. G., and G. E. Likens. 1990. Limnological analyses. Springer-Verlag Publishing, New York.

Willson, M. F., S. M. Gende, and B. H. Marston. 1998. Fishes and forest: expanding perspectives on fish-wildlife interactions. Bioscience 48:455–462.

Winer, B. J., D. R. Brown, and K. M. Michels. 1991. Statistical principles in experimental design. McGraw-Hill, New York.

Wipfli, M. S., J. Hudson, and J. P. Caouette. 1998. Influence of salmon carcasses on stream productivity: response of biofilm and benthic macroinvertebrates in southeast Alaska. Canadian Journal of Fisheries and Aquatic Sciences 55:1503–1511.

Wipfli, M. S., J. P. Hudson, D. T. Chaloner, and J. P. Caouette. 1999. Influence of salmon spawner densities on stream productivity in southeast Alaska. Canadian Journal of Fisheries and Aquatic Sciences 56:1600–1611.

Wootton, J. T., and M. E. Power. 1993. Productivity, consumers, and the structure of a river food chain. Proceedings of the National Academy of Science 90:1384–1387.

Chapter 10

Evaluating Fish Response to Culvert Replacement and Other Methods for Reconnecting Isolated Aquatic Habitats

George Pess, Sarah Morley, Philip Roni

Northwest Fisheries Science Center, National Marine Fisheries Service

2725 Montlake Boulevard East, Seattle, Washington 98112, USA

george.pess@noaa.gov

Introduction

The reconnection of isolated aquatic habitats is a common goal of many watershed restoration efforts. Previous chapters have discussed road improvements, floodplain restoration, estuarine restoration, improvements of instream habitats, and other types of restoration that include removal of artificial barriers to fish migration. For example, many road rehabilitation projects include removal or replacement of culverts that are impassable to fish. Instream and riparian projects often are completed alongside culvert removal projects. Estuarine and floodplain projects often include removal of levees or water control structures that impede fish access to important off-channel habitats. In this chapter, we discuss how to monitor and evaluate fish response to reconnection of isolated habitats or to the removal of artificial migration barriers. We provide an overview of the problem, discuss how methods and designs for monitoring fish response to removal of migration barriers might differ from types of restoration previously discussed, and provide examples and recommendations of what and how to monitor. We only briefly discuss physical monitoring, because it has been covered in detail in previous chapters. Hydraulic evaluations of different types of culverts and stream crossing are covered in texts and agency documents on engineering and fish passage design (e.g., Clay 1995; ODFW 2001; WDFW 2003).

Fish passage through culverts, tide gates, and other artificial barriers in streams and estuaries is critical to maintaining connectivity among habitats (Roni et al. 2002). Roads, culverts, levees, pipeline crossings, and other man-made stream crossing structures can block access for migratory fishes and other aquatic fauna, and can biologically disconnect large amounts of aquatic habitat from the river system. Such structures also can compromise delivery of materials, including sediment, wood, organics, and marine-derived nutrients, or, in the case of estuarine and off-channel habitats, the influx of water and nutrients.

The amount of stream habitat made inaccessible due to human infrastructure is daunting. There are an estimated 1.4 million stream-road crossings in the United States (M. Hudy, U.S. Forest Service, personal communication), and an estimated 2.5 million artificial barriers prevent fish passage in the United States (U.S. Fish and Wildlife, National Fish Passage Program, Arlington, Virginia, unpublished data). In Washington State alone, more than 7,700 km of historical salmon habitat is inaccessible to fishes because of impassable culverts or road crossings, despite state regulations that require road crossings to provide fish passage (Conroy 1997; Roni et al. 2002). Between 26 and 50% of the 10,000 culverts that exist in fish-bearing streams on federal lands in Oregon and Washington impede fish passage (USGAO 2001). In Oregon, forest landowners, state agencies, and federal agencies have identified almost 3,000 culverts on fish-bearing streams that are impassable to anadromous salmonids (OGNRO 2001). Of those, more than 900 locations throughout Oregon have been made more accessible to fish (OGNRO 2001). While massive efforts have focused on streams in the western United States and Canada, fish passage through culverts and other road crossings is a problem throughout North America (e.g., Warren and Pardew 1998; USGAO 2001; Langill and Zamora 2002), Europe (Yanes et al. 1995; Glen 2002), and, undoubtedly, worldwide.

Migratory species that use small streams for specific life stages can be particularly affected by culverts and other impediments to fish movement. For example, culverts can prevent adult coho salmon *Oncorhynchus kisutch* access to spawning grounds in small streams, limiting the upstream extent of habitat used and reducing the amount of marine-derived nutrients introduced in a river system (Gende et al. 2002; Roni et al. 2002). Similarly, culverts have been shown to impede the migration of resident rainbow trout *O. mykiss*, cutthroat trout *O. clarki*, brook trout *Salvelinus fontinalis*, and brown trout *Salmo trutta* (Belford and Gould 1989; Eaglin and Hubert 1993), and likely inhibit less-studied nonsalmonid species that have lesser swimming and leaping abilities than salmonids. Juvenile salmonids also can be blocked from moving upstream into tributaries and into winter rearing environments, such as floodplain channels (Peterson 1980). For example, in two watersheds in northwestern Washington, impassable culverts reduced potential juvenile coho salmon capacity by 30–58% (Beechie et al. 1994; Roni et al. 2002; Pess et al. 2003). Studies indicate that culverts can inhibit the movement of many aquatic and terrestrial vertebrates and invertebrates that use or migrate along stream corridors (Yanes et al. 1995; Vaughan 2002).

Similarly, tide gates or poorly designed culverts through levees and roads can prevent fishes from accessing estuarine habitats (Taylor et al. 1998). Off-channel and estuarine habitats often are isolated by the construction of dikes and levees (Beechie et al. 1994). An estimated 50% of the world's wetlands have been lost due to hydraulic isolation and land conversion (Dugan 1993). Thus off-channel and estuarine habitats lost as a direct consequence of this wetlands loss is thought to be one of the biggest losses of fish habitat in the United States and likely throughout the world (Dugan 1993). Only recently have considerable efforts been undertaken to reconnect or recreate important rearing and spawning areas for fishes and other biota in larger rivers and their floodplains in Europe and America (Buijse et al. 2002).

Water diversions reduce streamflows and can create barriers to fish movement through reduced flows and increased temperatures, particularly for coolwater fishes such as salmonids. For example, there are almost 76,000 permitted water diversions in Oregon alone, and some affect salmonids listed by the Endangered Species Act (OGNRO 2001). Less than 1,000 of these diversions are required to be screened, because they have flow greater than 30 ft³/s; however, only 5 have been screened to date (OGNRO 2001). Federal and state agencies developed criteria to exclude both juvenile and adult salmonids from being entrained in water diverted without being impinged on the diversion screens (NMFS 1997; CDFG 2000; ODFW 2001; WDFW 2003). Extensive studies on the effects of these diversions on the migrations of juvenile and adult fishes have not been conducted. There is increasing concern that water diversions create both seasonal hydrologic and thermal barriers to fish movement and migration, isolating fish from important habitats.

The reconnection of freshwater habitats is one of the more important efforts that can be undertaken to initiate the recovery of salmonid populations. Historically, fish passage structures also were installed at natural impassable barriers such as waterfalls. In some instances, these have been highly successful (e.g., Bryant et al. 1999). However, these projects are highly controversial, because they allow fish to access habitats or interact with populations and species that may have been isolated for hundreds or thousands of years.

In some cases, fisheries management agencies have used artificial barriers to isolate native fish populations from nonnative species to reduce hybridization, competition, and predation (Shafer 1995). However, the benefits of this strategy can be short term and can result in decreased native fish populations, increased vulnerability to stochastic environmental processes, and loss of genetic diversity (Novinger and Rahel 2003). Since we think improving fish passage at naturally impassable migration barriers should be discouraged for a variety of ecological reasons, we will focus our discussion on reconnection of habitats isolated by man-made barriers.

Inventories to assess isolation of stream habitats by anthropogenic barriers can be conducted by using physical criteria for fish migration blockages that have been determined for many highly migratory species. Identifying the amount of habitat affected or isolated typically involves little subjectivity. Determining whether a stream crossing is a complete (all species at all life stages or seasons) or a partial (certain species at specific life stages or seasons) barrier to fish movements can be complicated by physical variables, including the cumulative effects of other barriers within the watershed, seasonal changes in flow during fish migration, as well as biological variables, including the species, the abundance, the condition, and the life stage of the fish or fishes attempting passage. Software programs such as FishXing (USFS 2000) allow managers to determine the type of blockage a culvert may impose to different fishes at different life stages. Several states also have developed fish passage criteria for juvenile and adult salmonids that can be the basis for identifying fish blockages (ODFW 2001; WDFW 2003).

Combining these inventory results with cost estimates for restoration actions allows managers to rank the cost-effectiveness of individual projects to more effectively direct the expenditure of limited restoration funds. For example, Snohomish County Surface Water Management (SCSWM) combined eight inventories that identify isolated habitat in the Stillaguamish River basin from a variety of sources, including SCSWM, the Washington Department of Fish and Wildlife, the Washington State Department of Natural Resources, the Stillaguamish Tribe, and the U.S. Forest Service (M. Purser, SCSWM, personal communication). Three out of the five agencies doing inventories followed the Fish Passage Barrier Assessment and Prioritization Manual (WDFW 1998). Based on a 2002 inventory of 952 structures, 544 were identified as 100% passable to salmonids, 337 as impassable, and 71 as unknown due to no information (M. Purser, SCSWM, personal communication). One of the inventories has been used to evaluate the cost-effectiveness of reconnection projects based on the habitat area upstream of the project multiplied by the average life span of a blockage (~50 years) and divided by the cost of the project (Pess et al. 2003). These results allowed natural resource agencies to identify the most cost-effective projects for reconnecting blocked tributary habitats based on benefits to multiple salmonid species, as well as costs of reconstructing individual stream crossings (Pess et al. 2003).

Techniques to evaluate and to fix fish blockages have been summarized in book chapters, papers, and numerous agency publications (e.g., Furniss et al. 1991; Moore et al. 1997; Slaney and Zaldokas 1997). Roni et al. (2002) summarize the effectiveness of various stream-crossing structures with respect to juvenile and adult salmonid passage, as well as the transport of sediment and wood, and general impacts to stream channel morphology (Table 1). While most stream-crossing structures can be designed to provide fish passage for adult salmonids, more research is needed to identify the effectiveness of such structures on juvenile fish passage. A large portion of structures, however, do not allow for the transport of materials such as sediment and wood and, thus, disrupt natural processes (Roni et al. 2002).

Table 1.
Summary of various stream-crossing structures and whether they allow for fish passage (juvenile and adult salmonids) and the transport of sediment and large woody debris (LWD) or impact stream morphology by constraining the channel. (Modified from Roni et al. 2002.)

Stream-crossing type	Provides fish passage		Transports		Constrains
	Adult	Juvenile	Sediment	LWD	channel[a]
Bridge	Yes	Yes	Yes	Yes	No
Culvert					
Bottomless pipe arch	Yes	Yes	Yes	No	Yes
Squash pipe or countersunk	Yes	Yes	Yes	No	Yes
Round corrugated, baffled	Yes	Yes	No	No	Yes
Round corrugated, no baffles	Yes or no[b]	Yes or no[b]	No	No	Yes
Smooth (round or box)	No[b]	No[b]	No	No	Yes

[a]Depends on size of culvert or bridge relative to channel and floodplain width.
[b]Fish passage depends on culvert slope and length.

Although many fish blockages are in the process of being replaced (ODFW 2001) and isolated habitats are being reconnected, little has been done to document the results of such efforts in the published literature. The few examples that exist, however, do suggest a relatively large increase in potential fish production for a nominal cost (Roni et al. 2002). Monitoring of four types of restoration projects in the Snake River basin, Idaho, indicated that barrier removal accounted for half to more than two-thirds of the potential anadromous salmonids produced from the four project types, even though barrier removals were less than half of all the projects (Scully et al. 1990). Monitoring one year after a fish passage improvement project was implemented in one small stream in northwest Washington indicated that more than 90% of all spawning coho salmon occurred above the project, even though the majority of spawning area was below the project (Beamer et al. 1998). Pess et al. (2003) found similar responses to juvenile and adult salmonids in several tributaries of one watershed in the Pacific Northwest. Blockages that have cut off salmonid spawning and rearing for decades were used within the first year of blockage removal. Densities of adult and juvenile salmonid were one to two orders of magnitude greater after blockages were removed (Pess et al. 2003). In addition, several years of monitoring juvenile and adult fish populations above the corrected barriers revealed that restored stream reaches with higher habitat quality (e.g., greater density of pools and higher wood loadings) had average juvenile coho densities that were 2–4 times greater and redd densities that were 35 times greater than stream reaches connected with lower habitat quality (Pess et al. 2003). The relative benefits of reconnecting higher quality, more complex channels were greater than for other stream channels. This emphasizes the need to prioritize culvert and barrier replacement to maximize benefits and the need to quantify habitat amount and quality to help understand fish response to reconnection of isolated habitats.

Considerations for Monitoring

The initial step in any monitoring program is determining the project objectives and hypotheses to be tested (Table 2). Monitoring fish response to reconnection of isolated habitats provides one of the simplest and most straightforward cases for monitoring and evaluation. The hypotheses are typically whether fish now can access the habitat, what numbers of fish are using the habitats, whether a partial blockage to fish habitat exists, or whether the number of fish increase after improvements in fish passage. More detailed hypotheses could be defined to look at species composition, diet, seasonal habitat use, or attributes of physical habitat after change in watershed processes (delivery of wood, water, marine-derived and other nutrients, and sediment) after removal of barrier and reconnection of the habitat in questions. Similarly, the reconnection of habitats, whether in small tributaries, on floodplains, or in estuarine environments, lends itself well to some of the traditional study designs used in stream and watershed monitoring. Possible study designs, reviewed in Chapter 2, typically include before–after or posttreatment (retrospective) studies.

An individual fish barrier removal project within one stream reach or several fish barrier removal projects in one watershed would be best monitored by using a before–after or before–after control–impact design, and monitoring of fish species and abundance before and after replacement of an impassable culvert. For example, Glen (2002) monitored numbers of juvenile Atlantic salmon *Salmo salar* before and after an impassable culvert was replaced and found relatively rapid colonization of newly accessible habitats (Figure 1). The monitoring of several similar or several different types of fish barrier removal projects across different watersheds also could use a before–after design or include posttreatment collection of data on many sites (i.e., posttreatment design; e.g., Pess et al. 2003). In cases where habitats are completely disconnected from the stream network, such as a pond or estuarine slough isolated by a dike or road crossing known to be impassable to adult fish, simple posttreatment monitoring of fish colonization, or use of the newly accessible habitat may suffice. Partial blockages, such as culverts only passable at certain flows or stream reaches dewatered by seasonal water diversions, typically would require before and after monitoring to assess changes in fish movement and abundance. Similarly, monitoring of physical variables will require before and after data collection for both partial and complete barriers to transport of sediment, wood, organic matter, and so forth.

Assessing the effects of an individual project on an entire watershed requires estimation of fish abundance in each reconnected reach or area and a watershed-level assessment of population abundance. This last option requires considerable coordination and both extensive and intensive sampling, with ongoing status monitoring or trend monitoring at a population or watershed scale. That is to say, this would be most feasible where watershed-scale population estimates already are being made. For anadromous fishes, this could be relatively

Table 2.
Recommended steps in developing a monitoring plan for reconnection of isolated habitats, with specific examples given for replacement of a culvert on a small stream.

Step	Examples for small tributary culvert replacement
Identify project objectives	Increase coho salmon spawning and rearing habitat by (1) increasing habitat amount, (2) improving habitat connectivity, and (3) reopening existing high-quality coho salmon spawning and rearing habitat.
Develop project hypotheses	(1) Habitat amount will increase within study reaches as more small tributary habitats are made available, (2) habitat connectivity between the tributary systems and main stem will increase, and (3) coho salmon, as well as other salmonids, will successfully use new habitats for spawning and rearing.
Select appropriate spatial scales at which to monitor	At site scale, evaluate physical and biological differences between reconnected and reference channels. At reach scale, evaluate changes in relative abundance of tributary habitats and associated fish use. At basin scale, track changes in total smolt production and nutrient availability.
Formulate experimental design	Before–after design to evaluate changes in relative abundance of reconnected habitats and habitat connectivity between reconnected and downstream habitats. Posttreatment paired-site design to compare habitat quality and fish use between reconnected and reference channels.
Select monitoring parameters	*Physical*—measure habitat quantity and quality in reconnected and reference habitats. Measure habitat heterogeneity, wood abundance, and temperature regime in reconnected and reference channels. *Biological*—Measure invertebrate and fish abundance, community composition, and diversity in reconnected and reference channels. At a reach and watershed scale monitor smolt production.
Determine monitoring frequency and duration	Sample over multiple seasons to capture seasonality of fish use (e.g., juvenile overwintering vs. late summer spawning) and changes in habitat availability during high and low water periods. Monitor parameters at least twice annually after construction to identify potential design problems, then semiannually for at least 10 years to allow for response lag time.
Analyze and report	Where appropriate, use paired *t*-tests, analysis of variance, or other appropriate statistical tests to evaluate differences in means between before and after and between reconnected and reference monitoring parameters. Report results at regional and national conferences, post-project updates at relevant Web sites, publish initial results in technical report and final results in a peer-reviewed journal.

easily achieved by trapping out-migrating smolts from reconnected tributary habitats and trapping fish downstream in the mainstem river to estimate the total population in the watershed (Figure 2A). The proportion of the total smolt abundance in a watershed originating from various habitats then could be calculated (Figure 2B). While this is relatively straightforward, we found no published examples of this type of study. Determining the watershed effects of multiple reconnections requires assessing watershed-level population abundance alone.

Determining the length of monitoring will depend upon the goals of the project and the interannual and seasonal variation in fish abundance (Roni et al. 2002; see also Chapter 2). Reconnection of completely isolated habitat may not need to be monitored for more than a few years if the goal is simply to determine fish presence or absence. Fish often colonize new habitats relatively quickly (Iversen et al. 1993; Bryant et al. 1999; Glen 2002). However, if fish numbers are extremely low or if a culvert is only passable at some water levels or

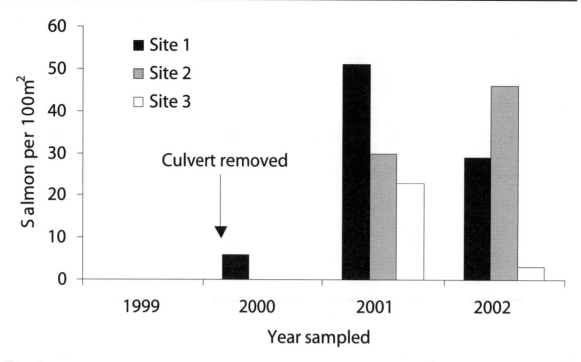

Figure 1.
Before and after monitoring of Atlantic salmon fry and parr of three sites in Wauchope Burn, Scotland, above a road crossing before and after an impassable culvert was replaced with a bridge (data from Glen 2002). The culvert had blocked upstream passage of Atlantic salmon for more than 30 years. Small numbers of juvenile salmon began moving upstream within 2 weeks of culvert replacement in 2000 (Glen 2002).

seasons, it may take several years for fish to colonize new habitats and monitoring may need to be long term. If the monitoring budget is limited, then another option is to wait and monitor only when appropriate flow conditions occur or when population levels have increased. Finally, if the project was addressing a partial blockage, then the goal is to examine a change in abundance, which may take several years to detect. Chapter 2 provides examples of how to estimate number of years or sites to monitor if an estimate of variability in fish abundance or parameter of interest is available.

The goal of most barrier removal and reconnection of isolated habitat projects is to provide habitat for fishes. We focused our discussion on salmonid fishes in particular because salmonids have been the focus of much of this work throughout North America and elsewhere. A successful fish passage project must get the fish to, into, through, out of, and away from the culvert or stream crossing. Chapter 8 discusses methods for sampling fish in detail. Electrofishing, snorkeling, floating smolt traps, and stationary trapping are some of the most common methods used to estimate fish abundance and species composition for barrier removal projects in streams (Figure 3). Fyke nets, seines, and various types of traps often are used in collecting fish in estuarine environments. Useful metrics are abundance, species composition, size and age structure, movements, and survival (see Chapter 8 for details). Fish movement is particularly important if there is concern whether culverts or other road-crossing structures are passable at all flows, seasons, or for every species and life stage. New tagging and remote monitoring methods allow monitoring of fish movements. For example, the U.S. Forest Service is using passive integrated transponder or PIT tags with detectors laid across the stream bottom or over the mouth of a culvert (Armstrong et al. 1996) to monitor fish movements through recently replaced culverts (B. Hansen, U.S. Forest Service, personal communication). These and other tagging and trapping technologies provide invaluable opportunities to monitor fish movements and survival through road and levee crossings.

In addition to benefiting fishes, culvert replacement or other barrier removal projects may benefit invertebrates and wildlife (Yanes et al. 1995; Vaughan 2002). For example, Yanes et al. (1995) found that culverts both provided and inhibited migration of many mammals and reptiles, and Vaughan (2002) suggested that culverts inhibit upstream movement of many aquatic macroinvertebrates. Depending on the objectives of the restora-

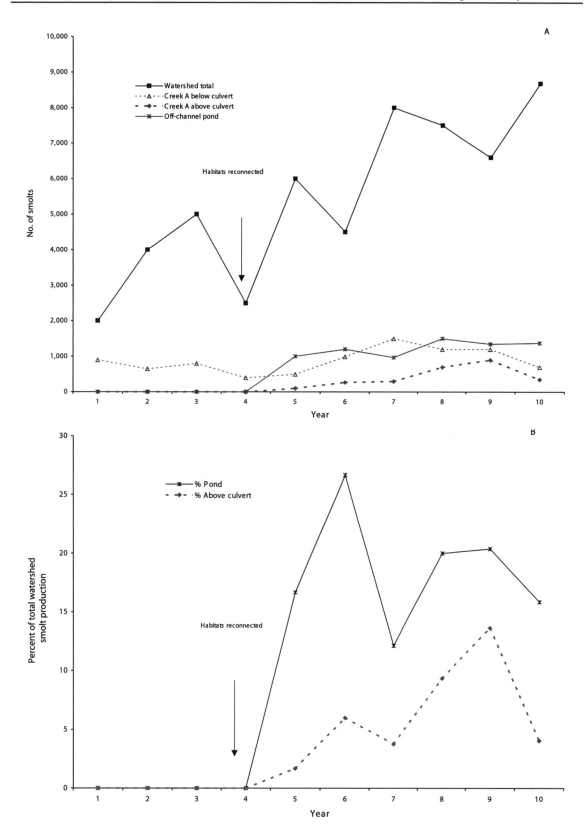

Figure 2.
Graph A is a hypothetical example of how to determine the effect of reconnected habitat on an entire watershed or population by using smolt counts from four separate smolt traps at main stem, upstream pond, and above and below an impassable culvert of a small tributary. Years 1–4 are before improvement of fish passage at off-channel pond and culvert, and 5–10 are after. Graph B indicates the percentage of total watershed smolt production from culvert replacement in Creek A and reconnection of off-channel pond. Data are for illustrative purposes only.

Figure 3.
Common techniques used to estimate fish abundance after culvert replacement or reconnection of isolated habitat, including (clockwise from top left) electrofishing, snorkeling, stationary and floating smolt trap.

tion and the hypotheses of the monitoring program, invertebrates and wildlife may be important parameters to measure.

Monitoring physical parameters of both stream crossing structure and physical habitat upstream and downstream of culverts is important for understanding the extent to which fish use newly available habitat. These parameters fall into two categories: measurements of the passage structure or former barrier location itself or measurements of the quality of the newly available habitat. For example, Pess et al. (2003) found that habitat-quality metrics (e.g., pool spacing, pool area, wood loading, amount of spawning gravel), combined with a stream classification system (Montgomery and Buffington 1997) based on a portion of these metrics, provide a basis for prioritizing which barrier removals would yield the most favorable biological response. They found that juvenile population size and adult coho salmon densities were greatest in pool-riffle and forced pool-riffle channels that have a stream gradient of less than 4%, a pool spacing of less than four channel widths per pool, and 4 to 5% of the total stream channel area in spawning gravels (Pess et al. 2003). For coho salmon, the relative benefits of reconnecting pool-riffle and forced pool-riffle channel types with more complex isolated habitat, therefore, greater than for other stream channel types such as plane-bed and step-pool channels. The differences in salmon densities were similar to what Montgomery et al. (1999) found with adult coho salmon and chinook salmon *Oncorhynchus tshawytscha*.

It is important to note that not all road-crossing structures will restore stream processes such as sediment and organic matter transport (Table 1). For example, when Wellman et al. (2000) examined the fine sediment and sediment accumulation above and below stream crossings (culverts and bridges) in Tennessee, they found that sediment accumulated upstream of culverts but not bridges and that culverts impeded transport of sediment but bridges did not. The objectives of a project will determine what stream processes are measured and over what time frame. For example, monitoring transport of organic matter (large woody debris or LWD) and fine and course sediment may be an important part of monitoring if one of the objectives of the restoration project is to restore LWD and sediment transport processes. Physical parameters that could be measured above, within, and below the stream-crossing structures' zone of influence include stream channel slope, stream flows at specified times of migration, sediment supply, wood loadings, channel cross-sectional area, and particle size distribution. Chapters 3, 6, and 8 provide detail on the types of physical parameters (e.g., habitat, sediment, wood, nutrients) that may be useful for various types of restoration projects, and these parameters often can be readily applied to barrier removal and reconnection of isolated habitats.

For culverts and other stream crossings, computer software is available to help estimate the ability of various species at various life stages and various flows to pass through culvert designs. One such program, FishXing, requires location, fish species of concern, culvert type and material, culvert inlet type and condition, culvert outlet type and condition, upstream and downstream channel width, channel slope, water depth, bank-full width, bank-full depth, channel roughness, and streambed elevation at specific points, such as the inlet, outlet, and tailout (USFS 2000). Choice of measurements for habitat quality of newly accessible habitat will depend on the types of habitat (e.g., stream, floodplain, estuary).

Summary

In this chapter, we provided an overview of barrier removal and reconnection of isolated habitats and summarized the considerations for monitoring fish response to these modifications. As with all restoration monitoring, having clear objectives and hypotheses is critical to a successful monitoring program. Evaluation of fish response can be as simple as determining whether fish use the newly available habitat or are able to access an individual site. Although determining the effects on the entire population can be more challenging, this can be achieved through trapping and estimating fish abundance at multiple locations at a reach or site scale and at a watershed scale to determine the proportion being contributed by newly available habitats. Some watersheds and states have large status monitoring and trend monitoring programs that provide the opportunity to link simple individual project monitoring to larger monitoring programs and to evaluate watershed-scale or population-scale effects for a relatively small amount of monitoring effort. Future research and monitoring should focus on determining the effects of an individual barrier removal project on a watershed or population. It also is important to monitor physical variables such as available habitat, habitat quality (e.g., pool number, frequency, LWD), factors such as channel slope and substrate type, and other factors that may affect the ability of fish to migrate through a passage structure. While culvert replacement and reconnecting isolated habitats are common restoration techniques and relatively easy to evaluate, few studies have been reported in the scientific literature. Today, there are ample opportunities for these types of studies, which could help answer some of the basic questions related to habitat reconnection and could contribute to the evolution of our methodologies.

References

Armstrong, J. D., V. A. Braithwaite, and P. Rycroft. 1996. A flat-bed passive integrated transponder antenna array for monitoring behaviour of Atlantic salmon parr and other fish. Journal of Fish Biology 48:539–541.

Beamer, E., T. Beechie, and J. Klochak. 1998. A strategy for implementation, effectiveness, and validation monitoring of habitat restoration projects with two examples from the Skagit River, Washington. Skagit System Cooperative, Challenge Cost Agreement 94-04-05-01-050, La Connor, Washington.

Beechie, T., E. Beamer, L. Wasserman. 1994. Estimating coho salmon rearing habitat and smolt production losses in a large river basin, and implications for restoration. North American Journal of Fisheries Management 14:797–811.

Belford, D. A., and W. R. Gould. 1989. An evaluation of trout passage through six highway culverts in Montana. North American Journal of Fisheries Management 9:437–445.

Bryant, M. D., B. J. Frenette, and S. J. McCurdy. 1999. Colonization of a watershed by anadromous salmonids following the installation of a fish ladder in Margaret Creek, southeast Alaska. North American Journal of Fisheries Management 19:1129–1136.

Buijse, A. D., H. Coops, M. Staras, L. H. Jans, G. J. Van Geest, R. E. Grifts, B. W. Ibelings, W. Oosterberg, and F. C. J. M. Roozen. 2002. Restoration strategies for river floodplains along large lowland rivers in Europe. Freshwater Biology 47:889–907.

CDFG (California Department of Fish and Game). 2000. Fish screening criteria. Online at http://www.iep.water.ca.gov/cvffrt/DFGCriteria2.htm [Accessed 3 Sept. 2003].

Clay, C. H. 1995. Design of fishways and other fish facilities. Lewis Publishers, Boca Raton, Florida.

Conroy, S. C. 1997. Habitat lost and found, part two. Pages 16–22 *in* Washington Trout, editors. Washington Trout Technical Report 7(1). Washington Trout, Duvall, Washington.

Dugan, P., editor. 1993. Wetlands in danger: a world conservation atlas. Oxford University Press, New York.

Eaglin, G. S., and W. A. Hubert. 1993. Effects of logging and roads on substrate and trout in streams of the medicine bow national forest, Wyoming. North American Journal of Fisheries Management 13:844–846.

Furniss, M. J., T. D. Roelofs, and C. S. Yee. 1991. Road construction and maintenance. Pages 297–324 *in* W. R. Meehan, editor. Influences of forest and rangeland management on salmonid fishes and their habitats. American Fisheries Society, Special Publication 19, Bethesda, Maryland.

Gende, S. M., R. T. Edwards, M. F. Willson, and M. S. Wipfli. 2002. Pacific salmon in aquatic and terrestrial ecosystems. Bioscience 52:917–927.

Glen, D. 2002. Recovery of salmon and trout following habitat enhancement works: review of case studies 1995–2002. Pages 93–112 *in* M. O'Grady, editor. Proceedings of the 13th International Salmonid Habitat Enhancement Workshop, Westport, County Mayo, Ireland, September 2002. Central Fisheries Board, Dublin, Ireland.

Iversen, T. M., B. Kronvang, B. L. Madsen, P. Markmann, and M. B. Nielsen. 1993. Re-establishment of Danish streams: restoration and maintenance measures. Aquatic Conservation: Marine and Freshwater Ecosystems 3:73–92.

Langill, D. A., and P. J. Zamora. 2002. An audit of small culvert installations in Nova Scotia: habitat loss and habitat fragmentation. Canadian Technical Report of Fisheries and Aquatic Sciences 2422.

Montgomery, D. R., E. M. Beamer, G. Pess, and T. P. Quinn. 1999. Channel type and salmonid spawning distribution and abundance. Canadian Journal of Fisheries and Aquatic Sciences 56:377–387.

Montgomery, D. R., and J. M. Buffington. 1997. Channel-reach morphology in mountain drainage basins. Geological Society of America Bulletin 109:596–611.

Moore, K. M. S., K. K. Jones, and J. M. Dambacher. 1997. Methods for stream habitat surveys. Oregon Department of Fish and Wildlife, Fisheries Division Information Report 97-4, Salem.

NMFS (National Marine Fisheries Service). 1997. Fish screening criteria for anadromous salmonids. Online at http://swr.ucsd.edu/hcd/fishscrn.htm [Accessed 3 September 2003].

Novinger, D. C., and F. J. Rahel. 2003. Isolation management with artificial barriers as a conservation strategy for cutthroat trout in headwater streams. Conservation Biology 17:772–781.

ODFW (Oregon Department of Fish and Wildlife). 2001. Guidelines and Criteria for stream-road crossings. Online at http://www.dfw.state.or.us/ODFWhtml/InfoCntrFish/Management/stream_road.htm [Accessed 3 September 2003].

OGNRO (Oregon Governor's Natural Resource Office) 2001. The Oregon plan for salmon and watersheds. Progress and reports. Online at http://www.oregon-plan.org. [Accessed 3 September 2003].

Pess, G. R., T. J. Beechie, J. E. Williams, D. R. Whitall, J. I. Lange, and J. R. Klochak. 2003. Watershed assessment techniques and the success of aquatic restoration activities. Pages 185–201 *in* R. C. Wissmar and P. A. Bisson, editors. Strategies for restoring river ecosystems: sources of variability and uncertainty in natural and managed systems. American Fisheries Society, Bethesda, Maryland.

Peterson, N. P. 1980. The role of spring ponds in the winter ecology and natural production of coho salmon (*Oncorhynchus nerka*) on the Olympic Peninsula, Washington. Master's thesis. University of Washington, Seattle.

Roni, P., T. J. Beechie, R. E. Bilby, F. E. Leonetti, M. M. Pollock, and G. R. Pess. 2002. A review of stream restoration techniques and a hierarchical strategy for prioritizing restoration in Pacific Northwest watersheds. North American Journal of Fisheries Management 22:1–20.

Scully, R. J., E. J. Leitzinger, and C. E. Petrosky. 1990. Idaho habitat evaluation for off-site mitigation record, Part I, Subproject I – Annual Report 1988. Prepared for U. S. Department of Energy, Bonneville Power Administration, Contract Report De-179-84BP13381, Portland, Oregon.

Shafer, C. J. 1995. Values and shortcomings of small reserves. Bioscience 45:80–88.

Slaney, P. A., and D. Zaldokas. 1997. Fish habitat rehabilitation procedures. British Columbia, Ministry of Environment, Lands and Parks and Ministry of Forests, Vancouver.

Taylor, D. S., G. R. Poulakis, S. R. Kupschus, and C. H. Faunce. 1998. Estuarine reconnection of an impounded mangrove salt marsh in the Indian River Lagoon, Florida: short-term changes in fish fauna. Mangrove Salt Marshes 2:29–36.

USFS (U. S. Forest Service). 2000. FishXing, software and learning system for fish passage through culverts. Sixes River National Forest, Arcata, California. Online at http://www.stream.fs.fed.us/fishxing [Accessed 3 September 2003].

USGAO (U. S. General Accounting Office). 2001. Land management agencies: restoring fish passage through culverts on forest service and BLM lands in Oregon and Washington could take decades. U. S. General Accounting Office, GAO-02-136, Washington, D. C.

Vaughan, D. M. 2002. Potential impact of road-stream crossings (culverts) on the upstream passage of aquatic macroinvertebrates. Report prepared for the U. S. Forest Service San Dimas Technology Center. The Xerces Society, Portland, Oregon.

Warren, M. L. J., and M. G. Pardew. 1998. Road crossings as barriers to small-stream fish movement. Transactions of the American Fisheries Society 127:637–644.

WDFW (Washington Department of Fish and Wildlife). 1998. Fish passage barrier assessment and prioritization manual. Washington Department of Fish and Wildlife, Olympia.

WDFW (Washington Department of Fish and Wildlife). 2003. Design of road culverts for fish passage. Online at http://www.wa.gov/wdfw/hab/engineer/cm/culvert_manual_final.pdf [Accessed 3 September 2003].

Wellman, J. C., D. L. Combs, and S. B. Cook. 2000. Long-term impacts of bridge and culvert construction or replacement on fish communities and sediment characteristics in streams. Journal of Freshwater Ecology 15:317–328.

Yanes, M., J. M. Velasco, and F. Suarez. 1995. Permeability of roads and railways to vertebrates: the importance of culverts. Biological Conservation 71:217–222.

Chapter 11
Monitoring of Acquisitions and Conservation Easements

Gino Lucchetti, Klaus O. Richter, Ruth E. Schaefer

King County Department of Natural Resources and Parks
201 South Jackson, Suite 600, Seattle, Washington 98117, USA
Gino.Lucchetti@metrokc.gov, Klaus.Richter@metrokc.gov, Ruth.Schaefer@metrokc.gov

Introduction

Effective restoration requires a holistic view of the watershed and, depending on the nature of impacts, a broad set of actions applied at multiple scales (May et al. 1997; Frissell and Ralph 1998). Structural solutions (e.g., riparian planting, adding wood to streams, fencing) and regulatory measures such as streamside buffers may not be sufficient or appropriate to protect sensitive habitats, key species, or more encompassing ecological processes (USCOTA 1989). Thus, acquisitions and conservation easements (ACE) that acquire critical habitat lands or that protect important ecological processes are valuable and, in some cases, essential tools in stream and watershed restoration. In spite of the potential importance of ACEs and the considerable past effort and ongoing interest throughout much of North America in acquiring them, little attention has been given to monitoring their effectiveness in meeting habitat- or species-based protection and restoration goals, or to methods of monitoring them. As with other management actions, without a solid monitoring program, the effectiveness of ACEs cannot be measured. Ultimately, if the habitat or species benefits of ACEs are not demonstrated, money is wasted and their value questioned, thereby risking loss of future funding and natural resource conservation. Monitoring also provides valuable information for future stream and watershed restoration actions.

There are two broad reasons for using ACEs to protect habitat. The first is to preserve a unique or valuable habitat or to acquire an area that has high natural potential for restoration. Within aquatic ecosystems, such areas often include high-quality stream reaches, springs, side channels, or confluence areas that provide critical spawning, nursery, or rearing functions. These areas also could be highly sensitive, irreplaceable wetlands, such as bogs and fens, or highly productive estuarine and marine habitats, including sloughs and eel grass or kelp beds. Such habitats tend to exhibit high biological productivity or species richness and often are critical for rare or endangered species. They also tend to be highly susceptible to development and other anthropogenic impacts.

The second reason for using ACEs is that they serve as buffers from human impacts or provide natural materials and processes necessary for adjacent targeted habitats to persist. Lands commonly protected for these purposes include upland forests, which can be important for their hydrological, geomorphological, chemical, and biological functions (e.g., protection of natural base and storm flows, slope stabilization, nutrient cycling, woody debris recruitment).

This chapter is intended to assist the reader in establishing a monitoring program for ACEs that may be part of a larger stream and watershed restoration strategy. Information on the types, the history, and the range of goals of ACEs is provided, an overview of issues and techniques applicable to their monitoring is presented, and several examples of how ACEs could be monitored are described. Acquisitions and conservation easements are found in a wide array of landscape settings and are acquired for equally diverse environmental purposes; therefore, there is no standard procedure for monitoring them. There are, however, common practical and technical issues related to their monitoring, such as establishing context (landscape, biological, ecological, and geomorphological) and basic monitoring concepts and activities (types, goals, objectives, study design, and field and analytical techniques) that should be considered in establishing a monitoring program. Consequently, this chapter is not a cookbook. Rather, it intends to provide contextual information as guidance in developing specific ACE monitoring plans.

Definitions and Types of Acquisitions and Conservation Easements

An acquisition (commonly called fee simple acquisition by real estate and land trust practitioners) is defined as the result of purchasing all rights an existing owner may have to the land, including that of "quiet enjoyment" in perpetuity. An easement is defined as a nonpossessory interest granted in the lands of another (Pestinger et al. 1991) established to obtain certain limited rights (e.g., development rights but never the right to quiet enjoyment) that often are in perpetuity but sometimes for only set periods of time. Easements are used in lieu of acquisition for a wide variety of purposes, ranging from temporary construction access and short- or long-term maintenance of a public facility, such as a road, a utility, or a trail to broad-scale, long-term natural resource conservation, such as protecting forest expanses to safeguard specific habitats and species along with the hydrology, sediment, and local climate-driven processes that affect them.

Choosing when and where to implement an acquisition or easement, or some combination thereof, can be complex. Conservation easements usually are obtained when acquisition is prohibitively expensive, is not needed to meet conservation goals, or is unacceptable to the landowner. Acquisitions can be a straightforward approach to land protection. But they also can be very difficult and time consuming to negotiate, especially if an owner is unwilling to sell the property. Conservation easements, on the other hand, are less costly up front and offer more flexibility for landowners and the agencies or nongovernmental organizations (NGO) that acquire them. They can, however, be equally difficult to negotiate and manage, and they may require additional monitoring for compliance to ensure the terms of the easement are being met.

There are three basic ways in which conservation easements are obtained. First, selected property rights are bought outright when a private landowner has lands of special value for natural resource protection or restoration goals, and those lands are not otherwise protected through a regulatory mechanism. Second, they are established as a regulatory condition of land development or to mitigate land-use impacts. Such easements typically are established as open-space tracts or native growth protection easements (NGPE) to protect sensitive areas such as streams, wetlands, and upland native vegetation or other critical fish and wildlife habitats. This type of easement usually is established in conjunction with subdivision, commercial, and industrial development. A third type of conservation easement is obtained through tax incentives or the transfer of development rights, in which landowners commit to certain land uses (such as forest management or native growth protection) that reduce the highest- and best-use basis for taxation. Examples of the third type of program are the King County Public Benefits Rating System and the Transfer of Development Credits programs in Washington State (King County 2001). Under the former program landowners receive a 50 to 90% reduction in taxes for voluntarily conserving and protecting land resources, open space, and timber. In the latter program, landowners can sell their zoned or vested residential densities (number of potential housing units per acre) to developers of projects within urban areas that are granted development density bonuses in exchange for purchase of such easements.

For more information regarding easements, especially how they are used by NGOs and legal, tax, and landowner issues, the reader is encouraged to contact organizations such as the Land Trust Alliance (Washington, D.C.; www.lta.org), the Northern California Regional Land Trust (Chico, California; www.landconservation.org), and the Cascade Land Conservancy (Seattle, Washington; www.cascadeland.org), among many others.

A Brief History of Acquisitions and Conservation Easements

Federal and state governments and larger well-established conservation groups have been acquiring land and easements for ecological purposes for more than 100 years in North America. Specifically, numerous federal agencies have purchased national parks, forests, and wildlife refuges for the protection of a wide array of ecosystems and their biota. Large, well-established NGOs such as the Nature Conservancy and the Audubon Society also have been acquiring and managing lands for ecosystem and species protection for anywhere from 50 to 100 years.

Increasingly, cities, counties, and other local jurisdictions, in addition to smaller, regionally or locally based NGOs, are devoting technical and financial resources to acquiring property and easements as part of a larger strategy for stream and watershed protection and restoration. This strategy also is being used to achieve species protection goals. Today, there are active land conservation efforts throughout the United States and in much of Canada. Over the last 10-year period (1991–2001), the Seattle-based nonprofit Cascade Land Trust acquired 3,278 ha (8,100 acres) at a cost of $50 million in three rapidly developing central Puget Sound counties (King, Pierce, and Snohomish). From 1995 to 2001, Portland (Oregon) Metro acquired 2,800 ha (6,920 acres) in 14 regional target areas, and six trail and greenway project areas for $98.2 million; another $22.5 million is still to be spent (Metro 2001). Furthermore, 10% of the 358,990 ha (887,082 acres) of conservation lands in the San Francisco Bay area have been protected with easements, two-thirds of which have been created since 1950 (BAOSC 1999).

One large-scale forest conservation effort is worth noting. The Pingree Conservation Easement in Maine was negotiated by the New England Forestry Foundation (NEFF) in March 2001 (Sader et al. 2002). Totaling 308,449 ha (762,192 acres), it is the largest easement in the United States. It ensures that 3,056 square km (1,180 square miles) of forest will be protected from development. The forest has been certified by the Sustainable Forestry Initiative, helping to ensure that timber harvesting will be conducted in a sustainable and environmentally sensitive manner. According to Sader et al. (2002), special features of this easement include 3,200 km of river frontage, 2,900 ha of wetlands, 110 remote lakes and ponds larger than 1.25 ha, 67 rare and endangered plant sites (including five sites with federally listed plants), and numerous other fragile and important habitats.

Setting the Ecological Context

Setting the ecological context of an ACE or a suite of ACEs can help clarify and guide subsequent monitoring efforts. Critical to this is understanding that ACEs, in essence, are pieces of habitat that often support sensitive, protected, or otherwise important species and biological communities. Therefore, they can be extremely effective components of stream and watershed restoration programs. Because many factors can make an ACE valuable, some level of monitoring may be useful (Table 1). To help the reader understand the ecological context of an ACE, this subsection summarizes some key ecological concepts and issues related to those factors.

Patches and Core Areas

Landscape ecology assesses the functional role of discrete patches (landscape heterogeneity) across landscapes (Farina 1998). Correspondingly, conservation biology uses the concepts of core areas, metapopulations, and source-sink dynamics to draw inferences about the uneven distribution of individuals of a given population or groups of populations.

Weins (1997) identified four aspects of patches: quality, boundaries, context, and connectivity. Patch quality can be characterized by availability of benefits (food, mates, or shelter) and costs (predation, physiological stress, competition). Boundaries affect the rate and timing of movements of organisms, materials, nutrients, or disturbances between patches. Patch context refers to the effect of the surrounding landscape on the functioning of a patch. And, connectivity is the degree of linkage among elements of an entire landscape. Weins said, "these features are defined by the structure of a landscape mosaic and by the responses of organisms to that mosaic structure." Thus, it is important to understand both the physical and biological context of an ACE patch.

Kaufmann (1962) described core areas as those places within a species range used more intensively than other areas and that contain the home sites, refuges, and most dependable food sources. Core areas have been widely used in describing relative use by wildlife (Samuel et al. 1985; Bingham and Noon 1997). The concept also has been proposed for management of threatened and endangered salmon (NMFS 1996).

Table 1.
Issues and variables to consider in monitoring acquisitions and easements.

Issues	Variables to assess
Landowner and human use	Existing and ad hoc trails, garbage dumping, artificial landscaping, unpermitted vegetation removal, tree cutting, etc.
Invasive and exotic plants	Species, number, density, dominance, and aggressiveness of species on or near site; level of threat, effectiveness of control or eradication methods
Habitat	Type, and area of habitat patches, structural complexity of habitats, connectivity with other patches, internal and external processes that form and sustain habitat patches
Land use	Extent, type, and intensity of land uses on and adjacent to the site and in the surrounding reach and watershed
Fish and wildlife use	Presence of key (rare, endangered, keystone, indicator) species; types of behavior (reproduction, rearing, refuge, migration); abundance, productivity, survival and growth rates of key species
Biodiversity value	On site and contributes to species and community richness, measures of biodiversity, native or other desired species
Restoration potential	Comparison of existing and predevelopment conditions, actions needed to improve or fully restore the site, reach or watershed conditions
Physiobiological processes	Hydrology, water quality, sediment and nutrient supply, large woody debris recruitment, location and rates of bank erosion and channel migration

Assessing differential use by species of certain habitats, river reaches, or subbasins within watersheds may help to define the location and extent of a core area. For example, Fukushima (2001) found that Sakhalin taimen *Hucho perryi* in low-gradient streams had a strong preference for spawning in reaches with high sinuosity. Geist (2000) found fall chinook salmon *Oncorhynchus tshawytscha* in the Hanford Reach of the Columbia River spawned preferentially in areas with hyporheic discharge into the river. And Pess et al. (2002) found adult coho salmon *O. kisutch* densities in the Snohomish River basin of Washington to be correlated with wetland occurrence, local geology, stream gradient, and land use. They found that median densities of coho spawners in forest-dominated areas were 1.5–3.5 times the densities in rural, urban, and agricultural areas. Furthermore, relationships between these habitat characteristics and adult coho salmon abundance were consistent over time. Such studies provide useful information to help identify core areas.

The extent to which an ACE encompasses or is part of a larger habitat patch or core area for a species or population is important to determine because it helps land managers understand the biological context and, therefore, the potential conservation role of an ACE. Effectively applying these concepts requires knowledge about the surrounding landscape and how species use an ACE. For example, does it contain all or just a portion of a species' core area? If the entire core area is within the ACE, is it of sufficient size and shape to have high-quality habitat for the species of concern? Is it connected via suitable, intact migration corridors to other core areas or key habitat patches? Clearly, local extinction probabilities increase proportionately with decreasing size and quality of habitat patches and core area, and with increasing edge habitat conditions and physical isolation. If the core area is partially outside the ACE or integral to a patch mosaic beyond the ACE boundary, are there barriers to fish and wildlife dispersal beyond the control of ACE management? Isolation of habitat patches used by interacting populations also increases the probability of within-patch extinction as metapopulation dynamics are altered or halted: recolonization processes may be slowed or stopped and migration reduced. Consequently, ACEs and respective patch selection for conservation should not solely be based on their unique characteristics but also on their contribution to the overall system, chiefly, how well the area functionally links with adjacent and discontinuous areas. For fish and wildlife, such functional links are determined by patch mosaics, size and core areas, edges and boundaries, and corridors and connectivity, all of which affect the life strategy of a species and the dynamics of a population.

Watershed Location

An ACE's location in a watershed plays a major role in its potential value for stream and watershed restoration and has a major bearing on the questions asked in a monitoring plan. Whether an ACE is located along a stream or in an upland area and whether it is in a headwater or lower watershed setting strongly affects its role and value. For example, a headwater ACE may play a greater or more critical role in stream hydrology and sediment routing processes than one located at or very near a stream mouth. Conversely, ACEs situated along or encompassing side channels, stream confluences, or estuaries often are sites of high direct use, productivity, and biodiversity for fishes and a host of other species.

Natural Disturbances

Wind, fire, drought, landslide, erosion, and other natural disturbances are important processes in shaping habitats (Benda et al. 1998; Wissmar and Beschta 1998; Reice 2001). Sometimes those responsible for managing ACEs view disturbances as threats to a site's integrity. However, at natural rates and magnitudes, such disturbances may be necessary to achieve certain biological goals with minimal cost and intervention. Flooding and lateral channel migration form and maintain complex substrate, in-channel, and channel-edge conditions, inputs of gravel, large woody debris (LWD; Bilby and Bisson 1998), and the formation of logjams, side channels, oxbows, and riparian wetlands used by a wide variety of invertebrates (Hershey and Lamberti 1998), fish (Reeves et al. 1998), and wildlife (Kelsey and West 1998). In terrestrial systems, fire is often a necessary prerequisite for the reproduction of some plants (e.g., lodgepole pine *Pinus contorta*, several oak *Quercus* spp., and fireweed *Epilobium angustifolium*). Many other plant and animal communities, such as the Douglas-fir *Pseudotsuga menziesii* and ponderosa pine *P. ponderosa* forests with deer *Odocoileus* spp., elk *Cervus canadensis*, cavity-nesting woodpeckers (e.g., pileated woodpecker *Dryocopus pileatus*), and owls (Strigiformes), and steppe grasslands with pronghorn antelope *Antilocapra americana*, bison *Bison bison*, raptors (Accipiters and Falconiformes), and grouse (e.g., sage grouse *Centrocercus urophasianus*) benefit from periodic burning (Thomas et al. 1979; Askins 2000; O'Neil et al. 2000). Wind and landslides also create mosaics of topography, soil, and vegetation that serve to maintain plant and animal diversity. Wind-caused blowdown recycles energy and nutrients through forests and adjacent aquatic ecosystems. Landslides and bank erosion replenish spawning gravel, woody debris, and other organic matter.

Exceptions to the value of natural disturbances are probably few and limited to only those situations where (1) an endemic and very rare species has become isolated to the point where extraordinary measures are necessary to protect it in situ or (2) where human life and property are at stake. In such cases, part of the monitoring should be focused on evaluating conditions that can help predict and avoid additional deleterious disturbances to the species or life and property in question.

Invasive Species

Acquisitions and conservation easements often are selected and justified for conservation because they provide functional linkages between aquatic and terrestrial ecosystems and habitats. As such, they can help decrease riparian and terrestrial habitat fragmentation, species isolation, and associated extinction mechanisms, such as inbreeding depression. Conversely, such transition ACEs may function as corridors for the dispersal of invasive species (Dawson 1994). Species from other parts of the world may cause environmental degradation or economic harm or threaten human health by displacing native species, altering predator–prey relationships, destroying crops, and decreasing ecosystem resiliency and native species populations (USEPA 2001a). Sometimes exotic species invasions are facilitated by deliberate introduction (e.g., planting purple loosestrife *Lythrum salicaria* or stocking waters with exotic fishes (Williams 1980; Nico and Fuller 1999) and amphibians (Jennings and Hayes 1985). In other instances, endemic species that are highly tolerant of degraded conditions become aggressive and invasive (Koch and Reddy 1992; Urban et al. 1993; Davis 1994; Scott and Helfman 2001).

The ecological impact caused by some aquatic invaders (e.g., purple loosestrife, reed canarygrass *Phalaris arundinacea*, spartina *Spartina patens*, common cattail *Typha latifolia*) and animals (e.g., zebra mussel *Dreissena polymorpha* and green crab *Carcinus maenas*) is considered so severe that major programs have been developed to eradicate or to minimize their presence. Scientists have linked exotic species invasions to 70% of the extinctions of native aquatic species documented during the past century (USEPA 2001a). Damages to landowners attributable to exotic species invasions currently total more than $1 billion per year in treatment costs and lost productivity. Moreover, this estimate does not consider the public costs of wildlife loss, displacement of endangered species, and reduced opportunities for fishing, hunting, camping, and other recreation (Pimentel et al. 2000; USEPA 2001a). Forty-two percent of U.S. endangered and threatened species have declined, in part, because of exotic species, and at least 3 of 24 known extinctions were wholly or partially caused by hybridization between closely related exotic and native species (Schmitz and Simberloff 1997).

Occasionally, acquired lands are devoid of invasive species; thus, a prime focus of monitoring is surveying the surroundings for invasive species, because any nearby infestations could readily expand their distribution into the ACE. It is critical to prevent infestation and to eradicate potentially aggressive species as soon as they are detected and when such invasions are small and more readily controlled. More often than not, however, ACEs have at least some degradation by exotic or invasive species. Consequently, the removal or control of invasive and exotic species as a restoration action may be a reason for its acquisition.

Human Impacts

Acquisitions and conservation easements are usually acquired to protect an area from human impacts, repair past impacts, or provide materials or processes important for a nearby habitat. Once acquired, however, there is often no guarantee that impacts will stop. ACEs in developed or developing landscapes may remain exposed to impacts caused by adjacent human activities. Land development can alter hydrology and sediment regimes (Booth and Jackson 1994; Schueler 1994; Booth and Henshaw 2001). Stress from habitat deterioration and anthropogenic actions may additionally increase the risk of disease (Denver 1997) and even the interaction of factors (Relyea and Mills 2001) to plants and animals using the ACE. Landscape fragmentation caused by clearing, buildings, roads, and other human infrastructure tends to isolate ACEs, decreasing their value as habitat patches for sensitive species and their connectivity with other patches. Even large expanses of forest, which may have considerable buffering capacity, can be affected by disease or other stress-mediated factors, such as far-ranging climate and air quality changes. For example, some national parks in California are affected by airborne pollutants from developed areas of the state (Sullivan et al. 2001). Also, in California, Sparling et al. (2001) provide evidence that wind-blown pesticides from the heavily agricultural Central Valley play a role in the decline of amphibians in Yosemite and Sequoia National Parks.

Locally, a variety of impacts can occur from the day-to-day activities of people living in or near ACEs. Examples of such impacts include ad hoc trail building, garbage dumping, pet intrusion, illegal clearing, and other anthropogenic encroachments. Relatively little study has been devoted to evaluating such activities or their impacts, but they can be a serious problem, especially in suburban and urban areas. For example, Baker and Haemmerle (1990) evaluated 34 randomly chosen sites comprising 62 NGPEs along streams, wetlands, and steep slopes in developing areas of western King County, Washington. They found that two-thirds of these sites had been altered, and, of those, 25% had been negatively affected. Moreover, the number and seriousness of impacts increased with the increasingly intense residential development near the NGPEs.

Developing a Monitoring and Evaluation Program

Monitoring Types and Purposes

MacDonald et al. (1991) identified seven types of monitoring distinguished more by the purpose than by the type and intensity of measurements. Of the seven, three (baseline, effectiveness, and compliance) are highly relevant for ACE monitoring. In general, monitoring an ACE would be done to address one or more of three basic questions: (1) what are the current site conditions, (2) what (if any) changes are occurring, and (3) if changes are occurring, are they consistent with the goals for the ACE?

The most immediate purpose for monitoring is for compliance to detect illegal encroachments and to ensure that easement conditions are being met. Assuming the site is protected from these impacts, the next purpose of ACE monitoring is to establish a baseline of the condition and variability of physical, chemical, and biological parameters. The third purpose of ACE monitoring is to assess an ACE's effectiveness in conservation goal(s) at the reach or the watershed scale. As with many other forms of natural resource monitoring, it generally is preferable to measure effectiveness by directly monitoring biological parameters (Karr 1998; Karr and

Chu 1999), such as the presence, the abundance, the diversity, and the use by key species of biota, rather than the physical and chemical condition of sites. An exception to this may be when an ACE is obtained for the express purpose of protecting a critical and unique habitat feature (e.g., a rare spawning site or nesting tree). Moreover, effectiveness also is best examined by assessing the cumulative effects of one or more ACEs over a stream or watershed and over a relatively long time period (Wissmar 1993). To accomplish such monitoring may require more baseline information than would be available to someone initiating a monitoring program for a single ACE or even a handful of ACEs. Thus, effectiveness monitoring may be best implemented as part of a larger watershed monitoring program. Ultimately, as more reach- and watershed-level data become available, effectiveness monitoring will play a larger role in assessing the functions and the values of ACEs and their cumulative contribution toward restoration on the reach and watershed scales.

Monitoring Goals and Objectives

Monitoring intention can be formulated as a broad goal, such as assessing the role of the ACE (or multiple ACEs) in stream and watershed restoration, or a specific objective, such as addressing the impact of a particular legal or biological issue (e.g., whether easement conditions are being met or whether a specific habitat type or function is protected). For compliance, the Land Trust Alliance (1993) operating manual outlines four monitoring goals: (1) to catch violations, (2) to develop landowner relations (both for educational purposes and to help avoid violations), (3) to save time and money (again, to catch violations before they become adversarial), and (4) to establish a record in case of court action. However, the manual provides no explicit monitoring guidance for evaluating ecological or biological condition or for determining effectiveness in achieving such goals.

For stream and watershed restoration, an ACE monitoring program might evaluate one or more of the following goals: (1) to preserve or to protect areas (aquatic habitats and the watersheds that sustain them) that are of high quality or importance for species protection (e.g., preserving the last best places or known critical nesting or spawning areas for rare and endemic species); (2) to acquire land or easements for an area that could be restored to a healthy, high-quality condition; and (3) to serve more comprehensive purposes such as the protection or the restoration of hydrology, water quality, sediment regimes, and other ecological processes critical for protection or restoration of biological functions and values. This latter goal requires ecologically appropriate, landscape-based restoration, which has come to be identified as the only viable way to achieve comprehensive and sustainable aquatic resource protection and restoration (Frissell and Ralph 1998).

When there is uncertainty about the goals of an ACE, steps should be taken to resolve or to minimize the uncertainty before any formal monitoring is undertaken. These steps should include obtaining site-specific scientific knowledge from local managers, NGOs, and the public; visiting sites, reviewing maps, and aerial and satellite imagery; and reviewing historical information, including any other existing information derived from previous site-specific, reach, or watershed surveys. These preliminary actions will help clarify the relevant issues inherent to each ACE, supply site-specific background needed to establish appropriate goals (and specific objectives), and help determine the monitoring requirements and increase the efficiency of future monitoring efforts. If such a process is not possible, the individuals responsible for monitoring should document their perception of the ACE goals as clearly as possible. These goals then will need to be transformed into clear objectives and hypotheses that can be tested to determine if the goals are being met.

However, determining habitat- and species-based objectives may be problematic for at least three reasons. First, the manager or the scientist may find that detailed technical objectives were not formulated to justify an ACE or that, to the extent an ACE has articulated goals, they may be vaguely defined or difficult to translate into specific objectives for establishing a monitoring program. For example, "protecting the last best places" or "preventing forest tracts from development" are common reasons for purchasing ACEs, but neither is sufficiently explicit for science-based monitoring. Thus, scientists must determine appropriate technical monitoring objectives to provide usable information with limited budgets. The Vermont Land Trust is a notable exception to this common lack of articulated goals. In that ACE program, an average easement contributes $7,000 to an endowment (Ratley-Beach et al. 2002), a portion of which is earmarked specifically for monitoring. Currently, the Vermont Land Trust endowment is about $5 million (P. Bristow, Vermont Land Trust, personal communication).

Second, ACEs usually are protective, hands-off actions, not typically classified or perceived as requiring active or goal-oriented management. Consequently, it can be challenging to identify the salient conservation goals for features or functions of the ACE, to select appropriate methods to quantify and to monitor these features for changes (trends) over time, and to use this information to determine whether goals and objectives are met. These initially vague programs are in stark contrast to other conservation programs that specify active restoration objectives, such as adding LWD to a channel or fencing off and planting a riparian area. In addition, conservation programs with specific objectives achieve results that are more likely to produce discrete changes; such programs also can measure beneficial or detrimental effects within a standardized experimental framework.

Third, ACEs often exhibit a high degree of variability in size, shape, and location; in physical, chemical, and biological characteristics; and in landscape, landownership, and land-use context. Thus, the full extent of an ACE's ecologically or biologically important functions and values may not be obvious. However, these are the functions that, when added cumulatively over the long term, are likely to have the greatest long-term management value (Wissmar 1993). This is especially true for many individual ACEs because each typically will be too small to meet all conservation needs. Cumulatively, however, they may contribute to these needs. For example, Booth et al. (2002) suggested that surface water management programs should preserve or restore a minimum of 65% forest cover in lowland watersheds of the Puget Sound region to provide adequate hydrologic functioning for stream- and water-quality protection and to meet flood hazard reduction goals. Because of socioeconomic and constitutional issues, the attainment of this level of forest cover in developing areas will likely require acquisition over time of a multitude of publicly held open spaces and easements from private landowners. Therefore, monitoring the preservation or restoration of a certain percentage and distribution of forest cover on a subwatershed or watershed scale may be preferred to monitoring individual properties.

Developing Hypotheses

Hypothesis setting and testing encourages managers and scientists to establish specific, quantifiable, and testable objectives. This increases the likelihood of obtaining useful, unambiguous results. Depending on the goals and the condition of an ACE, monitoring would be conducted to collect information to test the hypothesis that the ACE is being maintained at, or restored to, the desired condition. When the existing condition is satisfactory, the monitoring goal would be to collect information to test the hypothesis that site conditions are being maintained or perhaps improving. In this instance, an appropriate hypothesis to test is whether a habitat condition or species use has declined during the monitoring period. Conversely, for degraded sites where active or passive restoration is proposed, change toward a specific desired condition becomes the goal, and the testable hypothesis is whether the function (e.g., spawning, rearing, migration) is being restored to the desired level within the specified time frame. An example of this may be the removal of a culvert blocking salmon migration into a potential spawning stream encompassed by an ACE. The testable hypothesis is that fish migrate into and use the stream after the culvert removal and that they use the habitat in the numbers and timing expected.

On a larger scale, hypotheses should focus on broader biological outcomes, such as maintenance or restoration of species diversity, biotic integrity or abundance, and survival and condition of key species. Thus, an appropriate hypothesis may be that an ACE (or multiple ACEs) contributes directly to a specified amount of spawning, rearing, refuge, or migration use. A less desirable hypothesis may be that it possesses the surrogate physical characteristics necessary for these functions to be achieved at a desired level. Because many biological functions in a particular stream are tied to certain conditions in the surrounding watershed and landscape, it will be important to incorporate and to measure factors such as land use and land cover that describe the condition of adjacent landscapes as well.

Study Designs

Study designs provide a framework for data collection and analysis. They help to ensure efficiency in data collection and statistical rigor for the comparisons of data collected before–after (BA) a treatment (preferably with multiple replicates) or for comparisons of treatment sites with a control or a reference site or a set of reference conditions (before–after control–impact [BACI]). When feasible, study designs are best developed with some a priori knowledge of the natural variability of the data and the sampling error of the data collection techniques, as well as a good working knowledge of the site conditions, especially spatial and temporal diversity of habitat conditions and species use.

Because ACEs tend to be passive actions (i.e., their acquisition is not an experiment), monitoring of these sites tends not to fit into the standard BA, BACI, or extensive posttreatment (EPT) monitoring design discussed in Chapter 2. There often is no treatment other than natural, passive changes, due to time and vegetation succession (Berg 1997). Thus, one may expect monitoring designs for ACEs without active management to be less statistically complicated than for projects such as instream habitat, riparian revegetation, or stream fencing, in which a variety of treatments and response variables are measured and compared to pretreatment or control conditions.

This does not necessarily mean that the monitoring issues for ACEs are less complex, however. Instead, complexities may arise from high variability in ACE shape (linear, rectangular, round); size (less than a hectare to many hundreds or thousands of hectares); habitat type (instream, riparian, and upland); physical, chemical, and biological characteristics; landowner involvement (willing, begrudging, or hostile, and present or absent); and land-use context (urban, suburban, rural, forest, or agricultural).

Because of these complexities, rigorous experimental controls and replications may be difficult to implement for ACEs, and their monitoring may best be viewed as case histories following protocols described by Conquest and Ralph (1998). For such complex sites, the simplest BA design, in which each site is a case history, a comparison of ongoing conditions may be the most useful monitoring method to detect trends. Specifically, the "before" is the condition at the time of acquisition, and the "after" is the condition at whatever time interval is deemed appropriate for monitoring. Even this design should incorporate comparable reference or control sites to evaluate whether changes in the ACE are because of site-specific factors or regional trends (such as climate or air quality) that are assumed to equally affect all areas.

In lieu of a rigorously selected control or reference site, one could establish qualitative or quantitative performance measures for healthy habitat or properly functioning conditions against which the stream or watershed within the ACE can be compared, thus, enabling both an assessment for change and an evaluation against a set of reference conditions. For example, regional indices of biotic integrity that use information about species use of high-quality or pristine habitats could provide the basis to compare the condition of degraded areas (Karr and Chu 1999). For a program restoring ridge and slough habitats of the Florida Everglades, because of the lack of historical data, Trexler et al. (2003) suggested the following set of performance measures and targets for evaluating fish community response: (1) abundance (numbers and biomass of marsh fish), (2) size distribution (range and biomass of marsh fish), (3) relative abundance of centrarchids and chubsuckers Erimyzon spp., (4) frequency of nonnative species, and (5) contaminants (level of toxins in fish).

Time Scales

A key issue in monitoring is the length of time to conduct a monitoring project and the frequency of site assessment. As a general rule, the duration of monitoring and the frequency of assessment depend upon the monitoring goals, the nature and dynamics (i.e., the variability) of the parameters being measured, and the level of change accepted as a departure from the baseline or reference site condition. Naiman (1998) describes a variety of time scales over which stream and watershed processes occur that initially can be considered as meaningful units:
1.   Up to a year for microhabitat features such as substrate composition, vegetation, and detritus
2.   Several years for changes that occur within the habitat-unit scale
3.   Decades to a century or so for processes that occur on the stream-reach scale
4.   Hundreds of years to a millennium for changes on stream-segment scale
5.   Up to a million years for processes affecting an entire stream ecosystem

These suggestions indicate that the frequency and duration of monitoring is highly dependent on geographic scale: in general, the larger the site, the longer the period over which monitoring should occur. The specific time scale for monitoring often is obtained by a "power analysis" (discussed in Chapter 2; and MacDonald et al. 1991). This analysis assesses the trade-offs between variability in factors evaluated and the intensity of monitoring needed to detect a specified probability of change.

Parameters

Once the appropriate level of effort has been determined, appropriate parameters should be chosen for monitoring (see Table 1 for examples). MacDonald and Smart (1993) and Conquest and Ralph (1998) note that the best attributes to monitor are those that:

- Will change in a measurable way in response to a treatment (such as a land-use impact or active or passive restoration program)
- Are related directly to the resources of concern
- Are not likely to be overwhelmed by confounding natural factors of scale or time

In addition to these criteria, having clear, standardized data-collection protocols to ensure quality and repeatability is important. Besides these statistical criteria, selecting variables that can be cost effectively measured also is important because funding may preclude or influence the selection and the use of certain parameters.

Parameters can range from relatively simple, straightforward measures of a condition to those that are far more complex because they are a composite of parameters. Collecting data and providing a significant amount of basic information for simple parameters is usually less costly than for complex parameters. Simple parameters include area and length of discrete habitat units, reaches, segments, or patches; site topography (slope and aspect); air- and water-quality measurements; presence, spatial and temporal distribution, and abundance of key species; and the extent and condition of particular soil or vegetation types. Because of their basic nature, these attributes lend themselves to simple comparisons via tabulation, mapping, aerial and satellite imagery, or other types of census methods.

Composite variables are those that combine or are derived from simple variables and describe a more complex and integrated condition. Composite variables may include indices intended to understand and to evaluate a site's role in the context of a stream reach, a landscape, or a watershed. Typically, the variables describe physical complexity (e.g., age and structural complexity of terrestrial habitats, or structural components of aquatic habitats) and biological community attributes (e.g., species composition, productivity, and richness).

In landscape ecology, numerous indices are derived from the combination of individual land cover and other site variables (Forman 1995; Farina 1998). Foremost among these are indices that describe the fragmentation of landscapes from measurements of individual landscape elements. An example of one such composite variable is the related circumscribing circle. This variable combines perimeter, area and length of longest axis measurements of land units, and compares this value to that of a circle that can circumscribe the patch, thereby providing an index value of 0.00–1.00 as the patch approaches a circle and exhibits the maximum core area.

Another integrated variable method used nationally is the hydrogeomorphic habitat assessment method, which quantitatively ranks a wetland's different functions (Brinson 1993; Smith et al. 1995; Shaffer et al. 1999). For example, the extent to which a wetland provides a hydrologic function is determined, in part, by the combination of several individual surrogate variables, including bank-full width, channel width to depth ratio, average channel slope, average lateral slope, and others. For identifying functions for fish and other vertebrates in riverine wetlands, the hydrogeomorphic assessment method uses measures of species abundance and richness.

Indices of biotic integrity, which have gained wide acceptance, are composite variables that directly measure biological condition rather than surrogate habitat characteristics (Hilsenhoff 1988; Karr 1998; Karr and Chu 1999). These methods assess aquatic habitat condition by evaluating community species composition, foraging guilds, and health values.

The types of composite variables described above provide greater insight into functional relationships than those derived from the collection and tabulation of data for simpler individual variables. These variables also enable the deconstruction of their composite value to identify individual variables that bias the composite value.

Recommendations for Monitoring Acquisitions and Conservation Easements

At this point, the reader is presumably well informed about the goals of the ACE, has established testable hypotheses, and has obtained a map showing conditions in and around the site, including legal boundaries (preferably a legal survey), land developments (e.g., buildings, roads, utilities), features (e.g., streams, wetlands, and lakes, topography, vegetative cover), land use, species use, and other basic information. As MacDonald and Smart (1993) discuss, monitoring is a continuum of qualitative to quantitative observations tailored to the questions that need to be answered. The following suggestions will span that continuum.

Monitoring effort

The extent to which monitoring should be conducted depends on a variety of factors. Primary among these is the presence or potential use by a rare or otherwise valuable species or biological community. Other factors include the value of the ACE for restoring or maintaining watershed processes, size, and connectivity with adjacent habitats; the level of degradation; the extent to which passive or active restoration is needed and likely to be successful; and the level of threat from future impacts, cost, and practicality (Table 1; Figure 1).

The following three examples illustrate how these factors may be evaluated to determine the appropriate level of monitoring effort (Figure 1). In the first instance, an ACE with high biological resource and watershed process value (e.g., a set of springs in which high levels of spawning or rearing occur or that contribute high-quality water for downstream spawning or rearing), and a concomitant high threat of human-caused change would warrant a high level of monitoring effort in terms of frequency, detail, and amount of sampling over time. Conversely, a small (<0.2 ha) ACE, such as a wetland or stream corridor completely surrounded by urban development, degraded by severe hydrologic changes, with no potential linkages to larger, more productive habitats, low likelihood of restoration, and high cost and difficulty for monitoring, would receive minimal monitoring. In this case, additional information would not likely be of much value for future management. Similarly, but for different reasons, a large, pristine (or nearly so) ACE situated in a remote or rural area and with no restoration needs also may receive a relatively low level of monitoring, because it may be assumed that the site's large size helps to buffer it from change, while the low threat of degradation indicates that extensive information is not needed to manage the site. Such high-quality sites, however, may warrant significant assessment for their natural baseline or comparison value.

Frequency and time frame for monitoring

Depending on the factors influencing an ACE (human activities, exotic species invasions, natural disturbances), site conditions can change quickly. Consequently, a site with high sensitivity to change should be monitored annually or even more frequently, depending on the level of threat or immediacy of such problems or changes. Significant dramatic changes, such as those from fire, flooding, wind, and other natural disturbances, may warrant monitoring at the earliest possible time after the disturbance, because data collected immediately or very soon afterward may provide a valuable baseline against which to monitor subsequent recovery and to offer insight into processes normally unobservable. Other factors, such as species use, may change relatively slowly unless driven by human or natural disturbance; thus, for these variables monitoring once a year to once every several years may be reasonable. Reach- and watershed-level attributes, such as land use and land cover, typically undergo significant change over longer intervals than either of the parameters described above. Therefore, appropriate time frames for monitoring these variables would likely range from years to decades. Finally, subtle or broad-scale changes, such as species response to climate shifts, sublethal pollution, and gradual land-use changes, may require several decades to hundreds of years to reach detectable levels within an ecosystem. For example, long-term (decadal) climatic phenomena affect both fresh and marine waters and their productivity for salmon (NRC 1995). To track these types of effects, a monitoring program that spans at least decades (possibly even hundreds of years) may be necessary. These time frames may be reduced as predictive models improve for climate change, regional biological responses, and other large-scale phenomena.

Categorizing habitats and identifying parameters to measure

Categorizing or stratifying the types of habitats in and around an ACE, and the potential parameters for evaluating those habitats and the species that use them, can be helpful in subsequent monitoring. First, categorize the ACE and its habitats, land cover types, and land uses within and adjacent to the site according to its location within the watershed. Habitat should be stratified into biologically meaningful, discrete units that can be measured, grouped, or further reduced and ultimately compared and contrasted, based on biological functions and values. For streams, a basic demarcation is the classification and quantification of pools and riffles (Hawkins

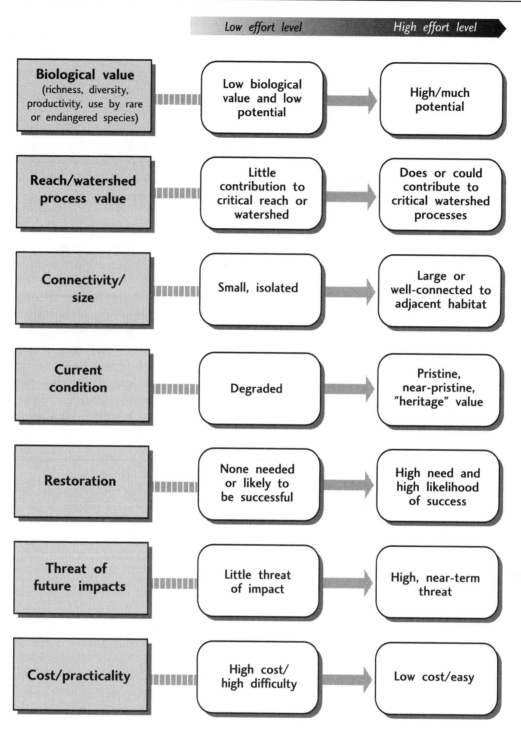

Figure 1.
Chart of factors to consider in determining appropriate level of effort for monitoring an acquisitions and conservation easement.

et al. 1993). Similarly, riparian and upland habitats can be classified in accordance with basic vegetation types, such as forest, scrub–shrub, grass, and barren areas. Depending on monitoring objectives, an even finer level of habitat classification may be required. For example, stream habitat units can be grouped by reaches or segments, based on gradient and channel morphology and valley confinement (Montgomery and Buffington 1993; Rosgen 1996). Riparian conditions can be characterized by forest type, density of vegetation, plant communities, soils, and animal use (Platts et al. 1997), as well as type and intensity of land uses. Instream conditions can be described in terms of the quantity, quality, and distribution of relatively simple habitat units (pools and riffles) and more complex subunits (substrate patches, pool tailouts, and riffle pocket water; Bisson et al. 1982;

Hawkins et al. 1993). Excellent comprehensive discussions of approaches to the measurement and assessment of aquatic habitat can be found in McMahon et al. (1996), Overton et al. (1997), and others. Classification schemes for wetlands also are available (Cowardin et al. 1979; Brinson 1993).

Once habitat is delineated to the level deemed necessary for monitoring (finer detail will be needed to make conclusions about certain changes), biological (vegetation, fish, wildlife, and benthic invertebrates), physical (flow, bank-full channel and wetted widths, substrate particle distribution, channel form, and hydraulic complexity), and chemical (temperature, dissolved oxygen, nutrients, anthropogenic compounds) conditions then can be collected, categorized, organized, and assessed. Ultimately, this information provides the basis for comparing changes in a site over time and with respect to a reference area or a prescribed set of reference characteristics (for an example, see NMFS 1996).

Riparian conditions and habitats can be assessed in terms of a variety of simple parameters, including width, slope, linear distance, location and area of vegetative communities, soils, distinct habitat types, and the type and intensity of land use. These simple parameters can be used to develop measures of structural complexity, habitat patches, species richness and diversity, and connectivity with other riparian systems or upland areas. Uplands such as midslope or ridge-top forests can be classified by their topography (e.g., slope, aspect), land cover (e.g., extent and perviousness of soil, age, type, and maturity of vegetative cover, extent and location of natural and artificial impervious surfaces), type and intensity of development (e.g., urban, suburban, commercial, industrial, rural, agriculture, forest production), and roads (e.g., distribution and density).

Delineation of physical habitat allows for meaningful classification of biological information. Consequently, once the basic template of habitat types is identified and described, the task of categorizing use by species becomes important. For vegetation as well as some animal taxa, standardized monitoring methods have been developed to document the distribution and abundance of species. In the Pacific Northwest, where salmon have been the focus of stream and watershed management for many years, reasonably reliable and detailed fish distribution maps may already exist. Nevertheless, it may be necessary to collect additional biological information, such as the location, the extent, and the degree of spawning or juvenile rearing, if those are the functions expected to benefit or change. A compendium of fisheries techniques edited by Murphy and Willis (1996) provides considerable guidance for accomplishing these tasks. For vegetation methods, Kent and Coker (1994) is a valuable resource as is Hicks (1996) for aquatic invertebrates. For vertebrates, seminal review publications include Heyer et al. (1994) for amphibians, Jones (1986) for reptiles, Ralph and Scott (1980) for birds, and Wilson et al. (1996) for mammals.

Data about the individual habitat or biological variables can be used to construct indices of habitat quality, species suitability, and ecosystem health. For animal communities, indices of biotic integrity (Karr 1998), which use information about the presence of pollution-tolerant and pollution-intolerant species, may be more meaningful in assessing biological condition and degree of impact than single species counts alone. Additional composite parameters relating habitat function and overall health to diverse anthropogenic actions have been developed for algae, vegetation, amphibians, and birds (Adamus and Brandt 1990; Adamus et al. 2001). For example, floristic quality assessments (Lopez and Fennessy 2002; Mushet et al. 2002) and bird indices of biological integrity (Adamus 2001) have been used in wetland habitat assessments and offer possibilities for monitoring the health of streams, riparian areas, and watersheds as well.

Characterization of the location, the area, the perimeter, and the condition of an ACE interior core and an edge habitat relative to key species needs also can be used to assess site value to respective species. Furthermore, measures of perimeter and internal area can be combined in various ratios and indices to assess whether a site is likely to meet its goals of providing habitats for species adapted to either edge or interior core habitats and to appraise overall habitat fragmentation.

Compliance and illegal activities

Monitoring for compliance with easement conditions and for illegal activities (clearing, building, and dumping) should be done on a regular (at least yearly) basis for all ACEs. This assessment is likely to be the least quantitative, least time consuming, and least costly. Because such information could have serious legal consequences, however, its collection should follow a rigorous and well-documented protocol and, to the extent practicable, follow accepted standardized procedures. To accomplish this, onsite and offsite impacts should be documented at the time of acquisition, including an inventory of the legal boundary and site conditions documenting encroachments and activities such as illegal clearing, trash dumping, trails, and pet impacts. Any subsequent problems or changes should be documented in writing and with dated photographs, in case legal action is required. The Land Trust Alliance (1993) provides good guidance for this type and level of monitoring.

Invasive and exotic species

The ACE and the surrounding area should be assessed for the presence and extent of invasive and exotic species. Lists of such species (sometimes referred to as noxious species) often are available from government agencies. The level of monitoring effort necessary will vary according to the extent of the problem, whether the species are creating, or have the potential to create, a problem in achieving ACE goals and, in some instances, whether a regulatory mandate for their control or other legal liabilities exist. If the presence of invasive and exotic species is determined to be of minor concern, then simply noting species, location, and relative abundance on a site map may suffice. Low abundance of these species does not necessarily mean the problem is minor; invasive and exotic species should be controlled at an early stage when there is still a reasonable possibility of their eradication, rather than monitored until they present serious ecological and control problems. In some instances, the species may already be a serious problem, and monitoring them and their impacts will be a major goal to track the success of eradication efforts. In these cases, sufficiently detailed information will need to be collected to make quantitative statements about their aerial cover and population trends. To do this, detailed maps of the location, abundance, and condition of each invasive and exotic species will have to be produced so that changes in their distribution and abundance can be tracked.

Natural disturbance

If an ACE provides a function deemed critical for a rare or endemic species and that function could be lost because of what would otherwise be considered a beneficial natural disturbance, or if normally beneficial disturbances cannot be tolerated because of concerns for human health and safety, then a survey of features that create or contribute to such disturbances needs to be conducted for the site and the surrounding area. For example, if fire is a concern, an assessment of dead and downed woody debris in or around the ACE may be of value to track fuel loading and to assess the potential danger and severity of fire. Periodic measures of fuel moisture levels also may be necessary to track the current fire hazard. Should a fire break out, data from such monitoring then can be used to develop protection or response plans. Another example of a disturbance-related threat is where a critical piece of habitat, such as a unique nesting or rearing habitat, is located near a meandering river and, thus, potentially threatened by channel migration. Floodplain and stream channel migration maps will need to be developed to assess the level of threat posed by this normally beneficial disturbance. Because stream channels often are highly mobile, such maps should be created periodically, especially following major flood events. The purpose of this mapping is to identify, ahead of time, the location and potential impact of a disturbance, so that protection and response plans can be developed. Similar examples of other disturbances could be given, such as those generated by severe winds, storms, and landslides. The long-term, adverse consequences of natural disturbances for locally adapted species are likely to be rare (Reice 2001). Resource managers often are risk averse, however, and may improperly advocate elimination or alteration of important natural disturbances in the name of habitat protection or to protect some other value (e.g., recreation or a desirable nonnative species for hunting or fishing purposes), when such disturbances are, in fact, beneficial, especially over long time periods.

Stream and watershed processes

Channel migration, streamflow dynamics, and sediment and nutrient routing profoundly affect instream, riparian, and upland conditions. These conditions often are modified by land use, and, in some cases (e.g., urbanization), modification is extreme. Thus, to help explain changes in ACEs, one may have to measure and model streamflow and wetland water depths and to compare them with precipitation patterns, rates of sediment and nutrient inputs, as well as the type and extent of land cover and use in the watershed. To assess hydrology, precipitation and streamflow gauges, stage gauges, piezometers, wells, and other instrumentation can be used to estimate precipitation, surface flow, and groundwater levels. Such information, when combined with land-cover and land-use information, can be used to construct and calibrate models to predict the hydrologic effect of changes in land cover. For sediment deposition, one may choose to map sediment sources and areas of active bank erosion and landsliding to construct a basic sediment routing model and sediment budget (see also Chapter 3). Modeling helps to determine if a stream channel is in a potentially sediment-rich or sediment-starved condition. Aerial photographs and satellite imagery are extremely helpful in broad-scale classification and measurement of land cover, vegetation patterns, and land use. Data for these factors will likely be a major requirement for the monitoring of most ACEs. Mapping and obtaining this information has become progressively more sophisticated, and depending on the area, there is considerable detail (on the order of 2–30 m^2 in detail) for demarcation of cover and land use. Furthermore, many jurisdictions have compiled geographic information systems (GIS) databases for zoning, parcel conditions, roads, and utilities.

Trends and effectiveness

Monitoring for trends and effectiveness is likely to be much more complicated, time consuming, and costly than monitoring for legal and compliance needs, because, to show trends, data must be collected in a statistically rigorous manner. If management has little need for statistical rigor, trends are quite obvious, or, if only gross trends are of concern to management, then low-cost, qualitative observations, using standardized criteria and protocols, may be sufficient if made by qualified persons, diligently recorded on maps, and backed up with photographs and good field notes. Conversely, if program managers need detailed information and inferences about trends backed by statistical testing, the sampling will have to be much more detailed and frequent.

Basic information needs for effectiveness monitoring are much the same as for trends. However, duration of monitoring will likely be shorter and frequency of measurement and intensity of data analysis higher than for trend monitoring (MacDonald et al. 1991). As with other monitoring, the focus should be on biological outcomes (Karr 1998; Karr and Chu 1999). Possible measures include changes in, or maintenance of, spatial and temporal use patterns, abundance, growth, survival, or productivity of a given key species, or changes in species composition and diversity at the community level. In some situations, however, it may be too costly or the species or habitat too sensitive to sampling impacts to obtain good or even minimally sufficient biological information to prove biological effectiveness. In such cases, physical or chemical surrogates with well-established linkages to biological outcomes may be the realistic choice.

Depending on management need, demonstrating effectiveness may be a relatively simple, low-cost effort or an extremely complex, costly endeavor. For example, if a key fish species' spawning site is protected by an ACE known to be sufficiently sized to provide the security and the food necessary for successful spawning, nothing more may be required than documenting that laws mandating habitat protection are being obeyed and current conditions are being maintained. However, monitoring of timing and distribution of spawning fish, egg survival, juvenile growth and survival, and other factors, as cost and time permits, would be the most direct and ideal method for determining successful management of the site. On the other hand, if an ACE has a primary objective of protecting some beneficial watershed process such as forest hydrology but that process is, in fact, affected by factors outside the ACE, it may be exceedingly difficult to definitively and directly show that a single ACE or multiple ACEs are having the intended effect.

For a more complex situation, evidence of effectiveness could show that a percentage of specific habitat functions, beneficial conditions, or habitat-forming processes provided by an ACE are being protected or are on a trajectory of restoration. For example, if a biological goal is to protect or to restore a fish species to a certain population level and the limiting factor is spawning habitat, then information on the amount of spawning habitat needed can be combined with knowledge about the conditions that create spawning habitat to assess those ACEs acquired to protect or to restore spawning. In this case, monitoring should focus on whether the desired amount of spawning habitat was provided and, in turn, that the intended number (or range) of spawners is, indeed, using the habitat. The latter may not be a good measure, however, if the original limiting factor assumption was incorrect, some off-site factor other than availability of spawning habitat is governing the population (for example, ocean productivity, overharvest, or off-site habitat impacts), or the inherent natural variability masks the value of spawning habitat.

Statistical concerns

There are a variety of sources that describe statistical methods for resolving the often difficult issues of determining sample size; sampling strategies, such as random versus regular sampling and stratification of sampling collection; and appropriate analysis techniques (see Brown and Austen 1996; Conquest and Ralph 1998; MacDonald et al. 1991; Kershner 1997). Generally, as variability (natural or otherwise) increases, more samples are required to make inferences. As noted earlier, the more information on spatial and temporal variability of a given parameter that is available before monitoring, the more confidence one will have in resolving statistical concerns such as sample size and frequency. It is highly recommended that a statistician be consulted before finalizing a sampling strategy and especially before formal data collection. Additional discussion of study design and statistical concerns is presented in previous chapters (see Chapter 2) and can be found in general (e.g., Sokal and Rohlf 1981; Zar 1999) and in specialized (e.g., Conover 1980; Elliott 1983; Bonham 1989; Brown and Austen 1996) statistical texts. The widespread availability of computers and statistical software has spurred the analysis of communities and complex ecosystems and, furthermore, has been responsible for a dramatic rise in specialized landscape statistics incorporating various complex multivariate techniques (e.g., Gauch 1982; McGarigal and Marks 1994; Farina 1998; McGarigal et al. 2000).

While statistical rigor in sampling and data collection usually is desired to make inferences with a known level of confidence, such rigor may not always be necessary. MacDonald and Smart (1993) describe a continuum of monitoring ranging from an informal walk through the site to carefully replicated, quantitative studies. Depending on the objectives of the monitoring, either approach can be valid. These authors also note that the informal approach can be extremely cost effective and can provide a range of learning experiences that may not be realized by focusing on a rigid sampling protocol. In contrast, more formal studies provide more defensible results.

Information collection and management

The time and the cost of collecting and analyzing data traditionally have hampered or precluded effective environmental monitoring (Minns et al. 1996). While these factors inevitably influence the level of monitoring that can be achieved, some of these concerns have been lessened over the past decade by the availability of powerful computers, digitized electronic information, and satellite imagery. These tools are especially valuable for ACE monitoring because some of the most valuable monitoring information is readily derived from satellite or aerial images of land cover and vegetation patterns. This information, in turn, is amenable to electronic storage, analysis, and dissemination by using digital images and outputs from computerized database programs.

Despite the availability of sophisticated information and analytical techniques, properly qualified and trained staff must verify or collect high-quality field data. In addition to the many excellent manuals and guidebooks available, many of which are referenced elsewhere in this chapter, it is becoming increasingly common to employ trained volunteers to collect field data during environmental surveys. A growing body of literature now exists on the training of volunteers, including aspects of quality assurance (USEPA 2001b). Often, ACEs are highly important to local residents, who are willing to devote time to become trained and to assist with data collection that will provide information that could support preservation and restoration of local natural resources. In some instances, volunteer-based data collection has been shown to be a reliable, cost-effective alternative to professional staff for this purpose (Canfield et al. 2002). In others, the cost savings are not as evident (Fore et al. 2001), but other benefits, such as public education and resource stewardship, may make use of volunteers worthwhile.

The availability of digitized information (especially satellite imagery), high-powered computers, global positioning system devices, and increasingly sophisticated mapping tools make the use of GIS highly valuable for efficient and effective monitoring (Johnston 1998). Although the establishment of a GIS database can be time intensive, once the data are entered, it can allow rapid, computer-driven analysis and evaluation of habitat data at any scale. However, a serious problem that can arise with GIS databases (and to some extent with all databases) is the tendency for the proliferation of multiple, uncoordinated, and, at times, conflicting databases. Users should develop clear goals and management protocols for the collection, use, and types of data that will be stored and analyzed in electronic format. Agencies and jurisdictions within an ecoregion should develop a common relational database for the storage and retrieval of mutually beneficial monitoring information.

Acquisitions and Conservation Easement Examples

To demonstrate how one might develop a monitoring plan for ACEs, a series of eight examples is provided. Table 2 provides a summary of each ACE's hypotheses, of potential issues, and of some suggested monitoring parameters. Below, we provide a description of each ACE and its surrounding landscape and resource values. Unless otherwise stated, goals and hypotheses are conjectural. These examples are provided because very little formal literature on ecological monitoring of ACEs exists. Of the literature the authors found, little or no specific objectives or testable hypotheses were provided, thus highlighting a common deficiency in ACE management.

With the exception of the Pingree Conservation Easement in Maine, the examples are drawn from the authors' experience in the Puget Sound region of Washington State. The six individual ACEs we discuss include two each (one urban and one rural setting) of wetland, small stream, and large river floodplain habitats, representing a range of habitats and resource values. Although derived primarily from the Pacific Northwest, these examples illustrate a range of monitoring issues common to ACEs.

Rural Wetland: Upper Bear Creek Conservation Areas 1 and 2

Upper Bear Creek Conservation Areas 1 and 2 are adjacent, forested, open-space tracts (totaling 40 ha) located to the east and southeast, respectively, of Paradise Lake in western King County, Washington (Figure 2). They were acquired as part of King County's Waterways 2000 Program (King County 1997a) to protect and to conserve natural resources, especially salmon and other aquatic-based species in nearby Paradise Lake and Bear Creek watershed, a 145-km² tributary to the Sammamish River in the Lake Washington watershed. Private land surrounding the lake is enrolled in the county's timberland and Public Benefit Rating System current use taxation program and, thus, is expected to remain rural and forested. Also, surrounding land use is rural residential, and the contributing watershed is mostly forested and rural residential (typically one residence per 2-ha plot or lower density). A gas transmission pipeline runs through the eastern edge of the conservation area. The pipeline creates a 16-m-wide corridor cleared of forest vegetation that is maintained as grass and used as a recreational trail.

Both tracts have high-quality mixed second-growth forest, with almost no exotic or invasive plant or animal species. The lake, however, does have a high population of nonnative bullfrogs *Rana catesbeiana*, because it was used historically to pen raise bullfrogs for the restaurant industry. Area 1 has several small, uninventoried forested wetlands and four small nonfish-bearing streams that drain to Paradise Lake and its wetland-dominated outlet channel. Area 2 comprises forested and scrub–shrub wetland at the outlet of Paradise Lake and about 0.4 km of Bear Creek downstream from the lake.

Paradise Lake and Bear Creek have high biological resource value, providing habitat for sockeye salmon *Oncorhynchus nerka*, coho salmon, and cutthroat trout *O. clarki*, as well as freshwater mussels *Margaritifera falcata* and *Anodonta oregonensis*, a variety of amphibians (e.g., northern red legged frog *Rana aurora aurora*, Pacific treefrog *Pseudacris regilla*, northwestern salamander *Ambystoma gracile*, long-toed salamander *A. macrodactylum*, Ensatina *Ensatina eschscholtzii*, and western red-backed salamander *Plethodon vehiculum*), resident and migratory birds (passerines, waterfowl), aquatic mammals (beaver *Castor canadensis*, otter *Lutra canadensis*, mink *Mustela vison*, and muskrat *Ondatra zibethicus*), and terrestrial mammals (black bear *Ursus americanus*, Columbian blacktail deer *Odocoileus hemionus columbianus*, and coyotes *Canis latrans*).

Goals and hypotheses

King County (1997a) has three goals for acquisitions in the conservation area: (1) maintain ecological integrity of the conservation area and enhance ecological quality where feasible, (2) provide for passive use and environmental education at targeted access sites while protecting outstanding natural features from overuse and disturbance in the remainder of the area, and (3) monitor key ecosystem processes and functions over time and take action where monitoring reveals existing or potential damage to natural resources. The county's monitoring guidance for these goals is general: recommending monitoring plant and animal species composition and distribution; water quality; stream, wetland, and riparian zone characteristics; incidence of invasive and exotic species; and anthropogenic impacts, including access, recreation, and infrastructure, such as the water supply pipeline along the eastern edge of Area 1. A hypothesis for this ACE is that conditions (plant and ani-

Table 2.

Summary of hypotheses and monitoring issues or parameters for eight examples of acquisitions and conservation easements (ACE). Unless otherwise indicated in the "Issue or potential parameters to measure" column, "human activity" refers to location and extent of impacts from human access points and trails; "vegetation" refers to location, maturity, and species composition of forest patches; "hydrology and water quality" refers to seasonal fluctuation in streamflow and temperature; "stream habitats and substrates" refers to location, distribution, and quality of pools, riffles, and spawning substrates; "aquatic habitats and substrates" refers to location, distribution, and quality of streams and wetlands; "snags and LWD (large woody debris)" refers to location, density, and condition of snags and woody debris in aquatic and riparian areas; "invertebrates, fish, and wildlife" refers to presence, abundance, and distribution of aquatic invertebrates, fish, amphibians, birds, and mammals, and to location and extent of salmon spawning and juvenile rearing; and "invasive and exotic species" refers to location and extent within and near the ACE.

Example	Hypothesis	Issue or potential parameters to measure
Upper Bear Creek Conservation Areas 1 and 2	Ecological conditions (plant and animal diversity, size, and condition of habitat patches)will remain stable or improve over time as plant succession proceeds.	· Human activity · Vegetation · Snags and LWD · Wildlife: presence, abundance, and distribution of amphibians, birds, and mammals · Invasive and exotic species
Wetland 90A	Bog's hydrology, water quality, and plant community will decline, and invasive species (especially *Spirea* spp.) will increase.	· Human activity · Vegetation: distribution and condition of endemic bog plants (e.g., Labrador tea, sphagnum) and invasive plants (e.g., Douglas spirea *Spirea douglassii* and cattail *Typha latifolia*) · Hydrology and water quality: seasonal fluctuations in pond level and pH · Wildlife: assess use by birds (e.g., warblers) as indicators of change · Invasive and exotic species
Lower Bear Creek Corridor	Salmon use will be maintained or increase as impacts of recreation and invasive and exotic species decrease. Wildlife use will be maintained or decrease due to isolation and fragmentation of surrounding landscape by urban and commercial development.	· Human activity: location and extent of impacts from human structures (roads, buildings), access points, and trails · Vegetation · Stream habitats and substrates · Snags and LWD · Invertebrates, fish, and wildlife · Invasive and exotic species
Rock Creek Natural Area	Forest condition will improve and fish and aquatic and riparian-oriented wildlife will remain stable or increase. If flow is restored, chinook, coho, and sockeye salmon use will increase.	· Human activity · Vegetation · Hydrology and water quality · Stream habitats and substrates · Snags and LWD · Invertebrates, fish, and wildlife · Invasive and exotic species
Duwamish Park	Salmon use will be maintained or increase as impacts of recreation and invasive and exotic species decrease. Wildlife use will be maintained or decrease due to isolation and fragmentation of surrounding landscape by urban and commercial development.	· Human activity · Invertebrates, fish, and wildlife · Invasive and exotic species

Table 2. continued

Example	Hypothesis	Issue or potential parameters to measure
Tolt-MacDonald Park	Vegetation maturity, forest complexity, and fish and wildlife use and distribution will increase over time.	· Human activity · Vegetation · Aquatic habitats and substrates · Snags and LWD · Invertebrates, fish, and wildlife · Invasive and exotic species
Bear Creek Watershed	Hydrology and water quality will be maintained or improve over time, high-quality aquatic habitats will be protected, and salmon use will be maintained or increase over time.	· Human activity · Vegetation · Hydrology and water quality · Aquatic habitats and substrates · Snags and LWD · Invertebrates, fish, and wildlife · Invasive and exotic species
Pingree Conservation Easement	Forests and aquatic habitat quality will improve and species abundance and diversity will increase as easement conditions and sustainable forestry are implemented.	· Human activity · Vegetation · Hydrology and water quality · Aquatic habitats and substrates · Snags and LWD · Invertebrates, fish, and wildlife: presence, abundance, and distribution of aquatic invertebrates, fish, amphibians, birds, and mammals; location and extent of fish spawning and juvenile rearing · Invasive and exotic species

mal diversity, size and condition of habitat patches) will remain stable or improve over time as plant succession proceeds.

Recommended monitoring

The current high quality of these sites and their high value for protecting and contributing to biological and watershed processes at both the local and watershed scale suggest that significant monitoring effort is warranted. To measure compliance, boundaries and human access points should be monitored for impacts at least twice yearly. Invasive and exotic species on and near the site also should be evaluated for their presence and threat through a general evaluation survey visit at least once per year with the greatest attention given to edges and maintained clearings, such as at access points and along the pipeline, which often provide the pathway for dispersal and establishment of invasive and exotic species.

Beyond compliance, monitoring should focus on detecting changes in the site's currently high-quality vegetation and plant and animal (specifically amphibian, because of the exotic bullfrog influence) diversity (Table 2). Use by key aquatic and terrestrial species (salmon, mussels, snails, sponges, amphibians, beaver, birds) should be tracked on and in areas adjacent to the site at least once per year at phenologically appropriate seasons, such as during spawning and nesting for salmon, amphibians, and birds. Finally, it can be expected that the high-quality forest cover of this site will help maintain the forest-based hydrology and water quality of the area. Monitoring of the ACE's contribution to forest cover in the watershed should be tracked by using satellite imagery and GIS database analysis.

Urban Wetland: Wetland 90A, Headwater Bog

This 1.6-ha bog is situated in the Snoqualmie Ridge urban planned development, a large, still growing, urban subdivision in the headwaters of Kimball Creek, a small tributary to the Snoqualmie River in the City of Snoqualmie,

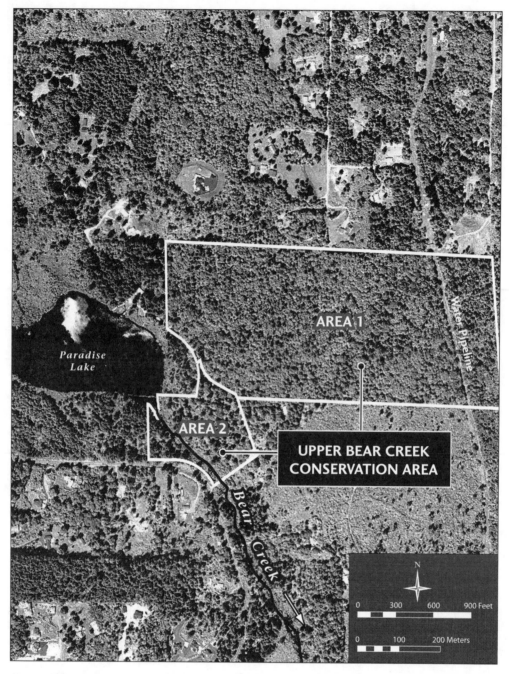

Figure 2.
Upper Bear Creek Conservation Areas 1 and 2 are forested wetland tracts. Bear Creek has high biological resource value. The contributing watershed is mostly forested and rural residential. Arrow points downstream. (Photo courtesy of King County Department of Natural Resources.)

Washington (Figure 3). As is typical of headwater bog systems, fish are not present in this wetland. The bog's outlet stream drains into at least two stormwater detention ponds before reaching known fish-bearing (mostly cutthroat trout) portions of Kimball Creek. In addition, because Kimball Creek is located upstream of Snoqualmie Falls, a 90-m-high anadromous fish barrier on the Snoqualmie River, it is not used by nor does it provide critical habitat for any rare, threatened, or endangered anadromous fish species. Nonetheless, like many bogs in the region, Wetland 90A is a relatively rare and irreplaceable system and, thus, a valuable resource in its own right.

The dominant plants found in this wetland include several sphagnum moss species *Sphagnum* spp., Labrador tea *Rhododendron groenlandicum*, bog laurel *Kalmia* microphylla, and round-leaved sundew *Drosera rotundifolia*.

Figure 3.
Wetland 90A, a headwater bog, is located near planned urban development. Like many bogs in the region, it is a relatively rare ecological resource. (Photo courtesy of King County Department of Natural Resources.)

Wildlife species are most abundant within the protective buffer edge, although passerine birds, including swallows (Hirundinidae), flycatchers (Tyrannidae), and warblers (Emberizidae), catch flying insects above the bog.

Goals and hypotheses

There are no formal goals for Wetland 90A, but the city of Snoqualmie's development standards require that adjacent developments provide a relatively high level of protection for bogs. As a result, stormwater runoff from the surrounding development into Wetland 90A is subject to a relatively high degree of stormwater detention and water-quality treatment (e.g., through detention ponds and bioswales). In addition, local residents are being educated about the wetland, and the edges of the buffer are marked to minimize encroachment. Regardless of these measures, a variety of impacts are already occurring even though the surrounding subdivision has not yet been completed. A paved trail around the wetland and an interpretive pier extending into the wetland already has been constructed within the buffer. Based on the authors' experience elsewhere, it is likely that this buffer will be increasingly subject to myriad anthropogenic impacts, including informal trail building, dumping of yard waste, vegetation clearing, and pet intrusion. Given Wetland 90A's condition and surrounding land use, a working hypothesis for this ACE is that the bog's plant community, water quality, and species use will decline and invasive species (especially Spirea spp.) will increase.

Recommended monitoring

Maintenance of the sphagnum-based plant community is a regulatory requirement and, therefore, is the main biological concern for monitoring Wetland 90A (Table 2). Monitoring fish and wildlife in Wetland 90A is a relatively low priority and may be unnecessary for fish because of the wetland's small size, isolation by urban development, and location well upstream from anadromous salmonid-bearing habitat. Thus, measurement of plant community attributes and the bog's hydrology and water quality are the basis of a monitoring program. Specifically, monitoring should focus on evaluating success in maintaining the quantity, quality, and distribution of key plants (such as *Sphagnum* spp., Labrador tea, and bog laurel), a few select bird species that use the bog (such as warblers and flycatchers), and hydrologic conditions (primarily water levels and hydroperiod) and water-quality factors (pH and sediment) that serve as indicators of bog physical habitat degradation and, if degraded, could have downstream effects. For compliance, annual assessment of human activity (trails, garbage, and pets) should be conducted.

Urban Small Stream: The Lower Bear Creek Corridor

This linear riparian corridor (100–150 m wide and roughly 3 ha²) straddles 0.4 km of lower Bear Creek in Redmond, Washington (Figure 4). As noted earlier, Bear Creek is a midsize stream that, in spite of its location within a landscape dominated by rural and residential land uses, possesses highly productive aquatic habitat. In contrast to much higher-quality areas upstream where there is less development, this lower reach has been adversely affected by commercial development, several arterial roadways, a state highway, and a short segment of paved trail in close proximity to the creek. High amounts of trash and pet waste are present in the corridor, and streambanks generally are eroded. Although a few alders and willows are present and some coniferous trees have recently been planted, riparian vegetation is highly degraded and monotypic, being composed almost entirely of Himalayan blackberry *Rubus discolor*, an exotic, invasive herbaceous shrub. The stream substrates are mostly sand and silt and, therefore, low quality salmon spawning habitat; however, salmonids do spawn in high densities upstream and modest densities downstream of the reach. Despite its condition, the stream reach is an important migration corridor for salmon and provides a modest amount of juvenile salmon rearing habitat. Primary wildlife value is for small mammals as a migration corridor and, to a limited extent, for passerine birds as nesting habitat. Aside from a relatively limited effort to plant native conifers, no large-scale restoration projects have been conducted within this reach. In part, this is because of the City of Redmond's interest in expanding an existing trail adjacent to the creek. Restoration has been deferred until trail location issues between the trail and fish interests have been resolved.

Goals and hypotheses

There are no formal goals for this ACE; however, the Bear Creek Basin Plan (King County 1990) calls for protection and restoration of the stream's aquatic habitats and species as high-priority goals. The highly urbanized setting for this reach limits its current resource potential and constrains much restoration potential as well. To the extent that it occurs, restoration is likely to be limited to localized improvements in riparian vegetation (reestablishment of native forest) and stream channel complexity (through some limited addition of LWD). The working hypothesis for this ACE is that while human recreation use and impacts will increase, plant communities will improve somewhat as native plants are reestablished. It is unlikely the invasive species will be eradicated completely, however. Habitat for salmon rearing and migration is likely to increase, while native wildlife use will, at best, remain stable or more likely will degrade further as surrounding development and human recreation increase and further isolate this reach from upland areas.

Recommended monitoring

Monitoring should focus on documenting and tracking riparian habitat (native and exotic species stand characteristics) and stream-channel physical conditions (channel complexity measures such as pools, riffles, and woody debris) that could be used to assess future conditions (Table 2). Human impacts (e.g., pollution, additional brush clearing) that could affect fish habitat also should be tracked. Unless large-scale restoration projects are anticipated for this site, monitoring at 3- to 5-year intervals may suffice to document further deterioration of this ACE and to develop restoration and other mitigation measures as needed.

Figure 4.
The Lower Bear Creek corridor, an urban small stream reach important for salmon migration, also provides a modest amount of juvenile salmon rearing habitat. Arrows point downstream. (Photo courtesy of King County Department of Natural Resources.)

Rural Small Stream: Rock Creek Natural Area

Similar to Upper Bear Creek Conservation Areas 1 and 2, the 56.6-ha Rock Creek Natural Area (RCNA) was acquired in two phases between 1996 and 1998 as part of the Cedar River Legacy program (Figure 5). The land straddles about 1 km of Rock Creek, a midsize (31 km2) tributary to the Cedar River in the Lake Washington watershed (King County 1993). The RCNA is composed of mature mixed forest dominated by relatively large second-growth conifers. Moreover, the incidence of invasive or exotic species is quite low and occurs only at the developed margins. This area is bounded to the west by urban development (city of Maple Valley, Washington) and elsewhere by rural residential lands, several hundred acres of which have been set aside by a developer as open space in exchange for higher development densities granted elsewhere in the county. The largest single development to the east is a school.

The creek is predominantly spring-fed with high-quality cold water and clean (low silt) gravel and cobble substrates. In a recent study of 22 Puget Sound lowland streams, it had the highest ratings for biotic integrity

Figure 5.
Rock Creek Natural Area is a forested area bounded by urban development and rural residential lands. The rural small stream supports highly productive salmonid runs. Arrows point downstream. (Photo courtesy of King County Department of Natural Resources.)

(May et al. 1997), suggesting that it is one of the least degraded creeks in the region. It supports highly productive runs of coho and sockeye salmon and cutthroat and rainbow trout *Oncorhynchus mykiss*. The primary concern for Rock Creek is the effect of municipal water withdrawals, which remove up to 70% of the late summer and early fall base flows. The withdrawal appears to eliminate use by spawning chinook salmon, which are believed to have historically used the system in modest (roughly 50–100 fish per year) numbers. Water withdrawals also reduce spawning habitat for sockeye and juvenile rearing habitat for the other salmonid species (King County 1998).

Goals and hypotheses

King County (1997b) has established a set of formal goals for the RCNA. These include (1) protection of physical stream habitat, (2) base-flow restoration, (3) low-impact passive recreation, and (4) environmental education. Given these goals, a set of hypotheses would be that upland and riparian forests will improve (i.e., become more like late-successional forest in diversity and structure), physical stream habitat and fish use will remain stable or will improve over time, water quality will remain high, invasive and exotic species will remain low and limited in area to developed edges, and impacts of human use will remain stable or will decrease. If base flow is fully restored, the Lower Cedar River Basin Plan (King County 1998) estimates that annual coho and chinook smolt production could increase by 11,700 and 2,900, respectively, and annual sockeye fry production could increase by 1.1 million. Without base flow restoration, the working hypothesis is that the value of the site for these uses should stay the same or improve slightly as forests mature and because surrounding development is not expected to change in type or intensity. For wildlife, use by riparian and aquatic-oriented species should remain stable or increase, while the effects of nearby development may reduce use by larger migratory animals, namely elk, and those with large core-area requirements, such as bear and cougar.

Recommended monitoring

The high biological value of the RCNA, the possibility of some level of flow restoration, and the proximity to urban development suggest that significant monitoring effort is warranted. For compliance purposes, human access and impacts should be monitored by field visits at least twice yearly. Invasive and exotic species on and near the site also should be evaluated through a general site visit at least annually, with the greatest attention given to the western urban edge, where homeowners use nonnative species for landscaping. This also is where two low-impact (narrow, unpaved) trails enter the site, potentially providing pathways for dispersal and establishment of invasive or exotic species.

Trend monitoring should focus on tracking the site's current high vegetation quality and plant and animal diversity by measuring vegetation maturity, forest complexity, and instream habitat diversity (as evidenced by habitat patchiness, snags, woody debris on the forest floor, pool and spawning substrate quantity and quality, and instream LWD) and use by key aquatic and terrestrial species (e.g., salmon, raptors, elk) in appropriate seasons, such as during spawning for salmon, calving for elk, and nesting for birds (Table 2). If flows are restored (by reducing or eliminating municipal water withdrawals), salmon use and productivity should increase commensurately. Finally, the RCNA's high-quality forest cover makes it valuable for maintaining the watershed's forest-based hydrology and high water quality. Thus, the contribution of this ACE's forest to the forest cover in the watershed should be tracked by using aerial and satellite imagery and GIS database systems.

Urban Large River Floodplain: Duwamish River Park

This small, roughly 1.5-ha park is one of the few pieces of shoreline without a structure along the otherwise highly developed lower Duwamish River (Figure 6). Purchased in 1916, it originally served as an urban park and has only recently been identified as a potential habitat restoration site in response to the 1998 listing of Puget Sound chinook salmon under the federal Endangered Species Act (ESA; USACE 2000). Most of the site still is maintained as grass and ornamental landscaping for passive recreation; however, there is a small but distinct strip of seminatural bank and edge habitat, especially when compared with the overly steepened, rock-lined banks that are prevalent almost everywhere else in this reach. Despite the level of development, the river supports robust runs of chinook, coho, and chum salmon *Oncorhynchus keta* and steelhead *O. mykiss* and cutthroat trout. It also is used occasionally by ESA-listed, threatened bull trout *Salvelinus confluentus*. As a result, the park provides habitat for migration and rearing of these and many other fish species. The park is not known to provide critical habitat (under Section 7 of the ESA) for any wildlife species.

Goals and hypotheses

There are no formal goals for this parcel of land. Given its small size and heavily degraded landscape, a modest goal of providing limited improvement of habitat for fish and wildlife along the river's edge may be the most reasonable. Commensurate with this goal, we hypothesize that salmon (juvenile rearing and adult migration) use will stay the same or will increase consistent with localized improvements (e.g., improvement in riparian vegetation and addition of LWD along the river's edge), while wildlife use is unlikely to increase due to the site's isolation. In addition, we hypothesize that impacts of invasive and exotic species and recreation will stay the same or decrease slightly as park managers change management in response to growing concerns about the river's value for fish.

Monitoring needs and recommended approaches

The ACE's small, highly altered, isolated, and constrained urban–industrial setting suggests that most, if not all, monitoring needs for this site could probably be met by a yearly site visit to document anthropogenic impacts and changes that may be occurring in shoreline vegetation or within aquatic habitat. Annual surveys

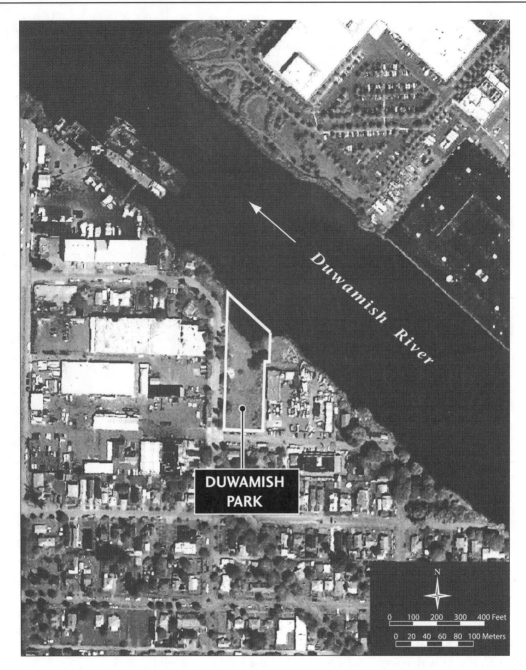

Figure 6.
The Duwamish River Park, a small area in a heavily degraded urban landscape, is a potential habitat restoration site. The park provides habitat for migration and rearing of salmonids and other fish. Arrow points downriver. (Photo courtesy of King County Department of Natural Resources.)

of juvenile and adult salmon use of shoreline also may be warranted, especially if a restoration or enhancement project geared toward protecting or restoring salmon were implemented at this site (Table 2).

Rural Large River Floodplain: Tolt-MacDonald Park

This 53-ha park encompasses the confluence of the Tolt and Snoqualmie rivers (Figure 7). Land uses at or near the site consist of a combination of forested natural areas, ball fields, playgrounds, campgrounds, and parking lots are within the 100-year floodplains of the Tolt and Snoqualmie Rivers. The park is used extensively year around for fishing, hiking, and playing. The vegetation within the forested portion of the park is a mixed second-growth forest dominated by black cottonwoods *Populus balsamifera*; exotic plants (mainly Himalayan blackberry) have invaded portions of the park. A state highway (the main arterial roadway for the city of Car-

Figure 7.
Year around land uses at or near Tolt-MacDonald Park are a combination of forested natural areas, recreational areas, and parking lots. Despite these impacts, this rural floodplain park provides habitat for a variety of fish and wildlife, including threatened chinook salmon and bull trout. Arrow points downriver. (Photo courtesy of King County Department of Natural Resources.)

nation, Washington) crosses the Tolt River about 0.5 km upstream of its confluence with the Snoqualmie River and splits the park. In addition, almost the full lengths of the banks of both river channels have been converted to levees and armored with riprap. Behind these levees are several remnant side channels, one of which was reconnected to the Tolt River in 1998.

Despite these impacts, the site provides extensive and heavily used habitat for threatened chinook salmon and bull trout, as well as for coho, pink *Oncorhynchus gorbuscha*, and chum salmon, and sea-run cutthroat and rainbow trout. In addition, a wide variety of wildlife species are found in the area. These include bald eagles *Haliaeetus leucocephalus*, black bear, deer, river otters, beavers, cougars *Felis concolor*, and bobcats *Felis rufus*. Reconnection and restoration of the additional disconnected side channels would add valuable fish habitat and would benefit many of the wildlife species as well.

Goals and hypotheses

There are no formal habitat or species goals for this area. A study is under way to evaluate reach-level restoration options for salmon habitat, including the feasibility of removing bank armor and relocating or eliminating levees to restore floodplain forest and aquatic habitat. Thus, restoration of native floodplain forest and habitat, either by active intervention or by changing park management to reduce ongoing impacts, may be a reasonable goal. The working hypothesis is that if human structures are removed or set back from their existing locations and native vegetation and remnant side channels are restored, vegetation maturity and forest complexity (patchiness, snags, woody debris on the forest floor, instream and off-channel LWD loadings), and fish and wildlife species use and distribution should increase over time.

Recommended monitoring

Given the site's moderate biological value and high potential for improved biological value, as well as its proximity to urban- and high-use recreational areas, a relatively high amount of monitoring effort is warranted.

The location, type, and abundance of native and nonnative plants and animals, and the impacts of surrounding land uses and human structures (trails, roads, ball fields, picnic areas, levees, and revetments) should be documented.

Trend monitoring should be conducted to assist in evaluating changes in these parameters over time that may occur as a result of restoration. Vegetation, land and recreation uses, and key aquatic and terrestrial species (primarily salmonids and birds) should be documented and tracked on and near the site at least once per year in appropriate seasons, such as during spawning for salmonids and nesting for birds. Floodplain and river-channel features, such as side channels, gravel bars, and LWD accumulations, also should be mapped and tracked for physical changes. Fish and wildlife use should be monitored at least yearly or more frequently if warranted by rapid changes in site conditions in response to active restoration.

Example of Multiple Acquisitions and Conservation Easement Watershed-Scale Monitoring—Bear Creek Watershed

The 145-km² Bear Creek watershed (Figure 8) is presented as an example of monitoring multiple ACEs on a watershed scale. King County's Bear Creek Basin Plan (King County 1990) calls for the protection and restoration of riparian and upland areas that sustain the creek's outstanding aquatic habitat. To accomplish this, zoning, regulations, and acquisition of land and easements have been used to protect high-quality aquatic, riparian, and upland forest habitats. For example, in 1993, the King County Council passed regulations requiring new developments to retain at least 65% of their land in an undisturbed (preferably forested) vegetated condition to protect forests for their hydrologic value. Currently, the watershed contains 1,561 ha of public and private open space. It also has 876 ha of land in current use taxation, a tax-based incentive program that provides protection as long as the owner remains enrolled in the program. Together, these ACEs total about 17% of the watershed.

Goals and hypotheses

The major goal of the Bear Creek Basin Plan is to protect forest-based hydrology and water quality, as well as discrete key habitat areas as a means of ensuring long-term sustainability of the watershed's salmon and other aquatic resources. Many other species, including a wide array of terrestrial wildlife, also would benefit from this goal. The working hypothesis is that riparian and upland forest maturity and complexity (patchiness, snags, woody debris on the forest floor), aquatic habitat quality (quality of pools and amount of LWD), and fish and wildlife species use and distribution should increase over time.

Recommended monitoring

Annual monitoring by using aerial and satellite imagery (taken at yearly intervals), combined with a GIS-based tracking system, is recommended to assess changes in forest cover, the extent of development and impervious surfaces, overlap of protected riparian areas with high-use salmon spawning and rearing areas, and overlap of forests and development with wildlife. Field monitoring should include yearly measurements of rainfall, streamflow, water-quality monitoring (especially of temperature, dissolved oxygen, and turbidity), range and degree of use by salmon, wildlife, and invasive and exotic species.

Example of Large Acquisitions and Conservation Easements, Multiple Watershed Scale Monitoring—Pingree Conservation Easement

The final example is intended to provide guidance for large areas comprising multiple watersheds. As the impacts of land development become better known and concern for land and species protection grows, it seems likely that the need for larger ACEs will become apparent, while the availability of such landscape deals diminishes every day, even as we seek them as a means of ensuring the protection of biological resources on watershed or larger landscape scales. The next 5–10 years offer the opportunity to acquire ACEs at the landscape level. Current trends in the northeast indicate that within 10 years, large blocks of land (10,000 ha and greater) will be split into smaller parcels and, therefore, will no longer be available for acquisition as large ACEs.

Clearly, the monitoring of large areas will include many of the approaches noted above, but it also will include more consideration of multiscale approaches (ground, aerial, and satellite) that achieve cost efficiencies on an

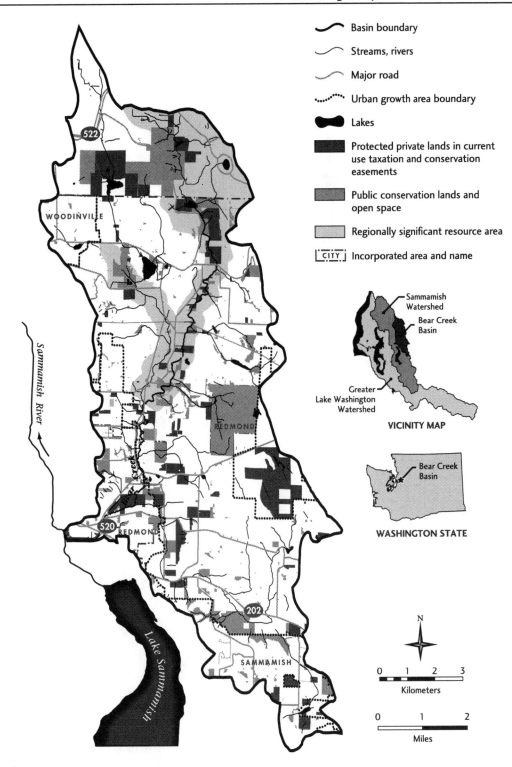

Figure 8.
Map of Bear Creek watershed shows locations of publicly held conservation and open space lands and private lands protected under current use taxation and conservation easement programs. (Courtesy of King County Department of Natural Resources).

increasingly larger scale. To demonstrate this, a brief summary is provided of the approach the New England Forestry Foundation (NEFF) has proposed to monitor its March 2001 purchase of the 308,449-ha Pingree Conservation Easement (PCE; Figure 9). To date, this is the largest easement in the United States (Sader et al. 2002). It encompasses a wide range of special features and conditions, including 305,750 ha (1,180 square miles) of forest protected from development, more than 3,200 km (2,000 mi) of river frontage, 2,900 ha (72,000 acres) of wetland, 110 remote lakes and ponds larger than 1.25 ha (3 acres), 344 km (215 mi) of lake

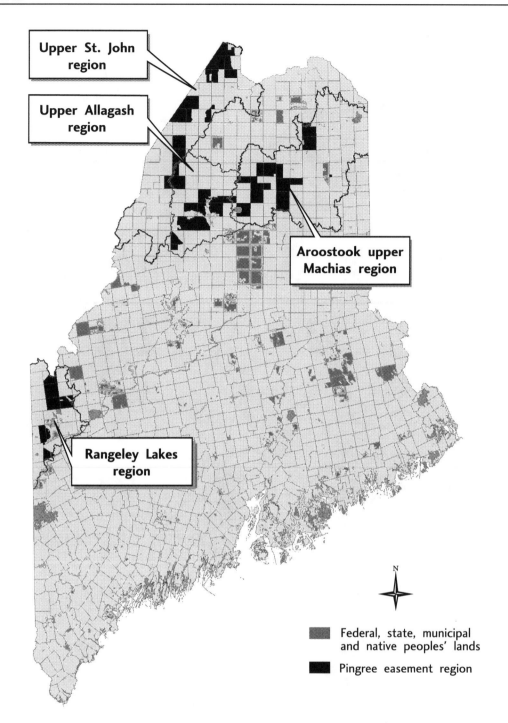

Figure 9.
Map of the state of Maine shows locations of the Pingree Conservation Easement regions. (Map provided by Keith Ross, NEFF, modified by King County Department of Natural Resources.)

and pond frontage, 67 rare and endangered plant sites, five active bald eagle nests, 10,040 ha (24,800 acres) of managed deer yards, 4,900 ha (12,264 acres) of fragile high-mountain areas more than 900 m (2,700 ft) in elevation, and a 1,200-ha (3,000-acre) limited harvest management zone along the St. John's River, managed in partnership with the Maine chapter of The Nature Conservancy.

Goals and hypotheses

The NEFF's goals for the PCE include working with the landowner to ensure terms of the easement are followed and to promote sustainable forestry practices. Although not explicitly stated by Sader et al. (2002), the inferred intent is to protect and to promote the long-term sustainability of the forest and its native plant and animal communities. Similarly, no discrete hypotheses were articulated, but it appears that the working hypothesis is that forests, aquatic habitats, and species abundance and diversity will improve as the new forest management regime takes hold.

Recommended monitoring

To monitor the PCE, the NEFF proposes to pay special attention to specific features, such as existing leases, structures, roads, gravel pits, riparian habitat, clearcuts, wetlands, and recreational use, as well as landscape-level attributes, such as forest diversity and ecosystem health and disturbance. The initial stage of monitoring will establish baseline documentation of ownership, historical data, legal condition, maps and descriptions of natural areas (streams, wetlands, lakes, forest types), anthropogenic features (roads, residences, outbuildings), and cultural resources. Subsequent monitoring will evaluate implementation of the forest management plan and effects on native plant and animal communities. After establishing a baseline, the NEFF proposes a hierarchy of remote-sensing and ground-visit activities. Initially (Level 1), medium spatial resolution satellite imagery (e.g., Landsat) would be used as a relatively quick, inexpensive (per unit area) coarse filter approach to detect change. This would be followed by either high-resolution satellite imagery or aerial photography sampling (Level 2) on sites either detected as disturbed in Level 1 monitoring or that are too small to be monitored with Level 1 technology. Level 2 monitoring will be done opportunistically and at a yearly or a longer frequency, depending on the diversity and structure indicators to minimize costs. Level 3 field visits are the most expensive (per unit area) form of monitoring and recommended on an as-needed basis to verify the condition of high-priority features detected at either Level 1 or 2 or to conduct sampling and monitoring that cannot be effectively done at the other levels. To date, the NEFF has committed $1 million for monitoring and, if necessary, to enforce easement provisions.

Summary

Land ACEs have been a strategy for natural resource protection for a century or more. Initially, and still substantially, ACEs were implemented by the federal and state governments and larger, well-established conservation groups. However, the use of ACEs has grown considerably in recent years with increased involvement by local (city and county) governments and locally or regionally based NGOs in species, stream, and watershed conservation efforts. Moreover, ACEs now are being acquired for a wider variety of conservation purposes throughout the United States and Canada. As human populations and their impacts on species, streams, and watersheds increase, preservation and restoration become greater concerns in conservation. More attention must be given to the active or the passive role of ACEs, especially where there is a need to protect important sites or processes from the impacts of development.

This chapter is intended to assist resource managers in developing an ecologically based monitoring program for a wide range of ACEs with equally diverse goals. Despite the potentially important role of ACEs in stream and watershed restoration, existing literature on monitoring them focuses on legal concerns, primarily enforcing terms of easements or detecting illegal activities. Little published information was found on the biological and ecological monitoring of ACEs. Therefore, this work is a first attempt to provide monitoring approaches and methods to ACE managers by providing an overview of issues related to setting the ecological context and to establishing the goals and objectives of ACEs, as well as study designs and parameters for monitoring them.

Because ACEs are acquired for a wide variety of reasons and in a multitude of settings, there is no single, simple framework or general set of goals for ACE monitoring. For each ACE, it will be necessary to determine its role in protecting or restoring species based on size, condition, landscape connectivity, species use of the ACE, surrounding landscape condition, threats to productivity, and potential for restoration or enhancement. Generally, larger ACEs in good condition and with good landscape connectivity will have higher conservation value and commensurately higher monitoring needs. Threat of development and invasive and exotic species impacts, and the need or likelihood of restoration also will affect the necessary level of effort, with those ACEs having higher threats and greater restoration needs requiring greater effort. Table 2 provides a summary of the hypotheses and some potential parameters that might be monitored for the examples discussed above. Activities in or around ACEs should always be monitored for compliance with laws, boundaries, and easement terms on a regular basis (at least yearly).

Our experiences indicate that most ACE monitoring has not led to significant changes that stem detrimental impacts on the resource(s) the ACE is "protecting." We strongly recommend that monitoring be coupled with action, that it be more than just describing baseline or changing (and often deteriorating) conditions or simply documenting extinction of species. Our review of ACE projects indicates that few have well articulated goals from which specific objectives and testable hypotheses could be derived. We recommend that ACE managers take the necessary steps to arrive at hypotheses, then use the prescribed monitoring principles and practices to test them. A well-designed monitoring program can demonstrate the habitat or species benefits of an ACE, can help justify the project's funding, and can provide valuable information for adaptive management and future restoration actions.

Acknowledgments

The authors would like to acknowledge King County for its support in the development of this chapter. Keith Ross of the New England Forest Foundation provided information on the Pingree Conservation Easement. Special thanks to Lindsey Amtmann for technical editing and reviews of previous drafts.

References

Adamus, P. 2001. Methods for evaluating wetland condition: #13 biological assessment methods for birds. U.S. Environmental Protection Agency, Office of Water, EPA 822-R-01-007m, Washington, D.C. Also online at http://www.epa.gov/owow/wetlands/bawwg/monindicators.pdf and http://www.epa.gov/ waterscience/criteria/wetlands/13Birds.pdf [Accessed 15 May 2003].

Adamus, P. R., and K. Brandt. 1990. Impacts on quality of inland wetlands of the United States: a survey of indicators, techniques, and applications of community-level biomonitoring data. U.S. Environmental Protection Agency, Environmental Research Laboratory, EPA/600/3-90/073, Corvallis, Oregon. Also online at http://www.epa.gov/OWOW/wetlands/wqual/introweb.html [Accessed 5 May 2003].

Adamus, P., T. J. Danielson, and A. Gonyaw. 2001. Indicators for monitoring biological integrity of inland, freshwater wetlands: a survey of North American technical literature (1990–2000). U.S. Environmental Protection Agency, Office of Water, EPA 843-R-01-Fall 2001, Washington, D.C.

Askins, R. A. 2000. Restoring North America's birds: lessons from landscape ecology. Yale University Press, New Haven, Connecticut.

Baker, C., and H. Haemmerle. 1990. Native growth protection easements: survival and effectiveness. King County, Department of Development and Environmental Services, Technical Report, Renton, Washington.

BAOSC (Bay Area Open Space Council). 1999. Ensuring the promise of conservation easements: report on the use and management of conservation easements by San Francisco Bay area organizations. Bay Area Open Space Council, report dated 14 May 1999, San Francisco.

Benda, L. E., D. J. Miller, T. Dunne, G. H. Reeves, and J. K. Agee. 1998. Dynamic landscape systems. Pages 261–288 in R. J. Naiman and R. E. Bilby, editors. River ecology and management: lessons from the Pacific coastal ecoregion. Springer-Verlag, New York.

Berg, D. R. 1997. Active management of riparian habitats. Pages 50–61 in K. B. Macdonald and F. Weinmann, editors. Wetland and riparian restoration: taking a broader view. Contributed papers and selected abstracts, Society for Ecological Restoration, 1995 International Conference, September 14–16, 1995, University of Washington, USA. U.S. Environmental Protection Agency, Region 10, EPA 910-R-97-007, Seattle.

Bilby, R. E., and P. A. Bisson. 1998. Function and distribution of large woody debris. Pages 324–346 in R. J. Naiman and R. E. Bilby, editors. River ecology and management: lessons from the Pacific coastal ecoregion. Springer-Verlag, New York.

Bingham, B., and B. Noon. 1997. Mitigation of habitat "take" application in habitat conservation planning. Conservation Biology 11(1):127–139.

Bisson, P. A., J. A. Nielson, R. A. Palmason, and L. E. Grove. 1982. A system of naming habitat types in small streams, with examples of habitat utilization by salmonids during low streamflow. Pages 62–73 in N. B. Armantrout, editor. Acquisition and utilization of aquatic habitat inventory information. American Fisheries Society, Western Division, Bethesda, Maryland.

Bonham, C. D. 1989. Measurements for terrestrial vegetation. Wiley, New York.

Booth, D. B., D. Hartley, and R. Jackson. 2002. Forest cover, impervious-surface area, and the mitigation of stormwater impacts. Journal of American Water Resources Association 38:835–845.

Booth, D. B., and P. C. Henshaw. 2001. Rates of channel erosion in small urban streams. Pages 17–38 in M. S. Wigmosta, W. E. Dietrich, J. Lewis, T. Dunne, D. R. Montgomery, editors. Land use and watersheds: human influence on hydrology and geomorphology in urban and forest areas. Water science and application, volume 2. American Geophysical Union, Washington, D.C.

Booth, D. B., and C. R. Jackson. 1994. Urbanization of aquatic systems—degradation thresholds and limits of mitigation. Pages 425–434 in R. A. Martson and V. R. Hasfurther, editors. Effects of human-induced changes on hydrologic systems, proceedings: annual summer symposium of the American Water Resources Association. American Water Resources Association, Jackson Hole, Wyoming.

Brinson, M. M. 1993. A hydrogeomorphic classification for wetlands. U.. Army Corps of Engineers, Wetlands Research Program, Final Technical Report WRP-DE-4, Washington, D.C.

Brown, M. L., and D. J. Austen. 1996. Data management and statistical techniques. Pages 17–59 in B. R. Murphy and D. W. Willis, editors. Fisheries techniques, 2nd edition. American Fisheries Society, Bethesda, Maryland.

Canfield, D. E., Jr., C. D. Brown, R. W. Bachmann, and M. V. Hoyer. 2002. Volunteer lake monitoring: testing the reliability of data collected by the Florida LAKEWATCH program. Lake and Reservoir Management 18:1–9.

Conover, W. J. 1980. Practical nonparametric statistics, 2nd edition. Wiley, New York.

Conquest, L. L., and S. C. Ralph. 1998. Statistical design and analysis considerations for monitoring and assessment. Pages 455–475 in R. J. Naiman and R. E. Bilby, editors. River ecology and management: lessons from the Pacific coastal ecoregion. Springer-Verlag, New York.

Cowardin, L. M., V. Carter, F. C. Goulet, and E. T. LaRoe. 1979. Classification of wetlands and deepwater habitat of the United States. U.S. Fish and Wildlife Service, Washington, D.C.

Davis, S. M. 1994. Phosphorus inputs and vegetation sensitivity in the Everglades. Pages 357–378 in S. M. Davis and J. C. Ogden, editors. Everglades: the ecosystem and its restoration. St. Lucie Press, Delray Beach, Florida.

Dawson, D. 1994. Are habitat corridors conduits for animals and plants in a fragmented landscape: a review of the scientific evidence. English Nature Research Reports, Report No. 94, Peterborough, England.

Denver, R. J. 1997. Environmental stress as a developmental cue: corticotrophin-releasing hormone is a proximate mediator of adaptive phenotypic plasticity in amphibian metamorphosis. Hormones and Behavior 31:169–179.

Elliott, J. M. 1983. Some methods for the statistical analysis of samples of benthic invertebrates. Freshwater Biological Association, Cumbria, UK.

Farina, A. 1998. Principles and methods in landscape ecology. Chapman and Hall, London.

Fore, L. S., K. Paulsen, and K. O'Laughlin. 2001. Assessing the performance of volunteers in monitoring streams. Freshwater Biology 46:109–123.

Forman, R. T. T. 1995. Land mosaics: the ecology of landscapes and regions. Cambridge University Press, Cambridge, England.

Frissell, C. A., and S. C. Ralph. 1998. Stream and watershed restoration. Pages 599–624 in R. J. Naiman and R. E. Bilby, editors. River ecology and management: lessons from the Pacific coastal ecoregion. Springer-Verlag, New York.

Fukushima, M. 2001. Salmonid habitat-geomorphology relationships in low-gradient streams. Ecology 82:1238–1246.

Gauch, H. G., Jr., 1982. Multivariate analysis in community ecology. Cambridge University Press, Cambridge, England.

Geist, D. R. 2000. Hyporheic discharge of river water into fall chinook salmon (Oncorhynchus tshawytscha) spawning areas in the Hanford Reach, Columbia River. Canadian Journal of Fisheries and Aquatic Sciences 57:1647–1656.

Hawkins, C. P., J. L. Kershner, P. A. Bisson, M. D. Bryant, L. M. Decker, S. V. Gregory, D. A. McCullough, C. K. Overton, G. H. Reeves, R. J. Steedman, and M. K. Young. 1993. A hierarchical approach to classifying stream habitat features. Fisheries 18:3–12.

Hershey, A. E., and G. A. Lamberti. 1998. Stream macroinvertebrate communities. Pages 169–199 in R. J. Naiman and R. E. Bilby, editors. River ecology and management: lessons from the Pacific coastal ecoregion. Springer-Verlag, New York.

Heyer, W. R., M. A. Donnelly, R. W. McDiarmid, L. A. C. Hayek, and M. S. Foster, editors. 1994. Measuring and monitoring biological diversity. Standard methods for amphibians. Smithsonian Institution Press, Washington, D.C.

Hicks, A. L. 1996. Aquatic invertebrates and wetlands: ecology, biomonitoring and assessment of impact from urbanization. University of Massachusetts, Amherst.

Hilsenhoff, W. L. 1988. Rapid field assessment of organic pollution with a family-level biotic index. Journal of the North American Benthological Society 7:65–68.

Jennings, M. R., and M. P. Hayes. 1985. Pre-1900 overharvest of California red-legged frogs (Rana aurora draytonii): the inducement for bullfrog (Rana catesbeiana) introduction. Herpetologica 41:94–103.

Johnston, C. A. 1998. Geographic information systems in ecology. Blackwell Scientific Publications, Ltd., Oxford, UK.

Jones, K. B. 1986. Amphibians and reptiles. Page 858 in A. Y. Cooperider, R. J. Boyd, and H. R. Stuart, editors. Inventory and monitoring of wildlife habitat. U.S. Department of the Interior, Bureau of Land Management Service Center, Denver.

Karr, J. R. 1998. Rivers as sentinels: using the biology of rivers to guide landscape management. Pages 502–528 in R. J. Naiman and R. E. Bilby, editors. River ecology and management: lessons from the Pacific coastal ecoregion. Springer-Verlag, New York.

Karr, J. R., and E. W. Chu. 1999. Restoring life in running waters: better biological monitoring. Island Press, Washington, D.C.

Kaufmann, J. H. 1962. Ecology and social behavior of the coati, Nasua nirica on Barro Colorado Island Panama. University of California Publications in Zoology 60:95–222.

Kelsey, K. A., and S. D. West. 1998. Riparian wildlife. Pages 235–258 in R. J. Naiman and R. E. Bilby, editors. River ecology and management: lessons from the Pacific coastal ecoregion. Springer-Verlag, New York.

Kent, M., and P. Coker. 1994. Vegetation description and analysis: a practical approach. Wiley, Chichester, England.

Kershner, J. L. 1997. Monitoring and adaptive management. Pages 116–131 in J. E. Williams, C. A. Wood, and M. P. Dombeck, editors. Watershed restoration: principles and practices. American Fisheries Society, Bethesda, Maryland.

King County. 1990. Proposed Bear Creek basin plan. King County Department of Natural Resources and Parks, Seattle.

King County. 1993. Cedar River current and future conditions report. King County Department of Public Works, Surface Water Management Division, Seattle.

King County. 1997a. Waterways 2000: Upper Bear Creek conservation area management plan. King County Departments of Natural Resources and Parks, Seattle.

King County. 1997b. Waterways 2000: Rock Creek natural area management plan. King County Department of Natural Resources and Parks, Seattle.

King County. 1998. Lower Cedar River basin and nonpoint pollution action plan: a plan adopted by the Metropolitan King County Council, July 1997. King County Department of Natural Resources and Parks, Seattle.

King County. 2001. Overview: King County ESA progress report 1998–2000, January 8, 2001. King County ESA Policy Office, Seattle.

Koch, M. S., and K. R. Reddy. 1992. Distribution of soil and plant nutrients along a trophic gradient in the Florida Everglades. Soil Science Society of America 56:1492–1499.

Land Trust Alliance. 1993. The standards and practices guidebook: an operating manual for land trusts. The Land Trust Alliance, Washington, D.C.

Lopez, R. D., and M. S. Fennessy. 2002. Testing the floristic quality assessment index as an indicator of wetland condition. Ecological Applications 12:487–497.

MacDonald, L. H., and A. W. Smart. 1993. Beyond the guidelines: practical lessons for monitoring. Environmental Monitoring and Assessment 26:203–218.

MacDonald, L. H., A. W. Smart, and R. C. Wissmar. 1991. Monitoring guidelines to evaluate effects of forestry activities on streams in the Pacific Northwest and Alaska. U.S. Environmental Protection Agency, EPA/901/9-91-001, Seattle.

May, C. W., R. R. Horner, J. R. Karr, B. W. Mar, and E. B. Welch. 1997. Effects of urbanization on small streams in the Puget Sound lowland ecoregion. Watershed Protection Techniques 2:483–494.

McGarigal, K., S. Cushman, and S. Stafford. 2000. Multivariate statistics for wildlife and ecology research. Springer-Verlag, New York.

McGarigal, K., and B. Marks. 1994. Fragstats: spatial pattern analysis program for quantifying landscape structure. Oregon State University, Forest Science Department, Corvallis.

McMahon, T. E., A. V. Zale, and D. J. Orth. 1996. Aquatic habitat measurements. Pages 83–120 in B. R. Murphy and D. W. Willis, editors. Fisheries techniques, 2nd edition. American Fisheries Society, Bethesda, Maryland.

Metro. 2001. Six years and 6, 920 acres: Metro's open spaces land acquisition report to citizens. July 2001. Portland Metro, Portland, Oregon.

Minns, C. K., J. R. M. Kelso, and R. G. Randall. 1996. Detecting the response of fish to habitat alterations in freshwater ecosystems. Canadian Journal of Fisheries and Aquatic Sciences 53(Supplement 1):403–414.

Montgomery, D. R., and J. M. Buffington. 1993. Channel classification, prediction of channel response, and assessment of channel condition. Washington State Department of Natural Resources, Timber Fish and Wildlife Agreement Report, TFW-SH10-93-002, Olympia.

Murphy, B. R., and D. W. Willis, editors. 1996. Fisheries techniques, 2nd edition. American Fisheries Society, Bethesda, Maryland.

Mushet, D. M., N. H. Euliss, and T. L. Shaffer. 2002. Floristic quality assessment of one natural and three restored wetland complexes in North Dakota, USA. Wetlands 22:126–138.

Naiman, R. J. 1998. Biotic stream classification. Pages 97–119 in R. J. Naiman and R. E. Bilby, editors. River ecology and management: lessons from the Pacific coastal ecoregion. Springer-Verlag, New York.

Nico, L. G., and P. L. Fuller. 1999. Spatial and temporal patterns of nonindigenous fish introductions in the United States. Fisheries 24:16–27.

NMFS (National Marine Fisheries Service). 1996. Coastal salmon conservation: working guidance for comprehensive salmon restoration initiatives on the Pacific coast. National Oceanic and Atmospheric Administration, Northwest and Southwest Regions of the National Marine Fisheries Service, Seattle.

NRC (National Research Council). 1995. Upstream: salmon and society in the Pacific Northwest. Committee on Protection and Management of Pacific Northwest Salmonids, Board on Environmental Studies and Toxicology, Commission on Life Sciences. National Academy Press, Washington, D.C.

O'Neil, T. A., K. A. Bettinger, M. Vander Heyden, B. G. Marcot, C. Barrett, T. K. Mellen, W. M. Vanderhaegen, D. H. Johnson, P. Doran, J. L. Wunder, and K. M. Boula. 2000. Structural conditions and habitat elements of Oregon and Washington. Pages 115–139 in D. H. Johnson, M. P. O'Neill, and M. Directors, editors. Wildlife-habitat relationships in Oregon and Washington. Oregon State University Press, Corvallis.

Overton, C. K., S. P. Wollrab, B. C. Roberts, and M. A. Radko. 1997. R1/R4 (Northern/Intermountain Region) fish and fish habitat standard inventory procedures handbook. U.S. Forest Service, Intermountain Research Station, General Technical Report INT-GTR-346, Ogden, Utah.

Pess, G. R., D. R. Montgomery, E. A. Steel, R. E. Bilby, B. E. Feist, and H. M. Greenberg. 2002. Landscape characteristics, land use, and coho salmon (Oncorhynchus kisutch) abundance, Snohomish River, Washington State, USA. Canadian Journal of Fisheries and Aquatic Sciences 59:613–623.

Pestinger, K. H. J., W. W. Pemberton, P. E. Leach, and P. Noffsinger. 1991. Land titles: course 801—United States student manual. International Right of Way Association, Torrance, California.

Pimentel, D., L. Lach, R. Zuninga, and D. Morrisson. 2000. Environmental and economic costs of nonindigenous species in the United States. BioScience 50:53–65.

Platts, W. S., C. Armour, G. D. Booth, M. Bryant, J. L. Bufford, P. Cuplin, S. Jensen, G. W. Lienkamper, G. W. Minshall, S. B. Monson, R. L. Nelson, J. R. Sedell, and J. S. Tuhy. 1997. Methods for evaluating riparian habitats with applications to management. U.S. Forest Service, Intermountain Research Station, General Technical Report INT-221, Ogden, Utah.

Ralph, C. J., and J. M. Scott. 1980. Estimating numbers of terrestrial birds. Studies in avian biology no. 6, proceedings of an international symposium, Asilomar, California.

Ratley-Beach, L., B. Wagner, and D. Bradley. 2002. Easement stewardship: building relationships for the long run. Exchange: The Journal of the Land Trust Alliance 21(2):6–10.

Reeves, G. H., P. A. Bisson, and J. M. Dambacher. 1998. Fish communities. Pages 200–234 in R. J. Naiman and R. E. Bilby, editors. River ecology and management: lessons from the Pacific coastal ecoregion. Springer-Verlag, New York.

Reice, S. R. 2001. The silver lining: the benefits of natural disasters. Princeton University Press, Princeton, New Jersey.

Relyea, R. A., and N. Mills. 2001. Predator-induced stress makes the pesticide carbaryl more deadly to gray treefrog tadpoles (*Hyla versicolor*). Proceedings of the National Academy of Science 98:2491–2496.

Rosgen, D. L. 1996. Applied river morphology. Wildland Hydrology Books, Pagosa Springs, Colorado.

Sader, S. A., K. Ross, and F. C. Reed. 2002. Pingree forest partnership: monitoring easements at the landscape scale. Journal of Forestry 100(3):20–25.

Samuel, M., D. Pierce, and E. Garton. 1985. Identifying areas of concentrated use within the home range. Journal of Animal Ecology 54:711–719.

Schmitz, D. C., and D. Simberloff. 1997. Biological invasions: a growing threat. In Issues in science and technology online, summer. Online at http://www.nap.edu/issues/13.4/ schmit.htm [Accessed 5 May 2003].

Schueler, T. 1994. The importance of imperviousness. Watershed Protection Techniques 1:100–111.

Scott, M. C., and G. S. Helfman. 2001. Native invasions, homogenization, and the mismeasure of integrity of fish assemblages. Fisheries 26(11):6–13.

Shaffer, P. W., M. E. Kentula, and S. E. Gwin. 1999. Characterization of wetland hydrology using hydrogeomorphic classification. Ecology 19:490–504.

Smith, R. D., A. Amman, C. Bartoldus, and M. M. Brinson. 1995. An approach for assessing wetland functions using hydrogeomorphic classification, reference wetlands, and functional indices. U.S. Army Engineers Waterways Experiment Station, Technical Report TR WRP-DE-10, Vicksburg, Mississippi.

Sokal, R. R., and F. J. Rohlf. 1981. Biometry. Freeman, New York.

Sparling, D. W., G. M. Fellers, and L. L. McConnell. 2001. Pesticides and amphibian population declines in California, USA. Environmental Toxicology and Chemistry 20:1591–1595.

Sullivan, T. J., D. L. Peterson, and C. L. Blanchard. 2001. Assessment of air quality and air pollutant impacts in Class 1 national parks of California. National Park Service Air Resources Division and Fish and Wildlife Service Air Quality Branch, Denver. Online at http://www2.nature.nps.gov/ard/pubs/careview/CAreport.pdf [Accessed 5 May 2003].

Thomas, J. W., R. G. Anderson, C. Maser, and E. L. Bull. 1979. Snags. Pages 60–77 in J. W. Thomas, editor. Wildlife habitats in managed forests of the Blue Mountains of Oregon and Washington. U.S. Forest Service, Pacific Northwest Forest and Range Experiment Station, Portland, Oregon.

Trexler, J. C., W. F. Loftus, and J. H. Chick. 2003. Setting and monitoring restoration goals in the absence of historical data: the case of fishes in the Florida Everglades. Pages 351–376 in D. E. Busch and J. C. Trexler, editors. Monitoring ecosystems: interdisciplinary approaches for evaluating ecoregional initiatives. Island Press, Washington, D.C.

USACE (U. S. Army Corps of Engineers). 2000. Green/Duwamish River Basin ecosystem restoration study: final feasibility report, October 2000. U.S. Army Corps of Engineers, Seattle.

USCOTA (U. S. Congress, Office of Technology Assessment). 1989. Technologies to maintain biological diversity. U.S. Government Printing Office, OTA-F-330, Washington, D.C.

USEPA (U. S. Environmental Protection Agency). 2001a. Protecting and restoring America's watersheds: status, trends, and initiatives in watershed management. U.S. Environmental Protection Agency, Office of Water, EPA-840-R-00-001, Washington, D.C.

USEPA (U. S. Environmental Protection Agency). 2001b. Moving into the mainstream, proceedings, 6th National Volunteer Monitoring Conference, U.S. Environmental Protection Agency, Office of Water, EPA 841-R-01-001, Austin, Texas.

Urban, N. H., S. M. Davis, and N. G. Aumen. 1993. Fluctuations in sawgrass and cattail densities in Everglades Water Conservation Area 2A under varying nutrient, hydrologic, and fire regimes. Aquatic Botany 46:203–223.

Weins, J. A. 1997. The emerging role of patchiness in conservation biology. Pages 93–107 in S. T. A. Pickett, R. S. Ostfeld, M. Shachak, and G. E. Likens, editors. The ecological basis of conservation: heterogeneity, ecosystems, and biodiversity. Chapman and Hall, New York.

Williams, M. C. 1980. Purposefully introduced plants that have become noxious or poisonous weeds. Weed Science 28:300–305.

Wilson, D. E., F. R. Cole, J. D. Nichols, R. Rudran, and M. S. Foster, editors. 1996. Measuring and monitoring biological diversity. Standard methods for mammals. Smithsonian Institution, Washington, D.C.

Wissmar, R. C. 1993. The need for long-term stream monitoring programs in forest ecosystems of the Pacific Northwest. Environmental Monitoring and Assessment 26:219–234.

Wissmar, R. C., and R. L. Beschta. 1998. Restoration and management of riparian ecosystems: a catchment perspective. Freshwater Biology 40:571–585.

Zar, J. H. 1999. Biostatistical analysis, 4th edition. Prentice-Hall, Englewood Cliffs, New Jersey.

Chapter 12

The Economic Evaluation of Stream and Watershed Restoration Projects

Mark L. Plummer

Northwest Fisheries Science Center, National Marine Fisheries Service
2725 Montlake Boulevard East, Seattle, Washington 98112, USA
mark.plummer@noaa.gov

Introduction

Evaluation of aquatic restoration typically focuses on examining physical and biological responses to single or multiple restoration actions. Efforts to restore streams and watersheds, however, are always constrained by budgets or other limitations on resources. These constraints force entities ranging from local watershed groups to the federal government to set priorities and to make choices among competing projects. Economics often is characterized as the "science of making choices," and, as such, provides insights into how to set priorities. In this chapter, I present and discuss several economic concepts that can be used to evaluate stream and watershed restoration projects.

Not all projects warrant a full exploration of economic benefits and costs. And in many cases, data on project costs and benefits, particularly the latter, are difficult to obtain. Nevertheless, familiarity with these concepts still can provide practical assistance in developing and evaluating a restoration program. In particular, economic evaluations can help set priorities for implementing projects.

The chapter begins with an overview of several economic concepts useful for an economic evaluation. I then discuss two frameworks for applying these concepts. Finally, I provide three examples from the Pacific Northwest that apply these frameworks to stream and watershed restoration projects.

Economic Concepts for Stream and Watershed Restoration

The use of economics for evaluating an individual project generally focuses on efficiency or the extent to which a project's benefits exceed its costs. This approach encounters resistance for many environmental projects, in part, because their benefits (and sometimes costs) are difficult to quantify. Even after acknowledging these difficulties, however, the traditional framework of economic efficiency can still contribute to the planning and evaluation of such projects, even if the entire framework is not always applicable (Huppert 2001).

Below, I discuss several economic concepts and how they apply to stream and watershed restoration projects. These concepts include
* Economic benefits and costs
* Benefit and cost metrics
* Total and marginal values
* Economic values and time

Applying these concepts prospectively to a restoration project can be difficult, often because data are not readily available. In all cases, however, some data can be gleaned from the project planning process (for costs) and the monitoring effort (for benefits), which will at least allow ongoing or retrospective evaluations.

Economic Benefits and Costs

The concepts of benefits and costs are central to economic analysis. In the context of stream and watershed restoration, their definitions are straightforward, although their quantification (discussed in the next subsection) may not be. In general, benefits are the favorable effects of a project. Some of these effects will stem from changes in fish populations of interest, but a project's benefits may not be limited to just these changes. Other species may benefit or favorable aesthetic changes may take place. A project also may have unfavorable effects (e.g., it might negatively affect some type of fish), in which case these can be counted as negative benefits.

The costs of a project are the value of the resources used to produce its benefits. In most cases, this value is adequately reflected by the project's budget (or the actual expenditures, if that amount is available), in which case, the budget is an accurate measure of the project's costs. An exception to this occurs when resources are donated and so appear to be free. Donated resources have a value not reflected in their zero price, and this value is not available to any other use if the resources are used in a particular project. The donated resource's value in these other uses is what economists call its opportunity cost: the value of a resource in its best alternative use. These costs should be counted as part of the project's costs.

Benefit and Cost Metrics

In traditional benefit-cost analysis, both benefits and costs are measured with the same metric: dollars. For the cost side of the ledger, using a dollar metric is mostly straightforward, especially when costs are measured simply in budget terms. For the benefit side of the ledger, using a dollar metric often presents problems because the favorable effects may come from enhancing a natural environment or from protecting an endangered species. Attaching a dollar value to these types of effects is difficult and rarely precise; even in cases where it is feasible, the exercise usually is expensive.

Despite these difficulties, there is a growing literature in economics on the dollar valuation of natural resources, including fish (Brown 2000). This literature covers resources that are (1) sold in a market (e.g., commercial fisheries), (2) used in a nonmarket setting (e.g., recreational fisheries), and (3) valued even in the absence of direct use (e.g., the aesthetic value of a landscape or the existence value of a species). The results are expressed in several ways:

- Value per day spent fishing for an individual species (Matthews and Brown 1970; Sorhus et al. 1981; Huppert 1989; Berrens et al. 1993)
- Value per day spent fishing in a general area (Vaughan and Russell 1982; Miller and Hay 1984; Sorg et al. 1985; Brown and Hay 1987)
- Value per fish caught (Johnson and Adams 1988)
- Value per fish before harvest (Olsen et al. 1991; Layton et al. 1999)
- Value per fisher for access to a fishery over a season (Layman et al. 1996)

The benefits of a restoration project need not be limited to improvements in fish populations. Such projects can improve the functioning and aesthetics of a watershed. Studies that have quantified these benefits in dollars include

- Value of improved water quality (Whitehead and Groothuis 1992; Qui and Prato 2001)
- Value of instream flows (Johnson and Adams 1988; Loomis and Cooper 1990)
- Value of restoring ecological functioning in a watershed (Gonzalez and Loomis 1997; Loomis et al. 2000)
- Value of river amenities (Kulshreshtha and Gillies 1993)

Nearly all these values are site specific, and the appropriateness of transferring those values to other sites is not always clear. Thus, the prospects of attaching dollar values to the benefits of individual stream or watershed restoration projects are uncertain, although they do provide a rough estimate for attaching dollar values to improvements in fish populations or, generally, to improvements in watershed conditions. Despite these problems, attempts have been made to evaluate restoration projects by measuring benefits in dollars, and some are discussed later in this chapter.

If a dollar metric is not practicable, the benefits of a restoration project can be evaluated by using either a technological or biological metric. A technological metric uses the physical processes the project is intended to affect to gauge its effectiveness. Table 1 lists several types of restoration projects with corresponding metrics that incorporate ecological and other functions to measure project effectiveness.

The examples in this table illustrate two fundamental problems with a technological metric. First, gauging the benefits in this way does not routinely enable a comparison across all types of projects. Each type of project has its own measure of success or failure, which cannot, in most cases, be used to judge whether one type of project will produce more or less benefits than another type. Second, these metrics do not allow an estimation of the cumulative restoration effect, as they cannot be summed or aggregated in some way. These related problems limit the ability of an economic or any other type of evaluation to set priorities among different types of projects.

For the purposes of conducting an economic evaluation and setting priorities, the ideal (nondollar) metric is a biological one. A biological metric uses changes in biological characteristics, such as abundance, survival, or growth of the species of interest or some other population or community common to a watershed. Such a metric can be applied to any type of project and, therefore, enables comparisons of, say, the effectiveness of large woody debris structures to grazing restrictions. These biological data are much harder to gather, however, and a considerably longer time span for monitoring is needed to overcome the relatively large interannual variation they exhibit (Korman and Higgins 1997; Ham and Pearsons 2000; Roni et al. 2003).

The more types of projects that are evaluated with the same metric, the greater is the scope for an economic evaluation. This consideration may play only a minor role in the choice of a metric, however. The project's ecological objective, as well as the monitoring and evaluation strategies appropriate for that objective, will help determine this choice. So too will budgetary constraints, which may limit monitoring and evaluation to certain forms. Nevertheless, the choice of a metric will affect how economics can be used as part of the restoration planning process.

Total and Marginal Values

It is common for an individual project's scale to be positively related to its total benefits and costs, at least up to a point. How benefits and costs change when scale or some other component of the project change is captured by what economists call marginal value. "Marginal" refers to the change in total benefits or costs when the scale or some other component of a project changes. As a rule of thumb, marginal benefits tend to decrease as an individual project grows larger in size.

Table 1.
Examples of technological metrics for measuring the effectiveness of different types of watershed restoration projects. (Drawn from Roni et al. 2002.)

Type of habitat restoration project	Technological measure of effectiveness
Fish passage improvements	Available habitat area
Road improvements	Fine sediment delivery Landslide hazard
Riparian restoration	Recruitment of large woody debris Stream temperature
Grazing restrictions	Sediment delivery Stream temperature
Instream habitat structures	Structural failure rate Pool frequency and depth
Carcass and other nutrient enrichments	Primary production Density of invertebrates

A common misperception is that the best scale for an action is the point where total benefits are maximized. This makes sense only if the resources used to produce those beneficial effects are "free"—that is, they have no economic value. If these resources are not free, the last small increments of biological productivity come at increasingly higher economic cost. Even if the benefits are not being measured in dollars, the value of these final marginal benefits is likely to be less than the marginal cost of obtaining them. If that is the case, the resources used to produce those benefits would be more productive if applied to another project.

It also is common to see benefits and costs in per unit terms, which is equivalent to specifying an average value and applying that figure across the range of possible project scales. This procedure is appropriate if the values are linear with respect to scale—that is, the average benefit or cost is constant across this range. This usually is not the case for the costs of restoration projects, nor is it often the case for their benefits. If these values are not linear in scale, the marginal value will not equal the average value.

To see the importance of this, consider an example of the average and marginal productivity of off-channel ponds in supporting juvenile salmonids. By using data compiled from several studies, Keeley and Slaney (1996) estimated a relation between the surface area of a pond and the number of salmonid juveniles present in the pond:

(1) $\log^{10}$ (fish number) = $0.51 \times \log^{10}$ (pond area) + 3.47

where pond area is measured in hectares. For the studies the authors considered, the density of fish in the ponds ranged from 0.02 to 5.40 fish/m², with a mean (across the studies) of 1.09 for all salmonids and 1.01 for coho salmon *Oncorhynchus kisutch*, the latter being the main beneficiaries of the ponds.

It is tempting to use one of these average figures to estimate the productivity of different-sized ponds simply by multiplying the average productivity by the size of the pond. Because the relation between pond size and productivity is nonlinear, however, using an average figure can produce highly inaccurate estimates. In this case, an increase in pond surface area increases the expected number of fish but at a decreasing rate. Using a constant average productivity will underestimate the actual productivity for smaller ponds and will overestimate it for larger ponds. For example, by using the average for all salmonids (1.09 juveniles/m²), a 300 m² pond would support an estimated 327 salmonid juveniles, while a 1-ha pond would support an estimated 10,900. By using equation (1) to estimate the same figures produces strikingly different results: 494 and 2,951 juveniles, respectively.

These differences underscore the importance of considering how size or some other measure of scale affects the benefits and the costs of an individual project. If there is reason to believe that benefits and costs are linear (or almost so) in scale, using an average will be appropriate. If this is not the case, using an average in place of the marginal value is likely to produce errors, sometimes substantial, in estimating the project's benefits and costs.

Economic Values and Time

Economic values are dynamic in two ways. First, inflation increases the nominal prices of goods and services, even though their real values may not change. This distinction—nominal for inflation-affected values and real for inflation-adjusted values—should be taken into account when a project's benefits and costs are spread across a number of years or when comparing benefits and costs from different historic periods.

The second dynamic feature of economic values involves discounting or adjusting future values to make them comparable to present values. Even in the absence of inflation, the real value of a beneficial action that occurs in the future is less than the real value of the same action if it occurred today. The percentage to which the future is discounted is determined by what is called the discount rate. While the formulas used to make these two adjustments are similar, they are distinct concepts that need to be treated separately.

Adjusting for inflation

Inflation adjustment takes two forms, depending on whether its consideration is prospective (projecting economic values into the future) or retrospective (comparing economic values over a historical time span). In a prospective framework, the simplest adjustment for inflation is to assume it will affect all economic variables equally, in which case, inflation effectively can be ignored. This does not set inflation to zero; instead, a prospective economic analysis focuses on real values instead of nominal ones, under the assumption that benefits and costs (if both are measured in dollar terms) will be equally affected by inflation.

For example, if a project produces annual benefits that are worth $5,000 today, that figure is used as the real value of its annual benefits over the project's life span (assuming the physical quantity or quality of the project's outputs does not change). Similarly, any annual monitoring and maintenance costs are set at their current amount, which then is used as the real annual value of those costs.

When historical benefits or costs are considered, some adjustment must be made for inflation if those values are from different years. This adjustment takes a simple form, using an index that measures the level of prices in various years (Gwartney et al. 1999). The index is set at a value of 100 for a base year; a value higher than 100 indicates that the level of prices is higher than the base year, while a value lower than 100 indicates that prices are lower. Adjusting a dollar value, V, to account for inflation then requires a value for the price index from 2 years: the original year, P_0, and the year that will serve as the standard for the cost comparison, P_1:

(2) $$V_1 = V_0 \left[\frac{P_1}{P_0} \right]$$

Adjusting for inflation encounters two possible problems. First, there are a variety of price-level measures one can use, each corresponding to a different measure of inflation. The two most common measures are the consumer price index, developed by the U.S. Bureau of Labor Statistics (USBLS 2002), and the gross domestic product (GDP) deflator, developed by the U.S. Bureau of Economic Analysis (USBEA 2002). In any case, the same measure of inflation should be used for all comparisons.

A second difficulty comes from possible changes in technology over time. Expressing the cost of historical restoration projects in current dollars implicitly assumes that those projects would use the same materials and construction techniques if undertaken today. If restoration techniques have improved over time, converting historical costs into current dollars overstates the costs of undertaking a project of that type today. Nevertheless, the adjustment will accurately reflect the cost of undertaking the given project today, which then enables a comparison of the project's cost-effectiveness with other projects undertaken during other time periods.

Examples of adjusting historical costs for inflation are in Table 2. These examples come from several restoration projects undertaken during the 1980s by the U.S. Bureau of Land Management (BLM) in northwestern Oregon (House et al. 1989). Inflation has increased nominal values considerably since 1981, but even within the 7-year period covered by the table, adjusting for inflation has important effects. In nominal value, for example, the 1982 Upper Lobster project is less costly than either the 1987 "J" Line or East Fork Lobster project. When the costs are converted to 2001 dollar values, the relations are reversed.

Discounting

Discounting is a process that reflects the fact that a beneficial or a detrimental action that occurs in the future generally is viewed as less valuable or onerous than the same action if it takes place in the present (Zerbe and Dively 1994). More formally, a discount rate, r, is used to convert a value that occurs t years in the future into a present value, PV:

(3) $$PV = \frac{V}{(1 + r)^t}$$

For a series of benefits that spreads over n years, the present value of the sum of this series becomes

(4) $$PV = V_0 + \frac{V_1}{(1 + r)} + \frac{V_2}{(I + r)^2} + \dots + \frac{V_n}{(1 + r)^n} = \sum_{t=0}^{n} \frac{V_t}{(1 + r)^t}$$

The initial value, V_0, usually is composed of costs that are incurred at the beginning of the project, as is the case for construction costs. The remaining values then are annual costs, such as maintenance and monitoring

Table 2.
Examples of the difference between the nominal (historic) and real (inflation-adjusted) costs of a watershed restoration project. (Project costs are from House et al. 1989.)

Project location	Year completed	Cost	
		Nominal	Real (2001 dollars)
East Fork Lobster	1981	20,000	34,243
Tobe	1982	15,800	25,709
Upper Lobster	1982	2,120	3,450
South Fork Lobster	1982	1,200	1,953
Little Lobster	1986	13,000	18,771
"J" Line	1987	2,400	3,357
Lobster	1987	10,600	14,827
Upper Lobster	1987	5,600	7,833
East Fork Lobster	1987	2,400	3,357

costs, and annual benefits. A technical but important assumption is that these annual benefits and costs occur at the end of each year, where "year" is measured from the completion of the project.

If each value V_t in the series of benefits is a constant, V, equation (4) simplifies to the following:

$$(5) \qquad PV = V \frac{1 - (1 + r)^{-n}}{r}$$

Another use for a discount rate is to calculate an annualized value, AV, which is a constant value for n years equal to the present value, PV, of a stream of unequal values, $(V_1, ... V_n)$. The annualized value then is given by the following formula:

$$(6) \qquad AV = PV \frac{r(1 + r)^n}{(1 + r)^n - 1}$$

This formula assumes that the annual value occurs at the end of each of the n years. Comparing a project's annualized benefits to its costs is equivalent to comparing the present values of those benefits and costs.

Two simple examples illustrate the importance of discounting. First, consider the present value (equation 3) of a benefit of $1,000 that occurs in a single year sometime in the future. Changing the discount rate and the year in which the benefit is received will change the benefit's present value, as shown in Table 3. Note how much the present value diminishes when a large discount rate is used for a long time period. For instance, $1,000 discounted at a 4% rate and received 10 years in the future has a present value of $676, while the same amount discounted at a 8% rate and received 50 years in the future has a present value of $21.

Next, consider how the growth in the present value of a series of benefits (equation 5) equal to $1,000 each year is a function of the discount rate (Figure 1). For even a small discount rate, the present value of the sum of the series falls rapidly below the undiscounted sum. This underscores an obvious but important point: discounting significantly reduces the value of benefits or costs that occur far in the future.

Just as there are real and nominal benefits and costs, so there are real and nominal discount rates, with each used when the corresponding type of value is used. The difference between the two rates is the inflation rate: a real discount rate effectively sets future inflation to zero, while a nominal discount rate adds a premium equal to the expected or assumed future rate of inflation. When discount rates are chosen by reference to current market interest rates, they are nominal, as they incorporate the market's expectation of future inflation.

Table 3.
Present value of $1,000 discounted at a given rate and received a given number of years in the future.

Years before $1,000 is received	Discount rate			
	2%	4%	6%	8%
5	$906	$822	$747	$681
10	$820	$676	$558	$463
20	$673	$456	$312	$215
30	$552	$308	$174	$99
40	$453	$208	$97	$46
50	$372	$141	$54	$21

While straightforward in concept, discounting is complicated in practice by two issues. First, the choice of a discount rate is not always obvious. The economic literature on this subject is voluminous (USEPA 2000). Much depends on the nature of the project—the extent to which its effects span multiple human generations, for example. But the overall conclusion is discouraging: there is no simple answer to the question of what rate to use. In some cases, however, a regulation or statute dictates the choice. Many benefit-cost analyses con-

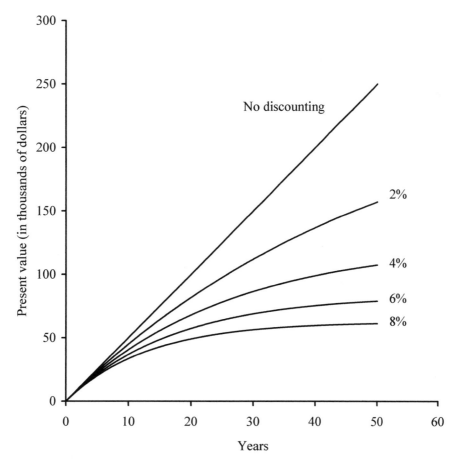

Figure 1.
The present value (sum) of annual payments of $1,000 over a given number of years. Each line represents the growth in this value as the sum of the annual payments accumulates over time. With no discount rate, the value of the sum grows linearly. With a positive discount rate, future payments are discounted below $1,000, so the sum of the payments falls below the undiscounted sum. This difference increases over time as well as with a higher discount rate.

ducted by the federal government, for example, use a discount rate set by the U.S. Office of Management and Budget (USOMB 1992).

A second issue that complicates discounting is the fact that the benefits of restoration projects usually are expressed in biological units, not dollars. By itself, this does not make discounting inappropriate. If two projects have identical dollar costs and biological benefits but one delivers those benefits sooner than the other, the notion that "sooner is better than later" still applies. If the biological benefits can be measured in quantitative terms and translated in principle into monetary values, it is appropriate to apply a discount rate to the stream of benefits (USEPA 2000).

Discounting is not without controversy, of course. When very long time spans are involved, for example, consideration of future human generations becomes important. This might be relevant for some restoration projects, such as riparian buffers, where the benefits (e.g., natural recruitment of large woody debris) may not come for decades. In most other cases, the relevant time frame is considerably shorter, because most projects have a life span measured in years or a few decades.

Economic Evaluations of Restoration Projects

Using the concepts discussed above may seem daunting, because the data to bring them to life are rarely fully available. Even when data are lacking, though, considerations of economic efficiency and effectiveness can improve project planning. In this subsection, I describe two frameworks that use these concepts. The frameworks can be distinguished by whether a dollar metric is used to measure project benefits or not. I then present three examples of how these frameworks can be applied to evaluate restoration projects.

The discussion below is aimed at using economics to evaluate an individual project (e.g., a single project to restore riparian conditions at a particular site) rather than an overall restoration program for an entire watershed or for choosing among restoration programs across multiple watersheds. Using economics in the latter cases is more difficult than applying it to an individual project.

For a restoration program covering an entire watershed, the biological effects of one project may be dependent on the existence or scale of other projects. For example, the effectiveness of a project that enhances rearing habitat may depend on another project that enhances spawning habitat. Similarly, a project's costs may be affected by how close other projects are both in time (i.e., whether they are built at the same time) and space (i.e., whether they are being built nearby). Several projects planned in the same area, for example, could use the same equipment and labor, which would allow economies of scale.

These interdependencies at the watershed scale complicate the estimations of project benefits and costs but do not make them impossible. If adequate data are available (usually a harder task for the biological benefits than for the economic costs), applying many of the principles discussed in this chapter at the watershed scale is feasible. The key difference would be accounting for the effects of one project on others and counting these effects as additional benefits (if the effects boost the productivity of other projects or lower their costs) and costs (if the effects are the opposite).

Similarly, applying economics to the problem of setting priorities across multiple watersheds also is possible, given sufficient data. If multiple watersheds support a single fish population, for example, the problem arises of how to allocate a limited restoration budget across those watersheds. Economics addresses this problem by casting it as one of constrained maximization: choose the set of projects that maximizes the biological benefits over all watersheds subject to the constraint of a limited budget. Use of this framework is beyond the scope of this chapter, however. For these reasons, I have limited the application of economics in this chapter to individual projects.

An Efficiency Framework

A project's efficiency is the extent to which its benefits exceed its costs (in present value terms, if they span more than one year) or its net benefits. Using efficiency to evaluate a project on economic grounds requires that both benefits and costs be measured in dollar terms. Economists use efficiency to judge the optimal scale of a project or set of projects, or the scale or set that maximizes net benefits. It also is used to judge whether a project is worth undertaking at all.

A simplified example illustrates these uses (Table 4). Consider a project for which scale is measured by kilometers of stream treated, and the benefits and the costs can be measured in dollars. For this example, the present value of the project's benefits and costs, both total and marginal, increase as the scale of the project increases. Total benefits increase up to 7 km of treatment, at which point (by assumption), the benefits are maximized. Total benefits exceed total costs up to 6 km of treatment, so net benefits are positive up to that point.

From an economic perspective, the optimal scale is 3 km, the point at which net benefits are maximized. Beyond this point, marginal benefits fall below marginal costs. In general, as long as marginal benefits are falling and marginal costs are rising as scale increases, the optimal scale is the point at which (in an ideal sense) marginal benefit is just equal to marginal cost.

Setting the optimal scale at the point where marginal benefit and marginal cost are equal always needs a check against net benefits if there are fixed costs. In this example, fixed costs of $2,000 instead of $500 would not change the relation between marginal benefit and marginal cost but would affect net benefits. At any scale, net benefits would be negative, indicating that the project is not efficient from an economic standpoint, though, it might be worth undertaking for other reasons.

A Cost-Effectiveness Framework

A different framework is used when benefits and costs are expressed in different metrics. In this case, economic evaluation weighs a project's ability to deliver biological benefits against its economic costs, less formally known as the project's "bang for the buck." A cost-effectiveness approach is most useful when a wide range of restoration projects is evaluated with the same biological metric. If not, projects that share a biological metric can be compared to one another in terms of their cost-effectiveness, but sets of projects that use different metrics cannot be compared.

Economists use cost-effectiveness in two ways:
- Given a limited budget, determine the set of projects that maximizes biological benefits, and
- Given a biological goal, determine the set of projects that minimizes the economic cost of achieving that goal.

Each of these frameworks uses the ratio of benefits to costs as the measure of effectiveness.
A cost-effectiveness framework is more limited than an efficiency framework, but it also avoids the problem of placing a dollar value on project benefits. It is useful for setting priorities when the restoration budget is limited or when a specific biological goal (such as abundance or population growth) is set. In general, projects with higher benefit-cost ratios should be given higher priorities.

Table 4.

A hypothetical example of how the efficient scale (km treated) of a watershed restoration project is determined. The project incurs initial fixed costs of $500 no matter what scale is chosen. Marginal benefit (cost) is the incremental benefit (cost) obtained from treating an additional km. Net benefits (total benefits−total costs) are maximized by treating 3 km.

Km treated	Total benefits	Total costs	Marginal benefits	Marginal costs
0	$0	$500		
1	$1,000	$600	$1,000	$100
2	$1,800	$750	$800	$150
3	$2,300	$1,000	$500	$250
4	$2,500	$1,350	$200	$350
5	$2,600	$1,850	$100	$500
6	$2,650	$2,550	$50	$700
7	$2,675	$3,550	$25	$1,000

A cost-effectiveness analysis cannot easily judge the optimal scale for a project, nor whether the project should be built at all. This is because a project's net benefits (if they could be calculated) and its benefit-cost ratio are not monotonically related. For example, in Table 4, the ratio of total benefits to total costs rises from 1 km to 2 km of treatment, then falls after that; however, net benefits rise from 1 km to 3 km, then fall after that. In general, the point where a benefit-cost ratio is maximized is not necessarily the same point where net benefits are maximized.

Moreover, if a project's benefits have multiple dimensions—for example, it improves habitat conditions for more than one species—cost-effectiveness loses its ability to prioritize projects unambiguously. To see this, consider three BLM projects undertaken in the 1980s in northwest Oregon (House et al. 1989). The projects increased the density of juvenile coho salmon, steelhead *Oncorhynchus mykiss*, and cutthroat trout *O. clarki* (Table 5). If the total number of salmonid juveniles is used as the biological measure of the project benefits, the Upper Nestucca project produced the greatest benefits, followed by the East Fork Lobster project and then the Lower Elk project. If the three species are considered separately, the East Fork Lobster project still produces more benefits than the Lower Elk project, because the first project produces more of each species than the second project. If either of these projects is compared to the Upper Nestucca project, however, their relative ranking is now ambiguous: while the Upper Nestucca project produces more coho salmon than the other two projects, it produces less steelhead and cutthroat trout.

This ambiguity can be resolved only by assigning weights to the individual species, in essence, creating a "benefit function" that aggregates improvements in individual species populations or, in general, the multiple dimensions of the project's benefits. The output of this function then can be divided by cost to gauge the project's effectiveness. One approach is to assign equal weights, looking only at an aggregate number. Alternatively, if the project objective is focused on a single species, that species can be assigned a relatively high weight, while other types of benefits are given positive but lower relative weights.

Three Examples of an Economic Evaluation

This section presents three examples of how to apply the above-mentioned economic concepts and principles to restoration project planning. A word of caution is in order: although based on actual data, the examples are, nevertheless, highly stylized and intended to illustrate how these concepts and principles can influence planning, not determine it. These examples are all drawn from projects intended to benefit salmon in the northwestern United States. This focus is not intentional but rather is due to the paucity of economic data for stream and watershed restoration projects. For whatever reason, salmon projects in the northwestern United States are an exception, with data available both in the published literature and through government sources. The limited focus of the examples, then, should not be taken to mean that the principles themselves are limited by species or geographic location.

Conducting a cost-benefit analysis

The first example comes from a project in Fish Creek, a tributary of the upper Clackamas River in Oregon (Everest et al. 1991). In the early 1980s, the U.S. Forest Service surveyed fish habitats and populations in this area, finding that off-channel ponds were limited in number but also were very productive for coho juveniles.

Table 5.
An illustration of how multiple biological outputs can present a problem for economic analysis. (Project outputs [number of fish produced] are from House et al. 1989.)

| Project location | Estimated juvenile production | | | |
	Coho salmon	Steelhead	Cutthroat trout	Total salmonids
Upper Nestucca	463	26	5	494
East Fork Lobster	350	49	27	426
Lower Elk	332	40	21	393

In 1983, the Forest Service undertook a project to develop a large vernal pool on a flood terrace next to the creek, following this with an evaluation of the ensuing smolt production from 1985 through 1987. Construction costs for the project totaled $24,330, and annual maintenance costs were projected to be $100 (both in 1983 dollars). The project evaluation estimated that the annual smolt production would be about 1,200 coho salmon.

By using these figures, the Forest Service conducted a cost-benefit analysis by attaching a dollar value to the estimated smolt production. The quantification of this value used the following series of calculations:

- 1,200 smolts × 7.5% smolt-to-adult return (SAR) = 90 returning adults,
- 90 returning adults × 0.88 harvest rate = 79 harvested adults,
- 79 harvested adults × 64% commercial catch = 51 adults commercial harvest,
- 79 harvested adults × 36% recreational catch = 28 adults recreational harvest,
- 51 adults commercial harvest × $10.37 per adult = $529 commercial value, and
- 28 adults recreational value × $107.00 per adult = $2,996 recreational value.

This series of calculations produces a total annual value of $3,525 (1983 dollars), beginning in the third year after construction when the first adults produced by the project would return.

Was this project economically efficient? An answer to this question comes from following these steps: convert the costs and benefits into current dollars, use a discount rate to calculate the present value of costs and benefits over the expected project life span, then calculate the net benefits of the project. The project is economically efficient if the net benefits are positive.

Converting the costs and benefits from 1983 dollars into 2001 dollars requires a choice of a price deflator and then the price levels from the 2 years (1983 and 2001). In this and the following examples, I use the GDP deflator (USBEA 2002), which uses 1996 as the base year and has a value of 68.86 for 1983 and 109.36 for 2001. Equation (2) then gives the value for the construction cost, annual maintenance cost, and annual benefits in 2001 dollars as $38,640, $159, and $5,598, respectively.

As noted before, there is no set rule for choosing a discount rate. In this example, I use 4% as the real discount rate and a 20-year period for the project life. Because a real discount rate is used, I treat all benefits and costs as real values as well and, therefore, do not incorporate any inflationary trends.

By using equation (4) and treating the construction cost as a cost incurred in year 0, the present values for total benefits and total costs are $65,519 and $40,798, respectively, for a net benefit of $24,721. Thus, given the economic values and other parameters the Forest Service picked for this example, the Fish Creek project was economically efficient. But how sensitive is this conclusion to variation in those economic values and parameters? Answering this question is important, because there will always be some uncertainty over these values. Conducting some form of sensitivity analysis can increase the confidence in any conclusions drawn from an examination of an individual project's economic efficiency (Merrifield 1997).

In the case of the Fish Creek project, the judgment that it was economically efficient does not hold up well if more recent data are used to set the levels of key parameters. For example, a SAR of 7.5% is much higher than recent data would support. Over the period 1991–2000, for example, the Oregon production index, a measure of marine survival, averaged 2% for coho salmon (PFMC 2002). Also, the harvest rate of 0.88 might be appropriate for a healthy wild or hatchery stock but is high for a threatened or endangered stock. And the economic values chosen in the original analysis are based on studies that are now outdated. More recent studies, even those that consider the value of all fish (not just those that are harvested), show values that are lower (Olsen et al. 1991; Layton et al. 1999; USACE 1999).

Substituting figures based on more recent data for the ones used by the Forest Service, as well as by using different values for the discount rate and the expected project life, can have a substantial effect on the project's net benefits (Table 6). Using more recent data tends to lower the net benefits, in some cases, making them negative and, therefore, the project inefficient. These results should not be taken as a judgment of this partic-

Table 6.
An example of how the economic efficiency of a watershed restoration project is related to the underlying biological and economic parameters. (Data for the base case are from Everest et al. 1991. Commercial and recreational harvested fish values are from USACE 1999.)

| | Present value of | | |
Case	Benefits	Costs	Net benefits
Base case	$65,519	$40,798	$24,721
SAR = 2%	$18,417	$40,798	-$22,381
Harvest rate = 50%	$37,412	$40,798	-$3,386
Harvest rate = 10%	$7,123	$40,798	-$33,675
Discount rate = 1%	$89,986	$41,506	$48,480
Discount rate = 7%	$49,183	$40,322	$8,861
Economic value per fish harvested:			
$9.54 (commercial), $54.20 (recreational)	$23,456	$40,798	-$17,342
Economic value per fish (all) = $50	$52,669	$40,798	$11,871
Economic value per fish (all) = $25	$26,334	$40,798	-$14,464

ular project. Instead, they underscore the importance of accurately estimating the values of key parameters, given the sensitivity of net benefits to variation in their levels.

Applying economic analysis to project scale

The second example considers how economic analysis can be applied to the scale (size) of an individual project. I use the case of an off-channel pond that can be used by juvenile salmonids, with the scale of the project measured by the pond's area. Keeley and Slaney (1996) estimated the relation between pond area and juvenile salmonid production, which can be converted into a dollar benefit function by following the same steps used in the previous example. No data exist on the costs of constructing and maintaining ponds of various scales, so I have created a cost function for illustrative purposes.

The calculation of benefits begins with the juvenile production function estimated by Keeley and Slaney (1996):

(7) Number of juveniles = $10^{3.47} \times$ (pond area)$^{0.51}$

where area is measured in hectares. For the annual value of adult fish, I use a 3% SAR and a value per salmonid adult (harvested or unharvested) of $50:

(8) Annual value of adults = $50 \times 0.03 \times$ number of juveniles

Substituting equation (7) into equation (8) gives the following relation between pond area and annual benefits (from adult fish):

(9) Annual benefits = $4,427 \times$ (pond area)$^{0.51}$

Costs have two components, which are assumed to take the following forms:

(10) Construction cost = $10,000 + $20,000 \times$ (pond area)^2
(11) Annual maintenance cost = $0.01 \times$ construction cost

Finally, these cost and benefit functions are converted into present values by using a discount rate of 4% and a time period of 20 years, with the benefits beginning in the third year.

The effect of the project's scale on its benefits and costs is shown in Figure 2, while Figure 3 shows the same for the project's net benefits, which reach a maximum at 0.7 ha. Larger ponds still have positive net benefits but are not as economically efficient as a pond of that size. From an economic viewpoint, the resources used to produce such larger ponds would produce greater value in other uses.

Again, this example is highly stylized and should not be taken as an exact method for determining the size or another characteristic of a pond, or the optimal scale or configuration of any other restoration project. What is important to see is how economic variables and variation in local conditions affect these choices. In general, changing the parameters that underlie the benefits and costs will change the optimal pond scale. For example, an increase in the economic value per adult fish increases the optimal scale, a decrease in the SAR decreases it, and an increase or decrease in the discount rate changes the optimal scale in the opposite direction.

These changes can be derived formally but mostly follow common sense. Any change that increases the benefits but not the costs of increasing an individual project's scale will increase its optimal scale, while any change that increases the costs but not the benefits of doing so will decrease its optimal scale. For a change in the discount rate, the predicted effects are more subtle but still straightforward. In general, the benefits of a restoration project are spread evenly over time, while the costs mostly occur in the present. Discounting reduces values that occur in the future more heavily than values that occur closer to the present, and this effect is magnified when the discount rate increases. A higher discount rate, therefore, reduces the present value of benefits by a greater amount than the reduction in the present value of costs. This reduces the net gain from increasing the scale of an individual project, making a smaller scale more efficient from an economic standpoint.

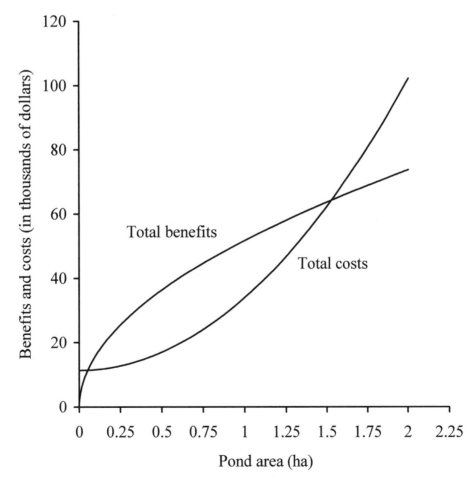

Figure 2.
The total benefits and costs of an off-channel pond project as the scale of the project, measured by pond area, increases. The benefits are based on Keeley and Slaney (1996); the costs are hypothetical.

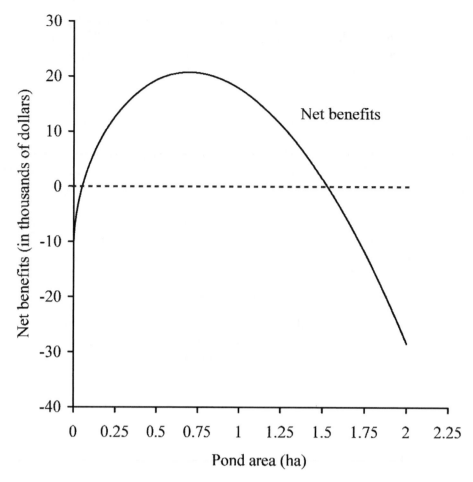

Figure 3.
The net benefits of a hypothetical off-channel pond project, calculated from the total benefits and costs illustrated in Figure 2. In this hypothetical case, net economic benefits are maximized at 0.7 ha.

Using cost-effectiveness to set priorities

The third and final example is based on the BLM restoration projects described earlier (House et al. 1989). The BLM evaluated each project's effectiveness in producing juvenile salmonids. By using these estimates and data on the project costs, this example shows how the cost-effectiveness of a project can be used to set priorities for project planning.

Central to this example is the choice of a metric for evaluating project benefits. I consider two possible choices, each based on data collected during the evaluation: the change in pool habitat (m²) and the change in total juvenile coho abundance over the treated stream length. Each of these metrics is used to evaluate the biological effectiveness of a project. The BLM accounted for the construction costs of each project in nominal dollars, as well as the estimated maintenance costs (1% of construction costs per year). After transforming these into 2001 dollar values, I calculated the annualized value of the costs by using a 4% discount rate over a 20-year period. Finally, dividing the biological effectiveness by the cost of the project for each metric then produces its "bang for the buck," or the biological benefit per dollar expended on the project (Table 7).

Setting priorities for this set of projects can be done in a number of ways (Table 8). The first two methods use the cost-effectiveness ratio based on the change in pool habitat (column A) and change in juvenile abundance (column B). The next two methods rank projects by their biological effectiveness alone—change in pool habitat (column C) and change in juvenile abundance (column D)—without regard to cost.

While not dramatic for this example, the four schemes do produce different results. One way of viewing these differences is to consider how a comparison of two projects is affected by changing the ranking scheme. With

Table 7.

Annual cost, biological benefit, and cost-effectiveness (biological effectiveness/annual cost) of 11 Bureau of Land Management habitat restoration projects, using two different biological metrics (change in m² of pool habitat and change in total juveniles over treated stream length; project data are from House et al. 1989).

Project	Annual cost	Biological benefit by using metric of		Cost-effectiveness by using metric of	
		Pool habitat	Juvenile abundance	Pool habitat	Juvenile abundance
Middle Nestucca	$2,572	8,671	15,789	3.37	6.14
Upper Nestucca	$6,638	21,984	42,136	3.31	6.35
Lobster	$1,239	3,215	1,158	2.59	0.93
Lower Elk	$3,017	6,810	15,277	2.26	5.06
Upper Elk	$2,689	4,639	5,308	1.73	1.97
"J" Line	$281	382	594	1.36	2.12
EF Lobster	$2,862	1,557	6,648	0.54	2.32
E. Beaver	$3,234	1,318	792	0.41	0.25
Upper Lobster	$655	176	104	0.27	0.16
Tobe	$2,149	218	1,382	0.10	0.64
Little Lobster	$1,569	-654	585	-0.42	0.37

11 projects, there are 55 unique pair-wise comparisons, where a comparison produces a relative ranking (i.e., one project is given higher priority than the other). Switching between the two schemes based on the cost-effectiveness ratios (columns A and B) changes 12 of the 55 pair-wise comparisons. Switching from either scheme based on the cost-effectiveness ratio (columns A and B) to the corresponding scheme based only on biological effectiveness (columns C and D) reverses 6 of these comparisons.

Because different priority schemes can produce different sets of ranking, the choice of a scheme should be carefully considered. If setting priorities is desirable because a budget constrains the number of projects that can be undertaken, project costs should be an explicit part of the priority scheme. The choice of how to incorporate a biological metric into the priority scheme will probably be determined largely by the project's objectives.

Table 8.

The priority ranking of 11 Bureau of Land Management habitat restoration projects, using four ranking schemes. The four schemes are (A) pool habitat cost-effectiveness ratio, (B) juvenile abundance cost-effectiveness ratio, (C) change in pool habitat alone, and (D) change in juvenile abundance alone. (Rankings are based on data from House et al. 1989.)

Project	Ranking scheme			
	A	B	C	D
Middle Nestucca	1	2	2	2
Upper Nestucca	2	1	1	1
Lobster	3	7	5	7
Lower Elk	4	3	3	3
Upper Elk	5	6	4	5
"J" Line	6	5	8	9
EF Lobster	7	4	6	4
E. Beaver	8	10	7	8
Upper Lobster	9	11	10	11
Tobe	10	8	9	6
Little Lobster	11	9	11	10

If the objective is clear and easily translates into a specific biological or technological metric, there is no need to test the sensitivity of priority ranks to different priority schemes. If the project's effectiveness can be evaluated with more than one metric, however, ranking projects with the corresponding priority scheme can reveal whether the project ranks are sensitive to the choice of a metric.

As indicated previously, setting priorities by evaluating the cost-effectiveness of a set of projects becomes problematic if the projects affect more than one species or population of interest. Also, if one project's productivity is related to another's—for example, an upstream habitat restoration project and a downstream fish passage improvement—the interrelations must be accounted for in considering each one's cost-effectiveness. Finally, this particular example has considered projects that all have the same form (instream structures). As noted before, evaluating the cost-effectiveness across a range of project types requires a common metric, such as the juvenile abundance measure of biological effectiveness.

Summary

Many of the concepts presented above are intuitive, although their formal application to stream and watershed restoration projects may not be. The availability of data will always constrain the application of economics. When data are scarce, the benefits of gathering enough to conduct a formal economic analysis may not outweigh the costs.

This chapter has primarily focused on the application of economics to individual projects, not to a restoration program that involves multiple projects covering one or more watersheds or regions. Applying economics at broader scales is challenging, because it involves assembling the most efficient set of individual restoration projects within a watershed or determining the best way to allocate a fixed restoration budget across watersheds. It also requires the availability of accurate data on the physical and biological effectiveness of single and multiple restoration actions, as well as the interactions among projects. These data typically have not been available historically. As they become available, economic evaluations at broader scales become feasible.

Economics has some valuable lessons for the planning and evaluation of restoration projects. Among the most important is that variation in benefits and costs, no matter how they are measured, affect the best configuration of a project or the best set of projects overall. Project costs should play a role in setting priorities, for ignoring them risks using scarce restoration resources inefficiently. Getting the "biggest bang for the buck" out of a limited restoration budget mandates attention to the economic concepts presented above.

Important too are some of the simpler concepts, such as marginal benefits and costs, and discounting. Paying attention to benefits and costs at the margin means that pushing a project's scale until its biological effects are exhausted undoubtedly pushes it too far. And a project that provides a given type and amount of restoration benefits more quickly than another project should be given a higher priority, a result suggested by a positive discount rate.

The circumstances in which economic considerations alone will be used to set restoration priorities rarely will occur. Nevertheless, economics highlights the trade-offs that, in fact, are present for any restoration effort that uses scarce resources. Understanding and applying the economic concepts and frameworks presented here can help set priorities and otherwise can contribute to the planning of stream and watershed restoration efforts.

References

Berrens, R., O. Bergland, and R. M. Adams. 1993. Valuation issues in an urban recreational fishery: spring chinook salmon in Portland, Oregon. Journal of Leisure Research 25:70–83.

Brown, G. M., Jr. 2000. Renewable natural resource management and use without markets. Journal of Economic Literature 38:875–914.

Brown, G. M., Jr., and M. J. Hay. 1987. Net economic recreation values for deer and waterfowl hunting and trout fishing, 1980. Division of Policy and Directives Management, U.S. Fish and Wildlife Service, Working Paper No. 23, Washington, D.C.

Everest, F. M., J. R. Sedell, G. Reeves, and M. D. Bryant. 1991. Planning and evaluating habitat projects for anadromous salmonids. Pages 68–77 in J. Colt and R. J. White, editors. Fisheries Bioengineering Symposium. American Fisheries Society, Symposium 10, Bethesda, Maryland.

Gonzalez, C., and J. B. Loomis. 1997. Economic benefits of maintaining ecological integrity of Rio Mameyes, in Puerto Rico. Ecology and Economy 21:63–75.

Gwartney, J. D., R. S. Sobel, and R. L. Stroup. 1999. Macroeconomics: private and public choice, 10th edition. South-Western College Publishing, Mason, Ohio.

Ham, K. D., and T. N. Pearsons. 2000. Can reduced salmonid population abundance be detected in time to limit management impacts? Canadian Journal of Fisheries and Aquatic Sciences 57:17–24.

House, R., V. Crispin, and R. Monthey. 1989. Evaluation of stream rehabilitation projects—Salem district (1981–1988). U.S. Bureau of Land Management, Technical Note T/N OR-6, Washington, D.C.

Huppert, D. 1989. Measuring the value of fish to anglers: application to central California anadromous species. Marine Resource Economics 6:89–107.

Huppert, D. 2001. The role of economics in habitat restoration. Pages 35–52 in S. T. Allen and R. Carslon, editors. Proceedings of the salmon habitat restoration cost workshop. Pacific States Marine Fisheries Commission, Gladstone, Oregon.

Johnson, N. S., and R. A. Adams. 1988. Benefits of increased streamflow: the case of the John Day River steelhead fishery. Water Resources Research 24:1839–1846.

Keeley, E. R., and P. A. Slaney. 1996. Quantitative measures of rearing and spawning habitat characteristics for stream-dwelling salmonids: guidelines for habitat restoration. Watershed Restoration Program, Ministry of Environment, Lands and Parks and Ministry of Forests, Watershed Restoration Project Report No. 4, Vancouver.

Korman, J., and P. S. Higgins. 1997. Utility of escapement time series data for monitoring the response of salmon populations to habitat alteration. Canadian Journal of Fisheries and Aquatic Sciences 54:2058–2067.

Kulshreshtha, S. N., and J. A. Gillies. 1993. Economic evaluation of aesthetic amenities: a case study of river view. Water Resources Bulletin 29:257–266.

Layman, R. C., J. R. Boyce, and K. R. Criddle. 1996. Economic valuation of the chinook salmon sport fishery of the Gulkana River, Alaska, under current and alternate management plans. Land Economics 72:113–128.

Layton, D., G. M. Brown, Jr., and M. L. Plummer. 1999. Valuing multiple programs to improve fish populations. Department of Economics, University of Washington, Discussion Papers in Economics, Seattle.

Loomis, J. B., and J. Cooper. 1990. Economic benefits of instream flow to fisheries: a case study of California's Feather River. Rivers 1:23–30.

Loomis, J. B., P. Kent, L. Strange, K. Fausch, and A. Covich. 2000. Measuring the total economic value of restoring ecosystem services in an impaired river basin: results from a contingent valuation survey. Ecological Economics 33:103–117.

Matthews, S. B., and G. M. Brown, Jr. 1970. Economic evaluation of the 1967 sport salmon fisheries of Washington. Washington Department of Fisheries, Technical Report No. 2, Olympia.

Merrifield, J. 1997. Sensitivity analysis in benefit-cost analysis: a key to increased use and acceptance. Contemporary Economic Policy 15:82–92.

Miller, J. R., and M. J. Hay. 1984. Estimating substate values of fishing and hunting. Trans-actions of the North American Wildlife and Natural Resource Conference 49:345–355.

Olsen, D., J. Richards, and R. D. Scott. 1991. Existence and sport values for doubling the size of Columbia River Basin salmon and steelhead runs. Rivers 2:44–56.

PFMC (Pacific Fishery Management Council). 2002. Preseason report I: stock abundance analysis for 2002 ocean salmon fisheries. Pacific Fishery Management Council, Portland, Oregon.

Qui, Z., and T. Prato. 2001. Physical determinants of economic value of riparian buffers in an agricultural watershed. Journal of the American Water Resources Association 37:295–303.

Roni, P., T. Beechie, R. E. Bilby, F. E. Leonetti, M. M. Pollock, and G. R. Pess. 2002. A review of stream restoration techniques and a hierarchical strategy for prioritizing restoration in Pacific Northwest watersheds. North American Journal of Fisheries Management 22:1–20.

Roni, P., M. Liermann, and A. Steel. 2003. Monitoring and evaluating responses of salmonids and other fishes to instream restoration. Pages 318–339 in D. R. Montgomery, S. Bolton, D. B. Booth, and L. Wall, editors. Restoration of Puget Sound rivers. University of Washington Press, Seattle.

Sorg, C. F., J. B. Loomis, D. M. Donnelly, G. L. Peterson, and L. J. Nelson. 1985. Net economic value of cold and warm water fishing in Idaho. U.S. Forest Service, Rocky Mountain Forest and Range Experiment Station, Resource Bulletin RM-11, Fort Collins, Colorado.

Sorhus, C., W. Brown, and K. Gibbs. 1981. Estimated expenditures of salmon and steelhead sport anglers for specified fisheries in the Pacific Northwest. Agricultural Experiment Station, Special report 631, Oregon State University, Corvallis.

USACE (U. S. Army Corps of Engineers). 1999. Economic value assumptions. Appendix 4. C, Anadromous fish economic analysis, Lower Snake River juvenile salmon migration feasibility study. U.S. Army Corps of Engineers, Walla Walla, Washington.

USBEA (U. S. Bureau of Economic Analysis). 2002. Table 7.1, Quantity and price indexes for gross domestic product, National income and product accounts tables. U.S. Bureau of Economic Analysis, Washington, D.C.

USBLS (U. S. Bureau of Labor Statistics). 2002. Table containing history of CPI-U U.S. all items indexes and annual percent changes from 1913 to present. U.S. Bureau of Labor Statistics, Washington, D.C.

USEPA (U. S. Environmental Protection Agency). 2000. Guidelines for preparing economic analyses. U.S. Environmental Protection Agency, EPA 240-R-00-003, Washington, D.C.

USOMB (U.S. Office of Management and Budget). 1992. Guidelines and discount rates for benefit-cost analysis of federal programs. U.S. Office of Management and Budget, OMB Circular A-94, 29 October 1992, Washington, D.C.

Vaughan, W., and C. Russell. 1982. Valuing a fishing day: an application of a systematic varying parameter model. Land Economics 58:450–463.

Whitehead, J. C., and P. A. Groothuis. 1992. Economic benefits of improved water quality: a case study of North Carolina's Tar-Pamlico River. Rivers 3:170–178.

Zerbe, R. O., Jr., and D. D. Dively. 1994. Benefit-cost analysis in theory and practice. Harper Collins College Publishers, New York.

Glossary

Acquisition: The purchasing of a piece of land for the protection or restoration of plants and animals. Commonly called fee simple acquisition by real estate and land trust practitioners, it is the result of purchasing all rights an existing owner may have to the land, including that of "quiet enjoyment" in perpetuity. Compare *easement*.

Adaptive management: An iterative decision-making process involving a cycle of planning, implementing, monitoring, evaluating, and, subsequently, reexamining and altering management decisions based on monitoring results.

Anadromous: An organism that migrates from the sea to freshwater for reproduction.

Anastomosing channel: A channel that branches and departs from the main channel, sometimes running parallel for several kilometers before rejoining the main channel.

Anthropogenic: Caused or produced by human action.

Autocorrelation: Correlation of a variable with itself over successive time intervals.

Bankfull width: Channel width between the tops of banks on either side of a stream; tops of banks are the points at which water overflows its channel at bankfull discharge. Contrast *wetted width*.

Basal area: Square feet of total base area of trees (usual at breast height) per unit area (typically acre or hectare).

Baseline monitoring: Characterizing existing biota, chemical or physical conditions for planning or future comparisons. Compare *status, trend, implementation, effectiveness, and validation monitoring*.

Basin: See *watershed*.

Bed load: Sediment particles resting on the channel bottom that are pushed or rolled along by the flow of water. Note that sediment can move between bed load and suspended load as the stream discharge changes. Compare *suspended load* and *wash load*.

Benthic: Of, related to, or living in the soil–water interface of a lake or stream.

Biodiversity: The number of different species of plants and animals in an environment during a specific period of time.

Biofilm: Community of microorganisms attached to a solid surface.

Biological integrity: The capability of supporting and maintaining a balanced, integrated, adaptive community of organisms having a species composition, diversity, and functional organization comparable to that of the natural habitat of the regions.

Biomass: Total amount of all living organisms in a biological community, as in a unit area or weight or volume of habitat.

Bioswale: Vegetated channel commonly used to remove pollutants in storm water runoff.

Biota: Flora and fauna of a region.

Bioturbation: Biological activities, such as burrowing and feeding in, at, or near the sediment surface, that occur and cause the sediment to become resuspended and mixed.

Blowdown: See *windthrow*.

Catchment: See *watershed*.

Channel bifurcation ratio: Number of first-order channels divided by the number of second-order channels, the number of second order divided by third order, etc. Bifurcation ratios provide insight into the maturity of tidal channel development. Compare *stream order*.

Channelization: Straightening, narrowing, and deepening of a stream channel to improve navigation, move water faster, prevent flooding of human infrastructure, provide for construction of infrastructure, or other human uses. Often includes removal of debris and channel obstructions that may impede flow conveyance.

Channel unit: See *habitat unit*.

Coarse sediment: Generally, greater than 2-mm diameter, which is gravel, cobbles, or boulders. Compare *fine sediment*.

Consumer price index (CPI): Measure of the average change in the cost of typical wage-earner purchases of goods and services expressed as a percentage of the cost of these same goods and services in some base period.

Control: A study location nearly identical to the treated location, with the exception that no treatment occurs. See also *reference site*.

Coppicing: Forest regeneration from vegetative sprouts from stumps, branches, or roots.

Core area: Part of a species' range that is typified by high and frequent use or that provides high-quality habitat for breeding, rearing, feeding, and other key functions necessary for a species' survival.

Creation (habitat): Construction of a new habitat or ecosystem where it did not previously exist. This is often part of mitigation activities.

Cross section: Profile of elevations perpendicular to the stream channel.

DBH (diameter at breast height): A measurement of tree diameter taken at breast height.

Discing: Mechanical site-preparation technique used to break up soil and plow existing vegetation into the soil. It usually is performed by towing a disc (a trailer on wheels with numerous sharp rotating discs that cut into the soil) behind a tractor.

Discount rate: Rate at which future dollars are discounted relative to current dollars.

Distributary: Branch of a river or a stream that flows away from the main channel and does not rejoin it. Also called distributary channel.

Drainage basin: See *watershed*.

Easement: In restoration ecology, it refers to acquiring a portion of the rights to a land to allow for, or protect from, a specific use. Technically defined as the nonpossessory interest granted in the lands of another, established to obtain certain limited rights (e.g., development rights, but never the right to "quiet enjoyment") that are often in perpetuity but sometimes for only set periods of time. Compare *acquisition*.

Ecoregion: Area determined by similar land-surface form, potential natural vegetation, land use, and soil; it may contain few or many geological districts.

Ecosystem: Dynamic and holistic system of all the living and dead organisms in an area and the physical and climatic features that are interrelated in the transfer of energy and material.

Effectiveness monitoring: Evaluating whether actions had the desired effects on physical processes, habitat, or biota. Compare *baseline, status, trend, implementation, and validation monitoring*.

Endangered species: Species in danger of extinction throughout all or a significant portion of its range. See also *threatened species*.

Endpoint: Composed of the variable, the sampling unit, and the statistic together. Often used to establish a quantifiable measure of success. For example, a water-quality endpoint might be a mean daily maximum temperature of 16°C.

Enhancement: To improve the quality of a habitat through direct manipulation. It does not necessarily seek to restore processes or conditions to some predisturbed state. Some practitioners call this partial restoration. Compare *rehabilitation* and *restoration*.

Estuary: Semienclosed coastal body of water at the mouth of a river, where the saltwater ocean tide meets the freshwater current.

Exclosure: Fencing an area to prevent (exclude) access of livestock or other ungulates.

Fine sediment: Generally, less than 2-mm diameter, typically composed of clay, silt, or sand. Compare *coarse sediment*.

Fining: Decrease in mean substrate particle size.

Floodplain: A flat depositional feature of a river valley adjoining the channel, formed under present climate and hydrological conditions, and subject to periodic flooding.

Fry: Brief transitional stage of recently hatched fish that spans from absorption of the yolk sac through several weeks of independent feeding.

Girdling: Removing the layer of bark and cambium around the circumference of a tree, usually performed in an attempt to kill the tree.

GIS (geographic information system): A computer system for assembling, storing, manipulating, and displaying geographically referenced information.

Glide: A shallow stream section (habitat unit or mesohabitat) with even laminar flow and little or no turbulence or obstructions.

GPS (global positioning system): A worldwide radio navigation system that uses a constellation of satellites and their ground stations as reference points to calculate positions on the planet for location or measurements.

Gramnivory: Seed eating.

Greenline: First perennial vegetation that forms a lineal grouping of community types on or near the water's edge, most often at or below the bankfull stage.

Ground-truthing: Field measurement of specific attributes that have been predicted from models, maps, or remotely sensed data for the purpose of assessing accuracy and precision of predictions.

Gullying: Erosion of soil by formation or extension of channels (gullies) from surface runoff.

Habitat: In this book, the term refers to the aquatic environment that fish experience and not those landscape processes or attributes outside streams that alter habitat conditions.

Habitat unit: Distinct geomorphically defined area within a stream reach, such as a pool, a riffle, a glide, etc. Sometimes called a *mesohabitat*.

Hydraulic head: Water elevation and water pressure.

Hyporheic zone: The saturated interstitial areas below the streambed and into the streambanks (or floodplain), where stream water and deep groundwater intermix and where a number of important chemical, hydrological, and biological processes take place.

Implementation monitoring: Evaluating whether the restoration project was constructed (implemented) as planned. Compare *baseline, status, trend, effectiveness, and validation monitoring*.

Large woody debris (LWD): Large piece of woody material such as a log or stump that intrudes into or lies entirely within a stream channel; LWD typically is defined as wood greater than 10 cm in diameter and 1 m in length, but other minimum size criteria also are used.

LIDAR (light detection and ranging): By using the same principle as radar, the LIDAR instrument transmits light to a target and receives reflected or scattered light back for analysis. The change in the properties of the light enables measuring some property of the target, such as distance, speed, rotation, or chemical composition and concentration.

Limiting factor: Factor that confines (limits) the growth of an ecosystem element.

Long profile (longitudinal profile): Longitudinal plot of elevation versus distance (gradient), typically along the *thalweg* of a stream.

Macroinvertebrate: Animal without a backbone, living one stage of its life cycle, usually the nymph or larval stage. Macroinvertebrates are visible without magnification, and many are benthic organisms (see *benthic*).

Main stem: Principle stream or channel of a stream network.

Marginal benefit: Increase or decrease in total benefit as a result of one more or one less unit of interest.

Marginal cost: Increase or decrease in costs as a result of one more or one less unit of output.

Mass wasting: Downslope movement of earth materials under gravity, including such processes as rockfalls, landslides, and debris flows.

Meiofauna: Benthic animals that can fit a mesh size of 1 mm and be retained on a mesh size of 42 µm.

Mesocosm: Surrogate for a real ecosystem that meets the requirement of being of sufficient size to contain all the components of interest while allowing "natural" behavior. In aquatic ecology, it often is an enclosed portion of a stream or other body of water or artificial stream channel, and may range from a few to several hundred square meters, depending on the ecosystem and organisms being studied.

Mesohabitat: Distinct geomorphically defined habitat area within a stream reach such as a pool, a riffle, a glide, etc. Often called a *habitat unit*.

Metapopulation: Network of semi-isolated populations, with some level of regular or intermittent migration and gene flow among them, in which individual populations may go extinct but then the habitat they occupied can become recolonized from remaining populations.

Metric: Standard of measurement or combination of parameters used as a standard of measurement. See also *parameter* and *variable*.

Microhabitat: Specific locations where organisms live that contain combinations of habitat characteristics that directly influence the organism's physiology or energetics in a small or restricted area. In fisheries and aquatic ecology, this typically is at a scale smaller than a *mesohabitat* or a *habitat unit* and may include preferences for substrate, velocity, depth, etc.

Mitigation: Action taken to alleviate or compensate for potentially adverse effects on an aquatic habitat that has been modified or lost by human activity.

Monitoring: Systematically checking or scrutinizing something for the purpose of collecting specific categories of data, especially on a recurring basis. In ecology, it generally refers to systematically sampling something in an effort to detect or evaluate a change or lack of change in a physical, a chemical, or a biological parameter. Compare *baseline, status, trend, implementation, effectiveness, and validation monitoring*.

Nutrient enrichment: Addition of organic or inorganic compounds to a water body to increase background levels of nutrients (e.g., phosphorous, nitrogen).

Overstory: Uppermost layer of foliage that forms a forest canopy. Compare *understory*.

Parameter: Quantitative physical, chemical, or biological property, such as water temperature or biota abundance, whose values describe the characteristics or behavior of an individual, a population, a community, or a ecosystem. See also *metric* and *variable*.

Parr: Young salmon during its freshwater residence between the fry and smolt stage and before the first seaward migration.

Photic zone: Upper layers of bodies of water into which sunlight penetrates sufficiently to influence the growth of plants and animals.

Population: Group of individuals of a species living in a certain area that maintain some degree of reproductive isolation.

Power (statistical): Probability of rejecting null hypothesis when it is, in fact, false and should be rejected. Typically denoted as $1-\beta$.

Primary production: Creation of organic matter (biomass) by photosynthesis or chemosynthesis.

Primary productivity: Rate at which organic matter (biomass) produced by photosynthesis or chemosynthesis is stored in an ecological community or group of communities. Compare *secondary productivity*.

Pseudoreplication: Use of inferential statistics to test for treatment effects with data from experiments, where either treatments are not replicated (though samples may be) or replicates are not statistically independent (S. H. Hurlbert, 1984, Pseudoreplication and the design of ecological field experiments, Ecological Monographs 54(2):187–211).

Rainsplash erosion: Transport of sediment by movement of water from precipitation, which typically causes soil particles to be splashed more on the downhill than on the uphill side of a slope.

Reach: A geomorphically similar stream section or a section of stream as defined by two selected points.

Redd: Nest in gravel, dug by a fish for egg deposition, and associated gravel mounds.

Reference site: Site in a relatively natural state, representative of conditions before human disturbance. See also *control*.

Reclamation: Returning an area to its previous habitat type but not necessarily fully restore all functions.

Rehabilitation: To restore or improve some aspects or an ecosystem but not fully restore all components. A general restoration term that can include habitat improvement, enhancement, or reclamation. Some practitioners call this partial restoration. Compare *enhancement* and *restoration*.

Remote sensing: Gathering data from a remote station or platform, as in satellite or aerial photography.

Restoration: 1. Returning the ecosystem to some predisturbed condition. Some practitioners call this full restoration. 2. A general term for referring to various enhancement, improvement, and rehabilitation actions. Compare *enhancement* and *rehabilitation*.

Riffle: Shallow section of a river or stream, with moderate to rapid flow and with surface turbulence.

Rill: One of the first and smallest channels formed by surface runoff.

Rilling: Removal of soil by water from small, well-defined, visible channels or streamlets where there is substantial overland flow.

Riparian: The banks of a river or the terrestrial aquatic interface. That part of the terrestrial landscape that exerts a direct influence on stream channels or lake margins, and the water or aquatic ecosystems.

Riprap: Layer of large, durable materials such as rock used to protect a streambank from erosion; also may refer to the materials used, such as rocks or broken concrete.

Road prism: Road surface and fill, and its geometry. Road prism removal includes excavation of part or all of road fill to restore natural drainage patterns.

Salmonid: Fish of the family Salmonidae, including salmon, trout, and chars.

Scientific method: Process of investigating a system by making initial observations, formulating hypotheses about the behavior of the system, making predictions based on these hypotheses, then designing and conducting experiments to test the hypotheses.

Secondary productivity: Rate at which primary (plant and organism) material is synthesized into animal tissue per unit area in a given time period. Compare *primary productivity*.

Sediment budget: Accounting of sediment sources and transfer processes in a watershed. The complete budget quantifies sediment sources, transport, and storage within a watershed, usually tracking each process of sediment production or movement separately.

Sediment supply: Supply of sediment to a river system, where it is carried in suspension (see *suspended load* and *wash load*) or on the bottom (see *bed load*).

Segment: Section of stream between two defined points.

Sheetwash: Surface erosion from water running off in sheets, distinct from channelized erosion in rills and gullies.

Side channel: a subsidiary or overflow channel branching from the primary stream channel, typically conveying a small fraction of the total stream flow.

Silviculture: In forestry or forest management, the care, cultivation, and harvest of trees. In restoration ecology, the term generally refers to planting, removing, or growing trees and other vegetation to restore certain forest characteristics.

Site: Place where a treatment or restoration activity may occur. Term can indicate a habitat unit or stream reach, depending on the coverage of the treatment or restoration activity.

Smolt: A young salmon just after the parr stage that has undergone the physiological changes to prepare it for its first migration from freshwater to the sea. A juvenile salmon in its seaward migration stage.

Soil creep: Gradual downslope movement of the soil mantle.

Source–sink dynamics: Interplay between high-productivity (source) and low-productivity (sink) areas in which excess individuals produced in a source area help maintain populations in sink areas through immigration.

Statistic: Numerical value such as standard deviation or mean that characterizes the sample or population from which it was derived.

Status monitoring: Characterizing the condition (spatial variability) of physical or biological attributes across a given area. Compare *baseline, trend, implementation, effectiveness, and validation monitoring*.

Stream order: A method of classifying streams based on size and number of tributaries. Typically smallest streams are given smaller numbers. For example, a first-order stream would be the smallest detectable headwater stream, a second-order stream would be formed by the formation of two first-order streams, etc.

Succession: Changes in species composition of plants and animals in an ecosystem with time, often in a predictable order. More specifically, the gradual and natural progression of physical and biological changes, especially in the trophic structure of an ecosystem, toward a climax condition or stage.

Suspended load: Part of the total stream load that is carried for a considerable period of time in suspension, free from contact with the streambed; it mainly consists of clay, silt, and sand. Note that sediment can move between suspended load and bed load as the stream discharge changes. Compare *bed load* and *wash load*.

Terrace: Exposed former floodplain deposit that results when a stream begins downcutting into its floodplain.

Thalweg: Line defining the lowest (deepest) points along the length of a stream.

Thinning: Removal of trees or other vegetation to allow for increased growth of other trees or vegetation.

Threatened species: Species not presently in danger of extinction but likely to become so in the foreseeable future. See also *endangered species*.

Tidal prism: Volume of water between mean higher high water (MHHW) and mean lower low water (MLLW).

Trend monitoring: Monitoring changes in biota or physical conditions over time. Compare *baseline, status, implementation, effectiveness, and validation monitoring*.

Tributary: Stream or river that flows into another stream or river.

Understory: Shrubs and smaller trees between the ground cover and the forest canopy. Compare *overstory*.

Ungulate: Any of a number of hoofed, typically herbivorous, quadruped mammals, superficially similar but not necessarily closely related taxonomically.

Validation monitoring: Evaluating whether the hypothesized cause-and-effect relationship between restoration action or other treatment, and physical and biological response were correct. Sometimes considered a part of effectiveness monitoring. Compare *baseline, status, trend, implementation, and effectiveness monitoring*.

Variable: Attribute that may assume any one of a range of values. See also *metric* and *parameter*.

Voltinism: Number of life cycles repeated annually.

Wash load: Relatively fine material in near-permanent suspension that is transported entirely through the system without deposition. Compare *bed load* and *suspended load*.

Watershed: Entire land-drainage area of a river. Also called *basin, drainage basin*, or *catchment*.

Wetted width: Width of the water surface within a channel. Contrast *bankfull width*.

Windthrow: Trees uprooted and felled, or branches broken and felled by strong gusts of wind. Also called *blowdown*.

Index